Brian Lamb is also the author of

*Booknotes: Life Stories, Notable Biographers on
the People Who Shaped America*

*Booknotes: America's Finest Authors on Reading,
Writing, and the Power of Ideas*

Also by C-SPAN:
Traveling Tocqueville's America

Who's Buried in Grant's Tomb? A Tour of Presidential Gravesites

BOOKNOTES:

STORIES FROM AMERICAN HISTORY

Booknotes
STORIES FROM AMERICAN HISTORY

Brian Lamb

PENGUIN BOOKS

PENGUIN BOOKS
Published by the Penguin Group
Penguin Group (USA) Inc., 375 Hudson Street, New York, New York 10014, U.S.A.
Penguin Books Ltd, 80 Strand, London WC2R 0RL, England
Penguin Books Australia Ltd, 250 Camberwell Road, Camberwell, Victoria 3124, Australia
Penguin Books Canada Ltd, 10 Alcorn Avenue, Toronto, Ontario, Canada M4V 3B2
Penguin Books India (P) Ltd, 11 Community Centre, Panchsheel Park, New Delhi – 110 017, India
Penguin Books (N.Z.) Ltd, Cnr Rosedale and Airborne Roads, Albany, Auckland, New Zealand
Penguin Books (South Africa) (Pty) Ltd, 24 Sturdee Avenue,
Rosebank, Johannesburg 2196, South Africa

Penguin Books Ltd, Registered Offices: 80 Strand, London WC2R 0RL, England

First published in the United States of America by PublicAffairs,
a member of the Perseus Books Group 2001
This edition with three additional essays published in Penguin Books 2002

5   7   9   10   8   6

THE LIBRARY OF CONGRESS HAS CATALOGED THE HARDCOVER EDITION AS FOLLOWS:
Booknotes : stories from American history / [compiled by] Brian Lamb
p.   cm.
Collection of essays by various authors based on interviews
originally held on the television program Booknotes.
Includes index.
ISBN 1-58648-083-9 (hc.)
ISBN 0 14 20.0249 6 (pbk.)
1. United States—History—Anecdotes.   2. Authors, American—Interviews.
I. Title : Booknotes.   II. Lamb, Brian, 1941–   III. Booknotes (television program)
E178.6 .B645 2001
973—dc21
2001048469

Printed in the United States of America
Designed by Robert C. Olsson

To
Carolyn Griffen Shatto
Jim Huston
John Splaine

And to the memory of
Cynthia Marshall

Great teachers, all.

Contents

Rebuilding America and the Gilded Age
1865–1901

Progressive Era and Reaction
1901–1929

Depression and War
1929–1945

Early Cold War
1945–1957

Social Transformation
1957–1975

The Culture Wars
1975–2002

Introduction

It's 6:45 A.M., Monday, June 3, 2002. In a cool and dark control room on Capitol Hill, C-SPAN technician Paul Munson watches the final few minutes of the 669th *Booknotes* interview. A graphic appears on the screen beneath the image of the speaker: Richard Posner, author of *Public Intellectuals: A Study of Decline.* Across the hallway, a second technician, Kris Gault, readies the final hour of that weekend's forty-eight-hour package for C-SPAN2's BookTV—Paul Jeffers, discussing his new book, *Theodore Roosevelt Jr.: The Life of a War Hero.* Books about political philosophy and political biographies on C-SPAN? Most people equate our network with live coverage of the U.S. Congress. How, then, did we become so involved with nonfiction books and their authors?

Book programming on C-SPAN has had an evolutionary presence, the beginnings of which date to 1986, when an invitation arrived at my office from Warren Burger, who had recently retired as chief justice of the U.S. Supreme Court. He was overseeing a task dear to his heart, the 1987 national celebration of the U.S. Constitution's bicentennial. Would I, the invitation inquired, join a group of media executives forming an advisory committee for the anniversary? I agreed, as much as anything, for an opportunity to observe the well-known chief justice up close. In one of our meetings, Mr. Burger spoke passionately about the enormous odds that faced the drafters of the Constitution two hundred years earlier. "If you want to get a better understanding of what it was like for them, read this," he advised, passing out copies of Catherine Drinker Bowen's 1966 classic, *Miracle at Philadelphia.*

At that point in my life, reading had become something I mostly did for work. Preparing for my role as an on-camera host, I faced a stack of daily newspapers, weekly cable trade magazines, and lots of news magazines. Books were a luxury for which I, like many people, reserved little time.

Wanting to be a good committee member, however, I set about reading Mrs. Bowen's book, quickly discovering that the chief justice was truly on to something. Her writing made James Madison, Ben Franklin, George Washington, and Alexander Hamilton, slowly threading their way through critical and contentious issues during a sweltering Philadelphia summer, real and human, not at all like the one-dimensional icons I'd studied in school. Reading about them lit a fire under me; I wanted to know more. Soon I was on I-95, heading north to Philadelphia to get a sense of Independence Hall for myself.

I returned to Washington wanting to share the experience with our C-SPAN audience. Learning about history, particularly the origins of the Constitution, it seemed, would help add context to our network's daily fare of national politics and government. We sent C-SPAN camera crews to record tours of Independence Park, interviews with historians, and reenactments by historical interpreters.

We also offered our viewers discounted copies of Bowen's book and gave away thousands of reprints of the Constitution. In June 1987, as the bicentennial drew near, we even subjected C-SPAN's own "founding fathers and mothers"—the CEOs of the cable television companies who, in 1979, had created our public affairs channel—to a board meeting-cum-history lesson, scheduling their annual meeting in Philadelphia. They dined at the same tavern frequented by the writers of the Constitution and were enlisted as the audience for a live conversation with Franklin interpreter George Archbald.

Reactions all around were positive and we decided to do more—more books and more history. So, while our camera crews and producers continued to ply the halls of Congress, C-SPAN also began to seek out more authors. The interviews led to new historical programming ideas: a 1994 conversation with Lincoln scholar Harold Holzer inspired the re-creation of the seven Lincoln-Douglas debates. Then, in 1997, our curiosity about the often-quoted Alexis de Tocqueville, prompted a nine-month series retracing the 1831–1832 tour of the new nation that inspired his political classic, *Democracy in America*.

The year 1999 brought our most ambitious books-and-history effort yet—a forty-one-week series of live telecasts that recounted the lives of the American presidents. Visiting birthplaces, gravesites, libraries, and other places associated with the nation's forty-one chief executives, we brought more than a hundred presidential biographers and historians to the screen, compiling a video record of more than four hundred hours of programming. That series is permanently archived on a Web site, *americanpresidents.org*.

In 2001 we were at it again with a series called *American Writers: A Journey Through History*. This project envisioned a thirty-eight-week televised tour of America based on the writings of American authors whose books chronicled or affected the times in which they lived. Forty-five writers such as Nathaniel Hawthorne, Harriet Beecher Stowe, Frederick Douglass, Mark Twain, Upton Sinclair, John Steinbeck, and Whittaker Chambers were on our list. We made it through to September 10 and the dawn of the twentieth century; after the terrorist attacks, we paused for six months to focus our programming on the federal government's antiterrorism efforts, and went on to finish the series in the spring and summer of 2002.

Books and authors have inspired more than just programming: A 1993 interview with historian Douglas Brinkley, who taught history to college students aboard a "Majic Bus," initiated the production of C-SPAN's own "school buses." Two bright yellow, forty-five-foot-long electronic classrooms have been on the highways ever since, teaming with our local cable affiliates to visit schools. In nine years, the buses have been in more than a thousand communities, introducing a hundred thousand or more young people to C-SPAN and our coverage of the political process.

The television series, the C-SPAN School Bus, and more have all germinated from our weekly author-interview program, *Booknotes*. Since April 1989, *Booknotes* has been offering one-hour televised conversations with nonfiction authors every Sunday night at 8 and 11 P.M., Eastern time. When the series marks its fourteenth anniversary on April 2, 2003, we will have interviewed more than 710 historians, biographers, memoirists, journalists, and policy experts. That's 710 distinct individuals—a *Booknotes* tradition stipulates that authors can be interviewed only once for this series, even if we didn't have the foresight to book them for their masterwork.

By television standards, *Booknotes* has a few eccentricities: It's taped in a small, black-curtained studio, devoid of any decoration. In recent years, we've started using robotic cameras, so the author and I can be alone in our conversation. Our goal is a program that emphasizes content rather than showmanship. In today's society, that's a formula almost guaranteed to attract a small audience; happily, it's also been an extremely loyal one.

Because *Booknotes* is such a simple production, most of the nearly seven hundred programs have gone off like clockwork. Former *Wall Street Journal* editorial writer Amity Shlaes experienced one of our exceptions: As we began our conversation about her book, *The Greedy Hand,* a technician pushed the wrong button, missing the first ten minutes of the interview. After we discovered the problem, she was gracious enough to come back to Washington, sit down in front of the cameras for a second time, and make it sound as if she hadn't already heard my questions.

Booknotes has also been the inspiration for a series of books, of which this is the third. Each has been a collection of essays developed from *Booknotes* interviews and relies on the same editorial concept: excerpted transcripts of the series' sixty-minute interviews, edited into essay form. To tell stories effectively, we omit my questions and often piece together nonsequential portions of the interviews, taking care to remain faithful to the author's intent.

Some readers may find it ironic that a TV network noted for showing events in their entirety has published three books of edited transcripts. We believe this editorial trade-off has given readers a greater selection of authors and stories. Readers who find themselves wanting a fuller picture, however, can find the complete transcript of every author interview on our Web site, *booknotes.org*.

While the format of these three books has been the same, the organizing theme of each is unique and reflects the evolution of my interests as a *Booknotes* interviewer. When I first began talking to authors, I was often amazed by the commitments people make to their scholarship. Many had embarked on years of painstaking research, not infrequently self-financed. These stories, demonstrating writers' love of their craft, form the core of the first *Booknotes* volume, published in 1997 by Times Books. Later, my interest in people who affect history grew, and the series moved more heavily into political biographies. Out of those programs came *Booknotes: Life Stories*, tales of seventy-five influential Americans, also published by Times Books, in 1999.

More recently, perhaps in an attempt to add context to current political situations, I have found myself looking for books that help explain the past. That created the organizing principle of this third book, *Booknotes: Stories from American History.*

This book was on the presses just shortly after September 11 and reached bookstores about six weeks after the terrorist attacks. Although we were initially a little wary about releasing a new book at such a time, the subject matter proved rather appropriate and, in fact, led to some interesting conversations with audiences and the press during our fall book tour.

From our opening event at the National Archives in Washington through stops at Books and Company in Dayton, Ohio, and the Selby Public Library in Sarasota, the questions never seemed to stray far from September 11; in response, I frequently found myself drawing upon statistics from several of our *Booknotes* authors:

• James McPherson reminds us of the Civil War's enormous casualties. Eighty to ninety percent of the soldiers, he explains, were volunteers. By the war's end in April 1865, 620,000 soldiers had died—fully two percent of the American population. "If two percent of the American population were to be killed in a war fought by this country today," McPherson says, the deaths would total five million. "One can readily imagine the impact . . . that number of deaths would have on American society today."

• Another half-million Americans died as a result of the 1918 influenza pandemic. Gina Kolata reports that the virus spread so quickly among America's World War I soldiers that their dead bodies were "stacked up like cordwood." For those with post–September 11 worries about the threat of biological attacks, it may not be reassuring to know that some of the viral genes that caused the epidemic still exist. They are stored under tight security, however, at the Walter Reed Army Medical Center in Washington, D.C.

• James Bradley tells of the thirty-six-day battle for Iwo Jima, an eight-square-mile volcanic rock in the western Pacific, during World War II. From this single battle, the death toll stood at 22,000 Japanese and 7,000 Americans, soldiers who were "just little boys," Bradley says. There were "so many dead, they couldn't bury them in individual graves."

Recently, I've had the chance to interview Diana Preston, who has written a book on the *Lusitania*, a luxury liner filled with civilians, which was torpedoed by a German U-boat on May 7, 1915, as it was steaming from New York to London. Twelve hundred passengers died in the attack; another 750 were rescued from the sea. It was an event that outraged Americans and helped draw the nation into World War I. "It was an enormous shock to the world," Preston said. "If you look at the press reporting on both sides of the Atlantic—complete shock, complete outrage, a sense of a barbarous, unprecedented act."

In the aftermath of September 11, in addition to our near round-the-clock coverage of the government's response to the attacks, our producers sought out writers who could help explain what had happened that day and, perhaps, why. We've included two of those interviews in this paperback edition—a chapter with investigative reporter Peter Bergen, who once interviewed Osama bin Laden, and a chapter with historian Bernard Lewis, who explains how the stage was set for the rise of Muslim fundamentalism. We've also added a chapter on another history-making event: the contested 2000 election between Al Gore and George W. Bush.

Every chapter in *Stories from American History* is new to the *Booknotes* trilogy. This book did bring us full-circle in one important way, however: The hardcover was published by Peter Osnos of PublicAffairs, who had published the first *Booknotes* book while he was the head of Times Books. Our PublicAffairs team included editor Paul Golob, who is PublicAffairs' executive editor, and assistant editor David Patterson. Paul and David helped us keep the best of the series' overall concept while freshening our approach to certain aspects. In publishing this paperback edition, Penguin Books helps bring *Stories to American History* to new readers, for which we thank them, especially our editor, Jane von Mehren, who is Penguin's editor in chief and associate publisher.

A small team of C-SPAN colleagues helped me assemble the essays for *Stories from American History*. Carol Hellwig took the leadership role on the editorial team, having assisted with our earlier *Life Stories* book. Joining her were Vanessa Melius, then part of our executive department staff, and Maura Pierce, our network's history producer.

Susan Swain, our network's co–chief operating officer, has very ably assisted with all three Booknotes books. Assuming the role of project director, Susan has done everything from pitching concepts to publishers, to writing and editing copy late at night. Her co–COO, Rob Kennedy, and corporate counsel Bruce Collins once again provided valuable assistance during the contract phases of this project. Lea Anne Long was another important member of our team, concentrating on the photo section, a feature that's become *Booknotes* series tradition. For this book, we've moved from portrait photos of our featured authors to photographs that help illustrate the stories.

The historical hunts that produce these photos can become a little obsessive for me. After listening to Jay Parini describe the life of Robert Frost, I decided to find the poet's Vermont cabin for myself. I flew to Burlington, drove a rental car to Ripton, Vermont, near Middlebury, and followed Parini's descriptions. At last, I found what I determined was the path to Frost's cabin, only to find a prominent "No Trespassing" sign. Hoping that an owner would conclude that a business-suited traveler in a rural spot meant no harm, I decided to ignore the sign and walked down the leafy path—exactly the kind Frost describes in his poetry. You'll see in the photo section that I finally found the cabin and took my shot.

If this is your first acquaintance with the *Booknotes* series, we welcome you. For returning readers or longtime C-SPAN watchers, let me briefly bring you up to date on what's happened at our network since the publication of *Booknotes: Life Stories*. We've grown: we now have 280 employees in our Washington, D.C., headquarters. C-SPAN transmits to 87 million homes, and C-SPAN2 can now be seen in 70 million cable and satellite homes. We also program nine Web sites; operate a full-time public affairs FM radio station in Washington, which launched nationally via two satellite radio services this year; and there's now a full-time digital cable channel, C-SPAN3, which televises a combined schedule of events from Washington and history programming. C-SPAN's former board chairman, Joe Collins, who was CEO of AOL-Time Warner Cable, and our current chairman, Steve Burke of Comcast Cable have given this channel a big boost by committing to carrying it to all of their companies' digital cable customers.

C-SPAN's growth, including our ability to incorporate books and history into our offerings, is a direct result of the continuing investment made by C-SPAN's affiliates. The cable television executives who founded C-SPAN twenty-five years ago had the vision to commit a portion of their channel space to noncommercial public affairs television. Their ongoing support of C-SPAN allows us to operate without seeking additional subsidies from the public, corporate underwriters, or the government. This gives us the ultimate editorial luxury—we are able to produce informative public affairs programming without having to deliver profits to a bottom line. Because of this, C-SPAN doesn't worry about generating ratings for its programming, doesn't have to grow earnings for investors, and doesn't need to televise underwriting spots for sponsors. There's probably not a journalist in the business who wouldn't like to be in our situation.

My path to journalism probably began in my hometown neighborhood in Lafayette, Indiana. A couple of years ago it was named to the U.S. Interior Department's National Register of Historic Places. An enduring memory is of the old bicycle bridge; many parents forbade their kids to cross it because it took us away from our secure environment. These restrictions only enhanced my curiosity about the world beyond, and that curiosity often got the better of me. That bridge has become my childhood symbol of access to the larger world.

Our neighborhood had street names like Kossuth and Shawnee. Our high school was called Jefferson and my favorite catfish restaurant was in Colfax, Indiana. Back then, it never occurred to me that each of those names had historical roots. As reading began to open the world to me, I made it a habit to inquire about the history behind place-names. Books became my bridge to intellectual experiences and, as I've described, to geographic ones, as well. I'm now a bona fide historical tourist who has visited the burial places of every U.S. president, all twelve presidential libraries, and even the forty vice presidential gravesites.

My colleagues and I hope *Booknotes: Stories from American History* will inspire its readers to their own intellectual journeys. Most of the featured authors' books are still in print, available at local bookstores or libraries. With luck, our brief excerpts will entice you to read more or even to get on the road and visit the historical places they describe.

When Don Hewitt, creator of CBS's *60 Minutes*, sat down for a *Booknotes* interview last year, he explained that the enduring feature of his program is that it tells three good stories every week. He made me realize how much I, as an interviewer, appreciate a good story and how I strive to produce a few in every *Booknotes* conversation. We've done our best to capture more than eighty good stories for this book. We hope you enjoy them.

Brian Lamb
June 7, 2002
Washington, D.C.

Revolution and Founding

1776–1815

———

A Shoemaker and
the Boston Tea Party

by

ALFRED F. YOUNG

On the evening of December 16, 1773, American colonists boarded three ships owned by the British East India Company anchored in the Boston Harbor and, as a protest against what they saw as unfair British trade practices and taxation, dumped the ships' loads of tea into the harbor. The Boston Tea Party didn't cause the American Revolution, but it was one of several significant events that served to widen the gap between the colonies and Great Britain. Alfred F. Young, a senior research fellow at the Newberry Library in Chicago, appeared on Booknotes *on October 15, 1999, to discuss* The Shoemaker and the Tea Party: Memory and the American Revolution, *published by Beacon Press in 1999. Mr. Young wrote about this historical event and others from the perspective of George Robert Twelves Hewes, an ordinary citizen of colonial America and a participant in the Boston Tea Party.*

GEORGE ROBERT TWELVES HEWES lived in Boston a good part of his life and was a shoemaker all of his life. He was active in most of the famous events of the American Revolution that took place in Boston: the Boston Massacre, the Boston Tea Party, and the tarring and feathering of people. He became a soldier and sailor in the Revolution and then left Boston, living out his life in country towns. When he was in his nineties, he was "discovered" in western New York; someone wrote a biography of him. He was brought back to Boston in 1835, where someone wrote another biography of him. He was the hero of the day for the Fourth of July. His portrait was painted and he became a celebrity.

This portrait portrayed him not as a shoemaker but in his Sunday best clothes, an old man leaning on a cane. The picture was called *The Centenarian* because Hewes thought he was ninety-nine years old, just on the verge of one hundred. He was wrong—off by six years. He was only ninety-three. I don't think it was an intentional lie, but he then passed into history as a nearly one hundred-year-old man and as the last survivor of the Tea Party. But he wasn't the last survivor; there were twenty-five others.

THE FIRST BIG ACTIVITY in Boston was around the Stamp Act, which was 1765–1766; an awful lot of working people were involved. The leader of the popular demonstrations was a shoemaker named Ebenezer McIntosh, who had formerly been leader of the annual November 5 Guy Fawkes Day ritual. He was chosen by the political leaders to help organize the demonstrations against the Stamp Act, an act of the British Parliament putting a tax on printed matter—newspapers, books, pamphlets, even playing cards and legal documents. It aroused a storm in the colonies.

The British repealed the Stamp Act because of the protest, but they insisted that they had the right to pass laws regulating trade in all cases whatsoever, including [implementing] new taxes. They passed new trade regulations and new tax laws. There was further protest of a much more violent sort. They sent troops to Boston to enforce the laws—some 4,000 troops to a city of 15,000, which means they were very much of a presence.

As far as I could figure out, Hewes had not been active in the Stamp Act demonstrations. He started talking about revolution at the point where the soldiers arrived in town, reacting very much to the personal things that took place on the streets. He saw a soldier hit a woman and rob her. . . He mended shoes for a British captain, and he was not paid. When he protested, the soldier involved . . . was whipped as a punishment. Hewes was appalled that he caused this man to be whipped, but this series of personal things aroused him against the soldiers.

Then there was an event which became famous. Soldiers moonlighted— they were allowed to take off-duty jobs. One evening [in March 1770] a soldier asked for work at a wharf ropewalk. The ropewalk workers told him where he could go, with a great deal of profanity. More soldiers came in and there was a fight between the ropewalk workers and the soldiers. Both sides were furious. Soldiers were beaten and vowed revenge. They were going to get even with the townspeople. The townspeople vowed that they were not going to take any more of this sort of stuff. That was the matrix of events leading to the killings on March 5, which became known as the Boston Massacre.

Hewes said that it all began on the night of the fifth with an apprentice boy yelling at one of the soldiers for not paying his master, who was a barber, for some work in the barbershop. There was a fight over this and there was a gathering of people. It was not a large crowd at first, but the people in the crowd were angry with the soldiers for hurting the apprentice boy.

People started throwing snowballs, which were probably laced with stones. The guard was called out, some six or seven soldiers, and they formed a circle to protect the sentry. Soon there was a larger gathering of townspeople, maybe a hundred or so, in the square. The townspeople taunted the soldiers too: "Fire. Fire. Fire. We dare you. We're standing in the king's highway. We have a right to stand here." The soldiers were restrained. At some point, there was a shout of "fire" and the soldiers fired. They shot into the crowd. Four people were killed and several others were wounded.

Hewes was present. He was not armed, but he came out because he knew his townspeople were under attack. As he remembered it years later, . . . one of the men, James Caldwell, fell in his arms, wounded. Hewes remembered, sixty years later, that he took Caldwell to Dr. Thomas Young on such and such a lane, and then he went to another lane to inform Caldwell's ship captain that he had been shot. Extraordinary.

There had been protests all over the colonies about the Stamp Act . . . but the [deployment] of the soldiers was only in the colony of Massachusetts. It did not arouse the rest of the colonies as much, although they were watching. The massacre, as it was called by the patriots, did arouse large numbers of people all over, who were frightened [by this event].

THE TEA PARTY was three years later, 1773. . . . By the time of that event, the British had withdrawn many of their taxes but kept the tax on tea. They had given a monopoly of the tea trade to the British East India Company, based in London, which drove out the intermediaries, the merchants in the colonies who were importing tea on their own.

The issue raised was the same old one: "We have the right to tax ourselves. You don't have the right to tax us." But another issue was also raised: "Are you going to give special favors to British interests—as opposed to American interests?" At that point the fear was, "Where is our taxation going? What's going to be taxed next?" As Samuel Adams said in the town meeting, "Will they tax our land next? Will they tax windows on our houses?" There was a general fear of taxes, which spread through the countryside.

The colonies resolved that they didn't want the tea imported, and elsewhere the ships were turned around and didn't land. But in Boston, the tea ships . . . were all stationed at one dock, Griffin's Wharf [ready to off-load their tea]. The patriots . . . began to hold giant meetings in what was the Old South Meeting House, starting a process of negotiation to get the ships out of the port.

The leaders stationed a small militia at the dock to prevent the tea from being landed. There were meetings all day on the fifteenth and sixteenth of

December 1773. As they were conducting negotiations with the royal governor, they sent a delegation from the meeting. These meetings were attended by Hewes and by apprentices and journeymen. Normally a large town meeting in Boston would draw five hundred, six hundred, or seven hundred people because you had to have a certain amount of property to attend. However, they cut the property qualifications and said the whole body of the people could attend. In came what gentlemen would call the rabble.

THE TEA PARTY began in the Old South Meeting House, where 5,000 people were meeting. They adjourned and the people designated to conduct the Tea Party marched from the Old South Meeting House down to Griffin's Wharf.

There were three tea ships, and about thirty people were designated by the leadership to board them. I call them "the invited." There was another group who sort of invited themselves, but they knew that something was brewing and were given word to be ready. Hewes was one of those. I call them "the semi-invited." Then there was another group, even larger, who invited themselves. These were young men—apprentices and journeymen who were carried away by the excitement of the day.

The officially designated parties dressed in Indian disguise with blankets and war paint. Hewes, who came along semi-invited, stopped at a blacksmith's shop and put some soot from the hearth on his face and carried a blanket. Only a handful of those who were at the Tea Party were disguised as Indians, but it came down in history that "the Indians did this."

They disguised themselves because what they were doing was very dangerous and illegal, and they pretended to be something other than what they were. "It's not us, it's Indians from someplace else, the Mohawks, who came in to do this."

They were afraid. They didn't know what would happen. There were British naval vessels in the harbor; the British admiral was on shore, watching. The people who were doing this didn't know whether troops would be landed to suppress this action. After all, three years before, there had been troops in the Boston Massacre, so they had this tradition of troops attacking civilians.

There were maybe 2,000 people standing on the wharf watching all of this. The royal governor had decided earlier he was not going to call out the troops. He did not want another bloodbath, as they had at the Boston Massacre. But the people involved didn't know this.

They began the action at 6:00 in the evening. At 12:00 midnight the tea had to be officially landed, so they were working very fast to throw it overboard. There were 342 chests of tea, and they were very heavy. They had to be raised on winches, broken open with hatchets, and then the tea was thrown into the sea. They worked, maybe 150 people in all, in absolute silence. There was moonlight and there were some lanterns, and all you could hear that night was some muffled orders from one person to another and the plopping of the tea and the tea chests into the water.

George Hewes was on board one of the ships. He later said he was appointed a boatswain, a person who blows a whistle to give orders to the other sailors. . . . He was snatched from the ranks and given a kind of field appointment as a quasi-officer. He was very proud of this and talked about it years later.

It took several months for the news to get back to London. . . . The British were furious. The rebels had not only destroyed 342 chests worth nearly £10,000 belonging to the East India Company, but they defied the royal governor. The British Parliament brought down all of its weight on Boston. They closed the port until restitution was made for the tea. They shut down the town meetings. They remodeled the central government, paying the salaries of royal officials out of the British treasury instead of the colonial government, so they could control them.

The impact was enormous. The port was closed and Boston depended on the sea for supplies. The cry went up all through Massachusetts, and in other colonies, to come to the aid of Boston. Others sent money. Small towns sent supplies of meat and grain and other foodstuffs to take care of the people. There was a sense of rallying to the defense of Boston.

As soon as the events in Boston got going, there was a struggle between conflicting groups. The leadership, people like Samuel Adams and John Adams, wanted to keep the so-called mob under their control. They wanted people to demonstrate under their leadership. They were very nervous about people demonstrating against the British on their own.

For example, tarring and feathering was usually carried out against customs officials or customs informers, and it was usually carried out by crowds heavily composed of sailors and people around the docks. This was not approved of by the leadership. [In fact] the leadership came out and tried to rescue the man who was being tarred and feathered by saying, "Leave him to the courts."

The motto of the leadership in the decade before the Revolution was, "No violence or you'll hurt the cause." "No mobs, no tumults"—that was their phrase. So they tried to control the activity. They didn't control it at the time of the Boston Massacre. That was a chaotic event, which nobody wanted to take place and was not orchestrated by the leadership. And, as soon as the killing took place, the leadership rushed out to assume command of the protest and to meet with the royal governor.

The same thing was going on as they reported the events. Paul Revere's engraving of the massacre was in tune with the way the leadership wanted people to see it, that is, the British shooting down a group of hapless civilians who were completely passive. The truth is that the civilians were quite aggressive against the soldiers.

From the beginning, there was a struggle to control what I call the memory of the Revolution. The leadership was very concerned with what people would think about Boston, which had a reputation as a mobbish town, and deserved it. But the leadership was trying to present the town as being respectable and having legitimate protest. . . . So they were able to control the Tea Party. That was the beginning of an effort to control the knowledge of what took place in the Revolution.

After the Revolution, that process continued of trying to control the knowledge of what happened. Conservatives in the 1790s, who would be called Federalists, were very uneasy with this tradition of the Revolution, which stressed popular activity.

The conservatives in Boston, for the longest time, didn't want to read the Declaration of Independence. They didn't read it at the Fourth of July celebrations. It was very anti-British, and the conservative Federalists were sort of sympathetic to the British. Secondly, the Declaration talked about all men being created equal, and about the right of revolution. In the 1790s, conservatives were very frightened of the French Revolution. They wanted to play down what we would call the popular, or radical, side of the Revolution.

In the course of that, they celebrated the Fourth of July, but they didn't celebrate the Tea Party; they didn't celebrate the Stamp Act demonstrations; and they certainly didn't celebrate the Boston Massacre. As we moved into the nineteenth century, the descendants of the leadership, people like Harrison Gray Otis and Josiah Quincy, after whom the market in Boston is named, presented a version of the Revolution that erased the Tea Party and the Boston Massacre; they erased the mob side of the Revolution.

[The Marquis de] Lafayette helped revive this hidden history of the Revolution. Lafayette came to Boston to dedicate the Bunker Hill Monument; that was the beginning of the movement. They began to celebrate, in the 1820s, fiftieth anniversaries. [The year] 1825 was the fiftieth anniversary of Lexington and Concord, the fiftieth anniversary of the Battle of Bunker Hill, then in '26, the fiftieth anniversary of the Declaration. These were called jubilees.

In the course of celebrating the jubilees, they wanted to bring out the old soldiers who still survived. At the dedication of the Bunker Hill Monument, they found dozens and dozens of old soldiers like Hewes who became guests of honor for the day. I think that was the beginning of the rediscovery of the men who fought the Revolution.

Declaring Independence

by

PAULINE MAIER

From September 5 to October 26, 1774, a group of delegates from every colony except Georgia met in Philadelphia in response to the British imposition of the Intolerable Acts on the colonists. Although declaring independence from Britain was not the purpose of their meeting—sympathies ranged from loyalist to rebel—they nonetheless passed ten resolutions enumerating the rights of the colonists, and they agreed to convene again if their grievances had not been satisfactorily addressed by the British. They met again in May 1775, and in June they appointed George Washington commander of the new Continental Army. On July 4, 1776, Congress issued the Declaration of Independence, a document signed by fifty-six men from all thirteen colonies. Pauline Maier, a professor at MIT, appeared on Booknotes *on July 1, 1997, to talk about* American Scripture: Making the Declaration of Independence, *published in 1997 by Alfred A. Knopf.*

KING GEORGE III was probably an insecure man; not the smartest man who ever walked on the face of the earth; a man who was probably somewhat bewildered by the rash of constitutional arguments that the Americans were putting forward. He was certainly deeply dedicated to his country and to his traditions. He was the third of the Hanoverian kings. His father had died. His grandfather still spoke with a deep German accent. [George III] spoke English well and was raised in England. He was a dedicated Englishman and stood for the rights of Parliament.

He thought that the welfare of Great Britain turned on its continuing hold on the American colonies. The colonies had become a major purchaser of British goods. That was clear. They had surpassed the West Indies, who were always the preferred colonies earlier on. But the Americans had come to import far more British goods. He thought, and this was his greatest nightmare, "If we lose the American colonies, we shall sink back into obscurity and be just a small, insignificant island once again." So he wanted to be severe in making sure that didn't happen.

[IN 1775 THERE WERE] probably about two and a half million people in America, small by today's standards, of course. There were thirteen colonies who were uniting for independence. The government was in a state of disarray. Some of these colonies still had their colonial governments in place, but not very many. In one colony after another, revolutionary governments had taken the place of the official crowned government. They normally took the form of an elected legislature, which wasn't called a legislature if it was extralegal; it would be a "convention" or a "congress." These bodies of elected delegates (and, if you will, of the people) were the operational government in most colonies.

A couple [of colonies] still had the old legal governments. Connecticut and Rhode Island were ever [loyal]—all their officials were always elected; they retained their traditional government. The royal governor remained a long time in Maryland and other places, so it was a kind of mishmash. But all of these colonies were sending delegations to the Continental Congress. The Second Continental Congress, which convened right after [the battle of] Lexington and Concord on May 10, 1775, was a jerry-built institution.

[The Second Continental Congress] met in Philadelphia. It wasn't meant to be a government [but] it soon became the first government of the United States. The delegates who were elected probably thought they were going to be like the members of the First Continental Congress—just coming together to discuss the situation, to see what could be done, to make some grand policy statements. They probably expected they'd be able to go home in under two months, as the delegates to the First Congress were. But the situation was entirely changed as result of Lexington and Concord.

April 19, 1775, is the conventional date for the beginning of the Revolutionary War. [After colonists and British soldiers fought at Lexington and Concord, Massachusetts] the Congress found itself the government of, for all practical purposes, a nation at war. Very soon they had to make decisions for the military and for Indian affairs. One topic after another fell on their agenda and they became the government of a country-to-be.

AS I CAME TO THE TOPIC of the Declaration, [I felt] it had been so glorified; was there some way we could get it down to earth? I thought that comparisons were always very useful, so I started poking around to see what I could find. I started coming across these state and local [documents]—what I call now the other declarations of independence—statements written by people in town meetings in Massachusetts or county meetings in Maryland or Virginia.

The ordinary people in these local events—men, of course, because politics was confined to men at this point—would meet and they would discuss the issues. They drew up documents that affirmed their support of independence and told their representatives in their state legislatures to support it, to try to get the instructions sent to the delegates to Congress changed so that they could vote for independence. They not only stated their views, they explained them. They were, in some cases, very moving and very eloquent documents.

One [such local document] really sticks in my mind, maybe because I had heard of the town, and it was one of the first I encountered. It was from Ashby, Massachusetts, which is north central Massachusetts, not a major town then. Mostly, they paraphrased the question that was submitted to them by the general court, but they said, "If Congress decides to vote for independence, then we, the inhabitants of Ashby, will most solemnly defend that decision with our lives and fortunes." It was very moving. These were farmers, in the boondocks by our standards, who had utter confidence that their opinion made a difference in the course of human affairs. And it was expressed with a simple eloquence that I found very moving.

I needed to figure out how these documents fit into the story. They were important because this government of the United States called the Second Continental Congress didn't have a written constitution. . . . They couldn't do anything that a majority of delegates were not authorized to do. So the real fight over independence was over getting proper instructions that would allow the delegates to vote for it.

Why did independence happen? I think a lot of accounts have a magic bullet simplification. . . . There was one man, Thomas Paine, who made an important contribution. . . . He published *Common Sense* in January 1776, and it opened a public debate over the issue [of independence]. Silence had reigned. People were hesitant to face up to it, although the events were going in that direction. It was published right after news of [a speech] the king [made] to Parliament in October 1775, where George III said, "These Americans, whatever they say, they're trying to be independent."

Somebody in Congress stood up and said, "We should disavow that," and the others said, "Wait a minute, let's just think this through." They'd also heard that, as the report went, the king's navy had burned Norfolk, Virginia. How long were they going to go on saying, "We don't really want independence" as the king piled one atrocity on the other? *Common Sense* was published at a point where the information arriving in America was starting to make the Congress think, "You know, maybe independence is where we're going."

Common Sense sold. It was offered at a low price. It had a kind of a language that common people could relate to, so it was enormously popular. There's no doubt in my mind that Paine helped change popular sentiment in favor of independence. What I found very interesting was that when these local people started explaining why they came to support independence, they came to Paine's conclusion but they didn't use his argument.

CONGRESS HAD THEIR debates in June. Robert R. Livingston of New York argued against independence while John Adams and Richard Henry Lee and George Wythe carried the burden of arguing in favor.

This was, remember, an age of oratory. Thomas Jefferson was well-known for being a very poor public speaker. John Adams said Jefferson rarely spoke more than three sentences together in public. His talents were in writing. The Congress, in a very interesting way, had a writers corps, people whom it could call upon to write its public pronouncements. John Dickinson of Pennsylvania was one of the favored writers and probably the most popular because he had written a set of essays (in 1767–1768) that had been widely copied in the newspapers, which, of course, were the television of the time, the public medium.

People thought John Dickinson spoke their thoughts and spoke them well, so he was very well-known. He used to write documents quickly and was senior to Jefferson, who, when he first came into Congress, was a rather young, unknown person, but whose talents for writing were known nonetheless. The Congress quickly grabbed onto [Jefferson to draft the Declaration].

[There's a debate about how much Jefferson relied on the arguments of John Locke for his draft.] Locke was a seventeenth-century Englishman who wrote the *Second Treatise of Government,* which, in a sense, defined principles widely shared by other Englishmen at the time, on the basis of the beginnings of government. He said that government is a human creation; it isn't based simply on the will of God. Rulers are the trustees of the people. If they violate the terms of that compact, the people have a right to overturn the government and found another.

This is the basic philosophy that came out in the Declaration of Independence. That doesn't mean that Jefferson cribbed it, however. What I've learned is that those ideas were known virtually everywhere. He could get them directly from Locke. He could get them filtered from a large number of other places. These were ideas that Americans encountered in the press and in sermons. Therefore, the lines that are most familiar to us didn't seem particularly noteworthy in the eighteenth century. Hardly anyone paid attention to them.

CONGRESS ADOPTED independence on July 2, 1776. It issued the Declaration on the fourth. After New York came in, the Congress then said, "It is now a unanimous declaration of the United States of America" and ordered the document put on parchment. It was only after it was on parchment and brought back to Congress on August 2 that they formally signed the document. . . . Congress didn't actually circulate a copy of the document with signatures until January 1777. Why? Well, this was a confession of treason. You were putting your head in the noose. And the war was going very, very poorly in 1776. Think of Washington losing on Long Island, retreating up Manhattan, retreating down the Jersey coast, crossing the Delaware. It looked real bad till the end of the year, until Trenton and Princeton. Only after Trenton and Princeton made it possible to believe that the Americans might win this war, only then did they circulate the document with their signatures.

AMERICANS ARE FOND of saying that these American revolutionaries were really a different order of men; that they were different than we are. John Adams was very anxious to say that was not true. He became upset at what he called the canonization of men like Washington . . . . He thought that it was important to grant esteem and fame to those who had contributed in an important way to the founding of their country. But he found the religious imagery unrealistic and discouraging to younger Americans who thought that they were, therefore, inferior to the founding fathers.

John Adams went to great lengths to tell younger Americans that his generation was no better than theirs; that, in fact, there was more talent in the country in 1820 than there was in 1776. "There weren't very many talented people around in 1776," he said, "which made it very easy to realize your ambition." There was a kind of healthy antidote to many of our modern mythologizing tendencies in the wisdom of John Adams.

We do ourselves a disservice by doing more than granting proper attribution to the founders for beginning a system. They were ordinary men who lived in extraordinary times and certainly made memorable contributions. We are right to regard what they did with a great amount of respect. Jefferson's draftsmanship, within the limits given him by the committee, was brilliant. But we should understand it in the context of the times and shouldn't overemphasize it, because it lets us off the hook. It says they did it all. We are responsible for maintaining the tradition.

Creating the Constitution

by

JACK N. RAKOVE

While Thomas Jefferson was putting the finishing touches on the Declaration of Independence, a committee headed by John Dickinson began meeting to draft the Articles of Confederation, a document needed to clarify the form and nature of this new government. Due to the Revolutionary War and many disagreements between the states, the Articles were not ratified until 1781. The war ended two years later in 1783. In order to amend the inadequate Articles, the Constitutional Convention convened in May 1787. At the convention, the Articles were abandoned and a new Constitution was written. The last of the original thirteen states to ratify the Constitution of the United States of America was Rhode Island in 1790. Ten amendments were ratified on December 15, 1791, and became known as the Bill of Rights. Eight of the fifty-five delegates attending the Constitutional Convention had previously signed the Declaration of Independence. Stanford professor Jack N. Rakove visited Booknotes *on May 28, 1997, and told us more about the creation of the Constitution. Mr. Rakove's book,* Original Meanings: Politics and Ideas in the Making of the Constitution, *was published in 1996 by Alfred A. Knopf.*

THE CONSTITUTIONAL CONVENTION met in Independence Hall, which was also the Pennsylvania State House where the Pennsylvania Assembly met. The convention sat there from May to September 1787, and toward the end of that period the Pennsylvania Assembly, the state legislature for Pennsylvania, was also due to meet.

There were fifty-five delegates attending, at one time or another, over the course of the convention, . . . thirty-nine of whom signed the document.

Some others left before the convention was quite done. Two of the New Yorkers, later Anti-Federalists, left: Robert Yates and John Lansing. Luther Martin, another Anti-Federalist, left. Some other delegates went back and forth for personal reasons. George Wythe from Virginia, who had been Jefferson's mentor as a law student back at William and Mary, left early because his wife was ill.

Others occasionally took leaves of absence, such as Alexander Hamilton and Gouverneur Morris, but came back. About fifteen or so were the really active speakers, and the others were either sitting on their hands or couldn't quite muster the temerity to actually say something. . . . Once the convention mustered a quorum—it took the better part of a fortnight after the appointed time—then it met in pretty regular sessions.

JAMES MADISON was the most important of the framers because of the crucial role he played at each of the major points in the process: calling the convention, framing the Constitution, ratifying it, deciding whether it made sense to add a bill of rights to it, and seeing what it meant in practice. He is also the most important point of entry for modern commentaries on the Constitution. To an extraordinary extent we rely on Madison for our basic insights into the original theories and ambitions of the Constitution.

Madison, with some misgivings, was one of the handful of crucial actors who decided it was necessary, although dangerous, to have a constitutional convention in the full, complete, ambitious sense of the term. In the 1780s, there had been a strategy for trying to reform the Articles of Confederation, . . . a very piecemeal process in which the Congress would propose individual amendments to all the states, which would have to agree unanimously.

Of course, that process always came a cropper because you could never surmount the unanimity hurdle. At some point, Madison and a handful of like-minded people decided, even though they thought the political odds were against them, to go for broke and risk having a general constitutional convention in the hope that having a fresh agenda would somehow free up the logjam of constitutional reform. That was step number one.

Step number two was Madison going into the convention having prepared himself in a very characteristic way—very carefully and very deeply. He read deeply and thought even more deeply about the fundamental problems of both the Articles of Confederation and the state constitutions and also, to some extent, the lessons of history. On that basis, and on the basis of his own experience as a legislator both in the Continental Congress and in Virginia, Madison understood the importance of trying to frame, if not control, the agenda.

There was a Virginia Plan partly because the other delegates hadn't shown up and the Virginians and the Pennsylvanians were sitting around in Philadelphia waiting for the other delegations to appear. They might as well do something, so they framed the Virginia Plan. In one sense, there was a kind of accidental quality to this. But at a deeper level, to get the deliberations going, Madison was really well aware of the importance of having some set of proposals prepackaged, to which others would have to react.

A number of the delegates going into the deliberations probably would have expected that the convention's business would have been confined to proposing some additional set of powers that could be safely vested in the existing unicameral Continental Congress. . . . However, anybody reading the Virginia Plan or hearing it read as it was first announced by Edmund Randolph, the governor of Virginia, would understand that it was, in effect, calling for an abandonment to the existing structure of the Confederation.

Madison's proposals (or Madison's scheme), as embodied in the Virginia Plan, basically called for creating a fully articulated national government. He called for a national government with three independent, constitutionally established branches with the authority to legislate, to execute, to adjudicate its own laws and therefore not rely on the states, as Congress had to do under the Articles of Confederation. That was about as fundamental, or as wrenching, a transposition as one could have imagined. It's clear that what the Virginians were proposing, what Madison was actively advancing, was not simply tinkering with or amending or strengthening the Articles of Confederation. They wanted . . . a freshly conceived government with powers that would go far beyond what the Continental Congress had ever been able to exercise.

The Continental Congress was headquartered in Philadelphia for most of the Revolution, but then it occasionally had to go on holiday to Baltimore and New York when the British got too close. In 1783 there was an ugly incident with the Pennsylvania militia, as soldiers complained about not being paid their wages. Congress took umbrage with this and went off to Princeton, which was too small, in the summer of 1783, later followed by Annapolis. It reconvened in Trenton late in 1784, didn't like it, then went on to New York. It stayed in New York through the first session of the new Congress in 1789.

The Constitutional Convention wanted the Congress to give an imprimatur—its of seal of approval—to the Constitution without tampering with it. They hoped it would then send it on to the state legislatures, which in turn would call the state ratification conventions, which would represent the sovereign people, whose approval would make the Constitution supreme law.

There were thirteen states in the union; fourteen if you wanted to call Vermont a state. Vermont was actually kind of an independent republic through much of this period. Some of the states were on the verge of break-ing up. Virginia was certainly getting ready to slough off Kentucky as an independent state.

Vermont was not part of the union, so they didn't have any delegates to the convention. The other state not represented was Rhode Island. Through-out the 1780s, Rhode Island had pursued what was sometimes characterized as an antifederal, antiunionist policy. Rhode Island had always been known as kind of an outlier. It was sometimes described as the home of Jews, Turks, and infidels because of its history of religious toleration. It was a quintessen-tial dissenting community. Rhode Island had been antifederal all along and didn't bother to send a delegation to Philadelphia. That actually had impor-tant implications for how the framers thought about the process of ratifica-tion.

Virginia was the most populous state, Pennsylvania was second, and Mas-sachusetts was third. The delegations varied in size, but that didn't really mat-ter because at an early point, after only a little discussion, the Virginians and the Pennsylvanians, while waiting for the other delegations to show up, dis-cussed what the rules of voting should be in the convention.

In the Continental Congress, the rule was one state, one vote, regardless of population. Madison, the Virginians, and the Pennsylvanians were intent on changing that rule of voting in Congress—in both houses of the new legisla-ture they wanted to create. The question arose, Would they also want to make the same demand for the convention itself? Would they want to have some scheme of proportional voting?

The Pennsylvanians said, "Let's force this issue at the start." Madison and the Virginians said, "No, it's better if we preserve the existing rule and try to convince the small states to give up their equal vote as we go along." So it was one state and one vote.

Some of the most important aspects of the Constitution were decided by very narrow margins. The one that I try to emphasize in my book—because in some ways I still find it offensive today—is what's known as the Great Compromise, occasionally misnamed the Connecticut Compromise. It gave each state an equal vote in the Senate and thereby preserved, at least to some extent, that rule of voting from the Continental Congress.

That was the principal issue that perplexed the convention from almost the first week of deliberations down to July 16, the day the so-called compro-mise was approved. It was approved by the narrowest of margins, five states to four, with one divided. Massachusetts, which was a large state and had always voted with the large states against equal-state representation in the upper house as well as the lower house, was divided. Elbridge Gerry and Caleb Strong decided, on the basis of compromise, to side with the small states; therefore, Massachusetts lost its vote. Or in this case, it meant you had a majority, five to four, with one divided to carry the so-called Great Compromise. It was about the narrowest victory possible.

There were a couple of other issues. [One] of Madison's pet proposals was to give Congress a negative on all state laws, which certainly would have made a major difference in the convention. That . . . proposal . . . was originally approved, then rejected after the Great Compromise, and then brought back fairly late in the convention. At that point there was a vote to commit. They sent it to committee, not to bury it but to refine it and bring it back. That one lost four to three, with two states divided.

Probably the most interesting [delegate] to speculate about is James Wilson, who was a very powerful legal mind, a Philadelphian, a Scottish immigrant, a lawyer who later served on the first Supreme Court. He was very much an elitist in his politics, especially in Pennsylvania, which had very sharp political divisions throughout this period; but he was also in his theory extremely democratic. In fact, he was probably the framer who was most consistently democratic in his thinking, [from] the first principles of popular sovereignty [to] consistently arguing for popular election of all the major political branches—not just the lower house, the House of Representatives, but the Senate, and probably the presidency as well.

GEORGE MASON was a fascinating guy. . . . Mason was a neighbor of George Washington's and was an old political ally and friend. He had a very powerful mind and was a person deeply faithful to the whole radical Whig tradition of Anglo-American political theory. They were the kind of people who would take really strong positions against the Stuart kings of the seventeenth century and tried to keep that heritage alive in the eighteenth century. Mason was a guy who didn't really like politics all that much.

He had a large family. He had nine kids and worried a lot about providing for them, so it was sometimes hard to get Mason to show up at the Assembly. But when he was there, he was always a force to be reckoned with. He was well-known in Virginia, and elsewhere, as the principal author of the Virginia Declaration of Rights, probably the most influential of the bills of rights that the Americans attached to their first constitutions—the constitutions of the separate states framed at the time of independence.

At the convention Mason played a very active role, and in many ways, a very productive role. He was certainly not a carping dissenter. But toward the end of the convention, he got very disillusioned about a number of particular points. He was most concerned about the initial minority position of the South, and he also professed to be somewhat disturbed about the composition of the Senate, whether it was going to be elected by the state legislatures.

Mason was one of the first to start speculating that the Senate was really going to be too aristocratic a body, more aristocratic than you would really want it to be, and that it might be able to consolidate power. There was a lot of speculation in 1787 and 1788, and I think Mason was a source of a fair amount of it, that the real locus of power in the new government would not be the presidency or the House of Representatives, but the Senate.

The Senate is the one branch of government that seemed to have all three forms of power. It had the authority to legislate, it shared executive powers with the president in treaty power and the power to make appointment, and it had judicial power as the court of impeachment. There was this image that the Senate was going to be the real locus of decision making. It was going to be too far insulated, too far removed from the real political life of the nation, too aristocratic, too potentially oligarchic in its character. Mason got a bee in his bonnet on these issues and he threw in the absence of a bill of rights as another legitimating point for his opposition. He was the most formidable of the three nonsigners.

"ANTI-FEDERALIST" is the conventional name given at the time and since to the opponents of the Constitution, . . . those who opposed its ratification or at least felt that its ratification should be hedged about by significant amendments at a very early, if not immediate, point. [Well-known Anti-Federalists were] George Mason and Elbridge Gerry, who was the nonsigner from Massachusetts. Luther Martin, who had been behind Madison at Princeton, was one of the delegates who left early, a kind of a militant states' righter of the first order, a very important politician in Maryland. George Clinton, the governor of New York, and Patrick Henry in Virginia were probably two of the most successful politicians in terms of having big popular followings. Richard Henry Lee in Virginia [was another Anti-Federalist]. Edmund Randolph . . . wound up being a Federalist—Randolph was a trimmer; he went back and forth and wound up finally supporting the Constitution.

ONE OF THE DEEP arguments in my book is that there is a fundamental element of Madison's thinking, particularly about the problems of rights, which provides a very powerful connection between the eighteenth and twentieth centuries. Madison's whole theory of rights circa 1787, 1788 was, "How do you protect rights? Where does the danger to rights lie in a republic?" He argued, with good reason, that the chief danger to rights would not come from a national government that was too powerful, as a lot of Anti-Federalists would have said. Instead, it would come from the processes of democratic politics as they would continue to operate within the states.

The real problem of protecting rights in the federal union would be to enable the national government to intervene within the individual states to protect individuals and minorities—that's Madison's language—against the "viceful" legislation he thought would be produced periodically at the state level. That is why Madison wanted to give the national government an unlimited veto over all state laws, in part so it could protect itself from the interference of the states, but also so the national government could intervene within the states in the name of protecting rights.

Depending on how you count, there were eighty-four or eighty-five [*Federalist Papers*]. They were originally published in the *New York Journal,* a thrice-weekly paper in New York. They were substantially reprinted in other papers across the country. Then the first bound edition, the so-called McLean edition, came out in the spring of 1788. It included the papers on the judiciary, which Hamilton wrote, and the famous Federalist 78, a statement of the theory of judicial review, which, I think, had not yet appeared in the newspapers.

There is a lot of debate about [the impact of *The Federalist Papers* on ratification]. One would want to be cautious about ascribing too much importance to them. They are especially valuable to us because they are the single most detailed, comprehensive, and, I would argue, lucid expositions of the Constitution we have. The fact that they're principally authored by Madison and Hamilton give them all that much more impact. But the flip side of that is precisely because there are so many essays and the series runs for so long— the arguments are, in some cases, so finely spun and so deep and rich—that I'm actually somewhat skeptical about the kind of impact they would have had at the time on ordinary readers and citizens.

I think the one statement that mattered most to ratification was a famous, much publicized public speech by James Wilson. The Pennsylvania delegate, the elitist democrat, if you will, gave a public speech right outside the Independence Hall, the Pennsylvania State House, on October 6, 1787. He made a number of very strong statements, including why there was no need for a bill of rights in the Constitution, why a bill of rights would have been superfluous and pointless. Wilson was identified as a framer, as not hiding behind a pseudonym. He was speaking in public and his speech was regarded as an authoritative early statement. Anti-Federalists started jumping all over it within a matter of days. If you had to pull one document out of the whole ratification campaign that had the greatest impact at the time, I think that's probably the one document. It's not Federalist 10 and it's not Federalist 51, the classic numbers everybody reads in college or sometimes even in high school; it's probably Wilson's public speech of October 6 that mattered most.

I WROTE THE BOOK largely not just to explain how the Constitution was adopted, which we already knew, but rather to explain why the kinds of appeals to the original intent or meaning of the Constitution are so difficult and so problematic. And yet, since they are so important, I wanted to work out a way of answering those questions that would allow us to come up with the best story we could provide of how the Constitution was framed—and also, what are its limits.

The Federalist Papers

by

ROBERT SCIGLIANO

Massachusetts, New York, Pennsylvania, and Virginia were critical to the passage or failure of the Constitution. New York was, perhaps, the most troublesome delegation of all. The New York delegation did not approve the draft at the Constitutional Convention in Philadelphia. Two out of the three delegates left in protest, which meant that Alexander Hamilton, the third New York delegate, could not cast the state's vote. A series of articles, collected as The Federalist, *or often called the Federalist Papers, were drafted by Hamilton, James Madison, and John Jay to help answer concerns about the Constitution and win the battle of public opinion in New York, which became the eleventh state to ratify the Constitution on July 26, 1788. On January 21, 2001, Robert Scigliano appeared on* Booknotes *to discuss a new edition of* The Federalist, *published in 2000 by Modern Library. Mr. Scigliano is a political science professor at Boston College.*

THE FEDERALIST is a collection of newspaper articles written during the ratification campaign for the Constitution in 1787 and the first part of 1788. The essays were put together in two bound volumes, and they were used during the ratification campaign in New York. They were published in the New York newspapers, and then they were sent down to Virginia to be of use in the Virginia ratification campaign. They had an extensive influence. . . . They provided arguments to the delegates supporting ratification [but they] also stated arguments that had to be met by the opponents to the Constitution. So they were part of a large dialogue being carried out in these two states, and also elsewhere, because they were reproduced in newspapers in other states at the same time.

Alexander Hamilton, . . . James Madison, and . . . John Jay [wrote them]. I name them in descending order of the number of articles that each wrote. Hamilton organized the project. He saw that the Constitution, when it came out of convention, was going to have tough sledding in New York, and the Anti-Federalists, those opposed to ratification, were already publishing in the newspapers. So he decided to organize a series of articles. He recruited his friend John Jay, and then he tried to get another friend of his, Gouverneur Morris—an interesting person, not known to Americans, even to many students of American politics, today. Morris declined the invitation. Then he went to James Madison, and Madison agreed, so the three of them formed a collaboration. They assigned the numbers more or less according to their interests and also to the time that they had available.

Madison was thirty-six years old when he began them. Depending on whose records you accept, Hamilton was probably thirty and Jay was forty-one. They were young men. The Constitutional Convention finished on September 17, 1787. Because they agreed to comply with the terms of the old Constitution, the Articles of Confederation, the Constitution was submitted to Congress with the request that Congress submit it to the states, with the request that the states call conventions of the people to consider it for ratification. That was done and sent out to the states toward the end of September.

Hamilton and Jay were on rather close terms. They were fellow New Yorkers, they were allies in New York politics, and their thinking was very close. Hamilton and Madison cooperated under the Articles of Confederation and the Continental Congress on various projects. They got together to propose a constitutional convention at the Annapolis meeting a year prior, but they were not close [then]. They got close for a period of time during the writing of *The Federalist*. I went back through their letters to see what their salutations and their closings were. As the collaboration proceeded, they dropped the formal closings, "your obedient servant," to "yours truly," and then "affectionately yours" and then simply "affectionately." So there is a period of time when they felt the closeness through their collaboration. That's before they pulled apart.

THE FIRST FEDERALIST paper was written probably in the early part of October. Hamilton had to go up to Albany to conduct court. He was a lawyer and made his living from the law then. According to a report, he wrote the first paper on his way down the Hudson River on a schooner. Whether that is true or not, we don't know, but it makes a nice story. It began then, and the last group of papers was actually published in a volume before they appeared in the newspapers. The last eight papers, published [in pamphlet form] at the end of May, were then printed in the newspapers going into July.

There were generally two or three Federalist papers a week published in the newspapers. [Later] Hamilton was trying to bring the thing to an end because the New York ratifying convention had already been elected by the people of New York, and it was due to begin its deliberations in a couple of weeks. So you find the papers lengthening at this time.

[Each paper was signed "Publius" because] it was common practice then not to use one's own name. My own belief is that writing for the newspapers was not quite proper; only later did political people sign their name. "Publius" itself was chosen because he was the defender of the Roman republic, the one who helped establish the republic. That was done for a political reason because there were charges by the Anti-Federalists that the Constitution was aristocratic or a maniacal document. Hamilton said, "No, Publius the author is the defender of a republic."

[They were not paid to write these articles, and the newspapers in which they appeared were] not necessarily [committed to the ratification of the proposed Constitution]. One of the newspapers stopped reprinting them because about twenty-seven of its subscribers wrote and said, "Why are you wasting all this time on that stuff?" [They were] probably afraid of losing their subscribers. There was one newspaper that switched the articles around and put them in a more logical position, and one article was cut in two because of its length. But other than that, the articles appeared in their chronological form.

Hamilton collected them and published them in book form. Both the newspapers and the original book had a number of minor errors in them. It was a rush job. In 1802 Hamilton supervised a new edition of *The Federalist* and that new edition provided [several] very small changes and corrections in the total number [of essays he had written]. In 1818 Madison provided additional changes for the numbers that he said that he had written.

These revisions improved the text in a number of very small ways, word selection, maybe a dropping of a word. For example, in Federalist 34, it always didn't quite seem right to me that Hamilton should say that under the republic, Rome reached the height of utmost perfection. There's an overstatement there. But in going through the revisions, I found that Hamilton's final determination was that under the republic, Rome reached the height of perfection.

VARIOUS ANTI-FEDERALISTS [wrote articles answering each Federalist Paper]. The two most prominent of the opponents—at least the ones that come to my mind—were the "Federal Farmer" and "Cato." In fact, "Cato" started writing before "Publius" got into the fray. There's some dispute as to whether "Cato" was Governor George Clinton of New York. It was thought that the "Federal Farmer" was one of the Lees of Virginia.

The Anti-Federalists claimed that they were the real Federalists. "We're the ones standing by the Articles of Confederation, our federal Constitution, and you have stolen the name 'Federalist' from us." There's some truth in that, and yet the Federalists' argument was that they had been in favor of strengthening the Articles of Confederation, getting a stronger federal government, and therefore they were the real Federalists. Hamilton also had a special definition of a Federalist, a person who could support a consolidated, unitary national government, so long as the states existed in some subordinate role within it. His was a special definition of federalism.

[THERE IS A GREAT dispute as to who wrote which articles] because the articles were written anonymously at the time. There was an agreement between the two main authors, Hamilton and Madison, that they would not disclose which one of them wrote which articles without the consent of the other. So far as I know, this consent was never sought by either one, nor given. . . . Their drafts never survived, and that would have helped us. If we could have had recourse to their drafts, we could have seen for sure which of them wrote which articles. Jay kept copies of his drafts, and so there was never any dispute as to which numbers Jay wrote. Jay's drafts are at the Columbia University archives.

I try [to differentiate between the writing of Madison and Hamilton]. You can't have too much confidence when friends of theirs had trouble determining who wrote which ones. Even though George Washington knew Hamilton well, because Hamilton had been his aide-de-camp, Washington wrote [a friend] asking, "Can you tell me who the authors of the individual numbers are?" Down in Williamsburg, Virginia, people said, "We know James Madison, he's really the author of these." Thomas Jefferson, who knew Madison well, said, "I know you wrote most of them."

That being said, I have certain indications of writing. Madison wrote in more detail, perhaps more digression. He made sure that the point was completely made and understood. Where Hamilton tended to be more direct, Madison was more theoretical. Madison more often started with a theoretical statement and then worked his way down to the practical situation. Federalist 10 is a fine example of that. Hamilton started with the problem. He may have generalized the problem, but he generally started with the particular.

Hamilton put more stress on ambition as a human motive than Madison. They both talked about ambition as well as interest. I drew a conclusion from this, [which] is for Madison, the human problem—that is, living at peace—was more within reach of solution if you could satisfy all interests. For Hamilton, the human problem was insoluble because you may have plenty, but there would be resentments, there would be ambitions and passions. He himself had kind of a noble ambition but still a lot of ambition.

THE FEDERALIST was written in late-eighteenth-century prose, which is quite different from our prose. They did not write down to their audience. My students like Number 1. It's the kickoff to the rest [in which they find some] interesting things. Certainly [they like] Number 10, Madison's famous argument [on factions]. Number 15 is interesting because it ends up with the nucleus of the Monroe Doctrine—that we could become the mistress in the New World. [They also study] the ones on separation of power, and checks and balances, 47 through 51; 62 and 63 on the Senate and why you need a Senate as a restraint on the House of Representatives. You learn a lot about the House in reading about the Senate. Then [there is] the great argument of Hamilton's on executive energy, Number 70, and the difficult but rewarding essay, Federalist 78, on the role of the judiciary and judicial review.

[THERE ARE MANY references in *The Federalist* to the government of Great Britain.] It was natural to make comparisons with Great Britain because the comparisons were meaningful to the people. Also, comparisons could be made to the favor of the Constitution. Federalist 69 compares the powers of the proposed American executive with the powers of the British king. It shows that the British [monarchy] was hereditary, [whereas] this office would be elected for four years. The British king could make treaties by himself; this office must make treaties with the consent of the Senate, and so on down the line. So it made a nice basis for a counterargument. Great Britain had been the enemy and was still unpopular in the minds of a number of people. That did not contribute to Hamilton's popularity because Hamilton was a great admirer of the British constitution. He said it was the best constitution that the world had seen.

ACCORDING TO MADISON, we are a republic because we rule through representatives. That, incidentally, for me is an indication that if we didn't know for other reasons that Madison wrote Federalist Number 10, we would know that Number 10 was his, since Hamilton did not accept that distinction between a democracy and a republic. For Madison, a democracy was direct rule by the people as in the Athenian assembly, and a republic was indirect rule, through a congress. In a New York convention, Hamilton called the Constitution a "representative democracy." Hamilton did not think that representation changed the character of popular rule very much, whereas Madison thought it changed it, perhaps in a decisive way. Therefore, for Hamilton, other means were needed to temper the wayward passions of democracy.

I think of Hamilton on one side and Thomas Jefferson on the other. Their positions were more clear-cut, boldly edged, whereas Madison wove a moderate position in between. There's a clear understanding of the need for executive power in Hamilton, clearer than Madison had, that this society could only be held together by an energetic government and that meant an energetic executive. Hamilton spelled that out in Federalist Numbers 70 through 74. [Hamilton believed in] the need for some flexibility in the powers of government. Hamilton was not a strict constructionist, as Jefferson was. Madison wove a position somewhere in between—the need for a national bank to consolidate the state debts and make them a national debt.

The writers of *The Federalist* believed that [financial] interest was an important motive of human contact. It had to be taken into account, it had to be restrained. Ambition and interest were the two great engines of human conduct for the famous, so they were sensitive [to that].

There is a certain hardheadedness in *The Federalist* with regard to human moral motives. The passage from Number 51, which says that "if angels were to govern men, neither external, nor internal controls on government would be necessary," indicates that. Hamilton, to make the point even more strongly, to hit the reader, said one must remember that "men are ambitious, vindictive, and rapacious."

One of Ronald Reagan's pet phrases [would] resonate with the framers: "Trust but verify." That idea appears in *The Federalist*. . . . There is virtue in human nature; we take that into account. But we can't put our full reliance on virtue. Virtue must be armed. It must be supported by providing for self-interest. For example, if you want the president to do his job against Congress and not just say the heck with it, you have to give him a motive for facing up to Congress. Give him a long enough term of office so that he'll be willing to defend his turf. Give him a six-year term, as some of the state governors did, he won't be concerned with braving it against Congress.

So much of *The Federalist* still is relevant today. They make their arguments with a clarity and with a profundity that you do not often encounter in political debates today. That's why thoughtful politicians will go back to *The Federalist* and other founding documents. For example, there was a great controversy over the extent of the president's power in foreign affairs and regarding the use of the armed forces, especially in the late 1960s and the 1970s. The best opposing arguments were made by Hamilton and Madison. So you learn something from reading their arguments. They were thoughtful.

Thomas Jefferson and Sally Hemings

by

ANNETTE GORDON-REED

Thomas Jefferson inherited 135 slaves when his wife's father died in 1772. One of them was Sally Hemings, the half sister of his wife, Martha. In 1802 James Callender, a political journalist, linked Thomas Jefferson and Sally Hemings in an article printed in a Richmond, Virginia, newspaper, suggesting that the two had an intimate physical relationship. Since then, their relationship has been the subject of much debate among Jefferson scholars. Annette Gordon-Reed, a professor at New York Law School, came to our studios on January 13, 1999, to talk about Thomas Jefferson and Sally Hemings: An American Controversy, *published by the University Press of Virginia in 1997.*

THE FIRST TIME I heard of Sally Hemings was when I was twelve. I read my parents' copy of Winthrop Jordan's book *White over Black*, and he has a chapter called "Thomas Jefferson's Self in Society." It discusses Sally Hemings, and I thought that was quite interesting. He mainly talked about Jefferson. He introduced Hemings as an individual who had been something of a problem in Jefferson's life and the controversy surrounding her. There was not much about her personally because there's not much known. . . . She was described by a slave, Isaac Jefferson, as being very fair-skinned, very pretty, with straight hair down her back. Most descriptions of her just say she was attractive, not anything more than that.

When I was fourteen, I saw a notice in a magazine about a book called *Thomas Jefferson: An Intimate History,* by Fawn Brodie. In that book, Brodie took the position that Jefferson's relationship with [his slave] Sally Hemings was a fact. At the end of the book, she reprinted the memoirs of Madison Hemings, the son of Sally Hemings, who said that Jefferson was his father.

[My research indicates thàt] Sally Hemings and Thomas Jefferson had seven children, four of whom lived to adulthood. . . . Jefferson's Farm Book mentions all of her children except one. There is controversy over whether or not she had a [seventh] child named Tom. Madison Hemings's memoir mentions that when she returned from France with Jefferson, where he was serving as minister to France, she had a child. He said the child died. There is one family who believes that this child did not die and grew up to be a man named Tom Woodson. I do believe that she gave birth to seven children, but the best information we have now indicates that only four of them survived to adulthood.

At Monticello there are rooms along the south pavilion outside of Jefferson's bedroom. That's where she lived, in the stone houses. She was never formally freed. She left Monticello after Jefferson died and lived with her sons in Charlottesville [for nine more years]. She lived to be sixty years old. . . . No one knows where she was buried. We know where two of her sons are buried. Eston Hemings is buried in Wisconsin. Madison Hemings is in Ohio; they know the cemetery, but the cemetery wasn't well kept, so they don't know the actual grave site.

SALLY HEMINGS's mother was a woman named Elizabeth Hemings. Her father was John Wayles, who was also the father of Jefferson's wife. Sally Hemings was part of the inheritance of Jefferson's wife. When his wife's father died, Jefferson came into possession of upwards of 135 slaves. One of them was Sally Hemings [who was then three years old]. A certain group of slaves, mainly Elizabeth Hemings, her children, and others—the ones that are most famous—came to live at Monticello.

Madison Hemings says that when Jefferson was in Paris, he sent for his younger daughter, Maria, to come to Paris with him. He already had his older daughter there. When he left for France he had three children, then his youngest daughter died. At that point, he decided to have the remaining child in the United States come to Paris with him. . . . Sally Hemings went to Paris as a nursemaid to Jefferson's youngest remaining daughter. Hemings was between fourteen and fifteen when she went.

[Jefferson's wife] had been dead since 1782—five years at this point. People who were at the deathbed scene said Jefferson's wife asked him not to remarry, indicating that she did not want another woman over her children. It didn't seem to be so much that she didn't want him to have anyone else, it was more that she had a fear about stepmothers. He supposedly agreed.

Madison Hemings said that Sally was pregnant when they returned [from Paris]. She returned in 1789, so she would have been sixteen or seventeen years old at the time, and he was forty-six. When they came back to the

United States, Jefferson accepted an appointment in Washington's government. He stayed at Monticello. His older daughter got married and then he went off to be in the government. Sally Hemings, as far as we know, remained at Monticello.

[THE FIRST PUBLISHED reference to the Thomas Jefferson–Sally Hemings connection] was in 1802 by James Callender. He was angry at Jefferson. He had been a Jefferson partisan. He was one of those people who were radical Republicans in Jefferson's party. Once Jefferson was elected president, Callender wanted to be postmaster of Richmond. As often happens to the people in a political party who are the attack dogs of the party, the candidates didn't think that he really had the temperament to hold office. He was good for being an attack dog; he wasn't good for being postmaster of Richmond. Jefferson denied Callender this position, and Callender was upset. He had heard these stories before and went down to Charlottesville and talked to people about it. He decided to print the story in the *Richmond Recorder*.

There was outrage on the part of some of Jefferson's partisans, but they defused the crisis by not answering it. After the initial printing of the article, there were a couple of sallies back and forth but Jefferson and his friends just defused the crisis by not talking about it. It eventually died down after a couple of years.

Despite this, Jefferson was reelected in a landslide [in 1804]. In 1805 in New England, the story resurfaced through Jefferson's political enemies. It never really made a difference in his political career, and it died down and came back periodically anytime anybody felt like attacking Jefferson or anybody associated with Jefferson.

THE FIRST PERSON to note [the circumstantial evidence connecting Jefferson and Hemings] was Winthrop Jordan in *White over Black*. We know the birth date of Sally Hemings's children because Jefferson marked them in his Farm Book, which was his record of his activities on his farm. You count back from the date of birth to their probable dates of conception, and he was there for each one of them. We have no record of her having any children or conceiving any children that were born when he was not there. So his presence is tied to the conception of each of her children.

[Jefferson biographer Dumas Malone] referred to their relationship as "alleged." He thought it was something concocted by Jefferson's enemies, that it was a huge misunderstanding. It was his view that instead of Jefferson being the father of Hemings's children, it was actually Jefferson's nephews who fathered them. It was a misunderstanding that Jefferson's political enemies capitalized upon.

My thesis is that Jefferson scholars, the people who had been entrusted with Jefferson's life, had dismissed [the Sally Hemings] story too quickly. In fact, there was abundant evidence that the relationship actually existed. By not paying attention to the black voices, the black people who spoke about this, they had denied people a full and fair opportunity to view the evidence.

DR. EUGENE FOSTER had the idea of taking the DNA test using a Y chromosome from a male Jefferson descendant [to compare it with the chromosomes from Sally Hemings's male descendants]. Because Jefferson had no sons with his wife, they used an uncle. The assumption is that Thomas Jefferson and his brothers were not illegitimate, that they were, in fact, both Jeffersons. They took a descendant from [Thomas Jefferson's] uncle Field Jefferson. They looked at the Y chromosome from an Eston Hemings descendant, a straight-line male. They compared them and found that the Jefferson chromosome had a very distinctive mutation they had not seen in any other Y chromosome. And it turned out that the Eston Hemings descendant had the exact same Y chromosome as the Jeffersons.

I think it proves that this Eston Hemings descendant was a Jefferson. That, with the other information we have, proves that Thomas Jefferson was likely the father of all of Sally Hemings's children. [It indicates that] Madison Hemings was a credible historical witness. I can't think of a historical witness whose story has been more resoundingly corroborated than his. It makes me believe that Madison Hemings was telling the truth when he said that he and his siblings were the sons of Thomas Jefferson and Sally Hemings.

The American and French Revolutions

by

ROGER G. KENNEDY

The French Revolution, beginning in 1789 and leading to years of turmoil in France, was inspired, in part, by the earlier American Revolution. Many Americans followed the events in France with great interest, and even today the two revolutions and their differences provide a study in contrasts. These two countries, their revolutions, and the relationship between them are the subject of Roger G. Kennedy's Orders from France: The Americans and the French in a Revolutionary World, 1780–1820, *published by Alfred A. Knopf in 1989. Mr. Kennedy, former director of the Smithsonian's Museum of American History, appeared on* Booknotes *on June 22, 1989, to discuss his book.*

THE FRENCH HAD a revolution two hundred years ago. Their revolution had an effect on us, and we have a feeling that our revolution had a little effect on them. . . . The Americans and the French have a kind of on-again, off-again romance. We started out with the French and Indian wars and burning villages and [the 1704 massacre in] Deerfield, Massachusetts, and every kid who learned American history thinks about those terrible Indians and those terrible Frenchmen burning us up. Nobody paid much attention to our burning them up, I'm afraid. They were the desperate enemy.

Then during the Revolutionary War, they were our allies in achieving our independence. People like the Marquis de Lafayette and Major Pierre-Charles L'Enfant, who laid out Washington, D.C., were our allies and our friends and our heroes. There were more Frenchmen at Yorktown than there were Americans—nearly three times as many. We had a romance that lasted from the end of our War of Independence, 1783, through the first year or two of the French Revolution, when we thought they were going to have a revolution like ours—a safe and sane, not too disruptive one. Then it got out of hand, and they cut off their king's head. Americans were shocked. We hadn't cut off our king's head. . . . There wasn't a king available to decapitate.

LAFAYETTE WAS ONE of those guys who made a great deal out of goodwill and being exceedingly sexy and handsome. He was not terribly bright. He was a noble soul with a poor grasp not on reality so much as possibility or what you could actually achieve. But the nobility is the center point of it, and he had a tremendous sense of the self-dramatizing possibilities of public life. He looked wonderful on a horse; he was very good in front of a crowd. He represented France at its most heroic to us. He also, of course, was aristocratic; he wasn't just some guy off the street leading a revolution. He was involved in a series of revolutions, but he was always a marquis. We sort of liked that. Our snobbish sense is drawn to that kind of thing. Lafayette had the great virtue of coming back fifty years after his chief exploits and making a tour. It was like Sarah Bernhardt's last tour. It was Lafayette's last tour; he went everywhere. He went anywhere that people would gather to lift a glass and celebrate the achievements of the grand old men. . . . That was a thoroughgoing desire to make an impression. He succeeded.

PIERRE L'ENFANT did a great job with Washington. He would have done an even greater job with the Capitol if he had finished its design. One of the things that's nice to know is that if you look at that immense central rotunda, which nobody knows what to do with, that was a L'Enfant idea. It was going to be the assembly of the people. We have Congress and the Senate and the Supreme Court, but that was the place for all the rest of us to raise our flags and make speeches. That is what that great hole in the center of the Capitol is for. That was L'Enfant's dream of an assemblage of the American people, a revolutionary idea.

AFTER THE FRENCH eliminated their king and had a profound social revolution, Americans . . . began—in differing degrees—to withdraw their sense of affinity to France. Then within a few years we went to war with France, though we never declared it. Between 1797 and 1799 the Americans and the French were in an active naval war in the Caribbean. The second independent republic in the Western Hemisphere was established by blacks in what is now called Haiti, formerly Santo Domingo. They declared their independence and achieved it by their own strength from the French and the Spanish, who had the other end of the island. They fought off a British expedition that attempted to put them back both in slavery and in colonial status.

The American government, then led by George Washington and Alexander Hamilton—the Federalists—many of whom were northerners and not slave owners, supported the black government led by Toussaint Louverture, the great hero of Haitian independence. In many ways we went to war with France . . . to defend the sea-lanes between us and that second independent republic. American ships fired on French ships and sank a lot of them. We actually battered the shore of Haiti with our naval guns to protect Toussaint's black army. That story, which is almost totally unknown to Americans, is not so well-known to Haitians either, because after 1800 a new American government came into power, led by Thomas Jefferson, and was largely dominated by the interests of southern slaveholders. That government reversed the position of the former American government and cut off aid to Toussaint. This same government entered into an agreement with Napoleon, then in charge of France, stating that we would not resist if the French sought to reestablish both slavery and colonialism in the Caribbean and our American fleet was withdrawn. The French succeeded in landing an immense force, led by Napoleon's brother-in-law and his sister.

They succeeded in defeating Toussaint, kidnapping him, and taking him to die in France, probably starving him to death. The long, desperate decline of the island of Haiti, one of the poorest nations in the world today (it was once one of the richest) began as a succession of expeditions and military campaigns that ravaged the countryside. The part of the story that is both intriguing and in some ways terrible is that the first independent republic in the Western Hemisphere, the United States, and the second, the independent country of Santo Domingo, now Haiti, did not form a continuing alliance.

If the two republics had formed an alliance, the whole history of independence movements in this country and this hemisphere would have been entirely different. However, we were still very much a slaveholding country, dominated by a government led by Mr. Jefferson. . . . Slaveholders simply could not tolerate the presence of a free, black, revolted-slave republic in the hemisphere. Therefore we formed an alliance of a more disagreeable sort at that time with a neocolonial, imperial French government to reimpose colonialism in the Caribbean. That was one of our sorrier periods.

The French didn't reappear as an imperial power in the Western Hemisphere until . . . after Waterloo, after Napoleon was defeated, finally, by the British and Germans. His whole staff college from the Battle of Waterloo came to Philadelphia, maybe twenty-seven colonels and seven or eight generals, intending to invade Texas. . . . [In 1818] they did, in fact, invade . . . [with] mostly generals, captains, colonels, and darn few foot soldiers. They had the beginnings of a successful alliance with pirates in the Gulf of Mexico, and these French, very distinguished military leaders, succeeded in building three or four forts along the Trinity River [in Texas].

At that point, the United States government and the French government were again in alliance against this collection of freebooting, independent Bonapartists, . . . who were trying to reestablish a government in Texas. This government would serve as the basis on which they could collect enough money from silver mines to liberate Napoleon from Saint Helena, the island in the south Atlantic where he was being held. . . . [It] was during our own Civil War that the French reappeared as a colonial power and installed Maximilian as the emperor of Mexico. That was a French operation, not a Spanish one. Maximilian was left in the lurch by Napoleon III, the emperor of France, in the 1860s. When we got through with our own Civil War, General Ulysses S. Grant and others made it clear to the French that we wanted no part of the reimposition of a French empire in the Western Hemisphere. We were almost at the brink of war when the French withdrew, leaving Maximilian to be dealt with by the Mexicans, who lined him up against the wall. A firing squad took care of the last French imperial adventure in the Western Hemisphere.

BETWEEN 1780 AND 1820 . . . the United States and France were both in the process of making constitutions. We made one; we created one. The French made a whole series of them. A story I like to tell is about Charles Maurice de Talleyrand . . . who had been present in the forming of the French Revolution and was then a very elderly gentleman. A guy saw him coming out of his carriage and said to him, "Sir, isn't this the forty-eighth government to which you have sworn final allegiance?" He said, "I believe it's the forty-ninth, and I do hope it is the last."

The Contested Election of 1800

by

BERNARD A. WEISBERGER

Informal divisions between what would become the nation's first political parties developed early in American history. During George Washington's presidency, the Federalists, who believed in an active federal government, and the Anti-Federalists (also known as the Democratic-Republicans or Jeffersonian Republicans), who advocated a limited federal government, began to establish themselves as features of the American political landscape. The founding fathers hadn't anticipated political parties when creating the Constitution, and the system in place led to a tie, as well as contention and confusion, in the presidential election of 1800. This election was the subject of historian Bernard A. Weisberger's Booknotes appearance on February 25, 2001, and Mr. Weisberger's book America Afire: Jefferson, Adams, and the Revolutionary Election of 1800, *published in 2000 by William Morrow. Mr. Weisberger lives in Evanston, Illinois.*

THE ELECTION OF 1800 turned out to be a test, the first real test, of the electoral system and the Constitution. The test was successfully passed, but only after great dangers and perils had been encountered.

Thomas Jefferson ran against [the incumbent president] John Adams. They happened to be vice president and president because of an unusual provision of the original constitutional method of electing presidents. This provision decreed that the electors should not vote for a president and vice president separately, but for two men. The one with the highest total would be the victor, and the runner-up would be the vice president. That provision was installed when the founding fathers had no idea there would be political parties. The situation of a president of one party and a vice president of another . . . didn't occur to them.

Jefferson, in his fifties, was a very tall, loose-jointed man, comfortable in his own body, with reddish hair turning to gray and rather sharp features with a prominent nose and cheekbones. He was a man who had an endlessly roving mind and a taste for making political and philosophical pronouncements that were sometimes much more radical than his actual views.

Adams is a wonderful story. [In the 1770s] . . . he identified himself with the revolutionary cause, went off to the Continental Congress and was an absolute workhorse there, and really the spark plug of a great many of the Continental Congress's efforts to carry on the revolution. It meant long, long periods of separation from both his home in Massachusetts and his wife, Abigail, whom he loved very dearly.

Then he agreed to go abroad to represent the United States in Europe and negotiate loans with European bankers. Domestic letters took anywhere from a week to four or five weeks to pass between parties, and several months to pass across the Atlantic. . . . It meant being really cut off and isolated from home. It meant serious risks of capture or shipwreck, but he did that, and when he came back, he was rewarded with the vice presidency. He served as president from March 1797 to March 1801.

[Adams and Jefferson] were fascinating people, and they were old friends who had been together in the Continental Congress. Both were on the drafting committee for the Declaration of Independence. They had both been ambassadors abroad during the Revolution, at a time when that meant a long, dangerous sea voyage. They were good friends, but they were very different in their views of human nature.

Adams was a conservative who didn't have a very high opinion of popular judgment. He did believe in self-government, but he also believed that, in the end, people were easily seduced by rank and riches and glamour. And he believed that society was in a constant state of class war; that the poor and the rich would always be trying to get the advantage of each other. So you needed a stable, steady government, particularly a strong executive, to hold them in check. While not particularly religious, he respected tradition and authority.

Jefferson, on the other hand, was much more of a philosophical than a governmental radical, as it turned out. Jefferson believed in the triumph of reason; he was a child of the Enlightenment. He was sure that if humanity got rid of all superstitions and idolatry (i.e., revealed religion and reverence for monarchy and aristocracy), the world would get better and better. He thought that in the mass of ordinary people, by whom he meant usually small landholders, there was a natural elite of intelligence, which could be brought out by a universal system of public education. And if such a system were in place, democracy could prosper without a great deal of authority, without a great deal of government. So there was almost an optimistic versus a hard-boiled view of human nature that separated them.

IN 1800 THE POPULATION was about 5 million, of whom about three-quarters of a million were slaves. . . . Mostly white males who had some property could vote. Each state set its own qualifications for electors. Most of them still had some property qualifications, but in many cases, it had gotten down to owning your own house or owning a house lot. It varied from state to state. . . . On the whole, scholars think that maybe as high as 60 percent to 80 percent of the white males were eligible to vote but, of those, probably only half turned out. It's very hard to get precise figures because, of course, statistics weren't kept then. But, in short, if you were white, and a man, and you had any kind of taxable property, you probably had a good shot at voting.

They elected the [president] in one way as we do now [but] in another, quite differently. Each state was to appoint electors equal to the size of its congressional delegation in any manner the state determined. In 1800 ten of the sixteen existing states actually had the state legislatures choose the electors. The other six chose the electors by popular vote.

Where the difference between then and now was—besides the fact that there was no general popular vote—the electors only voted for two men, not for a separate president and vice president. But it was like today's elections in that by 1800, the electors, who were originally envisaged as an independent body of people who would scatter their votes among a lot of potential candidates, . . . were already running on party slates. They were already simply registering the decision of party caucuses as to who the candidates would be.

OF THE 138 ELECTORS chosen in 1800, there were seventy-three Republican electors on Jefferson's side, who faithfully cast one vote [each] for Thomas Jefferson, and sixty-five [Federalist electors], who cast their votes for John Adams.

In a sense, the Electoral College was already being somewhat compromised from the original vision. But a glitch occurred in 1800 in that by then, both parties had a president-designate and a vice president–designate. It was understood who the number one and number two men were. But that meant, given the system, that the electors of your party had to agree that at least one of them would throw away a second vote—not vote for both men on the ticket. But the Republicans didn't do that in 1800, either through mismanagement or accident or fear that they weren't going to win if they didn't cast every vote for both men. All seventy-three voted for both Thomas Jefferson and Aaron Burr [the vice presidential candidate]. So the president and the understood vice president–designate came in a dead heat.

[Burr refused to concede, and according to the Constitution] the tie would have to be broken by the House of Representatives. In the House, each state delegation got one vote, and you needed a majority of nine. . . another provision of the Constitution, since changed, . . . caused still another problem because the Congress that sat in January and February of 1801 was not the [Republican] Congress that had just been elected. [It was] the lame-duck Congress that had been elected two years before, dominated by the Federalists.

THERE WAS A CONSTITUTIONAL mechanism for resolving a tie; however, what happened was a series of political shenanigans. The Federalist Congress did not want to yield power to this "upstart red Jacobin," Thomas Jefferson, so they contrived [a plan]. . . . Two states had delegations equally divided, so in effect, their votes were nullified. Six were controlled by the Federalists, and that meant they could deny Jefferson the majority [of nine out of sixteen] he needed. What they decided to do was to keep voting for Aaron Burr and block Jefferson's access to the presidency. So when Inauguration Day rolled around on March 4, 1801, they would presumably say, "Look, there is now a constitutional problem. There's a vacancy in the presidency not foreseen in the Constitution, and what we'll do is pass special emergency legislation to allow us to name a president, one of our own."

This was un-American or at least unconstitutional, and the Republicans responded to it, [but] not Jefferson personally. Jefferson and Adams took no part; . . . they remained on their aloof pedestals. But Republican Party leaders, including some Republican governors and congressmen, said, "Well, if you do this, we will either not recognize this usurpation and we will jail any federal officers who try to enforce federal law within our boundaries, or we will walk out of the union and call a new Constitution and perhaps form a new union, which will exclude the Federalist states." The Federalists, by the way, dominated all the New England states and a couple of the middle states. The Republicans controlled the South and West. So there was a sectional split, too.

The Adams Federalists (because Adams was essentially a moderate), rather than throw the country into turmoil, wanted some kind of assurances that Jefferson would not (a) wipe out the national debt that they had incurred, because Jefferson was constantly raging about the necessity to make government frugal and cheap, and (b) that he would not purge the civil service and throw out all the Federalist officeholders. There were only a couple of hundred of them at the time.

Jefferson never gave any formal assurances to that effect, but there was a wonderful moment, and one . . . I would have loved being a fly on the wall for. Jefferson and Adams met on Pennsylvania Avenue, both out for a walk, while the crisis was at its height in the House, and had a discussion. Adams said . . . that Jefferson could avoid a constitutional crisis if he would give some assurances that he wouldn't expunge the national debt, in Adams's words. Jefferson said, well, he didn't know about that, but he thought the

Federalists really ought not to risk breaking the country apart. And as for what he would or wouldn't do, he said, "Let my past conduct be the guide to what I'll do in the future."

The situation was finally resolved only by . . . some backstairs bargaining. We don't know for sure. But, in the end, after a week of furious balloting . . . the Federalists blinked. They let Thomas Jefferson take ten states and become the president.

On the morning of March 4, in 1801, . . . after the balloting was concluded and Jefferson was named president, John Adams got up. At 4:00 in the morning, he took himself to the stagecoach depot in Washington . . . and got on a coach. He was just a private citizen, a passenger on the start of his journey back to Boston. And Jefferson, in his turn, about 10:00 that morning, walked from his boardinghouse to Congress with no fanfare, no big inaugural parade [only] a small detachment of D.C. militia marching along in front of him, and there was a militia cannon salute when he entered the Capitol. But it was all done without fanfare. It was, indeed, a peaceful transfer of power. It was the first time in modern history, in a republic of any size, that as a result of a popular vote, one party had simply turned over the reins to another party that was radically different in its outlook on the country.

I don't know whether Jefferson thought Adams would be at the inaugural or not. Probably not. There has been some speculation that it was bad grace for Adams not to stick around, but there was really no precedent for it. The first two inaugurals had been Washington's. And Jefferson was at Adams's inaugural because he was vice president. [But] there was no precedent for the outgoing president to be present at the inauguration.

Adams was grumpy about the defeat, there's no two ways about it. [He had] run for reelection and been turned down. But I'm not sure whether [missing Jefferson's inaugural] was bad manners or just a deliberate attempt to show exactly what it did show: "I was the president but now I am a private citizen. I'm just one of you."

The Hamilton–Burr Duel

by

ARNOLD A. ROGOW

Alexander Hamilton was born in the West Indies in 1757 and immigrated to America in 1772 in pursuit of an education. Aaron Burr was born in 1756 in Newark, New Jersey. When they met for a duel on July 11, 1804, Hamilton was a former Revolutionary War general and secretary of the Treasury. Burr was a famous and respected soldier, a former U.S. senator, and the current vice president of the United States. Their friendship and duel is the subject of Arnold A. Rogow's A Fatal Friendship: Alexander Hamilton and Aaron Burr, *published in 1998 by Hill & Wang. Mr. Rogow, who taught political science at City University in New York, appeared on* Booknotes *on August 12, 1998.*

My book is focused on the duel in 1804 between Alexander Hamilton and Aaron Burr in which Hamilton was killed. But, more broadly, it's a biographical study of the two men and how their friendship developed the way it did.

I was fascinated by this duel and could not understand why these two prominent Americans, one the vice president of the United States, would fight a duel in which one would be killed, which would terminate the life of one and the political career of the other.

[Aaron Burr] is regarded as one of the great villains of American history. [However] Burr was quite an impressive man. He was a very open person and kind; he wrote letters to his slaves and servants, solicitous about their welfare. He was invariably polite to everyone. He was never known to make any statement about Alexander Hamilton [that was critical until after the duel].

I don't think I found a single statement of [Burr's] that was critical of Jefferson or Adams or anybody. He was sort of an easygoing person, basically. I would say that he was a Bill Clinton type. He enjoyed life. He did not have any great ideology or conviction about anything. He believed in "live and let live." And he thought Hamilton, right until almost the end, was a friend of his. Hamilton would come to dinner. Hamilton's daughter and Burr's daughter were friends. I'm still mystified as to how he got the reputation he has.

Alexander Hamilton was the first secretary of the Treasury under Washington. He was the most prominent Federalist politician of his time. Burr, at the time of the duel, was vice president of the United States under Thomas Jefferson. He had been a U.S. senator from New York and had been in the New York legislature. The two of them were the most prominent lawyers in New York State and two of the most prominent in the country.

In politics today, Aaron Burr would have been a Democrat; Alexander Hamilton would have been a Republican. [Hamilton] was big on the role of business and the industrial relations of America and measures to promote industry and manufacturing. He would not have hesitated to promote business and commerce and trade.

BURR CHALLENGED HAMILTON [to the duel]. It was in June 1804, in connection with remarks Hamilton had made about him at a dinner in Albany in February in the course of a political meeting that were leaked to the Albany paper. Hamilton said Burr was a "dangerous man." Someone who was present, a Dr. Charles Cooper, said that Hamilton had gone further than that and said something that was so despicable that he didn't repeat it in the letter he was writing about this.

There's speculation by author Gore Vidal with his novel *Burr*, a fictional statement, . . . that Hamilton said Burr had an incestuous relationship with his daughter Theo.

DUELING PROCEEDED with a provocation usually involving honor. The injured person could issue an invitation to the person who had dishonored or insulted him. The duel itself was often called an interview. . . . If it was accepted, then "seconds" arranged the details—the time, the place, pistols, and so forth.

The duel between Aaron Burr and Alexander Hamilton was on July 11, 1804, at Weehawken, New Jersey. [Dueling] was illegal in New York, and the chances of getting away with it were much better in New Jersey. In fact, Burr was subsequently indicted for murder in both states, but in New Jersey it was not pursued.

The duel was [set for] early morning, between 7:00 and 7:30. They had dueling pistols that had been modified. . . . Weights had been added to the fore ends to make them easier to balance and aim. The caliber was much greater than dueling pistols were supposed to be. [Theirs were] over .50 caliber. To give you an idea what that is, the heavy machine gun of World War II was a .50-caliber machine gun. [Theirs were] .55 caliber, roughly, . . . designed less for dueling than for killing. . . . The two men probably stood about ten or twelve feet apart, something like that. The usual command was, "Fire" or "Present" (pronounced prez-ent) or "Present" (pronounced preezent).

Hamilton was hit in the lower right side, fell, and was carried to the boat waiting in the Hudson River and taken to New York to the home of a friend. He was in considerable agony, and nothing, of course, was going to save him. He died the next day, thirty-six hours later.

[Hamilton's funeral was] very impressive. They had a procession of his coffin on a carriage and his general's uniform on the top of the coffin. He had been made a major general, a brevet major, two-star general, and was very proud of that. . . . July 14 was the funeral, Bastille Day. It happened to be the fifteenth anniversary of the French Revolution.

THERE WAS SUCH AN UPROAR that this was murder, that cold-blooded malice was involved. Some newspapers went so far as to say it had been plotted long ahead of any remarks Hamilton made in Albany, that Burr and his henchmen were out to kill Hamilton and destroy him. [Burr] was indicted in New York and New Jersey, and he took a boat toward New Jersey, *Perth Amboy,* and went into Pennsylvania. He thought he was going to be delivered by the governor of New Jersey back to New York for trial. It was one of the few times in his life he was just a bit anxious.

From Pennsylvania, [Burr] made his way south and found to his surprise he had more friends than he thought. The South generally did not have the high regard for Hamilton that people in the North did. Burr was more of a hero there and still is, as a matter of fact. And the general view, of course, was that Jefferson, later on in the so-called treason indictment, was framing him. That's a view that some southerners still have today.

After a pause in the South, he came back to preside over the Senate in his final days as vice president.

THE ACTUAL DETAILS of the duel are still contradictory and controversial. Hamilton had written before the duel that he would reserve his fire and give Burr a chance to reconsider, as he put it. When he was mortally wounded and they were taking him back to New York in the boat, he said, "Be careful of that pistol, that it will fire," but it had been fired. His brother-in-law and his second went to the dueling ground and said they found a branch of a tree twelve and a half feet [off the ground], about four feet to the right of where Burr was standing, that was broken off by Hamilton's bullet. But Hamilton's second claimed that Hamilton had fired involuntarily after being hit by Burr. In other words, the muscle finger hadn't pulled the trigger. It was discovered further that the gun had a hair trigger, meaning that all it took was a slight touch for the gun to go off.

One of the questions, of course, is, Did he touch the trigger too soon? Is that why the gun went off? Could he have—wounded as he was and dying the next day—had enough strength in his hand to exert a pull on the trigger to set it off high above Burr? Or was he aiming at Burr and just touched it too soon, as one of the dueling authorities said, and booby-trapped himself?

I think it is very possible [that Hamilton was essentially committing suicide]. He was very depressed. He'd lost his son in a duel less than three years before, possibly with the same pistol. Circumstances were very similar in terms of what was reported about the duel and whether his son fired or not. It was said by his [son's] second that he did not fire. Hamilton's son was his oldest and probably most beloved child of the eight he had. One consequence [of his son's death] was that his daughter Angelica lost her mind and would remain insane the rest of her life. She was never the same again. She talked about her brother all through her life as if he were still alive.

Several people knew [the duel was going to happen], including Hamilton's father-in-law and friends of Hamilton's. One of the mysteries of this whole thing is why no one tried to prevent it. And to my knowledge, no one tried.

ALEXANDER HAMILTON had been the secretary of the Treasury under President Washington for about four years and then resigned. He found it tiring. He was under attack, charged with corruption, with using inside information to benefit himself and his family, with trading privately in Treasury securities and so on. There had also been a scandalous affair that got into the public press.

Maria Reynolds said that Hamilton had colluded with her husband and that he had had an affair with her. She was a Philadelphia woman, who some say was a former prostitute, but turns out to have been born into a good family. . . . She was married to a man named James Reynolds who was in jail, along with some others, for speculation in Treasury securities and embezzlement. Her husband claimed that Hamilton . . . was a co-embezzler, in effect, and had been making money on his own as secretary of the Treasury. Hamilton wrote a long pamphlet saying that, "None of this is true. What I am guilty of is an affair with his wife, Maria."

Hamilton's friends were horrified. Not that it happened but that he wrote a pamphlet about it, confessing it. They thought this was one of the reasons why . . . the perception [took root] about that time that he was unstable. This perception grew in the years that followed because he did a number of very rash things.

[AMERICANS THINK of Alexander Hamilton as a martyr, but] I would call him a kind of a borderline type, in psychological terms, meaning that he was unstable. He was driven by ambition. He could be ruthless. He was certainly capable of dishonesty on a massive level. If anybody was dangerous in terms of what I think of as American ideals, it was Hamilton, not Burr.

It was Hamilton who said, "I have no use for democracy"; who made it very clear that he had no use for ordinary people. He thought children of a very tender age should work in factories. He horrified some of his own friends with some of his views. He was good about slavery. He did believe in the emancipation of slaves and believed that blacks should be serving in the army, to which the service was totally opposed. He had some virtues; but a martyr, no.

IN 1807 BURR was acquitted of a charge that he wanted to lead an army south and liberate or separate the western United States, west of the Mississippi and south into Mexico . . . and set himself up as a kind of leader, king, or something of the sort. [President] Jefferson led the charge. The key piece of evidence was a letter, now believed to have been a forgery, not written by Burr at all, but which Jefferson said was written by Burr. So he was in seven court proceedings, including one presided over by Chief Justice John Marshall, and in all of them, he was acquitted. [Burr lived] another thirty years [after this].

There wasn't anything made of [Aaron Burr's funeral]. For twenty years, there was nothing on his grave to indicate he was even buried there. There is now. There is an Aaron Burr Association with about two hundred members that is dedicated to promoting [Burr's] reputation. . . . [He is buried] in Princeton, New Jersey, not far from the graves of his father and grandfather, who were both presidents of Princeton, both ministers.

Most Americans think Alexander Hamilton was a martyr and that Aaron Burr was a villain. . . . I want them to have another look at Aaron Burr. I want them to see that Burr has been much maligned and deserves to be thought of in a far better way than he is. I want them to think that Hamilton was ruthless, totally ambitious, power-driven. He [was] certainly a brilliant man, maybe a genius. Burr was not a brilliant man. He wasn't that. Hamilton was important in terms of the nation's financial security at the beginning, and he deserves every kind of credit for that. Burr contributed nothing of any lasting importance. But for me, if I had to choose a dinner companion, it would be Aaron Burr.

The Slave Ship Henrietta Marie

by

MICHAEL H. COTTMAN

The Henrietta Marie *sank near Key West in 1700 after delivering African captives—slaves—to the island of Jamaica. The shipment of human cargo from Africa was a feature of early American life until a federal ban was placed on the importation of slaves in 1808. The* Henrietta Marie *was discovered in 1973 and is the earliest slave shipwreck identified by name. In May 1993 the National Association of Black Scuba Divers placed an underwater memorial plaque at the site of the shipwreck. The plaque faces the African shore and is inscribed with the ship's name and the following: "In memory and recognition of the courage, pain and suffering of enslaved African people. Speak her name and gently touch the souls of our ancestors." Michael H. Cottman joined us on June 21, 1999, to discuss* The Wreck of the *Henrietta Marie:* An African-American's Spiritual Journey to Uncover a Sunken Slave Ship's Past, *published in 1999 by Harmony/ Crown Books. Mr. Cottman is a writer in Washington, D.C.*

THE *HENRIETTA MARIE* is an extraordinary archaeological and historical discovery in America and, I dare say, throughout the world. This is the only slave ship in the world that's been scientifically documented, the only slave ship in the world from which artifacts have been recovered. More importantly, 7,000 artifacts were recovered from the ocean floor. Of those artifacts, more than one hundred were [pairs of shackles]. It's the largest collection of slave ship shackles ever found on one site—on one ship. So this particular ship, the *Henrietta Marie,* has just an incredible story to tell.

The *Henrietta Marie* was built in the early to mid-1600s. We believe it was a French ship that was a prize to the British because it actually sailed under

the British flag from 1697 to 1700. It was physically built, we believe, somewhere in France. It was eighty feet long and weighed about 120 tons.

Its purpose originally was slaving. It was a slave ship as far as we can trace
it back in 1697, when it sailed out of the Thames River into the English
Channel and into the Atlantic. . . . We were able to find the names of the
three ship captains. We were able to identify about twenty crew members on
board the vessel. The ship sailed out of London. From London it sailed to a
place called Calabar, which is now southeast Nigeria.

That's where the captains traded with African kings and chiefs for African
people. They traded with some of the trade beads that were actually found on
the wreck site. Among the 7,000 artifacts that were recovered, several—
maybe a couple thousand—were trade beads. These were glass beads that
were made in Venice, all different colors and all different shapes and sizes.
These beads meant different things to African chiefs and kings. Some
thought that they brought spiritual power. Some chiefs and kings thought it
brought great social status. Some just liked the way they looked and figured
they would adorn their bodies with necklaces.

AFRICAN MEN, WOMEN, and children were systematically packed into the
hulls of slave ships. The idea was, of course, to try to pack as many people in
to make that transatlantic voyage. The more people they packed in, the
greater the profits.

You can talk to historians who say anywhere from 6 to 10 [million people
were sold into slavery] and you can talk to people who say 10 to 30. I'll just
say millions, generations, of African people were sold into slavery.

Millions [died on their way to the West. On Goree Island, there was] a
place called "the Door of No Return," where the slave ships would pull up to
the back of the slave house. That was the door where African people were led
through to be taken onto dinghies—they called them longboats—and then
taken to the slave ships. It was the last time that African people would see
their families again. Generations of families were separated through that
door.

WE CAN SAY WITH certainty that the *Henrietta Marie* made two transatlantic voyages. The first one ended up in Barbados, where the captain sold
several hundred African people at public auction. The last trip that we can
verify ended in Port Royal, Jamaica, in May 1700. It unloaded 150 African
men and women and forty children, and tried to make a run back to London
to replenish supplies, re-outfit the ship, and then go back to West Africa. But
it sank in a hurricane. It was blown severely off course. It tried to drop three
of its anchors and ride out the storm. They were unsuccessful, and it was bro-

ken apart in pieces and splintered and crashed in an area called New Ground Reef.

THE WRECK IS LOCATED thirty-seven miles west of Key West, Florida, in about thirty feet of water on New Ground Reef. It makes a really incredible place to dive because it's such a shallow site. Divers and underwater archaeologists can actually work this site for hours and hours at a time without worrying about decompression sickness.

[The first time I came upon the *Henrietta Marie*] was an incredibly gut-wrenching, emotional experience. [I started diving to the wreck] back in the early '90s. The ship, in fact, was discovered in 1973 by divers working with the Mel Fisher Maritime Heritage Society. One of the people who located the ship is Moe Molinar, probably one of the only successful underwater treasure hunters of African descent.

Moe and a group of divers . . . were looking for a ship called the Atocha. . . . As Moe was underwater, sifting through sand and looking for glitter on the ocean floor, he discovered these encrusted shackles. He looked at them and knew that these were shackles used to bind wrists much like his own. But he didn't know the name of the wreck. He didn't know anything. He just knew that he had discovered some shackles and he was compelled by it. He'd found countless treasure on treasure ships, but this was an unusual discovery for him.

He put them in his dive belt and they took them to a warehouse, where they sat for years. In 1983 a group of divers went back out and discovered the ship's bell, which said *Henrietta Marie* on [the front and] on the back, 1699. It was a blueprint for us to start our research in London to try to piece together this transatlantic puzzle. This bell served like a black box in an airplane crash; they look for that black box to try and give them an idea of some of the last words or conversations from the pilot to the tower. This gave us a blueprint right back to London to start this research.

WE SPENT A GREAT DEAL of time [going] back and forth between the United States and Goree Island. . . . This is where we believe the *Henrietta Marie* docked to repair the ship. Then we made several trips to Jamaica and at least one or two to Barbados, and then countless trips back and forth to Key West to dive on the site of the wreckage.

We forged [a partnership between] the National Association of Black Scuba Divers and the underwater archaeologists in Key West, who happen to be white. This was an unprecedented union of people who came together to excavate and to examine a slave ship. Whites and blacks coming together to talk at a table is one thing. . . . It's even more complex and more challenging to be on a boat with whites and blacks discovering and excavating and examining a slave ship. We were out on a boat, thirty-seven miles offshore. It's not the kind of distance where you can come back and forth. We stayed on the boat for maybe three, four, five days in a row working the site and examining it. We'd come back on the boat and couldn't go anywhere. There was nowhere to go, so you had to talk. In fact, what we realized was that the ship, the *Henrietta Marie*, became this experiment on race.

The National Association of Black Scuba Divers and a number of archaeologists who helped us with this project, white and black, decided that we wanted to honor and commemorate the African men, women, and children who lost their lives on this ship. We decided to lay a monument on the ocean floor, a one-ton concrete monument with a bronze inscription, to commemorate the loss of life aboard the slave ship during the Middle Passage.

It took about four hours to get to the site of New Ground Reef [to lay the monument] because we were so weighed down and we had so many people. It took about four hours to actually get the job done, to get the monument on the wreck site. Then it took several hours to get back. So it was a daylong event.

[My fellow divers were] guys who were prepared for any encounter and any experience in the ocean. But what they could not prepare for, emotionally or spiritually, was what they felt laying this monument on this wreckage of this slave ship. When you ran your hands underwater, as I did, on this wreck and uncovered trade beads; when you ran your hands underwater on this site and raised planks of wood that once made up the hull of this vessel that carried these African people into slavery, you looked through tempered glass of the underwater mask at other divers. I looked at tears in the eyes of some of these divers, some of the most stoic individuals that I've seen in my life. [They] succumbed to this rush of emotion, being on the site of this wreck.

So it was indeed just a phenomenal opportunity to be a part of this examination of this ship. But there was also a spiritual aspect to it as well, just being bathed and baptized in the waters where so many atrocities took place, and to be around so many other men whom I respect in the dive industry and watch how they handled this rush of emotion that they experienced.

I THINK WE HAVE an incredible connection with the water, and that's something I write about. We were a people—African people—who were actually born on the water. We were born on the ocean. We were forced to cross this great divide. To this day, I think that the National Association of Black Scuba Divers [is] diving into the past but is also coming to grips with how we, as a people, started in the first place. We're exploring this vast ocean, an ocean we were forced to cross three hundred years ago to come to this new world.

How do we cross this enormous divide that clearly exists between whites and blacks? One of the ways we talked about doing this is through books and through real-life stories, being able to share things that happened in your life without beating people over the head with it, by understanding that when I came out of this process, I wasn't bitter.

There are a number of people who just don't want to deal with [the slavery issue] but I think when they learn more about what this is all about, they will learn more about the fact that African people came to this country to help build this republic that we now embrace and that we love. I think more people are more interested in learning about this particular piece of history. . . . It's a global story. It's a story about whites and blacks. It's our story.

The Young Nation

1815–1850

The First Generation of Americans

by

JOYCE APPLEBY

The census of 1800 reported 5.3 million people living in the United States—more than twice the number in the colonies at the beginning of the American Revolution. There were four cities with a population greater than 10,000—Baltimore, Boston, Philadelphia, and New York. Half of the population was under sixteen years of age. On June 18, 2000, Joyce Appleby, a UCLA history professor and author of Inheriting the Revolution: The First Generation of Americans, *published in 2000 by Belknap Press, appeared on* Booknotes *to tell us about this era and how this "first generation" helped shape the young nation.*

THOSE MEN AND WOMEN who were born between 1776 and 1800 . . . would not have had any contact with the colonial era. They would have none of the sensibilities of having been subjects to the king of England. They were the inheritors of the revolution. . . . This generation took very seriously the fact that they had inherited a remarkable revolution and they wanted to demonstrate to a world of monarchs and monarchies what democracy—what a democratic society—could truly be.

Thomas Jefferson's influence was the most pervasive in this generation. They frequently talked about him. As a hero, Henry Clay loomed large, as did DeWitt Clinton, because he was the one who championed the Erie Canal. Those figures in [this] generation are important. Andrew Jackson doesn't figure as a great hero. I'm sure he was to [some] people, but he doesn't seem to be among the people that I've read. But Jefferson was important because he so clearly articulated a different conception of what a republic could be, and he had a different vision of how human beings could participate in their society. People refer to him throughout this period.

IN 1800 ABOUT 6 MILLION people lived in America . . . . They lived in what you might call the Appalachian shelf—that Atlantic shelf between the Appalachian Mountains and the Atlantic Ocean. Once the Revolutionary War had been won, there was an outpouring of people from this little shelf— this confined area up and down the Atlantic Coast—into the western parts of the original states. Western New York was the frontier of the 1790s, in the early decades of the nineteenth century, but also western Virginia, western Georgia, western Pennsylvania.

Religion too was going through an exuberant period; it's what historians refer to as the Second Great Awakening; [there was] an emphasis on evangelizing, reaching out to people, on the personal experience of sin, about being an active soldier for Christ in society. . . . The people were moving west and there were no churches going with them; it was too expensive. The Episcopalian Church, which was the Church of England; the Presbyterian Church; the Congregational Church [which] was a dominant church in New England: those were the old-line churches. The Methodists were a new group that began in the bosom of the Church of England, but they broke with the Church of England; they broke with Episcopalians, became a separate Methodist Episcopal Church in America.

The Methodists and the Baptists had the means to reach the people in the West who were going without churches and after five, ten years, were unchurched. Their children were unbaptized. They were getting married without marriage ceremonies. There was a thirst for religion. You had these uneducated preachers; they did have a skill and a talent and a calling to preach. You had them going into the frontier, preaching, creating converts, and building new churches.

[The rush for temperance came from] the religious revivals . . . because you're not in control of yourself if you drink too much. The Revolutionary generation drank a lot. There was this desire for more control; [this desire for] control had religious impetus, but I also think it had to do with ambition. This was not an easy society to get ahead in; it took a lot of hard work. That was incompatible with drinking in the morning or drinking in the afternoon, whereas in the old society, in an artisan's shop, such as a printing shop, the youngest apprentice went out at 10:30 and came back with a bottle of liquor, and then at 2:00 they went out again. No one ever built a ship or raised a house without providing liquor for the workers; drink was implicated in all the everyday routines. It [eventually] became incompatible with many people's sense of how to get what they wanted, how to get ahead, how to activate their plans.

The Sabbath Crusade was [an attempt] to stop all business on Sunday. Most churches and churchgoers observed the Sabbath and didn't do any ordinary work on Sunday. But as the tempo of commerce increased, post offices stayed open on Sunday. The worst thing was that the Erie Canal ran on Sunday because you couldn't stop the Hudson River and the other rivers from flowing; you couldn't stop the canal. This upset people, and there was a move to get the federal government to enforce the Sabbath in the ways that it could. One of them was to not deliver the mail on Sundays, and this failed. The churches were beaten back by those people who argued that the government shouldn't interfere in this way.

The first Jewish congregation [in America] came in the seventeenth century, from Brazil to New York City. But the Jewish population was very small; real Jewish immigration didn't come until the end of the nineteenth century. There were some Catholics with the Irish population that came in the eighteenth century, but many more Scotch-Irish who were Presbyterians. Catholic immigration began in the 1840s, with the potato famine and other dislocations in Ireland, and then also in Germany. This also was a period with the lowest foreign-born population in American history; about only 3 percent were foreign, and most of those were slaves who came in with the brief . . . opening up of the slave trade [from 1788 to 1808. By contrast] by the end of the nineteenth and the early twentieth century, two-thirds of the people in American cities were either foreigners or foreign-born.

[AMERICANS IN THE 1820s and 1830s] farmed; . . . 85 percent of them lived in rural areas. . . . It was the beginning of a shift out of the rural areas and into commerce and into manufacturing, into the professions, into preaching, teaching, becoming lawyers. These were all growing because the society was becoming more intensely commercial. That was creating the need for an infrastructure of teachers. Literacy was moving up. The first railroad was 1830, the B&O—they were just beginning. There were canals. The Erie Canal was the great engineering triumph. It opened in 1825. And there were roads; there was a national road; there were post roads; there were toll roads. They were doing everything they could to connect the country in a transportation system. There was a steamboat [invented] that finally enabled the western farmers to get their boats back up the Mississippi and the Ohio.

There was a pretty high mortality rate. It was unusual to have a big family. The average number of children was about seven point something at the beginning of the nineteenth century, and it dropped to four by the end. There were some big families, but many children were wiped out by diphtheria or tuberculosis or cholera. It was a mixed picture; it was not even. That was true of just about everything about this generation.

The military was very small. It swelled at the time of the War of 1812. At the end of the war, there were about 70,000 in the army, but they quickly demobilized and got down to a force of about 14,000. West Point was founded in the first decade of the nineteenth century. What you did have was the military teaching men civil engineering. The army virtually lent civil engineers to railroad companies and to canal companies and to expeditions that found Yellowstone—Stephen Long's expedition. So there were many ways that military people participated in economic life.

In the North, almost everyone was educated, including free blacks who got three years of three months' schooling. That was the goal, to teach reading, writing, and ciphering. In the South, fewer would be educated, but there were lots of academies for planters' children. Teaching was the great bridge for talented boys and even some talented girls to get off the family farm. If they were good at book learning, they could become teachers, and then in a year or two they could move into one of the new areas, perhaps become a lawyer, move on to becoming a newspaper editor, a clerk in a store. It is fascinating what teaching offered young people.

YOU [ALSO] HAD the beginning of the state universities; there were probably thirty . . . by the end of the 1830s. The religious revivals inspired colleges [that were affiliated with different churches] because groups wished to have their boys and girls reared in their church and do their actual secular learning in a religious environment.

[The printed word had] enormous impact. Americans were knitted together [from all over the country by] print. Publishing and printing became cheap. America acquired all of the printing machinery to do its own printing. Literacy was high. The importance of commerce meant that boys and girls needed to learn to read and write. And then, reading was an entertainment. Eighty-five percent of them lived in rural areas, and books and pamphlets and printed songs brought the world to them.

There were lots of publishers, oodles of printers. . . . There were just hundreds and hundreds of printers and newspapers. In 1810 Americans were buying more issues of the newspaper than any country in the world regardless of size, regardless of population. It was just a phenomenon. . . . In 1810 there were 371 dailies in a country of 8 million.

[AFTER THE WAR OF 1812, veterans received 160 acres of land.] It created another surge forward into the West. Some veterans might have set up a store to sell the bounty; there was always a brisk trade in the paper involved in land. But most of them went west, and that was when you had these states of the Northwest and the old Southwest coming into the Union.

People moved west, in part, because of the Jeffersonian challenge that "Americans are ambitious because the lowest can aspire as much as the highest," which broadly challenged not only politics but the social forms of hierarchy. Also . . . there were 4 million of them on the edge of a very fertile continent, so they had the opportunity—indeed, everybody wanted to see them be ambitious. And then the nation was forming at a time of economic development, the beginning of industrialization, of trade, of finance, of the professions. So it was a very fortuitous convergence of developments.

THERE WERE SOME twenty-six states in the early 1800s. They were coming along very rapidly. Vermont came in, then [others such as] Ohio, Indiana, Mississippi, and Alabama. Voting was determined by states, so [suffrage policy] could be very different. Free African Americans voted in New Hampshire and Massachusetts all through this period. They voted in North Carolina, and then it was taken away from them. There was a movement to have white male suffrage, but in 1850 Virginia still had property qualifications. Vermont came in with no slavery and no property qualifications. So it was a patchwork quilt. But the move, the thrust, was for free white men to be able to vote.

Women could vote in New Jersey for a brief period if they had property and no husband. The way the law was written, there was a property qualification, but they didn't put in that you had to be a man, so women voted. Women only controlled their property if they didn't have a husband, so it was mainly wealthy widows who voted. Then that was changed; "man" was put in the law, and the vote was taken away from them.

SLAVERY WAS THE problem that they could not resolve. The founding fathers and the next generation knocked out slavery where it was weakest, and they left it where it was strongest. They almost made the Civil War inevitable by doing that.

There were reformers who took the initiative and abolished slavery in the North. The absence of slavery in the North not only meant they didn't have slaves, it freed northerners to imagine a world without slaves, to write critically of slavery. If slavery had still been in their midst in the North, you wouldn't have had people being so freely critical of it. So, I think it was both the absence in the North and the presence in the South that kept it in the public eye. Also, there were vocal antislavery people. Congress opened each session with a bunch of petitions, some of them from free blacks, some of them from Quakers. They couldn't get away from it. Southerners were just enraged that this, their institution, which they understood and wanted to wall off, was being examined and criticized by former slaves.

The American Colonization Society formed to resettle free blacks in Africa. They were actually the founders of Liberia on the west coast of Africa, as Sierra Leone was founded by Great Britain to provide a haven for former slaves that the British freed during the American Revolution. The Colonization Society attracted a lot of attention as a possible solution to the problem of slavery in America because the problem was twofold: it was not only the existence of this hideous and degrading institution, which was now being publicly exposed, but a problem of white America being disinclined to live in a biracial society. The thought was, What if we repatriate free slaves, send them back to Africa? A couple of thousand did go back and formed the nucleus of Liberia. But it was a fantasy solution. The population of slavery was doubling every twenty years. . . . There were a million slaves moving to 4 million by the time of the Civil War.

The impetus for northern abolition was very much a sense of the contradiction between [slavery and] the natural rights affirmed in America's founding, in the Declaration of Independence. It was a dramatic move. It was the first legislative act abolishing slavery in the history of the world. It's interesting that England gets credit for being the first country to abolish slavery because . . . actually the state of Pennsylvania, in 1780, was the first political unit to abolish slavery.

[Abolition] didn't happen in the South because there wasn't the same drive to do it. There were many more slaves in the South. About 40 percent of Virginia's population, which was far and away the largest state in the Union, was African American. South Carolina had a slave majority—more like 60 percent of the population. So there were many more complicated problems associated with abolishing slavery in the South. It didn't have the same group of antislavery reformers. But there was antislavery agitation in the South. The contradiction between slavery and the Declaration of Independence was evident and spoken about [there]. But it was just much more difficult. . . . In the North, there was a small free black population to grudgingly integrate into the white population.

Northern abolition was gradual [and] peaceful. Typically, a state would pass a law that would say: All slaves born after this date will be free when they reach the age of twenty-one for women or twenty-four for men. It would have been difficult to have a gradual emancipation in the South, or at least it would have strained the moral and economic resources of the South in a way that it didn't in the North.

IT WAS A VERY EBULLIENT economy; there was this release of ordinary ambition, and there was this scrambling for land. In the South you had a scrambling for land and slaves. But the southerners managed to keep this out of public view. In the North it was much more open, and this was new; this was novel. It wasn't refined. It wasn't restrained the way it had been, and people were shocked at this open avidity for gain. It came from the absence of restraints. It meant that people could follow their ambition and they could brag about it at the tavern, they could talk about it in the parlor. Maybe there were some people who were outraged by this; people of taste were offended. But the social arbiters had been dismissed. They had been sent home, sent away, and the public was pretty much open to whatever group was out there.

Writers Frances Trollope and Charles Dickens toured America at this time. They found a society that was intoxicatingly free. They saw things they loved. They loved this outpouring of human energy. They loved to see [how] these associations were forming. But they were appalled at other things, such as the scramble for money or the servants' lack of respect, which appalled everyone. Servants in America were saucy. They wouldn't accept the word "servant"; they were "help." That was an Americanism that the British thought was just ridiculous. So theirs was a mixed report. They saw a society in which all the arrows were not pointing in the same direction.

MY FAVORITE ASPECTS of this period are the voluntary association, the zeal of people getting together and forming a society to determine America's national character or to get rid of liquor or to honor the Sabbath or whatever. I like the idea that these people could move for women's rights, which happens in the next decade. I think that voluntary spirit was wonderful because it created a social integration that is sometimes lacking in our world today.

Celebrating Fifty Years of Independence

by

ANDREW BURSTEIN

On July 4, 1826, as Americans enthusiastically celebrated the fiftieth anniversary of the signing of the Declaration of Independence, they lost two of the last and most revered founding fathers—Thomas Jefferson and John Adams. In a Booknotes *interview recorded on February 14, 2001, Andrew Burstein, a professor of history at the University of Tulsa, described the state of the growing nation and the ways in which it marked its first significant anniversary. Mr. Burstein's* America's Jubilee: How in 1826 a Generation Remembered Fifty Years of Independence *was published in 2000 by Alfred A. Knopf.*

THOMAS JEFFERSON died at home at Monticello near 1:00 in the afternoon on July 4, 1826. He was surrounded by his servants and his family. John Adams died about four and a half hours later, around 5:30 in the afternoon at his home in Quincy, Massachusetts, surrounded by loving family as well.

I was curious about what they, at that time, described as the astronomical odds that Thomas Jefferson and John Adams could have exited the national stage, could have died on this glorious day—the fiftieth anniversary of America's independence. It seemed too good to be true, . . . a mystery that needed to be solved. John Adams's last words, as they've come down to us in history, were, "Thomas Jefferson survives." Too good to be true. I had to go back and find out who said what, when. Who recorded Adams's last words? Who was in the room? Who promoted it in the newspapers, in speeches? Our historic memory has been conditioned by the myths that were created by this generation—the generation of 1826, the sons and daughters of the revolutionaries. They needed to hallow the day, and what better way than to take John Adams's words?

He did, in fact, say something about Jefferson on his deathbed, but the words were indistinctly uttered. What I did was trace how the people of 1826 made sure that they bequeathed to history this wonderful providential occurrence.

The coincidental deaths of Thomas Jefferson and John Adams, on this date of national jubilee, caused the children of the revolutionaries to feel that the republic was, perhaps, immortal, that providence was looking down on them and blessing their efforts. [These are] people who have been forgotten but were headliners in their own times. They were the ones who enshrined the Revolution as we've come to appreciate it. The founding generation was a generation of geniuses. The [next generation of Americans] were the ones who honored their parents and . . . romanticized the idea of America.

THE UNITED STATES in 1826 was really at an enthusiastic moment in its history. The canals were being built. The Erie Canal had become operational in 1825, and on July 4, 1825, the father of the Erie Canal, DeWitt Clinton, broke ground on the Ohio Canal. This was thought to be the way [in which] the twenty-four states were going to be linked. Canal building seems rather pedestrian to us at this point, but at that time it was as enthusiastically greeted as space exploration is in our own time.

Americans believed in the idea of improvement. John Quincy Adams coined this as the era of improvement. It was before the industrial revolution, but Americans were very much on the move. They heralded the revolutionaries for having given them a sense of unity, of harmony among the states. If there was a political issue that dominated the scene at this time, it was to what extent should the federal government, representing all the states, make policy for internal improvements like canals, road building, and turnpikes and to what extent should the states be permitted to retain the full power to conduct internal improvements in their own states.

People wrote letters [then] and that was how all emotional information was conveyed, and all information was conveyed. The telegraph was still a couple of decades away. And they marveled at steamboats. This was the new means of getting people from one place to another faster, just as canals were another means of getting people to places that they would otherwise have to hobble to over tree-stumped, pockmarked roads.

It was [also] a violent society. When Americans think of the Wild West, they think of the period after the Civil War because we have Hollywood to give us our history. In fact, the Wild West was pretty tame compared with the way America was, particularly on the frontier, in the early nineteenth century.

IN 1824 . . . PRESIDENT JAMES MONROE, in his last year of office, invited the Marquis de Lafayette [back to America]. He spent a little over a year in advance of the national jubilee touring all twenty-four of the states. Lafayette was called "the nation's guest" because he was the guest of Congress, the guest of the Monroe administration, and he was the last surviving general of the war for independence. So, as Americans began to romanticize the upcoming jubilee of independence, nobody represented that historic moment, that nation-building moment, as [much as] General Lafayette.

[As a young man] Lafayette had been inspired by the American dream, the idea of helping liberty find itself. At the age of nineteen, he became a major general in the Continental Army. He was like a son to George Washington and he was an aide-de-camp to Washington for a period of time. He proved to be an able tactician as well.

Lafayette sailed on *La Victoire* to America in the dark days of the Revolutionary War. He fought at the undistinguished battle of Brandywine, where, in his first engagement, he was wounded. He was nursed back to health under the roof of George Washington, and that's where they became close. Lafayette was a nobleman and therefore able to go back to France and report on the patriotic cause. Perhaps more than anyone else, with the possible exception of Benjamin Franklin, he enlisted the French government in the American cause, which, of course, was the decisive reason for America's victory over Great Britain, winning its independence.

He was sixty-six years old in 1824. The Marquis de Lafayette was a hero to Americans. He had not been in the United States since 1784. Everywhere he went, people fainted at his feet, newspapers carried stories. James Fenimore Cooper, the distinguished novelist whose book *The Last of the Mohicans* was published in 1826—that year's best-seller—wrote for a newspaper called the *New York American.* [Cooper covered the reception given for Lafayette in New York City, noting] the lavish display, the tent and the thousands of people and the triumphal arc that were put together to welcome Lafayette to America. Everywhere Lafayette went, cannons roared and speeches were made and balls were held and everyone who was anyone came out to shake his hand.

[LAFAYETTE'S VISIT] was reported everywhere in the United States, including who toasted whom and what was said. The canals then replaced Lafayette as a major, if not the chief, issue. In turn, there was the election of 1824, and there were strong editorials in regional presses; different candidates were put forward and their friends would write supportive articles hailing them.

The election of 1824 didn't actually end until February 1825, when the House voted John Quincy Adams as president. Andrew Jackson had more popular votes but not enough votes to secure the election without it being thrown into the House, according to the Constitution. [Andrew Jackson received 43 percent of the popular vote and ninety-nine electoral votes; John Quincy Adams won 30 percent of the popular vote and eighty-four electoral votes. Then there was William Crawford, who got forty-one electoral votes, and Henry Clay, who got thirty-seven.] Clay was not part of the House runoff because he did not receive enough electoral votes. It was really between Adams and Jackson.

What happened was that Henry Clay, as an influential member of the House, former Speaker of the House, used his connections to arm-twist, to get his friends, North and South, to vote for Adams. Adams turned around and appointed Henry Clay secretary of state. This was then called the "corrupt bargain," and it hounded Clay for the rest of his career. He ran for president two more times and was soundly defeated both times, by Andrew Jackson in 1832 and James K. Polk in 1844. Adams became president and he was seen as an illegitimate president. Clay, however, was identified as the real villain in this drama.

JOHN QUINCY ADAMS was probably better prepared for the presidency than any president. He had been a professor of rhetoric at Harvard, who had published a book on rhetoric in 1811. He had grown up in diplomatic circles; as a teenager, he was accompanying the American minister to St. Petersburg, to Russia. Later, under President James Madison, he became the ambassador, or the minister, to Russia and was involved with Czar Alexander I in attempting to negotiate an end to the War of 1812. He was, at the end of the War of 1812, the American minister to Great Britain at a time when the British were dismissive of America, angry at America, in part for Jackson's magnificent victory at the Battle of New Orleans.

So, John Quincy Adams was in the heat of American political life at home and abroad for many, many years. In fact, while Jefferson had defeated Adams's father in the election of 1800 for president, John Quincy Adams, as senator for Massachusetts in the last two years of Jefferson's presidency, embraced Jefferson's foreign policy. As a result, the Federalists kicked him out of office, and he was out of a job, as his father had been eight years earlier. These irascible, cantankerous Adamses liked to be in the heat of things. They were diplomats who weren't very diplomatic.

Andrew Jackson, who had lost in 1824, . . . had such charisma and so many followers that when William Crawford's southern partisans disbanded (because Crawford suffered a stroke and was no longer capable of campaigning for the presidency) and the westerners who had supported Clay over Adams were dismayed by the corrupt bargain, they shifted their allegiance to Jackson. Everyone was up in arms about this so-called corrupt bargain. Jackson himself tried to remain aloof and allowed all his supporters in Congress to do his bidding for him and they made long, passionate, often angry speeches about the conduct of the current administration. The writing was on the wall early that Jackson had been robbed of election, that he would be the victorious candidate in 1828, and all he really had to do was sit pretty out in Tennessee.

In 1828 Andrew Jackson beat John Quincy Adams soundly. Adams only won portions of New England, his home area. Jackson won most of the country.

[OF ALL THESE CHARACTERS, I perhaps would have most liked to meet] William Wirt. He was a true romantic. He wrote a lot of newspaper essays and he gave [great] speeches, such as his joint eulogy in the U.S. Capitol in the fall of 1826, eulogizing Adams and Jefferson. He was a man who had a lot on his mind and dreamed of being a novelist. He wanted to give up the courtroom, give up his legal career, and become a professional writer.

What I wanted to bring to this book especially was to talk about the people who were important in 1826, who are no longer important to us, but who have, in fact, had a great impact on shaping our historic memory of the Revolutionary era. William Wirt, for example, was attorney general of the United States during the administrations of James Monroe and John Quincy Adams, so for twelve consecutive years he was attorney general. He argued some of the most important cases before the Supreme Court before and after his tenure as attorney general. Yet he was, perhaps more importantly, the author of a well-read biography of Patrick Henry, the orator who, some said, brought the Revolution into being; who cried, "Give me liberty or give me death." It was William Wirt, as a biographer, as a literary man, who gave us the Patrick Henry who has come down in history.

Jefferson, who was not a fan of Patrick Henry, once said that "he spoke as Homer wrote." So Henry was considered an orator of the finest quality, but [he was] vintage American in that his roots were obscure. He was one of these rags-to-riches types: an ill-educated frontiersman, a failed storekeeper who kept his law offices in a tavern in Hanover County, Virginia, but who somehow had a mesmerizing power that caused all the great minds, the geniuses, of the Revolutionary generation to pay attention to him. He was the uniter, he was the harmonizer. He was the man whose great speechmaking brought the revolutionaries together.

William Wirt presented it in such a way as to suggest that, without Henry, the Revolution may never have happened; that everyone else was too polite;

it needed a rough-hewn frontiersman like this. His book on Patrick Henry was published in 1817, . . . the same year that Wirt became attorney general of the United States, and it went through dozens of editions by 1826. The edition that I own is an 1833 edition, so it was published throughout the nineteenth century and read by many people.

.In fact, Henry's orations were never recorded, and the truth kept running away from Wirt as he wrote. He wrote letters to his friends deploring what he was doing. He knew that he had happened upon what I guess we could describe as a romantic truth, but what comes down to us as facts, in fact, were not facts. Wirt romanticized the Revolution, romanticized Henry, and he shaped future Americans' impressions of the Revolutionary generation.

THE FIREWORKS, THE "bonfires and the illuminations," to use John Adams's prediction for how the Fourth of July, 1826, would be celebrated, were comparable [to modern patriotic celebrations]. Everywhere you went, there were fireworks and parades and speeches. What makes this moment so special is that it was the consecration, the immortalization of 1776. These were the people, in 1826, who made the Revolution immortal. They were the ones who put the age behind them, finally, by declaring it a masterful age.

President John Quincy Adams . . . attended the celebration at the Capitol. There was a long parade, and he went in a carriage with military honors and thousands of people marching behind. He learned of Jefferson's death a couple days later. His father's death was anticipated because he received a letter just prior to the jubilee in which one of his relatives said it looked doubtful he would survive more than a few days, a couple weeks at most. So John Quincy Adams decided he would go home and try to make it back to Quincy, Massachusetts, before his father died. He left on July 7 and before he even got to Baltimore, the news had already reached the papers in Baltimore that John Adams had died on the Fourth of July as well. John Quincy Adams got home on the seventeenth of July, and for most of his journey he was aware he wouldn't be able to see his father again.

Tocqueville's
Democracy in America

---

by

HARVEY C. MANSFIELD

Alexis de Tocqueville was born into the French aristocracy in Paris on July 29, 1805. During the years 1831–1832 he traveled throughout America with Gustave de Beaumont as commissioners sent by the French government to study the American prison system. He wrote Democracy in America, *the result of his travels and observations, upon his return to France. Since the book's first publication in 1835, there have been several different translations of Tocqueville's work. Harvey C. Mansfield appeared on* Booknotes *on October 13, 2000, to discuss his translation with his wife, Delba Winthrop, of* Democracy in America, *published in 2000 by the University of Chicago Press. Mr. Mansfield teaches government at Harvard.*

DEMOCRACY IN AMERICA IS, at once, the best book ever written on democracy and the best book ever written on America. It's about the logic of democracy, which is best shown in America, and it's also about the peculiarities of America, the country where the Puritans landed, where Indians were mistreated, and where blacks were enslaved. America has its own characteristics, but it's a democracy. And for Tocqueville, especially, and perhaps still for us today, it represents democracy in the world. It's the most advanced democratic country. So if you want to look at democracy, you have to look at democracy in America.

Democracy is rule of the people, literally, but Tocqueville had a different understanding. He spoke especially of the equality of conditions in America; that people were similar to one another and if they weren't, nonetheless, they still regarded themselves as similar. He thought of it as a social condition more than as a form of government, though he certainly was interested in government, the government seemed to be a consequence of a democratic society.

TOCQUEVILLE WAS BORN in 1805 and died [in] 1859. He came to America in 1831. He lived [much] of his life [in] Paris because he was a member of the French Academy and hung out there, especially during the time of Louis Napoleon, when French republicanism was under a shadow and, of course, he had his ancestral estate in Normandy. He was Alexis de Tocqueville, and the "de" means "from." So he was from a place called Tocqueville, and you can still visit that place in Normandy.

[Tocqueville wrote *Democracy in America* when he was about twenty-five. At that age, a person's mind has not necessarily developed in reason as much as it could, at least] not in philosophy—not in political philosophy, especially. In mathematics, yes. If you're not a famous mathematician by the time you're twenty-five, I suppose you won't be one. But philosophy, especially political philosophy, depends on or uses experience. You have to learn what human beings are like. That's one point. And then another point is that with something like mathematics or different branches of science, you're on a frontier. Everything that's being done now is the best that's ever been done. But with political philosophy, that's by no means the case. What's being done now is not as good as what used to be done in the great books or in the classics. It takes a long time to develop a mature understanding of those books, reading them over and over, and teaching them helps as well. So you'll get better. And you would be at your best, I would say, in your fifties or sixties, even.

THE FIRST THING YOU might do [to study *Democracy in America*], just to get yourself interested, is to look at some of the most interesting parts, like the five chapters on women in the second volume, or the pages on American blacks in the end of the first volume, or the Indians. These are some of the most famous passages. His contrast between America and Russia, two democratic countries, which way will the democratic future take us? Toward America or toward Russia? [Russia embodied] a kind of democratic despotism, as he understood it. . . . I would [also suggest that a reader] go back to the beginning and spend a lot of time on the introduction.

[Today] the place of women is utterly different from what Tocqueville [described] in his book. We've gone to a kind of gender-neutral society in which women have equal rights in public as well as private. Tocqueville said in his book that the places of men and women in America were equal, but they had very different . . . destinies. Now that's no longer true, and I'm sure that would impress him.

He would also be interested in what's happened to black Americans. Tocqueville had a pessimistic view of what might happen. He was fearful of a race war, and, of course, we did have a war, but it wasn't a race war. So he would be very interested to see that blacks are somehow much more integrated as Americans than he would have expected.

The presidency has become still more of a tribune than it was when he saw it and therefore much more powerful, in a sense; weaker in another sense. He saw Andrew Jackson, and he didn't much care for Jackson. He thought that Andrew Jackson was a weak president. He is usually considered today by historians and political scientists to be a strong one, but Tocqueville's understanding of weak was somebody who went along with the people too much. So I think looking at the presidency today, he would say, "Yes, they're stronger in the sense that they occupy the center of the stage much more even than Jackson did, but weaker in the sense that presidents rely now on polls and focus groups."

Tocqueville saw the power of the judiciary. I don't think he would be surprised [at its power today]. He's famous for one of his remarks in that book—that in America, somehow every political question becomes a judicial one. I don't think he would be surprised at the fact that if you look in our generation, most of the big decisions that have been made as to how our life is actually lived—a great example, abortion—have been made by the judiciary.

[He would still call the House of Representatives "vulgar."] We've maybe polished up our act a little bit. We're not as coarse as we used to be. We don't drink as much whiskey. There are no spittoons in the halls of Congress, as there used to be. We're not as rustic, or not as many of us are farmers, and the farmers that we do have are businessmen now. So our life has become more industrial, more technological, more professional. But it still somehow remains deeply democratic.

[Tocqueville would probably believe] that television somehow heightens the effects of democracy. Who am I to put words in Tocqueville's mouth? But this is what occurs to me: that it makes government even more immediate, [but] that it substitutes . . . for a better and more active participation. It tells you what's going on—in Israel or in the Middle East or whatever. It doesn't tell you what's going on in Cambridge, Massachusetts. Well, there is a channel about that, but you're probably not going to be watching. So in other words, it doesn't tell you about problems that you can do something about or that you have a chance in your daily life to solve through association. Tocqueville is a great one for association. [Therefore, it] is probably bad that television is a substitute for association.

Liberals like Tocqueville's communitarian aspect, the fact that, as [Harvard professor] Robert Putnam says, Americans don't "bowl alone." And conservatives like his attack on big government. Tocqueville says that big government leads to a people that suffer under a mild schoolmaster—despotism, he even says. So somehow liberals and conservatives both like Tocqueville, but what that probably means is that they overlook the parts in him that go against what they like to believe.

[MY WIFE, DELBA WINTHROP, and I translated this from French to English.] It took us about five years. It would have gone more quickly if we had known at the beginning what we knew at the end, because you learn as you go along. My experience had been mostly with Italian. I've translated Machiavelli into English, which was, by the way, much harder than this. Neither of us are experienced translators, but we loved Tocqueville and we loved this book and we thought that the two preceding translations [were inadequate]. One . . . was made in Tocqueville's time by an English friend of his, a translation that Tocqueville criticized as being too aristocratic in tone, and the other . . . was done in America in the 1960s, and that's a little bit better, but it's not accurate enough.

All three [versions translated] the full book. The first one, by Henry Reeve, Tocqueville's friend, was quite loose and, for example, didn't even keep his paragraphs. Tocqueville's writing is peculiar to him because he had very long sentences and very short paragraphs. There were sometimes even one-sentence paragraphs. We thought that was very important for his style.

The more recent translator [was] the American George Lawrence. It came out in the '60s and is much more readable and more up-to-date than the Henry Reeve; but it's not as accurate as ours, and it doesn't have the notes that we had. Sometimes when he encounters a difficulty in the French, he makes a kind of end run around it instead of reproducing the difficulty. We think that if something's difficult to read in French, it also ought to be a little bit difficult to read in English.

Both of us speak [French but do not] write it well. Translating from English back into French—that we couldn't do. And that brings up a kind of secret of translation: that the language you really have to know is the one you're going into. There are obviously some puzzles in Tocqueville's text. It's hard in places to understand his French, but you can figure it out. The real difficulty is finding the right English for the French equivalents.

WE WANTED A MORE accurate translation, one with a few notes that would tell readers things they don't necessarily know, like when was the Hundred Years War, . . . and that would be more careful about Tocqueville's key terms.

He wasn't just an observer or a traveler; though he was those things he was also a thinker. He said, "I saw in America the image of democracy itself." That's a kind of theoretical statement.

[Studying Tocqueville's papers at Yale's Beinecke Library] didn't make much of a difference with our translation because we were dealing with what he actually chose to say. What they have at the Beinecke Library are his manuscripts, which are certainly wonderful to look at. He wrote on one side of the page, and then on the other side he put his footnotes and left room for other thoughts and for comments by his brother and his father, who read his text and made little criticisms. There's actually an edition in French which gives you in the margin these remarks by his family. Not many authors have that happen to them, to have your father and brother say what they think of you. So it's wonderfully interesting, but it wasn't all that much use to us as translators.

[THE REASON TO STUDY these classic texts is] to get beyond the newspapers and magazines. Most people read newspapers or watch TV, and if they want to get profound, they read magazines. But the people who write magazines have read these books, so if you really want to get back to the sources of things, you have to read the books of philosophy. That is where the ideas that get spread into the world first originate, and where they first originate is where they're most deeply and most often sharply stated. So it's to get back to the first source of things, . . . so that you don't depend on other people. It's a route to being independent or even free. A free person in the highest sense of free is someone who doesn't live off another person's word or doesn't live by the authority of his society and our society, the authority of public opinion. And the way to achieve this independence is by reading, especially, the great books, the classic books.

Slavery and the Civil War

1850–1865

Buildup to the Civil War

by

STEPHEN B. OATES

In 1792 Eli Whitney invented the cotton gin, which made it easier to process cotton on a large scale and had the unintended consequence of further committing the South to agriculture and a slave-based economy. A growing abolitionist movement, opposed to the practice of slavery and seeking to ban it, developed in the early 1800s. The stage was set for a national confrontation. On March 21, 1997, Stephen B. Oates, a history professor at the University of Massachusetts, appeared on Booknotes *to discuss* The Approaching Fury: Voices of the Storm, 1820–1861, *published in 1997 by HarperCollins.*

[AMERICA IN THE 1830S] was an extraordinarily decentralized agricultural country that was not even a country yet. It was more a loose confederation of localities and rampant localism; and only a handful of people, . . . like Henry Clay and Daniel Webster and a young Abraham Lincoln growing up, had any national vision whatever. [There was a] growing slavery problem. Eighteen thirty-one was the year of the Nat Turner insurrection. It was the year that William Lloyd Garrison started publishing his *Liberator*. Alexis de Tocqueville [touring America then] said this slavery thing would tear the country up.

[THE TITLE] CAME from my characters. Starting with Thomas Jefferson and all the way through to Jefferson Davis who said, "The storm has broke upon us," they used the metaphor of the sectional conflict as a gathering storm, an approaching fury, a coming tornado. They referred to it again and again, "The wind blasts of civil war now upon us.". . . These are people who lived with the weather constantly.

I started with Thomas Jefferson because Jefferson was slapping the side of his head, profoundly upset over the Missouri crisis of 1819–1820. It was the first crisis over the territorial issue of slavery, and it was a territorial issue that would ultimately smash up the nation. He was upset. He said the threats of disunion in 1820 caused him to look into the future. He foresaw the Civil War, saying, "My God, this country is going to have a blowup. When it hits us, it's going to be like a tornado." Those were his exact words. . . . He was the first of a whole line of seers who looked into the future and saw that this territorial issue and the issue of slavery in a nation based on the Declaration of Independence, this combustible issue, was going to blow the sections apart.

In the 1850s, we had a five-way fight going: We had Lincoln and the Republicans arguing with the southern Democrats. We had the northern Democrats, with Stephen A. Douglas, arguing with the southern Democrats through Jefferson Davis. And we had the abolitionists. There were arguments between Frederick Douglass and the political abolitionists and [between] William Lloyd Garrison, who was still in favor of nonviolent moral suasion, and the no-political-process abolitionism. All of that led to John Brown's violent abolitionism. I had a theme of abolitionism moving from nonviolent protests, to political process and protests, to violent protests.

HENRY CLAY WAS BORN in Virginia and migrated as a young man. A lawyer whose mentor was Thomas Jefferson, he went out to the brand-new state of Kentucky. He made his reputation and served . . . as a U.S. senator early in his twenties and speaker of the House [at age thirty-four]. He went on to become one of the great senior senators for the next thirty years.

He was a perennial candidate for president, and he probably should have been president. As he said, "I would have made the best president of them all." Now you have got to understand about Henry Clay; he would joke and say, "I've never met a man who was my superior." Then he would grin, but he meant it. The only reason he didn't make the presidency was because he lacked a military career. Had he been a famous general, he would have been in the White House, served at least once, maybe twice. I think he understood that the lack of military success was probably what doomed him.

The American Colonization Society was founded by Clay and a number of other guys in Washington, D.C., in 1819, for the purpose of removing the free black population from this country. It was a private organization. It got its funds simply by soliciting. It tried to get some money from the federal government and whatever philanthropic individuals would give it. Henry Clay became a leader of it. He was the spiritual founder. He served, eventually, as its president. He was also its most vigorous speaker and champion.

The Colonization Society was supposed to induce the southern states to abolish slavery by a gradual emancipation program because there would be a viable, workable colonization program underway by this organization. Clay had sponsored one of the groups of people pushing for gradual emancipation in Kentucky, and it failed. It failed because there was no colonization program. Most white people were not going to let blacks remain in this country free. If the slaves were liberated, they were going to have to be removed outside the country. Jefferson had argued that in the previous century, and Clay believed it too.

Clay claimed a whole lot of blacks went back to Liberia. But ultimately, . . . the actual number was around 10,000. In its first ten years, maybe a handful of thousand—3,000 or 4,000 was all. It had to be voluntary. As Frederick Douglass, the great black leader, pointed out, "This is our country too. Most of us are second-, third-, and fourth-generation black Americans, and we're not leaving."

NAT TURNER WAS A black fellow born in Southampton County, Virginia, in 1800, the same year Jefferson was elected to the presidency. He was a slave and was extremely bright and precocious. He learned how to read. He couldn't even remember how he did, but somehow he did. His old Methodist owner thought he was just the brightest little kid—"bright little darky" is what he called him. This young boy, by the time he was eight or nine years old, had memorized the entire Bible. The old master liked to trot out his little bright darky and show him off to itinerant Methodist preachers who came by to spend the night and drink some of the apple brandy that the old master made.

The master, the slave boy's grandmother and mother, and everybody else on the plantation said, "This boy's too bright to be a slave." The old white man said, "He'll never amount to anything if he remains a slave. He's too smart for it." So Turner grew up thinking there was a promise of freedom. But when he came to manhood, he was not freed. Turner's first master died, his son inherited him, and the son sent Turner to the fields. That started the rage and it went on. He got married; he had absentee children. The more he thought about slavery, the angrier he got. He found abundant examples in the Old Testament where slavery was supposed to be banned by the Scriptures. Then he finally got his insurrection—the rampage through Southampton County—in which ten children in Levi Waller's family were decapitated. The insurrection lasted just a couple of days. The superiority of white firepower, with the federal forces thrown in as well, put it down.

WILLIAM LLOYD GARRISON was the great founder of the immediate, nonviolent abolitionist movement started in 1831. When he started his *Liberator* [a daily newspaper] in Boston, he argued for nonviolent moral suasion. "We're going to appeal to slaveholders; we're going to appeal to the northerners, who are guilty of complicity to slavery and appeal to their conscience, and the country will all come together and abolish slavery.". . . Garrison had a column called "The Refuge of Oppression." He would quote southern newspapers and let southerners hang themselves by quoting some of the stuff they said in defense of slavery or some of the violence newspapers would admit to that existed inherently in the system.

Garrison . . . brought Frederick Douglass into the movement. He didn't make Frederick Douglass—Douglass made himself—but Garrison gave Douglass a great start. Douglass rapidly became one of the best-known orators in the abolitionist crusade. Garrison thought he had made Douglass and that Douglass was a loyal supporter. Garrison demanded loyal support. [He said,] "We're not going to have anything to do with churches. We're not having anything to do with governments. We're having nothing to do with the military. They're all corrupted by slavery.".

Douglass went to England and then came back home and told Garrison, "I think I'm going to open up my own black newspaper to show people that blacks can do this sort of thing." But Garrison said, "They've got a black newspaper. It's the *Liberator*.". . . Garrison and his friend in the movement, Wendell Phillips, dissuaded Douglass at this point from establishing a black paper, and they went on a tour together. But when Garrison fell sick, Douglass went back to Rochester, New York, and set up [his] paper to prove to the American reading public that a black man could not only write an intelligent and analytical and truthful paper but could manage it as a successful enterprise.

MOSTLY FREE NEGROES and the white and black abolitionists who followed Garrison [read the *Liberator*]. Black people read [the *Liberator*] too, [though] I think the *North Star* mainly appealed to black people. It was hardly ever a very viable source. It had fewer readers than the *Liberator* did. John Brown subscribed to Douglass's *North Star*.

John Brown was born in Connecticut, but he spent much of his time in Ohio. A go-for-broke typical businessman of the 1830s and 1840s: always on the lookout for the Big Rock Candy Mountain, moving back and forth for the next big fix. He was a speculator in land and in wool. This was a speculative time; everyone was doing it and going broke. Brown failed maybe more than the average guy.

He was humorless. He would not have known a witticism if it had come up and kicked him in the pants. He was a pious Calvinist of the old school and demanded that his children walk the righteous path. He got so horrendously upset if they strayed, questioned, or got off into some of the newer and less demanding forms of evangelical Christianity. He was profoundly upset about slavery because he thought that Jehovah, his God of the Old Testament, in a fit of anger, would simply wipe the United States out, since he believed that the Scriptures condemned slavery. Brown and his family would never get to paradise if that happened.

Brown was like an Old Testament warrior. . . . Brown's whole plan at Harpers Ferry was to have the two sections come to some kind of blow. He could not have foreseen the entire Civil War, but some mighty blowup of some sort in which slavery would die. He kept saying, "I'm going to be like Samson. I'm pretty sure I'm going to fail at Harpers Ferry, but I'll so polarize the country that the South is going to blame me on the Republicans and on the North. I hope it will polarize the sections worse than anything. I'll be like Samson, pulling the temple down."

JOHN C. CALHOUN was the chief spokesman for the slave South, particularly in the 1820s . . . to 1850. At one time, he was a nationalist and a presidential contender, but after the rise of abolitionism in 1831 and from then on, he was never a nationalist. The turn for him came with the fight over the protective tariffs in the 1820s and early 1830s. But with the rise of northern abolitionism, the horrific threat that [it] posed to the whole slave-based way of life of the South, he became the chief spokesman of the South in answer to the abolitionists.

Calhoun was the toughest to bring alive and the toughest to become empathetic with because the cause that he was defending is a loathsome cause for a twentieth-century sensibility. He was on the wrong side of history and he didn't know it. . . . He was the foremost leader of the new defense of slavery that emerged from 1831 until the end of the Civil War. Before then, southerners had defended slavery as a necessary evil. That was a Jeffersonian argument. But with the forces of abolition seeming to surround them— Mexico became an abolitionist nation, abolishing slavery in the 1820s; Great Britain abolished slavery [throughout] the empire in the 1830s; there was a powerful and potent northern abolitionist movement—southerners felt themselves a lonely slave outpost in a hostile world. With Calhoun, they pronounced slavery a positive good. It was good for the blacks and good for the whites and ordained by God from the beginning of time.

[I USED] STEPHEN A. DOUGLAS . . . to describe the 1854 Kansas-Nebraska Act. That was his baby. That was the act that started the inexorable drift toward civil war. I let him describe why he got that bill enacted and his incredible misperception about how it would be taken in the North. . . .

Stephen A. Douglas was one of the most profane men in politics, certainly in the nineteenth century. Even in speeches in the Senate, according to reporters, he was "damning" and "helling" and "goddamning" all the way through the speeches even with ladies present in the galleries. So I decided to honor his character and let him curse, and he curses with gusto.

Then I bring Lincoln in, because Lincoln responded to the Kansas-Nebraska Act. He was one of the northerners who were so upset they formed a brand-new political party, the Republican Party.

I don't have any doubt in my mind at all that there was an assassination attempt—a plot to kill President-elect Abraham Lincoln—in Baltimore as he came through in 1861 to go to Washington to be inaugurated as president. [As a precaution, his advisers insisted that he travel in disguise.] But, of course, the news leaked out that the president-elect had sneaked through Baltimore and the press made a field day out of it. . . . The *New York Times* and a number of other publications talked about how Lincoln was a coward and a baboon, particularly for coming in like that. *Vanity Fair* had a cartoon of a scarecrowish Lincoln in Scottish kilts dancing and sneaking his way [beneath] a cloak into the capital. The press really demeaned him for that.

His poor wife, Mary, . . . endured the worst episode of her life going through Baltimore. People were yelling and screaming, "Hurray for Jefferson Davis" and "Where's that Republican, Lincoln? Goddamn him! Bring him out! Show his face!" Mary said, "They were looking for you, Father," as she called Lincoln. "They were looking for you, and they leered at us and jeered at us. Oh," she said, "it was the most miserable experience I've ever had."

IN THIS BOOK I TRIED to show how the perception of events played such a crucial role in the coming of the Civil War: how southerners perceived northerners; how northerners perceived southerners; how some northerners perceived other northerners; how the northern Democrats perceived the northern Republicans. The way we perceive things causes us to behave the way we do. It causes us to act the way we act and causes us to think and say the things that we do.

In the second book of this series, some of the same players will return. Jefferson Davis and Lincoln will come back, . . . Frederick Douglass will come back. Then we'll have the generals added: Sherman, Grant, and Lee. And then I'll have a couple of northern women: Cornelia Hancock, a young Quaker nurse, who went to Gettysburg after the great battle there and worked for almost a month in a horrendous battlefield hospital. . . . And I'm going to use Mary Livermore, who was a great head of the Chicago Sanitary Commission and was one of the great businesswomen of the war who raised an enormous amount of supplies for Lincoln's army.

The last character to come on with a coda to wrap it all up is Walt Whitman, who gave a little-attended but profoundly moving and insightful talk
about Abraham Lincoln's death and what that meant for the coalescing of a
nation and the creation of a nation. It's a coda that talks about how the final,
agonizing, terrible death of Lincoln was what really finally brought us
together as a country.

Volunteer Soldiers

by

JAMES M. McPHERSON

The Civil War lasted four years and exacted an enormous toll on the nation. There were over 600,000 American casualties. Both sides were, after all, Americans. On March 21, 1994, James M. McPherson talked to Booknotes viewers about What They Fought For: 1861–1865 *(Louisiana State University Press, 1994), his examination of the lives and motivations of the fighting men of the war. Mr. McPherson teaches courses on the Civil War at Princeton.*

MY BOOK IS ABOUT what motivated volunteer soldiers in the Civil War to risk their lives, both Union and Confederate. Eighty to ninety percent of the fighting soldiers in the Civil War were volunteers—most of them volunteering in the first year of the war. It was a noncoercive, democratic society. The [mustering of troops] to fight the Civil War was a kind of do-it-yourself mobilization from the bottom up—from localities, counties, communities, and states.

During the Civil War, soldiers wrote an enormous number of letters home. Many of them kept diaries. Letters were not subject to censorship during the Civil War, and so the best place to go to find out what these men really thought they were fighting for—the purposes of their volunteering to fight and risk their lives—is to go to their personal letters to parents, wives, sweethearts, brothers, and sisters who were eager to hear about their experience as soldiers, and . . . are amazingly frank.

I've read an estimated 25,000 letters. I've actually read the letters or diaries—sometimes soldiers' collections contained both—of about 1,000 soldiers, 600 Union and 400 Confederate. That's about 800 collections of letters, I'd say, and the average collection [has] thirty to forty letters. Some are only a dozen or fifteen because many of the letters haven't survived. I've read some collections that have as many as 300 letters. A soldier was writing three or four letters a week, either to his wife or his mother or a family member.

The letters that really got me more than any others . . . were from two brothers. They were Quaker farmers from New York State and, of course, the Quakers were pacifists. They did not believe in violence, but in the Civil War some Quakers, including these two brothers, believed so powerfully in the goal of freeing the slaves that they actually enlisted to fight in the Union army. Both of them were killed during the war, and the letters that I found most moving were those that they had written to their mother in the months before they were killed—one was killed at Gettysburg—in which they explained why they were fighting.

The older brother said that a man risking his life for freedom is risking something more precious than life itself; we all have to die sometime and how better than by fighting for freedom. . . . After he was killed and the other brother was writing to his widowed mother to console her, he also wrote, "Oh, God, thy price for freedom is a dear one, but nevertheless we must pay that price." I found that powerfully moving.

THE CIVIL WAR lasted four years. It started in April 1861 and ended in April 1865; 620,000 soldiers died . . . —360,000 Union soldiers and 260,000 Confederate soldiers. To give you some idea of what kind of impact that war had on American society, with that number of dead, it amounted to 2 percent of the American population in 1861. If 2 percent of the American population were to be killed in a war fought by this country today, the number of American war dead would be 5 million. One can readily imagine the kind of impact that number of deaths would have on American society today.

The Civil War started primarily because, in the generation before 1861, an antislavery movement had grown in the North that attacked the South's "peculiar institution" as immoral, inhumane, and inconsistent with American ideals of liberty and the Declaration of Independence. . . . Only one-third of the Southern whites belonged to slaveholding families, . . . [but] Southerners—slave owners and the society that they ruled—felt increasingly defensive about this attack on the institution that underlay their economy and society. The Republican Party was founded in the mid-1850s on a platform of restricting the further expansion of slavery, as one of its leading founders, Abraham Lincoln, put it, in order to put slavery "in the course of ultimate extinction." He was a gradual emancipationist. When that party and that candidate won the presidency in 1860, the Southerners saw the handwriting on the wall. They had lost political control of the national government, and they feared that that loss of political control portended an eventual loss . . . of the institution of slavery.

They seceded to form an independent nation of eleven Confederate states, all of them slave states. The Lincoln administration refused to recognize secession as constitutional or legitimate. It argued that if any state or group of states could secede at will, then the United States had no national government; in fact, there was no such entity as the United States if [people] could get out of it at any time whenever they didn't like the outcome of a presidential election. The two sections were polarized over the issues of slavery and secession.

There were thirty-four states altogether. . . . Two other Southern states, Kentucky and Missouri, had a minority of secessionists who formed their own Confederate government and applied for admission into the Confederate congress and were admitted. So when you see the Confederate flag, it will have thirteen states, and the number of states that remained loyal to the Union was really twenty-three because Kentucky and Missouri were split.

ALL IT NEEDED WAS a trigger, an incident, to start a war. That trigger was the Confederate firing on Fort Sumter, the United States installation in the harbor at Charleston, one of the last such United States installations in the Confederate States still under [federal] control. That functioned very much on Northern public opinion like the Japanese bombing of Pearl Harbor did in 1941 on American public opinion. It caused a rise of war fever in the South and a counterpart rise of war fever in the North. As Lincoln said in his second inaugural four years later, "The war came and lasted four years, resulting in the destruction of slavery, the destruction of the planter class in the South, and the social basis for its rule of the South." It also resolved for all time the question of whether a state or any group of states can secede from the United States. No state has tried it since then.

At all times in the war, the Union army had at least twice as many men under arms as the Confederate army. The high point of the war for both of them in terms of number of men was in 1863 and 1864. By 1864, however, the Confederates had no more manpower on which to call. They had mobilized every white male between seventeen and forty-three, or forty-five in some cases, who was not lame or blind. Their numbers gradually began to shrink and by the end of the war, the Union forces outnumbered the Confederate forces by four or five to one.

The Lincoln administration's [early] war aims were to restore the Union and not to abolish slavery. One of the reasons was that Lincoln was trying to keep the border slave states like Kentucky, Missouri, and Maryland loyal to the Union, while at the same time trying to reassure Southerners in the Confederacy that their fears that he was going to precipitately attack slavery were wrong. He was trying to make it a war only for union and not for the abolition of slavery. As a consequence, the Union army and the Lincoln administration [initially] refused to accept black soldiers, since to enlist them, especially if they'd been former slaves, would be a sign that it was an antislavery war.

The Lincoln administration [subsequently] transformed Northern war aims from that of restoring the old union to that of destroying the old union and rebuilding a new one. . . . "Give the union a new birth of freedom," as Lincoln said at Gettysburg. Once that commitment had been made, which was the major, transforming commitment in the Civil War, the administration decided to enlist black soldiers. In late 1862, they authorized the first enlistment on occupied territory in South Carolina where the war had started, on the so-called Sea Islands off the coast of South Carolina.

ABOUT 180,000 BLACK SOLDIERS and an estimated 10,000 black sailors fought in the Union army and navy, all of them in late 1862 or later, except for some blacks who enrolled in the navy earlier. . . . The total number of men who fought in the Union army and navy was about 2.1 million, so the black soldiers constituted about 9 percent of the Union armed forces.

Black soldiers didn't fight in the Confederate army unless they were passing as white—some light-skinned blacks probably did. Some Confederate soldiers, especially officers, brought their body servants into the army, who in many cases had grown up with them and had been very close to them. On occasion, some of those body servants were known to have picked up a rifle and fought. But there was no official recruitment of black soldiers in the Confederate army until the very end of the war, when out of their desperate shortage of manpower, the Confederate Congress finally passed—by a single vote in the Senate in March 1865—the so-called Negro soldier bill, which provided for the enlistment of slaves to fight for the Confederacy. Appomattox came only a few weeks later, and none of these men were ever put in uniform to fight.

THE CONFEDERATE SOLDIERS were basically fighting for the independence of what they called their country—the Confederate States of America. They were harking back to the model of the American Revolution in 1776, when Americans had declared their independence from the British empire—seceding in the name of liberty, establishing independent, free government. The Confederate soldiers said they were doing the same thing in 1861—fighting for liberty and for self-government. They were defending their country against invasion by what they considered to be an alien power that no longer represented their interests. They compared Abraham Lincoln to King George III and compared the Congress in Washington to the British Parliament of 1776.

As the war went on, Northern armies did invade and occupy the South and destroy its resources, including, ultimately, slavery. Many Confederate soldiers became increasingly motivated by notions of revenge, of defending their homeland from these hated "Goths and Vandals," to use the terms they sometimes did. They were fighting a defensive war to protect their homeland and the independence of their country.

THE CONFEDERATE PURPOSE was not to invade the North and conquer and occupy; it was merely to defend its territory against Union invasion and conquest. The Confederate soldier thought that he was fighting for the same goals that his grandfather had fought for in the War of the Revolution in 1775 to 1783. The Union soldier had the same motive except that he interpreted the example of the American Revolution in the opposite way.

The Union soldiers said they were fighting to preserve the nation that was created in 1776—to preserve it from dismemberment and destruction. They too appealed to that model of 1776, and it was a powerful motive for Union soldiers. Over and over again you find in their letters the argument that "if we lose this war, if the Confederacy succeeds, it will establish a fatal precedent that will destroy the United States. We will no longer have a united nation. By definition it will be a disunited nation, and the next time that a disaffected minority loses a presidential election they might secede. All of the labor of our ancestors to set up this brave experiment in democracy in 1776 will have been proven a failure."

It's important to remember in understanding the Northern soldiers' perspective, that in the mid-nineteenth century the United States was one of the very few republics and by far the largest and most successful republic in the world. Most European countries were monarchies or empires. Other republics, such as those in Latin America, had usually succumbed to dictatorship. When Lincoln said at Gettysburg that this was the great test whether a nation so conceived and so founded could survive, he struck an important chord among the Northern people. That's what they were fighting for.

For Union soldiers, the question of whether they were fighting to abolish slavery—whether they were risking their lives to free the slaves—was a controversial issue, and it did divide the Northern soldiers at first. . . . By the latter half of the war many Northern soldiers, but not all, found themselves fighting for the freeing of the slaves. And of course, those who were more inclined to be sympathetic toward that at the beginning were those who were most committed to that as one of the Northern war aims.

OLIVER WENDELL HOLMES JR. was one of the most remarkable of Civil War soldiers, and one who is best known. He lived well into the twentieth century and knew Franklin Delano Roosevelt. He was still sitting on the Supreme Court at the age of ninety, [on the eve of] FDR's presidency. He was a young officer during the Civil War and had just graduated from Harvard in 1861, enlisted and was a lieutenant, then captain. He was wounded three times, ended up on the staff of the Sixth Corps Commanders in the Army of the Potomac in 1864, and then wrote eloquently about that experience after the war. He said, "It was given to us in our youth to be touched with fire. We really knew what passion was." He spoke to future generations, he lived so long after the war, about the meaning of the experience that he and his generation went through.

THE CIVIL WAR ended gradually. The principal Confederate army was the Army of Northern Virginia, commanded by Robert E. Lee. The Army of the Potomac, which had fought that army for four years, finally brought it to bay at Appomattox, and Lee made the decision to surrender on April 9, 1865, just five days before Lincoln was assassinated. That is often taken as the date that the Civil War ended, when the Confederate's principal army surrendered, but there were still several other Confederate armies in the field, and they surrendered one by one over the next couple of months.

In *A Farewell to Arms,* Ernest Hemingway writes about his experience in World War I, . . . a disillusioning experience for his generation. Thereafter every time such words as "glory" and "honor" and "the cause" came up, they were cynical about it. We are the heirs of that cynicism, especially we in the post-Vietnam generation. So when we read Civil War soldiers saying that they were willing to die for their country or to die for freedom, or that they were cheerfully risking their lives to preserve the existence of a democratic government in the United States, we need to overcome the barrier [of] . . . post-Vietnam cynicism about these idealistic motives. I'm convinced after reading these 25,000 letters that these soldiers—when they used these Victorian phrases—really believed in them. I have to believe that because so many of them gave their lives for this cause. These were volunteer soldiers. Most of the people I quote were not conscripts. They were not long-term, professional soldiers. They were citizen volunteers.

Women of the Slaveholding South

by

DREW GILPIN FAUST

On July 16, 1996, Drew Gilpin Faust appeared on Booknotes *and discussed* Mothers of Invention: Women of the Slaveholding South in the American Civil War, *published in 1996 by the University of North Carolina Press. When asked how she got interested in the subject, Ms. Faust, a dean and professor of history at Harvard, replied, "I am sure that the origins of this book lie somewhere in that youthful experience, and in the continued confrontations with my mother until the very eve of her death—when I was nineteen—about the requirements of what she usually called femininity. 'It's a man's world, sweetie, and the sooner you learn that, the better off you'll be.' . . . My mother was trying to make me into the lady she thought I ought to be. I think that confrontation made me very conscious about what it meant to be a lady in the South, and about some of the dilemmas that, one hundred years earlier, these women faced."*

THE "MOTHERS OF INVENTION" were white Confederate women who lived in [any of the 385,0000] slaveholding families during the Civil War. . . . These were women of an elite class, women who came from the 25 percent of Confederate society that was rich enough to own slaves. Many of them were well educated, some of them not so well educated, but they tended to be the most educated of the Confederate citizens. This is about their experiences in this time of crisis, and the ways in which they coped with the challenges of war and the transformations that it brought about.

We often forget the various dimensions that went along with ladyhood, especially in the nineteenth century. It very much meant someone who was privileged, someone who had enough wealth. In one moment in the book, I have a quote where . . . a woman during the Civil War has lost her slaves, and then she manages to get another slave, and she says, "Newport has taken the cooking, and we are all ladies again," thereby showing us that ladyhood depended on having a servant, in that instance. I think ladyhood in the Old South, or in the Civil War South . . . also depended on being white. Indeed, in my childhood, "lady" was a term that was applied to white women in 1950s and 1960s Virginia, not to black women, so that "lady" involved a racial definition as well as a definition of privilege or a certain kind of class status.

ONE OF THE MOST important realities in the Confederacy, and one of the most important realities for the women's experience in the Confederacy, was the extremely high rate of mobilization of white Confederate men. Because there were black slaves to do much of the nonmilitary labor, the Confederacy was able to draft men at a rate that was very unusual for any society. About three out of four white men of military age in the Confederacy served in the Confederate army.

The Confederacy passed the first conscription bill in American history in April 1862, and that original conscription bill was expanded in its inclusiveness until, by the end of the war, men from the ages of seventeen to forty-five were being drafted into the Confederate army. . . . Eighteen to twenty percent of Confederate men of military age were killed in the course of the war, and as many as 40 percent were either wounded or killed. The impact of this destruction on white families was enormous. Everyone had a family member who had been killed or wounded in the war.

The first impact of this on white women was that many of them reconsidered how they wanted to live. Did they want to stay there without their men? Did they want to move in with family members, with their parents or his parents? Did they want to move in with sisters? Households reshaped as a result of the war and as a result of the men departing. Almost immediately, the women had to confront the responsibility for managing the slaves who were left behind. Much of slave discipline, slave management, almost all of it in fact, had rested in the hands of white men. Even if the white women were responsible for the day-to-day direction of slaves in the household, they knew that the white man was there as a recourse, and usually as the source of the violence—the whipping, the beating, or the threats of violence that were at the foundation of the maintenance of the mastery over slaves.

Many white women had difficulty when they were forced to be the instigators of physical discipline and coercion of slaves. They were much more likely to do it in a fit of rage, to just lash out and hit a slave. There were some examples of women chasing slaves with shovels or brooms in fits of anger and frustration. But white women were very uneasy about the use of systematic, rationalized violence. They felt that this was something that was gendered as male. White women, ladies, were not supposed to do this. There was a tremendous ambivalence, concern, guilt, and unease about the necessity of disciplining slaves in this manner.

White women would turn to men who remained in the community—men who were exempt for one reason or another or over the age of conscription—and ask them to come over and discipline the slaves for them. The notion was that they would be a force for order, and perhaps could extend their maleness from their own plantation onto those of the plantations of white women who had been left alone by their own husbands.

MAKING SURE THAT the economic functions of the household were continuing in order to provide food and income for the family was an immediate problem as well. It usually depended very heavily on managing slaves, but it might involve other questions as well: Are we going to plant cotton? Are we going to plant corn? What are we going to do about the agricultural situation now that [Union] troops are nearby? Am I going to pick up and leave? Am I going to become a refugee and go elsewhere and try to take my family with me? These kinds of questions were an immediate challenge.

One of the richest sources of material for this book were letters to Confederate officials that are available in the National Archives here in Washington from women who plead for all kinds of assistance from the Confederate government. These letters cover a wide spectrum of class origins among Confederate women. Some of them are from complete illiterates. Some of them are dictated to neighbors, and so you know that these women are unable to write. One of my favorite of these letters is from a blind girl who writes in a kind of script that she's been taught in a school for the blind. Somehow that script coming out at you from the page almost makes her alive before you.

These letters give a very vivid portrait of the kinds of troubles and challenges that women are facing; they also give a vivid portrait of some of the failures of the Confederate government, because you'll read a letter to Jefferson Davis that just makes you want to weep. . . . I would almost burst into tears, I'd be so moved by these letters. Then I'd turn to the back page of the letter, and it would say "file." It wasn't answered. The plea was not dealt with. Simply, the letter was filed. So the breakdown in the trust, you can imagine, by this woman in this Confederate government, is just right there before your eyes.

One of the realities in the Confederacy was that paper was increasingly scarce as the war continued. We can see that represented in the changing nature of stationery in the course of the war. Sometimes by the end of the war, paper was things like wallpaper or sheaves taken out of books. People were struggling to find anything to write on. One of the ways they dealt with the paper shortage is particularly obnoxious to contemporary historians, because they'd write across the piece of paper, and then they'd turn it, and write on top of what they'd already written. And that is a real challenge for a historian to try to read.

[THE RELIGIOUS TRANSFORMATIONS in these women's lives were also significant.] There was a gradual confrontation with a newly distant God. At the beginning of the war, white women felt that the God of battles was on the side of the Confederacy. They found all kinds of citations in the Old Testament about hordes coming down from the north into Judea and God protecting his chosen people. They were very confident that God would be on their side. But as death tolls mounted, and as the war became more intense, and as the South lost battle after battle, they shifted to another interpretation of religion—a more Jobian interpretation: We're being chastened. God chastens those whom he favors. So we just have to wait for him to finish chastening us. We have to bear up under these punishments, and then everything will be all right.

When defeat finally came, I found many women who wrote with despair about loss of faith: How can I believe when God has done this to us? How can I continue to be a Christian under these circumstances? Most of these women came back to their faith, but they had to shift into a notion of a God who was not watching every sparrow that fell or every Confederate that fell. It was a God whose interventions were not as direct, a God who was a more distant kind of power.

[LIZZIE NEBLETT WAS one of my favorite characters] not because she's particularly admirable—there was much about her that one would deplore— but she was so frank in what she put into her letters. She talked about how she was afraid to have her husband come home because she didn't want to get pregnant again, and she was not going to allow him in the house unless he came home with some kind of birth control. She was very frank about this. She and her husband owned eleven slaves, so she was not a huge plantation owner. She wrote in great detail about her difficulties in managing the slaves, to the point that you got to know all eleven of them by name, and you could see the social dynamics in this slave community. She is, indeed, one of the women who was so troubled by the necessity, as she saw it, to physically coerce the slaves. She got a neighbor to try to help her.

Neblett got so frustrated about her inability to control her slaves that she turned to beating [her own child] a small infant under two years old. She took out some of her frustrations about her own inadequacies in this new role she was experiencing; as she called it, "trying to do a man's business," which she found overwhelming. Her actions with her own children were deplorable. Some of the violence she countenanced against her own slaves was deplorable, although she ultimately intervened to keep the white man she'd borrowed down the street from killing her slaves in order to set an example. She did intervene, but she also countenanced a good deal of extreme violence against these slaves that we would find very off-putting in our own twentieth-century values.

I FOUND A LOT OF anecdotal evidence [of women going insane during the war]—quotations of women who said they had gone crazy or they knew people who had gone crazy. The point I want to make in putting that evidence forth is to alert people to the tremendous impact the war must have had on the emotional and psychological lives of women who were really on the front lines. I make an analogy between what happened to civilians, who were mostly women in these Confederate towns and villages and countrysides, and the kind of understanding we now have of posttraumatic stress syndrome.

It applied both to Confederate men who were in battle and to white women who experienced war, particularly in some place like Winchester, Virginia, which changed hands dozens of times during the war. The war went on for four long years, and the psychological impact on both civilians and soldiers cannot be denied or underestimated.

One of the themes that white women dealt with was the departure of slaves. [The women] would get up one morning and the slaves would simply be gone. This started happening as early as 1861 or 1862, and after Lincoln's Emancipation Proclamation in 1863 it happened ever more frequently because they were guaranteed freedom when they got to Union lines. The motivation to pick up and go was greater than when they feared they might be returned to Confederate owners.

At the end of the war, there was a real renegotiation of labor arrangements in the South, and what evolved was ultimately a system of sharecropping and tenancy, and a whole new labor situation for the exercise of Southern agricultural efforts in the South. For white women of this class, the real renegotiation was about the issue of servants, and how they were going to be able to reestablish control over a black labor force that would help them out in the household. One of the primary commitments for these white women was not to have to do their own household labor, and they struggled at the end of the war to figure out ways to keep servants, to get servants, to continue to benefit from this kind of labor.

IN MOST CASES in the Old South, and in the earliest months of the Civil War, white women lived in households where they were mostly isolated from other white women. They lived perhaps on a farm or a plantation that was very distant from other farms and plantations. They lived with a husband and children and slaves, and perhaps some other family members—a maiden aunt or something, but there weren't concentrations of white women. And because the South had so many fewer urban centers than the North, it was hard to get access to other families. They were separated by the rurality of the South.

In the Civil War period, all of these women moved in together. They developed a new consciousness of womanhood, a new sense of solidarity, a new sense of gender identity, and new sense of bonds . . . between women. Out of this came a lot of organizations in the war period itself for hospital relief and so forth. After the war, things like temperance and the kinds of organizations that one saw in the North in the early nineteenth century grew out of this new female solidarity in the South.

IT WAS ESTIMATED that as many as four hundred women dressed up as soldiers and went off and served in the Confederate and Union armies. . . . Belle Boyd didn't dress up as a man, [but] she used her femininity, her female garb, as a way to hide her very male activities of spying and working on behalf of the Confederate cause. She was quite something. She gave information to Stonewall Jackson about Union troop movements, and when she was put in prison in Washington, she beguiled the manager of the prison, who bought her clothes and wanted to marry her. She was released and passed more information on to Confederate officers and was ultimately put on a boat by Union troops to be shipped north to prison. She then seduced and married the Union captain of the boat. She was forever using her ability to manage men in order to advance the Confederate cause.

MANY WOMEN BECAME really disillusioned. They began to focus on their personal needs, their families, loss of life, and their desire to have their husbands come home, rather than on the kinds of abstract notions of patriotism that had caught many of them up in enthusiasm for the war at its very beginning. There was a lot of abandonment of patriotism and a lot of focus on "just come home; we're probably going to lose this war, but whether we win or lose, it's not worth this tremendous cost in lives and destruction."

[After the war] there was a lot of discussion in the Confederacy about widows, who were seen as rather dangerous in the eagerness that many of them displayed to remarry. There was an active social network of these widows searching for appropriate men to attach themselves to. I argue that it was an indication of these women finding that they had a self-interest and that they were desiring beings. It was a rejection of the ideology of self-sacrifice that many of them were told to embrace, because they said, "I'm not going to sit around and mourn and pine forever. I have a right to happiness, and I want to find someone else."

Susan B. Anthony was an advocate of women's rights and women's suffrage in the North. I use her to contrast her notion of women's rights with some of the emerging sense of self that I saw in these white Southern women. Susan B. Anthony approached women's rights with a tremendous sense of opportunity, possibility, and optimism—"Failure is impossible." White Southern women came to a notion of themselves out of desperation, out of necessity, out of a need to protect themselves, and out of a real sense of the possibility of failure, a possibility that Susan B. Anthony didn't see as part of the expansion of women's roles and powers.

The Events of 1863

by

JOSEPH E. STEVENS

President Abraham Lincoln issued the Emancipation Proclamation in January 1863, freeing all slaves in territories held by Confederates. The Enrollment Act, a law granting the federal government enlarged powers to conscript soldiers, was also passed in 1863. Several of the Civil War's most infamous battles took place in 1863, including one that led to Ulysses S. Grant's rise to prominence. Joseph E. Stevens examined the events of that year in 1863: The Rebirth of a Nation, *published in 1999 by Bantam Books, which he discussed on* Booknotes *on May 14, 1999. Mr. Stevens is now a writer in Sante Fe, New Mexico.*

EIGHTEEN SIXTY-THREE was the pivotal year in American history [as] the country basically reinvented itself. There was tremendous military conflict but also a great deal of political change and social change. One of the biggest changes was the federal government becoming much more powerful and intrusive and state governments enjoying less power.

It was in 1863 that the federal government really assumed a position that it has increasingly had since then . . . in directing the tone and tenor of national life at the expense of the states. There was the passage of a national banking law. Before 1863, states chartered banks and each bank issued its own currency. You would have hundreds of different kinds of bills and coins and currency floating around from banks of who knows what quality, which really impeded interstate commerce. The national banking law allowed for a national currency, which was a big change in the economy.

Another big thing was conscription. Prior to 1863, the individual states had recruited soldiers and organized them into regiments, picked the com-

manders, done a lot of the equipping, and then sent them off. When the
Enrollment Act was passed, the federal government was saying, "We're going
to take charge of this now." Each state had a quota: "Recruit so many soldiers, but if you fall below that quota, we're going to send provost marshals
in, draft people, and take them."

EIGHTEEN SIXTY-THREE was the essence of the Civil War. It definitely was
the most important year. . . . At the start of 1863, the Confederacy was
extremely close to winning. In December 1862, Union forces had attacked
the Army of Northern Virginia at Fredericksburg and suffered a disastrous,
terrible defeat. The army was demoralized. People on the homefront were
demoralized. Politicians from both parties were pretty much ready to give up,
saying, "The Confederacy has won. We can't go on with this. We need to
negotiate a boundary." So . . . the Confederacy [was very close to] achieving
victory.

ABRAHAM LINCOLN HAD signed the preliminary Emancipation Proclamation in September 1862, after the Battle of Antietam, but he made it condi-
tional. He said if the South would agree to certain terms that it could be
withdrawn, but the deadline was January 1. The South rejected any sort of
negotiations, so Lincoln followed through and signed the Emancipation
Proclamation.

His objectives were twofold: One was to hurt the South militarily. There
were 4 million slaves. They were producing crops; they were being used to
dig fortifications and do all sorts of work that freed up the white Southerners
to [join] the [Confederate] army. So it hurt them militarily. More importantly, he wanted to change the political dynamic of the war. Jefferson Davis
and the Confederates claimed that they were fighting for liberty; . . . they
were [fighting] a second American Revolution. Lincoln felt that he was losing
the war of ideas, and by making emancipation a stated war aim, he could
then say the Union was fighting not just for union but for freedom.

U. S. GRANT WAS the most successful general in 1863. Before that, he had
been twiddling his thumbs, mostly, waiting [for a] chance. . . . His victory at
[Fort Donelson] really put him into the public eye. That was where he
became known as "Unconditional Surrender" Grant because he demanded
that the Confederates surrender unconditionally. This nickname was boffo
in the press . . . and that brought him to the attention of Lincoln and the
people at the War Department.

Grant's wife would be brought from Illinois when his aides became concerned that his drinking problem was getting out of hand. Apparently she

was the one who could crack the whip and keep him on the straight and narrow. She stayed at his headquarters. During the Vicksburg campaign, they
were living on board a steamboat. He had several of his children with him
too.

There was one rather spectacular incident during the siege of Vicksburg.
Grant . . . went on a tremendous bender for a couple of days. Fortunately, his
aides and the newspaper reporters who were accompanying him managed to
cover it up. If it had gotten back to Washington that he had this episode, he
might well have been relieved of command.

Vicksburg was the most important battle of 1863. By capturing Vicksburg,
the Union forces opened the Mississippi River to unimpeded river traffic,
and they also divided the Confederacy in half. It meant that Arkansas,
Louisiana, and Texas were cut off from the rest of the South. The South was
drawing a lot of its foodstuffs and horses for remounts from those areas. So
strictly from a strategic military standpoint, Vicksburg was the most important battle.

OF COURSE, THERE were all kinds of political battles going on through that
period. In a lot of ways, they are as interesting as the military battles because
there was this constant drumbeat, especially from the Democratic Party, to
negotiate peace. It is interesting to see Lincoln deflecting and parrying this
and keeping the war going.

The so-called Radical Republicans controlled the Congress. They also
tended to be very critical of Lincoln, feeling that he was not prosecuting the
war harshly enough. So Lincoln was in the middle, catching it from both
sides.

THE GETTYSBURG ADDRESS was in November 1863. After the Battle of
Gettysburg, the battlefield was just a ghastly scene, thousands of bodies of
soldiers and horses. Total casualties, killed and wounded, were probably
40,000-plus. It became obvious that something had to be done, or there was
going to be a terrible health situation with all these bodies lying around. So it
was decided that a national cemetery would be built there, and . . . a dedication ceremony was arranged. President Lincoln was invited to make a few
appropriate remarks. He was not the featured speaker at the dedication. That
honor went to a man named Edward Everett, who was the foremost orator of
the time. Everett gave a speech that went on for two hours that he had memorized. From all reports, the crowd—there were 20,000 spectators—was just
entranced with Everett's speech. Then Lincoln got up and read his ten sentences, 272 words, and sat down. And yet those words ring down the years,
and Edward Everett is long forgotten.

What Lincoln did was explain what all this sacrifice was for. Certainly that was something that needed doing—just the outpouring of blood was horrifying. There needed to be an exalted reason for this kind of sacrifice.

AS WE LOOK BACK at history, we feel that whatever happened was inevitable, and it's not true. The Confederacy could have won. And if it had won, we would be living in a very different country. That's really one of the amazing things about 1863 and what makes it such an important year.

Civil War Correspondents

by

JAMES M. PERRY

The demand for timely and accurate reporting from the front lines of the Civil War transformed American journalism. By making use of the telegraph, steam-powered presses, and steam locomotives, reporters were able to file stories of the day's events with unprecedented speed. Many accounts of Civil War battles turned in by these "specials," as the reporters were called, can be considered the battles' definitive histories. Still, the journalists, the immediate precursors of the modern war correspondent, were a motley bunch. On April 14, 2000, James M. Perry appeared on Booknotes *and told us a few of the stories from his book,* A Bohemian Brigade: The Civil War Correspondents—Mostly Rough, Sometimes Ready, *published in 2000 by John Wiley & Sons. Mr. Perry is a senior political writer emeritus for the* Wall Street Journal.

TODAY'S CELEBRITY JOURNALISM began [during the Civil War] for two basic reasons. One was the telegraph, of course. This was the first instant-news war in history, and the problem was very much like [what we have with] the Internet today. They could file immediately, and it caused the rush to be first. They would take these immense, long rides across broken countryside on horseback to get to the nearest telegraph station to file. The other [reason] was steam—the new [steam-powered] presses and . . . steam-powered locomotives. You could get on a train and go back to your own office pretty quickly and file the story that way, if you couldn't get on the telegraph. The army wasn't too keen on making the telegraph easily available to reporters. They preferred to reserve it for themselves as much as possible.

"Telegraph all the news you can get, and when there is no news, send rumors." They did a lot of that and the competition was ferocious. Remember how many newspapers there were. New York had eighteen daily newspapers at this time, and four or five of them seriously covered the war, mainly Horace Greeley's *New York Tribune,* James Gordon Bennett's *New York Herald,* and Henry J. Raymond's *New York Times.* The *New York World* had some serious correspondents in the field, and they were eager to get information and the telegraph made it so easy to do. . . . At the beginning of the war, Bull Run [was a] great Union defeat, and here's the headline in the *New York Herald:* "The Great Battle; Brilliant Union Victory," it says. "Capture of Bull Run's Batteries, The Rebels Routed and Driven Back to Manassas." That's what happened in the morning, but they filed so quickly that they didn't get what happened later in the day. The *Boston Journal* ran this headline: "By Telegraph; Great Battle Near Manassas Junction! The Enemy Forced to Retire; Three Masked Batteries Taken; Desperate Conflict." They filed prematurely.

HORACE GREELEY was a celebrity. He was known all over America. He was the owner and publisher of the *New York Tribune,* an erratic, strange character who was more interested in ideas than in news. His paper was almost comparable to a national newspaper except it didn't circulate in the South, where his views on slavery were anathema, of course.

James Gordon Bennett was also pretty well-known. He was probably the greatest genius we've ever had in American journalism. He founded the modern newspaper, warts and all, with lots of warts in his case. But he was very interested in covering the news; [he] had no interest in anything else, unlike Greeley. The other major publisher and proprietor was Henry J. Raymond of the *New York Times,* a more sedate figure, although there were some unusual things about him as well. Those three despised one another and were highly competitive.

Bennett was the oldest of the bunch. Bennett came from Scotland and he was probably the best educated of all the great proprietors. He trained as a Catholic priest in Scotland, came over here, and was well into his middle age at the time of the Civil War. Greeley was moving along in years too. Raymond was much younger. They are interesting, wonderful characters. I love characters and eccentrics, and the Civil War is just filled with them.

I'd done an earlier book on military history, and I kept bumping into war correspondents, Richard Harding Davis [who covered later wars, including the Spanish-American War and World War I] and others. . . . And then it dawned on me—the modern journalist as we know him today began in the Civil War, mostly with the North, though there were Southern war correspondents as well, but we don't know much about them.

THESE PAPERS WERE read by dozens and handed around. This was the bloodiest war we ever fought, in terms of casualties, and the one thing that makes the reporting so important is that the armies—both sides—did not report casualties. They didn't give out lists of who was killed and who was wounded. That was done by the reporters who collected the casualty lists and published them. So people would read them, particularly [when] a reporter was covering their own unit.

The Civil War correspondents named themselves the "Bohemian Brigade." They thought that they were bohemians surrounded by professional soldiers, and they were a little mischievous. . . . The "Jolly Congress" was a group of Europeans who came to cover the war, two reporters and . . . a lot of professional soldiers who came to observe the war. They traveled around in a group, just like the Bohemian Brigade—the *Times* of London, the *Illustrated London News,* and four or five soldiers over here to observe the war.

The western reporters were more true bohemians; they were more mischievous, they had more fun, I think. There were more rogues out there, perhaps, than there were in the East, although there were rogues everywhere. And the soldiers themselves were different. The western army was more relaxed; they were bigger and . . . stronger.

It's hard to define just what a reporter was. Some regiments would have an officer or somebody with them, sending material home to the local newspaper, and historians rely on those a lot. For the North, if you wanted to estimate the number of reporters, there were well over two hundred, surely. The South had maybe fifty to seventy-five. . . . Newspapers were desperate to find anyone to send into the field. . . . There was lots of criticism, particularly of the *New York Herald,* for sending these useless, hard-drinking characters, who did no good to anybody, out into the field. It was a raffish crowd.

THE SOUTH HAD few telephone wires, but the Southern newspapers did tend, in the latter part of the war, to depend on something called the Confederate Press Association, which supplied them with a very small amount of telegraph news every day, maybe less than 1,000 words. Some of these Northern reporters would take that long to write their leads.

A lot of stuff went on the telegraph that shouldn't have, a lot of it totally unreliable. My favorite [story] in the whole book was [from] the battle called Pea Ridge in Arkansas. There were only two reporters there, Thomas Knox [of the *New York Herald*] and a reporter from St. Louis. Pea Ridge was an important battle because it pretty much preserved Missouri for the Union cause. These two reporters got on their horses and [rode] two hundred miles to . . . file their stories. Knox filed a very short piece, just two hundred, three hundred words, with a map. And it turns out that the day before, two other reporters had holed up in a hotel room and made up the story of the battle, which ran for, oh, most of the whole page, and they'd never been there. They hadn't seen the battle at all. But they heard enough; they had a few reports on the battle. They talked to some people who knew the geography of where it was, and they put it all together. The *Times* of London called [their account] the greatest battlefield story of the war, and [those particular correspondents] hadn't seen a thing. They hadn't seen a shot fired at all.

MOST OF THE CIVIL WAR journalists were quite young—and strange. A lot of them went to college and they tended to go to small liberal arts colleges like Trinity and Beloit and Miami of Ohio and Amherst—Union schools. Only one of them that I could find actually went to an Ivy League school, a very good reporter named George Smalley, who stroked the first Yale crew in the first race against Harvard on Lake Winnipesaukee. He went on to Harvard Law School as well, so he had quite a distinguished academic background. [One of] my favorite reporters, the nicest one in here, is a very young man named Henry Wing, who was kissed by Lincoln—that was what he was most famous for. He was only eighteen when he went off to cover the war and that was after serving with a Connecticut regiment and being wounded at Fredericksburg. He had an amazing career.

They didn't get paid very much. That was, of course, the cause of some of them—out West, particularly—beginning to speculate in cotton and make money on the side. Of course they wrote books and had other sources of income, but there wasn't a whole lot of money. [Another] favorite, Franc Wilkie, was the most mischievous of all these correspondents; he [later] worked for the *Chicago Times* . . . for [Wilbur Storey, a man] so cheap that [he] invented tongs you could attach to the stub of pencils so you could keep using them after they were almost worn out.

Union General William T. Sherman hated correspondents and actually court-martialed one of them, [Thomas Knox]. In all of history, this was the greatest challenge to freedom of the press—particularly as far as war correspondents go—that ever happened. [Knox was tried and] could have been hanged.

One of the worst things the press does is pile on. This is an old tradition and it's a bad one, of reporters getting together, ganging up and piling on, and they did this with Sherman. They said he was insane. There was a piece that ran in the *Cincinnati Commercial,* "General William T. Sherman Insane," the headline said. And the story went on to say that he was a little bit crazy. He did have a history of serious breakdowns, and he was having one at this point, but they all finally piled on him then. He had to go home; he spent some time recuperating, came back, restored himself, and performed very well at a number of battles.

But then there was a battle at Chickasaw Bayou. It wasn't Sherman's fault that it turned into something of a disaster, but a couple of the reporters . . . wrote stories and you could tell that they were colluding because the stories were so similar. They started by saying that Sherman and his officers had been rifling their mail. And they had—Sherman's chief of staff, J. H. Hammond, had been rifling their mail. Then they said, "If Sherman and his people spent more time fighting the Confederates and less time trying to make life miserable for journalists, he might have won that battle." They finally concluded, again, that Sherman was insane.

It's no wonder that Sherman, who was not very pleased with them to begin with, began to think, "I can't put up with this anymore. I'm just not going to be able to do it." So he actually had poor Knox arrested and scared the man to death. Knox wrote a letter at one point and groveled to Sherman, saying he'd been all wrong and was sorry about it; [but] he didn't talk to the right people. The trial went ahead, full-dress officers in uniforms, swords, and sashes, a general in command. Knox was mostly found not guilty of the charges and Sherman was absolutely incensed. He wrote a wonderful letter expressing his distaste for this business, and he wrote one to Knox, who had asked to be reinstated, and said, "Come with us with a musket, come with us and join us in combat, come with us anywhere, but as a newspaper reporter, never." It's still one of the most stunning letters from a general to a reporter I've ever seen.

UNION GENERAL GEORGE Gordon Meade, the victor at Gettysburg, despised reporters and had an even bigger temper than Sherman. A *Philadelphia Inquirer* . . . reporter named Edward Crapsey . . . tried to do an analytical piece on the relationship between General Ulysses Grant and Meade. Grant, at this time, was the generalissimo in charge of everything, and Meade was in charge of the Army of the Potomac.

Crapsey [wrote] that there was a time after the Battle of the Wilderness when Meade wanted to do what all the other generals had done, which is retire and retreat. He said Grant intervened and said, "No, we will not; we will go on. Never again are we going to go back." Meade saw that as some reflection on his courage, got furious, had Crapsey arrested, [placed] backward on a mule, and ridden around the camp with a big sign on his back, saying, "Libeler of the Press." Some of the journalists became very upset by this, and Meade for months thereafter was never mentioned in the papers. They boycotted him. They just simply wiped him out because they were so furious.

MOST OF THE COVERAGE was directed out of . . . offices in Washington and just like today, they would have a bureau chief and . . . be assigned . . . to cover a [particular] corps or regiment or army. The smart ones tried to stay near the general's tent because they could see more of what was happening from that vantage point than they could out somewhere else with the troops.

Photography had been invented, but newspapers did not have the technology to print photographs, so there were no photographs in any of these newspapers of the Civil War, just drawings. Photographs would be published in books and then they would have shows in which they would display their photographs, but you couldn't get it on a newspaper press. The process of printing the same photograph over and over again overnight in thousands of copies wasn't yet possible.

WHITELAW REID STARTED with the *Cincinnati Gazette* and . . . wrote the monumental account of Shiloh, which was quite controversial because he was a wonderful reporter. I think he was the second best reporter after Charles Carleton Coffin [of the *Boston Morning Journal*] but Reid was grumpy. The first day of Shiloh was a bit of a disaster for the Union army, and when Reid wrote this huge 12,000-word story, he just kept going over and over again how they'd been surprised and shouldn't have been by the Confederate attack. They had been, but Grant didn't want to admit that and seemed very upset. So the story became quite controversial. Reid did that constantly. Even at the very end, the fall of Richmond, he was still grumbling about things not being the way they ought to be.

[THERE WAS ONLY one black correspondent] a very interesting man, Thomas Chester of the *Philadelphia Press*. . . . Richmond had just fallen, and Chester was [there]. His story was datelined, "Hall of Congress, Richmond, April 4th, 1865." [He wrote] "Seated in the Speaker's chair, so long dedicated to treason but in the future to be consecrated to loyalty, I hasten to give a rapid sketch of the incidents which have occurred since my last dispatch." Here is the Civil War's only black reporter, seated in the Speaker's chair of the Confederate Congress.

At this point, in comes a young Confederate officer, who sees Chester seated in the chair. Two other reporters [are watching]. This Confederate soldier says, "Come out of there, you black cuss." Mr. Chester raised his eyes, calmly surveyed the intruder, and went on with his writing. Later, when the guy approached him, Chester got up, gave him one quick punch on the nose, toppled him down on the floor, and continued with his story. Isn't that amazing? The only black reporter. It's just so dramatic.

I HAVE A CHAPTER in the book about two Northern reporters, Junius Henri Browne and Albert Richardson, who were captured [by Confederate troops while] trying to run past Vicksburg. They had a terrible time, spent [nearly] two years [in prison, including ten months] in one of the very worst prisons—Salisbury, North Carolina—where [conditions] were just appalling. . . . They were treated just like captured soldiers. They weren't considered to be noncombatants at all. They escaped, these two reporters, and made their way north, 340 miles in twenty-seven days. Sometimes they were on horseback, sometimes on foot. They were helped occasionally by loyal Union supporters they encountered. It was an extraordinary experience for both, and they both wrote books immediately. So things haven't changed entirely.

IT WAS A LITTLE UNFAIR to blame the worst sins of the press on the public. Even so, simply substitute today's gossipy and irresponsible Web sites on the Internet for the Civil War telegraph, and it becomes shockingly clear how little reporting the news has changed in 140 years.

Ulysses S. Grant's Military Career

by

BROOKS D. SIMPSON

Hiram Ulysses Grant was born on April 27, 1822, in Point Pleasant, Ohio. As a result of an error on his commission to West Point, Hiram came to be known as Ulysses S. Grant. After the Civil War, he was elected the country's eighteenth president in 1868 and served for two terms. Grant died of throat cancer on July 22, 1885, at Mount McGregor, New York. An estimated 1 million people turned out for the funeral procession to a temporary burial site. In 1897 President William McKinley dedicated Grant's Tomb, which overlooks the Hudson River in New York City, where he was finally laid to rest. Brooks D. Simpson explored Grant's life, his military successes, and personal shortcomings more fully in Ulysses S. Grant: Triumph over Adversity, 1822–1865, *published in 2000 by Houghton Mifflin. Mr. Simpson, a history professor at Arizona State University, appeared on* Booknotes *on May 30, 2000.*

ULYSSES S. GRANT was an extremely able commander who mastered the challenges that felled other men. His success was not inevitable by any means. He was a master at improvising and responding on the spur of the moment to changes in plan and changes in circumstances. He did that well. On the other hand, he played favorites and was sometimes a little too stubborn in not taking a second look at some people he did not like. Sometimes he was so interested in offensive action that he forgot that the enemy also had a will and might try to impose it on him. There were things that Grant did that weren't so shrewd.

GRANT WAS BORN IN Point Pleasant, Ohio, on April 27, 1822, the son of a tanner and businessman, Jesse Grant, and Hannah Simpson Grant. He grew up in south Ohio on the outskirts of a little town called Georgetown, not too far from Cincinnati. Not much is known about Grant's mother, Hannah. She was a very quiet, reserved person, and some people claimed that's where Grant got his own taciturn sense. Jesse Grant, on the other hand, was a boisterous businessman and was active in politics. He bragged openly about his son and made young Ulysses' life somewhat difficult at times. People looking to strike back at the old man found in his oldest son a rather vulnerable target. As a young man, Grant often found himself the butt of jokes.

Grant's father dearly wanted to get him an appointment to West Point. First he corresponded with a senator named Tom Morris, who said he must contact his local congressman, a fellow named Tom Hamer. Tom Hamer and Jesse Grant had been friends but had grown apart due to political disagreements. It was a very painful process for Jesse, a very proud man, to write to Tom Hamer and say, "Please give an appointment for my son, Ulysses, to West Point."

The request came to Hamer just as he was cleaning out his desk at the end of a session of Congress. He rushed through the papers and didn't know the boy's name, which was formally Hiram Ulysses Grant. Hamer filled out papers for Ulysses S. Grant, assuming that since everyone had always called the fellow Ulysses, that was his first name. He thought the middle initial, the S, would come from Hannah Simpson [Grant]'s name. That's how Hiram Ulysses Grant became Ulysses S. Grant.

Grant went to West Point and asked for an appointment for Hiram Ulysses Grant or Ulysses Hiram Grant. He was told, "The only appointment we have is for Ulysses S. Grant. If you don't like it, you can go home." He decided to stay.

WHEN GRANT ENTERED West Point, there were . . . seventy-seven in his class. Out of that entering class, thirty-nine received commissions four years later. Grant was ranked twenty-first out of thirty-nine. Usually we see [that cited as evidence that] Grant was a middling student. In fact, he survived, whereas a lot of other people were farmed out or couldn't make it.

Grant married Julia Dent in 1848. She was the sister of one of his West Point roommates, Fred Dent. . . . They had four children between 1850 and 1858. Julia Grant was an interesting person. She had a great deal of faith in her husband. On the other hand, she was also a slaveholder's daughter and had a very paternalistic, romanticized view of American slavery. She was . . . very much attached to her . . . father, creating some tensions in the Grant marriage. Grant himself was ambivalent toward his father-in-law. But Julia was one of the few people who had faith in Ulysses Grant even when things weren't going well.

[Prior to his marriage, Grant] got a series of assignments closer and closer to the Texas-Mexican border, as people awaited the outbreak of hostilities between the United States and Mexico. . . . James K. Polk had taken office as president in March 1845. The United States had already acquired Texas by annexation, but there were hungry eyes looking westward for other parts of what was, at that time, northern Mexico. There was a border dispute between Mexico and the United States about exactly where Texas ended and Mexico began. Polk moved very aggressively to place American forces in a disputed area. Grant was among the people in that contingent.

Grant was given various staff duties like regimental quartermaster and commissary officer at the beginning of the Mexican War. He was not given a command with a company at the front lines. But in many a battle in the Mexican War, when the firing started, Grant would make sure that his mules were in line and all the supply issues were taken care of. He'd ride off to the front and get himself involved as quickly as possible. You just couldn't keep him out of action once the firing began. He would pick up squads of troops, lead them forward, and basically act on his own as an officer. He was not supposed to do that.

He was supposed to stay behind, and he protested against that rear assignment as not giving him the sort of service he wanted to have. Nevertheless, it was probably a critical service for Grant's later formation because Grant began to understand the importance of logistics. He obtained the sort of experience that many Civil War generals did not have: How do you manage an army? How do you keep it supplied? How do you feed it? How do you move it forward? Grant got that experience during the Mexican-American War.

People saw him as a very courageous young officer. He did things under fire in the Mexican-American War that were pretty astonishing, taking advantage of his horsemanship and his ingenuity. He was known as a young, brave officer, but the Mexican-American War was filled with young, brave officers. There would seem to be nothing exceptional about him, except that he was cool under fire.

GRANT GOT OUT of the Mexican War in 1848, when the war ended with a formal treaty. . . . He came back to several postwar duty posts in Detroit and New York. Julia was with him in most of these places, [until] Grant was sent out to the West Coast in 1852. [Afraid the trip would be too risky] Grant advised his wife not to go with him, but rather to go back to live with her father and mother.

[In 1854] Grant decided to give up the service. He was very depressed from being apart from his family and missed his wife terribly. . . . By the time he resigned from the army in 1854, he was a captain. There were stories that drinking had something to do with it. He was probably drinking because he was depressed, but he resigned because he'd had enough.

GRANT STRUGGLED FOR several years as a farmer, a real estate agent, and several other minicareers that all ended disastrously for one reason or another. In 1860 he moved to Galena, Illinois, where he worked at a general store owned by his father and younger brothers. That's where he was at the outset of the American Civil War.

Galena was raising a company and parts of a regiment. . . . Grant had this reputation for being the man for the situation. . . . He wanted to fight. He thought he should be a colonel, that he had the commensurate military experience for such a position, but it took an awfully long time to get that commission.

They used him in all sorts of other capacities because of his administrative experience during the Mexican-American War. Grant found that all he was doing was filling out forms; he wasn't getting the combat command he wanted. Several times he was about to leave. He wasn't pulling strings, but he was making himself achingly available.

He got it because there was a very unruly regiment outside of Springfield, the Twenty-First Illinois, members of whom Grant had sworn in. . . . Grant, by this time, was doing odd jobs in Springfield, helping to run the clerk's office in the Old State Capitol. All of a sudden, people said, "Why not try Grant? Grant's been around." The men of the regiment had met him, so there was a fit.

Republican congressman Elihu B. Washburne was an early supporter of Lincoln who was instrumental in Grant's early career. When President Lincoln made available several commissions for brigadier generals from the state of Illinois, Washburne shrewdly made sure that his man, Grant, was included in that mix. So Grant earned his first star not because of anything he accomplished on the battlefield, but because he had a patron in Congress.

GRANT WAS A PIPE SMOKER. . . . The popular story is that in February 1862, at the Battle of Fort Donelson, Grant was off conferring with his naval counterpart, Andrew Hull Foote. When he came back to the battlefield, he found that his army was under attack. Grant had very little use for swords; he saw them as obstructions more than anything else. Foote had given him a cigar. Grant began to direct military operations not with a sword but with a cigar in his hand, pointing back and forth.

That image got back to the newspapers. Grant was one of the first great Union heroes of the war. People called him "Unconditional Surrender" Grant, giving his initials a new meaning from his surrender demand of the Confederate garrison. People began to send him cigars, and, sure enough, he became addicted to them. In many ways, Grant's calm exterior was the result of tobacco's calming influence on him.

[IN THE SPRING OF] 1862, Grant's forces were poised just above the border between Tennessee and Mississippi at Shiloh. Grant was not thinking too carefully about what the enemy was doing. His officer in charge of reconnaissance was none other than William T. Sherman; it was the first battle the men fought together. Sherman did not interpret evidence of Confederate activity very shrewdly, and on April 6, 1862, the Confederates launched a massive attack on Grant's encampment. It was a rather fierce fight. We think of Grant as an attacking commander, but in his early battles, he was involved in offensive campaigns where he was attacked by the enemy. He was attacked at Donelson and at Shiloh. Shiloh was a bloody battle, by far the bloodiest one in American history at that time. There was a search for scapegoats afterward. Grant came under heavy criticism. For a while, it looked like he might find that to be a very costly victory to his reputation.

THERE WAS EVIDENCE of Grant's drinking as early as the Mexican-American War. . . . He didn't need to consume too much in order for it to show. Just a couple of glasses might send him into an intoxicated state; he'd blush, his speech would slur, and he would look a little bit uncertain. It wasn't that Grant drank—lots of officers in the United States Army drank—it was that Grant couldn't hold his liquor.

There doesn't seem to be any truly harebrained thing that Grant did under the influence. There are all these stories that, while under the influence, he did this or that, but they always seemed to be fairly minor things. Defenders of Grant like to say this proves that Grant never drank when it was important. But when he was a major general and intoxicated, there were no lulls in the action.

The most famous story of Grant drinking during the Civil War happened during the Vicksburg campaign in June 1863. . . . He was going into enemy territory and was not feeling well. He had [apparently] taken a couple of drinks to make himself feel better, and it had a very negative effect. But a drunken general headed toward enemy territory during the Vicksburg siege was not a lark. That could have imperiled the Union cause.

VICKSBURG WAS A TOUGH NUT for Grant to crack. . . . It was the last major Confederate citadel on the Mississippi River, and he was frustrated in effort after effort to take it. There was a lot of press attention given to Vicksburg. Finally, he devised a campaign whereby he would cross the Mississippi south of the city, go first to the capital of Jackson, then go west toward Vicksburg itself.

It was a campaign of improvisation from the beginning. . . . He was out-numbered and had to live off the land. It was a very innovative campaign. Within weeks, he won five battles and laid siege to the city. It was astonish-ing. It is still held up in many circles as a model military campaign. What's interesting about the campaign is he didn't plan it from the beginning. He planned it in response to circumstances and what he saw in front of him.

IN OCTOBER 1863 Grant was given theater command and ordered to super-vise the relief of a besieged Union army in the city of Chattanooga. Grant came down, reinforcements gathered, and he launched an attack against the Confederate forces. It proved astonishingly successful, as much a product of luck as skill. Chattanooga, more than anything else, cemented Grant as the obvious top Union commander.

[In December 1863] Elihu Washburne and congressional Republicans [announced their intention to introduce a bill to] revive the lieutenant gen-eral rank, which had not been a full rank in the United States Army since the days of George Washington. They wanted Grant to fill it in part to take con-trol of the army away from people like Lincoln. Lincoln did not support the bill until he found out whether General Grant wanted to be president in 1864. Grant, very shrewdly, wrote letters to people who would see Lincoln [indicating that] he didn't have any presidential ambitions at all. . . . There were other messages leaked to Lincoln the same way, and Lincoln checked him out before he supported that bill.

Grant came to Washington in March 1864 to get the commission as lieu-tenant general, with a position as commander general in chief of the armies of the United States. At first, he didn't think he would stay. But after he checked the political situation in Washington and went down to visit the Army of the Potomac, he began to realize that he would have to stay with that army as much as possible to shield it from political interference from Washington.

The popular perception was that Ulysses S. Grant and Abraham Lincoln were very tight, that Lincoln had always chosen Grant as his general. That wasn't true. Lincoln often kept Grant at arm's length. He never went to the point of removing him, but he had doubts about his ability.

Mary Todd Lincoln had her own run-in with General Grant on April 13, 1865. Grant came to Washington right after Appomattox had shut down the war effort. . . . He rode around in a carriage that night for a grand illumina-tion in Washington. Mary Todd Lincoln was in the presidential carriage, and she became furious when people cheered Grant instead of the presidential carriage.

The Grants were invited to go to Ford's Theater the next day. Neither

[General nor Mrs.] Grant wanted to go out in public with Mrs. Lincoln around, so they [said they had to visit their children in New Jersey]. That's why they were not in the box at Ford's Theater the night [Lincoln was assassinated]. Abraham Lincoln was shot on April 14, 1865, and died on April 15.

THE END OF THE Civil War was a natural breaking point in Grant's career and his life. In 1865 he'd accomplished what he needed to accomplish. He thought that after the Civil War, he would be able to live out the rest of his life as a retired general basking in adulation. That was not to be.

Differing Perspectives on Abraham Lincoln

by

DOUGLAS L. WILSON
ALLEN C. GUELZO
LERONE BENNETT JR.

In presidential polls, Abraham Lincoln, America's sixteenth president, consistently ranks among the top five most admired U.S. presidents. Numerous books have examined his political and his personal life, and he continues to inspire debate among historians and the public alike. Several authors have visited us on Booknotes *and discussed the many different aspects of Abraham Lincoln. Those featured here are Lincoln scholar Douglas L. Wilson of Knox College in Galesberg, Illinois, author of* Honor's Voice: The Transformation of Abraham Lincoln, *published in 1998 by Alfred A. Knopf, who appeared on March 29, 1998; Allen C. Guelzo, history professor at Eastern College in St. Davids, Pennsylvania, author of* Abraham Lincoln: Redeemer President, *published in 1999 by Wm. B. Eerdmans Publishing Company, who appeared on April 16, 2000; and Lerone Bennett Jr., Executive Editor of* Ebony *magazine and author of* Forced into Glory: Abraham Lincoln's White Dream, *published in 1999 by Johnson Publishing, who appeared on September 10, 2000.*

DOUGLAS L. WILSON

Ann Rutledge was the most beautiful and most eligible young woman in New Salem, Illinois, when Lincoln [moved] there. But she almost immediately, by the time he knew her, was already engaged to another man. His name was McNamar. McNamar left town, saying he was going back east to get his parents, and he would come back and marry her. But he was gone three years and she apparently thought that she'd been deserted.

Lincoln, who apparently had a fondness for her all along, courted her, and she agreed to marry him. In the summer of 1835, which was a terribly hot, wet summer, there was a huge typhoid epidemic. She was suddenly taken ill and died in a few weeks' time. Lincoln was supposed to have taken this, according to the testimony of [his friends], very hard. People were afraid he was on the verge of insanity; that he was becoming suicidal. He was finally taken in hand by some of his closest friends, who looked after him for a few weeks until he began to come around.

MATILDA EDWARDS WAS a very beautiful young woman. She was eighteen years old in November 1840 when she accompanied her father, who was a state senator, Cyrus Edwards, to Springfield for the legislative session. She stayed with her cousin, who was Mary Todd's brother-in-law; in other words, she stayed in the same house that Mary Todd was living in. She apparently attracted the attention of practically every eligible bachelor in Springfield, and she got more than a few proposals, if we can trust the testimony about it. One of the people attracted to her was Abraham Lincoln.

Mary Todd came to live with her sister, Elizabeth Todd Edwards, in 1839—just as they were getting geared up for the 1840 campaign. That's how she knew Lincoln, because her brother-in-law and her cousins were all Whig politicians who were associated with Lincoln. We have testimony that Lincoln was fascinated by Mary, that she was a creature of excitement, that he would sit and listen to her talk, that they had a lot in common. Most people say they started seeing each other, and they became an item in 1840, and by the end of 1840, they were engaged.

But it's very hard to find the evidence for that. Mary's own letters suggest that she may not have been engaged to Lincoln. They may have had some kind of relationship, but she doesn't talk about it in her letters. What seems clear, if we can believe Joshua Speed, who was Lincoln's closest friend, is that after Lincoln and Mary were going together, Lincoln changed his mind and decided he wanted to take up with Matilda Edwards. Mary told him that this was dishonorable; he couldn't do this. He had a violent reaction to this, according to Speed, and he lost it again. They feared for his life; they were afraid he was suicidal.

Lincoln wanted out of their relationship and Mary resisted, and Lincoln began to sink into despondency. For a week in January 1841, he was dysfunctional. Then she presumably released him, . . . but she wanted him back. Lincoln felt guilty that he had made her unhappy by breaking up the relationship. This situation went on for a long time, almost two years, until all of a sudden, unbeknownst to most of their friends, they had been seeing each other and become reconciled. They announced they were going to get married that very day, [November 4, 1842].

Lincoln got himself into this entanglement with Mary Todd that he never really could get himself out of. The solution was to marry her. He apparently went into this situation where he simply couldn't function. . . . We don't know exactly what Lincoln did, but he says in a letter at that time to his law partner, who was in Congress, "I've been making a most discreditable exhibition of myself in the way of my hypochondriaism."

ABRAHAM LINCOLN'S EARLY life is a famous American legend and, in fact, it's really part of our national identity; we identify with Lincoln and his career. He is the person who rose from poverty and obscurity, gained a profession, gained a position in politics, became president and, many think, saved his country. We identify with that rise. There are important things about his rise that we don't know. We don't know how difficult it was. In this period, he went through great difficulty and struggle. A couple of times, he really had great mental problems. He was emotionally very vulnerable and seems to have just lost it. He had to struggle. The actual story doesn't belie the legend; it simply shows that there's a human being behind the hero.

ALLEN C. GUELZO

Lincoln, clearly, is a central figure in the central event of our history, which is the Civil War. The Civil War—and Lincoln articulated this better than anyone else—was the central testing event of the idea of a democratic republic. We take too much for granted today, in the twentieth century, that the idea of democracy is the ideal that everyone should aspire to. A hundred and thirty-five years ago that wasn't the case. There were very few republics, very few things that could be described as a democracy, and they were looked upon as chancy.

If you wanted stability, what you were supposed to have was a monarchy, an aristocracy, and a king who could guarantee stability, day in and day out. To be part of a democracy was to take a tremendous risk, especially in the United States, with a republic that was dedicated to a proposition that all men are created equal. That was really to put yourself at big political risk. The Civil War was the great testing event. It was the litmus test as to whether democracies could hold together or whether they were doomed just to fly apart into various kinds of special interests.

BY DISMISSING MCCLELLAN, Lincoln was taking the greatest political risk of his life and perhaps in the history of the republic. George Brinton McClellan, major general, United States Volunteers . . . had been recruited at the very beginning of the war after the terrible Union defeat at First Bull Run to take command of the Union armies. He was put in overall command of all the Union forces but he was also given specific responsibility for creating the Army of the Potomac, the Union army that would, . . . hopefully, defeat the Confederate army and capture the Confederate capital at Richmond.

McClellan took up his task in the summer of 1861. He built a wonderful army. He was a great organizer, a tremendously talented engineer. He was the kind of person who—if management consultants had existed in 1860—[would have] the resume that every management consultant in the country would take as an example. There was only one problem: He didn't like to fight, which is a strange thing in a general.

He was a comparatively young man, thirty-four, but he had talent coming out of every pore. And what's more, the army that he organized loved him. When he would ride down the ranks of men on review parade, they would cheer. One of his staff officers said that McClellan had this peculiar little way of taking off his cap and spinning it on his finger, that the men would just cheer about. On campaign, he would carry around a small printing press so that he could regularly print up and distribute bulletins and exhortations to the men in the ranks. When he took them on the great campaign in the spring of 1862, down to the James River peninsula, down to attack Richmond, the men were convinced that George McClellan was the greatest military genius of the age. There was only one problem: He might have been a genius but he was not a genius for achieving victory. And what's more, he had serious political disagreements with Lincoln.

McClellan was a Democrat; Lincoln was a Republican. McClellan was vehemently opposed to any movement, any twitch of a movement, in the direction of emancipating the slaves as part of the war. When that great Peninsula Campaign failed, when he won a half victory at Antietam in the fall of 1862 but let the Confederate army get away back into Virginia, that was when the rift became critical. Lincoln realized he was going to have to remove McClellan. McClellan was not going to win victories, and what's more, McClellan was not going to cooperate with him politically. But Lincoln knew that if he made any move to remove McClellan from command, there was that whole Army of the Potomac (120,000 men, when you counted up all the noses), there was a real chance that that army might have rallied behind McClellan, marched behind McClellan down to Washington, and been part of a coup d'état that would have made McClellan the temporary dictator of the United States for the view of achieving a truce and a negotiated peace.

People warned Lincoln about that. In fact, there was at least one staff officer on McClellan's staff who was cashiered for talking a little too freely about the plans they had for a coup d'état. But Lincoln finally did remove him, and the army cheered McClellan and said, "Lead us to Washington, General. We'll follow you." McClellan, whatever else he was, was not about to overturn his own government. He rode away from the army and made no attempt to lead a coup d'état. The army got a new commander and went back on campaign and had something to occupy itself with.

In those two, three weeks after Lincoln removed McClellan, there was nothing, nothing, that could have kept McClellan from saying to the army and his officers, most of whom he'd handpicked, "We're going down to Washington and we're going to sweep that baboon out of office and we are going to settle this civil war peacefully." That's why I say it perhaps was the most critical moment, not only in the war but maybe in American history.

Think what might have happened, first of all, if McClellan had done that and the Civil War had ended as a negotiated peace between two independent countries. And then think, too, what kind of political precedent would have been set for armies and generals to start interfering in the political process. We've seen enough of that in other places in the Western Hemisphere over the last 150 years to know what the United States might have been in for if that had happened.

Two years later when McClellan was put up as the Democratic candidate for president, he was beaten badly. Lincoln won 55 percent of the popular vote in the election of 1864, and maybe even more telling, Lincoln won 78 percent of the vote of the soldiers in the 1864 election. A lot had happened in two years, from the time when the army was cheering McClellan until 1864, when the army was cheering the man that they came to call, with reverence, Father Abraham.

LERONE BENNETT JR.

[The subtitle of my book] *Abraham Lincoln's White Dream,* means that contrary to what most people think, Abraham Lincoln's deepest desire was to deport all black people and create an all-white nation. It sounds like a wild idea now and it is a wild idea, but from about 1852 until his death, he worked feverishly to try to create deportation plans, colonization plans, to send black people either to Africa or to South Africa, or to the islands of the sea.

One of his greatest utterances—people quote it all the time [is] "We cannot escape history [we are] the last, best hope of earth." Lincoln said these words in a State of the Union message on December 1, 1862, in which he asked Congress to pass three constitutional amendments: one, to buy the slaves; second, to declare free all people who'd actually escaped; but the third one, his proposed Fifteenth Amendment, asked Congress to allocate money to deport black people to another place.

Almost everything I say here, I take from Lincoln or from documents of the time. It was not just [that] he wanted to push black people out; he had an idea of this great, giant vacuum sound, black people leaving and white people from all over the world coming in here and creating this all-white nation. As a matter of fact, in his "I Have a Dream" speech at Alton, Illinois, in 1858, he called for a white haven for "free white people everywhere, the world over."

Now these are Lincoln's words. And the interesting thing about that is he underlined these four words: free white people everywhere. He underlined them. . . . He was passionately committed to deporting black people and creating a white nation.

He believed that . . . was the only way to solve the race problem. I found that offensive and strange. Lincoln said over and over again he did not believe black people and white people could live together in equality in the United States of America.

THIS BOOK HAS BEEN attacked pretty harshly in some quarters, praised enthusiastically in others, but . . . I've not seen a single review which disagrees with any one of my four major points.

My first point is that the Emancipation Proclamation did not free black people. And it's doubtful if it ever freed anybody anywhere. Abraham Lincoln was not the Great Emancipator or the small emancipator or the medium-sized emancipator. Not only did the Emancipation Proclamation not free anybody, it [actually served to enslave some people] because Lincoln said in the document, which most people will never read, that he was specifically excluding certain slaves in southern Louisiana and eastern Virginia and elsewhere. Now why did he exclude these slaves in Louisiana? Because they were the only slaves he could have freed on January 1, 1863. The Union controlled southern Louisiana and New Orleans. The Union controlled eastern Virginia. Now on January 1, he could have freed these slaves. All he had to do was just not specifically exclude them.

Instead of freeing them, Abraham Lincoln, unfortunately, on January 1, said, "I'm not talking about you. You're the same as you were, as though this document never existed." So we have about 88,000 slaves in southern Louisiana and 33,000 or so in eastern Virginia, adding some 275,000 slaves in Tennessee who were not touched by it. All across the South, I estimate approximately 500,000 slaves were reenslaved or kept in slavery by the Emancipation Proclamation.

The second point is that Abraham Lincoln was a racist. I don't have any joy in making that [statement] but I think truth is important. He used the

N-word habitually, loved darky jokes, and black-based shows, and said in Illinois and elsewhere that he was opposed to black people voting, sitting on juries, intermarrying with white people, and holding office.

[Point number] three, [as I explained] Abraham Lincoln wanted to deport black people and create an all-white nation.

[Point number] four, and this is the controversial point . . . that Abraham Lincoln was, contrary to what all the historians say, an equivocating, vacillating leader who prolonged the war, delayed emancipation, and increased the number of casualties.

IF LINCOLN HAD NOT spent two years appeasing Kentucky, if he had mobilized 400,000 black soldiers and issued an emancipation order giving the soldiers freedom, the Civil War would have been over [in] two years, three years at most. . . . I don't understand the historians who say [Lincoln exhibited] great leadership. If Franklin Delano Roosevelt had conducted World War II as disastrously as Abraham Lincoln conducted the Civil War in the first two years, America would be a German protectorate today.

The Leadership of Robert E. Lee

by

H. W. CROCKER III

TOM WHEELER

A Virginian by birth, Robert E. Lee led the Confederate forces during the Civil War after turning down an offer to lead the U.S. Army. Lee's Army of Northern Virginia surrendered to Ulysses S. Grant at Appomattox Court House, Virginia, in April 1865. Although Lee was charged with treason, he was never tried. After the war, he served as the president of what is now Washington and Lee University in Lexington, Virginia. He spent the last years of his life urging his fellow Southerners toward reconciliation with the North. H. W. Crocker III, author of Robert E. Lee on Leadership: Executive Lessons in Character, Courage, and Vision, *published in 1999 by Forum/Prima Publishing, appeared on* Booknotes *on July 14, 1999. Mr. Crocker is the Executive Editor for Regnery Publishing. Tom Wheeler, president of the Cellular Telecommunications Industry Association, talked about his book,* Leadership Lessons from the Civil War, *published in 1999 by Doubleday, on* Booknotes *on December 1, 1999. Both authors discussed Robert E. Lee's capacity for leadership.*

H. W. CROCKER III

One of the things that . . . initially attracted me to Robert E. Lee was here was this man who combined the most daring battlefield maneuvers, who was an audacious and aggressive military commander, taking huge risks and always seeking to take the offensive whenever he could. But in his personal conduct with people he was incredibly gentle. He operated by suggestion rather than direct order if he could.

Lee's cause was the cause of constitutional government and the cause of people being allowed to determine their own destiny. When the Confederacy's distinguishing feature is identified as slavery, that's unjust because that's only true if America's distinguishing feature was slavery before the war. The South, at the outbreak of hostilities in the Civil War, was only upholding the status quo and upholding rulings of the Supreme Court on the issue of slavery.

ROBERT E. LEE was born in Virginia in 1807 at a place called Stratford Hall, which is down in the northern neck of Virginia. Stratford Hall was actually lost to the Lee family shortly after he was born.

Robert E. Lee was born into a world of grace—they were very gentle people. His mother's side was very well-to-do, from a famous Virginia family, the Carters—but . . . his father squandered the family fortunes [and] left the family when Lee was six years old. It was the last time Lee saw his father.

They moved to Alexandria, Virginia, in his boyhood. He went to West Point in the 1820s. He went back and became superintendent of West Point in the 1850s.

ROBERT E. LEE himself believed in the power of emulation. He believed you could study the lives of great men and learn something from them, not in the academic way but in a way that you would actually apply to your own life. . . . I cannot think personally of a better exemplar of mature leadership, of someone who showed us not only how to advocate useful principles, but somebody who actually lived them. Robert E. Lee lived it and even paid the price for it in some of the sadder parts of his life.

The price of having sided with Virginia during the war was that he lost everything. He lost his home; he lost his investments. One of his children died during the war, [along] with two grandchildren. He lost countless friends and saw the state that he valued [highest] among all other loyalties devastated by the war. His region, the South, was completely destroyed. A quarter of the draft-age men, white males in the South, perished in the war, either from combat or from disease related to combat. The industry of the South was famously destroyed. General Philip Sheridan said he'd so destroyed the Shenandoah Valley that a crow could fly over it and not find anything to eat.

He also paid the price in his career. He was a stellar officer during the Mexican War. Winfield Scott, then commander of all U.S. forces, thought that Robert E. Lee was the finest officer he had ever seen in the field, and he worked Lee practically to death. Scott kept him on horseback doing everything for days at a time, until Lee at one point actually received a flesh wound and collapsed, he was so exhausted.

At the outbreak of the War Between the States, Lee was offered command of the Union army. He was offered every professional ambition he could ever have wanted, and he turned it down. He turned it down saying, though opposed to secession, he could not consent to raise his hand against his family, his friends, or his native state. He would return to Virginia and share whatever Virginia was going to suffer and, save in defense of Virginia, he would raise his sword against no one.

Winfield Scott greeted him right after he made the offer [to lead the Union army] and when Lee told him of what he'd decided, Scott said, "Lee, you've made the worst decision of your life, but I feared it would be so." Then he turned around and told his colleagues in Federal service that the addition of Robert E. Lee to the Confederacy was going to be worth at least 50,000 men to the Southern cause. The job eventually fell to George McClellan, who was the first Union general Lee faced head-on in Virginia.

[When the Civil War began in 1861] the differentials between the North and South were on the basis of 2:1. The South was taking a much larger section of its draft-age population and putting them under arms. The North really had endless supplies of men. During the 1864 campaign, when Grant took command against Lee, Grant was losing casualties at the rate of 2:1; for every Confederate he killed of Robert E. Lee's, he lost two men. But he was able to win this endless war of attrition because Lee's resources were, more or less, static. When Lee's men were gone, they were not replaceable. It would have been an entirely different game if Robert E. Lee had had the same number of men that the North had.

ROBERT E. LEE was a man who believed in self-control. One of his famous dictums about leadership was, "I cannot consent to place in the control of others one who cannot control himself." He believed men's passions blinded their logic. They blinded their ability to make the proper decision. Robert E. Lee was very respectful, both of his superiors and of his subordinates.

Lee was a very humble man. . . . People noticed that ego was absent from his character. Fame didn't spoil him. . . . He embodied many Christian paradoxes. Among them was [the idea that] to lead is to serve. He never thought being a leader meant he had any claims over other people. He thought being a leader meant he was there to serve other people, to make them succeed.

LEE DISCOVERED THE GENIUS of Stonewall Jackson [when] Lee was still a desk officer, as he was at the beginning of the war. He was Jefferson Davis's troubleshooter in Richmond. And Lee saw this man in the Shenandoah Valley of Virginia, Stonewall Jackson, who was conducting all these independent operations that were stunning and befuddling Union forces [that were] much his superior in numbers, and was doing this largely on his own hook.

And Lee liked men like that. He liked men who could take the initiative.

[Lee and Jackson] had the greatest partnership of any two generals of the war. Stonewall Jackson was, in many ways, an odd man. He was known for being very dour, but there were actually many winsome, sweet things about him. He'd been a professor at Virginia Military Institute. He'd been a soldier before that; he'd gone to West Point. He served bravely in the Mexican War.

Lee joyously endorsed [Jackson's strategy at Chancellorsville]. That calm trusting to a daring subordinate was a hallmark of Lee for a couple of reasons: one is that he very much trusted Jackson. He believed in people; he didn't believe in numbers. When Lee first took battlefield command, which was during the Seven Days Campaign [east] of Richmond early in the war, the Confederate troops up to that point had been continually retreating, trying to find a good defensive position. They'd finally stopped within sight of Richmond, the capital of Virginia and the capital of the Confederacy.

When Lee called his first staff meeting, he wanted to know what the generals thought they should do, and they thought that they should retreat further. They were doing all these calculations, and he said, "Stop figuring. If you keep ciphering—we're beat before we even get started." He didn't believe in numbers. He didn't believe in textbook strategy. He believed to find the right man for the right job, you wanted him to be audacious and daring and you turned him loose. That's what he did with Jackson, and Jackson responded well to that sort of independent command.

Stonewall Jackson was killed, unfortunately, by friendly fire . . . at the battle at Chancellorsville. . . . One of Jackson's stratagems was that once you have your enemy flustered and on the run, don't let up, keep after them. He wanted to keep after them, even as darkness was falling, and he was looking out on a scouting expedition to find ways to keep the offensive rolling. As he was riding back, Jackson was actually shot down because he was mistaken for Federal cavalry. [As a result of the wounds] his arm was amputated and he died later of pneumonia.

This was a devastating blow for Lee. There was a famous quote where Lee said, "Jackson has lost his left arm, but I have lost my right." It was recorded by some that Lee—he was known as a religious man—never prayed harder than when he prayed that Stonewall Jackson might recover.

Lee [was rumored to have] said, "If Stonewall Jackson had been with me at Gettysburg, that battle might have gone another way." Lee wanted the same sort of independent operations he saw at Chancellorsville and couldn't get them done.

TOWARD THE END of the war Lee was always worried about his loss of officers The casualty rate among Confederate officers was extremely high. And Lee, at a couple points . . . during the Battle of the Wilderness in particular, was riding forward unarmed as the Union forces were pouring out, charging the Confederate line, as though he was going to stop them himself. He had to be grabbed and forcibly removed from charging the Federal forces. And he said, "All right, I'll go back if you men will charge in there and stop them." And they did.

Lee injured himself in a horse accident in the war. He developed heart problems. . . . It's hard to trace these things back, but the symptoms start hitting him during the war. During the battle of Gettysburg, he was famously not feeling up to par. As the war dragged on, it was obviously becoming more and more painful. It became hard for him to move. His breath was leaving him. He aged rapidly during the war.

SHORTLY BEFORE LEE rode into Appomattox Court House to surrender to Grant, he was talking to one of his young artillery officers, a man named Edward Porter Alexander, about what they should do. Lee always liked to talk. He generally knew what he wanted to do. He would talk it through with his officers to go through the different scenarios. Alexander, being a high-strung young man, said, "You know what we should do? We should become bushwhackers. We should wage a guerrilla campaign. We shouldn't give up." Lee said, "That might be very well for you and for me, for whom surrender is hateful. And it might be something we'd like to do for our own personal honor. But we can't think of ourselves first. We've already seen reprisals against civilians. We've already seen Sherman burning down Southern cities and destroying Southern property. This will only get worse. If we launch a partisan campaign, there'll be reprisals against civilians. We have to think first of the women and the children of the South."

[Lee surrendered to Grant at Appomattox Court House on April 9, 1865.] Lee was so taken by the generosity of spirit of Grant at the surrender that after the war he would not allow a harsh word about Grant to be said in his presence. This shows the spirit of Lee as being a kind, generous, forgiving man who bore no personal animosity, even against those he thought had been fighting against his native soil and countrymen.

HE DIED [AT AGE SIXTY-THREE] after coming back from a vestry meeting. It was a cold, drizzly day. He came home and suddenly just couldn't speak. He actually had sat down at the table to say grace, and no words would come out. He just sat there ramrod straight and was frozen. He didn't die immediately. There was a period where he was feverish. He actually did get his voice back a little bit. He spoke in monosyllables, and he did cry out a couple times. He called out for one of his officers, A. P. Hill, . . . who was dead already. [Some say] that his last words were, "Strike the tent," which is a fitting epitaph for him.

[His funeral] was a very big deal. He was obviously a hero to Virginia and to the South, but interestingly enough, Lee, before his death—and he died only five years after the war—became a national hero. . . . It is usually said that if you add up [the casualties in] all of America's wars put together, it's less than everybody who perished in the War Between the States. Yet before he died, a big New York newspaper, the *New York Herald*, was recommending that the Democratic Party nominate Robert E. Lee for president. This was when Robert E. Lee didn't even have his citizenship back yet. He couldn't vote. I really think that it's very few people who come to blows, come to warfare, who regard one of their former opponents as a hero.

TOM WHEELER

The word "audacity" [means] taking the bull by the horns, doing the unexpected. Audacity is a force multiplier. Robert E. Lee is a great example. He was always audacious. He was always on the offensive. It's hard to win if you're sitting back and playing defense. You need to make the other person respond to you. Lee was great at that.

Robert E. Lee [took risks] all the time. His biggest risk was probably Chancellorsville. He had a situation in 1863 where the Federal troops were on one side of the Rappahannock River, he was on the other, down by Fredericksburg, Virginia. The Union troops commanded by General Joseph Hooker were about 3 to 1 Lee's size. Hooker came up with a really brilliant plan where he brought about two-thirds of his force and flanked them around [Lee's troops]. The next thing you know, without Lee knowing it, Hooker was in the rear. Hooker had left men in Fredericksburg, so he had a vise that he could just squeeze Lee's army with. You would think that a commanding general would skedaddle. "How fast can I get out of this vise?" Lee left a handful of men to confront the guys at Fredericksburg and turned around and marched against Hooker, split his troops. You're never supposed to split your forces in the face of a superior adversary.

Lee got back to fighting Hooker, and what did he do? He split his forces again. He sent Stonewall Jackson on a flanking march with about two-thirds of Lee's force. That turned out to be very successful and proved to be decisive. But [there remained] the small force that Lee left down at Fredericksburg; suddenly the Union started advancing against that and the other half of the vise came back. What did Lee do then? He split this force again and went back down to deal with them and whipped them. And when he whipped them, he turned around and split again to go back. It was the most audacious military leadership. It was one of the great examples in all of history.

ONE OF THE THINGS that makes the leadership lessons of the Civil War so real to us today is that these were not professional soldiers, for the most part. At the beginning of the Civil War, the United States Army consisted of 15,000 men, most of whom were out fighting Indians, and four generals. At the end of the war, four years later, 1,000 men had worn general's stars. You look at even the great names: Ulysses Grant was a tannery clerk before the war. William Tecumseh Sherman was the president of the St. Louis Streetcar Company; Stonewall Jackson was a professor; even Robert E. Lee, who was in the U.S. Army at the start of the war, had never commanded men on such a scale.

So this was the last war fought by ordinary people, common people, people like you and me, who were placed into these kinds of situations and had to use their own best judgment, had to make their own leadership decisions. That's one of the most exciting things about the study of the war, and it's one of the things that we, today, can take the most solace in or learn from, because they were just like us. They weren't supermen; they were men who were placed in challenging circumstances.

Jefferson Davis and the Confederacy

by

WILLIAM J. COOPER JR.

A West Point graduate who served as a U.S. congressman, senator, and sec-retary of war, Jefferson Davis is most often remembered for the final politi-cal office he held: president of the Confederate States of America. As a U.S. senator, Davis argued that secession by a state was a constitutionally pro-tected but undesirable outcome. When his home state of Mississippi left the Union, Davis followed. His four years as leader of the Confederacy ended with the Confederate surrender, and Davis was soon imprisoned on charges of treason. Freed on parole after two years, Jefferson Davis was left with lit-tle money but an abiding American patriotism. Louisiana State University professor William J. Cooper Jr. appeared on Booknotes *on April 8, 2001, to discuss* Jefferson Davis: American, *published in 2000 by Alfred A. Knopf.*

"AMERICAN" is the best way to understand Jefferson Davis. Davis always thought of himself as an American. He thought of himself as a son of the rev-olution, both ideologically and biologically. His father had been a Revolu-tionary soldier. He looked at the Declaration and the Constitution as the true marks of the good American society. He believed in the things that most Americans of his time did—progress, economic growth, geographic develop-ment of the country. He believed in all those things, just as most other Amer-icans did and he never stopped believing in them. He is most famous for being president of the Confederacy, but he thought that the Confederate States was the last best hope for what he believed the United States of Amer-ica was.

Of course, one of the things in his Americanism was a belief in racial slavery. He didn't see any contradiction between America and slavery. Slavery had come through the Revolution intact. Slavery was protected by the Constitution. Davis believed that. Most all other Americans, South and North, believed that. The United States Supreme Court emphatically affirmed that. Davis looked at heroes of the nation—Washington, Jefferson, Madison, Andrew Jackson, Zachary Taylor, slave owners all—so he didn't understand why there had to be a separation over slavery. He rejected the notion that the country couldn't continue "half slave and half free," to use Lincoln's phrase, because it had been like that from the beginning. He thought it could continue like that for a long time.

There had been a law passed in 1820, the Missouri Compromise, which controlled how slavery could expand westward into the Louisiana Territory, which went all the way to Canada. The Compromise of 1850 . . . had to do chiefly with how the country was going to handle . . . the territory gained from the Mexican War, which included all of the current Southwest plus California. The fight was about slavery. Would slavery be permitted [in the new territory]? The nation had moved westward [since] the Revolution, crossed the Appalachian Mountains, crossed the Mississippi River. Slavery had moved westward all the way from the eastern seaboard to Texas.

Southerners wanted to take slaves out there. The issue was not so much whether they would take [slaves to the Southwest] but they wanted the right to take them. The Compromise of 1850 was no guarantee that Southerners could take slaves there. In fact, it was a guarantee that they couldn't take them to California. . . . Jefferson Davis opposed it bitterly.

When Davis started off, . . . he was chosen as an elector for the state of Mississippi in 1844. . . . Back then, you were expected to campaign. Davis went out and campaigned throughout Mississippi in 1844, just as if he were running for office himself. And he campaigned successfully. James K. Polk was elected president in 1844, a Democrat. The very next year, 1845, Jefferson Davis ran for Congress on a general ticket. Mississippi didn't have districts. The law permitted a state to have general tickets back then. So he had to campaign all across the state to get elected. He was elected to Congress in 1845. He resigned from Congress to go in the Mexican War. He came back from the Mexican War [and was appointed a U.S.] senator. Then at age fifty-one, he resigned to run for governor of Mississippi but was defeated. He became secretary of war in 1853 under Franklin Pierce. When Pierce's administration went out of office in 1857, Davis went back to the Senate. He was in the Senate when the Union broke apart in 1861. Then, of course, he became president of the Confederacy.

THE ATMOSPHERE [in 1860 when Davis was a U.S. senator] was one of tremendous political tension. The presidential election of 1860, most Americans felt, would be tremendously important for the future of the country. The Republican Party had run its first candidate four years previously and almost won. The Republicans were a sectional party. There were no Southerners in the Republican Party. The Republicans' whole strategy for winning was if you could carry the North, you didn't need the South. This was a new phenomenon in American history, and it frightened Southerners because they had always been instrumental in American political parties. They'd been at the top. The Democratic Party was their party in 1860, but the Democrats also had tremendous strength in the North.

But Northern and Southern Democrats were divided over personalities and divided over issues in 1860, so the Democratic Party split. There was a Northern candidate and a Southern candidate. As if three were not enough, there was a fourth candidate, because people who didn't like Republicans or Democrats, mostly old Whigs, put up a candidate. So, there were four people running.

Stephen Douglas was a Northern Democrat. Lincoln was the Republican. John C. Breckinridge was the Southern Democrat. And John Bale was the candidate of a group that called themselves the Constitutional Unionists.

Jefferson Davis supported John C. Breckinridge. Davis was also active in the effort to try to get all the opponents of the Republicans to unite behind a new candidate—that is, for Bale, Douglas, and Breckinridge to drop out— and to find somebody new and sort of neutral to come in and take the standard to run against the Republicans. That all failed.

[Lincoln won the election of 1860.] Mississippi seceded early in the month of January 1861. Davis had fought against secession. He believed it was constitutionally proper; that it was sanctioned by the Constitution. He never thought it was an unconstitutional act, but he never wanted it to come about. In fact, after Lincoln's election in 1860, the governor of Mississippi called together in Jackson, the capital of the state, the congressional delegation to consult with him about what he should propose to the state legislature. Among those people in that meeting, Davis was the only one who was not for immediate secession.

Davis went to Washington. He tried hard to find some way to come up with a compromise that would keep things going, at least for a while. Now, his compromise always had to be with a guarantee that the South could have its constitutional rights in the territories; that is, that there was a right for Southerners to take their slave property to the territories. Slavery was absolutely central in the Southern society and economy. Slavery was central in Southern political power because the Constitution, through the three-fifths provision, counted three-fifths of slaves for representation, that meant congressmen and votes in the Electoral College. Slavery was important for political power.

[Davis resigned from the Senate on January 21, 1861] after he received formal notice from Mississippi that the state had seceded. . . . The Senate was packed. . . . It was almost a spectator sport in this winter of crisis. He stood up and said it was time for him to say good-bye; that his state had seceded because the Constitution and the Declaration had been subverted by the Republicans, as he saw it. People knew his belief about secession; that even if he didn't think Mississippi was right, he would have to go, but he thought Mississippi had the right do what it did. And then he said good-bye.

[Three weeks later, Jefferson Davis] was chosen president of the Confederacy by a group of men who met in Montgomery, Alabama, . . . to create the Confederate States of America. Six states met then: South Carolina, Georgia, Alabama, Mississippi, Florida, and Louisiana. Texas also seceded, but the Texas delegates didn't get to Montgomery [until after] Davis was selected. The voting was [done] by state. Each state had one vote, and Davis won that unanimously. Davis brought to that office qualifications nobody else could match. He was elected for six [years], but the Confederacy didn't last but four.

[IT WAS VIEWED AS] a great victory for the Confederates when Virginia seceded. Virginia did not secede until after Fort Sumter, after Lincoln called for volunteers to put down the rebellion. But Confederates thought Virginia was the mother of the South; that Virginia was the home of the great heroes of the American Revolution. Richmond, Virginia, was the most important industrial city in the Confederate states. Montgomery wasn't big enough to handle the growth of the capital. So in May of 1861, the capital [of the Confederacy] was moved from Montgomery to Richmond, Virginia. They did not have a White House, but a mansion in Richmond was bought by the city and given to the Confederate states to use as an executive mansion.

[The Confederate States formed their own] Congress. In Montgomery, where the provisional congress met, there was only one house, unicameral. But when the provisional congress had run its course, the Confederate Constitution called for the election of a Congress. That was a bicameral Congress—House and Senate, just like the United States, and it met in the Virginia state capital.

[AT THE END OF THE Civil War, Davis went] on the run. He was trying very hard to get to Texas. He hoped to carry on the war in what the Confederates called the trans-Mississippi, that area west of the Mississippi River. He hoped to get there overland, or . . . at least to get to Florida and take a boat to Mexico and come up to Texas through Mexico. But he was captured by Union cavalrymen in south Georgia in May of 1865.

President Andrew Johnson and many other Northern leaders believed that Davis had been involved [in planning Abraham Lincoln's assassination]. There had been bad blood between Andrew Johnson and Jefferson Davis long before the Civil War, and when Davis got word that Lincoln had been assassinated, he expressed the opinion that neither he nor the South could expect much forbearance from Andrew Johnson.

They made him a prisoner, and he was taken up to Macon and put on a train and carried from Macon to Augusta, put on a boat, carried to Savannah, and eventually [he] ended up in Fortress Monroe, which is at the confluence of the James River and the Chesapeake Bay [in Virginia]. He was in prison there for two years, from May 1865 to May 1867. Initially, he was treated pretty harshly. He was brought in and they put irons on him. He fought that physically, the putting of irons on him, but that didn't last very long—at the most, for five days. But he was incarcerated in a casement, the inner walls of the fortress, and he had a steel door and had a sentry looking at him every second of every day. There was not one moment of privacy for anything whatever. That lasted until the fall. In the fall of 1865, he was moved into an apartment fitted for him in officers' quarters in a building at Fortress Monroe.

Davis was indicted for treason. He was never brought to trial. His captors couldn't decide what to do. The jury would have come from Richmond. They were afraid to bring him to trial, in part, because they were afraid a jury would acquit him, [that] the whole Northern rationale for fighting the war . . . would be thrown out by a jury. They didn't want to lose. They also had problems with the judges. The chief justice of the United States, Salmon P. Chase, sat on the circuit court in Richmond, and they were worried that Chase might decide for Davis. There were people inside the Federal government who felt that Davis should never be brought to trial, that the war was over and that he should be let go.

Ironically, Davis's attorneys were very afraid of a jury trial too. They were afraid that the jury would have on it people who were Republicans, even blacks, and they would vote to convict Davis, not on the merits of the case, but just on Davis.

IN MAY OF 1867, Davis was paroled. He went to Canada, [where] his family had been, for a few months, and then, desperate to try to make a living, he went to England trying to sell interest in Canadian mines. He was approaching sixty years old. He traveled in France and Scotland, but he stayed mostly in England. In England, he was royally received. Many in the English upper classes had been pro-contrarian in their sentiments, and Davis was lionized. But he and his wife had a serious problem because they had very little money, and Varina Davis especially was very anxious about getting involved in a social world in which she could not move as an equal, in which she could not reciprocate.

Davis was not succeeding in England, so he came back to this country. [Friends got him a job] but he was very unsure about getting into the insurance business. He [wondered] what people would think of him becoming "just an insurance man"—that his status would drop. His wife was concerned about that too.

[He spent the last twelve years of his life in Mississippi] writing *The Rise and Fall of the Confederate States*. . . . They were two fat, ponderous volumes, and they are dry. I was astonished that they had sold over 20,000 copies.

At the end of Davis's life, it was very sad; at the same time, it was very positive. . . . He was trying to farm his old plantation at Brierfield, which he had regained control of. He was having a most difficult time, no success at all, in making Brierfield run again. But at the same time, he was optimistic. He talked about the United States and its growing power and its glory and grandeur. He gave talks to young people, and he told them that they should revere their Confederate heritage, but they shouldn't be mired in the past. They should look to the future of the United States.

[Davis died at age eighty-one.] He had contracted serious bronchial difficulties, and it was probably pneumonia that killed him. He is buried [with] his wife and his children in Richmond, in Hollywood Cemetery.

JEFFERSON DAVIS WAS not a man of the twenty-first century; he was a man of the nineteenth century. I tried to understand him as a man of his time. . . . Jefferson Davis was [not] the most wonderful person who ever lived, [nor was he] the devil incarnate. He was a man who, like other men, had strengths and had weaknesses. And he lived through extraordinarily difficult times.

Rebuilding America and the Gilded Age

1865–1901

Frederick Law Olmsted and the Building of Central Park

by

WITOLD RYBCZYNSKI

Frederick Law Olmsted was an extraordinarily successful and influential landscape designer as well as a man of other careers and talents. With his partner Calvert Vaux, he designed what is arguably America's most famous urban park, New York City's Central Park, along with Prospect Park in Brooklyn and dozens of other parks, estates, and campuses. Witold Rybczynski's A Clearing in the Distance: Frederick Law Olmsted and America in the Nineteenth Century *was published by Scribner in 1999. Mr. Rybczynski, a professor of urbanism at the University of Pennsylvania, told us Olmsted's story on September 7, 1999.*

FREDERICK LAW OLMSTED and Calvert Vaux [worked on] Central Park. . . from 1858 to 1876. [The rest of Olmsted's designs] really come in categories. There are the famous public parks, like Prospect Park in Brooklyn and Montreal's Mount Royal Park. He did big parks in Chicago. Boston's Emerald Necklace is a whole series of public parks connected through the city that he designed near the end of his life. He designed the grounds of Biltmore House, the George Vanderbilt estate outside Asheville, North Carolina, which was the biggest house in the country and a beautiful estate. He was also the planner of Stanford University in California.

Perhaps his most important project, which we forget because it was a fair, was the Chicago World's Columbian Exposition in 1893. This was the biggest public event at the end of the nineteenth century in this country. A huge number of people visited it, and it was the first chance people in the United

States had to see a planned, total environment. This was a plan and landscape designed by Olmsted himself.

FREDERICK LAW OLMSTED had such a varied life before he started building parks. It made me curious as to what was it about him that enabled him to succeed at these enormous public works projects, coming out of a background in journalism and in farming. All of these things didn't obviously lead to [landscape architecture]. I became intrigued about the person himself, and what was it in his life that pushed him in that direction and that somehow formed him. He wasn't trained as a landscape architect at all. There was no such thing at that time.

Olmsted was born in Hartford [in 1822]. His father was born just outside Hartford into a farming family, moved to Hartford, started a hardware store, and was a fairly successful dry goods merchant. . . . He was a very important person in Olmsted's life. His mother died when he was only three years old. Olmsted had the great fortune to have an extremely supportive father who tolerated his long education and all of these diverse careers. He supported Olmsted financially and psychologically, and never forced him or pushed him. There was one exchange of letters where they were a little bit angry with each other, but they immediately made up. . . . This gave him that freedom to be very experimental with his life.

Olmsted had one brother to whom he was very close. . . . Tragically, his brother died of tuberculosis when he was thirty-two, leaving a wife and several children. His wife became Olmsted's wife; he married her about a year later. Some biographers feel he was doing his duty because she had several children, but I'm not so sure that's true. I think they really did fall in love. They had a very happy and long marriage. They had two children who survived and two who died. His son became a landscape architect also and was probably as famous if not more than his father in the twenties and the teens. . . . Olmsted's wife, Mary, was involved in his work. He asked her for advice about his projects. He gave her responsibilities to do things when he was traveling, regarding his work. They were very close.

He went to England as a young man on a walking tour, long before he had any thoughts of landscape architecture. He was enormously influenced by this experience of the beautiful English garden landscape. Every few years, he would go back to recharge his batteries. There wasn't much that someone like him could learn in America. There weren't other people doing it. But there were people planning Paris, there were people building parks in England, and these were the touchstones of his profession. He got to know these people and he would regularly go back. He had a great sense of time, so it was very important for him to see a park again and again as it changed, as the trees got bigger, as it grew into itself.

Olmsted was one of the early visitors to Yosemite; he was involved, actually, in studying how it ought to be turned into a public park, what later became a national park. It was his first experience of the big western landscape. He knew Connecticut, he knew New England, and he knew old England, ... but in the West, he saw this big American landscape. And the thing about his parks and landscapes is they have this great sense of expansiveness. They're big to begin with, but they actually look bigger than they are, and he did all sorts of tricks; he took a meadow that's a mile and a half long and made it look infinitely long.

HE GOT THE job as superintendent for Central Park in New York. Essentially, he was in charge of hundreds, and later thousands, of workers. It was all done by hand, with very little machinery. Then the Central Park Commission decided they needed to hold a competition for the actual design of the park, and he, like many employees of the park, entered the competition. He joined with Calvert Vaux and they won, partly because they really had an original idea for their design, and partly because Olmsted was very familiar with the park, having worked on it for about six months. He knew the topography; he knew the terrain.

He was thirty-five when he first got involved in Central Park. . . . When the Civil War broke out, he got a leave of absence—everybody thought it would be a short war. He [received] the leave of absence to get involved, but he had a limp [from a terrible carriage accident] so he couldn't serve [in the army]. Instead, he was asked to become the leader of the U.S. Sanitary Commission, to organize and run it, which turned into a much longer project as the war dragged on.

When war broke out, the Northern army consisted of volunteers. The army didn't really have the means to provide medical attention and food for the wounded. So with the collaboration of the government, this private organization was formed called the Sanitary Commission, which raised funds from volunteer efforts throughout the states and then used that money to deliver medical attention, food, blankets, to soldiers right on the battlefield. Olmsted organized it and then ran it for two years.

Henry Whitney Bellows, the man who founded the commission, needed somebody to be a CEO, and he knew Olmsted was good at organizing large things. It's something you came across a great deal in the nineteenth century. There were no specialists. Instead, there were these people who were good at getting things done and who were given large jobs. They were not necessarily trained for it, nobody was. So this was not unusual, that somebody was given a very large responsibility in a field that they hadn't had direct training for.

Olmsted was involved in the Peninsula Campaign. He had hospital ships that ferried the wounded from the [Virginia] peninsula all the way around to

Boston and New York. This was right at the beginning of the war. Later on he was at Gettysburg a day after the battle with wagons, hot soup, and blankets. The Sanitary Commission played a major role in keeping casualties down. It was an enormous undertaking. There were hundreds of doctors and nurses, and thousands of volunteers. This was all under his coordination.

[President Lincoln didn't like the Sanitary Commission.] He had a lot of trouble with it. It was very political. The Sanitary Commission had no confidence in the surgeon general of the army, and Olmsted and his colleagues set out to get the surgeon general replaced. The commission was a thorn in Lincoln's side because they were always lobbying him. . . . While the army accepted the Sanitary Commission, they were rather skeptical, especially at the beginning. They didn't like all these civilians messing around, but they appreciated all the voluntary efforts. They would rather have been given the materials. So there was a lot of friction there and Lincoln, of course, had bigger problems. He actually called Olmsted his "fifth wheel." It's clear the Sanitary Commission was crucial to the success of the war and to reducing casualties. The army was simply not in a position to deal with this huge volunteer army.

A SPLINTER GROUP, [the Liberal Republicans] formed in . . . the [1872] presidential election and felt that Olmsted might be a suitable person to be a vice presidential candidate. [Earlier] George Templeton Strong, who wrote a famous diary during the Civil War, thought Olmsted ought to have been secretary of war during the Civil War. He was a great man to organize things, and politics requires a lot of organization, so people turned to him after Central Park and after the Sanitary Commission. He declined the [1872 vice presidential] nomination.

Olmsted was always employed at Central Park as a civil servant, so he was an employee of the Park Commission and, ultimately an employee of the City of New York. When Tammany Hall came in, they basically fired Olmsted and Vaux. . . . When Boss Tweed took over New York politics, the Democrats pushed out the Republican appointees, like Olmsted and Vaux, and installed their own men. We have to remember that the park was an enormous job creation project, so there was a lot of pressure from people who wanted to get control over that. There were a number of years when Olmsted was not involved. Then the Republicans came back and he was rehired as architect for Central Park and was in charge of managing the park. And that continued, again, until there was another political change and he was finally fired. It was shortly after that that he finally left New York and moved to Boston. He had pretty much had it, I think, at that point.

CENTRAL PARK IS REALLY a magical landscape. First of all, we have to remember there was nothing there of consequence when he started. People look at Central Park and they imagine they're seeing a kind of natural, nonurban part of New York but, in fact, Central Park was very rough and rocky ground. There were a lot of swamps. It was not very good ground, which is why it was empty and cheap. The city needed to buy inexpensive land because they were buying so much, and this was not good agricultural land. There were some rocky outcroppings, not many trees. Everything we see other than the rocky outcroppings today was created—the lakes, all the thousands of trees that were planted, the meadows—all of that was a creation.

These parks would never be built today; they're much too expensive. Of course, New York was growing then, so there was a lot of money. These parks were not simply altruistic; they were also intended to raise property values and then pay for the park through increased property taxes. That actually worked. It worked in Brooklyn as well.

New York City had insisted that four city streets cross the park, so that traffic wouldn't be completely interrupted. One of the reasons Vaux and Olmsted won the competition was that they had the brilliant idea of sinking those streets below the park level so you wouldn't see the traffic, and that's what happens today. When you're in the park, there are bridges where you cross these streets but essentially you're unaware that there's city traffic crossing the park.

His idea of landscaping was obviously influenced most by the English picturesque landscape. Central Park is [over] seven hundred acres; it's a big park. Most of his parks are between five hundred and seven hundred acres. Most European parks arc much smaller than that. It has to do with the empty spaces that were available near American cities at that time. In 1858, about 300,000 people lived in Manhattan. By the time he got involved, the park had already been set in terms of its size. They had set aside seven hundred acres that were really not even in the suburbs. They were somewhere on the fringe of the city, with a view to the idea that the city would eventually grow and surround the park.

HAVING BUILT CENTRAL PARK, you'd think that would steer him into that profession, but it was not the case. He still wasn't convinced this is what he wanted to do. He kept getting pulled back into publishing—magazine publishing and editing—and it was only with Prospect Park, when he was forty-three years old, that he made the real commitment to become a landscape architect and planner.

Olmsted had worked as a managing editor and a publisher of *Putnam's*, which was a very important monthly magazine that published Melville and Emerson, an important literary magazine. It eventually failed, and he was interested in getting back into publishing. He met a man called E. L. Godkin, an Irishman, and they became very good friends and came up with this idea of what we would really call a news magazine, *The Nation*. It was a weekly newspaper that would have a little bit about politics, a little bit about culture, about economics, and various things. Godkin essentially worked as the editor and Olmsted was the publisher. They occasionally wrote for it as well and spent about a year or so doing that actively. Finally his landscape work grew too big and he had to step down from an active involvement.

My favorite of his parks is Prospect Park as a work of landscape art because I think he was much more experienced when he did it. It's a much more squarish piece of ground. It doesn't have this long skinny shape of Central Park. But Central Park is so wonderful today because of the way it's used. It's full of people. They're not doing the things that Olmsted imagined they would do; he never thought of Rollerblades or skateboarding or bicycling. The bicycle was invented later, but somehow that richness of activity is exactly what he wanted in his parks. . . . In New York, it's one of the few places where you get a real mixture of people. You don't get it in Lincoln Center or on the subway. But here, you actually get a total mixture of very rich, very poor, all sorts of people. Olmsted wrote about this very clearly. He said that in a park everybody should be seen mixing together. And these were, for him, not simply aesthetic places. They were also social places that were intended to be a safety valve for this industrial city that was just roiling around them.

After the Biltmore, he started having trouble with his memory. He decided he ought to step down from active practice, and he retired [in 1895] and then slipped into obscurity. He suffered from some debilitating disease [probably some form of dementia]. He spent part of his time living up in Maine, and eventually they had to put him in an asylum, tragically, whose grounds he had designed himself: McLean Asylum, outside Boston.

Olmsted died in 1903 when he was eighty-one years old. . . . He's buried in Hartford. It's a burying ground, a family tomb, and the biggest name is his father's name. At first I thought this was rather shocking. You don't even know this was the greatest landscape architect we've ever had. It just says "Frederick Law Olmsted." And then I thought it was actually quite appropriate because his father was so important in his life. So he probably would have liked that. He wouldn't have liked a big memorial.

The First Transcontinental Railroad

by

DAVID HAWARD BAIN

The first American railroad was composed of a mere thirteen miles of track and was formally known as the Baltimore and Ohio Railroad. The "B&O Line," as it came to be called, was begun by a group of Baltimore businessmen in 1828 and opened in 1830. At the time, turnpikes, rivers, and canals were the primary avenues for travel and transport. By the beginning of the Civil War, railroads had become a major American industry with many different companies and 30,000 miles of tracks. The first railroad to link the East to the West was completed in 1869, with the last spike hooked up to telegraph wires so that news of completion would reach both coasts as the spike was driven into the ground. The construction of this new transportation system and its impact on the country was the subject of David Haward Bain's January 20, 2000, Booknotes *appearance, when he discussed his book* Empire Express: Building the First Transcontinental Railroad, *published by Viking in 1999. Mr. Bain teaches English at Middlebury College in Vermont.*

AMERICA INVENTED ITSELF in the middle part of the nineteenth century. From the very beginning of [the transcontinental railroad project] in the 1840s all the way to the driving of the Golden Spike, the country really became what it is today. . . . It was like an express train.

I researched from 1842 to 1873, so this isn't just one of those narrow stories about the railroad. It's really a story about how America became what it is. By starting off in 1842, with Asa Whitney, the pioneer railroad promoter, I was able to take in all of the things that went on during his time and the years thereafter, issues like the Mexican War, the Civil War, the Plains Indian wars, the real beginning of the mercantile capitalist culture in America, and settlement patterns going westward. It was just a tremendously large story and it was all linked to the railroad.

THE TRANSCONTINENTAL railroad wouldn't have been built without public money. A good portion of the route was unsettled at that point, so it was supposedly federal lands that could be given over to the railroads in exchange for their moving westward and eastward. But even with subsidies according to the mile completed, it really was something that wouldn't have been done without the taxpayers' purse involved.

All of the people whom you see throughout the transcontinental railroad story were the founders of the Republican Party when it was formed for the presidential campaign of 1856. They were able to use those [political] connections over and over again to aid their private enterprises. . . . The idea of interlocking power was perhaps not the scandalous thing that it is today.

Representative Oakes Ames from Massachusetts was called the "King of Spades." He was heir, along with his brother Oliver, to a very large shovel manufacturing plant in Massachusetts that really took off during the California gold rush, so he became a very wealthy man. He went to Congress and was among the founders of the Republican Party. He was very highly placed. Ames knew Abraham Lincoln very well and they spent a lot of time together. Lincoln himself anointed Oakes Ames with the purpose of getting involved in the Union Pacific Railroad because the capitalists just weren't showing up to invest. It was really going nowhere after it was incorporated in 1862. Lincoln said, "Ames, take hold of this. It will be the biggest thing in the country." [Ames was able to focus on this] great national project right in the middle of the Civil War.

They had not been building [the rails] before [the Pacific Railroad Act of 1862]. It took about twenty years before they got to this act and it was a big political controversy: "Where are you going to put this transcontinental railroad? Where are you going to begin? Are you going to begin from Chicago or from St. Louis, or are you going to start down on the level of Atlanta?"

Senator Thomas Hart Benton of Missouri said, "It's got to go through St. Louis, and you won't get my vote otherwise." And the Illinois and Iowa people were saying, "It has got to go up on our level." It was just a complete stalemate for twenty years.

ABRAHAM LINCOLN WAS such an interesting character, as far as this railroad [was concerned]. He was like the godfather of the Pacific Railroad. If he had not thought of it as being a national priority, it wouldn't have gotten done during the Civil War. He insisted, on all sorts of levels, that it be given that kind of support. When he died, the railroad lost an essential kind of spiritual support that it had enjoyed under Lincoln.

[The Lincoln railroad car was built to honor his commitment to the railroad.] The Lincoln car was gilt, was furnished in silk drapery, and had beautiful hardwood appointments. Lincoln took one look at it and said, "I'll never ride in that car." So they retired it to the rail yard, and then when he was assassinated, that was what was picked to take him on this long, mournful route back home.

It was several weeks' worth of a funeral train that left Washington, D.C., and ultimately ended up in Springfield, Illinois. You can follow this route and see something about the state of American railroads at that time. It [traveled] from Washington to Baltimore up to Philadelphia, crossed the river, and on the Camden and Amboy, went up to New Jersey. Then it went on a barge to New York and up along the Hudson River and then transferred, by boat, over to the west side of the Hudson and so on. It took something like twenty-seven different railroads just to get that distance, and it really showed you what a crazy idea it was to have two railroads building 1,700 miles across this virtually uninhabited portion of the United States.

[PRIOR TO HIS DEATH] Lincoln had two big decisions to make in all this. One was the gauge of the railroad—exactly how wide should those tracks be? It was thought that five feet would be the best; the other route available was four feet, eight and a half inches. Now that seems like a small controversy, but it really depended on how many other companies in the United States had already committed to one gauge or the other. It was a hot political issue. Lincoln finally, in desperation, turned to his cabinet and said, "Well, what do you guys think about all this? What should we do?" He polled them, and they all wrote their nominations for what the gauge should be on little pieces of paper and put them in his pocket; then he made the decision that it would be on the five-foot gauge. It was basically an arbitrary decision that was later reversed by Congress to the four-foot-eight gauge. That had to do with the kinds of corporations that had already committed to that gauge.

The second decision was the Omaha decision: Where are we going to start this railroad? Lincoln had spread out a map of the Missouri River and was trying to decide. He saw Council Bluffs on the east side of the Missouri and Omaha on the other. He'd been hearing testimony for years about what the right way was and then finally said, "Well, I may get into trouble about this because I own a few building lots in Council Bluffs, but I'm going to put it in Omaha anyway."

[So] the Republican Party left in power in Congress after the beginning of the Civil War wrote the Pacific Railroad Act of 1862. It was a complex web of political and economic interests. . . . The Kansas and Missouri interests vied against the Illinois and Iowa and Michigan interests. Basically, it was the northern tier combined with the political powers of New York and New England, [who agreed that] Omaha on the Missouri River was where the Union Pacific would start.

THE CENTRAL PACIFIC Railroad started in Sacramento, California, and had to immediately address the Sierra Nevada Mountains, . . . how to get from the Sacramento Valley 7,000 feet up to the summit of the Sierras and then down, in some kind of a stately manner, into Nevada. . . . The two railroads were just built toward each other. [But] it took them years to do it. It was utterly impossible for them to find any labor in California because the mines paid so much better. So they began with the controversial idea of importing Chinese from Canton Province.

There were companies that were put together in order to bring them over. [The workers] were paid $30 a month. They had to board themselves and lived in camps alongside the track. When the snow got so bad . . . they would carve out entire galleries underneath the snow and live there for months at a time.

Ultimately, [there were] about 12,000 Chinese workers on the Central Pacific. It still took them quite a number of years to get over the mountains; they had to blast through tunnel after tunnel. It was quite a job.

The Irish worked out from Omaha. It was largely Irish because that was the available labor force at that time, but it was also made up of a lot of Civil War veterans who needed work, and a lot of other immigrants who were coming through. But it was predominantly Irish working out from Omaha—perhaps 10,000 at any time. Occasionally in the photographs you might see an African American face, but very, very rarely. There was some talk in California about bringing out large groups of freedmen after the war and putting them to work because they were having a lot of labor problems in California. It was something that never came to pass.

BRIGHAM YOUNG WAS one of the original incorporators of the Union Pacific in 1862, definitely a good guy, a very canny, political man. . . . He was very interested in getting the Pacific Railroad across so that the emigrants from Europe, who were coming over to join the Latter-Day Saints, would be able to get over, and so that they could take advantage of all the commercial prospects of having a railroad going through Utah.

The Promontory Spike was buried in the ground on May 10, 1869, in Promontory, Utah. They began this whole transcontinental enterprise without really having an idea about where they were going to meet. What it did was encourage a wild, speculative competition. By the time it got to be 1868 and 1869, the two competing railroad companies, the Central Pacific from California and the Union Pacific coming out from Omaha, were trying to grab as much territory in Wyoming and Utah—since they were being paid by the mile—as they could. So when the Union Pacific and the Central Pacific joined at Promontory it caused a national tumult of celebration. But it was also something that wasn't really planned for. The kinds of celebrities you might think would show up at a celebration like that just weren't there. It was a local thing.

THERE WAS A MAJOR scandal in Washington in 1872 during President Ulysses Grant's reelection campaign. Washington completely ground to a halt because of it. By then the railroad had become a major force in American politics and in American life. American imagination was taken up with the adventures that were going on out West. Suddenly to have that all come crashing down, to find out that major members of the Republican administration—senators, congressmen—all had feet of clay and had been enriching themselves for years on this, was quite a comedown.

Crédit Mobilier was a French corporation, and the name was appropriated for a very interesting corporate shenanigan. It was a corporation called the Pennsylvania Fiscal Agency, and Dr. Thomas Durant and several other people created it in order to be able to hire themselves to do the railroad construction and pay themselves at vastly inflated figures. If you're building westward out of Omaha and you're being paid at, say, $50,000 per mile by the federal government in securities, you try to do it as cheaply as you can. You hire a dummy corporation to do the construction and that way you hold all the cards. You can charge whatever you want.

Oakes Ames saw the whole notion of political influence being tremendously important, and he saw it as a perfectly natural thing to interest his colleagues in Congress indirectly in the Pacific Railroad so that they would vote the right way. Ames's brother became the president of the Union Pacific; Ames [himself] was a major stockholder in the Union Pacific and in the Crédit Mobilier. . . . He saw nothing wrong with that. He went among his colleagues and offered them greatly discounted securities in the construction arm of the Union Pacific, which was called the Crédit Mobilier of America. A number signed up and that was the root of the scandal. To his dying day, Ames said that he'd done everything with the best possible motivations and that the idea of personal enrichment was the farthest from his mind.

The laws weren't fully written at that point, but there was enough [evidence] to make a stink. . . . The congressmen also tried to cover it up as soon as they could. Some of them had the Crédit Mobilier stock assigned to sons-in-laws or partners or wives and so on. . . . I'm totally convinced that some of those connections have never been made and probably never will be made. In other words, the dummy owners of stock would have been maybe law partners or neighbors down the street. There's just no way to know how extensive this was.

[The House of Representatives] called hearings because of the newspaper scandals that had erupted all during the fall and because they had covered up, people like Congressman James Blaine of Maine, who was thought of as presidential timber, had covered up their involvement. And so the question became, Is any of this true or is just a political smear? They launched hearings in December and began to put everything together in January. The chairman of the committee was Luke Poland from Vermont. The hearings were closed when they began, and it was quite an unhappy thing as far as the press and public was concerned. The demand finally got to be so great that they opened it up. It was funny reading the transcripts and the newspaper reports of the whole thing. They were holding it in a small committee room and the place was so packed, it was like a New York City subway at rush hour. People were standing on chairs; newspaper correspondents sat on the arms of congressmen's chairs. It was quite a big thing.

The "Trial of the Innocents" was the name given to the Crédit Mobilier investigation by the *New York Sun.* It was supremely cynical and sardonic because they were a Democratic paper and very much against the Grant administration. There had been enough scandals and rumors leaking out about the first four years, so when this news about the Crédit Mobilier suit came out, they printed the transcripts in wholesale length throughout all of the newspapers. Every day, there would be something new about the congressional hearings and the Senate hearings. "Trial of the Innocents" was the running headline the *New York Sun* used because they knew that the conclusion was foregone.

Schuyler Colfax of Indiana testified. [He had been Speaker of the House and was then the outgoing vice president under Grant.] He took money and had to change his testimony when Oakes Ames showed up with a diary that [listed] names and dates and places. Journalists and congressmen were able to find out certain transactions that Colfax made at the bank that proved he had done it and then he had to admit to it. However, he wasn't punished. There were only two people who were punished, and the main person was Oakes Ames, who was cast out of Congress and censured.

Oakes Ames did end up with a lot of money in his pockets, [but] he was out of Congress. He had the tremendously successful shovel manufacturing company to go back to, but he was really a broken man and died within months of being thrown out.

They caught fewer than twenty-five [politicians who made money off the railroad], but a much larger number than that [were involved]. . . . Some of the names [include] Schuyler Colfax; Henry Wilson, who would be vice president in the next [Grant] administration; Oakes Ames, the Massachusetts congressman; and Senator James Willis Patterson from New Hampshire. The list went on and even included a lot of people who weren't actually culpable at that time, like [House Speaker] James G. Blaine of Maine, who was one of the largest politicians. This really was a stain that spread quite wide.

[REGARDLESS OF THE scandals the] American people fared positively because of the settlement patterns and the fact that the West was opened up by [the railroad]. Of course, there were a lot of very sorry chapters involving the Plains Indians and with the exploitation of the vast mineral wealth and water wealth out there. But we had a large, empty space that was still thought of, in most people's minds, as the great American desert, as it had been for fifty years, and [because of the railroad] this became the farmland and the ranch land of the West.

Grover Cleveland's Political Career

by

H. PAUL JEFFERS

Grover Cleveland was a president of firsts, the first president to serve two nonconsecutive terms, the first president to marry in the White House, and the first president to have a child born in the White House. Our country's twenty-second and twenty-fourth president was born on March 18, 1837, and served in office from 1885 to 1889 and from 1893 to 1897. On June 26, 2000, H. Paul Jeffers appeared on Booknotes *to discuss his Cleveland biography,* An Honest President: The Life and Presidencies of Grover Cleveland, *published by William Morrow that same year. Mr. Jeffers is a writer in New York City.*

WHEN GROVER CLEVELAND was running for president in 1884, Joseph Pulitzer wrote an editorial endorsing him, and he gave four reasons for wanting Cleveland to be elected. He said, "One, he's an honest man; two, he's an honest man; three, he's an honest man; four, he's an honest man."

Cleveland was born in Caldwell, New Jersey. His father was a Presbyterian minister assigned there. Cleveland spent about four years there and then his father, Richard Cleveland, was transferred to New York State, and that's how Grover wound up as a New York politician.

His first political job was as an alderman. He ran for alderman, and then he was appointed assistant district attorney in Erie County. He served for three years, ran for district attorney and lost, and then some years later—by default because no one else would run for the office—ran for mayor of Buffalo and was elected, a Democrat in a Republican city. He made such an impact there because he vetoed any bill that he thought was a blatant raid on the public treasury; his nickname was the "veto mayor." In 1882 the Democrats in New York were looking for someone to run for governor, and they said, "Why not this mayor of Buffalo?" He got nominated and won in a landslide.

Theodore Roosevelt was then a member of the New York Assembly. Cleveland was a Democrat; TR was a Republican. They formed an alliance on a bill called the Five-Cent Fare Bill, which was pending in the New York legislature, to force the transit companies in New York City to reduce their fare from ten cents to five cents. TR was all for it because he regarded the guys like [financier] Jay Gould and the people who ran the transit companies as thieves. He just wanted to stick it to them.

Governor Cleveland read the bill and decided that if it became law, it was a violation of the U.S. Constitution, and in fact, that it was no business of the state of New York to get involved in private contracts. So he vetoed it. That just stunned everybody, including Roosevelt, who rethought his own position and said, "You know, the governor's right about this. I was acting out of spite and not from the best interests of government." So TR threw his weight behind upholding Cleveland's veto, and Roosevelt delivered enough votes for the veto to be upheld.

Cleveland almost immediately called TR in for a meeting to talk about other things that might be of interest, particularly civil service reform, and they formed this amazing alliance. The prologue of my book is called "The Big One and the Dude." "The Big One" was the nickname for Grover Cleveland, and "The Dude" was the nickname applied to the young Theodore Roosevelt when he landed in Albany.

CLEVELAND WAS ELECTED president in 1884. He had been governor of New York for about a year and a half. He was defeated for reelection by Benjamin Harrison in 1888. . . . Cleveland had the popular vote, [but] Harrison had the electoral vote. Cleveland came back and ran again in 1892 and was elected. He is the only president to serve nonconsecutive terms. . . . He won all three elections in the popular vote. He lost to Harrison [in 1888] because he lost the state of New York, his own state, which threw it, in the Electoral College, to Harrison.

Cleveland was never a party machine man and, in fact, had been greatly opposed throughout his career when he ran for governor and served as governor by Tammany Hall, the New York City political machine. He was never friends with them. They never liked him, and they wanted him defeated. Another reason he lost New York when he was running for reelection as president had to do with positions he'd taken on the gold standard and particularly on tariff questions, which were important to New York, and they voted against him. . . . He lost narrowly, but he lost.

Knowing what kind of person he was depended on when you were around him. If you were with him in Buffalo, when he was a young man and an attorney prior to becoming mayor—and even when he was mayor—you would have spent a lot of nights in saloons and in German beer halls. You would have eaten a lot of sausage and sauerkraut, and you would have played cards throughout most of the night. There would have been a lot of bawdy jokes, and there would have been hunting and fishing expeditions in the Buffalo area.

When he became mayor, there was less of that because he was busy and spent long nights working as mayor. He wasn't out carousing quite as much. When he got to be governor of New York, he suddenly had a whole new cadre of friends. The politicians he met in Albany were a lot different from the ones he met in Buffalo. In Buffalo, you worried about water treatment and whether the sidewalks were broken and that sort of thing. In Albany, suddenly you're talking about taxes and the place of New York State as the primary state in the Union. There was a lot less carousing.

He was not a big social guy. For instance, in Buffalo he went to very few dances, or cotillions as they called them. He wrote a letter to his brother when he was elected governor, worrying about the requirements that were going to be imposed on him for socializing, and he did as little of that as possible. This became even more exacerbated when he became president of the United States, with a lot of formal dining for ambassadors and ministers. And he was a bachelor; there was no first lady [until 1886].

He married Frances Folsom—her nickname was Frank. She was born to Cleveland's friend and law partner, Oscar Folsom, in Buffalo in 1864. Cleveland was considerably older than she. Oscar Folsom was thrown from a wagon and killed; Cleveland became the executor of his estate and the ward to Frances Folsom. He bought her her first baby doll carriage, let her help write out some of the papers that he was working on when he was in his political offices, and basically raised her.

Everybody thought when he finally came to Washington as president of the United States that he would marry Emma Folsom, Oscar's widow. Cleveland said to his sister one day, "Why does everyone keep trying to marry me off to old women? Why don't they think that I might be interested in marrying the daughter?" She was twenty-one when they married. She had just gotten out of college.

He had proposed to her in a letter the year before that. She was visiting relatives in Scranton, and he wrote a letter proposing marriage. Very early on, when he was still in Buffalo and people were asking him, "Well, when are you going to get married?" his usual answer was, "I don't think I'll get married at all." But somebody asked him one day, "Grover, when are you going to get married?" Frances was in the room, and he looked at her and said, "Maybe I'm just waiting for my bride to grow up."

They had a very successful marriage and had five children. She turned out to be a really dazzling First Lady, although he didn't like the idea of her being called "First Lady of the Land." He just wanted her to be Mrs. Cleveland. But she took Washington by storm, pretty much the way Jacqueline Kennedy did in the 1960s.

Cleveland was very concerned about the publicity she was getting. He was furious whenever her picture would appear in a newspaper. He bought a property far north in Washington in what is now Cleveland Park, up near the Washington National Cathedral. They bought an old house, had it renovated, and turned it into a farm called Oak View. The newspapermen called it "Red Top" because it had a red roof. Whenever they could get out of the White House, that's where they went.

The White House then was not like it is today. Cleveland's office was on the second floor, which is where the living quarters were. When he decided to marry, he took one of the rooms that had belonged to his steward and had it made into a sitting room for Frances so that she would have something to do during the daytime. Once they got Oak View, they spent a lot of time there, largely because he wanted to get away from the press, which he hated.

When Cleveland ran for president in 1884, a political enemy of his in Buffalo who happened to be a minister, Reverend George Ball, wrote a piece for one of the Buffalo newspapers revealing the fact—and it was a fact—that ten years earlier, a woman named Maria Halpin gave birth to a son whom she named Oscar Folsom Cleveland. She claimed that Grover Cleveland was the father.

It was very interesting because Oscar Folsom had been Cleveland's best friend. Maria Halpin was a widow who had come to Buffalo from New Jersey and, to put it delicately, was a very friendly lady. She knew a lot of the gentlemen of Buffalo, including Cleveland, who was a bachelor, of course; Oscar Folsom, who was married; and a number of other of Cleveland's friends. There was a lot of speculation that the child was Oscar Folsom's and that Grover, being a bachelor and Oscar Folsom's great friend, basically stepped up to the plate and said, "The child is mine." The other story is that Maria Halpin really wanted to marry Cleveland and hoped to use the child as a way of coercing him into marrying her.

It all happened in 1874, and nothing was said about it [then]. The issue was never raised when Cleveland was mayor of Buffalo or when he was governor of New York. But when he ran for president the story broke, and it was a big scandal. The question was whether or not it would keep him from being elected president of the United States. When his political advisers came to him and said, "What's this all about, what's going on here?" he said, "Well, yes, it's true, and whatever you do, tell the truth." There was no attempt at cover-up, no evading it. He said, "Yes, I was the father of the child, but in all these ten years, I've been paying for its upkeep."

Some Cleveland supporters went to Buffalo, sort of a self-appointed investigating committee to look into this story and to prove certain aspects of the allegations—namely, that Grover had promised to marry her and then reneged on it—were not true. They dug all that information up, and they got the Reverend Ball, who first broke this story, to retract almost all of it. So in the end, while it caused quite a sensation, it really had no effect on Cleveland being elected president of the United States.

Another friend of Cleveland's, who was an editor of a newspaper in Buffalo, broached the idea that actually Cleveland claimed parentage in order to save the reputation of Oscar Folsom. Cleveland rejected that out of hand. But you can look at it two ways: either he was the father or he accepted the responsibility in order to save the reputation of his dead friend, of whose daughter he was the ward.

His political phrase, the one that sticks to him although it was put together for him by [a] journalist, was "Public service is a public trust." He believed that an executive, whether it was governor or president of the United States, was exactly that, an executive officer. His job was to see that the organization was run efficiently and that the stockholders' money, namely the taxpayer's, was not squandered or wasted. He also believed, as he said, "The people support the government. The government does not support the people."

The Events of the 1890s

by

H. W. BRANDS

The decade from 1890 to 1900 was tumultuous and, in the description of the historian H. W. Brands, "reckless." The Massacre at Wounded Knee, the last major armed conflict between Native Americans and the U.S. Army, claimed the lives of between 200 and 350 Sioux Indians; Ellis Island opened as a U.S. immigration depot—and over the next thirty years approximately 12 million immigrants would enter via the island; Wyoming became the forty-fourth state admitted to the Union, the first with female suffrage; and the Spanish-American War was fought and won in 1898. Mr. Brands, a history professor at Texas A&M, visited us on February 2, 1996, and told us more about The Reckless Decade: America in the 1890s, *published in 1995 by St. Martin's Press.*

AMERICA IN THE 1890s had a definite sense that something important was ending. The United States had, just a few years before, celebrated its one hundredth anniversary. There was a feeling, fairly well documented, that the frontier phase of American history was ending. During the 1890s, Frederick Jackson Turner popularized the notion of the American frontier as the formative influence in American history. The census of 1890 reported that the frontier had vanished, so Americans had this notion that they were running up against the end of their history as they had known it and were on the edge of something new.

Turner was a professor of history at the University of Wisconsin . . . and he had this belief that the frontier experience was central to American history. This was an innovation; it was a striking interpretation because it placed so much emphasis on the frontier. At the time Turner started teaching and writing, the center of gravity in the American historical profession was still in the Northeast, especially New England. People who taught in the Northeast tended to see the Puritan experience as the defining experience of American history. They tended to look more to the East than to the West. They looked for precursors to American democracy in European history.

Turner looked to the West. . . . He didn't deny that there were European antecedents to American democracy, but he asked the question: "Why is democracy in America so different from the democracies of Europe?" He said the basic reason was the frontier.

He pointed out that for three hundred years, from the seventeenth century almost to the beginning of the twentieth century, the free land out to the West [was] where people could go when life got hard in the East. They could put down new roots, and if those roots didn't sink too well, they could try something new. And that period had ended.

Nobody really noticed Turner, except a few people like Theodore Roosevelt, who was an up-and-coming member of the Republican Party, a civil service commissioner. He was quite taken by Turner's theory. Roosevelt and others thought that it was a reasonable and persuasive explanation of American history; it was also a way of extending the lessons of the American past into the American future. They agreed that the . . . notion of expansion to the West was the defining feature of American democracy and felt continued expansion was necessary to the health of American democracy. Until this time, expansion had taken place on the North American continent. But now that the continent was full, they would just have to continue to expand [beyond]. So Turner was adopted by a lot of people who had political agendas.

WILLIAM MCKINLEY was president from 1897 until he was assassinated in 1901. He was preceded by Grover Cleveland, serving his second term in office. Cleveland was preceded by Benjamin Harrison. The number of states went from forty-two to forty-five by the end of the decade. The population of the country was around 85 million in 1890 and grew to 95 million or so by the end of the decade.

Women could not vote, except in certain western states. The franchise was essentially an adult male business. There were not many residency requirements, so immigrants could vote almost right off the boat. That led to the rise of the urban political machines and a good deal of political corruption during the era.

Grover Cleveland described himself as "ugly honest." He was a reform mayor of Buffalo, New York, during the 1880s. He portrayed himself as the antidote to Tammany Hall, the notoriously corrupt political machine in New York City. In the 1880s, both parties were trying to put a little distance between themselves and the widespread graft that was quite common in American politics during the era of Reconstruction. He seemed to be an attractive candidate. He was fiscally conservative. He was a "solid gold Democrat" who stood for the gold standard, as opposed to the populist types, like William Jennings Bryan, who advocated the remonetization of silver at an inflationary rate. Cleveland was a conservative, establishment, eastern Democrat.

In the middle of Grover Cleveland's second term, from 1893 to 1897, there was a financial crisis in the United States. Over several months, the financial panic led to a severe drain on the American Treasury. The precipitating cause of the panic was nervousness on the part of British investors who had lent short-term in the American bond markets and wanted to get their money out. When they started pulling out, that sent bond prices down. Others who were watching the British realized that maybe it was time to get their money out as well.

The U.S. Treasury was committed to upholding the gold standard. If people wanted to convert their dollars to gold, then the U.S. government had to pay. It was generally thought that $100 million in gold was the necessary cushion. The Treasury reported periodically on the state of the gold supply. As more and more [investors tried] to get gold for their dollars, the Treasury gold supply dwindled.

President Cleveland decided that the only thing to do was to borrow money from the American private markets, which it had done before, but by some technique that would reassure investors. He felt obliged to call on J. P. Morgan, the founder of the House of Morgan. Morgan was the leading financier in the United States and the man who probably wielded more economic power than anyone else at that time.

Cleveland . . . asked Morgan what could be done. Morgan said that if the president desired him to do so, he could put together a bond package that would be sellable to British and other investors. Given the Morgan seal of approval, this would stop the panic.

Cleveland reluctantly went ahead with it. As a Democrat, he didn't like the appearance of being in hock to J. P. Morgan, who was one of the most unpopular figures in the country, especially among Cleveland's constituents. He knew that Morgan was going to make some money on this deal. Morgan wasn't doing this out of sheer patriotism.

The existence of the negotiations was common knowledge. Reporters hovered around the White House. They saw J. P. Morgan come out and asked him what happened. He was rather vague about it. Eventually Congress brought Morgan in and questioned him. Morgan refused to say how much money he had made off of this, claiming it was his private business.

DISTRUST AND HOSTILITY on the part of the aggrieved gave rise to a populist reaction. A populist is someone who appeals to the masses, who generally employs a rhetoric of distrust of groups that they identify as elite. And in a democracy like the United States, to be branded "elitist" is a serious charge. Populists portray themselves as the defenders of received values, of traditional virtues. They often tend toward demagoguery. In . . . the 1890s, they were quite taken by conspiracy theories. This was in line with their thinking that elites controlled the American political systems, the American economy. And there was a notion that if somehow the United States could simply get back to its populist roots, if the common people could once again take control of the political and economic system, then we would return to some golden era of American history.

William Jennings Bryan was a populist . . . and a career politician. He was elected to office [once] as a congressman. . . . He was nominated three times for president but wasn't elected. Finally, in 1913, he was appointed secretary of state [by Woodrow Wilson]. From the mid-1890s to about 1915, he was probably the most prominent Democrat in the country.

Bryan's "Cross of Gold" speech, which he gave at the Democratic National Convention in 1896, absolutely swept the delegates off their feet. They decided that a man with this sort of charisma was the person they wanted to lead them in the presidential contest that year. The "cross of gold" was a reference to the gold standard. Bryan gave a dramatic rendition of how the Republicans and all those who stood for the gold standard were trying to "crucify mankind," meaning the common people, "upon this cross of gold." He and various others persuaded the Democrats that the Democratic Party platform should come out in favor of "free silver"; that was their slogan. What they really meant was that silver should be coined again at a ratio of 16:1 to gold—sixteen ounces of silver to one ounce of gold.

Bryan contended that he and the Democratic Party stood for traditional values. They stood against the modernizing trends in the American economy that gave unprecedented power to people like J. P. Morgan. Bryan was one of the principal critics of the Cleveland administration for cutting this deal with Morgan. He was one of the figures insisting that Morgan should be forced to reveal how much money he made on [the gold bailout].

Bryan was essentially harking back to a golden age in American history and saying that those were the principles that the Democratic Party—the party of Jefferson, the party of Jackson, the party of the people—stood for. Bryan was a very good party man. He was tempted to bolt the party and join the populists, but his loyalty to his party was such that he stayed with the Democrats.

EUGENE V. DEBS [also] ran for president [several] times. Debs was one of the founders of the American Railway Union, which staged a sympathy strike in 1894 when George Pullman and his company, as a result of the panic of 1893, cut the wages of the workers at his plant in Pullman, Illinois. Pullman was a company town, portrayed as a model town. The workers found their wages cut by 25 percent. They felt especially bitter because Pullman, aside from being their employer, was their landlord. Even though he cut wages, he didn't cut rents. He maintained the fiction that his business as a landlord was entirely separate from his business as employer. The workers decided to go out on strike.

The American Railway Union had been founded that very year. Eugene Debs was trying to establish his credibility as a defender of the rights of workers, especially railway workers. Debs persuaded the leaders of the ARU to stage a strike in sympathy with the cause of the Pullman workers. This immediately caused the Pullman strike to become a major stoppage of train traffic from the West Coast to the East Coast. Members of the railway union refused to handle the Pullman cars, which were on nearly all the lines in the country. When the workers refused to handle those cars, they were fired by the railway managers. This would then cause the railway union to walk off the job in support of their own members who'd just been fired.

President Cleveland was not sympathetic to the cause of organized labor. At the instigation of his attorney general, Richard Olney, Cleveland took the side of the railway managers on the grounds that the strike was interfering with the delivery of the mail. They sought federal injunctions against the American Railway Union, ordering them back to work.

The union leadership defied the injunctions. Debs refused to order his men back to work. He was arrested but got out on bail. He was arrested again right away, at which point he realized that as often as he put up bail, he would be arrested again. So he stayed in jail and intended to fight the charge through the courts. Meanwhile, Cleveland decided to send in federal troops to suppress any violence connected with the strike. The governor of Illinois, John Peter Altgeld, didn't want them. Nonetheless, Cleveland sent in the troops over Altgeld's opposition. The troops arrived in Chicago, which was the center of railway traffic in the country and also the center of this strike. Sure enough, very soon there were widespread riots, arson, and looting. Much of Chicago was up in flames during that summer of 1894.

Eugene Debs was in jail for about two months before the trial began. The trial lasted the better part of a month. He was convicted and sentenced to six months in jail. They gave him credit for time [served] so he only had to serve three months beyond [his trial]. In prison, he obviously had time on his hands. He did a lot of reading, and he came out of prison far more radical than he had gone in. He was a left-wing populist when he entered prison, and . . . a socialist by the time he came out. [Debs later ran for president five times on the Socialist ticket.]

[AT THE OTHER END of the economic spectrum] greed took over as the primary motivating force, and a new ruling class of warriors and merchants, expert in the exploitation and the satisfaction of greed, came to power.

Andrew Carnegie was originally from Scotland. He came to the United States at the age of twelve, essentially penniless. He was the prototypical person who survived on pluck, luck, grit, and determination. He started out as a telegrapher. The telegraph industry was closely connected with the railroad industry. In the 1850s, a period of boom among the railroads, he realized that there was a lot of money to be made there. He bought an interest in a company that made iron bridges.

Carnegie realized that there was even more money to be made selling iron and steel to the bridge building companies and [to] the railroads, so he got into the steel business during the 1860s. He had a genius for business. He was an organizer. He wasn't a student of technology, but he insisted that the latest technology be employed to produce steel at the lowest cost. Carnegie's belief was that if you could produce steel efficiently, then everything else would take care of itself. He didn't worry much about marketing or the finances of it all. But he insisted on lowering the unit cost of steel production. . . . In 1901 Carnegie sold his share of Carnegie Steel, the major steel company in the country, to J. P. Morgan. He walked away with a quarter billion dollars in cash [and went] into philanthropy full time.

John D. Rockefeller did for the oil business in the U.S. what Carnegie did for steel. The oil industry in the United States began in the 1860s. . . . In 1859 a man in western Pennsylvania deliberately drilled for oil and found the first gusher in the United States. During the Civil War and the years after, the oil industry took off. Initially, oil was used as a lubricant for the railroad industry and refined into kerosene to light houses all around the country.

Rockefeller organized the oil business. Like Carnegie in steel, he brought down the cost of production and began to extend his business. He started out in refining [but] wanted to do more. He . . . extended so that he could control oil from the time it came out of the ground until the time it was burned in the kerosene lamp of some customer anywhere in the country. He had a passion for efficiency and believed that the highest efficiency would be achieved by what amounted to a monopoly. He wanted to drive all of his competitors out of business. . . . These people [Morgan, Carnegie, Rockefeller] were front-page news.

The 1890s was "the reckless decade," . . . a time when Americans seemed to be on the edge of something. They were somewhere between the past and the future, and there were a lot of ways in which Americans themselves thought they were living recklessly.

William Randolph Hearst and the Rise of Yellow Journalism

by

BEN PROCTER

The first newspaper to appear in the American colonies was a newssheet, Publick Occurrences, which was issued in Boston in 1690. It was suppressed after one issue because it was unlicensed and criticized public policy. Nearly two hundred years later, the press was thriving. The 1880 census recorded 11,314 different papers, and by the 1890s, the first circulation figures of a million copies per issue were recorded. One of the papers that hit that mark was William Randolph Hearst's New York Journal, *which he purchased in 1895. Hearst built a communications empire that included newspapers, magazines, radio stations, and news and motion picture syndicates. On June 12, 1998, Ben Procter, a history professor at Texas Christian University, appeared on* Booknotes *to discuss* William Randolph Hearst: The Early Years, 1863–1910, *published by Oxford University Press in 1998.*

WILLIAM RANDOLPH HEARST was a towering figure in the late nineteenth and early twentieth centuries. He was an individual who shaped both American domestic and foreign policies from the late 1890s to the early 1910s. He was an individual who thought he was responsible for the Spanish-American War. If he wasn't responsible, he helped mold public opinion in that direction—for the United States to intervene on behalf of justice and freedom for the Cubans.

He was a true progressive and would advocate many reforms that would come about in the early 1900s. But, as much as anything, he was the foremost communicator of his day. He [owned] eight newspapers in the five largest cities in this country [including the *San Francisco Examiner* and the *New York Journal*]—3 million readers. There was no radio or television—radio [arrived] in 1920 and television in 1939, but really after World War II. His effect upon American policies and the American way of life was tremendous.

WHETHER HE BEGAN the Spanish-American War or not, he thought he did. He called it "the *Journal's* war" in the newspapers, and he helped shape public opinion. Keep in mind that this was when the United States was still approximately 60 percent rural, and Hearst and Joseph Pulitzer [of the *New York World*] had the Associated Press wire. Therefore, what they said went out to all parts of the country in rural America.

I realized the type of journalism that Hearst had [created was a tabloid form of journalism] but I didn't realize how much [news] he fabricated in the Spanish-American War. As long as it was interesting, as long as it gained results, as long as it was entertaining, then he would accept it. . . . He was one of the forerunners of tabloid journalism.

He was the only one who printed the de Lome letter. [Enrique Dupuy de Lome was] a Spanish minister to the United States who criticized McKinley [in a private letter intercepted by Cuban spies]. Hearst put his comment on de Lome on the front page and tried to generate war. Five or six days later, when this story was about to die down, there was the blowing up of the U.S. battleship *Maine*. The [next day], he offered a reward. This was typical of Hearst. He offered $50,000 for the perpetrators who sank those glorious American sailors—264 sailors and two officers dead.

From that time on, his reporting was the most exciting historical fiction I have ever read. I read through the daily papers and would say, "Did that happen? That didn't happen." But I also said, "Isn't it exciting?". . . I read huge headlines that said, "Dewey on Way to Manila," and I said, "Oh no. You can't say that. The Spanish can read this." But I was caught up in it. Then the next day it said, "Dewey Will Attack the Philippines Soon," and I'd say "No." It would source a *Journal* correspondent with the Asiatic fleet and I realized he didn't have a correspondent with the Asiatic fleet. Of course, he guessed right in that case—they were going to Manila. They attacked on May 1, 1898, and destroyed the Spanish fleet. But in that same period, he also printed, "U.S. Army on Way to Cuba in May." That didn't happen until June. He guessed wrong then. But again, it was exciting.

IN OCTOBER 1896, Hearst produced a cartoon that [featured] Richard Outcault's *The Yellow Kid*. It was [one of the first] color cartoons, and it used a bright yellow. The comic strip character was a yellow kid who was a street urchin in Hogan's Alley, a slum in New York. The cartoon [spawned] the term "yellow journalism" because of Hearst's New York war with Joseph

Pulitzer for supremacy of journalism. Hearst wanted to call his exciting way of presenting news, entertainment, bold headlines, and salacious comments about individuals "new journalism." But it was already termed "yellow journalism" by Pulitzer because of *The Yellow Kid*. If the cartoon [featured a] purple kid, it would probably have been called purple journalism instead.

HEARST WANTED government by newspaper. . . . The *Journal* [advocated a variety of national policies—construction of a Nicaraguan canal, annexation of Hawaii, the maintenance of a mighty navy, the acquisition of strategic bases in the Caribbean] and later, within three or four months, he also said, "Keep the Philippines."

He also had an internal policy, which included his domestic policies for the United States, like direct election of senators; [public ownership of public franchises; graduated income tax; the establishment of great national universities at West Point and Annapolis; and national, state, and municipal improvement of the public school system].

He was always for the public schools and he wanted improvement. If education was the guardian genius of democracy, then he surely advocated for better schools and better teachers. He also identified his papers with the local scene and local sport and being part of the municipal [issues].

[One of his other internal policies was the destruction of criminal trusts.] There were huge corporations—Rockefeller's Standard Oil, Carnegie's steel company, which then became Morgan's U.S. Steel in 1901. . . . He would say, "Do away with the criminal trusts, those that infringe upon the rights of the American people." Then again, he had ideas about regulating other trusts so there'd be greater freedom, which is definitely a progressive idea.

He was an enemy of corporate greed, arrogant wealth, and of his own social set. [He had friends] but not necessarily of that set. . . . He was a rebel against his own upper class.

[AT HARVARD] Hearst was "rusticated." That's the sophisticated term, I suppose, for being kicked out. He knew enough to get by and was very bright. The first year he did extremely well and then he became more social, more prominent in activities. In 1884, the fall of his junior year, he ran the campaign for Grover Cleveland for president in the Cambridge community and at Harvard. The faculty became aware of him. The [previous] spring, he became the co–business manager of the *Lampoon*, a humor magazine. He did well on that, and it gave him the idea to go into journalism. But his grades suffered, and because he didn't show improvement, the Harvard faculty said, "You'll be rusticated."

WILLIAM RANDOLPH HEARST's father, George Hearst . . . had very little education, but he was a tremendous miner. When he was in Missouri in his early years, he was a lead miner. The Indians called him "Boy-That-Earth-Talked-To." He—and any number of his colleagues—would say that he could remember a rock formation that he had seen thirty years before, and still see it in detail exactly as it was.

George Hearst was surely successful. He obtained portions or all of one-sixth of the four greatest mines in this country. He had one-sixth of the Comstock Lode in Virginia City, Nevada, and after he ran through that money, by 1870, when he was broke or almost bankrupt, he then invested in the Ontario Mine [with only $600 to his name]. It was one of the great silver mines in Utah. Then, in 1877, for $70,000, he obtained a controlling interest of the Homestake mine in South Dakota. It was the greatest gold mine in this country. And, in 1881, [another speculator] Marcus Daly asked him if he would invest in what was known as the Anaconda in Butte, Montana. Within two years, the price of copper went up and he made millions. He never had to worry about finances ever again.

George Hearst became a United States senator from California, a Democratic senator, [in 1886]. He owned the *San Francisco Examiner* and used that to promote the Democratic policies and himself. California's Democratic governor, George Stoneman . . . appointed him when the Republican U.S. senator John F. Miller died. Back then you had indirect election of senators, and the California legislature elected George Hearst to [a full Senate term in 1887]. It's interesting that soon thereafter, William Randolph Hearst would come out for a direct election of senators as a reform, but not while his father was [in the Senate].

His mother, Phoebe Apperson Hearst, wanted her son to be a diplomat. His father tried to adhere to her advice and her wishes. George Hearst had a tremendous understanding of the land, so he offered William to be the manager of the Babicora Ranch, a million-acre ranch in Chihuahua, Mexico, that he owned. His son said, "I don't want that. Anybody could do that." He was then offered [the position of] manager of San Simeon, a 275,000-acre ranch [on California's midcoast]. He said no. Then came the pièce de résistance, which was to manage the Homestake, the gold mine. He said, "I don't want to do that [either]. I want to be manager of the *Examiner*."

George Hearst looked at his accountant and said, "How much would that cost me a year?" The accountant said, "It would cost you $100,000." George said, "Hell, that ain't no money." So, on March 4, 1887, William Randolph Hearst became the head of the *Examiner* at age twenty-three.

HEARST WAS UNIQUE. I've never found anybody that was so innovative. Sometimes his ideas bordered on genius. When he first started out at the *San*

Francisco Examiner, he said, "Get results." He said, "I want good writing. . . . I want the paper to be exciting. . . ." When stories would break, [he would say,] "Get the scoop and be the first." He always wanted to be the first, to be excellent.

Day after day after day, there would be key words in the *Examiner* that Hearst wanted in front page, second page, and third page headlines—[fatal, tragic, crimes, victim, suicide, slain, etc.]. Arthur McEwen, one of his first editors, called this Hearst's "gee-whiz journalism." . . . Hearst also said that reporters must focus on love and sex, tragedy and pathos, crime and violence. Overall, he advised, "Be sensational."

He had tremendous energy, not only when he was young but also at the *San Francisco Examiner* and when he first took over at the *New York Journal.* When he would get an idea, he would drum his fingers. Then, when he'd get the idea that he wanted to pursue, he would do a little dance and click his heels. The staff would say, "Ah, now the chief has gotten the idea. Now we're gonna proceed." Then it would be this insane asylum run by the mad overseer, or as one other said, "It was pandemonium with direction."

[Following his acquisition of the *New York Journal,* Hearst] loved to go to Broadway shows, and in 1897 he saw *The Girl from Paris.* Millicent Willson, who was sixteen, and her older sister, Anita, eighteen, were in the chorus line. He escorted both of them around for a number of years, until 1903, the day before his fortieth birthday. He was running for political office and he decided he needed a family. He loved Millicent and, therefore, he married her.

They had a very loving relationship from 1903 to about 1910. He met actress Marion Davies in 1915. Millicent was very supportive of him. Even in her interviews of later years, she was very praiseworthy and affectionate for him. She was a good politician's wife. She would go with him on trips and be supportive. Hearst was a tremendous philanthropist, and he would be Father Santa Claus and she'd be Mother Santa Claus and give out as many as 70,000 toys to New Yorkers on one or two nights. Millicent continued in that way [for several years].

HEARST RAN FOR political office for the first time in 1902. He ran for Congress [from New York City] and served in the Fifth-eighth and Fifty-ninth Congresses. He then decided he would run for president in 1904. He came in second [for] the Democratic . . . nomination. . . . Judge Alton B. Parker of New York defeated him. He then decided that he wanted to be [New York] governor. What he really wanted was to be president of the United States, but Hearst was the type of individual who never wanted to be second in anything. He wanted to excel and decided, therefore, that he really wanted to be governor.

In 1905, running for mayor, he fought against Tammany Hall, the great Democratic organization in New York run by Boss Tweed. . . . He thought he had the mayoral election won, and the first morning paper had [the headline] "W. R. Hearst Elected Mayor." Even with this close race, where there were stuffed ballot boxes and any number of his people beaten at the polls with clubs, they thought he had it won. There were two ballot boxes in his home district—about 8,000 votes—that he thought he would carry by 3:1, which would mean something like 6,000 votes to 2,000. They happened to be somehow lost in the North River in Manhattan, just happened to be dropped by the Tammany election judges. . . . He was defeated by 3,400 votes out of a half million cast.

However, Hearst gained tremendous fame from being the uncrowned mayor of New York in '05. He ran for governor in '06 [and was] defeated by 50,000. He would then run again in 1909 for mayor against a man by the name of William Gaynor, and came in third. That was his last real election where he headed a ticket. He would run again in 1910, one time, for lieutenant governor [on the Independence Party ticket]—that was the only time he did not campaign. He was defeated then also.

[A FEW YEARS after this last political defeat, Hearst] began building San Simeon. San Simeon is the Hearst castle on, as he called it, Enchanted Hill [down the coast from San Francisco]. They have an archives there of people who visited . . . in the 1920s, '30s and '40s, reminiscing about what Hearst was like and what they did at San Simeon when he [and Marion Davies] invited actors and actresses there. . . . It was estimated that over the next thirty years, he spent $1 million a year on San Simeon—on collections and . . . valuables for the castle. He then went into the movie business, which was really not his forte.

Hearst met Marion Davies while she was in the Ziegfeld Follies and fell in love with her. He wanted to divorce his wife, Millicent, but she would not give him a divorce. Therefore, Marion lived in California, . . . literally the mistress at San Simeon. They hosted the Hollywood crowd there for the next thirty years. He built up his collections there and built this huge castle with all of these artifacts, antique furniture, and beautiful paintings of the old masters. . . . It is one of the grand structures in the United States. It was donated to the University of California in [Hearst's will, but the regents declined the gift. It opened as a California state park in 1958.] They run tours there three times a day.

IN HIS DAY, Hearst was as well-known as Theodore Roosevelt. You could not ignore him. He was controversial. He ran the newspapers in the five largest cities—always with the name Hearst on them. I found in one newspaper—the *New York American* in 1904—his name printed eighteen times. And because of the AP wire, he was well-known. You could see how other Democrats as well as Republicans feared him—he was a potential enemy or a potential candidate. His papers made news. . . . At his height, he had twenty-eight newspapers. Everything seemed to have his stamp on it. . . . He was the greatest publisher in this country in this period of time and the greatest communicator in journalism.

J. P. Morgan, National Banker

by

JEAN STROUSE

John Pierpont Morgan, financier and art collector, was born in 1837 in Hartford, Connecticut. In 1857 he began working for the New York City banking house of Duncan, Sherman & Company, and three years later he joined his father's firm, J.S. Morgan & Company. In 1901 he was the guiding force behind the formation of the U.S. Steel Corporation, the first billion-dollar corporation in the world. New York-based writer Jean Strouse joined us on April 20, 1999, to discuss her biography, Morgan: American Financier, *published in 1999 by Random House.*

THE MAIN THING that J. P. Morgan did from about the 1850s to the 1890s was raise money for railroads and then watch over that money for his clients. There was not enough capital in America in the middle of the nineteenth century to build enormously expensive railroads; it had to come from Europe. European investors who had been burned by reckless buccaneers in the 1830s and '40s weren't about to send more money 3,000 miles across the Atlantic without some guarantee that it would be safe. Morgan, in New York, working with his father in London, provided that guarantee. That meant essentially finding sound properties, which meant having good information about what were good railroads, and then taking what they called moral responsibility for watching over the capital that their clients had [invested].

Say a railroad, for which the Morgan bank had sold bonds, went bankrupt. Morgan would take charge of the bankruptcy. He would fire the managers, hire new ones, reorganize the company, restructure its finances, appoint a board of directors—including himself, often—and stay on the board of the directors, watching over the company's finances until the whole thing was restored to financial health. This reorganization [of railroads] came to be called morganization.

Once the essential railroad structure of this country had been built, which knitted the country together into one economic and geographical unit, he turned to industrial corporations. He put together the first billion dollar corporation, U.S. Steel, in 1901. He organized General Electric in 1892. One of his partners put together International Harvester, and they did the financing for AT&T. Most of those companies are still around. GE was the only stock listed in the first Dow Jones industrial average published in 1896 that is still [there] one hundred years later.

THE SPAN OF MORGAN's lifetime was the period in which America had no central bank, and he really took it upon himself to act as the unofficial lender of last resort, a federal reserve. He was trying to control the [economic] panics and to keep the economy stable so that we wouldn't go through these terrible cycles of irrational boom and then terrible bust and depression.

The 1873 panic was set off officially by the failure of a railroad, the Northern Pacific, and then Jay Cooke, the leading banker in Philadelphia, failed as a result of that. European conditions had started it off, and then the Cooke failure set a match to the tinder of the situation here [in America].

The 1893 panic was a whole different set of circumstances. Morgan took it as his public responsibility to try to mediate this a little bit. He raised reserve funds among himself and several other bankers to try to supply liquidity when there wasn't enough, which is what happened. Suddenly, all the money left New York and there wasn't enough for people to meet their obligations.

The most dramatic panic was in 1907, when a trust company failed and the dominoes started to topple. Morgan by this time had just turned seventy and . . . was off at an Episcopal convention in Richmond, Virginia. Teddy Roosevelt was president. There was no real authority in the federal government at this point to handle a crisis like this.

Morgan seemed to be the only person who had the ability and the means to [stabilize the economy]. His partners sent him cables in Richmond . . . about this developing situation, but they didn't want him to come back early because they thought that would spook the already scared market. If everybody knew that Morgan had left this convention to come back to Wall Street, the panic would get even worse. He waited until the convention was over, took a night train, arrived at his library on Sunday, and spent the day in his library surrounded by his partners and lieutenants, who briefed him on the situation.

They did research [on] the institutions that were in jeopardy and decided which ones were not in very good shape and should be allowed to fail, and which ones they ought to really bail out. For the next three weeks, teams of financiers worked around the clock and Morgan raised hundreds of millions of dollars to try to calm this panic. Finally, by the end of three weeks, he had. But [the process] involved shoring up the stock exchange and these individual trust companies. At the end of that first week, [the city of] New York . . . came to him and said, "Mr. Morgan, we can't meet our payroll obligations and we're going to be bankrupt by Monday." He managed to manufacture $100 million of clearinghouse certificates that essentially kept New York City going through the weekend.

MORGAN HAD AN INHERITED skin condition called rhinophyma, which is excess growth of sebaceous tissue. In his fifties, it turned his nose into a hideous purple bulb. It looked like an alcoholic nose, although that was not the cause of it. W. C. Fields had something rather similar. It could have been corrected during Morgan's lifetime by surgery but, for various reasons, he chose not to do that. . . . It was a very big fact in his life because he was so public and constantly meeting new people. He would glare at you when he met you because you couldn't look at him without looking at his nose. His handshake and his imposing glare was kind of daring people to flinch or to react, or in some way not deal with his nose.

His first wife was Amelia Sturges. She was the daughter of a prominent New York merchant and patron of the arts named Jonathan Sturges. Morgan fell in love with her shortly after he moved to New York, when he was twenty years old in 1857, and courted her for a couple of years. They were engaged in 1860 and were going to be married in October of '61. That winter before their wedding, she came down with a series of colds and a bad cough that would not go away. By the summer, she was so sick that she said, "I don't think I can marry you. We should postpone the wedding." He said, "Nonsense, we'll take you to the sun in the Mediterranean and fix you right up."

They were married in October of 1861 in her parents' parlor in New York. She was so frail, he had to hold her up at the altar. She also kept the veil over her face during the ceremony because she felt she was so thin that she wasn't pretty anymore. He took her to Paris, where lung specialists diagnosed her with tuberculosis, which came as a shock to him. They then went to Algiers and then to Nice, where he rented a villa. . . . Eventually, he asked her mother to come stay with them because she was getting sicker and sicker; he felt he couldn't nurse her himself. Amelia's mother came over, but in February of 1862, Amelia died—four months after her wedding. He was heartbroken, obviously, and in some ways never really got over that loss. She was a very lively, intelligent, curious, wonderful girl. I kind of got to know her as he got to know her, through her letters and diaries. She died at the age of twenty-six.

[Morgan was twenty-four.] He never had to find out what that marriage would have been like; it was preserved in amber for him at that youthful stage.

Morgan came from a wealthy family, and his father, by this time, was working as a merchant banker in London. Actually, both sides of his family came to America before the Revolution, so they were really members of the American patriciate. . . . He and his father hated the idea of the Civil War because it was going to disrupt business. They were doing cotton trading with England and trying to build America with European capital. But the war interrupted commerce. It interrupted all sorts of other things. They weren't terribly interested in the issue of slavery and the moral cause of the Civil War. They were more interested in keeping business going. [The 1863 Conscription Act allowed] for a substitute to fight in the Civil War. [By paying] a fee of up to $300, somebody else would go in your place, which is what Morgan did. Many other men did that as well. It sounds to us like shirking, and certainly many men who didn't fight felt guilty about it for the rest of their lives. It was, at the time, quite an acceptable thing to do in certain classes and for certain people.

Junius Morgan staked the future on his son and on America. He was very supervisory, censorious, and critical of his son, and determined that his son was going to be an upright man with a solid-gold reputation. Pierpont [did] not follow in the paternal footsteps early on. He was much more likely to take risks, to speculate. Junius wouldn't hear of that, and he was furious whenever Pierpont took a speculative flyer. At one point, Pierpont bought five shares of stock in something called the Pacific Mail Steamship Company and Junius hit the roof and said, "How could you be so reckless and crazy?" Pierpont ignored him and kept the stock for a little while and then sold it at a loss. But if he'd held it for ten more years, he would have done just fine.

MORGAN'S SECOND WIFE was Frances Louisa Tracy, whom he married in 1865, right after Lincoln was shot and the war was concluded. It was an okay marriage for maybe ten or fifteen years. They had four children. But very quickly, it became clear that they had very different tastes and very different instincts. He loved New York and throngs of people, he was a workaholic, and he liked activity and travel—adventurous travel. She was much more domestic and quiet. She liked being home with the children, she wanted to leave New York for suburban New Jersey, and she wasn't very interested in art—Morgan was passionate about art. So after about fifteen years, he kept the Atlantic between them. They lived separate lives after about 1880. He went off to Europe in the spring and summer with a party of friends and traveled around. Sometimes he would take one of his daughters, and then later he would take a mistress. When he came back from Europe, he sent his wife abroad in the fall and winter with one of their daughters, a chauffeur, and a paid companion.

Divorce was really not an option in that world. Some people did, but it was very scandalous and shocking. Interestingly enough, it was more disruptive for the woman. Women were objects of scandal, even if they had done nothing wrong. A couple of the people the Morgans knew who did get divorced moved to Europe, just because it was a much more accepting and forgiving society. Also, in professional terms, Morgan was a conservative banker with a reputation for integrity. Divorce didn't figure into that picture.

Edith Sybil Randolph was his first mistress I was able to find anything out about. She was a widow, very beautiful and younger than he. It was 1890, so he was about fifty-three and she was probably in her late thirties with two children. Morgan was with her for about five years—traveling to Europe with her, seeing her in New York, and taking her on his yacht cruises. In his wife's diaries, there were rather sad entries about Mrs. Randolph being around at a lot of Morgan's parties. . . . In one of her diaries, it said, "Spoke to P. about Mrs. R." That's the last mention of Mrs. R. in Mrs. Morgan's diaries. That was a fairly dramatic moment.

He then had to keep it more secret. He was much more of a European than an American puritan about all this. The European aristocrats had mistresses. They would travel to other friends' country houses and stay in European hotels. They trusted their friends not to talk. It was accepted, especially in the Prince of Wales's set. The prince had women with him [when] he traveled, and everybody knew; nobody really talked about it. Morgan did more or less the same thing. But once his wife found out, it was a problem. The other problem was that Mrs. Randolph was relatively young and not wealthy. She needed a husband, and Morgan was not going to get divorced.

THE MOST INTERESTING woman in his life, to me, and the one I had the most fun figuring out, was Belle da Costa Greene. She was his librarian. He was a fabulous art collector, and he concentrated in New York on rare books, illuminated manuscripts, and prints and drawings. He built a library to house them between 1902 and 1906. Charles McKim [designed] the library and it's still there on 36th Street and Madison Avenue. By the time the library was almost finished, he decided he needed a librarian to manage and catalog the collections and help him buy new ones. He was introduced to Belle Greene by his nephew, Junius Spencer Morgan, who was a serious bibliophile and connoisseur of books and prints and drawings. Junius introduced him to this young woman who was working at the Princeton University Library as a clerk. She said she was twenty-two years old [but she was actually twenty-six].

She immediately took charge of Morgan's literary collections and disciplined dealers who were charging him too much, organized the collections, . . . somewhat limited Morgan's voracious tastes, and put things in order. She was a wonderful, flamboyant character. She supposedly once said, "Just because I am a librarian doesn't mean I have to dress like one."

But who she was—her background—was not clear. . . . I found out by a combination of luck, accident, and the pathological curiosity that takes over biographers' lives that her father was the first black man to graduate from Harvard. His name was Richard Theodore Greener. He graduated in 1870, and had six children, including Belle. Her mother was African American as well. I found Belle's birth certificate, actually, in Washington. It tells her birth date and lists C for colored. . . . Her mother was very light-skinned and [so her] children were very light-skinned. They invented the name da Costa to explain their exotic looks. Belle passed as white for the rest of her life, as far as I know. I don't think Morgan ever knew that she was black.

I don't think Morgan would have done anything if he had known. Once she became indispensable to him at his library, he would have appreciated that and he might have even admired her for it. On her own intelligence and initiative, she created a life for herself that few women of that time, black or white, could have imagined. She was just remarkable. I say this about Morgan not minding, because one of the surprises for me in this story was what a meritocrat he turned out to be, even though his reputation was [that of] an imperious snob who dealt only with the WASP-ocracy. The reputation of the Morgan firm was certainly as blue-blooded as you could get, but he was constantly on the lookout for interesting people who were competent, talented, wanted to do interesting things, and had new ideas. He set them up with the resources to do what they were good at.

RELIGION WAS EXTREMELY important to Pierpont Morgan. It's hard to talk about because, like everything else, he doesn't say very much about it. But he joined St. George's Church in New York, which is a low church—Episcopal parish—and was hugely committed to it. He was a very religious man. He went to church a lot. He read the prayer book and the Bible on his own. He contributed hundreds of thousands of dollars—$200,000 in 1887 alone—to the church. He attended the triennial conventions of the Episcopal Church, which are the debates of the clergyman about church policy. Most laymen would have found that incredibly boring. Morgan, in the middle of his busy schedule, took off three weeks every three years and listened in on these debates.

He helped subsidize a new edition of the *Book of Common Prayer*. He could quote you anything you wanted from the Bible. Many people who disapproved of his career thought it was hypocritical of him to be so religious and to be what they called a robber baron. I don't actually think he was a robber baron, and I don't think that his religion was about trying to pass through the eye of the needle. It was a very deep-seated, passionate connection for him, and it expressed a lot of things that he couldn't express on his own.

THE PUJO COMMITTEE was a [congressional] investigation into whether or not there was a money trust in control of the American economy. The hearings were held in 1912, but the impetus for it really came from the Panic of 1907, [which] Morgan single-handedly stopped. . . . For a moment, he was a national hero. World bankers and international statesmen saluted him with awe for having been able to do this. But the next minute, America and this nation of Democrats was quite horrified that one private citizen had that much power. It aroused America's long-standing distrust of private bankers and concentrated wealth. It led to the setting up of a national monetary commission and eventually to the Federal Reserve. And in 1911–1912, it also led Morgan and the men he was close to to try to concentrate a lot of financial power in their hands, because they did not want a situation like that panic to happen again.

By 1911 it was thought in much of the rest of the country that [Morgan and his cohorts] were running a money trust and that they had a stranglehold on credit and the availability of money in the country. So a congressional committee headed by Louisiana representative Arsène Pujo began to hold hearings in 1912, and Morgan was called as a witness in December of that year. He was the star witness. He was obviously the man they thought was running the money trust. [The hearings were] a very dramatic ending to his life.

[After he testified] he went to Egypt, as he did every winter during the last few years of his life. While he was on the Nile, he had a nervous breakdown. He'd had depressive episodes his whole life. They started in his early twenties and he never knew when [one] was going to come. [They were] truly terrible. He did what he could to ward them off, but the worst depression of his life came on the Nile after the hearings. His friends got him from the Nile back to the Grand Hotel in Rome, and he died in Rome on March 13, 1913. . . . His body was sent back to New York, and in April of 1913 his funeral was held at St. George's Church in Manhattan. The burial took place in Hartford, Connecticut, where he was born. He was buried near his father and mother.

WHEN HE DIED, he was worth approximately $80 million. That's a little low because it was valued for estate purposes. There was no federal estate tax at the time, but there was a New York state inheritance tax. . . . Today his fortune would be about $1.5 to $3 billion. It was a lot of money, but not nearly as much as people imagined and not as much as other wealthy men at the time had. . . . John D. Rockefeller, . . . when Morgan died, was already worth almost a billion 1913 dollars. This is an apocryphal story, but I have to tell it anyway, because it's too good. Supposedly, when Morgan died, Rockefeller read about his net worth of $80 million in the *New York Times,* shook his head, and said, "And to think he wasn't even a rich man."

Morgan's will opened with a resounding declaration of his Episcopal faith that Christ had died for his sins. [It stated] something to the effect that "I leave my soul to the hands of my redeemer, who may wash it in his blood and bring it cleansed before the throne of our Heavenly Father." Much was made of this, as you might imagine, in the press. Preachers, that Sunday, all over the country, were quoting this. One irreverent newspaper—it might have been the *Evening Post*—said, "Well, this is all well and good, but it shouldn't lead us to conclude that godliness is profitable." But a paper in Texas—reading those words in the will, and the fact that he'd left everything to his son—printed the headline, "Morgan leaves soul to Maker, money to son."

Progressive Era and Reaction

1901–1929

The Crusades of Ida B. Wells

by

LINDA O. McMURRY

Ida B. Wells was born a slave on July 16, 1862, in Mississippi, six months before Abraham Lincoln signed the Emancipation Proclamation. Segregation, the legally enforced separation of blacks and whites, and lynchings, the public murder of black Americans by white mobs or gangs, were features of the South that Wells knew as a young woman. She became a journalist crusading on the behalf of integration, antilynching efforts, and other progressive causes. On August 9, 1999, Linda O. McMurry appeared on Booknotes *to discuss* To Keep the Waters Troubled: The Life of Ida B. Wells, *published in 1998 by Oxford University Press. Ms. McMurray is a history professor at North Carolina State University.*

IDA B. WELLS was born in 1862 in Holly Springs, Mississippi. . . . She was a very attractive woman with an undercurrent of sorrow. . . . There was a lot in her life to be sorry about. Both of her parents and one of her siblings died in the yellow fever epidemic of 1878. Her father was a Mason and so the Masons showed up at their house and said, "We're gonna farm this child out here and this child out there." Wells just shook her head and said, "No. It would have just destroyed my parents to know the family split up. If you can help me find work, I'll take care of them.". . . So, at sixteen, she took over her the care of her siblings and became head of the household.

She started out in Holly Springs, getting a teaching job out in the country near there. Then, in 1881, her aunt invited her to come to Memphis. At first, she wasn't able to get a job teaching in Memphis, so she was teaching in Woodstock, which was nearby. The two boys, by that time, were old enough to be apprenticed out and to be somewhat on their own. Her two youngest sisters came with her to Memphis and lived with their aunt, . . . but Wells was the primary support for the family.

IDA WELLS'S FIRST MAJOR event came two years after moving to Memphis, when she rode a train between Woodstock, where she was teaching, and Memphis, where she was living. At that time, segregation was just in the process of being established. She always got a ticket and rode in the ladies' car. One day they came and told her to move from the ladies' car. She refused, and one of the men reached over to grab her and throw her off the train. She bit him. That didn't get much publicity, but it does illustrate her temperament. Not only did she refuse to leave the train willingly, but she sued the railroad company and won.

It was eventually overturned on appeal, but she won initially, and that got a lot of publicity in the black press. It launched her career into journalism, because she began to write articles about her suit. [Then] she began writing articles on all kinds of things for the various black newspapers of the time, and many of them had national readership. She assumed the name "Iola" and became pretty well-known as a black journalist. She didn't use her full name, maybe because she was a little bit concerned about the impact those editorials might have on her teaching career if it was widespread knowledge. But she never did check her pen for anybody. She eventually did get fired from teaching because she criticized the school board for some of its actions in a newspaper.

THE TURNING POINT for her on the whole issue [of black–white relations] was the lynching of three of her friends in Memphis in 1892. It also was a key factor in the change of the course of her career. These three individuals included Thomas Moss, to whom she was close enough to be the godmother of his child. They were lynched primarily because they opened up a supermarket in competition with a white supermarket. These were young men who were very respectable, worked hard, and were making themselves economically important and independent. And they were lynched because they were successful. That caused Wells to turn her considerable anger toward antilynching violence.

She began to refute the myth that had been perpetrated to justify lynching by white mobs, which was that black men were so bestial that they had to have the restraining hand of the white mob to keep them under control. Rape was [often] given as the major reason for lynching. With the lynching of these three people, Wells knew that rape was not in any way involved. She began investigating and discovered that rape wasn't even a charge in the vast majority of lynchings.

Wells . . . wrote an editorial in the *Memphis Free Speech*. . . . She implied that this cry of rape could be a source of embarrassment for white women, because many white women were willing participants in sexual liaisons with . . . black men and didn't raise the issue of rape until afterward. Needless to say, her editorial infuriated white Memphis. She was out of town at the time. They came to the offices of the *Free Speech* and ran her partner out of town. Eventually all of her presses were confiscated, and she was told by people in Memphis that she should not come back.

WHEN WELLS WAS run out of Memphis, she moved to New York. She became affiliated with the *New York Age*, which was a leading black newspaper. The fact that she was in exile added to the interest of her story, so that she began to give lectures. Her writing was the thing that was most effective because she could only give a limited number of speeches. She published numbers of pamphlets, as well as newspaper articles and so forth, but her speaking was very important as well.

T. Thomas Fortune was the editor of the *New York Age*. He became a mentor early on in the course of her journalism career. T. Thomas Fortune also was a founder of the Afro-American Council. Wells was involved in the founding of that organization as well as just about every major organization that had to do with black rights, [including] the NAACP, the National Association of Colored Women, and the Niagara Movement.

WELLS FINALLY FOUND her soul mate, Ferdinand Barnett, when she . . . moved to Chicago. He was a lawyer and an activist, and also owned a newspaper, the *Chicago Conservator*. She'd had problems with men. She was afraid she would lose her independence if she became too closely involved or especially got married. But Ferdinand Barnett was the exception.

She was thirty-three when she got married. She had four children and two stepsons. It was an unconventional marriage for that time. They were temperamentally opposite. Barnett was very easygoing and there was nothing easygoing about Wells-Barnett. She did not take his name; she hyphenated her name as Wells-Barnett. He was supportive of her . . . as militant as she was. He hired a housekeeper to do the housework and did most of the cooking because he liked to. He hired nursemaids to go with her so she could continue her lectures.

They were Republicans, like most African Americans at that time. The Republican Party was identified as the party of emancipation and was more supportive of black rights than the Democratic Party for most of that period. That began to shift with the New Deal and Franklin Roosevelt's election.

NOTHING WAS TOO big or too small for Wells to tackle. She's best known for her antilynching efforts, but she was a strong lobbyist in Illinois and took part in campaigns to turn back every attempt to segregate Chicago schools. She established the first black women's suffrage group in Illinois. She was very active in the fight for women's rights, as well as for black rights, but she always put race concerns over gender concerns.

One of the things that I think is significant about Wells that this book captures is that most of the labels are far too simplistic. She did believe in the self-help [philosophy] of Booker T. Washington, in some ways, but she didn't believe in his accommodation. She believed in separatism in some ways, but she remained a committed integrationist. There were a lot of ambivalent feelings among much of the black elite about what were the appropriate tactics and she, essentially, was for anything that worked.

SHE DIED AT AGE sixty-nine from uremic poisoning; it was fairly quick. She'd been deteriorating but just the year before, she ran for the Illinois state senate and lost. So, she was active up until practically the day she died.

Wells was exasperating because to the day she died, she was uncompromising. . . . Some degree of her temperament was inherited, but a lot of factors played into it. She was the oldest child. After her parents' death, she had to become the head of the household. She was angry because she was expected to play both gender roles. She wouldn't consciously admit it to herself, but she balked at that. She was also angry at the treatment that African Americans got. She really was just uncompromisingly militant. She felt that there were battles worthy to be fought, even if you couldn't win them. That's what she did all her life.

The Celebrity of Helen Keller

by

DOROTHY HERRMANN

Helen Keller was born in 1880 and at the age of nineteen months was rendered deaf and blind due to a fever. She was unable to communicate until her parents hired Annie Sullivan, a top graduate of the Perkins Institution for the Blind in Boston, to tutor the six-year-old Helen. Sullivan became Keller's remarkably effective teacher. As an adult, Helen Keller became an advocate for the deaf and blind and helped eliminate the institutionalization of the disabled. She received awards from around the world for her work on this and other causes, including the Presidential Medal of Freedom, America's highest civilian award. Dorothy Herrmann appeared on Booknotes *on September 17, 1998, to discuss* Helen Keller: A Life, *published by Alfred A. Knopf in 1998. Ms. Hermann is a writer living in New Hope, Pennsylvania.*

ANNIE SULLIVAN and Helen Keller were never parted. Only death parted them. Their relationship was very complex. It was a very strengthening relationship, but it was also a suffocating relationship. Their strange bond meant that they could not really lead independent lives; it was Annie Sullivan's devotion to Helen that, in the end, wrecked her marriage to John Macy. But overall, both women would have been diminished without this intense relationship. There's never been another relationship like the relationship of these two women in history or literature. Mark Twain, their good friend, didn't even consider them two separate beings. He said, "It takes the two of you to make a perfect whole."

HELEN KELLER WAS the world-famous deaf-blind writer and essayist, . . . a woman who spent almost her entire life, from the time she was nineteen months old, in darkness and in silence, and yet she accomplished many amazing things. She wrote many books, among them the famous *The Story of My Life,* which was her autobiography. She graduated from Radcliffe College. She was the first deaf-blind person ever to graduate from college. She was also an advocate for the blind and the deaf-blind. Yet interestingly, as famous as Helen Keller was, . . . many people are only familiar with the early part of her life; the part that William Gibson portrayed so compellingly in [his 1962 film] *The Miracle Worker.* Also, ironically, because Helen Keller was so revered in her lifetime, many people had ceased to regard her as a real person; that's why I wrote my book, to find the real woman behind the myth.

Helen Keller was born in 1880. . . . At the age of nineteen months she suffered a disease that at that time was known as "brain fever." . . . To this day we don't know what that disease was, whether it was scarlet fever, which was very prevalent at the time, or spinal meningitis, or rubella. Whatever this disease was, it completely wiped out her hearing and her sight. As a result, she could not speak, although there was certainly nothing wrong with her vocal cords.

Annie Sullivan was Helen Keller's teacher. She was a very young woman when she went to Tuscumbia, Alabama, where Helen was born. It's in a rural part of Alabama. Annie Sullivan came from a background that was really as horrendous as Helen Keller's. Her parents were illiterate Irish immigrants who came to Massachusetts after the great famine, and her mother died of tuberculosis at the age [of twenty-eight. Almost all] her brothers and sisters also died at young ages, and then her father abandoned the family, and Annie and her young brother, Jimmie, were placed in an almshouse in Massachusetts, where Jimmie subsequently died.

Annie was in a unique position to understand Helen because she was half blind herself, and she suffered from a viral disease of the eye that, until 1937 with the advent of sulfa drugs, was responsible for much of the blindness in the world.

[I VISITED] THE FAMOUS pump that Helen Keller reached her hand under and felt the rushing water and, for the first time, realized that it had a name and connected the rushing water with the word.

Helen was six and a half then, but the process had been going on for some time before she made the connection. Helen was just beginning to realize that these intriguing finger actions that Annie Sullivan was making on her hand might have a meaning. She began to become dimly aware of their connection with the outside world, but the water pump was the first time she was able to make the connection. In her book, *The Story of My Life,* Helen gave the impression, which she later corrected in another memoir, that once she had made this association she immediately grasped everything. That was not the case. First, Annie Sullivan taught her nouns, then she taught her adjectives, then she dropped in the verbs. It wasn't until many months had passed that Helen was able to ask the simplest type of question.

I THOUGHT SHE LIVED in this silent black pit, but that was far from the case. She had a very interesting world she lived in and it was filled with vibrations, with smells, and with taste. And, of course, after Annie Sullivan broke through to her, in the next few years, she learned braille. Before braille was standardized, she learned many other types of raised print. So she had a great deal of information at her disposal.

SHE WAS A WOMAN who became world famous shortly after the "miracle at the well" mainly because of Alexander Graham Bell, who was very interested in her. Bell invented the telephone partially as a hearing aid. He had a deaf mother and a deaf wife, and he wanted to use what had happened in Tuscumbia, the so-called miracle at the well, of Helen understanding language, to promote awareness of the deaf and his theories of teaching them.

The other person who certainly promoted Helen Keller was Michael Anagnos, director of the Perkins Institution for the Blind [in Boston, later] in Watertown, Massachusetts, which, by the way, was the first school for the blind in the United States. He pronounced Helen to be a prodigy, so when people heard about what had happened at Tuscumbia and then, with the influence of these two important men, especially Alexander Graham Bell, Helen was world famous.

But then, shortly after that, she sent Anagnos a little birthday gift, which was supposedly an original story she had written. . . . He pronounced the story . . . without parallel in the history of American literature. Unfortunately for Helen Keller, that story was a plagiarism. It was plagiarized from one of Margaret T. Canby's children's stories. [Canby was] a famous children's author of the period. After that, people began to suspect Helen Keller of being a fraud.

Helen Keller [plagiarized this story] *The Frost King,* probably around 1891. . . . As a biographer, one of my great challenges [was] in discussing her relationship with Annie Sullivan. [I had to find out] who was doing what in this relationship. Was Helen Keller really a genius through which Annie was her instrument for expressing that genius? Or was Annie Sullivan the genius and Helen Keller her mindless puppet? Certainly after *The Frost King* incident, there were many people who accused her of being Annie Sullivan's puppet and [suggested] that she was mindless.

THIS MAY COME AS a shock to many people who have seen *The Miracle Worker,* but Annie Sullivan did get married. She married a man by the name of John Macy, an instructor of English at Harvard, who was brilliant and handsome. He helped Helen edit *The Story of My Life.* He was much young than Annie Sullivan and only a couple of years older than Helen. They married when Annie Sullivan was about forty years old, and it had to be one of the strangest marriages on record.

[The relationship between John Macy and Annie Sullivan] started at Radcliffe College. Annie Sullivan was having additional problems with her eyesight, and getting Helen through college was quite an ordeal because she had to literally spell everything into her hand. It was a very difficult time for both women, and John Albert Macy stepped in. He learned the manual finger language so as to be able to communicate with Helen.

Then he and Annie Sullivan fell in love and were married a few years later. She was forty, he was about twenty-eight years old, and it was said that he married, in essence, two women. For years there's been speculation about which woman he was really in love with.

Helen Keller never married, and this was one of the tragedies of her life. She said once that, "If I could see and hear, I would marry first of all." She had one very tragic love affair and her family broke it up.

It was with Peter Fagan, who was her young secretary [and also a] socialist. It was 1916; Helen was thirty-six years old at the time, and she was an extremely beautiful woman. In her day, people always talked about Helen's spirituality and how she reminded them of some religious figure but, in truth, this was a physically gorgeous woman with a beautiful figure. She had long chestnut hair, gorgeous legs—but her family, especially her mother, did not want her to marry. But Helen managed to defy both her family and Annie Sullivan. This was the one time she really did turn against them, and she and Peter Fagan had a love affair, and then they were going to be married, and they went to the city hall in Boston and applied for a marriage license. Mrs. Keller, Helen's mother, got wind of it, and told Helen that she could never see this man again. But Helen was not to be stopped. She and Peter Fagan devised this very elaborate scheme where he would kidnap her and then they would be married by a friend. But again, the Keller family thwarted their getting married.

One night, when she was back in Tuscumbia, Alabama, she went out on the porch and met with Peter Fagan. How she got these messages to him nobody has ever able to figure out. Helen's sister and brother-in-law woke up and realized she was communicating with Peter Fagan, and they drove him off the property with a shotgun. Then, sometime later, they woke up—several months had passed—[because] they heard a noise on the porch, and there was Helen with her bags packed and she was waiting for him, and he never came. Then she really didn't have any choice but to resume her very cloistered lifestyle.

HELEN SUPPORTED THE Russian Revolution and the Bolsheviks. Ironically, Helen Keller had to compromise throughout her life. There is this discrepancy about her political beliefs, if one studies them. On one hand, she denounced many capitalists, and yet she also accepted money from them throughout her life. . . . Because Helen was unable really to provide for herself because of her disability, she was forced to accept pensions from people like Andrew Carnegie. This humiliated her on many levels, but yet she couldn't do without that type of help, not only from Carnegie but from John D. Rockefeller and from Mark Twain.

John Macy was a socialist, quite a violent socialist, and he wrote a book called *Socialism in America*. He ranted and raved against the capitalists of the time, and it is debatable whether Helen Keller would have become such a rabid socialist had she not met John Macy. He was a tremendous influence on her, but once she was exposed to socialism, it was something that she believed in her entire life. She eventually did tone down her speeches and her writings about socialism because, among other things, she was a very practical woman. She had to earn a living, and there was a time when, for her to have been such an outspoken advocate of socialism, would have gotten her into a great deal of trouble, and she was smart enough to know that.

During the late '30s and '40s, she supported a number of organizations that were later assumed to be Communist-front organizations. But there's no evidence that she was ever a card-carrying Communist. . . . She supported the Industrial Workers of the World, a militant [labor] union. She was very violent in a lot of her political opinions and supported actually rather violent measures. When the fight for women's rights occurred, she supported—I believe there was a British suffragist named Mrs. Pankhurst, who wanted women to smash windows and things like that, and Helen supported her wholeheartedly. Interestingly, though, Annie Sullivan did not support Helen in these beliefs, nor did her family. They were aghast at her radicalism.

Of all the roles that Helen Keller played in life of a handicapped whiz kid, a lecturer, a writer, an advocate for the blind and the deaf-blind, I think she enjoyed her vaudeville career the most. Vaudeville, of course, was quite a tasteless entertainment at the time that she was in it. She was supposed to be the inspirational act, but she was the exception. Besides the usual circus performers and jugglers, there were people that had been in prison, who had been pardoned because they had lovely voices. They were on the vaudeville circuit. There was an acquitted murderer at the same time that Helen performed, who had led a very bizarre double life as the husband of a woman in one city and the wife of a man in the other. Annie Sullivan was very mortified by having to go on the vaudeville stage, and they did this because they desperately needed the money. Their film, which was made in 1918, *Deliverance*, was a box office flop, and they needed money desperately. But Helen felt the opposite. She loved being around the people she called her fellow citizens and she loved the rush and the glare and the noise, as she put it, of the vaudeville stage.

AFTER ANNIE SULLIVAN's death in 1936, Helen Keller lived near Westport, Connecticut, and had a large and very comfortable house that she shared with Polly Thompson [her second companion]. But then in 1946, a fire devastated her home and many key papers were lost. We're not exactly sure what those papers were. Even people who were extremely close to Helen Keller have no idea of what precisely was in that house, but it can be assumed that Anne Sullivan's correspondence to her husband was destroyed in that fire, as was Helen Keller's correspondence with . . . Peter Fagan.

Polly Thompson . . . was very loyal to Helen. She accompanied her on many of her travels because Helen, in her later years, was a fund-raiser for the American Foundation for the Blind, and she traveled worldwide to raise public awareness of the needs of the blind. She was, however, not the brilliant teacher and companion that Annie Sullivan was to Helen Keller. She did not have Annie Sullivan's flair for making the world stimulating, this outside world that Helen Keller never saw or heard.

HELEN KELLER's LAST years were sad. She suffered a stroke when she was about eighty. Then she developed a diabetic condition and lapsed into senility. So it was a very slow deterioration for her. But she was never afraid of death and she wasn't afraid of aging, and she died a very peaceful death. She just drifted off in her sleep, said people who were close to her at the time. . . . She lived until 1968, an incredible eighty-eight years having [her] condition.

Helen Keller's body was cremated and then, following the funeral service, [buried] at the National Cathedral [in Washington, D.C.]. It was an enormous service. Many deaf-blind people and blind people with guide dogs attended her funeral, many dignitaries of the time. Here was a woman who had led such a life of quiet, and if you visit her grave at the cathedral, you find that it's filled with sound, because there are many schoolchildren who come through to see her grave.

The 1918 Influenza Pandemic

by

GINA KOLATA

The armistice ending World War I was signed in 1919. The year before the war ended, 1918, saw not only a huge number of war casualties but was also the year of one of the deadliest viruses in history.

In September 1918, Dr. Victor Vaughn, acting surgeon general of the army, received orders to proceed to Camp Devens near Boston, where the deadly strain of influenza first appeared in America. On the day he arrived, sixty-three men died from the virus. In October alone, 195,000 Americans fell victim to influenza and 1.5 million would die by the time the pandemic ran its course. Gina Kolata, a science reporter for the New York Times, *came to* Booknotes *on January 19, 2000, to discuss* Flu: The Story of the Great Influenza Pandemic of 1918 and the Search for the Virus That Caused It, *published in 1999 by Farrar, Straus & Giroux.*

THE INFLUENZA PANDEMIC OF 1918 . . . was the worst infectious disease epidemic in recorded history. It killed so many people that if something like that came by today, it would kill more people than the top ten killers wrapped together—1.5 million Americans or so.

Historians keep ratcheting upward the number of people who died worldwide. People now think that 40 million is an underestimate, which used to be the median estimate. Most recently there was a meeting of historians and other people who were interested in this flu in South Africa. They think that the true number of deaths worldwide was closer to 100 million and that possibly 20 million died on the Indian subcontinent alone.

With the 1918 flu, people would die very quickly, almost overnight, because their lungs would fill with fluid. You would have a young person who would start to feel sick and, within hours or a day or so, would be gasping for breath. Their skin would turn dark because their blood wasn't getting enough oxygen. One person described it as mahogany spots on the cheekbones, and then the dark color started to spread. We don't see that today. Today you feel very ill, and some people die, but nobody's getting this sort of instant death.

In a typical flu season today, [0.1 percent of the people who get the flu] die. Most of them are very old or have some other chronic medical condition that weakens them. In 1918 [a vast majority] of them were under age sixty-five. It was a very peculiar death curve, shaped like a W. The very young died, then people between the ages of twenty and forty died in huge numbers. That's the middle of the W. Then at the end of the W, some of the old people died.

Every year, the flu comes through a population and burns itself out. The 1918 one did that too. It infects everybody who's been exposed to it, and then it mutates. It changes itself a little bit and then it comes back again. If people are vulnerable to it, it will infect them.

We get the flu when somebody around us has it and they cough or sneeze. You usually breathe it in, or you get the virus on your hands and you touch your nose or mouth. It has to get into your lungs. The reason you tend to get it in the winter is that you're inside more. There are more people coughing and sneezing, and the virus lives longer in the air when the air's dry. So we get it in our winter, and in the Southern Hemisphere, they get it in their winter.

INFLUENZA IS A SIMPLE little virus. It has eight genes and only lives in human lungs. While it's there, its only job is to take a lung cell and make it into a virus factory. The virus gets in, just like every other virus, and takes a cell's machinery and forces it to make new viruses. Then the cell dies and the viruses escape and infect a new cell. It's a simple little thing.

The first time the flu came into the United States in a big way, it showed up at a place called Camp Devens, near Boston. At the time, people thought that it might be germ warfare because they couldn't believe it was something like the flu. Many people insisted on putting the word influenza in quotation marks. It was during World War I and there were rumors that there had been a greasy cloud floating over Boston Harbor with these germs in it, or that maybe the Germans had put something into Bayer aspirin that would kill people. When it arrived at Camp Devens, it was the most horrible thing that anybody had ever witnessed. So many young soldiers were dying that they had to have special trains to take away the dead. The bodies were stacked up like cordwood, as people said when they were there.

It was so shocking that the surgeon general sent a contingent of three of the leading doctors in the United States to Camp Devens. One of them later wrote in his memoirs that he couldn't even bear to think about this thing. In the fall of 1918, the deadly influenza virus demonstrated the inferiority of human inventions in the taking of human life. He said the memories were burned on his brain and that he would like to remove them if he possibly could. When these doctors wanted to see an autopsy, there were so many dead in Camp Devens that they had to step over the bodies just to get into the autopsy room. The bodies of the dead hadn't been removed yet.

When they watched an autopsy take place, the military doctor opened the chest of a young man who had died. There were his lungs, sodden and heavy in his body, filled with fluid, totally useless. The man had essentially died because his lungs had filled with fluid. A doctor there, who had been pretty much imperturbable, nothing could shake him, turned and said, "This must be a plague." He could not believe it.

THERE IS A MILITARY warehouse—people have described it as the Library of Congress of the dead—started by Abraham Lincoln. Every time a military doctor does an autopsy, he's supposed to put some of the tissue and the person's medical records in this big warehouse. When people died of that flu in 1918, doctors took little snippets of their lung tissue, soaked them in formaldehyde, wrapped them in paraffin and sent them to the warehouse. At the end of this century, Dr. Jeffery Taubenberger at Walter Reed Army Medical Center put in a requisition for some people who had died of that flu, asking if he could find some lung tissue with viral genes in it. Inside that lung tissue, after all these years, was still that flu virus from 1918.

Taubenberger [was working at Walter Reed in the] Armed Forces Institute of Pathology. He's a civilian. He's got M.D. and Ph.D. degrees, so he's both a medical doctor and trained as a Ph.D. scientist. He stumbled into this kind of a career. He's a brilliant man who always asks the right questions, but he's an outsider to the flu field.

Johan Hultin is a pathologist. He's Swedish. He came to this country as a medical student, and he was just going to study for one year at the University of Iowa. He was a real adventurer, so he decided that he and his wife, before he started school, would travel to all fifty states. They got a car and started driving around and they ended up in Alaska. While he was in Alaska, he met a paleontologist. He and his wife spent the summer with this paleontologist, going around with him on his travels.

The next year in medical school, visiting virologists said, "There was this terrible tragedy in 1918. The only way we're ever going to know what happened is if somebody could find someone who was buried in the permafrost where the ground never thaws and their lungs are still frozen. Then maybe we could get the virus out and find out what it was." So Johan Hultin said, "I know this paleontologist. I can find out where the Eskimo villages were and get a map of the permafrost. I could go up there and actually find a flu victim."

It was an amazing adventure. Hultin was still a young student. [In 1951] he went to three villages in Alaska where he thought maybe he could find some bodies from the 1918 flu. It was like the three bears: the first one wasn't right and the next one wasn't right; but in the third village, the mass grave was exactly right. This little village was called Brevig. He said to the Eskimos, "There was a terrible tragedy in 1918 and I'd like your permission to dig in this grave and to try to find some flu victims so that I can get that virus. We could make a vaccine and you will never have to suffer like this again." They told him it was okay to do it. The story of how he did it is an adventure in itself, but he did manage to get some frozen lung tissue from 1918 flu victims and bring it back with him to Iowa, where he tried to grow it.

Today, it's horrifying to think that someone was trying to grow the 1918 virus, but he hadn't really thought very carefully about the consequences. He was growing it in chicken eggs, which is to this day how they grow flu viruses. He kept injecting chicken eggs with the lung tissue hoping to grow that virus. Nothing happened, so he concluded it was dead, but he never forgot that grave and the 1918 flu. He always swore that one day he would go back there, when science advanced enough, so he could do something with that tissue and try again to solve the mystery of the 1918 flu.

[In March 1997] Johan Hultin saw Jeffery Taubenberger's article in *Science* magazine, where Taubenberger said, "I have this sample from the warehouse. I can start to pull out these genes." Hultin wrote him a letter and said, "I think I could get you another sample. Would you be interested?" He carefully tried to explain who he was so Taubenberger wouldn't think he was crazy. Taubenberger wrote back and said, "Of course, I'm really interested."

Hultin paid for [another trip to Alaska] by himself. It cost him about $3,200. The next week he was up there with his pickax, sleeping on the floor of the one-room schoolhouse on an air mattress, ready to dig in those graves. He got the permission of the Eskimos. He did it all by himself [back in 1951]. This time they gave him four teenagers to help him dig, which helped him a lot.

Hultin did dig into that grave again, and he did get a sample. He divided it into four pieces . . . put it in a preservative, and sent it to Jeffery Taubenberger. Being Johan Hultin, everything was done on a low-tech scale. He decided this was a really precious sample of lung tissue and he didn't want to trust the mail. . . . One piece was sent UPS, [two by] Federal Express, and the other one Express Mail. . . . They all got to Taubenberger. Taubenberger found the viral genes in there and started working on them.

They know it was a flu virus that caused the influenza of 1918. There are only eight genes in a flu virus. At this point, they have three lung samples from people who died in 1918 who have those genes in them. Getting them out is pushing the limits of molecular biology and takes a long time. They describe it as putting together a mosaic, a very detailed mosaic, piece by piece, to put those genes together. They've gotten three of the eight genes completely put together now. They chose them in the order of the likelihood that they were an easy answer to what made that virus so deadly. . . . Unfortunately, the first three genes have [only] told them that it's a flu virus, that it's related to bird viruses and pig viruses, but they have not provided the answer yet to why it was so dangerous.

There are two big differences [between the 1918 flu pandemic and what might happen today]. One is vaccine. In 1918 there were no vaccines. Now the big fear everybody has is if they see a virus like this coming, . . . people will think that scientists are just crying wolf and will not be vaccinated.

The second big difference is antibiotics. A lot of people who died in 1918 died because of the flu itself. But others got very ill from the flu, and while they were sick, bacteria came into their lungs and they died of bacterial infection. People still die of bacterial infections today when they get the flu, but we have antibiotics now. They make a huge difference in the death toll.

EVERY TIME I SPEAK to scientists about the 1918 flu, I say, "Are we going to see another flu like this?" And they say, "Yes, we just don't know when," because there's no way of predicting what's going to happen when and how the flu virus is going to mutate. It's definitely important to try to understand how a flu virus can turn into such a killer. If they can't find out by looking at all eight genes of this 1918 virus, at the very least, they'll be able to do experiments that can say, . . . "What does it do? What can you do to protect yourself? How do you stop this virus?"

Langston Hughes and
Carl Van Vechten

by

EMILY BERNARD

In the 1920s, New York City's Harlem neighborhood attracted African Americans with the promise of jobs and a way out of the segregated South. It was the heart of a new movement, first called the New Negro Renaissance and later known as the Harlem Renaissance—a flowering of black art, culture, and literature. Emily Bernard's Remember Me to Harlem: The Letters of Langston Hughes and Carl Van Vechten, 1925–1964, *published by Alfred A. Knopf in 2001, tells the story of two of the renaissance's most prominent figures, and their friendship, through the letters they shared. Ms. Bernard, an assistant professor of Afro-American Studies at Smith College, discussed their relationship in a* Booknotes *interview on March 12, 2001.*

THE HARLEM RENAISSANCE was a cultural movement that took place in urban centers like New York and Philadelphia and Boston and Chicago during the 1920s. [It] coincided with the period known as the Great Migration. In the late teens and early twenties, scores of black people were coming from the South, from ravaged, politically repressive situations, to urban centers like New York, Chicago, Philadelphia, looking for work. There was a push-pull situation with black people needing to find alternatives beyond the South and urban industries needing labor. That was the situation that created the bulk of black people in [places] like Harlem that then gave way to something like the Harlem Renaissance.

But the situation in the North was, of course, not the promised land of equality and liberty. Often black people came to the North and found that jobs that were promised them were not to be had. They found an equal amount of repression politically, also violence. So the situation was not what had been promised, but it still was a time when black people, like every other American, were benefiting from that postwar economy, and so there was a lot of conspicuous consumption and a lot of good hopes and a sense of possibility for black people as well.

HARLEM IS IN MANHATTAN, Upper Manhattan. Harlem has had a lot of different incarnations over the course of its lifetime. Before it became the "Black Mecca," as it was called during that period, it had claimed numbers of Dutch residents, German residents, Irish residents. So it's had a lot of different manifestations.

It still has a lot of the same flavor [today] as it did in the '20s. You can still go to the street called Striver's Row, which was the home to Harlem's elite. You can still see the magnificent architecture there, and it still claims a lot of black luminaries. But, of course, it's seen a lot of economic devastation since the booming economy that made it flourish during the early '20s.

[LANGSTON HUGHES was born] in Joplin, Missouri, in 1902. . . . His mother was Carrie Clark, someone who had a lot of ambitions. She wanted to be an actress and she would have roles in various performances. She ended up having an important role in a Harlem production. She wanted a lot for her son but wasn't able to provide him with any real stability, because she divorced her husband in the teens. Langston Hughes ended up having a nomadic upbringing with Carrie trying to find work in various situations and living with family members. James Nathaniel Hughes was Hughes's father. [He] was a very difficult man. Hughes writes about him in his 1940 autobiography as being someone who just didn't want to identify with black Americans at all and had a real disdain for African Americans. This caused Hughes a lot of inner turmoil that he wrote about in *The Big Sea*. It wasn't an easy upbringing for Langston Hughes.

Langston Hughes was very important. He was one of those rare writers who really reached out and was understood and appreciated by an enormous spectrum of readers. He'd go to college campuses all over the country and people would recite his poetry to him. He's a hero among black people; people who didn't have means to collect maybe a range of books and who were familiar with Langston Hughes. He was a folk poet. He was a poet of the people, as he called himself . . . and he was beloved all over the world.

Carl Van Vechten [author of *Nigger Heaven*] was about twenty-two years older than Langston Hughes. He was born in Cedar Rapids, Iowa, to parents who were very prominent members of the community. His father was an insurance broker and quite well-to-do. He was also someone who was sympathetic to black rights and used some of his money to help found a school for free black children at the turn of the century. His mother was a separatist who was interested in women's rights to vote. It was that kind of situation that led to a lot of early curiosity on the part of Carl Van Vechten, a lot of his interest in looking outside of the mainstream for a different evidence of culture.

Carl Van Vechten lived at 150 West 55th Street. This was the home that was referred to by [journalist] Walter White as the "midtown branch of the NAACP." . . .. Van Vechten literally brought uptown downtown, and vice versa. These were two different worlds. He always lived in these elite, mostly white neighborhoods, but he physically created a kind of integration by bringing black people to his home and by shepherding whites to Harlem.

The title *Nigger Heaven* refers to an ironic term that was used among black people around the time period of segregation. It refers to segregated situations in public theaters. Black people were forced to sit in the balconies, sitting, at an interesting vantage point, over the heads of white people but yet forced to sit in segregated and "inferior" seating. Van Vechten meant it to be an ironic comment on the situation of blacks in America, on segregation and the cruelties and absurdities of segregation and racism.

[Carl Van Vechten and Langston Hughes] met in 1924 for the first time. They met at a benefit party at Arthur "Happy" Rhone's nightclub on Lenox Avenue and 143rd Street in Harlem. The first time they met, Van Vechten was just then discovering this cultural flowering called the Harlem Renaissance. It was just being initiated at that time.

Van Vechten was brought to the party by Walter White, who was another gatekeeper of the period, a journalist, someone who was very politically active. Walter White [was a black man] who actually looked white and did a lot of research on lynching, using [his nearly] white skin to help him infiltrate various goings-on in the South. They became friends first, and White introduced him to everyone. That night in 1924, Van Vechten met Langston Hughes and the first night, he recorded his name as Kingston Hughes. It wasn't until several months later in 1925, when they met again—it was at another benefit party—that they developed their real friendship.

Langston Hughes was not very big. I don't even believe he was six feet tall, another contrast to Van Vechten, who was quite tall and gangly and imposing as a figure. Langston Hughes was none of those things. He was very handsome and as beautiful a spirit as he was a person to admire.

I knew about the black artists who had become well-known during that period, but I had never heard about this white person. The more I read about Carl Van Vechten, the more I learned about his relationships with black writers. I became interested in the interrelations between whites and blacks during this period and how difficult it was for black people to wrestle with these questions: What is white influence and what relationship does it have to our art? Does it take something away from the integrity of black art or is it, in fact, just a necessary evil? Is it possible for these kinds of relationships to exist without certain power imbalances naturally taking place? Those are the kinds of question that I wanted to pursue and Van Vechten brought it all to the front.

ZORA NEALE HURSTON is another amazing figure from this period. She . . . came to Harlem in the 1920s and was different from the elite group of the Harlem Renaissance writers in that she was less interested in affecting prim and proper airs. She was a folklorist and she wrote folk plays and poetry and collections of materials. She was impatient with the prissiness that characterized the other writing and attitudes about the Harlem Renaissance.

CHARLOTTE MASON was another notorious patron of the Harlem Renaissance. She stands in important contrast to a figure like Carl Van Vechten. She was from one of the most wealthy, elite families in New York, a white woman who considered the Vanderbilts new money. She was from that station in life. Her first passion was Native American culture and she became interested in things black in the 1920s and developed relationships with Alain Locke, who was one of the gatekeepers of the Harlem Renaissance. Alain brought her to Langston Hughes and Zora Neale Hurston. She had her charges call her "Godmother" and they actually kneeled before her. She sat on a throne in her lavish apartment in New York and had them kiss the ring and pay that kind of respect to her. Mason was someone who enjoyed having that almost master–servant relationship with her black protégés. She and Hughes had a very wrenching relationship and [eventually had a] falling out. . . . He was very emotionally dependent on her, attached to her. If you read his letters to her, which are at Yale's library [along with his letters to Carl Van Vechten], you see how he needed some parental guidance that he looked for in Mason, and she at some point just rebuffed him entirely.

Mason did give Hughes money. . . . She had a contract with him. I believe that Hurston received a little more money than Hughes did. But the contract was amazing in its detail, where he could publish, where he couldn't publish. Hurston had to come up with receipts for everything she spent money on down to her stockings, down to her shoes. . . . Both Hughes and Hurston would write to Mason asking for just enough money "so I can get a new pair of shoes." She was relentless in the control she exercised over her black protégés.

[LANGSTON HUGHES's poem "Advertisement for the Waldorf-Astoria"] not only caused such a stir in Hughes's personal life but also had professional reverberations throughout the course of his career. It was a beginning of Hughes's interest in his professional career to incorporate some more political sentiments. It wasn't the first political poem he wrote, by any means, but I think it was one that had many reverberations for him. He called it the poem that ended his relationship with . . . Charlotte Mason, but it actually wasn't. He wrote the poem after they'd already broken off.

In his autobiography he uses it as a signal poem that created a lot of chaos in his life. It's a poem that Van Vechten had a lot of problems with and it was representative of Van Vechten's distaste for Hughes's political poetry. Their correspondence about this poem gives you a sense of how they differed. They couldn't have been more different politically.

Hughes wrote about this beautifully and eloquently in *The Big Sea*. He wrote about how, at this point in his life, he was at a crossroads. He was being supported by this patron who lived in another world all to her own. Yet as he went to the Park Avenue home, and he saw outside of the window people huddled in the corners—it was the Depression and there were numbers of people on the streets who were absolutely destitute—the contradiction was something he just could no longer bear. It was no longer possible for him, poetically, to leave those observations out of his work, the kinds of contradictions that the Waldorf presents. How was it possible to have this kind of opulence when so many people in the country had lost everything?

It did have some impact. There were letters, of course, in support of the poem. Hughes was certainly not alone in his searing indictment of the Waldorf-Astoria. But you see in their correspondence that Van Vechten was really bothered by the poem. He goes to great lengths, even years later, to say to Hughes, "The Waldorf has these good qualities, and it gives these jobs to people, and it's one of the greatest employers here in New York." He was very defensive and it certainly became a little burr in the relationship between Van Vechten and Hughes.

Hughes was very active in the [politically radical] John Reed Clubs and he flirted pretty seriously with communism at different points in his life. . . . Hughes never formally affiliated himself with communism, and it's something that became a tender issue when he was called before the House Un-American Activities Committee to testify in the 1950s.

[In 1953 Hughes] was called to testify and his testimony was very careful. He very, very painstakingly avoided affiliating himself with communism, but he also avoided repudiating it. . . . He certainly . . . enjoyed affiliations with Communists in the United States. When he was in Russia [in the 1930s], he explored those kinds of impulses. But as time went on and he'd suffered politically and professionally from his affiliations, he distanced himself more and more.

There was a group that was going to go over [to Russia] and do a film called *Black and White*. It never got off the ground, but he had a lot of experiences and wrote to Van Vechten about them. Those letters are a wonderful contrast of Van Vechten's very—in some ways—sedentary and parochial life in New York. While Hughes was traveling and trying to understand himself and have global contacts, Van Vechten was living in his parlor in New York.

[About his Russian experience, Hughes wrote,] "There it seemed to me that Marxism had put into practical being many of the precepts which our own Christian America had not yet been able to bring to life. For in the Soviet Union, meager as the resources of the country were, white and black, Asiatic and European, Jew and Gentile stood alike as citizens on an equal footing protected from racial inequalities by law."

JAMES WELDON JOHNSON was a central figure during the Harlem Renaissance and beyond. He was an educator, a lyricist, the coauthor with his brother Rosamond of "Lift Every Voice and Sing," which now is called the black national anthem. [They collaborated on their first] book of American Negro spirituals in 1925, which was really a signal collection. They put together black spirituals and gospels and work songs and talked about how this is our contribution to American culture. James Weldon Johnson was also the author of *The Autobiography of an Ex-Colored Man*, which was the first modern novel authored by an African American. It was first published as an autobiography in 1912 and then reissued actually at the behest of Carl Van Vechten as a novel in 1927.

James Weldon Johnson died tragically in a car accident in 1938. After that, the Library of Congress approached his widow, Grace Nail, to contribute her husband's papers to the Library of Congress. That gave Van Vechten the idea, because he was as close to Grace Nail as he had been to James Weldon Johnson, to . . . create an archive, a place where you could build on this collection and maybe even create a chair of African American literature. Years before it actually would ever happen at Yale, he predicted that it might happen.

VAN VECHTEN WAS determined to get Hughes to collect his materials and send them to Yale. . . . You can read letter after letter of this nudging, nudging. . . . If Van Vechten hadn't done that, we wouldn't have this collection.

There was an interesting self-consciousness that happened between the two of them. In the later letters, after Van Vechten had come up with this idea to create the James Weldon Johnson collection, he was beseeching Hughes, "Please send your letters to me." He wrote to Hughes, "You have to write me back because our letters are historic. Our letters are going to mean something . . . for future generations." There is a funny letter where Hughes said, "Well, if you hadn't told me that, I would tell you this scandalous story that happened," and then he proceeded to tell it.

The Scopes "Monkey" Trial

by

EDWARD J. LARSON

In the summer of 1925, in Dayton, Tennessee, John Scopes, a biology teacher in the local high school, was brought to trial for violating the state of Tennessee's statute banning the teaching of evolution in the schools. The State of Tennessee v. John Thomas Scopes, *which quickly became known as the "Monkey Trial," focused the nation's attention on Scopes, Dayton, the issues at hand, and the battling attorneys William Jennings Bryan and Clarence Darrow. Bryan, whose official role was to aid the state prosecutor, a well-known populist and the Democratic Party candidate for president in 1896, 1900, and 1908. Darrow, the famous defense attorney, had defended such controversial figures as James and Joseph McNamara, labor activists accused and eventually convicted of bombing the* Los Angeles Times *building, and Nathan Leopold Jr. and Richard Loeb, sentenced to life in prison for a "thrill killing." On July 14, 1998, Edward J. Larson visited us on the* Booknotes *set to discuss his Pulitzer Prize–winning* Summer for the Gods: The Scopes Trial and America's Continuing Debate over Science and Religion, *published by Basic Books in 1997. Mr. Larson teaches history at the University of Georgia.*

THE SCOPES TRIAL [took place in] 1925. America was in the middle of the roaring twenties [and] . . . into media sensation, and this was the greatest media sensation of a media sensation-loving decade. It was also a time when we were deep into the Republican Party's "Return to Normalcy," [a phrase] coined by the late president Warren Harding. But then Calvin Coolidge was president and there was a reaction. It wasn't long after the Red Scare. It was a time when America was changing—jazz music was king, women's suffrage was brand-new, teen smoking was widespread, dancing—all these changes were coming, America was urbanizing. Before, we'd been a rural people. . . . With that reaction [to change] came the rise of fundamentalism and religion, which was a reaction to modernism and liberalism within the church.

The trial was in Dayton, Tennessee, a small town in Republican East Tennessee in the rising hill country, a new town that hadn't been around [long]. It was founded about twenty-five years earlier when the . . . railroads [pushed] through the Tennessee Valley. . . . [There were new] coal mines and . . . a blast furnace. [The valley was open] to strawberry production because they now had trains that could carry strawberries up north without spoiling. And there was an influx of Scottish immigrants to work in the mills there.

But Dayton wasn't your classic Old South; it was New South caught up in the turmoil of changing times. By 1925, after a boom at the turn of the century when it was founded, it was caught in an economic recession. The big blast furnace had closed down. The population had declined by half. It was a town in economic turmoil.

It was known as the "Monkey Trial" because what was being challenged was the idea . . . "Did humans evolve from monkeys?" [Tennessee had been the first state to pass an antievolution law four months before, in March 1925.] There were wonderful cartoons during the trial, [in which] when the verdict was announced and Scopes was convicted, you see all these monkeys in a tree jumping up and down, saying, "Hooray, we're not related to William Jennings Bryan."

John Scopes was a new teacher in Dayton, twenty-four years old. . . George Rappleyea, who invented the trial, . . . was the local manager of a coal mine who'd [hailed] from New York City and had read [in the *Chattanooga Times*] the offer by the American Civil Liberties Union (ACLU) to challenge the new Tennessee antievolution law.

[THE ACLU WAS] founded [as the National Civil Liberties Bureau in 1917] when they focused on defending antiwar activists. When they decided to broaden out and defend free speech more generally, they took the name the American Civil Liberties Union. By 1925 their commitment was in defense of the First Amendment, especially free speech and the right to assemble. That brought them head-on into opposition to something like an antievolution law, which was limiting academic freedom and free speech by teachers.

The ACLU had been dogging the efforts [in Tennessee and other states] to pass laws against the teaching of human evolution in public schools. That had been William Jennings Bryan's crusade. He'd come close in several states. Wherever he was trying, the ACLU would appear to try to stop the legislation. The first success after a two-year-long crusade came in Tennessee.

Rappleyea, this Yankee who was down there running the coal mines in . . . Republican East Tennessee, was opposed to the law. He saw this offer in the local paper for the ACLU to represent any local teacher who was willing to challenge the law. He thought that was a great opportunity to strike at it. So he tried to think, "How can I get the town to go along with me?" How he could was the idea of publicity, bringing publicity to the town. Remember, the town was in economic decline and it was in Republican East Tennessee. It was not Bryan country. The county where Dayton is had never voted for [the Democrat] William Jennings Bryan in any of his three campaigns for president. It had always gone for the Republicans, McKinley or Taft.

Rappleyea went to see the superintendent of the public schools and the president of the school board. He convinced them that this would be a great way to put Dayton on the map, to bring this trial down because this would certainly be a media sensation. The ACLU was willing to defend any teacher willing to challenge [the law] so they tried to figure out what teacher could they get. The biology teacher was also the school principal, and he had a family and . . . was a middle-aged man, and they thought, "Oh, well, the controversy just wouldn't be appropriate."

So they struck upon the idea of [drafting] John Scopes. Now the problem was [Scopes had] never taught biology, so he'd never violated the law. He was the general science teacher. He was also the football coach. But the idea was a test case, so it didn't matter that much. They sent a messenger out to get him . . . and brought him down to the local drugstore . . . where people hung out, which was owned by the president of the school board, Fred Robinson.

They . . . presented the option; remember, this is [Scopes's] boss asking. It wasn't [like] the scene from *Inherit the Wind* where a mob led by a fire-breathing fundamentalist minister dragged him out of his classroom. No, it was the summer; he was brought in from a tennis game. Here were his school superintendent and the president of the school board and George Rappleyea, the manager of the coal mine, plus a couple other figures—the city solicitor, Sue Hicks, and his brother Herbert Hicks. . . . They asked him, "Would you be willing to stand for a test case?" He was young. He had no particular plans to stay in town. He was up for an adventure.

Scopes had gone to college at the University of Kentucky. He was from Illinois. In fact, he was from the same town as William Jennings Bryan— Salem, Illinois. William Jennings Bryan had delivered his high school commencement address.

Scopes's father had been a labor organizer—an immigrant, a labor organizer, a radical, a socialist, an avowed atheist. He had been impressed when the president of the University of Kentucky had stood up to William Jennings Bryan and fought the passage of an antievolution law in Kentucky and won by one vote in the state legislature. So when the offer was made, "Will you stand for a test case?" [Scopes said yes.] Everybody knew he hadn't actually violated the law, but you [didn't] need to actually have . . . taught to bring a test case. They were originally envisioning what's known as a declaratory judgment action.

But Scopes said yes, and so they nominally arrested him. He never went to jail. The statute didn't call for a criminal penalty. It was a $100 fine if you were convicted. [Then Scopes] went to . . . play tennis. [The gathering] broke up. One of them called the ACLU, and the other ones at the meeting called the local newspapers—the Chattanooga, Nashville, and Knoxville newspapers. From the beginning their idea was publicity.

Lucille Milner was the secretary for the ACLU [in New York]. She worked for Roger Baldwin, the founder of the ACLU. It was her job to clip newspapers. . . . The ACLU hadn't reached much beyond New York. It was only about seven years old at the time. . . . She ran across the notice that Tennessee had passed the antievolution law and passed it on to Roger Baldwin. Immediately they knew they had another case.

Baldwin called together the ACLU board and drew in their consultants. Felix Frankfurter, the great Harvard Law School professor who went on to be a famous Supreme Court justice, was very active. He was consulted, [as were] a variety of different attorneys in New York: Sam Rosensohm, who was very active with the ACLU, and Arthur Garfield Hays, who ended up coming down to the Scopes trial.

When the great editor H. L. Mencken protested a censorship law in Boston by selling a banned book in Boston Common, Arthur Garfield Hays went with him, also peddling banned books in Boston. Hays went out to the coal mines to be . . . with the miners when they were in some bitter strikes [in Pennsylvania]. That was a great story. He was warned, "You can't go out there. . . . They'll tar and feather you, and they'll castrate you." His eyes got big and he said, "Well, that'll be interesting," and off he went. [During a] strike in Jersey City, . . . he went . . . there and climbed on top of a car and gave a speech. . . . So he was a man of action, he loved adventure. He didn't want to be bored. When you read his autobiography and various letters he wrote, the place he loved most was when he was at Dayton with Clarence Darrow.

CLARENCE DARROW—what a man! He was probably one of the greatest, if not the greatest, criminal defense lawyers in American history. He grew up in Ohio, . . . [lived in] Michigan, . . . then went to Chicago to be an attorney. He started off as a classic Democrat. In fact, he was nominated for Congress. He would have won, but he was too busy campaigning for the presidential ticket led by William Jennings Bryan. He lost [his nomination to Congress] by about a hundred votes.

But Darrow became increasingly concerned about government excesses. This was when the [1886] Haymarket Riot was put down and during the [1894] Pullman Strike. He defended [labor leader] Eugene V. Debs and became increasingly associated with defending labor at a time when labor was being sorely oppressed. He represented a series of great labor cases [including] the McNamara brothers and the bombing of the *Los Angeles Times* building. In that case there were questions about how Darrow handled it, . . . issues of perjury. For a while it dimmed his reputation, but he came back after that, mostly representing murder defendants because he was deeply opposed to capital punishment. . . . The Leopold-Loeb case . . . was his most famous until he handled the Scopes case.

The puzzling thing is that both Darrow and Bryan had two hats; they were famous for two reasons. As a defense lawyer, Clarence Darrow would hold the role today of an F. Lee Bailey. But he was also America's leading critic of revealed religion. In that sense, he would also hold, maybe, Carl Sagan's role.

Darrow wrote a book, and he [lectured] on the Chautauqua circuit at that time, which was before television. He was a very popular Chautauqua circuit speaker on the dangers of religious fundamentalism, the dangers of religious zealotry, the foolishness of aspects of the Bible. He would call Christianity a slave religion. By that sense, he meant it enslaved its followers, and that it would lead to war and destruction, conflict, exploitation. One of his biographers, Clarence Tierney, said, "He was the village atheist on the national scale."

William Jennings Bryan was also a mix. He had been nominated three times for president by the Democratic Party, the only person to be nominated three times and lose. He was a progressive and a populist. William Allen White, the famous [newspaper] editor from Kansas, said that "William Jennings Bryan was the closest thing to socialism the American mind could tolerate." He was the most radical person who ever came close to being president. He was a strong believer in controlling big business, nationalizing railroads, nationalizing industries, . . . breaking the gold standard, and helping the common people. That stayed with him. He remained a progressive throughout his life. He was a fierce opponent of Coolidge and Harding and the Republican administrations of the 1920s. He was a pacifist who campaigned against World War I, against militarism, and for disarmament.

Bryan was also a great orator. He was most famous because he could put these ideas into words that people would buy. I'd have to compare him with someone like Jesse Jackson today.

Bryan was also a fundamentalist. Back then, fundamentalism was a much broader term. It was more like saying you were a traditional, Bible-believing Christian as opposed to being a literalistic fundamentalist. He didn't believe in a six-day creation 10,000 years ago. He believed the Earth evolved over eons and eons of time. He wasn't, in that sense, a narrow fundamentalist, but a devout conservative Christian. He had held the number-two position in the Northern Presbyterian Church, the United Presbyterian Church.

He also wrote a weekly column that was published in most newspapers in the country called "Bryan's Bible Study." He wrote many books about religion. In that sense, trying to think of a person like that today, I might think of Charles Colson, who is an evangelical religious spokesman but not a minister; a lay spokesman who is widely known and has a regular radio show. Bryan combined two roles: a leader of the Democratic Party, committed Democrat, liberal politician, but allied with conservative forces due to his religious beliefs on some issues.

The Scopes trial lasted essentially a week, [starting on July 10, 1925]. . . . It was thought it was going to last a long time because Clarence Darrow was famous for using days to assemble a jury. He had a different strategy here that made it much shorter: Because it was a trial geared for the national media, he wanted to expose to the public that these jurors didn't know anything about evolution. The idea was to show the specter of having a trial where the merits of a scientific theory [are judged] by people who didn't know the scientific theory.

WHAT THEY WERE concerned about was the idea that species evolve from earlier species, and their main concern among this group was human evolution; that is, that humans are not separately created by God but evolved from, as they would say, lower types of animals. They . . . talked about apes and monkeys, that was the theory, but, ultimately, [it went] all the way back to one-celled organisms.

THIS WAS THE FIRST broadcast trial in American history. It was not viewed at the time as a serious trial. It was viewed as a media event, even by the judge and the participants. That's why the city held the event. Interest in the trial grew steadily in the two months before it was launched, especially after William Jennings Bryan and Clarence Darrow volunteered to participate. WGN, which is the radio voice of the *Chicago Tribune*—WGN stands for World's Greatest Newspaper, the nickname of the *Chicago Tribune*—. . . had arranged to broadcast the trial live. They hung special phone lines from Dayton up to Chicago to carry the radio broadcast; then they needed to put microphones up. They had never broadcast this sort of event before, and so they thought it would be better to have three microphones. In reality, it caused a cross-wave in the sound. But they had three large microphones and they wanted to put them in strategic locations, which meant they had to move the jury box. It was symbolic of the whole trial that they moved the jury box out of the center stage of the trial and put microphones in. . . . From those microphones, it was broadcast live nationwide via WGN. It was also broadcast out into auditoriums around town where an overflow crowd could listen.

The entire event was filmed on newsreel cameras. The cameras were left right in the courtroom. They built the first airplane airstrip in Dayton. They cleared a cornfield out near town, and every day planes would fly in and pick up the newsreel footage and fly it up to northern cities. It was shown at night in Cleveland, Detroit, and New York and then recopied and sent all over the country so the entire country could watch the trial. [So] not only was it broadcast live on the radio, but it was in the movie halls all over town that night or the next day. That shows the level of interest in this. . . . And these were new things. They'd never broadcast a trial; they'd never filmed a trial before.

MOST OF THE BATTLES were fought over legal issues, such as whether the judge would rule that a law was constitutional or whether the expert witnesses could testify. . . . The entire prosecution case was a half hour. They brought in a couple of school students to testify that Scopes had taught evolution. They established the case that he taught it and then they rested their case. Then . . . the defense . . . tried to bring in expert witnesses, great scientists from around the country, to explain what evolution was and to show why a law against it would be unjust and improper.

The jury only met for about twenty seconds. They had to get out of the courtroom. The courtroom was so packed that it . . . took them about fifteen minutes . . . to be led out through all these people. They never went to a jury room because that was all filled with press people working up their material. They just stopped in the hallway and agreed [to abide by] Clarence Darrow, who had asked them to convict Scopes because they wanted to appeal to a higher court. They all just acknowledged that they agreed right there in the hallway, and then they filed back in through the crowd and issued their verdict.

The law said that it was a crime for a public schoolteacher to teach the theory of human evolution in public schools. . . . That's why the defense tried to argue that the theory of evolution isn't in conflict with the biblical story of creation, because you could believe that God used evolution as his means of creation.

[The judge ruled] that evidence, which they wanted to get in, . . . was not relevant. The law was clear. The law said you couldn't teach human evolution. . . . There was uncontroverted testimony that Scopes had done it. The defense never put Scopes on the stand because he'd have to admit that he never taught evolution. They wanted to keep that out because they wanted a clean case. . . . Both sides wanted a clean case.

So there was a conviction. It was listed as a misdemeanor, and the potential penalty was from $100 to $500. The judge had told them that the jury could impose whatever amount of money they thought fit. If they were satisfied with a $100 fine, then they didn't need to come back with an amount, and he would impose the minimum sentence. It was the exact same fine that liquor convictions carried in the state—this was during Prohibition—so it was handled like a bootlegger case.

Bryan had said when he arrived in town that he was there not to try John Scopes but to defend the people's law. He was a majoritarian who believed in populism, and the people wanted this law. He was there to defend the law and, if Scopes was convicted, he would put up the money [for Scopes's fine]. In the end, . . . H. L. Mencken, who represented the *Baltimore Sun,* actually paid the $100.

Bryan was planning to give [his closing speech for the Scopes trial in] a nationwide series of speeches. . . . He [delivered] it twice in two other small towns in Tennessee, a week after the trial. The trial finally ended on a Tuesday. He gave the speech on Thursday and Friday, spent Saturday preparing the speech for publication as a booklet at a press down in Chattanooga, and then went back to Dayton, planning to leave the following day. He died [in his sleep while] taking a nap on Sunday afternoon.

[At his death, Bryan] was a national hero. He was carried [to Washington, D.C.] in a special train car for burial at Arlington National Cemetery, which many people thought was ironic, since he was a pacifist and opposed entry to World War I. It was like the train that carried Lincoln home—people just lined the train tracks by the hundreds of thousands to watch the train go by with the body of William Jennings Bryan. [It was] not the William Jennings Bryan of the Scopes trial; the William Jennings Bryan they remembered was the great commoner who had run three times for president, their spokesman. At every town [in which the train] stopped, people would file by the casket. . . . Then he lay in state in Washington, D.C. Six senators were his pallbearers, and other governors and leaders served as honorary pallbearers. He was carried down to Arlington National Cemetery, where he was buried under a speaker's podium. It's the stump of an oak tree, where an orator would stand.

THE SCOPES CONVICTION was appealed [to] the Tennessee Supreme Court, which struck it down . . . on a technicality: that the judge had imposed the sentence rather than the jury. . . . The theory that everyone said and no one denies, was that it was just a subterfuge on the part of the court to get rid of this silly case. They wrote a decision saying, "We're overturning the conviction, overturning the $100 fine, but we're upholding the law as a valid judgment of the people," directing the prosecutors not to reindict Scopes. "Never," they said, "never bring another case under this statute. Save the peace. To preserve the peace and dignity of Tennessee, don't ever prosecute this law again."

After [the trial] was over, Scopes got a scholarship to Chicago, collected by the ACLU. He went to the University of Chicago, became a petroleum engineer, . . . and looked for oil in Venezuela. He then ran an oil refinery in Shreveport, Louisiana, where he lived until he died [in] about 1970.

[In Dayton] they've taken the basement and first floor of the courthouse . . . and turned it into a museum. They [conducted] this trial for publicity, and it was a success. Not only did it make them famous then, but it's the only reason they're famous now. The town attracts people because of its Scopes connection. This trial has resonated through America for seventy-five years. And now they have a museum, they have a festival every year, and [at William Jennings Bryan's request, Bryan College, a school to teach truth from a biblical perspective].

Al Smith and the 1928 Election

by

ROBERT A. SLAYTON

Alfred E. Smith, the Democratic candidate for president in 1928, worked as a reform-minded public servant in his beloved New York for most of his life. The son of immigrants, he became a county sheriff, spent twelve years in the state assembly, was president of New York City's board of aldermen, and served four terms as governor of New York. After losing the 1928 presidential election to Herbert Hoover, he served as president of the Empire State Building. On March 16, 2001, Robert A. Slayton appeared on Booknotes *to discuss* Empire Statesman: The Rise and Redemption of Al Smith, *published that year by The Free Press. Mr. Slayton is a professor of history at Chapman University.*

A L SMITH was a great American who is not that well-known anymore; perhaps he should be. Al Smith was a four-term governor of New York. He, in New York State, created the modern system the state is governed by. He was the 1928 candidate for president on the Democratic Party ticket, the first Roman Catholic to ever run for president. And most important of all, he was a spokesman for democracy and pluralism in a very tough time called the '20s.

Smith was the great spokesperson for the immigrants, for tenement dwellers. . . . He considered himself to be Irish, but technically speaking, on his father's side, the grandparents were German and Italian. He was considered, prior to John Kennedy, the best-known and most important Irish politician in the U.S. on a national level. . . . He summed up the changes going on in America and he became a lightning rod.

He grew up on the East Side, very close to the Brooklyn Bridge. He didn't know his father all that well. His father died when he was young. . . . His mother raised him. She was a quiet, strong Irish woman. She, more than anybody, was the person who gave him his sense of integrity and honor.

He had to drop out of school in seventh grade. He did not have a grade school diploma. . . . He entered the workforce. That gave him [work] experience, [and] it also became part of the story of Al Smith, the self-made person.

He was about five-eight or five-nine. He had a clear face. He had a beak of a nose. If there was one thing that got your attention when you met Al Smith, it was his voice. It was deep, it was gravelly, and he had a terrible New York accent. . . . He had the real McCoy when it came to accents.

He was a fabulous speaker, but not an eloquent one. He could pull an audience in. I interviewed people who saw him speak and they said, "My God, the guy would be talking on the New York state budget and he'd have us enthralled, on the edge of our seat."

IN 1911, IN MARCH, a fire broke out on the eighth, ninth, and tenth floors. . . . of the Asche Building near Washington Square in New York, . . . where there was a sweatshop, the Triangle Shirtwaist factory; it made ladies' garments. [There were] long tables and every couple of feet was a station where the women worked. There was a sewing machine and below it was a box holding lint, and there was oil dripping into it. When the fire broke out, it was absolutely catastrophic. A hundred and forty-six people perished in the fire. These women were standing there on the top floor with their hair burning, making the horrible choice of whether to jump to their death or get burned alive.

Al Smith led the investigation, along with [State senator] Robert Wagner Sr., into the Triangle Shirtwaist fire. As a result of the work they did and the legislation they introduced into the New York State Legislature . . . the way Americans lived all across the country [changed]. They started to introduce the modern fire code. When you go into a movie theater, which has to be dark by the very nature of it, and you see that lit exit sign, that was Al Smith and Bob Wagner's work. When you look at a building, there's always a fire door that exits out. One of the things they found in Triangle was that the door pulled in, and it had a doorknob. The problem with that is if you've got a lot of people burning and terrified, you might not be able to pull it in. . . . So now all fire doors have to go to the outside, and they have what's called a panic bar. . . . That was from Al Smith.

IN 1924, RUNNING for the governorship once again, he was in Buffalo, New York, [making a] speech about a Ku Klux Klan christening. The image was in many ways a horrific one. There was a hooded Klansman holding an infant to his breast while a minister performed the rituals. Smith said, "This is horrible. This is taking an infant and breathing into her the spirit of hate and war." He referred to it as blasphemy. He then gave the line that I think is the best statement of his values, of his contribution to America. . . . He said, "The Catholics of the country can stand it; the Jews can stand it; our citizens born under foreign skies can stand it; the Negro can stand it; but the United States of America can't stand it." He really rose above just being another politician.

IN 1924 HE ALMOST got [the presidential nomination]; 1924 was a very unique, strange moment in American politics. In the 1920s ours was a nation split by very deep social cleavages. The 1920s was the decade when the Klan was at its height. It was not a southern institution, as it would be later during the civil rights movement. We had the Sacco and Vanzetti trial [where two Italian anarchists were found guilty of murder and executed]. We had the Scopes trial. In 1924 the Democrats showed up at Madison Square Garden in New York and these two wings of the Democratic Party—the rural wing coming out of the days of William Jennings Bryan, represented that year by a man named William Gibbs McAdoo and the new immigrant urban wing led by Al Smith—just clashed head-on. The convention deadlocked just horribly. It went 103 ballots; mercifully, a record that will last, we hope, for all time. Nobody has even come close to that. They eventually, just for the sake of getting out of there, named a dark horse candidate, John W. Davis, a Wall Street lawyer.

[IN 1928 SMITH ran as the Democratic candidate] against Herbert Hoover. He wanted to run a traditional presidential campaign, and instead he ran into one of the great buzz saws in American presidential history; 1928 was a very hate-filled campaign. Americans were told and they believed by the millions, that if a Roman Catholic was elected, immediately all Protestant marriages would be annulled; the children would become illegitimate on the spot, and the pope was going to come over [to America]. They actually showed pictures of the building of the Holland Tunnel, and it had the caption underneath saying, "This is the tunnel they're building right now in secret between Rome and Washington to bring the pope over for Al Smith."

In Daytona Beach, Florida, the school board handed out a card, officially, to every schoolkid that they had to take home to their parents that said, "If Al Smith is elected president, you will not be able to have or read a Bible." This was going on, and it was not just an attack on Al Smith; it was not just an attack on Roman Catholics; it was an attack on Al's people, [the immigrants]. They would continually talk about the "scum from Europe living in the cities," and eventually he had to deal with it. He honestly didn't want to, but he had to. This was his life; this was what he represented; these were his people.

Al Smith went into Oklahoma to deliver a traditional address, and as he came over the border, there were burning crosses around his train. He tried to laugh it off, but his heart was bleeding. He turned to [his close adviser] Joseph Proskauer, who was Jewish, and said, "Hey, Joe, how'd they know you were on this train?" He tried to laugh it off, but he was really serious inside. He went in that morning and dictated an entirely new speech. He stood up there and said he knew all about this talk. He knew all about what was going on, and, frankly, he knew what it was about. There was a long pause—he was a very skilled orator—"It's nothing more or less than my religion." A hush came over everything.

People . . . in the Smith family talked about their parents telling them about listening to this speech. They thought they were going to hear a shot ring out. They thought explosions were going to go off, that the guy wasn't going to make it out of there alive. This was in the middle of fundamentalist country. Just prior to Smith's arriving in Oklahoma City, the minister of the largest congregation in the city had said, and I'm quoting, "If you vote for Al Smith, you're voting against Christ, and you'll all be damned." And Al Smith walked into this kind of arena and said, "I know it's about my religion."

He then gave this talk where he said, "You can't do this in America. This is America, and we have certain values, and you just can't do this here. This is not right. This is not what it's supposed to be about." He said, "Look, I'm prepared to win or lose in November, and that's fine. If you want to vote against me because you don't agree with my positions, so be it, but not over this, because this isn't America; this isn't what we stand for.". . . This was where his destiny caught up with him. He had been advocating on behalf of these people ever since his early days in the New York State Assembly, and now it was creating this crisis, and he stood up for what he believed. It was a great moment.

In 1928 Al lost and lost unfairly and horribly. He was deeply hurt. No politician ever wants to lose an election; that's a given. But Al not only lost it, he lost over issues that he didn't think were fair, because he was a Catholic, because he was a New Yorker. If he had lost it because of prosperity, because Americans had voted for a different idea on tax policy, so be it. It wouldn't be pleasant, but it would be livable. But they were making snide remarks about his wife. They were getting up and saying, "Can you imagine somebody looking like that as First Lady?" That was hard. That was really tough.

SMITH HAD A UNIQUE trio of very, very close advisers. One was a man named Joseph Proskauer who was an eminent judge and a funny fellow.

Proskauer was a very gruff man. Lawyers hated going before him on the bench because if you weren't completely up to speed, if you weren't doing brilliantly, he would interrupt you and literally take over your case. He fell in love with Al Smith and vice versa. A strange, gruff man, and yet the bond was very deep. Second was Belle Moskowitz, who was his campaign manager. Proskauer was his éminence grise, his thinking man. Moskowitz ran everything on the day-to-day level. The third was Robert Moses, who went on to become [New York City's famous] parks commissioner and power broker. . . . Moses was a nasty man at times, to put it very mildly. And all his life, Smith's affection for Moses was very deep. . . . Robert Moses worked for every governor of New York from Al Smith through Nelson Rockefeller and he called all of them by name or by "Mister," except for one, and that was Governor Smith. That was the only individual he would grant that title to.

[All three of Al's top advisers were Jewish.] What it said about Al Smith was two things: One is his slogan, "Let's look at the record." He was picking people, as well as fashioning his own life, on the quality of their work. . . . The other thing that it said about Al Smith was that he was a champion, to use a modern-day term, of pluralism.

HE WANTED [the nomination again] in 1932. He really, really wanted it. He wanted it for very emotional and personal reasons. He wanted to end the sadness. He wanted to finally go back to the America that was good and just and that would vote for him and would reject the bigots. . . . Keep in mind, too, in '32, it was pretty clear it was going to be a Democratic year—it was the height of the Depression. And the party said, "God, the last thing we want to get into is another fight like we had in 1928."

He won a couple of states. He was a player at the convention. That's about it. Here comes Franklin Roosevelt, a fresh face, a young face, a fabulous politician in his own right. He just ran right over Al.

Here was this guy who he honestly felt affection for, but he didn't respect, and that guy not only got the presidency, but within one hundred days, he was the great national hero. He became a symbol, I believe, to Al Smith of the shallowness of the American people, a shallowness that had hurt him so badly in '28 and had now elected this fop, this dilettante, which is how he perceived FDR. . . . For a while, Smith turned horribly on FDR.

In 1935 a group of very rich Republicans formed a group called the American Liberty League to fight the New Deal. It was mostly about keeping their perks in place. They said they were on behalf of all Americans, but they were on behalf of rich people. It was led by and financed by the Du Pont family. Jim Farley, who was Roosevelt's campaign manager, said it was a classic Du Pont product, a lot like cellophane in that it was totally transparent. Here was

Al Smith, who wound up giving the great speech for them—this is early in '36—where he just about called the New Deal a Communist plot.

From the standpoint of drama, you have an amazing moment here. A guy like Al Smith, who grew up on streets where the Democratic Party wasn't a political organization, as most of us think of it today, it was a social club. It was an act of faith. You don't turn on your party when they're enjoying triumph like that. That's like turning on your church. Why did he do this? I honestly believe it was because, by then, he wasn't seeing Franklin Roosevelt, the man; he was seeing Franklin Roosevelt, the symbol of the shallowness of the American people. He just flew into a rage, and it was a blind rage.

There was only one person who really could get Al Smith and Franklin Roosevelt back together, and that was Adolf Hitler; both of these two men basically stood for the same sense of human decency, and both instinctively and initially looked across the ocean and said, "That's wrong. That's just wrong."

AL SMITH'S GREATEST contribution . . . was that in this harsh decade of the 1920s, there was nobody at that high a political pulpit who stood up and said, "These newcomers, these people, they're Americans. We have to accept them as Americans and that we have to continue to do that with newcomers, with new kinds of people." That was his greatest contribution, not whether he won or lost.

Edward L. Bernays and the
Birth of Public Relations

by

LARRY TYE

*Public relations, more commonly known by its acronym PR or even "spin,"
is the business of creating public understanding of or goodwill toward a
person, firm, or institution. Public relations has become a prominent feature of our modern media landscape. Edward L. Bernays, generally credited as the "father" of public relations, was born in Vienna, Austria, in 1891
and soon brought to the United States by his immigrant parents. As a young
man, he founded the country's first public relations firm, where he continued to counsel clients even beyond his hundredth birthday.* Boston Globe
reporter Larry Tye appeared on Booknotes *on August 30, 1998, to discuss*
The Father of Spin: Edward L. Bernays and the Birth of Public Relations, *published by Crown in 1998.*

Edward L. Bernays was around for most of the twentieth century. He
had a big influence on what happened starting in the 1920s and until he died
in 1995. In the 1920s, Bernays led the campaign to get American women
smoking. In the 1950s, he led the campaign that overthrew the leftist government of Guatemala. He worked for General Electric and did lots of things,
the most notable of which was the fiftieth anniversary of the invention of the
electric lightbulb. He helped publicize Thomas Edison and the whole GE
operation.

Whether he's the father of spin depends how we define "father." If it's
defined as the "first," it's clear that there were somewhere between six and
twelve people who were out there before he was, essentially doing the things

that constituted public relations. If "father" is defined as somebody who was the spiritual, emotional, and scientific originator of a lot of the things we think of today as public relations, then Bernays was the one. He was also best at crafting his own legacy. He continually insisted with the press that he was the father of public relations and if you repeat things often enough, they take on a certain truth.

Eddie Bernays was born in Vienna. He came over on the boat when he was one. He spent the next sixty-something years in New York and retired in Cambridge. He was a graduate in agriculture from Cornell. . . . His parents basically pushed him into agriculture. They came over as immigrants and believed the surest way of ensuring your family's future was studying agriculture. . . . [But] after spending all that time in the fields with cows and manure, he decided he never wanted to see another farm in his life. He came out with what he felt was a much more important lesson: that people's behavior could be dramatically influenced. He was somebody with a certain kind of charisma who wanted to get into the field of dealing with the public.

SIGMUND FREUD WAS Eddie Bernays's uncle. He told him exactly how to understand human psychology and how to use it. While Freud was using psychology to try to free people from their emotional bonds, his nephew took a different lesson from it. He used psychology and an understanding of why people behaved the way they do to help tie them to his clients, be they companies or politicians. He was a brilliant student of his uncle's but did things with his psychology that might have made his uncle turn over in his grave.

EDDIE'S WIFE, DORIS, was the first American woman to have a passport issued in her maiden name. She went for most of her life by Doris Fleischman and never took his name. That created wonderful waves in the feminist movement in America. It also did wonderful things for him in attracting attention to them, and that was what he tried to do through much of his life.

His wife was an intriguing character. If "mother" means not only the spiritual leader but also means the first, she was probably the mother of PR, even if he wasn't the father. He described their relationship over the years as being full and equal partners at home and at work. He was right that she was a partner in business. She was wonderful at advising him. She was a better writer than he. She would put a stop to some of his more outlandish schemes before he embarrassed himself. . . . Their business was always called Edward L. Bernays, Public Relations; she was never given credit, she was never given a name on their shingle. . . . While she was his partner at work, at home she was doing everything. She was taking care of the household, managing the staff and raising their two daughters, Doris and Ann. She was expected to be a partner at work when he wasn't one at home.

Bernays didn't believe in God, but more importantly, as part of his whole worldview, he saw the world as something he could mold. He was the PR man who could come in and tell us how to look at things, how to behave, how to believe. The idea of religion, that things were already set in some sort of divine order, was contrary to everything he believed. So he never had any use for religion and disparaged it. When his daughter asked him at about age five, "What am I?" he said, "You're nothing. You are what you want to be."

HIS MOST DRAMATIC campaign, selling cigarettes, was in 1929. American Tobacco, which was the biggest tobacco company, had managed to crack the male market for their products, particularly for Lucky Strikes, their number one seller. But they couldn't reach women. They went to Eddie Bernays, who went to see a disciple of his uncle's, Dr. A. A. Brill, and said, "What is it that cigarettes represent symbolically to women? Why aren't they smoking cigarettes?" Brill said, "It's very simple. Cigarettes are a male-imposed taboo. Men have convinced women that it's unladylike to smoke cigarettes."

Bernays thought that was brilliant. He went out and arranged for a dozen debutantes on Easter Sunday 1929 to march down Fifth Avenue holding what he called their "torches of freedom.". . . Bernays had his secretary, Bertha Hunt, send a telegram to these women, asking if they would join in doing something that would strike a blow for women's freedom. He found them by going to the editor of *Vogue* magazine, where he got a list of these wonderful debutantes. She simply took her telegram, sent it out to all these women, and got enough of them to agree to participate that he knew he had an event. They stage-managed for these women exactly what they ought to do, how to come down the church steps, just what to do in lighting up the cigarettes. And he warned the press beforehand to what was going on. So everything was perfectly scripted, except for the fact that nobody knew who the scriptwriter was.

The newspapers couldn't resist. The next day, just about every newspaper in America and across the world had a picture of these very elegant debutantes marching down Fifth Avenue on Easter Sunday with a cigarette dangling from their hands or their mouths. They called it the "Torches of Freedom Parade."

That helped launch an entire movement of women in the '20s and '30s seeing cigarettes as a sign of liberation; instead of being something that was seen as a taboo for women, they became a positive social value. Women, in large numbers, followed men into smoking.

During the years in the 1920s and '30s, when he was helping sell American women on smoking cigarettes, there were scores of inconsistencies that came up. . . . At the same time he was trying to pitch cigarettes to women, he was telling his young daughters at home any time they found their mother's cigarettes to break them in half and flush them down the toilet.

He had evidence then, the earliest evidence, of some of the potential health threats of cigarettes, and he helped his tobacco company client either rebut those or, when they could, cover them up. And yet, sixty years later, he was working with the American Cancer Society, helping them try to wean women from these habits that they had formed. He was telling the world, when they asked, that he had never understood the health risk of cigarettes when, in fact, he had evidence as early as the 1930s. There were incredible inconsistencies throughout most of his campaigns, and we can see it in the cigarette campaigns.

BERNAYS WORKED FOR more than thity years for Procter & Gamble, and he decided, again in the 1930s, that you had to take a symbolic and psychological approach in trying to sell a product. They were trying to sell Ivory Soap, and what he did was launch a campaign based on soap sculpting. . . . Bernays decided that little kids were never going to like the idea of cleaning up with soap, but he also understood that you could sell soap by convincing kids that they had to talk their mother into buying a particular brand when they were at the market with her.

By the end, he got millions of young kids all across the country competing by sculpting the only bar of soap that was acceptable in the contest, Ivory, into everything from the Statue of Liberty to Calvin Coolidge. The kids became wed to the contest, they became wed to Ivory Soap and Bernays got large retainers for thirty years from Procter & Gamble.

Calvin Coolidge had inherited an image problem while in the office of the presidency. Teddy Roosevelt's daughter had coined a phrase about Calvin Coolidge that stuck in the American public's mind and the press's mind, that he had a personality so sour that he was weaned on a pickle.

Bernays tried to sweeten things up. He arranged for a trainload of starlets, along with the famous entertainer Al Jolson, to come from Broadway in New York to Union Station in Washington. They were picked up by Cadillacs and brought to the White House, where they spent the morning eating breakfast with the president and singing and dancing with him. One of my favorite newspaper headlines ever was in the *New York Times* the next [day] . . . "President Almost Smiles." Eddie Bernays had managed to lighten up this seemingly dark president and several months later, he was reelected. Clearly, Bernays doesn't deserve all the credit, but he helped people see this guy as a human being for the first time. Coolidge thought he helped him a lot. The White House paid [Bernays's fees].

BERNAYS, FOR THE FIRST time in American history, broke down voters by everything from their ideology to their religion to their race. He decided that if you broke the electorate down in these ways, you could fashion various kinds of appeals to various voters. This was in the days before scientific polling, but he was essentially structuring a campaign in the same way we do today; that you have all these interest groups out there, and you fashion a pitch that appeals to each interest group.

Bernays did it for William O'Dwyer [mayor of New York in 1940] and for other candidates. He helped father the whole notion of [what we call] "spinning" today—political spinning of polling and of scientific research. Bernays always believed that behind every campaign, critical for the PR man, was an understanding of psychology, sociology, and history. This was what he called the science of PR. He wanted to combine that science with an art form of brilliant stunts. Together, he felt, you had a new profession of public relations.

Bernays understood the symbolic power of words; he understood that you couldn't pick words out of the air. You had to test their impact. He would often go to disciples of his uncle and ask them to help him understand the symbolic value of different approaches he was trying to use in campaigns, including the symbolic value of words. . . . [Bernays created] a list of words [for use] in campaign brochures for various clients. . . . Each of those words was not only powerful but was an action-oriented word. He believed that words ought to convey action in a way that every writer understands today, that you want things to be in an active tense and you want real power behind the words.

THE UNITED FRUIT COMPANY, based in Boston, was the biggest fruit company in America. It had what it called "banana republics" across Latin America, which meant it had these countries where it was the biggest employer, the biggest landowner, and the countries were always compliant. The whole republic seemed devoted to their crop of bananas and their other crops. In the 1950s in Guatemala, they ran into a problem. A leftist government was elected that started changing things. It encouraged workers to push for higher wages. It expropriated some of United Fruit's land. The company was very worried about what would happen there and the precedent this could set in the rest of Latin America.

They brought in their PR guy, Eddie Bernays. He understood that you couldn't just deal with Guatemala in a vacuum, you had to work through the press and the public in making Guatemala symbolic of something bigger. And the bigger thing at the time that was sitting there staring him right in the face was the cold war. Guatemala suddenly became defined for the press, through Bernays, as a little country one hundred or so miles from our southernmost point that was a bastion of Soviet influence which might let the Russians gain a foothold in our continent. This was scary to the American public and scary to the American government. The U.S. government ended up working with United Fruit in orchestrating a campaign to overthrow the Guatemalan leftist government. Done incredibly efficiently, it set some dangerous precedents but changed things in Guatemala.

The Middle American Information Bureau was a . . . front group, one of many that Bernays set up through his career, [designed] to get out supposedly neutral information on what was going on in Latin America generally and specifically on Guatemala. In fact, it was Eddie Bernays and the staffers he had hired [who were] putting out the propaganda. If a client was willing to pay enough money, [Bernays tried to create a front group] and he had over four hundred clients over the years.

WALTER LIPPMANN WAS one of a series of philosophers, starting with some people in France, who understood and were trying to come up with theories to explain how you controlled the masses of the public, how you generated some social cohesion. It was a time when the world was worried about communism and other forces that seemed to be taking the masses and steering them in directions that seemed to present a social threat to the established order in America. Lippmann and others were trying to tell the public and, more importantly, tell our leaders, that there were ways of uniting people behind the goals they thought were socially useful and important. There were ways of using symbols, whether it was the printed word or the new communication media, the motion picture, making them capture certain symbolic values, certain social goals you thought were good.

Bernays was intrigued by symbolism. He was intrigued by it at one level with his uncle, Sigmund Freud, and at the sociology level with Walter Lippmann. Lippmann was somebody he never credited much but who helped him form his whole idea on how public relations could perform this role of social cohesion.

He died of old age. Things just gave out at the end. At 103, he died quite peacefully. . . . A number of people claim to have been with him at the very end, . . . trying to sort out who was actually there was unclear, but he had family very close around him at the end and a couple friends.

HE LEFT BEHIND an incredible written legacy. He wrote fifteen books and scores of articles. His autobiography was more than five hundred pages. It recounted, in excruciating detail, every significant and insignificant event in his eighty-year career. Reporters were so used to calling Bernays the father of

PR, and he outlived all of his would-be competitors to the throne. When he died, the *New York Times* and every other major newspaper in America, in his obit, declared him the father of PR. He would have loved that because it was a title that he tried to win for 103 years.

Charles Lindbergh's Reluctant Public Life

by

A. SCOTT BERG

Charles Augustus Lindbergh was born on February 4, 1902, in Detroit, Michigan, the son of a Minnesota congressman. His overnight flight from Roosevelt Field in Long Island, New York, to Paris on May 20–21, 1927, in his single-engine airplane, The Spirit of St. Louis, *was the first solo nonstop flight across the Atlantic. Lindbergh was immediately the most famous man in the world. He met Anne Morrow, the daughter of the U.S. ambassador to Mexico, on his goodwill tour and they married in 1929. Although they were extremely private people, the Lindberghs were unable to escape public attention and even notoriety. Their first son, also named Charles Augustus, was kidnapped from their home in New Jersey in 1932 and later found dead. Press coverage of the kidnapping and subsequent trial was overwhelming. A. Scott Berg, a Los Angeles-based writer, joined us on* Booknotes *on November 20, 1998, to discuss these and other stories from his Pulitzer Prize–winning* Lindbergh, *published in 1998 by Putnam.*

CHARLES LINDBERGH is part of our national fabric. As Americans, we are almost born, genetically coded, to know something about Lindbergh. Even young people who don't remember him or know much about him do somehow know the name. They know he flew to Paris. They know a baby was kidnapped. It was remarkable for me to find that. The other thing I have always found is the polarity that exists about Lindbergh. There are people who still absolutely worship this man and there are people who utterly demonize him. They think he is one of the horrors of the twentieth century. What I have found is that he was neither a god nor the devil. He was a flawed, mortal human being.

CHARLES LINDBERGH was born in Detroit, Michigan. His mother's family were doctors in Detroit, but they moved as soon as he was born to the main residence, where the Lindbergh parents had been living, in Little Falls, Minnesota.

LINDBERGH NEVER REALLY lived anywhere. The Lindbergh family had residences here and there. . . . He had a very peripatetic childhood. He was a lifelong vagabond.

CHARLES LINDBERGH went to the University of Wisconsin at Madison in body, though not much in mind. He was kicked out of school his sophomore year. He was a terrible and totally distracted student. He loved his Excelsior motorcycle and rode that motorcycle from Minnesota to Madison, Wisconsin, when he started school. When he flunked out, he rode it to Nebraska, where he learned how to fly.

The great flight on the *Spirit of St. Louis* was from May 20 to 21, 1927. It was a big deal, make no mistake about it. This was one of the great milestones of the century, and with good reason. First of all, it was a great feat in transportation. It was a genuine act of heroism.

This twenty-five-year-old boy went up in a flying crate. Most people, especially if you haven't been to the Air and Space Museum to see it, don't realize this was a canvas plane. . . . It was put together with spit and glue and piano wire and canvas. Somehow, this flying gas tank, with one engine, was going to carry him across the ocean. It not only knitted the two continents together—Europe and North America—but it brought the whole world together geographically and in spirit because everybody shared in this feat.

There were no stops. That was part of the feat. There had been a $25,000 prize sitting on a table to be awarded to the first person or persons who could fly nonstop between Paris and New York in either direction. And, indeed, several people had tried and killed themselves in the attempt. Several people had already flown the Atlantic, but they had gone from Canada to Ireland. Nobody had done the great leap. Nobody had picked up the prize. Lindbergh raised the $10,580 he needed from a half dozen businessmen in St. Louis, hence the name *Spirit of St. Louis.* That gave him the plane and allowed him to make the flight.

The plane was built in San Diego by Ryan Aircraft, a small aircraft company. There were bigger airplane manufacturers at the time, but they wouldn't sell their plane to Lindbergh because . . . they figured this was a suicide mission. "We can't risk our company name on a twenty-five-year-old flyer who looks [like he's] nineteen." All he had ever done was fly the air mail between St. Louis and Chicago. "We can't chance that." So he had to look around for a small company that would make a plane affordable and available.

It was a single-engine plane and was literally nothing more than a gas tank. There is not a wasted ounce on that plane. It was simply gasoline. Lindbergh himself sat in a wicker patio chair because that was the lightest chair they could put in the plane that was comfortable enough to accommodate him for thirty-three and a half hours. He trimmed the borders off the maps he took just to save a half ounce here, a half ounce there. He took no food other than five sandwiches and a canteen of water.

His altitude varied. Sometimes he would go as high as 11,000 feet to get over clouds he had to surmount. Sometimes he would go as low as ten feet above the water. The biggest obstacle in the flight to Paris was sleep. He fought sleep for thirty-three hours. He flew so low that the spray of the Atlantic would come into the plane to wake him up.

There is another reason this feat is so remarkable and why it still lives with us: I honestly believe that, even more than the astronauts, Lindbergh was the first human being to leave the planet. Other people had gone flying, but they were either over land or, when they were over water, they were in communication with somebody. Or they were flying with somebody. Lindbergh was solo. He was completely alone in the universe.

He left in the early morning, local time, at 7:51 A.M., from Roosevelt Field, Long Island. . . . He landed at Le Bourget, France, at 10:24 P.M. the following night, Paris time.

Even before the plane came home, a wonderful man at the Smithsonian Institution in Washington named Paul Garber, who had a lifelong fascination with aviation, began trying to get hold of that airplane. He knew the significance of it. The Smithsonian got hold of it about five months after Lindbergh made his flight. Lindbergh came home, did a goodwill tour of the forty-eight states, went to Central America, Mexico, flew around the Gulf and Caribbean, and then ultimately gave the plane to the Smithsonian, where it is to this day.

CHARLES AND ANNE MORROW Lindbergh had an extremely private wedding. They did everything they could to run away from the press, and they pulled off a secret wedding. Even the people who were invited didn't know they were showing up for a wedding that day. Twenty-five of their closest family and friends showed up for what they thought was a lunch, and suddenly the minister walked in and performed a marriage ceremony.

She had been a writer at Smith College, and this was, too, another one of the great myths and ironies in the Lindbergh story, this marriage which had often been held up as a great storybook romance. It began that way, but was full of twists and turns. It became rather cold and dark in places.

Charles Lindbergh was an extremely domineering, dominating husband, but ironically it was he who brought the writer out in her and almost forced her to publish, forced her to become Anne Morrow Lindbergh. He almost turned her into a feminist. . . . She's obviously a wonderful writer and always had the talent, but I'm not sure she always had the temperament to put the material out there. He got that out of her.

THEIR FIRST SON was born in 1930. He was kidnapped March 1 of 1932 and was found about ten weeks later, half buried in a ditch about seventy-five feet off a back road in New Jersey, just a few miles from the Lindbergh house.

Coverage of the kidnapping was journalism, mass hysteria, at its all-time low. [There was a picture of the body, but] I didn't publish it. I had access to the picture, but I thought, "Boy, what's the point of a picture of a dead baby?" It wasn't widely published, but it was out there. It was a picture one could buy on the street, in fact. I think that was the ugliest moment of his life and he carried that with him all his life. Whenever anybody talked about the press, he would say, "Don't talk to me about the press. They took a picture of my dead baby."

Bruno Richard Hauptmann was the man apprehended, tried, and executed for kidnapping and killing the Lindbergh baby. He went to the electric chair in New Jersey proclaiming his innocence. He never admitted it; in fact, he left a magazine article to be published after his execution suggesting they had killed the wrong man. Indeed, this has kept speculation going. It has kept the debate going for sixty years now.

THE SUPERINTENDENT of the New Jersey state police was a man named Colonel Norman Schwarzkopf. The colonel is dead, but his son, the general, lives on. I went to talk to General Schwarzkopf, who was not yet born [at the time of] the crime, but I wanted to see what it was like growing up in the Schwarzkopf household. Did that Lindbergh crime loom? Did it linger in the house? And, indeed, it did. This was the great event in Colonel Schwarzkopf's life. This was the crime of the century, make no mistake about it, and this was the man who ultimately brought a man, quote, "to justice." A lot of people think they brought the wrong man. I don't think that. But Colonel Schwarzkopf was convinced this was the right man.

I THINK THE KILLING was accidental, but I think the kidnapping was premeditated. Kidnapping had become the crime du jour back in the '30s. This was the Depression. Kidnapping seemed like a neat, easy, clean crime. Parents let their children play on the street, play in sandboxes, play in the park. It was very easy to come along and snatch a child. Write a ransom note, there would be a quick exchange of cash, in most cases, and that was that.

I believe the baby was stolen by a man who climbed up a ladder that was leaned against their house outside of Hopewell, New Jersey, a dream house that Charles and Anne Morrow Lindbergh had just built for themselves. I think the kidnapper climbed up that ladder, snatched the baby out of his crib, and while coming down the ladder—it was a rather crude homemade ladder—put a lot of force on the first rung and the ladder split. I think the baby, which was in a burlap sack, was either swung against the stone wall of the house or dropped two stories below to the hard ground and was killed instantaneously.

I talked to the nurse, who was a Scotswoman who had barely been in this country when the Lindbergh baby was kidnapped. She fled the country to Scotland. Her life was, in many ways, ruined and certainly changed. She never fully recovered. The attitude I got from her was "if onlys." "If only we didn't do this that night. If only we didn't turn on the light. If only we didn't stay in the house that night and stayed instead with Mrs. Lindbergh's mother, where we had been staying." Sixty years later, to be carrying that around, is such a heavy burden.

I spoke to Anne Morrow Lindbergh about this. It did come up. She raised the subject at one point. This was the great tragedy of her life, obviously. She was still in her mid-twenties when this occurred. It was her first baby. I don't think one ever gets over that.

Anne Morrow Lindbergh had five children after the kidnapping, so she had six children altogether. Today, they are scattered. There are three sons, and there were two daughters. One daughter, also named Anne, died a few years ago of cancer. She was a rather gifted children's book writer. Another daughter, Reeve, is also a children's book writer, but has written a novel based, in large measure, on her parents called *The Names of the Mountains*. . . . The firstborn after the kidnapped child was Jon, who has spent his life mostly in, or under, water. The middle is Land, who is a rancher. And the youngest son, Scott, is an animal behaviorist, who lives now in Brazil. They are all great combinations of each of their parents. It's a very strong gene pool, and I saw all aspects of both parents feeding into all five children.

IN 1936 LINDBERGH went to Germany at the invitation of the American embassy in Berlin. The military attaché to Berlin, Major Truman Smith, was deeply concerned about the buildup of the German military, and he felt, as many did, that Germany was building up this huge air force, this Luftwaffe. But nobody knew how big or how powerful it was. Major Smith had a great idea. He thought, "I'll bet if we could bring Charles Lindbergh over here, the Germans would be so proud of what they had, they'd show off all their stuff." And, indeed, they did. So Lindbergh came over and paid six visits and got to visit just about every place he wanted to see.

Metaphorically speaking, in October of 1938, [Hitler's number two man and air minister] Hermann Göring hung a medal around his neck. There was a party at the German embassy. It was a stag night. The party was given by the American ambassador. The last guest to arrive was Göring. He walked right up to Lindbergh, talking in German with somebody translating along the way. A man opened a box that had the Service Cross of the German Eagle inside. It was presented on behalf of Hitler himself. Lindbergh accepted it and later went home that night—they were staying in Berlin. He showed it to his wife and she took one look at it and said, "the albatross." She knew there was something that was going to plague her husband for the rest of his life about that medal. And, indeed, it did.

He insisted it didn't become a plague. He said he never thought twice about it. But the truth of the matter was that Lindbergh came back to America shortly thereafter, in early 1939, to start speaking out against American intervention into a war he felt was about to break out, what became the America First movement. He gave about fifteen speeches on behalf of America First, a much misunderstood movement.

To my amazement, the roots of America First were on the Yale campus in New Haven. About a half dozen students got together, not to protest the war but to say what Lindbergh believed, that "this is a European war going on and the best thing America can do is stay out of it. Let them duke it out, and let us defend America first." Lindbergh believed the most important thing America could do at that time was build up an armed forces, especially an air force. He felt we had a very incomplete air force in 1939 and 1940. Indeed, the U.S. government was only just starting to wake up, largely because of Lindbergh's call to arms.

Almost his last America First speech [was] given in Des Moines, Iowa, in September of 1941 when he said, ["I'm not attacking either the Jewish or the British people. Both races I admire."] I think Charles Lindbergh just hanged himself with that speech, which was three months before Pearl Harbor. The great debate of American intervention, one of the great debates in American history, was going on. Lindbergh had been winning that debate against Franklin Roosevelt. Lindbergh was trying to keep America out of the war but was beginning to lose ground and popularity. He felt he had to drop a bomb to wake everybody up, and that was what he dropped in September of 1941: naming these groups who wanted to get in, talking about these races—the Jewish race and the British race.

He had no idea what the reaction was until he arrived in Massachusetts, where there was practically a lynching mob. Even people who had supported America First suddenly distanced themselves from Charles Lindbergh. It was not only because there was something deeply anti-Semitic about those comments, but because there was a genuine segregation in his mind of two different Americas. "'There's my America, and there's the Jewish America." This was largely an anti-Semitic nation, but what did him in was that his speech was un-American. It violated the melting pot theory—E pluribus unum.

I think he was an unconscious, genteel anti-Semite. I truly believe that Lindbergh believed he was not anti-Semitic. He believed in that speech. He thought that he was expressing great tolerance toward the Jews. But in talking about them as a separate class, he was revealing a kind of segregation, separate but equal.

Franklin Roosevelt would not let him go on active duty [during the war]. There was such enmity between Lindbergh and Roosevelt as a result of this great debate, this America First debate, that when Pearl Harbor was bombed and Lindbergh tried to volunteer, Roosevelt said, "There's no way Lindbergh can serve."

Lindbergh found a way to serve without uniform. He became a technical representative for United Aircraft and went over to the South Pacific and flew on fifty bombing missions without a uniform. He was somehow strafing Japanese targets and actually downed a Japanese Zero himself. He faced death several times.

Right after World War II, literally a week after V-E Day, the Truman administration . . . embraced Lindbergh and began to bring him back. Franklin Roosevelt, Lindbergh's great enemy, had died. Eisenhower made him a general, in fact. Lindbergh spent much of [the rest of] his life traveling around the world on U.S. government missions. He was on the Air Force Academy's site committee and on antiballistic missile committees. He did all sorts of work for the government.

[AT THE AGE OF seventy-two] Lindbergh was suddenly given a two-week death sentence from a doctor while he was in New York City. He had had cancer a little earlier, but they thought he had licked it.

[Against his doctor's orders] he spent the last ten days of his life in Hawaii. He planned his dying and his death with the same precision he planned his trip to Paris. It was just another flight for Lindbergh, complete with checklists. He wanted his three sons there digging a grave, which was in a place he had selected, all according to his design. He even planned the drainage in the grave and what stones were to be used to line it. Literally, the minute that grave was finished, that night, Lindbergh died.

There was a whole plan on what the family was supposed to do for the next few hours, how to get his corpse into the ground. They did it with absolute precision. At first, it made Anne a little crazy. She wanted to have a few hours—or moments, even—just to be alone and mourn, but she followed the checklist.

She realized why as they were driving off from their small service in a tiny church outside of [the town of] Hana and the first news trucks were driving in. Lindbergh knew, as he had been chased all his life by the press, he would be chased the moment he died and that his family would have about a two-hour window. This was Lindbergh's final embrace of his family, saying, "You're going to have to do this quickly so you can have a private moment." And that's just the way it happened.

The Roosevelt Dynasty

by

PETER COLLIER

Theodore Roosevelt served as president of the United States from 1901 to 1908. He was an enormously popular and visible American before, during, and after his time in office. His younger relative, Franklin Delano Roosevelt, became president in 1933 and remained in office until his death in 1945, a longer tenure than any other president. The close, often battling, Roosevelt clan was one of the most powerful American families of the first half of the twentieth century. FDR married his fifth cousin, Eleanor, in 1905, and there were other fifth-cousin marriages in the family. When he visited us on the set of Booknotes *on August 7, 1994, Peter Collier said that a Roosevelt of the time, if asked about these marriages, might have answered, "'Well, who else was there? That's the story of this family that there were, in a sense, only Roosevelts." Mr. Collier is the publisher of* Encounter Books *in San Francisco. His book,* The Roosevelts: An American Saga, *was published by Simon & Schuster in 1994.*

THE ARC OF THE ROOSEVELT family in America is really a remarkable story because it begins with probably the most clannish, tribal family, not in the narrow and semineurotic way as the Kennedys, who have taken that kind of tribalness to an extreme, but tribal in the sense of a tremendous closeness in this Dutch American family. This arc begins with one great man, Theodore Roosevelt, stepping inside history—not just deciding to live with history the way most of us do, but stepping inside and trying to bottle the lightning of history, as it were. The story that begins there completes itself in the generation of Franklin and Eleanor's children. These children . . . sold out the family. They were so angry, so filled with a vendetta against Franklin and Eleanor that they sold every scrap of privacy, writing bitter memoirs, giving bitter interviews. It completed this tragic arc that defines the Roosevelt family.

[If the Roosevelts were alive today, with contemporary media coverage] I suppose that they would be relentlessly picked at, their foibles, their peccadilloes. . . . Franklin probably would have been particularly vulnerable because he was, like John F. Kennedy, tremendously protected by the press in his own day. He was generally photographed from the waist up. It was considered bad taste to allude even visually or through imagery to his paralysis. There was a lot that went on in his private life, [including] the fairly well-known affair with Lucy Mercer Rutherfurd that was the storm that finally levered him and Eleanor apart That was known and never reported. And his flirtatious behavior with other women whom Eleanor bitterly referred to as "his blondes" was fairly well-known and never reported. So I think by today's standards he would be fair game.

Theodore Roosevelt [had] the first family with really boisterous young children to inhabit the White House, the first family that was clearly a nuclear family in a time when America was shifting from being the extended family of the frontier and the plains to the nuclear family of the big cities. He came along at a time when the press had really come of age in America. There were wire services, so that details of his intimate doings and those of his really charming children, all of whom were major figures in the American imagination at the turn of the century, could be reported to every hinterland in America. The press was obsessed with Theodore Roosevelt and followed him very closely because he was, really, in his own time, a larger-than-life character.

Theodore Roosevelt, of course, left the presidency in 1908 and lived until 1919. From the day he left the presidency until the day he died, there was a pool person, a member of the press, stationed in Oyster Bay where he lived, who got up every day and sat around the telegraph office there waiting to transmit news of what Theodore ate, said, thought, felt, and experienced. He continued to have this magnetic hold on the American imagination.

Part of the story was Alice, his daughter. She had this long antagonism with her cousin, Eleanor. They had certain similarities in a way. Alice was the daughter of Theodore by his first wife, who died tragically when he was a young man twenty-five years old. She died right after Alice Roosevelt was born, hours later. Theodore was a young promising Republican legislator in the New York state assembly. He came rushing home to see the birth of his daughter and saw his daughter, but saw also his first wife dying. She died in his arms a few hours later.

This became part of that remarkable epic of self-creation which is Theodore Roosevelt, which began when he was a young man, a boy of eight or nine years old, feeling so sick from asthma that his parents feared he might die. At one point his father came to him, in a fairly famous story, knowing that he had this charisma and magnetism, told him that he needed a vessel to contain this luminous intelligence, said, "You have the intelligence, but you must make your body." In other words, you must make the container that will allow you to survive. Theodore manfully started working out in this gymnasium, creating himself. This process of self-creation kept going; right after his wife died and Alice was born, for instance, he was so heartbroken he just threw up everything and left for the Badlands of North and South Dakota, in a fairly famous episode, and became a cowboy. He . . . found in that American frontier the strength to go on, the strength to feel that he could survive and, indeed, not only endure but prevail, to use Faulkner's words, among those rough-hewn American frontiersmen.

He had six [children]. He had two daughters, Alice and Ethel, and four sons. They all married except Quentin, who was really on the verge of marriage. He had been engaged to Flora Whitney and then died in aerial combat before he got a chance to marry her.

[Teddy Roosevelt's sons] Theodore Jr., Kermit, and Archibald Roosevelt were major figures in their own day, [but] were elbowed out of the way in the really significant drama of this family, which was an almost Homeric civil war between the two branches that erupted after Theodore's death; that is, the Oyster Bay branch, his own children, and the Hyde Park branch, the family of Franklin Roosevelt and Theodore's beloved niece Eleanor, who was the daughter of his much-loved brother, Elliott.

Elliott Roosevelt, Theodore's brother, had been considered more promising when the two of them were young. But as Theodore got his body, got his health, he really outstripped Elliott so significantly that Elliott wilted in his shadow and became a drunk, self-destructive, and died early, leaving this remarkable, physically unattractive but emotionally expansive young woman Eleanor behind, an eight- or nine-year-old who was passed around then like a bad penny from aunt to aunt inside that Oyster Bay family and finally married Franklin, this pampered only child of the Roosevelt family that had moved up into the Hudson River Valley in Hyde Park.

[Theodore Roosevelt] sent his four boys [to fight in World War I], one of whom was perhaps his favorite child, Quentin Roosevelt. His very poignant love story with Flora Whitney is a kind of Capulet and Montague story because of Theodore Roosevelt's well-known distaste for those he called the malefactors of great wealth; that is, the plutocrats whom he really despised because they had done, he felt, nothing with their lives. He initially felt that way about the Whitney family, but he came to admire them in a way, particularly Gertrude Whitney, the mother of Flora Whitney who had started [the Whitney Museum].

[Quentin Roosevelt and Flora Whitney were] a perfect metaphor of what war does to people, how it blights their hopes. Quentin was Theodore's son who was lost in the war in a dogfight over France after shooting down a German airplane. The other three boys came home war heroes, and Theodore Jr. came home ready to seize the legacy of his father and to move toward the White House to become the next [President] Roosevelt. He assumed that he would have a good shot at it, but there was this other Roosevelt in the way. That was Franklin, who had spent the war at home as assistant secretary of navy under the Wilson administration, an act Theodore Roosevelt Jr. always thought of as treachery. In fact, Franklin had always wanted to be, in a way, the surrogate son of Theodore and had fed him private information from this listening post inside the Navy Department during the war as a kind of mole. He too felt that the Wilson administration was dragging its feet. The stage was really set in 1920 for this contest between Theodore Jr. and Franklin.

[Of Theodore's children] only Theodore Jr. ever ran for political office. People often said that Alice would have made a great president, which she probably would have. But Theodore Jr. really followed his father's footsteps. He ran for the assembly in New York and was elected overwhelmingly and became a maverick assemblyman the way his father had been. He became assistant secretary of the navy as his father and Franklin had been; it was almost like a Roosevelt family sinecure. In 1924 he made the decision to run against Al Smith for the governorship of New York, to take the bit in his teeth and to go for it.

Eleanor and Franklin, . . . that affair with Lucy Mercer having ended any kind of husband-and-wife relationship between them, had perfected the beginning of a political partnership. Both, for their own reasons, saw that Theodore Jr.'s ambitions had to be beaten back. When Theodore Jr. finally made his run for the governorship of New York in 1924, which he figured would be his stepping-stone to the presidency as it had been for his father, Franklin was really on the shelf, suffering the aftereffects of polio. It wasn't clear that he would ever become a political factor again.

Eleanor, in a most uncharacteristic gesture, set out to destroy the political hopes of her cousin Theodore Jr. As he went around the state of New York campaigning, she followed him. She had a car made with a papier-mâché bonnet in the shape of a teapot in order to associate him with the scandal of Teapot Dome. . . . Every place he spoke, Eleanor showed up with this teapot-shaped car spouting steam. She would speak afterward with some of her lady friends indicating that she felt he was not a chip off the old block, that he was an immature and easily used man. It was really a baptism into politics for her. It was also a subject that she was always embarrassed about forever after. She could never explain satisfactorily to anybody else, least of all to herself, why she had stepped forward. This shy, retiring woman who had been oppressed by her mother-in-law, who had been a semi-orphan, dependent on the kindness of strangers all her life, had stepped up and smacked her cousin viciously.

THERE HAD ALWAYS been a symmetry between . . . Alice and Eleanor. Alice had been semi-orphaned by the death of her mother at her birth, and Eleanor had been semi-orphaned by the death of her father when she was nine years old. They grew up in that same family together, passed around. . . . There was both this competition and thwarted love that existed between Eleanor and Alice. . . . In some sense their story together was of the tortoise and the hare, because Alice began way, way ahead of Eleanor and then Eleanor gradually overtook Alice and became a fairly famous newspaper columnist while Alice's own column was stillborn. . . . Alice was picked up to do a column too, but that incredible wit and vivacity that she had didn't translate itself to the printed page.

Alice Roosevelt was [known as] Princess Alice. She was the most eligible woman in America. She had people following her doings, her quick, biting wit. . . . She was paired in the public imagination with every eligible crowned head of Europe; they had her marrying royalty. But she finally found herself, after a long period of eligibility, marrying this squat, charismatic, but not particularly handsome congressman from Ohio named Nicholas Longworth, who was a powerful figure in the House of Representatives. . . . Longworth had a strong resemblance physically to her father, and people at the time noted that. They had a vexed relationship which paralleled that of Franklin and Eleanor, although it had less depth to it obviously, less depth of field, because Nicholas Longworth was a very famous womanizer.

In one particular case [Alice] found that he had been [caught] flagrante delicto in their own bedroom. She knew the woman, a society dame. Alice wrote her a bitter letter [saying,] "I found your hairpins in my bed." This woman, Cissy Patterson, wrote her back a letter saying, "Yes, and if you look hard, you'll find my underwear up on the chandelier." So their relationship was carried on at that kind of a level. . . . Nicholas Longworth became Speaker of the House and had a lot of enemies [there]. One particular congressman, knowing his reputation for being a philanderer, thought to have the best of him one day and came up to Nicholas as he was sitting at the Speaker's desk and said sneeringly, looking at his bald head, "Your head looks like my wife's behind." Nicholas looked at him, everybody waiting for his answer. He rubbed his head and said, "Yes, it feels like your wife's behind too." That was his way of dealing with these rumors, which was to say yes.

Alice saw Eleanor outstrip her and become First Lady. There had always been this competition between them, and Alice always was fairly vicious to Eleanor. She had this imitation she would do of Eleanor with a bucktooth look, making her chin recede, and she did it in front of all audiences. In fact, Eleanor, with this self-lacerating quality that she had, would invite Alice to the White House and at some point during the evening would say, "Alice, don't you think it's time that you did your imitation of me now?" And Alice would oblige and do this terribly wounding imitation of her facial inadequacies. She did this on into her nineties, when she was still a major society figure in Washington. . . . She died at the age of ninety-six, still obsessed with Eleanor. Eleanor was long gone, and as Alice was wondering in senility, she would ask, "Where's Eleanor? What's Eleanor doing?"

[FRANKLIN AND ELEANOR had five children.] Their son John only had two marriages; the rest had from three to five. Franklin Jr. and Elliott both had five marriages. There were suicides of spouses. That Roosevelt family was a tough act to be in, not because of the demanding, moral imperatives—the way it was in the Theodore family—but because of the moral degeneracy and the moral chaos. For instance, Ethel Du Pont, whom Franklin Jr. married, came to live briefly in the White House in the late '30s. The White House maids always talked about her walking around looking distracted and pulling her hair out as she heard rumors of her husband, Franklin Jr., having brought women into the White House itself to be with. It was a hothouse atmosphere that these Roosevelts inhabited.

In 1939 President Roosevelt was fielding all of the world's problems, trying to maneuver the United States into the European conflict, trying to still be, as he put it, "Dr. New Deal" at the same time. Probably his most intractable problem for all his life was his own children. These were the children of basically a loveless relationship with Eleanor, although it was a tremendous partnership. . . . Elliott was probably the most attractive, charismatic of the boys in a certain way. He was the one who most voiced the resentment of his generation for his parents. . . . That generation spent its life complaining about its parents, Eleanor and Franklin, obsessed with the coldness that they had exhibited toward them, obsessed with the fact that they had not gotten the kind of spiritual and emotional nourishment that they expected.

LIKE ALL THEODORE's sons, Theodore Jr. was pushed to the margins by Eleanor and Franklin in the '30s. He really became a reflexive critic of Franklin and Eleanor. He saw Franklin in the New Deal, as he put it, making himself into an American Mussolini. Rather than guide his efforts by what he thought, everything was instinctively opposed to what Franklin thought and what Franklin was doing. Theodore Jr., and to some degree his brothers, became the disloyal opposition. A lot of the opposition of the New Deal coalesced around them, and Theodore Jr. particularly spent the '30s really attacking Franklin and Eleanor. He was kind of the pit bull of the Republican Party during those days. In fact, his father's widow worried that he was allowing himself simply to become a pawn in their hands.

When war was in the offing, uncharacteristically, given the fact that he was Theodore Roosevelt's son, Theodore Jr. became part of America First, became perhaps the most effective spokesman against the involvement in the European situation, and yet, as one of Theodore Roosevelt's sons, when it became clear to him four or five months before Pearl Harbor that there was going to be a war come what may, he immediately, even though he was in his mid-fifties, enlisted.

He had maintained his commission from the time when he was in World War I. He enlisted and came back in as a general. He became one of the few fighting generals in the American army. He fought through North Africa, through Italy, and at the age of fifty-seven on the eve of D day, this man crippled by arthritis, having to use a cane to get around, demanded that General Eisenhower allow him to go ashore with the first wave at Utah Beach. He said, "My men expect it of me. I'm the son of Theodore Roosevelt." He struggled ashore there on his cane on Utah Beach that morning and stood there on the beach shuttling his men back and forth to a seawall for protection from the German fire. He stood there with the bullets zinging around him, smiling that famous smile of his father's, that famous Roosevelt dentition.

General Omar Bradley, when asked at the end of his long military career what the bravest thing he'd ever seen in his military life was, he said without hesitation, "Theodore Roosevelt Jr. at Utah Beach." Theodore Jr. got his men together, broke through the German lines, pushed quickly into the inland part of France, rushing to keep a German counterattack from forming and died a few days after Utah Beach of exhaustion, heart failure. He spent himself to the maximum. Indeed, he found a kind of closeness at the end of his life, as all the Roosevelt boys did, with Franklin, who also proved to be that real surrogate son of Theodore that he had always wanted to be. He spent himself too. He died, as the Roosevelts say among themselves, spending and being spent. . . .

JOHN GABLE, WHO is the head of the Theodore Roosevelt Association, who, I would argue, knows more about the Roosevelt family than anybody in the country, said of this book, "Well, this is the rest of the story." I think that's probably right. Everybody knows the story of Theodore Roosevelt. It's become almost a myth, and, like a myth, it bears retelling over and over again because it's always interesting. The same is quite true with Eleanor and Franklin. The story, yet to be done, is of the most interesting marriage in American history and the people who inhabited this dark undergrowth of hidden, denied, suppressed emotion filled with suppressed and oppressed love and also a kind of anxiety and despair about each other, a feeling that they could never have their lives dovetail. That marriage has been written about, notably by Joseph Lash, but I think it still bears constant reexamination as we change as a society. It's a kind of constant that, in a way, defines us by what we say about it. But what had never been done before is following out the arc of this entire family.

One of the upshots of having done these books—I don't know if it is a cause or an effect, actually—is an appreciation of family, particularly in our own time when families are an endangered species. I appreciate the ties, the thick loyalties, the tragedies. These families that I have written about have victors and victims. The psychological toll that families sometimes [exact] has led headless and thoughtless, and ultimately irresponsible, critics to criticize American families.

Depression and War
1929–1945

The Great Depression and World War II

by

DAVID M. KENNEDY

In 1929 Herbert Hoover was president of the United States. The country's population was over 120 million, and the annual per capita income was $750. On October 29 of that year, commonly called Black Tuesday, the stock market took an unprecedented dive. Although a number of factors contributed to what would become known as the Great Depression, Black Tuesday is generally considered the starting gun. By 1932, approximately 10,000 banks had failed and 16 million Americans—about one-third of the available workforce—was unemployed. In that fall's presidential election, Franklin Delano Roosevelt promised the American people a "new deal" and defeated Herbert Hoover. In 1939 Adolf Hitler's German forces invaded Poland. The United States began to emerge from the Depression as it built up its armed forces to prepare for war. On December 7, 1941, Japanese carrier-based planes attacked the U.S. Pacific fleet at Pearl Harbor. The United States declared war on Japan on December 8 and within a few days Germany and Italy, the other Axis powers, declared war on the United States. Stanford history professor David M. Kennedy covered the world-altering events of the Great Depression and World War II in Freedom from Fear: The American People in Depression and War, 1929–1945, *published in 1999 by Oxford University Press, and on* Booknotes *on June 8, 1999.*

THERE IS NO QUESTION that these two events, the Depression and World War II, were the most deeply formative events in the history of American society. . . . They made us who we are as a people and as a country.

When I was writing this book, I set the scene in the 1920s during the Herbert Hoover administration and the onset of the Depression. [I wanted to] avoid doing what most writers have done about this issue: to describe the

Depression and Hoover's failed attempt to deal with it, and then bring Franklin Roosevelt onstage. The implication is that at the moment everything was hunky-dory again and we were on the road to recovery. In fact, the Depression persisted until 1940 or even 1941. By some measures, rather obvious measures, in fact, Roosevelt was no more successful in licking the Depression than was Hoover. The unemployment rate never went below 14.3 percent in the two Roosevelt New Deal administrations.

Lorena Hickok . . . was a reporter—one of the few really prominent women news reporters of the era—who got very close to Eleanor Roosevelt during the presidential campaign of 1932. She was assigned to cover Eleanor during the campaign. In a sense, she lost her professional journalistic objectivity and became more of a flack for Eleanor Roosevelt than a reporter. It became impossible for her to work as an objective journalist any longer, so Eleanor got her a job as a kind of roving field reporter for Harry Hopkins, the chief federal relief administrator in the New Deal. Her assignment was simply to drive around the country and write back to Hopkins about what it looked like out there and how the relief programs were working or not working.

The upper Midwest and the South were the two regions where she spent the most time, but she also traveled the Northeast and even the far West. . . . Something happened to her when she was out on the road in Depression America. She came to an understanding that the misery she was looking at was not simply the result of the Depression, but the accumulated misery and suffering of generations of wild, unregulated industrial revolution. She was looking at the old poor, not just the Depression poor. She came to an understanding that the issues that had to be addressed were not just relief from the Depression, but really some far-reaching structural reform that would deal with the accumulated problems of a century's worth of unbridled industrial revolution in the United States.

ANOTHER IMPACT ON the Great Depression was the Versailles Treaty. The big four negotiators of the Versailles Treaty, of course, were the American president, Woodrow Wilson; the British prime minister, David Lloyd George; the French premier, Georges Clemenceau; and the Italian premier, Vittorio Orlando. Orlando was really a minor player in this, but he nevertheless had one of the so-called big four seats at the Paris peace talks. The negotiation took place at Paris and the document was signed at Versailles.

The great product of the negotiation, particularly from the American point of view, in 1919, was that all the signatories agreed to create this new thing called the League of Nations. Of course, Woodrow Wilson was the great champion of creating this new institution. One of the bitter ironies of the end of World War I was that the American Senate rejected the treaty that would have taken the United States into the League of Nations. The United States retreated rather markedly from the limited, tentative internationalism that Woodrow Wilson had tried to promote. That was the first big breakdown of the treaty mechanism—the Americans refused to enter into the League of Nations.

The most penetrating analysis of the Versailles Treaty . . . was written in its immediate aftermath by a British observer who was there for most of the negotiations—the famous economist, John Maynard Keynes. [He wrote] a wonderful book called *The Economic Consequences of the Peace.* The central argument of that book was that the Versailles Treaty perpetuated in peacetime the greatest economic and political crime of the war, which was the economic division of Europe. Europe, before 1914, had been quite a functionally unified continental economy—lots of international trade and capital flows and so on. It really functioned as a single economic unit to a considerable degree. The war disrupted all that.

There were also punitive measures imposed on Germany by the treaty: reparations payments, the suppressing of the German coal and steel industry, taking away from Germany control over her own inland waterways, her own merchant marine, taking away her colonies. All of these flowed from the treaty. Keynes said this was an insane perpetuation in peacetime of the economic disruptions of the war by formal treaty arrangement. He predicted that the treaty would sow the seeds of another war, and he was absolutely right.

World War I was an immense perturbation of the international environment—a great disruption. It was against the backdrop of that lingering disruption that the subsequent history played out—the history of the Depression, the history of the New Deal and, of course, the great sequel to World War I, which was World War II.

I WAS ABLE TO locate where Adolf Hitler, Winston Churchill, Franklin Roosevelt, and Joseph Stalin were at the moment they heard of the end of World War I, in November 1918. . . . Hitler was recovering in a hospital in Pasewalk in the eastern part of Germany. He had been gassed in a later phase of the war in a British attack. The gas temporarily blinded him and he was sent to this recovery facility in the eastern side of Germany in a hospital with a lot of other recovering war wounded. A chaplain came to tell him and the other men that the German government had surrendered, even while the German army was still intact in the field.

Though there was some controversy about the reliability of Hitler's memory of this moment, it was more or less the moment when he and others began to think they had been betrayed by the civilian leadership. This was the great stab in the back. They were enormously resentful of the wastefulness of their sacrifice and the sacrifice of their comrades in arms. If not precisely at that moment, certainly shortly thereafter, Hitler set himself on the track of trying to avenge this great injustice to the German veterans and the German people. Throughout this whole period, between the end of World War I and the conclusion of World War II, he was the single actor who, more than anybody else, drove the action and disrupted the scene. World War II was his war to a disproportionate degree.

Hitler wrote *Mein Kampf* in the early '20s, and among the people who read it early on was Franklin Roosevelt, well before Hitler came to power. It convinced him that, as he said, "Hitler is a madman." But neither he nor anybody else could anticipate just how influential this madman would be. They regarded him at first as an aberration when he came to power. But then he closed his fist over the entire apparatus of government in Germany, made the whole country subservient to his will, and made more trouble for the world than anybody could anticipate.

Churchill was a minister in the British government, and because he was such a wonderful writer and a great documenter of his own life, he was the easiest to fix in time, most reliably. He was in his office in London looking down onto a street below. He knew that Big Ben was going to ring the chimes at 11 A.M., on November 11, 1918—the famous eleventh hour on the eleventh day of the eleventh month. He recorded in his own memoirs how he looked down onto the street and first saw one girl all by herself come out of a storefront or an office building, and then suddenly hundreds of other people poured out of these buildings and celebrated the end of the war. Then he told us what he was thinking at this moment. Of course, the first thing he was thinking was how glad he was that it was all over. But he also said something to the effect that a knell rang in the ears of the victors, even in this moment of celebration. He knew that the war did not settle all the problems it had caused and the future most likely held considerable trouble. So his is, in a sense, the most prophetic and tragic view of what the next couple of decades would hold.

FDR was assistant secretary of the navy. In fact, just months before the armistice, he had traveled to the front in France and made a whirlwind tour of the battlefield. He later referred to that tour quite often, particularly in the presidential campaign of 1940, when he repeatedly said, "I have seen war. I know what war can do. I hate war." Well, that was kind of true. He'd seen some very safe areas of the front. He had not really been exposed to any particular danger. But he had seen some of the destruction of the First World War in France. But on November 11, 1918, of course, he was in Washington, D.C., and actually it was not he but Eleanor who recorded in her autobiographical writing how they felt at the moment of the armistice and what a celebration it caused.

Joseph Stalin, at the end of World War I, 1918, was a little more difficult to place precisely. But just before November 11, 1918, he'd been in the city that was then called Tsaritsyn. It was later called Stalingrad and still later called Volgograd. He had been a political commissar there and his job was to punish political enemies, which he did by murdering them. Probably at the moment of the armistice, he was back in Moscow. His precise whereabouts are a little illusive. But he was clearly, at that moment, one of the leaders of the Bolshevik Revolution and part of his responsibility was to extinguish as many political opponents as he could get his hands on.

ROOSEVELT, AS EARLY as 1935, began to understand that the United States had to somehow find a way to put its weight on the scales to check aggression, particularly Nazi aggression in Europe and Japanese aggression in Asia. But the Congress and the country did not necessarily agree with that. In fact, they rather deliberately disagreed with it. Much of Roosevelt's effort as president from 1935 right down to the end of 1941 and Pearl Harbor was a presidential civics campaign to educate the American public, and through the public, the Congress, about the necessity to break out of this isolationist mold and somehow play a part in this international scene.

As Churchill later explained to his war cabinet, Roosevelt said he would wage war but not declare it and that he would become more and more provocative. Everything was to be done to force an incident. The president made it clear that he would look for an incident that would justify him in opening hostilities.

Churchill at that moment was talking about the Atlantic, of course. That remark was made in August of 1941, after the Argentina Conference and well before Pearl Harbor. At that time, the Roosevelt administration was trying to decide whether or not, or how, it could escort the merchant marine convoys that were taking lend-lease goods to Britain. There was a lot of American munitions of war and material flowing to Britain, but the Lend-Lease Act of March 1941 explicitly prohibited American naval vessels from escorting these merchant ships that were carrying goods to Britain. There was an obvious problem here. Congress had authorized the expenditure of money in lend-lease to get the goods to Britain, but it stopped short of taking measures to ensure the goods actually got there by protecting them from German submarine attacks. Roosevelt was turning every which way looking for a legal means to get these ships protected. He began to convoy, through a lot of convoluted devices, declaring first Greenland and then Iceland as part of the Western Hemisphere. He arbitrarily said they were part of the Western Hemisphere so American ships could go out that far without violating the provisions of the Lend-Lease Act. It was an egregious fiction, but he did it anyway.

He expected, and so did Churchill, that at some point, the Germans would attack an American naval vessel and that this could be used as an occasion for Roosevelt to go to Congress and ask for a declaration of war. Woodrow Wilson had done this in April of 1917, after the German submarine sinkings of American ships.

There were several naval incidents that followed. German submarines attacked the *Reuben James,* the *Kearney,* and the *Greer* in the fall of 1941, but Roosevelt did not use these sinkings as an occasion [to go to Congress]. To use Churchill's language, he didn't call them an incident that demanded that the United States declare war on Germany. There was a question about why Roosevelt still, at this late date, was hesitating to use one of these incidents to go to war with Germany. The answer seems to be that he was not ready for war. It wouldn't have done any good to declare war because he didn't have an army to fight with, and he didn't have much of a navy, either. So what good would a declaration of war do? It would just unleash the Germans to undertake absolutely unrestricted attacks on American ships.

Roosevelt's prolonged indecision and his ultimate deviousness in implementing the escort policy have exercised generations of critics. The most famous episode, or the more sensational episode, where Roosevelt is frequently accused of deception, is the Pearl Harbor attack. But the reality is that there has never been a scintilla of credible evidence brought forward to persuasively argue that Roosevelt knew in advance about the attack on Pearl Harbor, and certainly not that he contrived to have that happen. We have to remember that he was dealing here with a public and with a Congress that had repeatedly made clear its isolationist commitments and its deep desire not to get drawn in to this European conflict.

ROOSEVELT ONCE SAID, when he was a much younger man, "No man who has tasted public life will ever willingly give it up." I think he was really married to the idea of himself as the first citizen of the United States and the president of the United States, and it was just psychologically impossible for him to give that up. I think it was irresponsible of him to run for a fourth term. He knew he was ill. Some of his intimate associates knew he was ill, and yet he persisted. To compound the irresponsibility, he paid the most minimum kind of attention to who would be, most likely, his successor. He could not help but understand that whoever was his vice presidential running mate in 1944 would almost certainly become president before that term of office had expired. But, in fact, he did not give much attention to the selection of Harry Truman. He scarcely knew Truman before 1944, and he didn't tell Truman some of the most important facts he needed to know to be a responsible president. He never told him about the Manhattan Project, about the atomic bomb project.

This was not Roosevelt's finest hour. A more responsible leader at that moment would have stepped down. To be sure, it would have taken a tremendous psychological effort to give up power at the moment, on the eve of victory in this war. Clearly, the war was winding down by that moment, and he knew that if he just held on a little longer, the laurels of victory would be his. You can imagine how psychologically difficult it would have been for him to step down at that point, but I think a wiser and more responsible leader would have, or, at a minimum, would have . . . prepared his successor better.

In the end, Roosevelt conveyed a rather Pollyannish message that he repeatedly told the American public: that the postwar era would be an era of cooperation between the western allies—Britain and the United States—and the Soviet Union. What he was hoping for was to somehow domesticate Joseph Stalin and bring the Soviet Union into the family of nations—making it behave itself as a responsible international partner. But in no way did he prepare the public for the kind of confrontation with the Soviet Union that formed what's known to history as the cold war. There was no hint publicly from Roosevelt that there might be difficulty in this relationship.

However, we also know that inside the Grand Alliance—Britain, the United States, and the Soviet Union—there was one strong, unmistakable signal . . . that Roosevelt understood there was likely to be trouble in that relationship after the war. He quite deliberately and repeatedly refused to share with the Soviets the secret of the Manhattan Project, the atomic bomb project. That was an Anglo-American project. The British, in fact, early on in the war, came to Roosevelt and said, "You know, we think the terms of our treaty relationship with the Soviet Union require us to tell them that we're working on this weapons project," and the Roosevelt administration said, "Oh, no. If you insist on telling the Soviets, we're gonna cut you—the British—out of the project. We'll do it all ourselves."

Harry Truman walked up to Stalin during the Potsdam Conference and nonchalantly said, "Hey, by the way, we have a new weapon." Joseph Stalin tossed it off and didn't pay any attention. It was a moment that has long puzzled historians because there was a lot of the preparatory work for the Potsdam meeting. Truman was quite clearly thinking how he could use the fact that the United States now had a successfully demonstrated nuclear device because he got news of the successful test of the first atomic device at Alamogordo, New Mexico, during the Potsdam Conference. He had clearly been thinking, "How can I use this to get some leverage with the Soviets?" or, as he put it in his own Missouri vernacular, "How can I get a hammer on those boys?" Then the moment came when he could raise the hammer or use the weapon in some way, diplomatically, and he didn't.

Henry Stimson later said, "What we now call conventional bombing," that is, prenuclear, "killed nearly a million Japanese, before the atomic bombs were dropped." One single raid on Tokyo, the night of March 9, 1945, killed 90,000 people. That was [more than] the people killed at Nagasaki—about 75,000—and approached the number killed at Hiroshima, which was 130,000. There was great drama attached to the two nuclear attacks—the Hiroshima and Nagasaki bombings—but they represented no crossing of a moral threshold. They represented a technological novelty, a more efficient instrument of mass destruction.

IN 1945 FDR WAS inaugurated for the fourth time on January 20; the Yalta Conference convened in February; FDR died on April 12; Benito Mussolini was shot on April 28; Hitler committed suicide two days later on April 30; on May 8, 1945, the war in Europe was over; and shortly thereafter, the Churchill government was rearranged in England, and Churchill was out of power by July of 1945. In the middle of the Potsdam Conference, Churchill had to give up his chair and Clement Atlee became the new prime minister. The remarkable thing was that in all the great belligerent states on both sides—victors and losers alike—the only state that maintained a kind of evident political continuity was the Soviet Union. Stalin stayed in power. The United States had a new president, Britain had a new premier, the whole German system was smashed, the Japanese system was smashed, and the Italian system was smashed. Out of this diplomatic and political rubble, people were obliged to reconstruct the world. It was really quite extraordinary that they did it as well as they did under those absolutely chaotic circumstances.

The Early Days of
Soviet Espionage

by

ALLEN WEINSTEIN

At the end of World War II, U.S. government cryptographers began decoding thousands of Soviet wire cables intercepted as part of a secret program during the war. The decryption of the so-called Venona files uncovered the existence of Soviet spies in the United States during the 1930s and 1940s. Although the American people were not aware of the Venona files, the nation's postwar relationship with the Soviet Union had quickly turned competitive and into a "cold war." The American people became more suspicious and less tolerant of the left and of American Communists than they had been before the war. Some politicians, including Richard Nixon, then a congressman from California, and Senator Joseph McCarthy of Wisconsin, rode this suspicion to a higher public profile. Allen Weinstein, founder and president of the Center for Democracy in Washington, D.C., told us more about these events as he discussed The Haunted Wood: Soviet Espionage in America—The Stalin Era, *published by Random House in 1999, in a* Booknotes *interview on January 27, 1999.*

THE HAUNTED WOOD [comes from] a poem of W. H. Auden called "September 1, 1939." The lines "Lost in a haunted wood, children afraid of the night who have never been happy or good" seem to apply to many of the characters [involved in Soviet espionage].

[In the 1930s] most of the agents in the United States or Britain or elsewhere who worked for [the Soviets] were ideologically motivated. They were antifascist. They were members of the Communist Party or they were people of the left. . . . American counterintelligence was virtually nonexistent in the 1930s. The FBI was focused, if it was focused at all, on Nazis and on fascists. They weren't really looking for this kind of espionage at that time.

[IN THE 1930s] we were in the middle of the depression decade; millions and millions were unemployed. There was a very significant reform current, some of which was liberal and went into the New Deal to achieve reforms through government. There were a number of Democratic Socialists who opposed from the left. There were also a number of members of the Communist Party during this decade, perhaps even hundreds of thousands of Americans, who went in and out of the Communist Party, some of whom became fodder for recruiting by the Soviet espionage networks.

Almost none of this was known in the '30s. When [the media did cover these issues] it tended to be discounted as the ravings and rantings of anti-Soviet Americans. After all, we had not recognized the Soviet Union for a good long period, from the 1917 revolution until Roosevelt recognized them in 1933. All of this [the espionage and our awareness of it] really opened up in the early to mid-thirties. We were also not their enemy at the time. That's another point that has to be kept in mind. We were, from their point of view, a listening post. They could get terrific information from our State Department or other government agencies and people they had there about Nazi Germany, about Japan, about countries that they did feel threatened them.

THE OFFICE OF STRATEGIC Services (OSS) [was created] during the period of American entry into the Second World War . . . when Roosevelt asked his old friend General William Donovan to organize this foreign intelligence entity. It lasted until about a year after the Second World War and was disbanded when it became clear that President Truman wanted to take another tack with intelligence.

The OSS [did not] get along with the FBI very well. J. Edgar Hoover's nemesis in the American government was General Donovan, because General Donovan had the right to engage in foreign intelligence work all over the world except Latin America. The FBI retained Latin America. Hoover and Donovan fought, especially when Donovan came to an agreement with the head of Soviet intelligence, General Pavel Fitin, to exchange information during the war. That drove Hoover up the wall. He lobbied the Joint Chiefs of Staff. They opposed the agreement. Franklin Roosevelt basically compelled Donovan to back away from any formal agreement with the NKVD, . . . the predecessor agency of the KGB. . . . But during the war, there was a lot of informal cooperation. What Donovan did not know was that his agency was heavily infiltrated by Soviet agents during this period.

There were allegations and charges [of infiltration both] during the war and after the war. But the first major batch of materials with credible evidence of this came out when the Soviet archives were opened and when the Venona archives were opened.

The Venona archives were intercepts done by [the predecessor of the National Security Agency] the U.S. Army Signal Security Agency, during the Second World War of thousands upon thousands of documents, cables sent by Soviet officials in this country back to Moscow, including about 3,000 intelligence cables. Many of these cables had never been deciphered, but the ones that were deciphered showed significant evidence [that there were] a number of Soviet agents in this country.

The Venona archives were deciphered at the end of the Second World War at a place called Arlington Hall in suburban Virginia, near Washington. A number of very talented code breakers worked on them over a period of over twenty years. . . . Apparently, according to Senator Daniel Patrick Moynihan's book, *Secrecy*, they remained a secret even from President Truman during his presidency. We didn't know about the Venona program. Finally, Senator Moynihan and others on this commission on government secrecy . . . persuaded the CIA and the National Security Agency to release the materials. Most of them came out in 1996.

J. ROBERT OPPENHEIMER was the . . . chief organizer of scientists at the time of the atomic bomb, the Los Alamos Project, during the Second World War. He was a Berkeley physicist, a brilliant figure. He was accused in some recent books . . . of having been involved, however wittingly or unwittingly, in espionage for the Soviets. We turned up no evidence of that and, in fact, most of the material we turned up suggests that they did try to recruit him on several occasions, unsuccessfully. But there's one cable [from the Venona archives] that described him as a secret member of the compatriots, as they called it, of the American Communist Party. That could have been a misjudgment. It could have been an error on the part of the person sending the cable. But as far as espionage is concerned, there's no reason that we found to question the loyalty of Oppenheimer.

WHAT [ALSO] EMERGED from the files is that [convicted spy] Ethel Rosenberg, who did not even have a code name . . . appears to have known what her husband was doing, appears to have maybe met a Soviet operative or two. [But] Ethel Rosenberg was not significantly involved, to the extent that the Soviet documents show, in the espionage activities of her husband. Her husband, Julius Rosenberg, was a very active agent, mostly on nonatomic matters. . . . Julius Rosenberg persuaded David Greenglass's wife, Ruth, to bring to David Greenglass, who was Ethel Rosenberg's brother and a machinist at the Los Alamos Project, a proposal that he begin to work for Soviet intelligence. He agreed to work for the Soviet networks [in 1944 and 1945].

David Greenglass provided the Soviets with sketches of the lens mold of the bomb and other things. Greenglass was arrested [and charged with espionage six years after he began spying]. In order to save his wife from arrest, he basically told the FBI all they wanted to know about Julius Rosenberg, his brother-in-law, and how he, Greenglass, had been recruited. The FBI arrested both Julius and Ethel Rosenberg. They were tried and convicted. They were sentenced to death and they were put to death in 1953 despite enormous protests, not only from Communists but from many, many non-Communist figures—not so much of the fact of convicting them but of their death sentence.

THE HOUSE UN-AMERICAN Activities Committee (HUAC) began in 1938, initially under the chairmanship of a conservative Texas Democrat named Martin Dies. HUAC performed for the galleries. It was much more concerned with what it could do by bringing people into open hearings—often before private hearings had established whether there was a need for open hearings, so it significantly damaged a range of reputations. Did it deal with some people who were members of the Communist Party? Sure. Did it add anything to what the FBI was already doing? Not to any significant extent that I've been able to find.

One of the frequent complainers and critics of the House Committee on Un-American Activities, as he was of Senator Joseph McCarthy's efforts on the Senate side, was [FBI director] J. Edgar Hoover. Real investigative work is private work. It is quiet work. It is work that needs cooperation from a maximum number of sources. That's not normally done in front of television lights.

RICHARD NIXON [as a member of the House committee] turns out to have been remarkably dogged and stubborn in the case [of suspected spy Alger Hiss]. He stuck to the case at a time when other committee members were willing to drop it because they really saw no way of dealing with the conflicting testimony by Alger Hiss and [his accuser] Whittaker Chambers. Nixon, on the other hand, wanted to continue pursuing this. . . . There were times during this case when, despite what he wrote about himself in his memoir *Six Crises*, Nixon was not calm, cool, and collected. He panicked whenever it appeared that Hiss had an advantage on something or Chambers may have lied about the date of the microfilm. Nixon hit the ceiling. But by and large, he stayed with this case. I suppose to the extent that the case helped make his reputation in California, that was understandable.

The gardens of subversion that Senator Joseph McCarthy pursued were by and large imaginary. There weren't 205 or however many Communists [he alleged were] here and there. But there were some real agents [working in the U.S. government]. There were some people who, in fact, worked for the Soviets. It was McCarthy's political good fortune at the time to seize upon the Alger Hiss case because his first speech, his famous Wheeling, West Virginia, speech, came only days after Hiss's conviction in early 1950. But in retrospect, McCarthy added little except mayhem to that process.

YOU PROBABLY HAD [the greatest number of] Americans working for Soviet networks during the Second World War. They wanted everything. They wanted materials on the different war weapons of one sort or another, everything from airplanes to radar to other things. They wanted information on government policies all through the government. . . . They accumulated a stunning array of material during the Second World War from their American agents in Washington.

[Among the agents was] Harry Dexter White, a leading official in the Treasury Department, helping to shape postwar plans for Germany, helping to shape postwar plans of U.S. assistance to the Soviet Union and other things. [State Department official] Alger Hiss certainly was another one. If Hiss had not been dogged by these accusations of Communist involvement because of Whittaker Chambers's defection back in the late 1930s, which finally got some serious attention from the FBI beginning in 1945, Hiss might very well have gone on to be secretary of state in another administration.

[There was also] the so-called Silvermaster network, run by a man named Nathan Gregory Silvermaster, who was not a major figure himself but had a significant number of agents working for him in the OSS and Treasury, at State and elsewhere. Silvermaster drove our puritanical Soviet friends up the wall because he was living at home in a ménage à trois. He and his wife and another agent in his network all lived together, apparently quite comfortably and happily. At the end of the war when things got a little pressured and he thought it might be time to leave this [operation], he persuaded the Soviets to give him the down payment on a farm.

I SUPPOSE THE MILESTONE [which caused many Americans to leave the spy network] was the Nazi-Soviet pact. A number of individuals recognized the cynicism of Joseph Stalin and those around him in aligning with their worst enemy simply to preclude an immediate attack. Many [agents left] because of the purge trials, which killed millions and millions, including a number of these intelligence officers.

250 / Allen Weinstein

ONE THING [I learned from writing this book was] that one must take these people on their own terms. . . . You had murders, suicides, love affairs—people with flaws like the rest of us who were struggling to fulfill what they considered to be their commitments or ideas. If they were Americans working against our government then, obviously, they were traitors. The word has to be used. But if they were Soviets, the Soviets came here and they fell in love with this country, many of them. . . . What Soviet intelligence ran up against over and over and over is what I call the stubborn individualism of American realities. Their agents were simply not very disciplined during most of this period.

The Nurses Captured on Bataan

by

ELIZABETH M. NORMAN

Bataan is a peninsula in the Philippines between Manila Bay and the South China Sea. It is a mountainous, hot, densely jungled place. It is also the location of one of the worst American defeats of World War II. On April 9, 1942, U.S. and Filipino forces on Bataan surrendered unconditionally to the Japanese. What followed was the infamous Bataan Death March. More than 70,000 already weakened Allied POWs were forced to walk over sixty miles to a Japanese prison camp at Cabanatuan on the coast of Luzon. Thousands died along the way of sickness and starvation or at the hands of their captors. It was not only fighting troops who became prisoners of war. A group of nurses, who continued to save lives in the worst of conditions, also became prisoners of the Japanese. Elizabeth M. Norman appeared on Booknotes *on July 22, 1999, to discuss* We Band of Angels: The Untold Story of American Nurses Trapped on Bataan by the Japanese, *published in 1999 by Random House. Ms. Norman is an associate professor of nursing at New York University.*

THIS STORY IS ABOUT the army and navy nurses who were in the Philippines when World War II began, who surrendered to the Japanese and were the largest group of American women POWs in the history of our country. . . . There were seventy-seven prisoner of war nurses, plus twenty-two who got out.

Helen Nestor, or Cassie, as she was known, lived in Pennsylvania, not far from Philadelphia. She embodies to me who these nurses were—she was bright, funny, the most humane person, and underneath it all, a very brave and courageous woman.

252 / Elizabeth M. Norman

She was a daughter of Italian immigrants and grew up in Massachusetts in a town called Bridgewater. She wasn't a particularly scholarly child—a bit of a tomboy, as she called herself—but she decided to go to nursing school because she liked working with people. She graduated in 1938, and at that time nurses were able to join the Red Cross. The Red Cross was almost used as a reserve force for the army nurses. When things began to build up in the early 1940s, Cassie became a member of the Army Nurse Corps, reserve status. She went to work in Massachusetts at an army base and really had an itch to get out of Massachusetts and see the world. She volunteered for duty in the Philippines, and as she said to me, "I wanted to have an adventure. I had a little bit more than I bargained for."

She arrived in the Philippines in late October of 1941, and the war started there on December 8, 1941. It was the same day as Pearl Harbor, but across the international date line. . . . She was there a whole five weeks before the bombs started to fall. The first day of the war she wound up volunteering for duty in Clark Air Field in the Philippines, which was destroyed. In the blink of an eye, she went from a fun-loving, very nice young woman to a nurse who was working in an operating room with trauma and damage she never thought she would see.

The first bombs fell in the Philippines about six hours after they started to drop on Pearl Harbor, so it was almost immediate. The first bomb dropped in a place called Baguio, which is in northern Luzon, at a small army camp. There was an army nurse there named Ruby Bradley who was up that morning getting ready for a routine surgical case. She said she was scrubbing in the operating room for a hysterectomy when a soldier came to the door and said, "Stop. There's not going to be any surgery today." She couldn't figure out what was going on. He said, "Go to the surgeon's office." She went over to meet the surgeon whom she had worked with, and he said, "Look, I've just been notified they've bombed Pearl Harbor. They may bomb us at any time." At that moment, they heard the drone of the planes. They went to the window, looked out, and there was a whole squad of Japanese Zeros coming in on the base dropping bombs.

She and the surgeon ran to the operating room. The casualties were enormous. The first case to come in was a little boy. He had been out walking with his mother that morning—just a normal Monday morning—and he was in very bad shape. He was in shock and he was blue. They tried to revive him any way they could, but they weren't having any success. The surgeon turned to her and said, "Look, we've got too many people to deal with here. We've got to let him go." Ruby—and I understand this as a nurse and a mother—just couldn't do it. She said, "Please, one more try." He said, "You do something" and handed her the needle, which they often will inject into the heart to get it going. The needle is about six inches long—it's not like one we'd usually get put in our arms. She couldn't do it. She looked across the operating room and saw a bottle of whiskey, which was sometimes used in the old days as a stimulant. She put the stimulant on a piece of gauze with some sugar, stuck it in the baby's mouth; he started sucking and was revived by the whiskey. They operated on him and saved his life. The next person to come into the operating room was his mother, who was screaming and crying, "Where's my baby? Where's my baby?" Ruby went up to her and said, "Do you hear him? He's just fine."

WE WERE COMPLETELY unprepared for the Japanese attack. The Americans had a sense that we were an omnipotent power. We had won World War I and we had gotten out of the Depression. No one would ever attack us. General Douglas MacArthur and his strategists were watching the Japanese . . . but they miscalculated. They thought the Japanese were going to attack perhaps in April or May of 1942, not December of 1941, and they didn't have the resources there. They did not foresee the disaster at Pearl Harbor, which temporarily annihilated our fleet. . . . Our troops weren't trained properly. A lot of the reservists—like Cassie—arrived in the fall with barely enough time to get acclimated to it.

GENERAL MACARTHUR was in Manila the day the war broke out, in his suite in the Manila Hotel. For whatever reason—and other historians have written books about it—there was a delay in letting the troops know exactly how near the Japanese offensive might have been. So Clark Field was destroyed. Baguio was bombed. Everything happened. And MacArthur was in his headquarters at that time.

He left Manila for the island of Corregidor, which is in the mouth of Manila Bay, and was there from December until March, when the president ordered him out of the Philippines to Australia. The controversy . . . is that the troops—and these nurses were with the troops—were fighting in the jungles of Bataan and on Corregidor, and MacArthur left, and he left his troops. There's a lot of feeling about that. Some people think, "Well, he was just obeying orders, so you can't fault him." But other people say, "Wait a minute; he left. He took people with him and left seventy-seven women behind to surrender to the Japanese." These were American nurses with absolutely no training. They didn't even have uniforms to go into the field, and he left them behind.

The nurses were able to get some canvas shelter halves for some protection, but they hung their clothes from vines and they put their bed legs in tin cans so the ants wouldn't crawl up them. They were camping in the most rugged sense you can imagine. [All of the patients] were outside. . . . In the event of a retreat, they planned to take the troops to Bataan, but they under-estimated the fact that there'd be civilian refugees with them and that there would be incredible casualties. [Bataan Hospital No. 2] wasn't planned until after the war started. There was no place to put it. They literally bulldozed land out of the jungle. . . . They had open latrine pits until an engineer came and put some seats over them to deal with the flies and the dysentery.

They did bring supplies with them, and they had quite enough anesthetics at first . . . . Toward the end, there were so many casualties, so many surgeries, that they ran out of the typical anesthetic and had to use ether, which goes right back to the Civil War. You drip ether over a gauze to put a person out. It was a very crude way to anesthetize somebody. The nurses said sometimes they had to start surgery prior to the anesthetic taking [effect] and [the patient's scream] was an awful thing to have to hear.

ON BATAAN, MALARIA was epidemic; everybody pretty much had it. They [also] started to suffer from dengue fever. All the tropical diseases you can imagine, the nurses and the troops had. [Malaria brings about] high fever, shivering, sweats, and an inability to eat. You can't sleep. . . . But because everybody had malaria on Bataan, and because they didn't have enough qui-nine, everybody just went to work. The nurses got up and they went to work. One of them said, "I learned when I was in the operating room to take one hand that was really shaking from my malaria and contaminate it by steady-ing myself [so that I could] use my other hand to help the surgeon."

THEY WERE ON Bataan right from the beginning, from Christmas of 1941 until the night they knew they were going to surrender, which was the night of April 8; April 9 was the surrender.

It was traumatic. The chief nurses of the two hospitals were called in by their physicians, who ran to them and said, "You've got ten minutes. Tell the nurses to grab whatever they can and be ready to leave." What was wrenching about this—and to this day, almost fifty-five years later, they'll cry about it—they had to leave their patients. They literally had to take off their operating room gloves, maybe grab a shirt off a clothesline, and go. It killed them because there's nothing worse for a nurse than having to abandon her patient.

AFTER MAJOR GENERAL Edward King [the senior American officer on Bataan] surrendered to the Japanese on Bataan, the Japanese wanted to cap-ture Corregidor, so they turned their guns toward Corregidor. They wanted to get the American troops out of Bataan as quickly as they could. Some-thing, however, happened at that point that no one has really fully described. They took the troops from the point of the peninsula, the tip near Corregidor, and started to march them off the peninsula. Our American troops didn't have enough food or medicine during the four-month battle from January to April, so they were not in good physical shape to begin with. That's a very arduous walk along the coast and the Japanese were moving them quickly. They didn't feed them. They didn't give them water. It was tropical weather. If a man fell by the wayside, he was most likely murdered. Why they didn't put them on the trucks, why they didn't slow the pace down, why they didn't feed them or give them water, no one knows. It was one of the great atrocities of World War II. The distance was sixty-five miles. There were about 72,000 troops on the death march. They figure about 20,000 died on the march. The vast majority were Filipinos, but there were many, many hundreds of American men who died.

After Bataan fell on April 9, 1942, the nurses were sent off the Bataan peninsula across two miles of water to this island fortress of Corregidor, which had long been an American stronghold. They were underground in this cavern of labyrinth-like tunnels that the Americans had built. They probably would have gotten all the American women out of the Philippines, but the Japanese blockade was too great. Our fleet was sitting at the bottom of Pearl Harbor. There just wasn't the time or the resources to get them out. Therefore, you had these nurses on Corregidor when the Japanese troops landed on the island. General Jonathan Wainwright [MacArthur's successor] knew that if he didn't surrender the forces, who were horribly outnumbered, there was going to be a bloodbath.

Corregidor looks like a tadpole, and at the very tip of the tadpole there was an airfield. [In the late '20s, early '30s] they were having trouble getting supplies to the airfield, so the original intent was to blast this tunnel through Malinta Hill and put the trolley on it so they could ferry supplies from the main base to the airfield. Then they started to build other laterals off the main lateral, where they stored supplies, and in the event of an emergency, they knew they'd be safe. It was a bomb shelter.

The nurses were inside the tunnel and rarely saw night and day, so they had an underground molelike existence. One of the problems with Corregidor, not surprisingly, was that they had a lot of respiratory ailments, breathing that air in the tunnel, and they developed terrible blisters from the heat and humidity.

The nurses were in the tunnel on Corregidor until the surrender on May 6. When the Japanese saw the nurses, they were shocked. They did not know what to make of them. At first, they thought they might have been camp followers, because there were no Japanese women in the military. So they said, "You stay in the hospital tunnel with the physicians and take care of the patients," and left them there. They moved all of the men out into prison camps except for the physicians and enlisted men helping in the hospital, but kept the nurses underground for about seven weeks. The nurses said that it was a very hard time. They were only allowed out for fresh air one hour a day. They couldn't speak to anyone unless they were spoken to. They had to bow. It was really the beginning of what they saw as the humiliation of being a prisoner of war.

[Eventually] they moved the nurses to Manila and put them in a university called Santo Tomas University, which the Japanese had turned into a civilian internment camp for enemy aliens—English, Dutch, French, Canadians, and Americans—who were in the city on business. They chose to put the American nurses in that camp and, in a sense, saved their lives. Conditions were very bad in Santo Tomas, but they never approached the depravity of the military camps like Cabanatuan and Bilibid.

The university was completely surrounded by a wall and iron gates. It was almost uniquely set up to be a prison camp. It was a sixty-acre site, so they could easily wall the prisoners off. They put 3,800 people in that camp, and there wasn't enough room. It was terribly overcrowded. What the Japanese allowed the [prisoners] to do is build shanties, and those were the shacks you would see right by the wall, where people could at least go in during daylight hours to have some free time.

The first two years at Santo Tomas—1942, 1943—they had civilian Japanese running the camps. They allowed the prisoners to barter with the Filipinos to bring goods in. If you had money, you could supplement your diet and be okay. In 1944 the military took over running these camps. It was a change in policy out of Tokyo. They cut off all contact with the outside world. Food was running short, and they just started offering less and less food to these people to live on. By 1944, they were down to less than 1,000 calories a day. People were dying of starvation. The nurses themselves were very sick with beriberi and pellagra. Beriberi is a protein deficiency. There's a wet beriberi where your limbs swell up enormously and you can't move. It's almost like an elephantitis; and there's a dry beriberi where you don't swell up, but you almost can't walk. Your nerve endings are so tender, it's difficult to do anything.

There was a very active underground that involved certain Filipino priests. For a long time, the priests—and it's a Catholic country, so there were a lot of them—traveled between the military and civilian camps and carried medicines hidden in things, and money because money bought things in prison camps, so it was very valuable. The nurses would also hollow out fruit and put medicines in there to hide them. It was very ingenious what they did.

LIBERATION CAME ON February 3, 1945. It was very dramatic. The Americans were very worried about these prisoners. They were afraid the Japanese were going to have a mass execution. One night, the First Cavalry spear-headed through enemy territory into the camp. They crashed down the gates.

The women told me that story. They clearly remembered it. [At the time] there was nothing in their lives anymore, so they used to like to watch the sunsets for a little bit of beauty. Well, that night they were ordered inside. [From their rooms in the prison camp] they heard this terrible crash and smelled something strange, which turned out to be gasoline. The tanks crashed down the iron gate and pulled right up in front of their dormitory. People were afraid to come out. Then a soldier jumped out and said, "Hello, folks." At that point, people swarmed out of their rooms, surrounded the troops and somebody started to sing "God Bless America." They were moved by the American flags on the tanks. They had been so isolated and alone for so many years, it was just wonderful to see.

Carl Mydans from *Life* magazine had been in the Philippines when the war began. He had been on Bataan and Corregidor. He was able to get out. However, he wanted to go back because he had many friends in that camp. He went in with the troops and took some wonderful photographs. He said that this liberation was probably the most moving thing he'd ever seen as a war correspondent. The people were living skeletons, and they were just so glad they survived. . . . Every nurse survived the prison camp, and these were camps where hundreds of people died. So they did something right.

The toughest moment for me [writing this book] was watching the women cry. I didn't think you could cry over memories that were fifty-five years old. That was very difficult for me to watch, because of their sense of loss—and they lost a lot in the war. They lost their youth, many, many friends, their physical health, in some cases their emotional health, and they would cry about it. As a human being, that was hard to watch.

These women forged paths that nobody even ever imagined women could forge—nurses. When they were liberated, they all received a Bronze Star and the appropriate medals for the Pacific theater campaign. The men who served with the two head nurses—Maude Davison and Laura Cobb, who led the navy nurses—put them up for higher medals. They felt their leadership, through the battles of Bataan and Corregidor, and then in the prison camps, was exemplary.

They were not bitter. I expected to find that from day one—anger at the Japanese. If there's any bitterness, it was toward our unpreparedness for the offensive. They don't regret what they went through. They feel they learned a lot as human beings. They're not a bitter group, which was surprising.

The main thing I want people to take from this book is what these women have showed us. They were there. They didn't ask to go to war; the war came to them. And they served well. They stayed at their posts, and they did their jobs as well as any man. . . . These women showed us that the idea of courage and bravery is certainly genderless, and they tell us that women alone can survive in the worst of circumstances.

The Creation of the Withholding Tax

by

AMITY SHLAES

Although taxes and tax collectors have been around for thousands of years, the beginning of our present-day income tax began with the ratification of the Sixteenth Amendment to the U.S. Constitution in 1913. The amendment authorized Congress to tax the incomes of citizens. That year, 350,000 citizens filed returns, bringing the government revenues of $28 million. No one with an income below $5,000 had to pay taxes—a large exemption at the time. The federal government did not begin withholding, or taking money directly from paychecks, until 1943. Financial Times *consultant Amity Shlaes appeared on* Booknotes *on March 18, 1999, to discuss* The Greedy Hand: How Taxes Drive Americans Crazy and What to Do About It, *published by Random House in 1999.*

THE FIRST TIME we had the income tax was [from the Tariff Act of] 1913. Interestingly, Republicans played a big role and they should be blamed for that. They were, perhaps, fighting worse things. They said, "Let's do our income tax so we won't have an even higher income tax put through by Democrats." But a very important Democrat, Bourke Cockran, a leader of the time and a very articulate man, said that he didn't want too much progressivity. He opposed progressivity because he said one of the big engines for social order in America is the hope of success.

The important thing to know about that first tax code is that the top rate was 7 percent. There was a suggestion at the time that there should be some kind of law saying, "don't let the tax rate go above 10 percent." They didn't pass that legislation because they thought it was too ridiculous—taxes would never go above 10 percent. What a silly idea, and an unnecessary bit of legislation. Yet very soon, once government had this tool, taxes went up extremely high. They've been up as high as 91 percent.

WITHHOLDING ONLY STARTED on March 15, 1943. The income tax, although it did exist and although there were very high rates for many years, was not a mass tax. Relatively few Americans paid it. Then along came the war. We had World War II and this national moment when we wanted to pull together; we had to win, had to beat back the Japanese, had to beat Hitler. So, a broad-based income tax was passed for the first time. Roosevelt led it. Congress agreed. They say that's when the class tax became a mass tax.

But the question was, Could people pay it once a year? Could they come up with the money? What if they didn't have the money? This was particularly acute because a lot of people were going into military service at that time. They might be earning less in the military than they had been in the year previous, and yet they would owe a tax bill for the earnings on the year previous. . . . There was a panic and they said, "Okay, let's switch to withholding, where we start to collect automatically. Let employers be the handmaiden of government. They'll collect it." That was the plan.

Beardsley Ruml was a marketer and was also on the board of directors of the New York Fed, a Macy's executive, a think tank guy. He said, Let's not call it "withholding" or a "collection at source," or the technical names we have for this kind of tax collection. Let's call it "pay as you go." It sounds nice. Perhaps he was inspired by his experience in retail too. He figured out that people didn't mind paying little by little what they might object to paying all at once. There was a very interesting political event [surrounding this] which was that they did not just pass a law creating withholding; they gave voters a sweetener. They said, "We're going to grant a general tax amnesty for the year prior to 75 percent of what you owed. . . . You can forget about paying that, while we put in this new withholding [plan]." It's not as if there wasn't political resistance to withholding, but it came attached with this big sweetener. And it was during the war, when everyone wanted to go along with the effort. Interestingly, I think a lot of people thought withholding would end with the war. But, of course, it stayed. There were a few lonely tax protesters who tried to fight after World War II ended to lower taxes or to get rid of withholding.

MY PUBLISHER, Random House, and I wanted a title for this book that reflected people's frustration and rage [with income taxes]. But I wanted one that came from history; I wanted it to be from our own experience. *The Greedy Hand* comes from Thomas Paine, one of the publicists who wrote at the beginning of our country's founding. In *The Rights of Man* he wrote of "the greedy hand of government, making our prosperity its prey." I thought that was particularly apt for now, because we are quite prosperous as a people and government is taking a greater share of our money than it ever has before. The federal government takes over 20 percent of the gross domestic product of the economy in taxes, which is the highest rate since Beardsley Ruml. I had a nice talk with Eric Foner, the editor of Thomas Paine's writings, and we talked about how Tom Paine knew about taxes. It turned out that he was an excise man: a professional tax collector. So, of course, he knew about the greedy hand. He had been the greedy hand, measuring beer casks to collect excise taxes on alcohol.

PROGRESSIVITY [HAS BECOME] central to our lives. We don't all understand it. It says that as you earn more, your tax rate goes up. For the last dollar you earn, you pay the top rate. The more you earn, the worse you're punished, and interestingly, this is the centerpiece of our modern tax law. Very few people dare question it.

Raising the Flag on Iwo Jima

by

JAMES BRADLEY

Iwo Jima is the single largest volcanic island in the western Pacific Ocean, covering eight square miles. In 1891 the island was annexed by Japan and eventually became the site of a Japanese air base. During World War II, U.S. Marines captured the island on February 23, 1945, in a battle that resulted in 6,891 American deaths and 18,700 wounded. Only 212 of the 22,000 Japanese troops defending the island survived. James Bradley's father was one of the six men who raised the American flag on Iwo Jima, an image captured on film that has become the most reproduced photograph in history. Mr. Bradley, who lives in Rye, New York, appeared on Booknotes *on May 25, 2000, to discuss* Flags of Our Fathers, *published in 2001 by Bantam Books.*

I DIDN'T WANT to write a book; I wanted to find my father. He died at the age of seventy in 1994, and he had never talked about [raising the flag at Iwo Jima]. I phoned my mom after he died and said, "Mom, there must have been some pillow talk. Tell me what Dad told you about Iwo Jima." She said, "Well, that won't take long. He only talked about it once—on our first date for seven or eight disinterested minutes. Never again did I hear the words 'Iwo Jima' from your father."

My brother, Mark, was searching in my father's office suite and opened a secret closet door. In that closet were two cardboard boxes—plain and ordinary, like [my father] John Bradley. But in those boxes, we were surprised to learn, my dad had saved fifty years of Iwo Jima memories. At the bottom of one of the boxes was a letter he had written home to his parents three days after the flag raising. In that letter, he wrote, "I had something to do with raising an American flag, and it was the happiest moment of my life."

I cried when I read that letter, wondering, "What's going on here?" It was a fifty-three-year-old mystery. Everyone knew the famous photo; no one knew the boys [who raised the flag]. I'm a son, I have a degree in Japanese studies, and I knew nothing about who my dad was on February 23, 1945. So I picked up the phone and called mayors' offices, sheriffs' departments all across the country, and said, "You've got to tell me where the relatives of these boys are. I have to find out who my father was."

So [this process] was a search for my father. I did not intend to write a book but the stories got so good, I thought it was my duty to write them down. . . . The stories are about six nice young boys [who were captured in the most reproduced photo in history]. They were Depression-era boys who were rushed off to war. They would not have been warriors and they would not have been in uniforms, but something kind of big happened.

THE GUY [PHOTOGRAPHED] putting the pole in the ground was Harlon Block. He enlisted with all the senior members of his high school football team, where he was an all-state pass catcher. They were going off to just another great, glorious, patriotic game. It didn't work out that way. Harlon died March 1, 1945, with his intestines in his hands. His last words were, "They killed me."

The next guy was Doc Bradley. His real name was John Bradley, my father; but at that moment he was Doc Bradley on Iwo Jima. There were five marines and one navy corpsman. My dad was the navy corpsman. [How's this for] a humble guy: my dad was [dead and buried] in the ground, and my father's former captain, Dave Severance, from Iwo Jima, phoned my mother and said, "Mrs. Bradley, condolences. Are you aware that your husband is one of the most decorated veterans of World War II, and that he won the Navy Cross, second only to the Medal of Honor?" You know what Betty Bradley said, with her husband in the ground, "No." He kept it secret from his family, wife, and community—the Navy Cross. I told that to Senator John McCain. He shook his head and said, "If you weren't his son telling me, I wouldn't believe it."

The press would tell you that Ira Hayes was an alcoholic Indian. I did the interviews and didn't hear that from any of the people who knew him. What I heard was, "Here was an honorable warrior." He was a Pima Indian, a very upper-crust, peaceful, relatively wealthy tribe—they had ruins when Rome was young. Ira Hayes was an honorable warrior. Yes, he drank a little too much. However, I wish the public would get off his back for having a drink and take a look at a guy who engendered respect from everyone who knew him. Ira had ten years to live from the day the flag was put up.

Ira Hayes was in jail fifty-one times in his life—twice before he enlisted in the marines and all the others afterward. His life was impacted not by the photo but by a quote. After Harry Truman told him in the Oval Office that he was a hero, Ira Hayes said, "How can I feel like a hero when 250 of my buddies hit the beach with me and only twenty-seven of us walked off alive?"

Rene Gagnon was behind John Bradley in the photo, obscured. If you took that helmet off him at the moment this picture was shot, you'd find in the webbing a photograph of his girlfriend. Rene needed it for protection because he was scared. You see, that boy was nineteen years old. In 1979, at the age of fifty-four, he was found dead in a basement of an apartment complex, where he was the janitor.

His son phrased his life after the war as "stop-and-go heroism." He'd get a phone call, "Oh, Mr. Gagnon, it'd be a wonderful day for our community and a great honor if you'd come and address us." Hard to turn down. There were parades and applause, majorettes and the mayor, and the key to the city. Then he'd go back to an ordinary life.

My hero was Mike Strank. If you talk to guys in their seventies who knew Mike, they would say, "This is the finest man I ever met." They said he was "a marine's marine." I didn't know anything about the military, and I thought a "marine's marine" was a Rambo, a John Wayne, a killer. No. He was the grizzled leader. They called him "the old man" because he was already twenty-five. But what Mike was all about was caring for little boys. He had seventeen-, eighteen-, and nineteen-year-olds in his care. He would say to them, "You do what I say. You listen to me, and I'll get you home to your mothers." So when they would do dangerous things on Iwo Jima, like . . . getting shot, he'd say, "Your mom wouldn't like that."

If you look at the photo, Mike is captured in a characteristic pose. You can't see him; all you can see is his right hand. Where is that right hand? It's not on the pole . . . it's around the wrist of Franklin Sousley. He's helping a younger boy raise a heavy pole—characteristic of Mike, a marine's marine. My hero, a guy who had a photographic memory. He could have been governor of the state, but instead, with friendly fire, he had his heart ripped out on March 21, 1945.

Franklin Sousley was a fun-loving Hilltop, Kentucky, hillbilly. He was fatherless at the age of nine, dead on Iwo Jima at the age of nineteen. The story was that when the telegram came to the Hilltop General Store, a barefoot boy ran it up to his mother's farm. The lore is that the neighbors could hear her scream. I didn't say "cry," I said "scream"—all night and into the morning. The neighbors lived a quarter of a mile away.

Three of the six were killed on Iwo Jima: Mike Strank, Harlon Block, and Franklin Sousley. Franklin Sousley's last words were, "I'm okay." The three that came back as immortal heroes were John Bradley [who died in 1994], Rene Gagnon [who died in 1979], and Ira Hayes [who died in 1955].

THEY RAISED THE FIRST flag at about 10 A.M. on February 23, 1945. Why was that important? . . . Iwo Jima was part of the sacred realm; the mayor of

Tokyo was the mayor of Iwo Jima. So this was the first [foreign] flag raised over Japanese territory in 4,000 years—very, very important. The island went nuts. My dad's flag raising was just a replacement flag raising. It was insignificant.

The reason for the replacement flag raising had to do with the secretary of the navy, James Forrestal. Forrestal said to Holland "Mad" Smith, the general, "I want to go onto Iwo Jima." This was a bad idea because wherever you stood, you had a good chance of dying. But he was secretary of the navy and he insisted. So General Holland "Mad" Smith took the secretary of the navy onto the worst D-Day beach of World War II. Forrestal saw the first flag go up and he said words to the effect, "Boy, I'd like that as a souvenir."

That message was relayed to Lieutenant Colonel Charles Johnson, my dad's colonel, who with his flap flipped up, potbelly out, and cigar, said, "To hell with that," and other things I can't say. He said, "That flag is going down into the battalion's safe. We're keeping that flag, not any souvenir hunters." So he said, "Put up a replacement flag.". . . All this happened within three to four hours.

Lou Lowery took the photograph of the first flag raising. The photo was developed, but it just didn't create a sensation like the replacement flag raising. . . . They cropped the photo of the replacement flag raising to get it into the newspapers, and that crop became the most reproduced image in the history of photography. It appeared on February 25, 1945, and was taken by Joe Rosenthal, a five-foot-four guy who jumped on, I believe, four D-Days in the Pacific to take pictures. He was an American hero. He got up there on Mount Suribachi, with this big, bulky, Speed Graphic camera. Out of the corner of his eye, he saw some action [and took the shot]. He didn't even focus it. People say the photo was posed, which is ridiculous. Joe was so far away he couldn't even yell to the guys. They didn't know there was a photographer.

He barely got the shot. He thought at that moment that he had blown it, so he asked the lieutenant to pose eighteen guys underneath the flag when it was up, and he took a posed, gung-ho shot. My dad and three of the flag raisers were in it—Ira Hayes, Mike Strank, and Franklin Sousley.

Joe saw that one and thought, "Oh, this'll make a hit back in the United States, this posed shot." His film went to Guam. They sent the flag-raising photo to New York and it was sent all over the place. Joe didn't see it because it was 1945 and he was in Iwo Jima. He received a telegram from the AP that said, "Congratulations on that great shot" and Joe thought, "That was that posed shot I took."

He flew to Guam seven days later. Members of the press ran out of the Quonset hut and said, "Joe, did you pose it?" And Joe said, "Yes, of course," because he was thinking of the posed shot. An NBC guy heard that and said, "I'll get the scoop." He went back and wired New York, "Rosenthal posed the shot." There began the myth—the myth that the most reproduced photo in history was a posed shot.

WHEN THAT FLAG WAS raised, it was just the start of the battle. It was a thirty-six-day battle. It started on February 19, and the [flag raising] was February 23—five days into the battle. They took the high ground, Mount Suribachi, and, logically, they thought, "We won the island." They didn't know there were 22,000 Japanese in an underground city.

The island is six hundred miles south of Tokyo. It's one of the ugliest rocks you could possibly visit. It's a closed Japanese base. You can't get on unless the president, or somebody, figures out how to get you on there. . . . It's only five miles long. Normandy beach was hundreds of miles. The Japanese were in Mount Suribachi—seven stories of catacombs with ventilation systems, food to last for months, and ammunition behind seven-foot walls. They backed in tanks and only had holes for the turrets. So when my dad and those other boys ran across this volcanic ash sand, they couldn't see anybody. But there were 22,000 guys underground. America didn't understand that.

I was in the hospital there that was forty-five feet underground. They had hospital beds cut into the volcanic rock. You could drop a nuclear bomb and it was not going to disturb a scalpel forty-five feet underneath solid rock. An American surgeon set up a table when he was operating on boys. He got tired, went to sleep one night and heard Japanese voices. He scratched underneath the tarp and found he was atop a Japanese conference room. Twenty-two thousand Japanese living underground with 80,000 Americans above them. Amazing. I interviewed guys who never saw a live Japanese soldier.

The 22,000 Japanese had to die. Most of those guys supposedly "captured" were Korean laborers, slave laborers who gave themselves up. The Japanese who were "captured" generally had a hole in part of their body and maybe half of their blood system was already out of their bodies, and they were unconscious. The Japanese were not surrendering. Germans surrendered. Italians surrendered. English surrendered. Americans surrendered in World War II. The Japanese, no.

About 7,000 [American] boys died; so many they couldn't bury them in individual graves. They had to bury them by row and they had a draftsman marking the lines.

What I learned about my dad was that he was a twenty-one-year-old boy running through bullets to save lives. He probably held two hundred to three hundred kids in his arms as they died. And, when they died on Iwo Jima, they wriggled in pain. . . . [My dad was really badly wounded too.] If you had ripped his pants off, his legs would have been all chewed up with shrapnel.

Eyewitnesses said that he would not treat himself. He was crawling, with his bloody legs, to care for other guys around him.

Ralph "Iggy" Ignatowski was my dad's buddy. He was tortured underground for three days and when the Japanese gave the body back by tossing it up mutilated, my dad was called to examine the body. My dad told me just a little about it, in about a minute of an anguished gush when I was a little boy. It didn't mean anything. I didn't have the sensitivity to understand what he was talking about. Later, the other guys who saw the body talked to me as they would [have talked to] a son.

[The stories of torture] made the Americans very afraid. They were just little boys. I didn't detect any anger, however. It was amazing. I interviewed hundreds of Iwo Jima vets, and it was all about buddyhood. It was about love. I thought hate won the battle of Iwo Jima; I didn't realize it was love. It was a bunch of boys who bonded, and they loved each other. When their best friend got killed and they described it, they didn't say, "Then this Japanese"—no, no, no. They said, "And then Marty got it in the head and I held him and I said, 'Marty.'" It was all about their buddies and about love. They were fighting for each other. Corpsman Robert DeGeus says in my book, "It wasn't about valor or fighting or bravery. It was about helping your friends."

AFTER THE PHOTO was taken and the war was over, my father came back and there was the bond tour. The bond tour raised $24 billion in just sixty days. What did that mean? Now the president can take your taxes and fight anywhere he wants. Back then, the war was not in the federal budget, so the president had to go out and make appeals across the country to the populace. "Please approve what we're doing by buying a bond." A bond could be bought for $17. If you kept it for ten years, it rose to $25. The program also soaked up the economy's extra money because there were no goods to buy, and it kept inflation down. Brilliant.

There were six bond tours—huge extravaganzas, like a Rolling Stones concert moving across the country. The American public was a little tired and they didn't have a lot more money. Roosevelt said, "We'll have the photo as a symbol. Then we'll get the six guys who raised it." Well, only three came back: my dad, Rene Gagnon, and Ira Hayes.

They were brought to the White House—my dad was on crutches and full of shrapnel—and were told, "You used to work for the War Department; now you work for the Treasury Department. You fought for a mountain in the Pacific; now you're going to fight for a mountain of money." And they put those three boys on a bond tour that went to cities across the country. In Boston, 200,000 people stood in a sleet storm for hours just to get a glimpse.

In Houston, the police put roadblocks outside the city because the crowds were so huge that they were afraid to gridlock the town.

Hundreds of thousands of people jammed into Times Square. In Chicago, they closed the Loop because so many people were coming in. They filled stadiums. People were wild about that picture—like Beatlemania—and they dug deep in their pockets and contributed $26.3 billion.

Let me put that into context. Harry Truman's entire budget was $56 billion; that was all the dollars he got to play with. The bond tour raised about 47 percent of that in two months just with some young kids talking.

Then, later in 1954, came the actual dedication of the Iwo Jima statue. The sculptor, Felix de Weldon, was in the navy [in February 1945], working on a mural of the battle of the Coral Sea. Then, over some type of machine, the photo came through the day before the American public saw it.

He abandoned the picture he was working on as an artist and took some clay—he couldn't get his mind off the photo. He stayed up all night, and the day that America saw the photo, Felix de Weldon already had a lump of clay that was the statue.

My dad started teaching me about fame at the age of nine. I was trained how to handle Walter Cronkite's producers when I was a little kid. My dad would be sitting right there at the table and the code was, "He's in Canada." The *New York Times* would call and I would say, "No, sir. I'm sorry, thank you for calling but my father's fishing in Canada. Well, no, there's no phone up there. No, we don't know when he's coming back." And he'd be sitting right there. My dad never fished; He never went to Canada. If he spoke, he understood he created a headline. That headline would obscure who he thought were the real heroes, the guys who did not come back.

I think "up there," where those six boys are, they are happy that the book is out because it does something my father could never do—shine the light on all the heroes.

My daughter had a school assignment to write a letter to someone you admire the most. So Alison Bradley, at the age of fifteen, chose her grandpa, who had been dead for three years.

Statesman, scientist, printer and writer Benjamin Franklin, cast in bronze by George Lundeen, at the headquarters of the Printing Industries of America in Alexandria, Virginia.

ABOVE Hamilton Park in Weehawken, New Jersey, across the Hudson River from Manhattan, overlooks the site of the famous duel between Alexander Hamilton and Aaron Burr. Behind John Rapetti's bust of Alexander Hamilton is the New York City skyline.

OPPOSITE Each year, about 4 million tourists visit the Lincoln Memorial on the National Mall in Washington, D.C. Inside is this nineteen-foot-tall, 175-ton Colorado Yule marble statue of Lincoln sculpted by Daniel Chester French. The memorial to the sixteenth president was dedicated on May 30, 1922.

Photograph by Victoria Martin

ABOVE   The Railroad Heritage Mural painted by Connie Burns Watkins of
Paragould, Arkansas. Dedicated in 1990, this 205-by-25-foot mural took eleven
months to paint and is located in downtown Paragould.

OPPOSITE   The railroad track in Paragould, Arkansas, was built to carry cotton
from Texas to St. Louis in the middle of the nineteenth century. Peter Marshall,
the author's grandfather, worked on this railroad in the early 1920s. J. W. Paramore's
Texas and St. Louis small gauge rail line intersected with the St. Louis and Iron
Mountain Railroad headed by Jay Gould in the northwest corner of Arkansas.
People living at the junction named their new town Paragould in honor of the
two railroad presidents.

Theodore Roosevelt has been honored in Washington, D.C., with an eighty-eight-acre, federally preserved island on the Potomac River, across from Rosslyn, Virginia. Heavily wooded and full of walking paths, Roosevelt Island also memorializes the twenty-sixth president with this statue created by Paul Manship.

La Cambe is a five-acre cemetery for Nazi soldiers located near Omaha Beach and Pointe du Hoc in Normandy, France. Crosses made from black lava mark the graves of 21,160 German soldiers killed during World War II while fighting the Allies along fifty miles of Normandy coastline.

...398–1902 ✕ BOXER · REBELLION · 190... ...RAGUA · 1912 ✕ VERA · CRUZ · 1914 ✕ HAITI · 1915–1934 ✕ SANTO · DOMINGO 1916–1924 ✕ WORLD · WAR...

...ADA · 1983 ✕ PERSIAN · GULF-I... ...PANAMA · 1988–1990

IN HONOR AND
OF THE MEN
UNITED STATES MA...
WHO HAVE
THEIR LIVES TO TH...
SINCE 10 NOV...

ABOVE This house at 219 North Delaware Street in Independence, Missouri, was home to Harry and Bess Truman throughout their married lives. Built by Bess Wallace Truman's maternal grandfather and now managed by the National Park Service, the Victorian-style house is just a short distance from the Truman Library, where the former president maintained an office after his White House years.

OPPOSITE This seventy-eight-foot-tall bronze memorial, overlooking Washington, D.C., in Arlington, Virginia, honors the World War II soldiers who raised the flag on the island of Iwo Jima during the battle there in February 1945. Dedicated by President Dwight Eisenhower on November 10, 1954, the statue is the work of the artist Felix de Weldon, who sculpted the scene in clay just seventy-two hours after seeing a photograph of the flag raising. It took hundreds of artisans eight years to finish the memorial.

ABOVE This memorial was commissioned by the North Vietnamese to mark the capture of the most "prized" POW of the Vietnam War, Lieutenant Commander John McCain, a Navy pilot, at Truc Bach Lake near Hanoi on October 26, 1967.

OPPOSITE This wooded path (*bottom*), near Robert Frost's home in Ripton, Vermont, was a regular source of inspiration for the New England poet. Walkers taking "the road less traveled," will find the little cabin (*top*) where Frost spent many summers writing.

ABOVE   In 1963, Martin Luther King, Jr., wrote *Letters from a Birmingham Jail* after being arrested for leading civil rights protests in Birmingham, Alabama. This bronze cast of his jail cell door is displayed at the Newseum in Arlington, Virginia, and stands on a concrete slab the actual size of the cell in which Dr. King was detained.

OPPOSITE   The Edmund Pettus Bridge in Selma, Alabama, became part of American history on March 7, 1965, when a group of civil rights activists marching from Selma to Montgomery were stopped on the bridge by Alabama state troopers dressed in riot gear. Nearly 80 of the 500 unarmed marchers were injured in the confrontation.

ABOVE The thirty-seventh president, Richard Nixon, was born on January 9, 1913, in this farmhouse in Yorba Linda, California. His father, Frank Nixon, had built the house a year earlier from a catalogue kit. The Nixon Birthplace and Presidential Library complex is located about thirty miles southeast of Los Angeles.

OPPOSITE (*Top*) Rancho del Cielo, or "Ranch in the Sky" in Santa Barbara, California, where Ronald Reagan spent 364 days during his two-term presidency. The Reagans purchased this 688-acre ranch in 1974. (*Bottom*) This highest point at Rancho del Cielo overlooks the Pacific Ocean. Whenever Ronald Reagan was at the ranch, a Secret Service agent manned this sniper's nest.

Hoosiers, such as the author, can learn about history from the names of local institutions. Clockwise from top left: the town of Lafayette honors the French marquis who assisted in the Revolutionary War and toured the country in 1824; nearby Colfax memorializes Schuyler Colfax, speaker of the House and vice president to Ulysses S. Grant; Lincoln School, a grade school in Lafayette, is a tribute to the sixteenth president; and the street corner that was home to Bill and Opal Lamb, the author's parents, commemorates the Shawnee Indian tribe that had previously inhabited the land and the Hungarian democratic activist Louis Kossuth, who made a celebrated tour of the U.S. in the mid-nineteenth century.

The World War II Generation

by

TOM BROKAW

World War II lasted from 1939 to 1945, involved every one of the world's major powers, and was the most destructive war in history. At war's end, however, the United States had become a superpower. Tom Brokaw's The Greatest Generation *collects the life stories of Americans who fought in the war and those who supported the effort on the home front.* NBC Nightly News *anchor Tom Brokaw appeared on* Booknotes *on January 13, 1999, to discuss his book, published by Random House in 1998.*

THE WORLD WAR II generation is the greatest generation any society ever produced. They came out of the Depression with all that economic deprivation, went beyond their own shores to help save the world from fascism, came back, and rebuilt their enemies. They built the country we have today, married in record numbers, went to college in record numbers, kept their values, never whined, and never whimpered. They were not perfect. They were very slow on racism. McCarthyism reared its ugly head after they got back from the war. They were very slow on gender equality but once they got it, they really did get it. That generation, as much as any other generation, was whole. Everybody was involved: men, women, the older and younger ends of that generation, they all participated.

JOHNNIE HOLMES WAS raised in northwestern Chicago, in Evanston. He didn't know much racial discrimination growing up in that community, which is the home of Northwestern University, and then he went into the army. As he said, "I told my mother I wasn't gonna let the army break me. I was gonna let it make me." He became a member of the 761st Tank Battalion. He saw really god-awful racial discrimination, both [around the nation] and abroad. When he came back, he led a distinguished life in Chicago working for the city. Now he works for his Catholic church as a volunteer. One of the things he says is that "I made a deal with God. If he would let me come back, I would then do his work." And he said, "For everybody I killed in Europe, I think I've helped ten more here at home."

TOM BRODERICK WAS the only son of a Chicago Irish American family. His father had a small trucking business. He was in premed when the war broke out. He joined the merchant marine and got accepted to the academy. The Merchant Marine Academy was on a long, boring cruise across the Atlantic, as he described it. He decided that he wanted something more exciting, so he went into the airborne. Everybody tried to talk him out of it— his parents, his draft board, the merchant marine. He said, "No, that's what I'm gonna do."

In the Battle of Arnhem, he was shot through the head. He was blinded. They didn't tell him that he was going to be permanently blinded, and so he came back in quite a rage. When his children had gotten to an age where they understood that their father was blind, he would tell them this story: "Your grandmother took me to Lourdes hoping that there could be a miracle." And he said, "Just before they put the holy water on my eyes, I said, 'Lord, I know that we don't always get what we want, but what we deserve, and what I really need is a good woman.'" He met Eileen, his wife, not too long after that and they raised seven children. He built a very successful business.

His children got in touch with me to talk about him. One of his sons said that when Vietnam veterans were sent over to the house by the VA, "they would get out of the car looking suicidal, but Dad would sit on the porch and talk about White Sox baseball and Mom would get a case of beer. He'd walk them through the house and talk to them about what they could do with business. By the end of the evening," this son would say, "I'd hear laughter and reason for life to go on again."

Dr. Charles Van Gorder jumped on D-Day and did something unusual. They decided not to set up well behind the front lines; instead they were going to jump into the middle of the action and set up a MASH unit so that he could operate on young men. He was operating on them. By 9:00 in the morning, they had hundreds of casualties. He was captured later as a prisoner of war and almost died a couple of times during that experience. He and his closest friend, John Rodda, kept each other alive.

They made their way back through Poland and came back. They were going to go to fellowships in New York and have big, distinguished practices. He went to visit his family down in Andrews, North Carolina, and saw that they needed a physician, so he got his friend and they went down there to set up this very small clinic. They were the doctors there forevermore. They delivered all the babies, set all the bones, and built a hospital. What these people did when they came back was really what has made this country what it is today.

ART BUCHWALD IS VERY close to our family; he's like an uncle. Buchwald is the world's most unlikely marine. At Parris Island he was trained by a drill instructor named Pete Bonardi who called him "Artie Brooklyn." He was sure that Art was going to die because he couldn't do anything right; he was on demerit all the time. But Art got back after an undistinguished military record and went to USC and became famous as a columnist. *Life* magazine said, "We want you to go back to Parris Island." He found Pete Bonardi to take back with him. They had a wonderful week. Art still couldn't do anything on the obstacle course or with weapons or anything else, but it was a big laugh.

A few years later, someone called and said, "Art, your friend Pete Bonardi's dying of cancer." Art got out one of the photographs from the *Life* magazine series and said, "To Pete Bonardi, you made a man out of me; I'll never forget you" and sent it off to Pete Bonardi. His wife told Art that he hung it above his bed so everybody could see it. And when he died, he asked to have that picture buried with him.

I tried to describe that story over the phone to my daughters. I couldn't get through it because, to this day, it says to me what that generation did for each other. Here is Art, who became a very famous, celebrated newspaper columnist and was moving in the highest circles of Washington and Paris. Pete Bonardi came back to be a security agent at the World's Fair. But at the end of their lives, they were like this because of those formative experiences that they had.

I WENT ON MEMORIAL DAY eight or nine years ago to see my father's surviving brother. This was at the family homestead founded by my great-grandfather, this little town called Bristol, South Dakota, which was an intersection of two lines of the Milwaukee Railroad, north and south, east and west. They built a little railroad hotel and the family lived there, eleven brothers and sisters. Pretty raucous group, but wonderfully cohesive in terms of family. John was the surviving brother and had been in the navy during the war. He said, "We have to go put the flags out on the graves. I've given up that assignment to this young farmer south of town who is a Korean War veteran and he was supposed to do it. I don't know whether he knows where all the graves are."

I walked down with him to a small cemetery in Bristol, South Dakota, and stood on a knoll and looked at these two men, each clutching a fistful of small flags, going from grave to grave, putting them on. The great gray, late spring South Dakota sky was stretched out behind them. It was a moment of epiphany for me. I thought of all the sacrifices that had been made just in that community in wars, and of the people who had stayed behind and kept the community going, kept the country going together. These men were paying homage to them, as men and women will forevermore in that community.

These cemeteries are magnificent. They really are wonderfully maintained. And it's not just the Americans who maintain them, but in Holland, for example, or in the Philippines or in France, the local people are so grateful and still work on those cemeteries to make sure that they are impeccably kept up.

When you go there, it's a leveling experience. It's emotional and it really does bring you to your knees. Bill Mauldin [an American cartoonist who created sardonic cartoons of the enlisted man's life] tells this wonderful story about the dedication of Colleville-sur-Mer, the cemetery in Omaha Beach. A general had his back to the cemetery because that was where the speaker's platform was. He turned to the dignitaries looking out at the cemetery and he said to them, "I mean no disrespect, but I want to address my men." And he turned around and made his speech to those thousands of white crosses, saying, "I'm sorry I couldn't keep you alive." Mauldin, as I saw him tell this story on a PBS show, broke up, and with good reason.

I DIDN'T HAVE A military career. It's curious that I didn't because I grew up in such a quasi-military environment. I always thought I would probably have a professional military career. I wanted to go to Annapolis to the Naval Academy. . . . When I graduated from college, everybody was going off to the army ROTC. I was recruited by the navy and passed all the officer candidate school exams. I thought I was going to become a naval officer in Rhode Island, at Newport, and do my training. But I had flat feet and at the last station of the physical they said, "We can't take you." So I went out and volunteered for my draft examination and they said the same thing, "Well, those feet are flat." So, I don't have any military experience, which I regret. I don't regret not getting shot at or making the sacrifices that young men did in Vietnam, but I think that it is one of life's experiences, for males especially.

I have a lot of neighbors in Montana and up in New England who are Vietnam veterans and they are the staff of the community. They are ranchers and they run building supply companies and they are the first selectmen, and so on. One of the lessons of Vietnam is that the men who went and came back, a lot of them wanted to get involved in their communities. They didn't want there to be a time in their lives again when they didn't have a say in what happened to them.

Vietnam veterans deserve more attention than they are getting. That, too, is worthy of a book called "Coming Home" or however you want to describe it. There is something that can be done between those who did not go [to Vietnam] and those who did go and how they are joined in communities all over America now without knowing that. They are not talking about Vietnam together, about what motivated them.

The Great Black Migration

by

NICHOLAS LEMANN

In 1900 approximately 90 percent of black Americans lived in the South. That statistic began to decline in the first half of the twentieth century. Thousands left the South and moved north in the "great migration," as it came to be called, hoping to find a better life. This migration from the largely rural South to the more urban North led to a new set of opportunities—and challenges. One such person was Ruby Lee Haynes. Nicholas Lemann, a staff writer for The New Yorker, *appeared on* Booknotes *on March 21, 1991, and shared Ms. Haynes's story with our viewers. Mr. Lemann's* The Promised Land: The Great Black Migration and How It Changed America *was published in 1991 by Alfred A. Knopf.*

THIS BOOK IS ABOUT the migration from the rural South to the urban North. Ruby Lee Haynes is the heroine of my book. She was part of four great migrations. . . . Her first migration from the hills to the Mississippi delta to be a sharecropper; second migration from the drafty, unheated sharecropper cabins on the plantations into the town of Clarksdale, Mississippi. Then the third migration was to Chicago, Illinois. That was the big one; She lived in Chicago for about thirty years. Then the fourth migration was back to Clarksdale around 1980.

The hardest thing was finding my main character. . . . I went through church records and social welfare agency records; I got people to take me around Chicago and Clarksdale, looking for somebody who had lived through X amount of history, number one. . . . I needed somebody who was from Clarksdale, had lived as a sharecropper, and had moved to Chicago. I wanted somebody who had lived in high-rise public housing in Chicago, because part of this whole story is how that housing was built and how it declined. You had to have been through the Stations of the Cross to qualify for my book. Then, also, not only did you have to live through all the stuff, but you had to be a very extraordinary person with an unusual memory and unusual storytelling ability. A lot of people qualified, but they couldn't remember it all.

AFTER SOME MOMENTS of despair that I would never find somebody like this, I met a guy named Benny Gooden who is described in the book as the "richest black man in Clarksdale." He was the public housing king of Clarksdale. He had become rich by building privately and managing HUD subsidized housing projects. They were excellent projects. He was viewed, as many people like that were, in the white community as a poverty pimp. But he was beloved in the black community because he ran good projects, he knew everybody who lived there, and he lived in the same neighborhood where his projects were. He went to church with Ruby Haynes.

Ruby has an unbelievable memory. She's one of those people who can remember every phone number of every place she has ever lived, every rent check and how big it was, dollar amounts of everything, everyone's name. She can recreate each scene in her life, playing all the parts. She's amazing.

SHE HAS HAD AN incredibly eventful life. She was born in 1916. The first great migration she took part in was a migration of southern rural blacks, who were living in the hills of the South, eking out an existence as small farmers in the sharecropper system, which existed on big plantations. When she was just born, a white labor recruiter came to the town where she was living [in Kemper County, Mississippi]. And [the recruiter] talked her grandfather into the idea that if he moved down to the Mississippi Delta, which was the home of fabulously rich soil and big cotton plantations, that he would make a lot of money. It wasn't true, but he believed it.

Ruby's grandfather carried her as a baby down to the Mississippi Delta, so that was the first great migration. She lived, for the first twenty to twenty-five years of her life, in the sharecropper system.

SHE LIVED ON A succession of plantations all through the 1920s and 1930s as a sharecropper, staying with various relatives, chiefly her mother. She was born to a teen mother who wasn't married. Ruby didn't meet her father until she was about twenty. She shuttled back and forth between her mother's home and her grandfather's home, and both her mother and grandfather themselves moved among plantations a lot, which was very typical. Very often sharecroppers moved every single year from plantation to plantation.

SHARECROPPING WAS the successor system to slavery in the South. The way it worked was a sharecropper lived on a plantation and [did] not own the land, but was given a plot—fifteen acres was a typical size—on a very big plantation of thousands of acres. The farmer provided housing, feed, and seed, and the sharecropper raised a cotton crop. At the end of the year, the crop was picked, ginned, weighed, sold, and they split the proceeds fifty-fifty.

This system doesn't exist anymore. It died mostly in the 1940s. When Franklin Roosevelt was president, there started to be a lot of liberal pressure against the sharecropper system for a bunch of reasons. It was a very unfair system, and rightly considered to be cruel and inhumane. It was a system of rural serfdom, the kind of thing you don't think of happening in twentieth-century America. . . . The invention of various machines, in this case the mechanical cotton picker, ended the sharecropper system. It took away the need for hand labor in the fields, especially on big plantations.

AFTER THE SHARECROPPER system began to die out, Ruby moved in a second great migration into the nearest sizable town, Clarksdale, one of the bigger towns in the Delta.

SHE WAS ONLY married once. However, she comes from a world in which nobody ever got married. . . . There was a tradition of common-law marriage that she grew up with, in which people would either get married or not have a marriage ceremony and move in together. This was a time in the 1930s, when the only people cohabiting in America were poor, rural black folks, as opposed to now, when everybody is. So it was an unusual habit at the time, but very pervasive in her world.

She has had eight children, and only one was born in wedlock. The father of the younger four was her ultimate husband, Luther Haynes; several of her children were the product of these shorter-lived, common-law marriages. [Out-of-wedlock] children were the rule in the world she grew up with, and became also the rule in the Chicago ghetto, as they are now.

IF YOU'RE WRITING the story of this great migration, Chicago is mythic. . . . Chicago is a big, industrial, brawny city, and during the time of this book it's really the capital of black America. The South Side is probably the biggest contiguous black neighborhood in America, was then and probably is now.

[RUBY MADE HER third migration to Chicago in 1946 to make more money as a janitor. In the 1940s] close to 1.3 million black Chicagoans lived on the city's South Side. [Even today] the South Side of Chicago, is huge. It has a lot of different neighborhoods. That is one key to understanding it. It is not just the slums. It has some of the worst slums in America. It has the biggest high-rise public housing project in the world, the Robert Taylor Homes. It also has vast, huge middle-class to upper-middle-class black neighborhoods. It has the whole gamut of experience. It is a very varied place.

THERE'S AN OFFICIAL number and an unofficial number of people in Chicago living in public housing today. There are a lot of different numbers. It's something over 100,000 people though some people think as much as 250,000 people. . . . Officially the population of these projects is almost completely women and children. Unofficially, there are a lot of men living there, but they're not official residents and they're not paying rent. . . . Some of the houses are being paid for and some aren't, but primarily the federal government pays for them. You pay a rent, but it's a very low rent, and the rest is picked up by a federal subsidy.

[OVER THE YEARS] she became, for reasons described in the book, quite bitter about Chicago. She felt it had let her down and hadn't turned out the way she had hoped it would. Like many of her friends, poor black women, she has had many, many problems with men. She can talk to you for hours about no-good men. So, when she got to an age when she just didn't try to date anymore and didn't try to meet men, she says, she became much happier. She feels now that all of her romances in her life always went awry and left a bad taste in her mouth.

NOBODY HAS READ this book and said, "This is the welfare queen of Chicago. To heck with her.". . . And this is one thing that has pleased me about the reaction to the book. Very often, people have reacted to her life story by saying, "This is somebody who has had a real tough life and who should have had a lot more help than she had."

WITHOUT QUESTION, President Lyndon Johnson did the most to help her life get better. Mrs. Haynes's grandchildren are all in Head Start, a program that Johnson started. Her basic benefit on Social Security is higher now, thanks to Johnson and succeeding presidents. If she gets sick, she is taken care of through Medicare and Medicaid, a Johnson program. Some of her grandchildren are going to end up going to college. The grants they get will probably be grants that were instituted by Johnson. If she gets sick, she can go to Clarksdale Hospital. The reason she doesn't have to ride on the back of the bus anymore and the reason she can vote is because of the Civil Rights Act of 1964, and the Voting Rights Act of 1965, both passed by Johnson. [Numerous people] live where they live today because of the Fair Housing

Act of 1968, also passed by Johnson. There isn't anyone close; there isn't any second place. Lyndon Johnson did the most for black America in the panoply of white American politicians.

You can question Johnson's motives, but he did decide, for whatever reason—and Robert Kennedy did too, both after the John Kennedy assassination—that they were going to become crusaders on this issue. On all these issues, the record of Robert Kennedy is better than that of John Kennedy. There has been a lot of ex post facto mythmaking about John F. Kennedy and civil rights, mythmaking by the Kennedy circle, especially Arthur Schlesinger. Acting out of sincere admiration, they have remade him, in death, into a civil rights president. He did propose the Civil Rights Act, although the consensus is he would never have been able to pass it. . . . But on the whole, first of all, he just didn't "get" that race was a great moral issue in America until very late, if he got it at all. He was very worried about the March on Washington in 1963 and would have preferred that it not happen. He was not thrilled about all the civil rights activity that Dr. Martin Luther King was doing in the South; he was always urging him, "Go slower, take time." He was not a crusader on this issue.

The Moynihan Report (1965) was a government report called *The Negro Family: A Case for National Action,* written by then assistant secretary of labor, Daniel Patrick Moynihan. Most government reports are totally ignored, but the Moynihan Report was incredibly controversial. This report said the black family was falling apart and said it in very dramatic, one might even say overdramatized, terms. It produced a furious reaction in the nascent black power movement and in the academic, intellectual left, which was also just coming into being. Moynihan's assertion, made quite casually and off the cuff in the report, had a paragraph that said slavery destroyed the black family. This led to a whole shelf of books by historians written between 1965 to about 1980, proving that slavery didn't destroy the black family. That is why I say it was an incredibly refuted document.

Moynihan was wildly attacked after his report came out. He was pilloried. He was booed and hissed and called every name in the book. . . . It was not polite debate. This was a very angry time in America, 1965 and '66. Moynihan became very bitter, and he became obsessed with the danger posed to America by these forces that had gone after his report, namely, the interlocking directorate of the black power movement and the academic, intellectual left.

THIS BOOK IS ABOUT the migration from the South. I was trying to understand inner-city ghettos through the lens of the great migration and all the changes that happened in those city neighborhoods over the years since

World War II. . . . The issue of ghettos is on everybody's mind. . . . But there isn't a good way to talk about it. Everybody's stuck. The same arguments are being used, chasing each other in circles. My hope is that this book will create a history of ghettos. That it will allow people to come afresh to the discussion and start thinking about it again.

Early Network News

by

SALLY BEDELL SMITH

DAVID BRINKLEY

PETER JENNINGS

In the middle of the twentieth century, two networks—CBS and NBC—dominated television news. ABC was the last to enter the business, but its newscast soon became competitive with its two older rivals. In the following chapter, several authors paint portraits of the news business at the three networks. Sally Bedell Smith, a writer living in Rhode Island and New York City, tells the story of the patriarch of CBS, William S. Paley, in her book, In All His Glory: The Life of William S. Paley, *published by Simon & Schuster in 1990. She appeared on* Booknotes *in November of that same year. Then, two longtime network news anchors, David Brinkley, of NBC and later ABC, and Peter Jennings, who has anchored ABC's nightly newscast since 1983, discussed the news business in excerpts from their books:* David Brinkley: A Memoir, *published in 1995 by Alfred A. Knopf, and* The Century, *coauthored by Mr. Jennings with Todd Brewster and published by Doubleday in 1998. Mr. Brinkley visited us on December 10, 1995; Mr. Jennings appeared on* Booknotes *on December 27, 1998.*

SALLY BEDELL SMITH

William S. Paley was a broadcaster who had enormous influence over a medium that had a great effect on our lives. What was most intriguing about him was that his own personal identity was so bound up in the identity of CBS and the Tiffany network. He was a pioneer of broadcasting.

Paley's interest in radio began when he and his father were still in a cigar business together. His father and his uncle bought an ad on a little, struggling radio station in Philadelphia while Bill Paley was away on vacation. As the head of advertising, Paley was quite furious at them for having done this. At the same time, some friends of the Paley family were buying into this network that became CBS, and they proposed that Paley be the president of this network because he was young and energetic and dynamic. He said at that time, "I don't want anything to do with this little pip-squeak network." But his father asked him to supervise a network show that their cigar company was going to sponsor, and so Bill Paley ended up going to New York and overseeing the show.

This was his first exposure to the world of radio and to the world of show business. He was absolutely captivated by it. He also saw the power of radio to sell products to the American public, and that power caught him. When it came time for him to have an opportunity to invest himself, to take over the stake that the friend of the family had, he leapt at it.

FROM THE VERY beginning, Paley was masterful at public relations. One of the first people he hired when he bought into the struggling network that became CBS back in 1928 was the father of public relations, Edward Bernays. Bernays guided him very carefully in those days and taught him to develop an image for CBS that would distinguish it from NBC, which was far larger and stronger than CBS.

One of the important components of that was a commitment to public affairs. For the most part, CBS Radio was putting on programs that were pretty middlebrow and pretty ho-hum. It had the good sense to develop this public affairs commitment. This was very good, because it mollified the regulators in Washington who were leaning pretty hard on the emerging networks, fearful of their power. So, it gave them a good impression. It also created a good impression on the audience and it rubbed off on Paley as well.

The idea that Paley didn't get involved in CBS News at crucial times . . . simply isn't borne out by the record. Going all the way back to the 1930s and '40s, after CBS had devised a set of rules governing [on-air] commentary, is when trouble began. In the '30s Paley would frequently give time to advertisers who espoused very conservative views on the air. At the same time, he was currying favor with the Roosevelt White House.

At some point, they realized that sponsors liked a far more neutral environment for their messages, and so CBS said commentary couldn't be too opinionated or too sharp. When commentators would go over that line, they would be punished or dismissed. It began with [CBS commentators] H. V. Kaltenborn in 1940 and Cecil Brown in 1942. Elmer Davis ran afoul of Paley constantly. Paley said he used to have lunch with him every three weeks to persuade him not to go so far in his commentaries. Edward R. Murrow, for a while, was held apart because of his friendship with Paley. After the war, William Shirer went too far and he was dropped. Howard K. Smith and Eric Sevareid both got into hot water with Bill Paley because they had gone too far with their commentaries; Smith had to leave as a result. Eric Sevareid and Paley had a Mexican standoff, and Sevareid pulled back. As a result, Sevareid stayed on the network.

In the early 1970s it was Bill Paley himself who abolished instant analysis after Vice President Spiro Agnew had highly criticized it; six months later, he somewhat embarrassingly reinstated it. Some of the people who were privy to that decision said his friend Averell Harriman had criticized CBS for not doing analysis of speeches. But Paley didn't want opinion [on the network] at all. It just so happened that a lot of reporters who came out of the World War II experience were, I suppose you might say, liberals. It was really their criticisms of the administration that bothered him more than anything.

AFTER WORLD WAR II, when Edward R. Murrow was at his absolute peak, he was a hero because of the way he brought the war home to the American people and the eloquence of his reports from London during the Blitz. What Bill Paley did when Murrow came back home was he made him an executive. He took him and put him in the front office. He was a star player. It was an extremely unhappy period for Murrow. He was very uncomfortable working as an administrator. He did develop some good programs, but it was during that period that he had a terrible falling out with William Shirer when Shirer was doing too many pointed commentaries on the air.

Shirer was the author of *The Rise and Fall of the Third Reich* and had gone all through World War II with Ed Murrow. They were very good friends. After the war, Shirer did a program on CBS and took on members of the administration. This was a time, of course, at the height of the Cold War. The blacklisting had begun. The witch-hunting had begun. Joseph McCarthy was on the rise. Sponsors were getting very nervous and were sending letters to CBS addressed to the "Communist Broadcasting System."

Paley was obviously very sensitive to this. The advertiser of Shirer's show came to Paley . . . and said, "I don't want him. I want a more neutral commentator on the air." So Shirer was told he was losing his time slot, and he had the temerity to go on the air and announce this, that he was being removed from his time slot because a soap company had this kind of power.

Paley was sitting in his country house on Long Island listening to this broadcast. He was furious at the insubordination of it, and the next day convened a meeting at CBS's headquarters and said, "This man has to go." Murrow, to his credit, tried to defend him on the grounds of loyalty and many years of service to CBS, but Paley would have none of it. Murrow was put in the terribly uncomfortable position of devising a cover story, and the cover story was that Shirer just hadn't been doing his job; he'd been doing his commentaries out of the clippings and he wasn't performing up to snuff. It tore Murrow up. It was a terrible thing for him to have to do. After that he was disillusioned with the role of administrator and asked to go back on the air.

[PALEY'S] AGE SPANNED the century. He was born in 1901, and he was there at lots of important periods in our history—sometimes in very unusual ways. When you think of the 1930s, you always think of the Depression, and when I explored the life that he and his friends led in the 1930s, it was a luxurious, sybaritic life that was so far above the hardships that everybody else was going through at the time. That was one of the many contradictions of him, that he could be so rarified and associated with high culture and high society, but at the same time he had a very earthy side to him, which may have explained why he could understand mass audience programming.

DAVID BRINKLEY

[In the early days of radio, after 6:00 P.M., the radio announcers had to wear tuxedos] at NBC. It was a requirement because NBC then was the foremost network. It is the oldest network. For a time, CBS, in many ways, was better, particularly in news. But NBC and RCA, which owned it then, were the foremost forces in broadcasting. It was a chairman of RCA who thought of the idea of radio—of having a little box in your house that would bring you news and music. David Sarnoff was his name, and he, very busily and eagerly, later worked on developing television. The system we use today is the RCA system.

John Cameron Swayze started his nightly newscast in the late '40s. Cigarette manufacturers were the advertisers on the first television news program. They called it the *Camel News Caravan,* advertising Camel cigarettes, and the advertiser was R.J. Reynolds Tobacco Company. They always wanted that spelled out meticulously.

The other requirements were that Swayze have a lighted cigarette in the ashtray beside him on his desk while he was on the air so the smoke would float up. Another requirement was that we could never have news film showing a No Smoking sign. And the other was that nobody was allowed to smoke a cigar, with one exception and that was Winston Churchill. He was a hero of such magnitude at that time that even an advertising man dare not mess with him.

The war was barely over. There were still a lot of American soldiers around the world and the Reynolds people, each week—I guess the others did too, though I don't know about it—sent out thousands of cartons of free cigarettes to the American soldiers. Each week during that time, they had Swayze announce (and when I filled in for him, I had to announce) that the R.J. Reynolds Tobacco Company is sending X thousand cartons of Camel cigarettes to our boys around the world. They thought that was their patriotic contribution to the war. And we all did it. You had to hold up the carton at the end of the program, which I did once and got it upside down, which made them furious. But that was the first advertising on a news program on television.

[IN 1956 NBC PAIRED me and Chet Huntley for a nightly newscast that lasted fourteen years.] We didn't see each other much because he always lived in New York and I've always lived in Washington—still do. So we were not what we used to call "stone buddies" because I didn't see him that much. But when we were together, we got along just fine. I deferred to him and he deferred to me, and we worked together at conventions for hours and hours and days and days, in pretty close quarters, a glassed-in box usually up in the ceiling of the convention hall. I talked when I felt like talking and he talked when he felt like talking, and it just worked fine. Nothing was planned. There was no schedule; there was no script; it was all ad lib. Not everybody can do it, but we could do it and did it very well.

People began shouting at me in the streets. "Good night, David. Good night, Chet." They still do, a little bit. It's dying out now. That's when we knew the program was catching on. We had several arguments about the closing words of our news show. Huntley didn't like "Good night, David; good night, Chet." He thought it was sissified. I thought it was kind of silly saying good night to each other instead of saying good night to the audience. But the producer won; Reuven Frank is his name. That came to be the sign-off and it worked, because it became part of the language.

I was in a railroad station and a nice, gray-haired lady came over to me and said, "Aren't you Chet Huntley?" I said yes, partly because it didn't make any difference. We were like twins, almost. And she said, "I think you were very good, but I cannot stand that idiot Brinkley." I've never forgotten that and I never will.

PETER JENNINGS

[When I got into this business more than] thirty years ago, I was a very small fish and living, as we all did, in the shadow of Chet Huntley and David Brinkley and Walter Cronkite. What I do remember thirty, forty years ago was how people looked to the three networks—two networks, really, NBC and CBS; ABC being a nonstarter at the time—for this sort of centrality in life. I think it is still true.

I came to America in 1964 as a reporter determined to go and see the rest of the world. I got offered a job by ABC. I was so intimidated by the notion of coming to New York the first time that I said no. I woke up about six months later in a cold sweat and said, "Oh, God, what have I done?" And I wrote them and said, "Could I change my mind?" But I wanted to see the rest of the world, which was a very distinctly young Canadian thing to do. I came here, was plunged immediately into the coverage of civil rights in the mid-1960s. I worked here for five, maybe seven years, then went and spent almost twenty years in the rest of the world, always at ABC's behest.

My challenge when I first came to America was to work in every one of the fifty states, a silly challenge, but an interesting one. It kept me going. And then I became overwhelmed by the notion of learning as much about the country as I could as I went along. If you work in television, one of the things we fail to do, is to show Americans about their country, and I've always wanted to do that.

When I came here and was assigned to cover the civil rights movement, I realized how complicated it was, how much pain there was involved for all concerned in the country. Somebody asked me the other day what I thought was the saddest thing of the century; I was caught slightly off guard and gave some gratuitous answer about how man is still killing man with such vigor at the end of the century. The saddest thing of the century, of course, is that America has not managed to solve its racial problems.

[I grew up] in this little English town in western Quebec. I was interested in being a broadcaster [like my father]. My father was not only very good but did a lot of live broadcasting, describing the opening of Parliament and the visits of kings and queens. The Canadian Broadcasting Corporation did a lot of live broadcasting, took it as a public service to cover great events, and if you wanted to get ahead, if you wanted to do well, you had to describe things, and not talk too much over the sound of the horses' hooves.

So he sent me out one night as a kid, as an exercise, to go and describe the sky. I went up and stood on the little veranda outside my parents' bedroom, and looked up at the sky and said, "Yeah, man, look at that, blah, blah, blah." I was downstairs in five minutes. My father said, "Well, that was rather quick." And he taught me a great lesson, which I'm now trying to pass on to a lot of other younger broadcasters. He said, "Go up and look at the sky again and imagine that it's a pie, and just take a little slice of it and describe the slice. Then take the next little slice next to it and describe that, and then talk about the relationship between the two slices, and you'll begin to describe events and affairs and you'll begin to have some notion of context." And he was right.

It taught me very young that the most exciting thing in the world for a broadcast journalist is to go on the air and do a live event. You're totally in command. There's nobody who can tell you to shut up; they can cut your microphone but it's basically your decision about where you go and what you cover. But if you don't have a sense of context and if you have no history, forget it.

I'm rather struck by how many children of journalists or broadcasters end up going into the business. My instinct is to say I rather hope [mine don't] because the business has changed so much. When I was a young reporter and going off to Egypt, for example, they'd say, "Go do a thing on Egypt." And you could go up and down the Nile for two or three days, talk to local politicians, have a couple of good meals, take your time and file from Egypt. The CNN-ization of the world, not to mention what the rest of us have had to respond to in technological terms, means you're in Cairo today and Calcutta tomorrow and that's very hard. So I'm not sure I want my children to live a life that wouldn't give them the leisure of learning as much as they could about the local culture.

I ALWAYS THINK, when I come to Washington, about the *Challenger* disaster because I was here when the *Challenger* blew up. . . . I had been waiting to see President Reagan in the White House. I rushed to the bureau and was on the air for eleven and a half hours. When it was over, I went back to the hotel to come upon the bulldog editions of the *New York Times* and the *Washington Post*. And I was struck ("God, they've got thirty pages on this story") by how the country must have been moved by watching the television.

I went to see Dan Boorstin, who was then the librarian of Congress, and asked him to put this in some perspective for me. And he said, "Television is what we have to replace the campfire. At the time of Western development, when the people had a disaster on the wagon train, they sat around the campfire. Now people sit around television." They still do. They sit around more [networks now] but in the event of a national [story] people gather . . . around the television sets to have this shared experience.

Early Cold War

1945–1957

Five Men Who Shaped the Post–World War II World

by

DAVID FROMKIN

America's post–World War II role on the world stage was to a large degree established by a group of men whose decisions and actions shaped the course of the historic events of the twentieth century. These men included Franklin Delano Roosevelt, Harry Truman, Dwight David Eisenhower, George C. Marshall Jr., and Douglas MacArthur. In a Booknotes *interview on September 6, 1995, Boston University professor David Fromkin discussed this influential generation and how U.S. foreign policy evolved under their leadership. Mr. Fromkin's book* In the Time of the Americans: The Generation That Changed America's Role in the World, *published by Alfred A. Knopf in 1995, examines the history of America during a period of growing international influence.*

THIS BOOK IS A generational history. It's about American leaders who were born in the 1880s or early 1890s, and who played a role throughout the twentieth century. It ends on Inauguration Day, 1961, when . . . Eisenhower's generation handed over the torch to the younger generation, Jack Kennedy's.

The United States came out of this generation very well indeed. These were years in which America had tremendous challenges, the enormous two World Wars, the Great Depression, the Korean War, and the outset of the Cold War. Coming up against each one of these enormous challenges to our national prosperity, our greatness and, in some cases, to our existence, the United States always rose to the challenge and produced great leaders. . . . Five were among the most prominent and typical. . . . They had the character to win and to do things the right way, and they had courage. Theirs is a success story due to the qualities of courage and character they had.

[THE FIRST OF THE five is Franklin Delano Roosevelt.] In the whole of history, FDR is the most difficult character to write about. He was a man of immense contradictions. I don't know any biographers of Roosevelt who felt they got the whole man or found his secret. Roosevelt was an aristocrat; he was born [in 1882] to a wealthy and prominent family. As a young man, he seemed to be intellectually shallow. He wasn't very good at school nor was he interested in serious things. Even after he embarked on his political career and became president of the United States, many came away from conversations with him thinking he had very little intellect and didn't seem very serious.

FDR began his career as a lawyer but didn't spend many years at it. [In 1910 he] ran for state senator from his county in New York [and served one term]. Then he went to Washington as assistant secretary of the navy [from 1913 to 1920], in which capacity he served during the First World War. He ran [unsuccessfully] for vice president in 1920. After a bout with polio, he returned to politics and ran for and won the job of governor of New York [and served from 1928 to 1932]. Then [in 1932 he] ran for the presidency and was elected for an unprecedented four terms.

In the great strategic decisions of the Second World War, on the big things, FDR was just about always right even when the most accomplished of his professional advisers were on the other side. He was a true mystery, but he had a magic personality. He is endlessly fascinating to think and write about.

[THE SECOND MAIN character is Harry Truman.] Truman was deceptively simple; he made himself seem simple. He was a very engaging and smart person. He had much more depth to him than he let on. He played the part of an ordinary man to perfection. But he was not an ordinary man.

Truman [was born in 1884 and] had lots of jobs. He didn't have the money to go through college, so he worked as a bank clerk. He was a farmer; he also speculated in mineral leases. In the First World War, he went into the army as a citizen soldier. When he came back with a partner, he went into the haberdashery business and tried to make a success of that. But his successes came when he went into public life. He became a judge [in 1922], and he ran for the Senate [in 1934]. He made a name for himself as a senator. During the war, he headed a committee that looked into the industries that were supplying the war effort, and did an outstanding job. [I don't think he] made any mistakes.

Truman didn't really know FDR [when he was nominated as his vice president in 1944]. As a matter of fact, Roosevelt had intervened against him the last time he ran for the Senate. He knew very little about Roosevelt's foreign policy or what commitments had been made or about the various secrets that the president had in the running of the war. [After FDR's death in 1945, Truman served as the thirty-third president until 1953.]

[THE THIRD MAJOR character in this generation is Dwight David Eisenhower.] He was so different from Truman in so many ways. [Ironically] he was also much like him in that Eisenhower pretended to be unable to speak or write clearly. He also played the part of a plain old good guy, and he too was a man of great depth. As the thirty-fourth president, he was very much in charge of his presidency while allowing others to be out front seeming to make the decisions, but he [really] made the decisions.

Eisenhower was [born in 1890. He was] a professional soldier who went to West Point. In the First World War, he was a drillmaster. Even though he wanted to, he never got overseas. He was in the peacetime army and served as an aide to General Douglas MacArthur. . . . He was the American general in command of our first Atlantic campaign offensive by leading our troops into North Africa in 1942. As commander of our attack on France and Western Europe, he won the war in Europe. He was president of Columbia University [from 1948 to 1953]. But [Truman called him back to be the] NATO commander [from 1950 to 1952] after the war. Then he ran for the presidency [and served from 1953 to 1961].

Harry Truman called Eisenhower back because we really needed him to serve in Europe as our NATO commander when NATO was being set up. He also called George Marshall back because he was needed during the Korean War. He had been in retirement. Both men just came back, put on their uniforms, and went back to work. This was a generation that believed strongly in service to their country.

[THE FOURTH MAJOR player was George Marshall.] He was a person of great character who impressed himself on his contemporaries by force of his virtue and character. He was a great organizer and a great administrator. He played a tremendous role in the winning of the Second World War.

George Catlett Marshall Jr. was [born in 1880. He was] also a professional soldier but he didn't go to West Point; he went to Virginia Military Institute. He served in the First World War as a much admired and highly effective staff officer to the American commander, General John J. Pershing. Just before the Second World War, he became America's chief of staff in the U.S. Army and organized our victory in that war. [During the Truman administration] he became both secretary of state and later the secretary of defense.

As secretary of state, Marshall set forth the plan to save Western Europe in a speech at Harvard. President Truman named the plan for him, in part out of admiration and generosity for him, and in part because Marshall had played a major role in getting together the various groups that conceived of this plan. Western Europe was then in dire straits economically, and therefore socially. Society had broken down and so had the link between the countryside and the city. The farmers kept the food and didn't send it in to the cities because they didn't have faith in the money with which the cities could pay. In 1947 people starved during what was the coldest winter within memory in Europe, and there was the threat of a Communist takeover.

But beyond that, it was simply the fact that our friends and allies were simply going under. Marshall's plan proposed that the United States put up the seed money, the pump-priming money for these societies to get on their feet. The key element of the plan was that the Europeans themselves would have to create the plan for their recovery. We would back them, but they had to create the plan. It wasn't a plan [in which we said,] "You do this because this is what we want you to do." Marshall had the wisdom to see that if these people were going to stand on their own feet, they had to make their own plan and their own decisions. What we would do is simply give them the bridge financing so that they could do it.

It seems to me that none of Marshall's serious mistakes mattered. He was wrong in thinking that the Russians had no chance when Nazi Germany invaded Soviet Russia in 1941, but his superior, President Roosevelt, [thought they] did. Time and again, in the Second World War, on several really big things, Marshall was wrong. But it didn't matter [because] his boss, the commander in chief, Franklin Roosevelt, made the right decision by not following Marshall's advice. I don't think that anything on which he was very wrong had consequences.

[THE FIFTH IMPORTANT person was General Douglas MacArthur, who] was a fascinating figure and a man of genius and brilliance. He was a flashy, colorful character who lived an extraordinary life. He was amazingly courageous on the battlefield. His was an extraordinary persona, a persona that he and his mother worked hard at creating.

Douglas MacArthur [was born in 1880 and] was a professional army officer throughout his life, until retirement. He went to West Point, graduating in the top of his class, and he achieved the highest grades of anyone since Robert E. Lee. He served in many posts. From the beginning, he did heroic deeds, beginning in 1914 with a visit to Mexico. He was a courageous battlefield general in the First World War and he was our general in the Philippines at the outbreak of the Second. He was in command of the southern part of the Pacific campaign in the Second World War and he was in Japan. He was our initial commander in the Korean War, and then he retired to a job as chairman of the board of a large corporation, Remington Rand, Inc.

General MacArthur's greatest mistake was in the Korean War. He didn't stop at the waist of the peninsula [above the thirty-eighth parallel] after he had won great victories at Inchon. He could have stopped but he went ahead to the Yalu frontier and set up an enormous disaster, which clouded his reputation. . . . There's a spot where the mountains go down on a north-south basis, and if you're a commander going there, you don't want to get in that position because you have to split your troops. But he did and he shouldn't have. He went all the way up to the Chinese border, although there were signs that if he did so, they'd come in against us with their limitless manpower. . . . Had he stopped where he should have stopped, he would truly be remembered as one of the great generals.

THIS GENERATION HAD two mentors, two poles of discourse and thought. One was a Republican, Theodore Roosevelt, the other was a Democrat, Woodrow Wilson. They learned from both.

The Unlikely Kennedy–Nixon Friendship

by

CHRISTOPHER MATTHEWS

Richard M. Nixon and John F. Kennedy first met on January 3, 1947, as freshmen U.S. congressmen, thirteen years before their historic presidential debate in 1960, the nation's first televised presidential debate. Though the two men would each serve as president of the United States, they left very different historical legacies. Columnist and MSNBC Hardball *host Chris Matthews appeared on* Booknotes *on June 9, 1996, to discuss their relationship as recounted in his book,* Kennedy and Nixon: The Rivalry That Shaped Postwar America, *published by Simon & Schuster in 1996.*

THE KENNEDY-NIXON story is the story of our century. I think it's the best story since World War II in American politics.

From 1952 through 1972, the whole twenty-year span, through the shank of the Cold War, the heart of it, Richard Nixon was on the Republican ticket in all but one of those years. It was an astounding run. People try to deny Nixon's role in history. [People also misremember] . . . Jack Kennedy. You have to put Kennedy in perspective. He had people working for him who played tricks politically. He had hardballers working for him. He was a tough political customer. He was not a flower child. He was a Cold Warrior and a tough-as-nails politician. . . . He was not a victim. Sure, he ended up getting shot by Lee Harvey Oswald, or someone helping Lee Harvey Oswald, but no one will tell me that Jack Kennedy was a victim in life. He was a winner. And I think Watergate has to be put in perspective. The deeds that led to Watergate, the motives behind it and the actual conduct of the Nixon presidency, did not jump out from nowhere. This was an escalation in American politics all through the '50s and '60s and '70s. It was getting nastier and nastier, and the stakes were getting bigger. What presidents were willing to do, from wiretapping to whatever, was getting worse. Nixon ended it because he showed that it had gotten out of hand.

WE ALL KNOW THE story of *PT-109*. Jack Kennedy was the hero of that because he was this fabulous swimmer who saved his crew after their PT boat had been cut in half by a Japanese destroyer. Well, only about a hundred miles away in the Solomon Islands at that time, Richard Nixon was a supply officer in the navy, running what was called Nick's Canteen, which is where Nixon used to play poker. Nixon was so successful playing poker at his canteen that he came back from the navy with $10,000 in his kitty. Nixon was this sort of a Sergeant Bilko character; he had his card games. And there's Jack Kennedy out saving his crew. It's quite a comparison.

I compare the two to Mozart and Salieri. Let's just talk about Nixon because he's more understandable to most real people. It's almost impossible for us to imagine what it was like to be Jack Kennedy, but we can all imagine being Nixon: extremely hardworking, he could have easily had a scholarship to Harvard or Yale when he was a kid in high school, but he didn't have any money, even to pay for transportation to come back East. He ended up going to Whittier College, worked like mad there, worked like mad through Duke University Law School, got out of Duke Law, third in the class, hardworking all the time.

Nixon finally got into Congress and was a very hard worker, caught Alger Hiss red-handed, the only guy to ever catch somebody that big. Joe McCarthy never caught anybody. Nixon actually caught a real Communist and became a household name, became a U.S. senator in his thirties. He [became] vice president of the United States, a reelected vice president by the age of forty-three, an incredible political success story by his mid-forties. John Kennedy was a guy who had been very sickly most of his life. He had Addison's disease. His skin would change color radically. He always looked very ill when he was a congressman and a senator. People like Lyndon Johnson used to say, "Sickly, sickly, yaller, yaller, how can this guy be president?" Nixon never thought that Kennedy would overtake him.

So in a way, it's like the tortoise and the hare. Nixon was the tortoise who was working his way up slowly to be president by 1960, and Jack Kennedy was the hare that just came out of nowhere. Nixon was Salieri, the court composer. If you remember the movie *Amadeus*, Salieri was the hardworking guy who knew what the public wanted, who knew what the aristocracy wanted to hear, and always composed according to the conventions. He was a very talented composer. Along comes a genius, a fop, who chased women under tables . . . Jack Kennedy: no one thought he was a genius to talk to, but when he got on a platform and gave a speech, he spoke like Churchill . . . . So it was a battle between talent and genius, Nixon being talent, Kennedy being genius. To this day, when you hear Kennedy's speeches, you're hearing Mozart. "Ich bin ein Berliner." "Ask not what your country can do for you." Those words ring through us, even today; they have power. You can't think of a line Richard Nixon ever spoke.

THE ONE THING [these two men] agreed on, and the country agreed on from 1945 to the 1970s—and still agrees on—is that we had to stop world communism, but they agreed about it from different perspectives. When you said the word "freedom" to Jack Kennedy, he had a very clear idea of what it meant. It meant girls; it meant fun; it meant the good life. Communists were going to take that away from people. They were going to make them live like robots, like prisoners. Jack Kennedy knew what that meant. He had a very tangible, tactile sense of fun. To Nixon, it was more of an ideological thing. Nixon saw communism as a threat to the working middle class that he had grown up with, the small grocer, the small businessman. His first exposure to communism was going over in 1947 and talking to small businessmen in Eastern Europe, and being impressed by how angry they were about the Communist takeover.

Jack Kennedy ran for office in 1946 as a fighting conservative. He was more Irish than he was a liberal. If you look at the Democratic Party in the 1950s, there were the regular, organized people from the big cities—Irish, Italian, black, or whatever—and then there was the intellectual elite led by Adlai Stevenson and Eleanor Roosevelt. Jack Kennedy was not part of the Roosevelt-Stevenson crowd; he was part of the regulars. He was also very fond of southerners. His best friend in the Senate was George Smathers of Florida, a segregationist. He was very comfortable with southern members, and I think he did very well in 1956, when he ran for the vice presidency, with the South. The Texans all came out for him. He was a conservative by Democratic standards of those days. When he was getting too many letters from people saying, "Why don't you be a real liberal?" he said, "Why don't you just tell them I'm not a liberal and to stop bothering me?"

KENNEDY AND NIXON first met on January 3, 1947, swearing-in day. . . . Both these fellows were coming aboard as U.S. congressmen. They met at a National Press Club reception for returning GIs from World War II who had been elected to Congress. . . . Billy Sutton, who was press secretary to Jack Kennedy, freshman from Massachusetts, introduced him to Richard Nixon, the freshman from California. Jack Kennedy said, "You're the guy that beat Jerry Voorhis, aren't you?" Nixon said, "Yeah." And Kennedy said, "That's like beating John McCormack up in Massachusetts. How's that feel?" Voorhis was a big New Dealer, a five-termer, probably the most respected member of the House. . . . Kennedy was so impressed that this guy had knocked off the big guy, and Nixon, of course, not very good at small talk, says, "Well, I guess I feel great." That's all he could come up with.

IN APRIL OF 1947, . . . they were both freshmen. They were the two hottest shots in the U.S. Congress. A Pennsylvania congressman, a Democrat named Frank Buchanan . . . was asked by a local civic group in western Pennsylvania, McKeesport, to invite the most promising young Democrat and most promising young Republican to come up and debate the hottest issue of the day, Taft-Hartley, which was [a bill on] labor reform. They both went up together, and Nixon debated just as he had done in school, man to man, took on Kennedy point by point. Kennedy ignored Nixon and talked directly to the hall, just as he did thirteen years later in their nationally televised great debate. Kennedy was a charmer. Nixon got the audience very angry because he took the side of business against labor and got all the labor guys mad at him. They were heckling him.

What was interesting was, afterward, the two of them went off for a snack at the Star Diner, which was right next to the railroad tracks, and had this late dinner together. Apparently, according to the guys who were there, they were really friendly. What really struck these guys was, first of all, here was the one aristocrat, Jack Kennedy, and the other guy who was a middle-class sort of guy, yet you couldn't tell them apart—who was the well-born guy, and who was not the well-born guy.

When they came back on the train, they flipped a coin for the top bunk. . . . It's almost right out of *North by Northwest.* In the top bunk was Jack Kennedy, lying there. In the bunk below him was Richard Nixon, talking about the coming threat in Europe that had just been given its name the week before by Bernard Baruch, the "Cold War." Two navy officers who had both fought in the Pacific and didn't want to see [war] again; both had seen Hitler's march through Europe, didn't want to see Stalin's march through Europe; both Cold Warriors as the term had just been coined, arguing about what should be done. I think about the greatest political poster of all times: a picture of those two bunks, with the one guy sitting up there talking with the other guy, having a bull session as the train rolled on to Washington, the *Capital Limited.*

IN THEIR FIRST YEAR, Kennedy was on the third floor of what's now the

Cannon Building, and Nixon was on the fifth floor. He used to call it the attic, his office up there, a little low-ceiling office. Jack Kennedy apparently stopped by the office. He knew Nixon was about to go on his first-ever trip to Europe as a young man, and he dropped off some names of some people Nixon might look up in Europe. One of them was his sister, but then there were three other women he gave the names of, too, which apparently completely amazed Nixon. He didn't ever call them up. But that's how Jack Kennedy behaved. I thought it was a wonderful way of describing their relationship. . . It's just real. At that time Jack was thirty and Nixon was thirty-four.

JACK KENNEDY WAS a leader. I think the country saw him as a leader. When you met him, your first instinct was to try to get this guy to like you. People wanted Jack Kennedy to shine on them. He made people do more work in that department than he did. He didn't make any effort to try to win people over; he wanted them to win him over, and so he was a leader. He was the kind of guy that would be the club leader anywhere. In high school, he was the guy who organized the Muckers Club, to raise hell up at Choate, to bring down the old order of the prep school. But he was also a troublemaker, Jack Kennedy. He was the kind of a guy that loved taking on the Capitol Hill establishment or the old street corner gang in Cambridge, Massachusetts, that Tip O'Neill was part of, or the labor unions. He was very independent. So he was a combination of a leader and a troublemaker, which is very interesting, and his presidency reflected both of those. I'm not sure he would be nice to people; unless you were among his blessed circle of friends—a very small circle of friends like Ben Bradlee—you were not really of interest to him.

Nixon, on the other hand, comes across in history certainly as the only president to ever be forced to resign and therefore was disgraced. Nixon was probably a nicer person to be with, and this is a great irony. . . . All these fellows [still around Washington today] that worked with him found Nixon to be personable and generous and caring.

[WHEN NIXON SERVED as Eisenhower's vice president, he had a Capitol Hill office across from then Senator John Kennedy.] Bob Thompson, who was a Hearst reporter who had spent a year working for Jack Kennedy's staff in 1959, told me how . . . he used to see this happen like a ritual: Nixon would come out of his office, the vice president's office, and almost as if God had said, "Let's see them come out of the offices together," Kennedy would come out of his. Nixon would be kind of deflated because here's this gleaming Adonis that Kennedy had become in the late '50s. His back problem had been solved; his cortisone shots had filled out his face. He looked great. He never looked better, in fact, than he looked in 1960. And there's Nixon [who telegraphed that he was thinking,] "What's this? Do I have to confront this every time I come out of my office?" I think it was an amazing physical intimidation that went on.

RICHARD NIXON WAS president back in 1971. He was still in pretty good shape. Watergate was well ahead of him. He was looking forward to his reelection campaign, but the responsibility fell to him to hang the first Jackie and Jack pictures in the White House—those incredible pictures we see today of Jackie looking almost like a stem of a flower and Jack looking very ponderous and serious. Jackie was, of course, invited down and didn't feel comfortable coming in a big crowd, so the Nixons invited her for a special showing and dinner afterward. . . . It was a wonderful evening, I guess. The two Nixon daughters, Julie and Tricia, met them at the White House elevator in the family quarters and took them on this great tour, and Pat took Jackie on a tour and showed her what she had done with the White House since Jackie had restored it, and then Nixon joined them for dinner.

John Jr. told me that he had made a bet with his sister, Caroline, that he was not going to spill something. He was ten years old. Lo and behold, John Jr. spilled his milk on Richard Nixon's lap—right on his lap—during dinner. Of course, Nixon was the gentleman and didn't make much of it, but John lost his bet. But what I thought was really the grabber and which convinced me there were a lot of levels to this relationship between John Kennedy and Richard Nixon, was that after dinner Richard Nixon took the two Kennedy kids back to the Oval Office, where they used to play. We've all grown up seeing those pictures of John Jr. playing under the desk. . . . He wanted them to see where they used to play with their dad. Now, the Nixon daughters made a point of not joining them. They left Nixon alone with the two Kennedy kids because they knew how powerful this was to him.

My hunch is if Richard Nixon did not have a reservoir of regard for John Kennedy, no matter what had come between them between '60 and '63, if he didn't have a reservoir of regard for the guy from their first fourteen years of having a relationship, 1946 to 1960, he couldn't have done this. I think he really liked Jack Kennedy. I think he wanted Jack Kennedy to like him. Sure he envied him; everybody envied Jack Kennedy. Everybody felt that Jack Kennedy didn't give them the attention they deserved and was cruel to them. But I think Nixon was as smitten with Jack Kennedy as anybody on earth, and that's a great irony of history.

Lucius D. Clay and Postwar Berlin

by

JEAN EDWARD SMITH

General Lucius Dubignon Clay is best known for organizing the airlift of supplies into West Berlin during the Russian blockade after World War II. With the support of Presidents Truman and Eisenhower, General Clay was able to assist Germany in many ways and became a trusted symbol of the American presence in postwar Europe. In a Booknotes *interview on September 24, 1990, Jean Edward Smith, a political science professor at the University of Toronto, told us more about his biography,* Lucius D. Clay: An American Life, *published by Henry Holt and Company in 1990.*

IN 1948 THE RUSSIANS blockaded Berlin. The leadership in the Defense Department and the State Department felt that Berlin was untenable. The military, in particular, felt that they were holding a situation that the Russians could take if they wished and, to avoid that embarrassment, the city should be evacuated. Lucius D. Clay, on his own authority as military governor, organized the airlift.

He called Curtis LeMay, who was in charge of the air force in Europe at that time, and simply told LeMay to start flying supplies into Berlin. I asked General Clay if he had cleared that with Washington, and he said, "No." He thought this was within his authority as commander in chief, and so he never asked Washington for permission to organize the airlift. Problems arose that summer, though, and in the fall because he didn't have enough airplanes. In order to mount the airlift effectively, he really needed just about every plane the air force had in its strategic reserve. He came back to Washington in August of 1948 to try to get the planes.

President Truman invited him to come to a meeting of the National Security Council. Clay made his pitch. According to Clay, every member of the National Security Council—the secretary of state, the secretary of defense, the air force generals, General Omar Bradley, everyone—spoke against it. They talked about the risk involved in deploying everything. Clay said he thought he'd lost, that he was not going to get the planes he needed. He said President Truman simply overruled them, gave him the planes, and authorized him to announce it that night.

The airlift defeated the Berlin blockade and was the decisive turning point in postwar Europe. The Berlin blockade in the beginning of 1948 marked the Soviets' furthest thrust of Communist imperialism, if you will. Clay stood up to that and, by so doing, reversed the momentum in postwar Europe. That's certainly why he was respected in Berlin and in the U.S. as well.

JUST BEFORE THE currency reform in 1948 he also started the Free University in Berlin. The traditional Berlin university, the principal German university, the Humboldt University, was located in the Soviet sector, over in East Berlin. They were being placed under considerable political pressure, and dissatisfied students and professors wanted to found their own university in the West. Clay's university staff, his staff in German education and military government, said, "You can't do that. The problems of establishing German universities are so complex that you can't really do it."

Clay didn't accept that and commissioned the people who wanted [a new university]. They met with him, and he said, "Fine, go ahead," and gave them permission as military governor to do so. He checked it out with Herman Wells, another of Clay's aides who was president of Indiana University, and Carl Friedrich from Harvard. They suggested to Clay to go ahead, so he did. Clay, on his own authority as military governor, authorized these dissident professors and students to organize a new university, and found the money for them in the military government. . . . Again, I said, "General Clay, did you clear that with Washington?" He said, "Oh, no, that was in my authority as military governor."

Clay admired the German people. There's no question about it. But during his entire time there he kept them at arm's length. He refused to have any social contacts with even the highest-ranking Germans in military government or the administrative presidents of the provinces because, knowing the Reconstruction period in the South, he thought they would be termed collaborators. He thought he was doing them a favor by keeping them at arm's length, although he said, "I don't really think they understood that."

THE FIRST TIME THAT General Clay had ever gone to Berlin was 1945, just after the war was over. . . . He was among the first to go to Berlin, where the seat of the Allied government was in 1945. . . . General Clay strongly believed in German unity. In 1945 and 1946 and through most of 1947, he kept pressing for German unity. He was against dividing East and West. . . . He was Rooseveltian in his views toward dealing with the Soviets. In fact, in late 1946, he and Vassily Sokolovsky, his opposite from the Soviet Union, had reached an agreement whereby in return for raising reparations payments to the Soviet Union, the Soviet Union would agree on free elections and a unified Germany [but it was never acted upon]. In some respects, it was not much different from the deal consummated in 1989. The Soviets in 1946 were just as interested in economic reconstruction as they are today.

General Clay was originally Eisenhower's deputy governor in Germany for military government. Eisenhower was the supreme Allied commander. Eisenhower was succeeded as supreme commander by General Joseph McNarney for a brief period, and then, in early 1948, Clay became commander in chief of U.S. Forces in Europe and military governor [of the U.S. zone in Germany].

Clay insisted when he went over that military government was not really something the army should be involved in for very long. He therefore organized, with Eisenhower's approval, a command structure in which the military government reported to General Eisenhower on a parallel basis with the military forces. So, in effect, General Eisenhower had two deputies: Bedell Smith for the military forces was his chief of staff, and General Clay was, in effect, his chief of staff for military government.

General Clay stayed in Germany from 1945 until the establishment of the Federal Republic, the West German government, in 1949. . . . When he came back from Germany, he addressed both the House and the Senate—not in a joint session. He addressed each one separately. He wasn't told he was going to Congress until he was halfway back on his flight, so he prepared his speeches and gave them extemporaneously as he always did. [In New York] Clay was given a ticker tape parade, not because he had won a military victory but because he had won a victory without going to war.

After that, Lucius Clay retired. He retired from the army in 1949 with the establishment of the West German government and the lifting of the blockade, and he became, within a short time, president and chief executive officer of Continental Can Company.

THE BERLIN WALL, when it was built on August 13, 1961, succeeded in stopping the refugee flow from East Germany and arrested the hemorrhaging that was taking place. No one anticipated what the result would be in West Berlin—an absolute panic set into the city. West Berliners thought they were being abandoned by the United States. It was to arrest that panic that General Clay was sent back. He had written to the president offering his services. He had supported Nixon in the 1960 election, but he wrote to President Kennedy to offer his services.

General Maxwell Taylor, who was in the White House as Kennedy's principal military assistant, called Clay immediately and invited him down to Washington. He came down and met with the president, and as the situation went from bad to worse in Berlin, the administration decided the best way to bring it under control was to send Clay back. They were reluctant to do that for a couple of reasons: Clay was prominently identified with Eisenhower, and to pick a Republican like Clay—one of Eisenhower's old warhorses— looked, at first, like maybe there was some plausibility in the Republican claim that Kennedy was in over his head.

Clay was sent back because he was [seen as West Berlin's] savior. There was a serious crisis of morale in West Berlin and the most effective symbol of American resolve to convince Berliners that they were not being forsaken was to send General Clay back. I think the second reason he was sent was because Sam Rayburn, Speaker of the House, told Vice President Lyndon Johnson that if he was going back to Berlin, he should take someone with him who knew what the situation was. Rayburn strongly suggested that he take Clay with him. Rayburn and Clay had known each other for almost thirty years at that point.

When Clay went back in 1961, he did what he was sent back to do. He convinced Berliners that they would not be abandoned. By the spring of that year, he had brought a very difficult situation under control.

I FIRST MET CLAY at the time of the Berlin crisis in 1961. Any student of history had known about General Clay and the Berlin Airlift and the postwar period in Germany, [but] I had not met him before then. My impression was of a very decisive man who knew what he was doing, a very generous man, and a man far different from most military men I had met. I had served in the regular United States Army in the field artillery. General Clay was a much broader-gauge person, much more politically astute, and certainly much more articulate.

Paul Cabot, managing director at First Boston Corporation, said, "Lucius was the most arrogant, stubborn, opinionated man I ever met." He was that, too; there is no question about it. He was most stubborn about his own snap judgments. When you command in the army for thirty years and then run Lehman Brothers and Continental Can, as General Clay did, your doubts seem to be filtered out by that experience. He was stubborn and decisive. Ninety percent of the time that was beneficial. Ten percent of the time, he probably blew it.

IN 1971–72, CLAY participated in the Berlin Accords. He was one of the elder statesman advisers [and part of a] group that President Nixon felt it was important to touch base with before agreeing to anything about the two Germanys.

Clay was firmly convinced that German unity was the appropriate organization for Germany. He was deeply committed to teaching democracy in Germany by his own personal style. He was convinced that this effort had been successful, and I think he would have no doubts whatsoever about the political future of a united Germany.

Truman Defeats Dewey

by

ZACHARY KARABELL

As the votes in the 1948 presidential election were being tallied on November 2, 1948, newspapers and polling organizations predicted that Republican candidate, Thomas E. Dewey, would be America's next president. Over 48 million people had voted in the election and to their surprise the next morning, Harry Truman had won. The Chicago Tribune *had even printed up the November 3 edition of the newspaper with the headline "Dewey Defeats Truman." A photograph of the smiling Truman holding up the mistaken headline quickly became a popular symbol of Truman's good humor and the flaws possible in reportage. In a* Booknotes *interview on June 4, 2000, New York-based writer Zachary Karabell shared stories from this contest and famous error. Mr. Karabell's book* The Last Campaign: How Harry Truman Won the 1948 Election *was published in 2000 by Alfred A. Knopf.*

THE "DEWEY DEFEATS TRUMAN" photograph was perhaps the greatest miscalculation by a newspaper in American history, and is attributable to the long-lasting enmity, if not hatred, that the publisher of the newspaper, the *Chicago Tribune,* had for Harry S. Truman. The McCormick publishing empire had spent a lot of time and energy to try to make sure that Truman was not reelected. They obviously were hoping that they would be victorious and jumped the gun a little bit.

THERE WERE A LOT of main figures in the Democratic Party in March, April, and May of 1948 who were very vocal about dumping Truman. There was a "Dump Truman" movement up until the beginning of July, where they were trying to draft Dwight Eisenhower, of all people. Eleanor Roosevelt thought Truman was just not a very good leader, in spite of that very touching moment where she's supposed to have said to him when Truman assumed the presidency in 1945, "How can we help you, Mr. President?" She found him a weak leader. She wasn't as vocal as her son, James, the Democratic Party head in California, who was determined to remove Truman from the ticket.

Thomas E. Dewey had been governor of New York, and he had also been the Republican presidential nominee in 1944 and had performed much better against Roosevelt than a lot of people had imagined. Roosevelt was still immensely popular. World War II was going on. The fact that Thomas Dewey was able to run a pretty credible campaign against Roosevelt in 1944 was something that led him to become the nominee again in 1948.

NOT EVERYBODY WHO ran for president in 1948, as now, appeared on the ballot in every single state. There were four or five major candidates who appeared in the ballots in most states, and you had the two main party candidates. You had Harry Truman for the Democrats, and Tom Dewey, the boy wunderkind governor of New York, the Republican standard-bearer that year. Two parties had splintered off from the Democrats; one to the left, led by Henry A. Wallace, who was head of the Progressive Party, and the other led by the governor of South Carolina, Strom Thurmond, who was part of a party that was referred to as the Dixiecrats. They preferred to think of themselves as States' Rights Democrats. Also on the ballot in a lot of states was the old-time Socialist, Norman Thomas, who had run for president numerous times before. He ran once again to oppose Wallace from the left, the kind of anti-Communist Socialists. And there were a number of more marginal rump candidates. There was a Prohibition candidate, who actually did pretty well in a few states. There was a white supremacist candidate, who ran in the South. And there was a Greenback candidate. So there were twelve, all in all, but there were only five that really had national prominence.

POLLS PLAYED A HUGE role [in the 1948 election], both in the ways in which they were used by Thomas E. Dewey and the ways in which they were used and then proven wrong by the press. Dewey was one of the first poll-driven candidates. He watched his poll numbers. He believed them and he believed he was ahead. He was told by the Roper Organization and by the Gallup Organization that he was leading in all measures. He and his team developed a campaign strategy designed to maintain that lead, a lead they perceived themselves to have because the polls were telling them so.

The pollsters were saying that they had developed a scientific polling and that they had learned how to poll [since] particularly, the experience of 1936. There had been a real debacle in '36 [when the *Literary Digest* wrongly forecast that Alfred Landon would be president]. This was a time when people were touting new technologies and everybody had appliances. This age of scientific "golly, gee willikers" was really quite prominent in the culture. The idea that you could predict an election was seen as somewhat exciting, and people really gravitated toward that.

Arthur Krock, the famous columnist for the *New York Times,* later recognizing how wrong the polls were, said that "Tonight, we shall dine on crow" and took full responsibility for lending credence to what had been wrong poll numbers. Not a single newspaper, columnist, or pollster writing in 1948 got it right. There was one unofficial poll taken by the Staley Milling Company in Kansas, which had these things called Pullet Atoms, a feed for livestock. They printed up two types of feed bags, one was an elephant and one was a donkey, representing Republicans and Democrats. They told people to buy the feed bags based on the party they were going to vote for. And come late October 1948, Truman was ahead fifty-four to forty-six. So the Pullet Atom poll called the election right. Other than that, not only did none of the polls have it right, but none of the columnists and none of the people writing about it had it right. No one thought Truman was going to win.

On election night, Truman pulled up the covers and went to sleep. The commentary was that he seemed to be leading in the cities for which there were early results, the kind of northeastern belt, New York, Boston, Washington. But one of the major commentators at the time, H. V. Kaltenborn— who was known for having a pretty staccato voice—said, "While Truman is ahead in these areas, we fully expect that as the vote comes in from the Midwest and the West, this will quickly turn to Dewey's advantage. A Dewey victory is still all but assured."

[IN THE END, THERE were 303 electoral votes for Harry Truman, 189 for Thomas Dewey, 39 for Strom Thurmond, and none for Henry Wallace.] Certainly the size of the margin [was surprising] relative to the expectation that the figures, at least in the Dewey-Truman race, would be either reversed or show even much more of an advantage for Dewey. So the very fact that you have that electoral vote disparity, with Truman coming out on top, was astounding at the time. The fact that Wallace won none is less surprising, but it was a time when Wallace was expected to do considerably better. Certainly in the spring, he thought that he could pull as many as 10 million votes. It wasn't clear which states he had a chance of actually winning. Some thought perhaps he would do well in New York and Pennsylvania. He was anticipated to get more votes, but not necessarily more electoral votes.

In the South, one of the peculiar things was that while the Thurmond ticket did capture four states, plus one electoral vote from Tennessee, in two of those states, the people who were voting actually thought they were voting for the Democratic Party. One of the electors refused to cast the votes for Truman and cast it for the States' Rights ticket. In Mississippi, the States' Rights Dixiecrats had managed to control the state Democratic Party machinery and placed Thurmond's name instead of Truman's [next to the Democratic Party icon]. Truman didn't actually appear on the ballot. And in Louisiana, [the state Democratic Committee] in one of these infinitely complicated backroom deals [also voted to list the Dixiecrat candidates next to the traditional symbol of the Democrats]. It was a way for the party machinery to really stick it to the governor, Earl Long.

Truman had made a very dramatic civil rights message in February of 1948, which precipitated the Dixiecrat revolt. By the summer of 1948, the party around Truman preferred to let the civil rights issue be quiet. Truman had made his statement and created an executive order desegregating the military [but] wasn't really going to take much more action on it. Minneapolis mayor Hubert Humphrey wasn't content with this and was determined that there would be a strong language in the Democratic platform about civil rights. Humphrey knew, as did everyone else, that if there was language on civil rights inserted into the platform in such strong terms, that would lead to the southern Democrats around Strom Thurmond walking out of the convention hall and forming a rump political movement.

Strom Thurmond was the governor of South Carolina and was very popular. Part of the story of 1948 that is very illustrative for the present is the degree to which these coalitions didn't necessarily fall in neat little left and right cookie cutters. It's true that the Dixiecrats were heavily states' rights and represented a kind of Civil War redux. It's true that they had a real element of racism in them. But it's also true that people like Strom Thurmond and his running mate, Governor Fielding L. Wright of Mississippi, were known as southern progressives. These were people in favor of rural electrification and roads and education. They were very much seen as liberal progressives in a domestic sense in the South, at the same time being quite to the right on states' rights and race relations.

The fact was, though, that these southern "conservatives" or the people represented by States' Rights, were always strange bedfellows with the northern wing of the Democratic Party. The wonder of the New Deal coalition was that it brought southern Democrats and northern and midwestern Democrats together. That was always Roosevelt's incredible magic, to create this coalition. The Dixiecrat revolt in 1948 was the first major crack in what a lot of people have called the New Deal coalition that pretty much collapsed in the late '60s and reached its final moment in Lyndon Johnson's Great Society and then fell apart; then the South became largely Republican.

MOST OF US NOW, particularly in the past ten or so years, are influenced by a particular image of Truman as a scrappy fighter, a kind of honest, straight-talking man from the plains representing traditional and simple American values. That picture, in a lot of ways, was confirmed to me [in my research]. But added to it was the degree to which he was a tried-and-true liberal, the ways in which Truman was part of a long tradition of what a lot of people call "agrarian populism," kind of anti–Wall Street. The political spectrum really has shifted between then and now. That struck me, as much as he's become an icon for recent political parties, the degree to which his message would find a lot of opposition in today's political climate. That's something that tends to be overlooked.

The other thing that struck me about him was the degree to which he was a street-fighting, tough-talking politico. He was really willing to pull out the stops and ruthlessly attack his enemies, or his perceived enemies, in order to win electorally.

Truman undoubtedly was an extremely effective attack dog, who really lit into Dewey. He didn't talk much about any of the other candidates. He let other people do the talking for him. But when it came to Dewey, he ridiculed him as a stooge of Wall Street. He ridiculed him as being a man without opinions. And, finally, he compared him as being such a weak character supported by such an odious set of invisible forces behind him that it was a little bit like Germany on the eve of the rise of Hitler or Italy on the rise of Mussolini. [He suggested] that Dewey would be a conduit to fascism in the United States. This kind of critique, of a cabal that was going to rob the American people of their birthright, resonated with a lot of people in the United States then, as it does now. It effectively weakened Dewey in the election and generated a lot of passion for Truman.

But there was a price to pay. This was a strategy born out of weakness. Truman pulled out all the stops because he felt like he had very little to lose. [Losers] break the rules. There's no point in obeying them because if you obey the unwritten rules of civility, you're going to lose anyway. So why not just do what you can? . . . Truman did that and it worked, but I think the Republicans perceived that this was really foul play and that Truman, in breaking those rules, certainly didn't deserve fair play as president. They unleashed their own attack dogs against the Democrats in the form of Senator Joseph McCarthy.

Television would have made it more difficult for Truman to campaign the way he did because the downside of speaking plainly is that you galvanize people who agree with you and you alienate people who disagree with you. You have got to be willing to accept that trade-off. That was a trade-off Truman could easily accept. Because if you made a speech in a small whistle-stop town in Idaho in 1948, only your audience heard it. There was no twenty-four-hour news cycle. There were no TV cameras waiting to endlessly replay what you said. So you could tailor your message much more locally. What works for potato farmers in Idaho may not be a palatable message to steel-workers in Pittsburgh in 1948. . . . The problem with the twenty-four-hour news cycle in television is that what you say in one place, you're essentially saying in every place. And that leads to a kind of leveling out, a more generic way of speechifying because you don't want to run the risk of alienating people simply to gain the allegiance of a thousand.

THIS WAS ONE OF the last great railroad campaigns. This was the primary way that Dewey and Truman saw the country and met people. They each had their presidential cars. Dewey's was optimistically named the *Victory Special,* which I think may have dissuaded people from being quite so optimistic in the future about naming their cars. Truman's was a little more elliptically named the *Ferdinand Magellan,* and was an old outfitted car from the 1920s, very sumptuous. It had been used by Roosevelt. [Harry Truman was out there all the time in that railroad train.] Dewey was almost as active. I think he covered maybe 10,000 fewer miles. Dewey gave a lot of speeches, a lot of what would have amounted to the same thing that Truman was doing in his famous whistle-stop campaign. He would pull up at a small town and go to the back of the platform and make his speech. Henry Wallace, all in all, traveled more than any of them, although Wallace didn't have his own private train in quite the same way. Wallace went by bus and occasionally plane and occasionally train.

WALLACE HAD A REAL martyr complex. By the end of the summer—late August and September—it was very clear that the Progressive Party was not only not going to be a significant vote-gathering force, but that it was everywhere in disrepute and retreat. But Wallace persevered. He thought he was fighting the good fight. He was going to lead the Gideon's Army. He kept quoting from the Bible and kept making increasingly less veiled allusions to himself and Christ and talking about being crucified for his beliefs. It's almost as if he went out of his way to generate that. He traveled through the South in August and into the fall with a mixed-race entourage. This was a guaranteed way of getting angry southerners gathering to heckle him, jeer him with hatred because he would appear with African Africans on the platform. He would insist on eating in mixed-race situations, which just wasn't done. The kind of animus that confronts Wallace is familiar to us from the civil rights struggles of the late '50s and the '60s. Wallace received a lot of attention in *Time* and *Newsweek* and in the major radio programs for his attacks. If anything, he received a sort of grudging admiration from some people for being willing to state his beliefs in the face of such anger and hatred.

ALL OF THEM, in some ways, impressed me. The level of what I considered to be engaged debate on the substantive issues that each of the candidates put forth at various points was something I found compelling. Dewey certainly least so, at that level. By the fall, there was very little that Dewey said that was particularly compelling or particularly specific. In fact, the reporters on his train were so numbingly bored that a few of them tried to get over to the Truman campaign train. Reporting on one of his speeches, one of the reporters said something like, "Mr. Dewey announced that he was for prosperity and peace. And though he didn't say so specifically, it can safely be assumed that he is also against sin."

But Dewey, in the spring, when he was running against a primary opponent, Governor Harold Stassen, a Republican from Minnesota, actually took a really principled stand against a bill that was rumbling through Congress to outlaw the Communist Party. While Dewey was very much in favor of monitoring Communist Party activity, he said that he would not be in favor of outlawing the party, that the United States was a country that supported freedom of expression and a multiplicity of views, even those that people found disagreeable. This was a risky position to take in the climate of 1948, particularly with someone like Stassen, who was thundering for this bill, as was Richard Nixon, who was then a congressman from California.

ONE OF THE FASCINATING lessons, if you can say that about 1948, is the degree to which the perception of being packaged—which Dewey was widely derided as being—was a real liability. It turned people off from him. They didn't know who Dewey was. Dewey is an immensely perplexing figure in the light of history, as he was at the time—and somewhat impenetrable. It's hard to know why he rose as high as he did. It's almost like those pictures you see of your relatives in the 1970s wearing those loud polka-dot ties and those striped shirts and you wonder how anyone ever thought that looked good. Similarly with Dewey, it's hard to imagine why he was seen as such a viable candidate because he seemed so pallid when he was actually campaigning.

WHAT'S INTRIGUING ABOUT 1948 is the degree to which there was consensus that government was a good thing and a progressive force in American life. Most of the Republicans of this time could only say, "We should halt the New Deal" or "We should cease the expansion." But the spectrum was fully in support of an activist government.

The Rise and Fall of
Joseph McCarthy

by

ARTHUR HERMAN

Senator Joseph McCarthy was born on November 14, 1908, in Grand Chute, Wisconsin. He served as a judge in his home state, enlisted in the marines during World War II, and was elected to the U.S. Senate in 1947. During his first term as a senator he made a speech in West Virginia claiming that a specific number of Communists had infiltrated the U.S. State Department. He soon became America's most prominent red-baiter, working to expose Communists, real or imagined, to the nation. During a series of televised hearings, McCarthy's hard-charging style led Joseph N. Welch, the U.S. Army's attorney, to ask McCarthy, "Have you no sense of decency, sir?" This remark broke McCarthy's career. The Senate later formally censured him for his conduct. Arthur Herman, coordinator of the Smithsonian's Western Heritage Certificate Program, explored McCarthy's life when he appeared on Booknotes *on January 4, 2000, to discuss* Joseph McCarthy: Reexamining the Life and Legacy of America's Most Hated Senator, *published by The Free Press in 1999.*

[J]OSEPH MCCARTHY was most visible] from 1950 to 1954. His was a very sharply defined career, meteoric. It started in February of 1950, when he made his famous speech at Wheeling, West Virginia, accusing the State Department of harboring Communists and Communist sympathizers. Then it really came to a crashing conclusion in December of 1954 when the Senate censured him. That really was the end of Joe McCarthy as a public figure.

Joseph Raymond McCarthy was from Wisconsin. He grew up in the farming communities that surrounded Appleton, Wisconsin. . . . It's now mostly strip malls. The farms have receded as the suburbs have expanded outward. But at the time, it was farming communities heavily populated by the children of Dutch immigrants. The Irish McCarthy clans were rare. There weren't a lot of Irish Catholics in Wisconsin at the time, but there were a lot of Catholics. In that sense, the McCarthys were a part of this homogeneous rural community.

JOSEPH McCARTHY HAS always been a kind of shadowy figure in the history of Wisconsin politics. Wisconsin is a very progressive state. It's the place where William Proxmire and Gaylord Nelson were senators, and has a long and proud history of progressivism in its politics. Joe McCarthy was always kind of Banquo's ghost at the feasts. No one really wanted to talk about how he became a senator and reelected as a senator from the state. It was a very murky part of this whole political heritage of Wisconsin.

The other issue that intrigued me about Joe McCarthy was the whole question about American communism and the so-called Red Scare, and the 1950s probes into anticommunism. The first book that really got me interested in it, oddly enough, was Victor Navasky's *Naming Names*. He is the publisher of *The Nation*. What most impressed me about [*Naming Names*] was the human side of the story that he was capturing, the human tragedies of these figures who had become caught up in the Communist Party and in the accusations about their membership and their links to the party in the 1950s.

JOE McCARTHY SERVED his country in the Pacific [in World War II]. He did have experience flying in missions, including combat missions, but that wasn't his principal role. He exaggerated the number of missions he flew for political purposes. In the postwar period, right after World War II, to have been a combat hero was a ticket into politics, [like] John F. Kennedy, for example, and *PT-109*. Many of McCarthy's fellow members of the class of '46, who came to Washington with the 1946 Republican takeover of both the House and the Senate, were war veterans. McCarthy was part of that group. McCarthy saw the political opportunities that came with that war experience, and he cashed in on them.

McCarthy's first public job was working as a district judge in Shawano County, Wisconsin. It was an elected post. It's there that he really learned about how successful he could be as an elected official and in running in popularity contests against other candidates. He really didn't know that much about the law. He had a law degree from Marquette, but he didn't have the kind of lengthy experience that we normally associate with people who sit on the bench in county circuit courts.

It's significant because his first public job was really his last one, until he became senator. In other words, he moved directly from his experience serving as county judge to the U.S. Senate. There was no in-between as a state senator, as a legislator or a member of the House of Representatives. This is important for understanding why McCarthy created so much friction with his colleagues in the Senate and with the political establishment. He never learned the kinds of skills that are required to be a legislator. He was, in a sense, propelled by the election of '46 into the U.S. Senate and into an environment with which he was not very familiar and about which he developed a great contempt.

McCARTHY WAS A WARM, engaging, intensely physical man. He was the kind of person who cornered you and buttonholed you at a party, took hold of your lapel, and had his arm around you from the other side. He was charming and engaging, and he had a gruff and rather vulgar sense of humor. He was the kind of person who was very popular in male locker rooms and in barrooms. Most people—even his political opponents—found him to be a very likable individual. The one problem he had was this ferocious temper, which could flare up at unexpected and unpredictable points. This intensely physical man suddenly losing his temper, blowing up at imagined slights and insults, and firing back at people with really harsh and nasty personal attacks made him very difficult to deal with as a senator. People didn't want to touch him, didn't want to deal with him.

McCARTHY WAS THE youngest senator when he took office in 1947. He was born in 1908 and he would have been thirty-nine. But just to make sure that people understood that he was, in fact, the youngest senator, in his official biography he knocked off a year from his birth date to make himself even younger, to appear as a fresh, young blood, the young maverick arriving in the U.S. Senate.

The Republicans [controlled the Senate from 1947 to 1949]. It was a stunning . . . change from Democratic dominance of all the branches of government since Roosevelt's New Deal. . . . When McCarthy came in, although he was a junior senator, he came in as a member of the party in power.

JOSEPH McCARTHY originally was a Democrat. He had voted for Franklin Roosevelt, as his father had and as most Wisconsinites of a working-class, rural background had. He first ran for offices, in fact, as a Democrat. It's quite possible that he would have continued as a Democrat, but the opportunity came up to challenge a popular Republican senator from Wisconsin in the primary, and McCarthy realized that this was his opportunity. By switching parties he could really give his political career a boost.

THE RELATIONSHIP BETWEEN the Kennedys and the McCarthys is a very interesting one. It really is rooted in a shared Irish Catholic heritage and a similar outlook on issues such as communism, such as the Cold War, and in a mutual liking. McCarthy, for a period of time, became a part of that Hyannis Port entourage, playing softball with the Kennedys. Joe Kennedy, in particular, seemed to have had a strong liking for Joe McCarthy and always hoped that McCarthy would marry one of his daughters. They had other ideas about the subject. Bobby Kennedy was only in his mid-twenties when he came on as legal counsel for McCarthy's Committee on Investigations when McCarthy became chairman in 1953. He put Bobby Kennedy into that very important slot.

MCCARTHY INITIALLY went on a couple of small committees [like] the Committee for the District of Columbia. They were very small posts. But the other position he got was on a committee that had been very active during the war period, the Committee on Government Operations and its permanent Subcommittee on Investigations. It was this committee that, ironically, Harry Truman had used to build his political career by investigating corruption and overspending and cooking of the books by various government departments, including the U.S. Army. It was now in the hands of Republicans. It was going to become an instrument for examining what Republicans were convinced had been twelve years of Democratic corruption, of wheeling and dealing and of allowing America's large government agencies to become centers of political patronage.

The committee, in the hands of the Republicans, and particularly its Subcommittee on Investigations, very quickly became a key instrument in conducting investigative probes: "What have the Democrats been doing in those twelve years of power? What kinds of abuses are we looking for? What kinds of problems have been lurking there in the corners that we now are able, as Republicans, to bring to light?" It was in that background that McCarthy got the impetus for this idea of using investigations into Democratic malfeasance and misfeasance in government departments as a way of straightening out problems, but also of building his political career.

[State Department official] Alger Hiss had been convicted of perjury and was in prison [as a result of those investigations] . . . Richard Nixon was, at that time, about to launch his run for the U.S. Senate. He was going to use the name that he had made for himself, the fame that he had gained by prosecuting the Hiss case, and . . . translate that into political success to the next level, moving from the House to the Senate.

Nixon's success in becoming a national figure through the Hiss case and then winning in a landslide victory in November and being elected to the

U.S. Senate were powerful incentives for McCarthy to try the same thing. He thought to himself, "Here's the way in which you raise yourself from relative obscurity into national fame and become a pillar of your party."

In the end, it was a misleading example because the people that McCarthy pointed his fingers at were not Alger Hisses. He got himself out of his depth in the accusations he made.

THERE WAS A LIST which had been prepared by a House committee in 1946 of people working in the State Department whose personnel files committee members had gone through. They found various things that were disturbing about many of these people who were on the State Department payroll— some of them were members of the Communist Party, others were associated with Communist Party members. This was a period of time in which the conflict with the Soviet Union was just starting to heat up, [as was] the question, "Where are these people's loyalties, with us, the United States, or with our erstwhile ally during the war, the Soviet Union?" The list was put together and presented to the State Department with a nasty note saying, in effect, "Why are these people still on the payroll here if we find ourselves in the midst of a conflict with the Soviet Union?"

The State Department wrote back a reassuring letter saying, "Well, in fact, a lot of these people have been removed from the State Department. There are still some who are left, whose cases are still pending for investigation. We'll get to them as soon as we can." The number of cases that were left was fifty-seven.

[Senator McCarthy gave a speech in Wheeling, West Virginia, on] February 9, 1950. It was a speech for the Lincoln Day celebrations organized by the Ladies' Republican Club of Wheeling. Lincoln's birthday was traditionally an opportunity for Republican officeholders to give a speech about Republican principles, about the great traditions and heritage of the Republican Party and then, of course, to associate themselves with the figure of Abraham Lincoln. . . . McCarthy was invited to give the speech. He was, at that time, still a very obscure senator, . . . somebody who was struggling for a way to make a name for himself.

McCarthy got a speechwriter, a journalist by the name of Ed Nellor, to do the speech for him. In fact, it seems to have been Nellor who suggested doing a speech on Communists in government, in the State Department. In drafting the speech, at various points where it would mention specific numbers, for example, listing the number of people living under communism in 1945, Nellor or a typist would insert a [temporary] number and then later on plug in the exact numbers in preparation for the speech. What seems to have happened is that the number 205 was simply inserted into the slot where 57 would eventually go. In fact, when the speech was handed out to reporters, the number 205 was crossed out and the number 57 was substituted for it.

This is one of the most famous, notorious speeches in the twentieth century and we have no recording of it, only the memory of those who heard it. McCarthy, in the course of reading a speech, was never somebody who followed the script very closely. He was always ad-libbing. What seems to have happened is that he read the number 205 the first time around instead of the number 57.

McCarthy would always insist that the number 57 was the number that he had cited because there was some—although flimsy—documentary evidence to support that number. Under oath he would deny to Senate committees the fact that he had ever said 205. Later on, Democrats in the Senate were looking for ways to get McCarthy out of the Senate, [to] either expel him or censure him. The possibility that Joe McCarthy had committed perjury by telling a Senate committee that, "I never said 205, but rather 57," would . . . [aid them in] proving that McCarthy was, in fact, a liar. Democrats scrambled for years to try and find a copy of it, in the hopes that perhaps someone, somewhere, had recorded this at the radio station or during the course of it, so that they could prove that McCarthy had used the number 205.

[ON FEBRUARY 22, 1950, A] special Senate committee was set up to investigate McCarthy's charges against the State Department headed by Millard Tydings, a senator from Maryland. The Tydings Committee came out with a report that basically exonerated all of the [people] whom McCarthy had named as being either Communists or Communist sympathizers. . . . McCarthy accused Tydings and the Democrats who controlled the committee of conducting a whitewash, of using it for partisan purposes. With any kind of objective look at the Tydings report and the way in which they systematically ignored the evidence that was presented, not just by McCarthy but by their own investigators, you have to say that in this case, at least, McCarthy had something of a point.

ROY COHN WORKED as McCarthy's chief legal counsel when he became chairman of the Subcommittee on Investigations in 1953. He was a brash, precocious, street-smart kid who actually did know his way around the anticommunism investigations and the investigation of domestic subversion. He is, more than any other person, responsible for McCarthy's fall—that is, every other person except Joe McCarthy himself. McCarthy became absolutely mesmerized by Cohn's brilliance, his audacity, his seeming grasp of what was essential and how to get things done, and Cohn gave him consistently disastrous advice. He really pushed McCarthy off into a series of investigations that would cost McCarthy first of all, his public support, but then also cost him his career. McCarthy's investigations of the Voice of America, for example, and his investigations of the U.S. Army, which led directly to a confrontation with the Eisenhower White House . . . were done at the behest and at the urging of Roy Cohn.

NINETEEN FIFTY-FOUR was the year of . . . the famous Army-McCarthy hearings. A lot of people have a misconception about the Army-McCarthy hearings. They assume that it was McCarthy investigating the army that was being televised for the nation to see. In fact, it was McCarthy who was in the hot seat. It was McCarthy who was accused of allowing his staff members, including Roy Cohn, to blackmail the army by threatening investigations in order to get [Cohn's close friend] David Schine, special treatment as a new draftee into the army.

[IN DECEMBER 1954, Joseph McCarthy became the sixth senator censured in the history of the Senate, by a vote of 67 to 22.] There were a lot of senators who voted for censure who had their doubts about the grounds for doing so, but there had to be a way to stop Joe McCarthy. He had simply gotten out of control and really stretched the envelope of the institution by his excesses and by his reckless accusations. But the effect it had on McCarthy, the tremendous physical and mental decline that McCarthy suffered as a result of it, came as a shock to everybody.

[When] McCarthy's death came so quickly after the censure, there was a feeling on the part of the Senate [that they should] make amends by giving him a funeral [service in the Senate Chamber], which would ordinarily be reserved for Supreme Court justices or for presidents.

The legend is that McCarthy's disgrace and his censure drove him to the bottle and that he killed himself in the process. But, in fact, his drinking had really begun long before that, during the period of time in which he was at the height of his popularity and the height of his notoriety. The tremendous quantities of alcohol that he consumed as he responded to the tensions and the pressures of the national celebrity that had been thrust on him did physical damage that was irreparable. After the censure he didn't seem to have drunk quite as much as he did before. A lot of people who met him during that period of time describe him as being a moderate drinker. But the truth is that the physical damage had already been done by the time of his censure, and he went into a physical and mental tailspin after that.

MCCARTHY WAS ONLY forty-nine years old when he died [in 1957]. The death certificate says hepatic liver failure, and it does seem that hepatitis was the immediate cause of death. But there's no doubt that the liver damage he suffered was the result of his chronic drinking.

ONE OF THE ACCUSATIONS constantly made about Joe McCarthy was that he played fast and loose with the facts, that his accusations really lacked substance and were, in a sense, exaggerated by a hysterical rhetoric about the threat, about Reds under the bed and Soviet spies in the White House and control from the Kremlin. I'm not the first to point out that much of that playing fast and loose with the facts and much of that hysterical rhetoric was employed by his political opponents as well. And one of the things I want to make clear to people who don't remember the time, is the degree to which we have to realize that this was a bitterly partisan era. Emotions ran very, very high about how to conduct the Cold War, about how to deal with the threat of Stalinism, both abroad but also at home. You had American soldiers dying in Korea. The Korean War formed the vivid backdrop for all of McCarthy's career. There was a bitter, bitter partisan battle in Washington, in which people were prepared to say almost anything . . . to smear their political opponents. McCarthy did it, and his Republican allies did it.

You also have to remember that the Democrats were quite prepared to do the same thing. And they often did against McCarthy, calling him a Nazi sympathizer, talking about his investigations as posing a threat to American democracy and so on, charges which really don't, in the light of historical evidence and historical perspective, hold any kind of water.

VERY OFTEN PEOPLE write books because they want to read the book that they're going to write, and this was my case too. I wanted to read a book about Joe McCarthy. McCarthy was a way in which all of these kinds of issues about the 1950s—about what America was about, [about] domestic communism and its role and place in American life, . . . and the Cold War— could be reexamined in a single form. And, from the point of view of human tragedy, the story of Joe McCarthy is a tragedy. It really is a tragedy that in many ways he brought upon himself, but it's a tragedy all the same.

The New York Intelligentsia

by

NORMAN PODHORETZ

The "New York intellectuals" were writers and critics who wielded an enormous amount of influence in the American cultural life of the 1950s and 1960s. Norman Podhoretz, an editor-at-large at Commentary *magazine, moved in these circles until his increasingly conservative political views led to his estrangement from the people he calls "The Family." Mr. Podhoretz appeared on* Booknotes *on February 17, 1999, to discuss* Ex-Friends: Falling Out with Allen Ginsberg, Lionel and Diana Trilling, Lillian Hellman, Hannah Arendt, and Norman Mailer, *published in 1999 by The Free Press, in which he describes this experience.*

THERE ARE FIVE or six major characters in this book, and then there are bit players who make cameo appearances, strut and fret their hour upon the stage. Writer Norman Mailer is the only one of the major ones still alive, and I didn't see him for many years. Many of the others who are still alive, the minor characters, to this day are not on speaking terms with me and vice versa. I have a house in East Hampton, Long Island, where a lot of literary people, people in the arts, also have houses. If we happen to bump into one another on the beach or in the supermarket or in a restaurant, we pretend not to see each other. And that's after thirty years.

The reason [for this split] was politics. . . . Even at my most radical—and I was pretty radical in the mid-sixties—I always loved this country. I loved America. I still love America. I loved it for what it had done for me, personally, as a poor kid growing up in Brooklyn, the son of Jewish immigrants from Eastern Europe. It sent me to Columbia, sent me to Cambridge University, gave me a magazine to run. I also loved it because I thought it was built on the most precious political institutions that the world had ever seen, institutions that were also much more vulnerable than people thought and that needed to be defended and protected. I was a bit of a utopian, like all the members of the left, [and though there] were a lot of things wrong with America, I thought everything could be perfected within the going system. That was one of the arguments that I had with my fellow leftists. They thought this country was so rotten that nothing but a revolution could save it. Some people actually threw bombs; they took that idea of revolutionism seriously. Those who did throw bombs were apologized for by some of my fellow intellectuals who didn't throw bombs.

I have a complicated political history. . . . In the late 1950s, I moved from what you would, in those days, have called a liberal position to a radical position. There's no other way to say it—except the immodest way—I was one of the early intellectual leaders of the new radical movement that was just developing in the late '50s. It didn't even have a name; later people called it the New Left or the Movement or the Counterculture.

I used to go to meetings at which there were [maybe] six people, and I would never have dreamed that within five or six years, the ideas that I was helping to disseminate and develop, both through my own writings and through *Commentary* magazine, of which I became the editor in 1960 at the age of thirty—that by 1965, these ideas would have swept the country, especially the young people, and almost assume the status of conventional wisdom. This was an enormous surprise to me. I was one of the leaders of the movement intellectually. I was never much of an activist. I don't like marching, and I don't like demonstrations particularly.

Most of the work I did was through . . . the things I published and edited in *Commentary*, though I would make a speech occasionally here and there. But as the '60s wore on, I grew more and more disillusioned with the way the movement I had helped to create was developing. And as my disillusionment grew more intense, . . . I began breaking ranks. . . . It was a nonnegotiable difference, not just of opinion about small matters or particularities, but of the whole sense of life, the whole sense of the world. It mainly focused on the nature and character of American society.

When I broke ranks with the left, I had a lot of arguments in private with my friends, all of whom were to one degree or another associated with that movement. [Those arguments] erupted into the public arena. They attacked me; I attacked them. They considered me an apostate, someone who leaves a church, converts to some other religion. What a lot of people don't understand today and can hardly remember even if they were alive then is that . . . ideas about the arts, literature, painting, and [politics] were held with a veritably religious intensity by this world in which I lived, the world of so-called

New York intellectuals or "The Family," as I've called it.

So it was no small matter to break. It was considered an act of treason from a political point of view. I was a traitor to my class, as they say about Franklin Roosevelt, but I was also an apostate and a heretic with respect to the true faith. Apostates are always hated much more than people who are there the whole time. So I was hated much more than people who were then to the right of me, like Bill Buckley, since he had always been an enemy. I was a new enemy and I regarded all my old friends as a continuing threat to much of what I now believed and held dear.

I MET ALLEN Ginsberg when I was in college. I was a freshman, and he was a senior. He was the poetry editor of the Columbia College literary magazine, and I was a kid out of Brooklyn. Like all aspiring literary writers, I wrote poetry. He published a couple of my poems, and that's how our association began.

But our roads diverged after college, within ten years of leaving Columbia. I was a young and upcoming literary critic, fairly well established because I was quite precocious. And he, by then, was the leading figure of the Beat Generation school of writers. His most famous poem was called "Howl," which began, "I've seen the best minds in my generation go mad." America drove all the best people crazy. That was basically the position. That came out in the late '50s.

[When we met] I was politically moving to the left and he was way to the left. He was, in fact, what we later called a red diaper baby, the son of a Communist. His mother had been a member of the Communist Party. He was not himself a Communist, but he was a far left. He remained on the far left in a kind of nonsectarian way.

So we broke. We had already sort of drifted apart, but then I wrote a series of articles attacking the Beat Generation and its work, not so much his own poems because I thought he was very talented, but especially the novels of Jack Kerouac. Kerouac was his best friend and was the novelist of the Beat Generation, as Allen Ginsberg was the poet of the Beat Generation.

They summoned me. Kerouac's girlfriend called me up and said, "Come down and have tea with us," which was a euphemism in Greenwich Village. I got all dressed up in a suit and tie because I didn't want to seem to be going down to enemy territory in their uniform. . . . I got there, and first they wanted me to smoke marijuana with them. That's what they meant by tea. I had no moral compunctions, but I refused; I was not going to play the game by their rules. We had this long and very intense argument, both about literature—they accusing me of being Philistine about their work—and also about the doctrines that they were preaching through their literary works.

We got nowhere. I didn't convince them; they didn't convince me. At a certain point in the evening I left, with Kerouac, to go to see somebody else, and as I left, Ginsberg yelled at me, "We'll get you through your children." I already had children, by the way. He was an early out-of-the-closet homosexual and a preacher of the superiority of homosexuality to heterosexuality. So there was a double meaning in that.

What happened after that was that we'd see each other from time to time. Unlike the other characters in this book with whom I was intimately friendly, I wasn't with Allen. But I discovered from his writings and interviews [that] he continued throughout his entire life to have this fantasy about me. He was constantly arguing with me in his own head, as he himself said, and in his dreams. He finally became a kind of Buddhist late in life; [he was] born Jewish. But he finally said that I had become a sacred object to him because who else would he have to bang his head against if I hadn't been in the world.

LIONEL TRILLING WAS one of the great literary critics of our age. He also wrote fiction, a very famous novel called *The Middle of the Journey*, in which Whittaker Chambers of the Alger Hiss case was a character. As he later said, I was Trilling's best student or favorite student at Columbia. Then in later years we became personal friends.

Diana Trilling was his wife, a critic in her own right, [though] nothing near as distinguished or eminent. But, for a long time, she reviewed novels for *The Nation*, a weekly magazine that still exists, and she wrote some other [things]. I became a kind of surrogate son, really. They had a son quite late in life, and I was very close to both of them in my twenties, especially after I got out of the army, which was in just about the very end of 1955.

I always went too far for the Trillings. At first I went too far left, and then I went too far right. I was never, except for about five minutes in the '50s, exactly where they thought I ought to be. So I was always getting into trouble with them, and somehow they felt betrayed because I was supposed to be carrying Lionel's legacy forward, both as a literary critic and in my political views.

But the point about [both] the Trillings [is] they were what we used to call hard anti-Communists, but they also regarded themselves as liberals and members of the community of the left. Diana, particularly, was always terrified at being associated with the right because she was so strong an anti-Communist. Some of the strongest anti-Communists were people on the left. Ex-Communists who remained on the left became Trotskyists or Social Democrats of one kind or another and hated communism because they thought it had betrayed the idealistic hopes of the Russian Revolution. But they never moved to what they considered the right. For them, that would have been an act of apostasy, which is indeed what they accused me of committing when I moved to the right.

Diana outlived Lionel by twenty-odd years; Lionel died in 1975 at the age of seventy. Diana lived into her nineties and died only a few years ago. Lionel and I never broke. We just slightly drifted apart, and I thank God that we never broke because I still have very strong feelings about him. But no question, a coolness developed between us. Diana and I did break definitively because she thought I had gone too far to the right and because she considered that I had been untruthful about what Lionel had said to me and represented for me.

WHEN I SAY political disagreements, I mean something broader than what people mean when they talk about politics in Washington. I really mean something like a philosophy of life. The people I talk about in the world that I try to evoke in this book were passionately interested in politics, but they were just as passionately and perhaps more passionately interested in the arts, especially literature and painting. It was out of this world that the Abstract Expressionists were discovered.

[Today] there's no real sense of bloodthirsty passion behind these arguments, whereas in the early '50s, people got literally into fistfights—I'm talking about grown men—over whether a particular novel or poem was good or bad. . . . There's something quite wonderful about the passion behind this. . . . Of course, I'm nostalgic. Even though I came to disagree with almost everything most of those people believed in and tried very hard to argue against it, I find myself nostalgic for a world in which ideas and the arts were taken as seriously as they were. . . . Even though . . . I think it did a lot of harm in many ways, harm that . . . I participated in doing. I've spent the last thirty years trying to undo it.

I tell these stories and I talk about these friendships as a way of trying to relate in more vivid terms the political and cultural history of the era through which we have all lived, and try to elucidate the issues that were important, that were matters of life and death. My lesson in the end was that . . . I think this country is a precious asset of human civilization, and politically speaking—not culturally, but politically speaking—it compares to fifth-century Athens as a culture. It is a society that we must cherish and defend with all our hearts and all our souls. The lesson I learned from being a radical and turning against radicalism was that it was my duty as an intellectual to defend this country and its institutions, which intellectuals have not done for the most part for 150 years. Mostly they've been sour about this country from one angle or another.

The second thing I come away with is that it's very, very important to have a literary intellectual community such as I grew up in, in which the assumptions behind the conventional wisdom are constantly being scrutinized and argued about. We have policy wonks by the thousands, but we have very few intellectuals who talk about the assumptions that lie behind the policies that the wonks are arguing about, who see these questions in a larger political, philosophical, and cultural context. So we need that, and it's a shame that we've lost it.

Social Transformation

1957–1975

Orval Faubus and the Desegregation of Central High School

by

ROY REED

With Brown v. Board of Education *of Topeka, a 1954 case presented before the U.S. Supreme Court, the court struck down a Kansas statute permitting cities of more than 15,000 to maintain separate black and white schools and ruled that all segregation in public schools is inherently unequal and denies black students equal protection of the law as guaranteed by the Fourteenth Amendment to the U.S. Constitution. In 1955 the court implemented its 1954 opinion by declaring that federal district courts would have jurisdiction to enforce the desegregation decision. Some states and local communities either refused to comply with the federal orders or sought to delay them. When, in 1957, Arkansas Governor Orval Faubus called out the Arkansas National Guard to prevent the forced integration of Central High School in Little Rock, President Eisenhower responding by sending in federal troops. Roy Reed, professor emeritus at the University of Arkansas at Fayetteville, appeared on* Booknotes *on August 9, 1998, to discuss* Faubus: The Life and Times of an American Prodigal, *published by the University of Arkansas Press in 1997.*

THE YEARS 1957 AND 1958 were when Orval Faubus was most prominent in this country. In September of 1957 [as governor of Arkansas] he called out the Arkansas National Guard to stop the integration of the largest high school in the state, Central High School. President Eisenhower eventually had to send in federal troops to enforce the desegregation of that school. As a result of that action, he became known around the world—hated by millions of people, adored by other millions. But that's when he made his mark. . . . In the 1950s, he was one of the most famous men in the world. He was notorious for a number of years and then almost completely dropped out of sight. He did not deserve to be forgotten—whether he was a villain or a hero— however you might choose to look at him.

THE "SOUTHERN MANIFESTO" came in 1956—a year before the events of 1957. This was when the real massive resistance took hold in the South. It was a document drawn up by some of the more rigid segregationist members of the United States Congress; Strom Thurmond was prominent in this. The manifesto said, in effect, that the Supreme Court decision *Brown v. Board of Education,* ordering school desegregation, was illegal. It was unconstitutional, a misreading of the law and history, and ought to be resisted by every lawful means.

All but a handful of southern senators and representatives signed this manifesto because the pressure to sign built up to the point where it would have been political suicide not to sign it. J. William Fulbright signed it with great reluctance and only after getting [its language modified] to some extent. Brooks Hays, a famous liberal of the time and president of the Southern Baptist Convention back when it was a liberal organization, had to sign it. He hated it and regretted it the rest of his life.

THE SCHOOLS OF THE South were ordered to desegregate, but it was proceeding at a molasses pace. Little Rock had a school superintendent named Virgil Blossom who had come up with a voluntary plan of desegregation. It was very cleverly drawn and it was cynically designed to keep segregation, for the most part for years to come, by token integration of one high school. Then, after years, it would proceed to the junior high level, then to the elementary level. The Blossom Plan had been tested in federal court and approved. Virgil Blossom made hundreds of speeches to civic clubs around the town, promoting the plan. The general opinion in public was that it was going to succeed because there was no way it could fail.

There was no organized opposition until just weeks before the opening of school. Then the Capital Citizens Council, a small organization with maybe only five hundred members at the outside, began to agitate. They brought in Governor Marvin Griffin from Georgia, a very well-known segregationist, to speak at a rally, and he whipped up the crowd. There were other developments along the line and Governor Faubus began to get nervous. Faubus had kept his hands off and, from all indications, was going to have nothing to do one way or the other with the integration of Central High School. . . . Faubus was midway through his second term as governor of Arkansas.

Faubus called out the Guard September 3, the night before school opened. Things rocked along in a kind of limbo for about three weeks. Then there was an abortive meeting between the governor and the president at Newport, Rhode Island. [The president's staff] had to get Ike off the golf course to come to this meeting. They thought they had an agreement. Well, Eisenhower apparently thought he had persuaded Faubus to go back home and use the state guardsmen to protect the nine Negro children.

Faubus's view of it was that they had no such agreement; that, in fact, he felt tricked by Eisenhower's attorney general, Herbert Brownell. He thought he had talked the president into agreeing to a delay, to give everyone time to cool off. Delay was what Faubus was angling for from the beginning; that's what he really wanted more than an explosive confrontation. But Brownell told Eisenhower, "No, you can't grant a delay. That's not in your power. This is a court decision and has to be carried out."

Eisenhower finally had to [place the Arkansas National Guard under federal control] after there was violence; nobody was killed, but there was a good bit of very troubling violence in the streets and around Central High School. Segregationist mobs, who came to forcibly keep the nine black children out of the school, succeeded. The assistant police chief, one of the great unsung heroes of our time, a man named Gene Smith, had to spirit these kids out from the basement of the school in unmarked cars with their heads down so the mob couldn't get at them. . . . They were about to be killed by this mob, and he got them out at the last minute. The violence had reached the point where there was simply a breakdown in law and order, and the president had to send in the 101st Airborne to restore order.

The crowd was egged on by invective from strategically placed leaders. "I hope they bring out eight dead niggers," one leader shouted. The Reverend Wesley Pruden of the segregationist Citizens Council was more circumspect. He limited himself mainly to quiet words of assurance to the members of the mob, although once when the crowd rushed to the barricades, he raised his voice, "That's what we gotta fight, niggers, Communists, and cops." . . . Incidentally, that language was taken directly from old files of the FBI, which did a very thorough investigation of the trouble at Little Rock.

When Faubus called out the National Guard, he justified it on the grounds that he was preventing violence, that he had advance information that there was going to be bloodshed at Central High School; that there were caravans of men, armed to the teeth, heading for the city, and that the stores around Pulaski County had sold unusually large numbers of pistols, knives, and other weapons to young white boys and black boys that they intended to use against each other in the school.

The FBI investigated that claim of impending violence and found it to be essentially without base. There was no unusual sale of knives. Even the leader of the state Citizens Council, a man named Jim Johnson, told me, "There were no caravans. We made the governor believe that there were caravans, but there weren't any." The FBI established that this entire pretext for calling out the National Guard was simply not true.

GENE SMITH WENT on to be police chief and, within a very short time, found his own life in desperate circumstances, partly because of the pressure he had been put under from segregationists. Old friends of his who were segregationists began calling him a traitor—called him at home. He took to drink; he was always bad to drink, as we say in the South, and it got worse. He became a drunk and eventually, according to one source, actually threatened to kill Orval Faubus in a fit of anger one night. His wife stopped him. But one night he got out his pistol and shot his wife and then, after pacing the floor the rest of the night, put the gun to his own head.

THE PRESS WAS, BY and large, on the side of integration. They brought to the nation's attention this rather troubling development. Of course, there had been other developments across the South as the movement began to gather force. Martin Luther King had already successfully concluded the Montgomery bus boycott and was a growing figure in the nation's consciousness. By 1957 the civil rights movement had a pretty good head of steam, but it hadn't really had any great breakthroughs, especially in the field of school desegregation. That's why Little Rock was significant—this was the first big test of the Supreme Court's 1954 desegregation decision. The supposition was that this was going to work in Little Rock because it was a moderate upper South town. The press took a great interest in it before September on the theory that they were going down there to cover a success story; Little Rock was going to show the nation how a moderate southern city with a reasonable leadership could make integration work. Then it blew up in our faces, and some of the press found that it was covering quite a different story—a story of rebellion.

ORVAL FAUBUS, in the American mind, as far as he's remembered at all, is thought to be a raving segregationist on the order of George Wallace before Wallace repented, back there with Leander Perez and Ross Barnett and all those old enemies of civilization, as they were thought to be. Faubus is simply lumped in there with the rest of them.

I believe that Eisenhower was more of a segregationist than Faubus. Of course, I did not know President Eisenhower; . . . but from history I've read, from biography, I'm pretty sure that he, in his personal beliefs, was more nearly a segregationist than Orval Faubus. Faubus was not a segregationist; he simply was not.

Faubus's sin was not that he was a segregationist, but that he was cynical and that he was opportunistic. He was the consummate politician who dealt with pressures in the way that politicians always do. He finally gave in to the pressures of the moment, then catered to the mob instead of to good sense. . . . This country ought to . . . . be a little more indulgent with our politicians. We've come to think of politics as evil and smelly, and we have no patience with politicians because they compromise. Well, of course they compromise, and they sometimes compromise on principle. Faubus did, but he was not an evil man. He was simply a man caught up in events and overtaken. I wouldn't excuse what he did. He made a terrible mistake. He did the wrong thing.

He was a broken man during his last years. After he left the governor's office, he had no occupation he could go back to. . . . In fact, at one point, he was in debt several hundred thousand dollars, that largely because of a personal change in his life. He divorced Alta Faubus, a woman he had been married to for thirty-seven years, after he took up with a woman much younger than himself; [he was] swept off his feet in a kind of classic love affair of an older man falling head over heels for a younger woman. She turned out to [be] . . . a very expensive second wife, not in her tastes but because she suffered bad health and ran up enormous doctor and hospital bills. Then he got sick, and her children caused problems for him. And all the way around, it was a very expensive marriage. He was in debt and never really got out of debt the rest of his life until just shortly before he died.

I'm not sure I learned anything [about Faubus] that was terribly surprising, except this: that I liked him, in spite of all my instincts and in spite of his politics, which were always repugnant to me, right to the end of his life. In spite of personal things about him that I learned in the interviews, I found that I could not help liking the man. I suppose that's simply an indication of what a masterful politician he always was, even in his later years.

LITTLE ROCK NOW is very like dozens of other American cities: troubled; the public school system in a kind of a mess—struggling. It was integrated before Faubus left office, more or less successfully in the context of the times. But it has been under federal court order almost continuously for all these forty-one years, like a lot of other cities. You can't say that integration has succeeded very well there, just as it has not succeeded in a lot of other places, which, of course, is not at all to suggest that the attempt should not have been made. It was the right and proper thing to do. [But] it caused a lot of trouble, a lot of angst, and it still does.

Lyndon Johnson and the 1960 Election

by

ROBERT DALLEK

Lyndon Baines Johnson, America's thirty-sixth president, was born in 1908 near Stonewall, Texas. As a young man, he worked as a day laborer and a schoolteacher before entering politics as a congressional aide and New Deal official in the 1930s. He won his first political office in 1937 in a special election for a seat in the U.S. House of Representatives. Johnson was the first congressman to enlist for active duty in World War II and served in the navy until President Roosevelt ordered all congressmen back to their elective office in 1942. LBJ later represented his home state of Texas in the Senate before his election as the vice president in 1960. He was sworn in as president of the United States on Air Force One *after John F. Kennedy was assassinated in 1963. Boston University history professor Robert Dallek appeared on* Booknotes *on September 22, 1991, to discuss* Lone Star Rising: Lyndon Johnson and His Times, *published by Oxford University Press in 1991.*

INITIALLY, Senate majority leader Lyndon B. Johnson viewed John F. Kennedy as a pretty lightweight senator, and he was startled that Kennedy was going to be the [Democratic] presidential nominee in 1960. He kept saying, "How could they give him the nomination? He needs some gray in his hair. He's just a kid." [Johnson and his friends] used to refer to Kennedy as the "boy." He would go around complaining, "Jack Kennedy was out there kissing babies while I was getting the laws passed." He was always frustrated by the fact that Kennedy got the nomination. Of course, the relationship changed once Kennedy became the nominee and Johnson became his running mate. But Jack Kennedy was sensitive to Lyndon Johnson's situation. He knew it was a very difficult transition for Johnson to make because he knew that Johnson was such a powerful, dominating, overbearing character.

There is a wonderful anecdote about the election of 1960: the evening of the election, Johnson called up Kennedy and said, "Jack, I see that I'm winning Texas, you're losing Ohio, and we're doing all right together in Pennsylvania." It was the residual anger and feeling that he had that, "Gosh, I deserved to be the nominee at the front of the ticket and Jack Kennedy should have been playing second fiddle." Kennedy, though, was sensitive to him during Johnson's vice presidency. [This was] not true of Bobby Kennedy because he and Lyndon had quite a fierce struggle going back to at least 1955.

The origins of that Bobby-Lyndon animus [go back to] the fall of 1955. Joe Kennedy sent [former Franklin Roosevelt aide] Tommy Corcoran to Texas to ask Johnson if he would consider running for president and if he would take Jack as his running mate. If he would, Joe Kennedy promised to put up, or get, the $10 million to $12 million that it would take to run a presidential campaign. The Kennedys wanted, of course, to get Jack on the ticket as a prelude to running in 1960. The reason they wanted Johnson to run was because they knew that Adlai Stevenson, if he got the nomination again, would be beaten very badly by Eisenhower. They anticipated that Johnson would make a much better run for the presidency than Stevenson [in 1956], and this would undercut the charge against Jack Kennedy that his Catholicism undermined the ticket in 1956.

Now Johnson understood all this, and he knew the Kennedys wanted to use him as a stalking horse, and so he said, no, he was not going to run for president [in 1956]. He made noises about it at the Democratic convention that year, but he was really looking to 1960, also. Corcoran described in a manuscript memoir how Bobby Kennedy went into a rage when he heard that Johnson turned his father's offer down. He was infuriated that Johnson should turn down his father's generous offer. That was the beginning of their anger. Then in 1959 Bobby Kennedy went to see Johnson at his ranch and said, "Are you running for president?" Johnson said, "Oh, no," and lied to Bobby. Johnson insisted they go out deer hunting and . . . gave Bobby a big shotgun. Bobby Kennedy fired it off and the kickback hit him in the forehead, knocked him to the ground, and cut his forehead open. Johnson reached down with his hand, pulled him up, and said, "Son, you've got to learn to handle a gun like a man." So there was not very good blood between them from very early on in the 1950s and '60s.

It's ironic that the Kennedys were trying to get Johnson to run for president in 1956 with Jack as his running mate. . . . And, of course, in 1960, we end up with the exact reverse ticket. . . . Johnson forever after 1960 put out that he didn't want to be vice president, that he had to be almost dragged, kicking and screaming, into the nomination, and that he was very reluctant to take the office, which is not true. Johnson was avid to get the vice presidential nomination in 1960. The reason he was so drawn to it was because he knew he was finished as an effective majority leader. A number of liberals had been elected to the Senate in 1958, and that made Johnson's life difficult as majority leader. He also knew that if a Democrat won in 1960, it was going to make it awfully hard for him to be more than an office boy, so to speak, or a messenger boy for the president.

So Johnson decided, once he realized that he couldn't get the nomination for president, that he would go for the vice presidency. [House Speaker] Sam Rayburn carried the message to [Massachusetts Democratic Congressman] Tip O'Neill, and O'Neill carried it to Jack Kennedy, and Kennedy talked to Rayburn, and 'round and 'round it went until Johnson ended up as the nominee. Johnson's hope was that he could convert the office into something it had never been before. Indeed, this is what is striking about Lyndon Johnson: every major office he had held in his career, he converted into something it had never been before. He became the director of the Texas National Youth Administration in 1935 and very quickly became the best state director of the National Youth Administration in the United States and was recognized as such by the Roosevelt administration. Then [in 1937] he became a congressman and was an extraordinarily effective and successful congressman. He became a senator [in 1949] and . . . was the greatest Senate majority leader in the country's history. That office hadn't been a terribly important office before Johnson took it over, so he thought he could also take the vice presidency and turn it into something that it had never been before. He turned out to be wrong on that count, but it was the first time in his career he made that error in judgment.

IF YOU MET Lyndon Johnson, you would never forget him. He did some of the most outrageous things. He was terribly vulgar and crude. There was partly purpose to this, though; he was implanting himself in your memory. You had to remember Lyndon Johnson. He identified with disadvantaged people who were needy the way, in a sense, that he was needy, and he worked very hard throughout his career to serve them. I don't want to paint a picture of a saint. Believe me, this man was intensely ambitious, but . . . he loved to marry his ambition to his ideals. He was a magnificent scoundrel, a self-serving altruist, a man of high ideals and no principles, a chameleon on plaid. He was a man of many contradictions and a man with vision.

A picture was [taken of Johnson and Franklin Roosevelt] in 1937 after Johnson won his first congressional race. What comes to mind is the two great titans of politics of the twentieth century in American history, Johnson the young man. There's a wonderful story about that: Roosevelt met Johnson in Texas in May of 1937. He went back to Washington and talked to Tommy

Corcoran . . . about this young new congressman he had met. He said he really enjoyed meeting him. If he hadn't gone to Harvard, Roosevelt said, "that's the kind of young politician I would have been." He predicted that Johnson was the kind of man who was going to become president of the United States in future generations—someone from the South or the West. Roosevelt was anticipating the rise of the Sunbelt, the rise of the Southwest to power in American history and Johnson as a representative figure from that region who could hold power.

Johnson was such a controversial figure and there was so much animus, which still exists toward him. . . . In November 1988, Lou Harris did a poll and asked a cross-section of Americans to evaluate the last nine presidents from Roosevelt to Reagan in eleven different categories. [For example] who was the greatest in foreign affairs, in domestic affairs, who will go down as the best of these presidents in history, who was the greatest moral leader? Johnson came in last, tied for last, or near the bottom in every single category. When they asked who was the greatest moral leader, John Kennedy came in first. Johnson came in dead last with 1 percent of the vote. Even Nixon beat him out, getting 2 percent.

It has a lot to do with the memories of Vietnam, the anger over the defeat in that war, Johnson's manipulation of the Congress and of the public, a kind of stealth that people feel he practiced. But it also has to do with the fact that currently big government is in bad odor. Ronald Reagan told us in the 1980s that government is not the solution; government is the problem. People identified Lyndon Johnson with big government. They also see him as the consummate politician, which he was. He is now back in focus again because people—at least old-fashioned Democrats—are drawn perhaps to his agenda, to the kind of liberal programs that he was so powerfully committed to. Johnson is the last great Democratic leader to have made great advances on these liberal social justice programs.

There are lots of unpleasant things about Johnson, but I also see him as a man of great vision and thoughtfulness about what needed to be done to change the South, to improve [living] conditions, and to bring the South into the mainstream of American economic and political life. This is what Johnson wanted to do from very early on in his career—this was the impulse that came out of the New Deal. In 1938 there was a famous report issued by the New Deal saying that the South was the country's number one economic problem and that changes had to be made. Johnson saw this. He jumped onto this report and tried to use it as a springboard to help the South. The objective was to take these New Deal programs and build a new infrastructure in the South, to change the condition of the tenant farmers, improve the standard of living of laborers, and in that way help the South's economy and bring it into the mainstream of the country's life.

There was something else Johnson understood early on, which was that the South couldn't do this fully until it ended racial segregation. He understood that segregation in the South not only segregated the races but segregated the South from the rest of the nation. So, from early in his career, he was thinking about this. This is not to say that Lyndon Johnson got on a soapbox in 1937 or '38 while running for Congress and began shouting in Texas, "Let's have a civil rights bill that will overcome segregation."

He was too much the politician to ever do that. What he did was behind the scenes. For example, when he was the state director of the National Youth Administration, he would occasionally spend the night at a black college. He wanted to see how the programs were working and how they were helping the young black students. If this were known in this era of strict segregation, it would have been a severe injury to his chances for running for a congressional office. But he did it out of compassion, and was not doing it because New Dealers were so committed to black rights at this time; they were not. The Roosevelt administration was not making great advances at all on the civil rights front.

Johnson did this out of genuine compassion for the suffering of these people. When he went to Congress, one New Deal farm administrator said, "Johnson began to raise unshirted hell about the fact that black farmers were getting a smaller share of the pie than the white farmers." In 1938 the first Federal Housing Act passed, and Johnson was one of the three congressmen who took advantage of it. He got public housing for Austin, Texas, and he wanted to have public housing built not only for poor whites but for blacks and Hispanics. He told the city fathers, "This is what you've got to do. Let's go for this, and we'll improve the well-being of the poorest people in our city." There was a genuine compassion on this man's part.

Lyndon Johnson was also an extraordinary operator. My favorite story is about Johnson going to visit Harry Truman in the waning days of Johnson's presidency. He met with Truman in Independence, Missouri, and said to him, "Harry, you and Bess are living in this old house here in Independence. You're getting on in years. You may become ill. You ought to have an army medical corpsman living here at the house with you." Truman was supposed to have replied, "Really, Lyndon! Can I have that?" Johnson supposedly said, "Of course, Harry. My God, man, you're an ex-president of the United States. I'll arrange it." About six months after Johnson got out of the White House, a reporter caught up one day with him at the ranch and said, "Mr. President, is it true that you've got an army medical corpsman living here on the ranch with you?" Johnson said, "Of course it's true. Harry Truman has one." He sure knew how to pull the levers of government and pull the strings, as they say.

Robert Frost and the Kennedy Inauguration

by

JAY PARINI

Robert Frost wrote some of America's most loved poems. He also served as a presidential goodwill ambassador to Brazil and Russia, taught literature, and farmed for most of his life. At the age of eighty-six, Frost braved the bitter cold to read his poem, "The Gift Outright," at John F. Kennedy's 1961 presidential inauguration. Frost's performance stole the show. Jay Parini, an English professor at Middlebury College, examined this complex man in Robert Frost: A Life, *published by Henry Holt and Company in 1999, and* discussed Frost on Booknotes *on September 12, 1999.*

BEFORE ROBERT FROST, poets were invisible on the political landscape. We did not have, in the twentieth century, a national bard until Frost came along. . . . The fact that Presidents Eisenhower and Kennedy admired him and were willing to support him in his ventures was very important.

[Congressman] Stewart Udall was a friend of Frost's and suggested to John Kennedy that Frost read at the inauguration. Kennedy's first response in a memo back to Udall was, "What? That old scene stealer? They'll forget that I've just been elected president and that's all they'll talk about in the papers the next day," which was true, in fact. A big headline in the *Washington Post* the next day said: "Old Poet Steals Heart of America." That was something Kennedy had wanted to do.

Kennedy, of course, finally assented, and Frost came out to read a poem [at the inauguration]. He got up onstage. It was blustery and cold, a bitterly cold day. Frost had no hat on. He was well into his eighties, almost ninety.

He suddenly pulled up his sheet [of notes] and couldn't read because the sun was glaring on the paper. Lyndon Johnson, the vice president–elect, came over and shielded the paper with his top hat. Robert Frost said, "Oh, I can't read it—the sun and glare, I can't do it." Then there was this amazing moment when Frost very melodramatically crumpled the paper and looked up into the sun and began to recite from memory, as though he hadn't recited the poem a thousand times before from memory. . . . [He began "The Gift Outright."] "The land was ours before we were the land's." He looked up as though he was trying to struggle to retrieve from memory these lines. You know, for twenty years now, I've listened to tapes of Robert Frost reading his poetry as I've jogged and I could never tire of hearing him mouth these words over. He got it, you know. He really is the voice of American poetry.

[FROST LIVED TO BE] eighty-nine and was vigorous to the end. It was only a few months before his death in 1963 that John Kennedy sent him as a good-will ambassador to Russia, and he had an incredibly powerful head-on conversation with Nikita Khrushchev.

Frost had taken ill in his last days in Russia. He was desperately eager to meet Nikita Khrushchev. Khrushchev was not too far away, on a summer holiday, so he came over and visited Frost in his hospital bed.

Frost went to Russia because he suddenly got a letter from the State Department saying, "You were so successful as a goodwill ambassador to Brazil." He'd gone to a big conference in Brazil where he represented the U.S. government as a cultural ambassador. They said, "Why not go to Russia? We're at the height of the Cold War now, and we think that it might break the ice." They love poets in Russia. In fact, they loved Robert Frost in Russia.

The day Robert Frost arrived, there was a huge front-page article in *Pravda*: "Robert Frost is a true poet of the people. He is a farmer. He's a real working man." It's true. Frost's greatest poems are about working people and they're about simple people and they're about working. Most of his great poems involve [everyday tasks like] chopping up wood in "Two Tramps in Mud Time" or "Mowing," about mowing the grass, or "Putting in the Seed" or . . . "After Apple-Picking." Frost had done all these things. He kept a farm until the end of his life, even in the last years, in Ripton, Vermont. He always had a stand of apple trees and a big garden. He was a farmer much of his adult life.

FROST WAS ACTUALLY a very unpolitical man. I won't even say apolitical. He was actively against politics in some ways. When [poet] Ezra Pound was put in the St. Elizabeth's Mental Hospital, he was convicted of treason. Ezra Pound had been a fascist. He'd been an acolyte of Mussolini. He'd been in

Italy making broadcasts against the Americans and British and Allied forces. Ezra Pound was a pretty crazy fellow and a traitor. Robert Frost was one of many writers—including Ernest Hemingway, T. S. Eliot, and Robert Lowell—involved in trying to spring "Old Ez," as they called him, from the prison.

Ezra Pound was one of the founding poets and thinkers of modernism. He was an American poet who moved to London in the early part of the century and befriended T. S. Eliot, James Joyce, and Gertrude Stein. He really supported and buoyed up and systematized the aesthetics of this modernist movement in poetry. He was the ringmaster of modernism in literature. He was very kind to Robert Frost.

When Robert Frost was totally unknown, aged thirty-eight, he sailed with no books published, no money in his pocket, with a young family and nothing but the hope of a song in his pocket, to London. He met Ezra Pound at a party, and Ezra Pound took up Frost and promoted him. He helped him get his book published and reviewed his first books of poetry, not once but three times. So Frost felt forever an indebtedness to the great help he had gotten from Ezra Pound.

Frost was the point man because Frost knew Eisenhower and people in the Eisenhower administration. It would take somebody with real ties to the White House. . . . The people surrounding Eisenhower had great respect for Frost. It took Frost to spring Ezra Pound from St. Elizabeth's.

Frost always hated liberals. . . . If Frost had any politics at all, it was a kind of fierce independence and individualism. He was kind of libertarian in a way. One of his best poems is called "Provide, Provide," and it ends, "Better to go down dignified with boughten friendship at your side than none at all. Provide. Provide." Whenever Frost read that poem, he would say to the audience, "And if you don't provide for yourself, somebody else is going to provide for you, and you might not like it." He was anti–New Deal . . . and he rather despised urban liberals.

Frost was . . . hesitant about getting the government involved in anything. But he always said if you're going to spend government money, he thought you might as well spend it on poetry as opposed to guns.

FROST WANTED everything both ways. Frost was himself a lousy student, did not like the discipline of the classroom, and did not like orderly knowledge . . . . He got out of high school at the age of eighteen in 1892. Then he went on to a few months at Dartmouth, dropped out, worked for a while, then went down to Harvard for a year and a half and then dropped out. That was it. That's all the college he ever had.

Frost lived the life of a subsistence farmer and supported his farming with a little bit of teaching at the Pinkerton Academy and then later at a normal school, which was a kind of school for teachers in New Hampshire. By the time he was thirty-eight, he had nothing published. He had no money. He had four kids, quickly growing, eating a lot of food. He sold the farm and took off for England. It was in England in 1914 and early 1915 that he really pulled his books together, his first two books, got them published first in England, and was essentially discovered.

[When he returned to the United States, he taught beginning in] 1917, when he was made a professor at Amherst. . . . He was very rarely not connected to a college [but] the only college where he taught seriously was Amherst. He had an ongoing post at Amherst throughout much of his life. In the late teens and through the twenties he taught fairly seriously at Amherst and then sometimes at the University of Michigan. There was a little stretch when he taught at Dartmouth as the George Ticknor Fellow. There was a little stretch when he was a visiting writer and did some teaching at Harvard. Then in the summers, he often lectured at Middlebury College's Bread Loaf Writer's Conference.

Frost was a very learned man. He just wore his learning very, very lightly. He was trained in Latin. He read *The Aeneid,* Catullus, the great Latin poets in the original, right to the end of his life.

FROST SAID, "Poetry is all about stumbling your way into these little moments of recognition, not great truths." He said, "Great truths are for religions and cults. Let Jesus and let the Buddha have the big truths. For the poets, we have these little momentary stays against confusion, these recognitions, these illuminations, which we piece together to create a sense of self and to create a spiritual life."

Frost had a very sad life. He said life was chaos and we work our way through chaos. Frost's poetry is often very, very dark. When you think about it, his life was quite chaotic. . . . Frost was fairly depressive through most of his life, either exhilarated manic or somewhat down. He oscillated back and forth between those two poles. His wife, Elinor, was sick much of the time, as he was himself. His son Carol committed suicide. His daughter Irma was hospitalized and died in a mental institution. His beloved daughter Marjorie died from complications of childbirth. His beautiful little child Elliott was a young child of four when he died from an infection. There was one familial disaster after another.

To look at Frost's life, the wonder is that he got through it at all, and the wonder is he got through it with so much buoyancy and so much spirit. Every poem written was essentially a triumph over the chaos that surrounded him. Frost saw his life as this very tangled wood. You look at a poem like "Directive," and it's essentially a guide to Frost's work. He talks about a brook that is really the source of all poetry. It's the Helicon, the stream that flows off the Greek island of Parnassus, in his mind. He says, "Here are your waters and your watering place. Drink and be whole beyond confusion."

FROST WON FOUR Pulitzer Prizes for poetry, which is a record, beginning in 1924 with *New Hampshire* and *West Running Brook,* and so forth, right up through *A Witness Tree.* He won Pulitzer Prizes for almost all of his major books after *New Hampshire.* It's quite a record.

THIS WAS A man of total contradiction. He just reveled in contradiction. He liked to have everything—to have his cake and eat it too. If any man ever did want to have everything always at once, it was Robert Frost. He wanted to be the poet of the people and the totally independent bard.

The Cuban Missile Crisis

by

DONALD KAGAN

In 1962 American spy planes discovered that the Soviet Union was placing armed nuclear missiles in Cuba. The ensuing round of high-stakes diplomacy and military bluffing and threats, the Cuban missile crisis might arguably be the closest the world has ever come to nuclear war. Donald Kagan's book On the Origins of War and the Preservation of Peace, *published by Doubleday in 1995, examines war—the rationales, the lessons, and the costs—by looking at four wars and the Cuban missile crisis. Mr. Kagan, a professor at Yale, told us more about the crisis and his book during a* Booknotes *appearance on March 12, 1995.*

THE CUBAN MISSILE CRISIS [took place] in October of 1962. President John F. Kennedy announced on the twenty-second of October that the Russians were in the process . . . of placing missiles in Cuba with nuclear warheads that were capable of striking the largest part of the United States. They were doing this, in Kennedy's word, "clandestinely," and they were doing it after having lied about it repeatedly over a stretch of time. That combination of circumstances made it seem alarming to a variety of people, including Kennedy. He ended up taking the mildest line toward it, but, of course, he understood how serious it was.

[My book focuses on] two ancient wars, two modern wars, and the missile crisis, where there's a happy ending. . . . I find that there are very interesting analogies between the First World War and the Peloponnesian War, . . . in which the Athenians and the Spartans were the major opponents, . . . and the Second World War and the Punic War, . . . between Rome and Carthage. . . .

[I wanted] to see if [it was possible to] learn anything useful about things we are interested in today by examining experiences of human beings at different periods of time, different places, and different kinds of societies. Is there anything common?

There have been basically rational reasons that have motivated people [to go to war], like wanting more land or a better economic situation. These were widely thought to be the important things. What I find in every case is that something that Thucydides [an Athenian nobleman and historian who lived in the middle of the fifth century B.C.] called "honor" is the decisive element. That sounds a little surprising to us. But if you think of honor—if we were to translate it into a current idiom—it very often . . . means a sense of being valued, a sense of being respected, a sense of prestige; these are things that matter. This is present in just about every case [of war].

MATERIALS HAVE COME up about the Cuban missile crisis within the last four years that have totally changed my impression of what happened. . . . There are now tapes that are publicly available and transcripts of them, of what Kennedy and his advisers said to each other . . . during the missile crisis in the White House while making those decisions. We have it with the bad grammar and the er's and the uh's, . . . exactly what they said to each other.

Kennedy gathered [a group] around him to give him advice and to consult with him in managing the crisis—[it was known as] the Executive Committee of the Security Council [or ExCom]. . . . It wasn't an automatic group that already existed. Most of the important officials of the government who were relevant . . . were involved, but also there were people of considerable experience . . . who were not part of the government, . . . Dean Acheson, a former secretary of state [for example]. The rest were active participants in the government at the time.

President Kennedy secretly taped those sessions, and that is another interesting and wonderful part about it. He was the only one who knew that the tape was going, though probably [his brother, Attorney General] Bobby Kennedy knew; he generally knew everything that Jack did. . . . [The tapes are] in the Kennedy Library . . . and, through the Freedom of Information Act, people have been able to get hold of them before they would have otherwise been released.

The first critical thing that happened . . . that was unpredictable (and Thucydides would have said immediately, "Most things are unpredictable") is that [Soviet premier] Nikita Khrushchev made a judgment. He said, "I can solve a lot of my problems—domestic, foreign policy, military—if I can plant these missiles in Cuba." The question that next must have occurred to him was, "Can I get away with it?" The critical answer was that he thought,

"I can get away with it because my judgment of President Kennedy is that he will let me."

Then comes the interesting stuff that Thucydides would have had comments about. . . . How did he come to that conclusion? The answer lies in the track record that Kennedy had accomplished in the rather short time that he had been president, beginning in January of 1961 down to the time that Khrushchev made that decision in the spring of 1962. The Bay of Pigs disaster was the first step. . . . Kennedy inherited a plan from the Eisenhower administration to get rid of Castro in Cuba by having Cuban exiles land there supported by American forces; he changed it, watered it down, and then let it happen.

But when the critical moment came, Kennedy backed off and allowed the invaders to be either killed or captured. The lesson that everybody got from that, pretty much—certainly we know Khrushchev did—was that Kennedy was . . . weak and indecisive, the kind of guy you could push around. Kennedy himself feared that that was the impression that had been given . . . . A second thing was Kennedy and Khrushchev had a summit conference one-on-one in Vienna in the spring of '61, and we now have what is obviously a very reliable record of what was said there too. It's an astonishing conversation in which Khrushchev really treats Kennedy very roughly.

Dean Rusk, the secretary of state at the time, made a comment that one thing you never do in diplomacy . . . is use the word "war," but Khrushchev used that word many times in the course of that conversation. . . . We now know that Kennedy said to *New York Times* columnist James Reston right after he came away from the last session with Khrushchev, "He beat the hell out of me." His own reading of it was that he was very worried that Khrushchev had come away with the sense that this was a guy who could be pushed around. He was right.

FOR YEARS, I HAD been teaching the Cuban missile crisis pretty much in accordance with what I now would call the official Kennedy administration line. Basically, I believed the accounts of [Kennedy aides] Arthur Schlesinger and Theodore Sorensen, and Bobby Kennedy's very influential memoir of [the crisis,] *Thirteen Days.* It was a very important book. Now I know not merely that there were the biases and the prejudices that [affect] any participant in a historical event. [Additionally] on the twenty-fifth anniversary of the Cuban missile crisis, there were conferences held at different places with the participants in the events and a number of other people who knew about it, and these have been wonderful sources for what went on. People reminisced as to what had gone on; Russians, Americans, and Cubans . . . exchanged with each other, asked each other questions, and answered the questions.

In one of those discussions, . . . Sorensen admitted . . . that at a critical moment in the crisis, in an exchange between . . . Anataoly Dobrynin, the Russian ambassador to the United States, and Bob Kennedy, Bob had formally included the trade of the Cuban missiles for the Turkish missiles. Sorensen admitted that he, as editor of [*Thirteen Days*], edited that part out. He said he did so because it was a secret not only from the country, but it was a secret from most of the players; there were only a few people who knew about it. That shows you what the problem is with the documents before you get behind the first range. I used to believe the story as told by them, which more or less was a picture of this brave, tough president who managed to work his way out of the crisis by a combination of toughness and moderation and care in controlling the level of escalation. There is no question that who gets the story out there really makes a difference [in the historical view of an event].

After reading all the new material, I came away [with the impression] . . . that they got into the crisis because there was a lack of toughness, [especially as] perceived . . . by Khrushchev. . . . During the crisis the president was actually prepared to make just about any concession rather than use military force at any point. What forced him to take as hard a line as he did was the fact that there was dissension within the ExCom. There were important players who just wouldn't have it, who were insisting on military action someplace down the road.

The single biggest lie . . . was at the end of the story when Defense Secretary Robert McNamara was asked in a Senate hearing specifically, "Had there been a deal to trade the Turkish missiles for the Cuban missiles?" He said, "No, absolutely not," and it is now absolutely clear that there was a very specific, clear-cut deal in which that trade was made, only the promise was that the Cuban missiles would come first and the Turkish missiles would come later.

[Members of the ExCom were saying, "This is a national problem, not an international problem"] or to put it another way, this is a domestic political problem. This was the line taken very much by McNamara and by Kennedy, and supporting that view very strongly was Sorensen. That, to my mind, was one of the problems with their perception of what was happening. They didn't really think this was serious. Both Kennedy and McNamara have been quoted, accurately I'm sure, to say, "It doesn't matter whether you're hit by a missile that comes from Moscow or one that comes from Cuba," and if you believe that, then there was no reason to get excited if Khrushchev put missiles into Cuba. The only reason they saw a problem was that they would be beaten to death by their political opponents if they didn't do something about it.

To me, that is a stunning failure of understanding international relations and power politics, which are the realities out there. Thucydides would have held his head in pain at that statement because they were wrong. . . . They were wrong because everybody else in the game perceived that it did make a great deal of difference. For one thing, there were some very practical matters. At that time, as best we can figure out, the Russians seemed to have had about twenty operational missiles that could have hit the United States if launched from Russia. We had hundreds and hundreds [that could hit them]. But not only that, it is hard to know what their missiles would have hit; they were very poorly aimed and so on. The goal was to put forty missiles in Cuba, which would have doubled their actual payload capacity, but they couldn't miss from Cuba. So the issue, as some Russians have pointed out, was, it doesn't matter how many missiles you have; it's how many missiles can you deliver. Suddenly the balance of power was changed really very significantly by what the Russians could actually do.

Second, whatever we might say about it, everybody in the world would have said, "The Russians have just changed the situation. They're stronger now; the Americans are weaker now." So everybody's reaction to power would have changed. Finally, Kennedy's own credibility would have been so severely damaged.

In a funny way, there didn't turn out to be a turning point in a way that you would have anticipated it. [Nobody] pulled back from the terrible brink and said, "Now, let's not do dangerous things and stop being rivals and be friends," which was what a lot of people hoped would be the result immediately. Nor, on the other hand, did it create a tremendous [ongoing] crisis. What happened was that the Russians kept on going, doing what they were doing, namely, relying on force, attempting to increase their missile capacity, and doing so with great success over the next decade or so. But the McNamara doctrine that emerged from it, based on what they called "minimal deterrence," was that we didn't need to worry about that, that it didn't matter if the Soviet Union came to have as much nuclear missile power as we did or even more, so long as we had enough to do a lot of harm to them. The trouble was . . . that we accepted the concept of minimal deterrence but the Russians didn't. They thought they could gain politically around the world by increasing their actual power, and they did.

Martin Luther King Jr.'s Letter from a Birmingham Jail

by

ANDREW YOUNG

Andrew Young was deeply involved in the civil rights movement of the 1960s. He headed the Southern Christian Leadership Conference and was with Martin Luther King Jr. the night he was assassinated. Mr. Young, now the chairman of GoodWorks International in Atlanta, visited us on the Booknotes *set on April 3, 1994, and told us the story of Dr. King's* Letter from a Birmingham Jail, *a letter that would become one of the most influential documents of the movement. More stories from the movement followed as Mr. Young discussed his autobiography,* A Way Out of No Way: The Spiritual Memoirs of Andrew Young, *published by Thomas Nelson Communications in 1994.*

MARTIN LUTHER KING JR. went to jail in Birmingham, Alabama, in 1963. He went to jail because there was nothing else to do. We'd been demonstrating in Birmingham for over a month; there were hundreds of people in jail. We'd run out of bond money to get people out. There were people, black and white, urging us to call it off and just say that we'd failed.

I was thirty-one. Martin and I had known each other since 1957. We'd been on a panel together at Talladega College in Alabama while I was pastoring in Thomasville and he was pastoring in Montgomery. [Our wives] Jean and Coretta knew each other because they both grew up in the same little town of Marion, Alabama.

[At this time] I was living in Atlanta and was assigned to work with Martin Luther King and the Southern Christian Leadership Conference [SCLS]. I was on a grant from the Field Foundation. I was on the staff of my church, the United Church of Christ, the Board for Homeland Ministries. My job was to teach people how to read and write so that they could teach their neighbors.

John Lewis was then president of the Student Nonviolent Coordinating Committee and was with us in Birmingham. Jesse Jackson was still in Chicago in school in '63 and Hosea Williams was still in Savannah. Birmingham was our first success story. It was largely the work of the SCLC and the Student Nonviolent Coordinating Committee.

That was just about the time we met Fannie Lou Hamer. In fact, [Mississippi SCLS representative] James Bevel was in Mississippi with his wife, Diane, and they recruited Fannie Lou Hamer. While we were in Birmingham, we brought her over from Mississippi to Dorchester Center in McIntosh, Georgia, just south of Savannah. She was one of those that we gave this one-week training course to. While we were in Birmingham, she was coming back from a meeting that we'd had there, and she and Annelle Ponder and Lawrence Guyot and several others were arrested in Winona, Mississippi.

This is when she was beaten very badly. I went to get her out of jail on the day that [NAACP state director] Medgar Evers was killed. All of this was happening around the same time. Martin went to jail in the midst of that atmosphere, when everybody was telling us, "Look, it's not going to work. Nonviolence won't work. You have to quit. Call this off. You're getting too many people hurt, people are getting killed."

Martin thought about that and said that the only thing he could do was go to jail with them. He went to jail on a Thursday. That weekend, the ministers—the local white clergy—had in the Sunday newspaper a full-page ad blaming Martin Luther King for the racial troubles in Birmingham and saying that he should leave town and let them go back to their old, peaceful ways. He was furious. He was furious not at what they said, because everybody had been saying that, including some black people. He was furious because these were the clergy. These were the Episcopal bishop, the Jewish rabbi, the pastor of the largest Methodist church. These were people whom he felt, if they were true to their own biblical traditions, should understand what he was doing. So he wrote a letter to them.

He didn't have any paper in jail, but somebody had slipped him a *New York Times*. He started writing around the margin of the *New York Times*. Unfortunately, it wasn't a Sunday *Times*. The *Times* printed down South is rather thin, so he didn't have much space. When he finished writing around every scrap of paper that was blank on the *New York Times,* he started writing on toilet tissue. He normally fasted when he went to jail. He took only liquids. So there's no question but that he was in a heightened state emotionally and spiritually. [The words] just poured out. He had nothing to turn to, nobody to quote—he wrote it strictly from his own heart and mind.

When he got it out of there, we paid to have it published in the *Birming-ham Post-Herald* as an answer to the ministers. The Friends Service Committee picked it up and called and asked could they publish 50,000 copies and we said, "Sure." So, they published 50,000 copies and distributed it. From then on, it just took on a life of its own. It was probably the first time that anybody had actually sat down and put in writing the specific plight of black Americans in a systematic and logical way that ordinary white people could be at least encouraged to read and understand.

IN 1964 I GOT BEAT up by white officers in St. Augustine, Florida. I always saw that as contributing significantly to my maturity and awareness. It was kind of a Klan mob. For me, it was a realization that if you were going to be free, you had to be willing to walk in the face of death and stand up and take whatever happened. There's a sense in which today's young people have to make that same decision. It's not necessarily a racial decision. But long before our civil rights movement, someone said, "A coward dies a thousand deaths, and brave men, only one." One of the things I learned from the movement that I think everybody has to ultimately learn is that you can't live your life unless you have some ability to cope with the phenomenon of death and what's beyond death. Martin Luther King helped us do that. Martin Luther King used to say all the time, "If you don't have something you're willing to die for, you're not fit to live anyway."

I got a civil rights bill out of my beating. It was right about the time that the civil rights legislation was being passed. The fact that we had those demonstrations that got so violent and emotional reminded people of what had happened in Birmingham, and made it a little easier for Lyndon Johnson to cut off the Senate filibuster and pass the Civil Rights Act. I got beaten in June. The Civil Rights Act was passed on the second day of July, 1964.

I was courting trouble. I was putting myself deliberately in the path of violence because black people were always in the path of violence secretly and silently. They suffered in silence. We, through the demonstrations, deliberately took on the lot that ordinary people lived and put ourselves in their places as a means of change. Martin used to say you had to bring the evil to the surface, that racism was almost like a boil, that if it stayed under the surface, it infected your entire body. In order for it to be healed, it had to be brought to the surface where the healing light of truth, or in the case of the boil, the sun, would help it to heal. So we were doing this quite deliberately.

MARIAN WRIGHT EDELMAN, who is now with the Children's Defense Fund, had come to him in Atlanta with four men from Mississippi. These men who came with Marian were in their forties and fifties and hadn't worked in twenty years. They hadn't worked because government policy had paid the landowners not to grow food or fiber. So while the money went to the people who own land, all of the people who worked the land were left poverty-stricken; they didn't want to be on welfare. They'd worked all their lives; they wanted to work. Most of the younger people had moved to the northern cities without adequate educational preparation and created the problems that we now see in our northern cities. Martin understood that and said, "We need to get hold of this quick."

So, at Marian Edelman's invitation, we began to organize the Poor People's Campaign, which was not just black poor. We had white poor from Appalachia, we had American Indians, we had the Hispanics from out West—Cesar Chavez was part of it. We had a wide variety of urban poor who were represented in the makeup of that campaign. We didn't expect to succeed. We likened our plight to the bonus marches in the Depression and figured we'd get run out of Washington, but we hoped to establish an agenda that the next president would have to address. We expected that next president to be Robert Kennedy, and then he was killed. Then we hoped it would be Hubert Humphrey, because he understood the cities and he'd been responsible for much of the civil rights effort in the Democratic Party. He also understood poverty around the world. But by that time, people were so disillusioned; we couldn't get it together after Martin's death.

I WAS WITH MARTIN Luther King from Birmingham right on up through that evening in the Lorraine Motel [when he was assassinated]. After Birmingham, we became fairly close, and I began traveling with him. Though I was working with the church, . . . I changed from director of that voter registration project and became the executive vice president of the organization of which he was president. So I was running his organization from '64 to '68. [That night when he was killed] I was there with him. In fact, we were on the way out to dinner.

[His murder has stayed with me all my life.] I don't know whether I've dealt with it adequately yet. The week leading up to that day, he'd been very depressed. He was depressed because of the violence that occurred in Memphis. It was the first time where people in the march actually participated in breaking windows in violence. Later we found that some of those people were actually paid by the FBI to help disrupt that march. We didn't have any reason to suspect that at the time.

The 1963 Birmingham Church Bombing

by

DIANE McWHORTER

In 1963 Birmingham, Alabama, had a population of about 120,000 people, 40 percent of whom were African American. The city's racial divisions prompted Martin Luther King Jr. to call it "the most segregated city in America." Journalist Diane McWhorter now lives in New York City, but grew up in a prominent white Birmingham family, largely sheltered from stories of the Ku Klux Klan and racial violence. As an adult, she became interested in the civil rights struggle that took place in her own backyard. Ms. McWhorter described that tumultuous era and told us the story of the infamous bombing of the Sixteenth Street Baptist Church, a bombing in which four black children died, in a Booknotes *interview on April 11, 2001, about her book* Carry Me Home: Birmingham, Alabama—The Climactic Battle of the Civil Rights Revolution, *published by Simon & Schuster in 2001.*

IT WAS SEPTEMBER 15, 1963, and the schools of Birmingham, Alabama, had just been desegregated over the previous couple of weeks. John F. Kennedy was president and George Wallace was governor [of Alabama]. Wallace had called out the state troopers to try to block the young schoolchildren from entering the schools in Birmingham and had given a signal to the segregationists that they could go ahead and do what was necessary to stop the desegregation.

What became the Civil Rights Act of 1964 was being debated in Congress at the time. And it looked like it might be a losing proposition. George Wallace had been up screaming about it, [calling it] the "civil wrongs bill."

As a result of the big demonstrations there with the police dogs and fire hoses that [previous] spring, the Klan realized that their franchise was running out, and they were going to do anything to stop integration from coming about. They ended up bombing the church to do that.

That September day, on that Sunday morning, the Sunday school was winding down. A lot of the kids' Sunday school classes were taking place in the basement and a few girls went into the bathroom to primp. This was 10:15 in the morning. Normally these girls would have gone to a drugstore to get a Coke before the church service, but on this day the pastor was inaugurating a Youth Day because he was trying to breathe new life into the congregation, which was sort of stale and stodgy. Three of the girls were wearing white for their roles as ushers for Youth Day and they were going to be singing in the choir. Denise McNair, Carole Robertson, Addie Mae Collins, and Cynthia Wesley were primping [in the bathroom] because they wanted to look really nice. They were combing their hair in the mirror. One of their Sunday school classmates came into the bathroom and said something like, "They need you to get back to Sunday school class because those who don't obey the Lord live only half as long."

[A few minutes later] at 10:22, a bundle of dynamite that had been against the east wall of the church exploded. It blew out a man-sized hole in the wall of the bathroom, blew the clothes off the [four] girls, stacked them like cordwood under debris, and killed them all. One had been decapitated.

Most of [the descriptions] were actually from FBI documents of interviews with witnesses on the scene because the families have a hard time talking about it. . . . The pastor, when he came upon the girls, didn't recognize them because he thought they looked like women in their forties. And he couldn't figure out who they could be because he knew that there had just been kids downstairs. The . . . dry cleaner across the street from the church came up and he looked at the foot of one of the girls, and said, "Lord, that's Denise." It was his eleven-year-old granddaughter, Denise McNair.

That was the first time the pastor realized they were children. I think the father of Cynthia Wesley also recognized her shoe sticking out from the sheet in this makeshift morgue at the hospital. So those clothes had been their last thought on earth, and had ended up being blown off them, in one case, but identifying them [in another].

The area was sealed off. The white people were more worried about rioting blacks, it seemed, than they were about the victims. . . . I found out from my mother's date book that I had been in a civic production of *The Music Man,* the musical, and my rehearsal that night was canceled because we were afraid that the black people would be out in the streets hurting white people. As it turned out, two more black children were killed that day, one by a police bullet and one by two white teenagers who happened to ride by a paperboy and shot him off the handlebars of his bike. So it was a really tense situation.

A lot of people thought that blacks had bombed their own church in order to get publicity for the movement. That was a very popular theory among thinking people, as well as among the nut cases.

Ironically, Sixteenth Street was the seat of the [black] bourgeoisie, and they had been pretty hostile to Martin Luther King Jr. They had made their accommodations with segregation and didn't want to rock the boat. They had too much to lose. It was the masses who didn't have to risk that much in order to participate in the struggle. Reverend Fred Lee Shuttlesworth, the leader [of the black] masses, was very unpopular with the black middle class. There was a big division between the black [middle and upper] classes and the black masses. The masses were called "them asses" because they were an embarrassment to the striving elements of the community who had really made great strides and really didn't want to risk that. Sixteenth Street was very much in that tradition, and they had let the movement use the church grudgingly.

MARTIN LUTHER KING came back to town. President Kennedy's emissaries came back to try to keep the peace, and there were high-level meetings at the White House that night to try to figure out how to deal with the situation, whether troops should be sent in or just how to keep a lid on things.

The FBI called out a manhunt that they were comparing to [the search for John Dillinger in the 1930s] to try to find them. And they did quite a thorough job, except that because they were afraid that [Klan informant] Gary Thomas Rowe might have been involved, they told him to stay away from the scene for a week because they didn't want him to show up in somebody else's investigative files. When they were showing pictures of suspects to witnesses, they did not show Rowe's picture or a picture of his car. They were concerned that he might have been involved because he had been involved in other terrorist actions that the Klan had carried out. I concluded that he probably wasn't involved in the church bombing. I'm not sure whether he knew about it or not, but I don't think he took part in it.

J. Edgar Hoover was a pretty bad guy, and part of it stems from the fact that he was a totally bureaucratic creature. It seems as if his main goal in life was to protect his bureau from any kind of criticism. So whenever [the FBI] would come under criticism from somebody, he would try to find a scapegoat. As it happened, in several instances that scapegoat was Martin Luther King Jr. Hoover had gone off on this vendetta against King that was so ugly compared with the fact that . . . Gary Thomas Rowe, . . . was being shielded by his bureau. Because they were afraid that Rowe's cover would be blown, [the FBI] shielded [Rowe] and his Klan brothers from prosecution for various crimes. So the combination of going after King and then protecting the Klan is one of the ugliest chapters in the history of the Justice Department.

The Birmingham police were in cahoots with the Klan. They had a long tradition of collaboration, and even some of the members of the klavern [a small group of Klansmen] who perpetrated the bombing had been under the protection of the police. So that investigation was flawed, as well as the FBI's initial investigation.

[Prosecutors] took a long time to bring any case [to court] for several reasons. One is that the evidence is just really weak. The arch perpetrator of the crime, "Dynamite" Bob Chambliss, was convicted by the state of Alabama in 1977, but they never could build enough evidence on the four other chief suspects in the crime. Nobody involved in the case has ever talked about it. So we may never know what really happened leading up to that explosion.

The five main suspects . . . were suspects virtually from day three. [The state] could not build a case against them. Nobody talked. The physical evidence in a bombing is always virtually nonexistent because it is blown up. Sometimes there's evidence of a timing device, but rarely. The investigation went through fallow periods and then some eager police chief or attorney general would reactivate it and then come up against the same problem, which was lack of evidence. . . . Most of the evidence [against two of the men consists of] self-incriminating statements they've made to third parties. There's really no new evidence about the crime itself. [Editor's Note: The case was reopened and in May 2000, Thomas Blanton and Bobby Frank Cherry were charged with four counts of murder. Juries found both men guilty.]

THE KLAN WAS A very interesting terrorist arm of the establishment for a very long time. It had started out in the '20s, in earnest, oddly enough, as the liberal arm of the Democratic Party. It was this insurgent, radical, populist incarnation of the have-not bids for power over the previous couple of decades. That explains how Hugo Black, the great civil libertarian Supreme Court justice, had his political career launched by the Klan, because he was part of this insurgent arm of the party.

[The segregation establishment in Birmingham] went back to its industrial base. There was a very strong economic motive to enforce segregation rigidly, to foment racial strife. What it boiled down to was keeping the labor force divided so that they could keep wages down, they could have the white workers identified with management, and they would tar the union . . . to try to repel whites from joining.

Hugo Black became a New Dealer and Supreme Court justice. In the meantime, the Klan became the terrorist arm of the anti–New Dealers. They were to fight the union, to tar it with racism, while it was trying to promote social equality among the workers. And then finally, the heavy manufacturing industrialists who owned the city [of Birmingham] had encouraged this because the last thing they wanted was a strong organized labor. So they encouraged the terrorism to disrupt labor. And then finally, in the late '50s, the terrorists became bad for business because the economy was changing—it was moving away from heavy manufacturing toward service. And the industrialists, the business community, started disavowing the Klan, but it was too late. They let this force loose in the community, and they couldn't call it back. And then it led up to the church bombing.

The Klansmen were the dregs of the society. They were the most threatened by integration because they [were afraid they] might actually lose jobs to black people if they weren't systematically discriminated against. And also because it was their way of feeling important, that they were better than somebody. I think it's called a narcissism of small differences, that the closer you are together, the more you make of these tiny differences.

THE TYPICAL REACTION [to my book] and this sums up Birmingham: "Why do you want to drag that up again after thirty-eight years? Why do people care about Birmingham?" The white people in Birmingham haven't quite gotten that this was the most important place and the most important story in American history, perhaps. Finally, I came up with an answer, which was: "Would you question why people would want to read about Gettysburg?" And they say, "No." And I'd say, "Well, this is the Gettysburg of the second Civil War. This is the turning-point battle."

I think finally people are beginning to accept that it's just not going to go away; history was made here, and people are always going to be interested in it. The other reaction I have gotten has been shock that all this went on, tracing all the sources of the system back to the New Deal and the labor movement and the antilabor resistance has been a big shock to a lot of people.

The Kennedy Years

by

BEN BRADLEE

Ben Bradlee was the Washington bureau chief for Newsweek *magazine when he first met John F. Kennedy. During the course of Kennedy's presidency, Bradlee had to learn how to juggle the sometimes conflicting roles of Kennedy family friend and responsible journalist. In 1965 Bradlee became managing editor of the* Washington Post. *He was executive editor of the* Post *in 1971, when the paper published material from the Pentagon Papers, a secret government study on America's involvement in Vietnam. The Justice Department obtained an injunction against the* Post *and the* New York Times, *attempting to prohibit the papers from continuing to publish from the Pentagon Papers on the grounds of national security. The Supreme Court denied the Justice Department's injunction in* New York Times Co. v. United States *(1971). On October 29, 1995, Mr. Bradlee appeared on* Booknotes *to discuss his memoir,* A Good Life: Newspapering and Other Adventures, *published by Simon & Schuster in 1995.*

I FIRST MET John Kennedy] pushing baby carriages in Georgetown on a Sunday afternoon in 1959. I think I was pushing one; I can't remember whether he was. We had young children together, and he had moved to the same block as I. We ended up in his backyard and in his garden, and we were talking and then we actually happened to go to a party that night together and we ended up as friends.

I think Jacqueline Kennedy had trouble with [the fact that I was a newsman and a friend at the same time]. I had trouble with it for a while. Everybody had trouble with it until it became natural. I never dissembled. . . . I worked for *Newsweek* then. I occasionally wrote things that displeased him and ended up in the doghouse at least once for three months, compared to seeing him once or twice a week.

[My friendship with John Kennedy] gave me a profile, it sure did, but there was a little rub to it. There were people saying that I went bail for Kennedy and I didn't tell the truth [about] all I knew about Kennedy, which is not true. But that was the minor, minor downside of the relationship.

You can't assign a guy to cover a politician and [not understand] that that person will get close. You've got to get close to know them. You've got to get close to the politician and to the people around him or else you won't know him. You won't be able to report accurately. I don't see how you can say, "Get close, but don't get too close. As soon as he really gives you something good, bail out."

There were a great deal of self-regulatory mechanisms in that relationship. If you think for a minute that my colleagues weren't reading every word in *Newsweek* about Kennedy, and if they had found some consistent exclusives—God, I can imagine Hugh Sidey, who was my opposite number at *Time*, going both to the president and to [White House press secretary] Pierre Salinger saying, "Why the hell are you giving Bradlee all that good stuff, and you don't give it to us?"

The second, self-regulatory thing is the reporter himself. I don't want to go through life and end up in history as a bagman for any man. They used to call them "coat catchers" in Boston. You know, the guy takes his coat off, and there's somebody around there to catch his coat. The third regulatory force is the editors. They know of the relationship because it has to be public knowledge. You have to tell your editors that you've developed this relationship. They loved the skinny I was getting out of the White House. They just loved it and they dined out on it, but they went through everything with a fine-tooth comb.

I FOUND OUT [that President Kennedy was having a relationship with my then-wife's sister, Mary Meyer,] after Mary was murdered on the towpath in Georgetown. We received a call that same night from a friend of ours, who was Mary's close friend, who told us of the existence of a diary. That phone call came from Japan; Mary had expressed a desire that, "If anything ever happened to me, that [my] diary be destroyed."

[My wife and I went to find the diary and found a man also looking for it.] James Jesus Angleton, who at that time, and for many years later, was in the CIA. He wasn't quite the ogre that he became painted as. He was . . . intensely involved in his job. He was a great fly fisherman. He raised orchids. He was a great admirer of Elvis Presley. He was an all-around interesting man. . . . We were all friends together and his wife, Cicely Angleton, was a particular friend of Mary Meyer. She too had been told of the existence of this diary, and that if anything happened, it should be destroyed. Mary wanted it destroyed.

We soon divined that was why Angleton was there, but how he got in we didn't know because [the door] was locked. We found [the diary]. We didn't find it in Mary's house; we found it later in a studio, and we found Jim Angleton trying to pick a lock to get his way in. We were all more naive in that way. Mary Meyer was an artist and artists have things called paint books; the pages are quite a high-quality paper, thicker. And most of the pages had swatches of paint on it and then slight descriptions of how that color was achieved. She was a colorist. That was the school of painting she belonged to; color was particularly important.

[On] a couple of pages, maybe a dozen in all, there were some handwritten descriptions—no names—of what was obviously an affair with the president. [I personally saw the diary, which is now] burned. But it took a long time to get burned because [my wife] Tony thought that she had no skills at destroying documents. I'm sure she didn't consider giving it to me to destroy, so she gave it to her friend, who was a member of an organization that presumably was very good at destroying things. She gave it to Angleton to destroy, and he said he would.

Then two years later, when the president's affair with Mary Meyer became public, Tony wanted to know why. She saw Angleton and said, "You didn't destroy that document, did you?" And Angleton said no, that he hadn't. So no one knows what Angleton did with that thing, but he gave it back to Tony and she then destroyed it in a fire.

[They never convicted a killer in Mary's death.] There was a trial and the jury acquitted him. She was murdered on the C&O Canal towpath, and a man was found about fifty feet away crouching in the Potomac River. He said that he was fishing and had fallen in. Nobody believed him, but he was acquitted. He had been identified only by one person, and that person was looking across the canal into the afternoon sun. His lawyer was able to create a reasonable doubt.

We were left to work out how the news had changed our opinions of President Kennedy and Mary Meyer. The answer for me was not all that much. They were attractive, intelligent, and interesting people before their paths crossed in this explosive way and they remain that way in my mind. I never heard Kennedy lie about [the affair]. Nobody ever asked him. The rules sure changed afterwards, but the number one item on the journalist's agenda was not to pin some sexual escapade on the president. There were really other things that had higher priorities.

I think two things [changed the media's approach to this]. One is the counterculture that was born in this country in the '60s changed Americans' attitudes about sex, among other things. They changed American attitudes on all institutions. And then Watergate [changed things] when government people started to lie. Put those two things together and people said, "By God, presidents aren't going to lie to us anymore, and especially about sex."

I never discussed women with John Kennedy. Imagine having dinner with your wife and the president and his wife . . . I don't know all the things you're going to talk about, but I know one thing you're not going to talk about, and that is extracurricular fooling around by either one of you. It's not going to happen. So I did not know. People have trouble believing that, but it's the truth.

[Jackie stopped talking to me] about three weeks after the assassination. We spent a couple of weekends with her right after the end of November and then what we had together as a foursome didn't show up again as a three-some. She moved to New York, anyway. . . . She never was happy in Washington after that and left. And she didn't like the book I wrote about Kennedy. She just said she thought the language wasn't bright and that Kennedy and I, having been in the navy at a time when vocabularies are being formed, we used four-letter words, not with any sense of what they meant, [but] I reported that. Excuse me.

[She passed me a couple of times and wouldn't acknowledge me after that.] That happened twice. To go from as close as we were to the deep freeze is unnatural. It hurt me. I could live with it; I didn't want to recreate [our friendship] because times change and the caravan moves on, but I didn't want us to be, in any sense, hostile.

THE PENTAGON PAPERS were a 7,000-page [secret] study commissioned by [Lyndon Johnson administration secretary of defense] Robert McNamara to explore how come we got into Vietnam. The study stopped in 1969. In 1971 the *New York Times* got a copy of them, 7,000 pages, and they worked for months on it. The word on the local grapevine was that the *New York Times* had a big, big story, and they were going to bust in on the *Washington Post,* and we were going to quiver there for days. It was a big, big story because Vietnam was such a powerful story at that time. There were three or four stories a day on page one about Vietnam for years.

We finally published [material from the Pentagon Papers report] five days after the *New York Times.* We published, I think, three days' worth before we got enjoined [by the courts, to temporarily cease publishing] just the way the *New York Times* had been enjoined. The case was going from Judge Gerhard A. Gesell's court, the district court, up to the appeals court.

We thought that somewhere along the line there was going to be some late at night appeal to the chief justice by the lawyers for the government when we won [in the appeals court]. So we sent two reporters out [to the home of Chief Justice Warren Burger] that night just to wait to see, so that we'd know who and when and what was happening. After waiting a while, they went up and rang the door. This is one of the great sights that I conjure up in my life.

[It was] twelve o'clock at night. And the chief justice came down in his night robes, his jammies, with a gun. He didn't know who the hell was out there. There was this very dicey conversation while these two reporters established their identity to the justice's satisfaction and . . . he said, "Well, go down to the end of the street and wait there." The guys at the *Post* wanted to run that story. We were on our way up to the Supreme Court with an appeal, and I just didn't want to anger the chief justice. I kept it out of the paper. I'm not particularly proud of that, but we did it. Nick Von Hoffman, who was a columnist, sneaked it in [after the courts ruled in favor of the *Post*].

[THE FIRST THING I'd tell students interested in the press and politics is] tell the truth, and most politicians don't. A lot of newspapers don't because they don't know the truth. That's really the jam we find ourselves in. The best newspapers are trying to find the truth, and we have a limited amount of time and limited sources. If the president of the United States looks you in the eye and says he can't tell you the truth . . . because it involves national security, you've got to run it. But it's a lie.

The Warren Commission

by

ARLEN SPECTER

*John F. Kennedy, the thirty-fifth president of the United States, was assassi-
nated in Dallas on November 22, 1963. President Lyndon B. Johnson
signed Executive Order No. 11130 on November 29, 1963, creating the U.S.
Commission to Report upon the Assassination of President John F. Kennedy,
popularly called the Warren Commission after its chairman, Earl Warren,
chief justice of the United States. The commission determined that Lee
Harvey Oswald acted alone in shooting President Kennedy and that no
conspiracy existed between Oswald and his killer, Jack Ruby. Many people
were unsure of the commission's findings. Arlen Specter, a young assistant
district attorney from Philadelphia, served on the staff of the commission.
Now a U.S. senator from Pennsylvania, Specter described the group's findings in his book,* Passion for Truth: From Finding JFK's Single Bullet to
Questioning Anita Hill to Impeaching Clinton, *published by William
Morrow in 2000. During a* Booknotes *interview on January 23, 2001,
Specter talked about his experience on the Warren Commission and how its
conclusions continue to evoke skepticism.*

As you know, there's been enormous controversy about what the
[1963–1964 Warren Commission, which investigated the assassination of
President John Kennedy] has done. I could sense at the time that when we
had closed hearings and the people did not know what we were doing, that
we had to be as meticulous as we could be. One of the reasons that I wrote
this book—and I've been urged to do so for a long time—[was] to recount
what we did on the Warren Commission.

There were seven members [of the Warren Commission; they] were John

J. McCloy, former president of the World Bank; Allen W. Dulles, former director of the CIA; Richard Russell, a Democratic senator from Georgia; John Sherman Cooper, a Republican senator from Kentucky; Hale Boggs, majority leader in the House, a Democrat from Louisiana; and Gerald Ford, a Republican representative from Michigan. I was one of the young lawyers on the Warren Commission staff; I was thirty-three when I joined. I went to Dallas with Chief Justice Earl Warren to take [Lee Harvey Oswald's killer] Jack Ruby's testimony, among a number of things. After I'd won a big case in Philadelphia prosecuting Teamsters, Attorney General Robert Kennedy wanted me to join the prosecution team against Jimmy Hoffa, and I declined. But six months later, when President Kennedy was assassinated, I was asked to be one of the young lawyers [on the Warren Commission], where I developed the single-bullet theory.

[When] we went to Dallas, they wanted to keep as small a group as possible, and I was odd man out. I was the only fellow excluded. So I was sitting watching a baseball game in the sheriff's office in the Dallas jail. San Francisco was playing Philadelphia that day. Chief Justice Warren, who was a Giants fan, and I had speculated about the game coming down.

When it started, before Warren could call the meeting to order—and I read this in the notes of testimony because I was . . . involuntarily watching the game instead of [being in the room]—Ruby said, "How do you know I'm telling the truth? I want a lie detector test." Warren responded, "Well, Mr. Ruby, if you want a lie detector test, of course, we'll give you a lie detector test." Later I went back as the commission representative when his lie detector test was taken.

Partway through the proceeding, Elmer Moore of the Secret Service came [out] to me and said, "Arlen, they want somebody Jewish in the room. Jack Ruby wants somebody who's Jewish." So I walked in and sat down, about as far as I am from you. There was a court reporter taking notes. . . . [As] I [sat] there, Jack Ruby was mouthing the words, "Are you a Yid?" "Yid" is a word for Jew. And I sat there. I'd been chief of the appeals division of the DA's office, and I know when they typed it up what it would look like in print. So I said nothing. He leaned over again [and mouthed the words]. And I sat there. Again, "Are you a Yid?" Fortuitously, the court reporter ran out of paper.

Jack Ruby called the chief justice and me over into a corner. He said, "Chief, you got to get me to Washington." And Warren said, "Well, I can't do that." Earl Warren, for all of his greatness, did not respond well when something came up on the spur of the moment. Joe Ball walked by, one of the senior lawyers, and he started to listen in. He thought, "If Arlen Specter could be in this, half my age, why am I not there?" Ruby looked over at Ball and said, "Are you Jewish?" Ball said, "No." So Ruby said, "Get out of here," and Ball did what he was told. Ruby said to Warren, . . . "They're cutting off the arms and legs of Jewish children in Albuquerque and El Paso and you've got to get me to Washington."

About this time, the court reporter had her [paper] back in the machine and Ruby went back and sat down. Seated in the back of the room were Gerald Ford and Joe Tonahill, Jack Ruby's lawyer. Tonahill did such a great job. Tonahill handed Gerald Ford a note, and Ruby saw this happen. Ruby said, "I want that note." It's hard to picture this. I describe it in some detail in the book, but Ruby was in charge. He just dominated the whole proceeding. . . . Gerald Ford jumped up, walked up, did what he was told. He handed the note to Ruby. Ruby [was] trying to read the note, [but] he couldn't read it. So the chief justice of the United States took off his glasses and handed them to Jack Ruby and Jack Ruby put on the chief's glasses and read the note. The note said, "You see, I told you he's crazy." Ruby threw the note down; he didn't care anything about that. And the proceeding went on.

Later, when we took his polygraph, he denied having any connection with [accused president Kennedy shooter] Lee Harvey Oswald or being involved in a conspiracy. He said it was a very emotional thing when he read about the assassination and knew that Mrs. Kennedy would have to come back to testify [in Dallas when Oswald went on trial]. He knew the police in Dallas because he ran a strip joint there; he brought them sandwiches and coffee, ingratiated himself because he didn't want to be arrested. That morning, he walked into the jailhouse and everybody knew him. And, on national television, as so many people know, he pulled out a revolver and put it in Oswald's stomach and murdered him. The lie detector examiner, who went with me to take his polygraph, thought Ruby was telling the truth when he denied any involvement in the assassination. But when the report got to J. Edgar Hoover [the director of the FBI], Hoover decided that it was not valid because of Ruby's mental state.

My own evaluation was that, although Ruby was delusional at times . . . he knew what he was saying. On our trip back, the polygraph examiner, Bell P. Herndon, told me that he thought Ruby knew what he was doing, [that he] was telling the truth. But when Hoover got hold of it, Hoover ran the show and said it wasn't to be used. What I did in writing up the report was to put the whole section in and put the tapes in so that they could be examined historically. History, not Hoover, can be the judge.

I WAS NOT PERMITTED to see [the autopsy photos of John F. Kennedy] at the time, nor was anybody on the staff or the commission with the possible exception of the chief justice. I was very unhappy about that and wrote a very strong memorandum to [former U.S. solicitor general] James Lee Rankin, who was the general counsel, complaining about it, that although we had the autopsy surgeon's testimony, that the photos and the X rays were corroborative evidence, and we should have had them. I thought the Warren Commission would be subject to a lot of justifiable criticism.

I first saw [the autopsy photos of President Kennedy] in 1999, when I made a special trip to the archives. . . . I saw the small bullet hole in the back of his head, which was fatal, blew out the top of his head. I saw the top of his head, that thick head of hair; he was a handsome young man. I saw the bullet hole in the back of his neck, the bullet that hit him first and then went through Governor John Connally. I think Chief Justice Warren did not want the pictures shown because they might get into the public domain—so much does, as you know. People would not have the picture of Kennedy as a handsome, vibrant young man, but instead with significant wounds and part of his head shot off. It was rumored that Warren did look at the photos and X rays. But that was no substitute for having the staff look at them and have them examined and have testimony and have the other commissioners see them.

[The Kennedy autopsy had been conducted in] Bethesda, Maryland, [and was] very controversial, because the autopsy surgeon, Dr. James Humes, burned his notes. [It is] inexplicable that the notes would be burned on such a major event. When I wrote this book in collaboration with Charles Robbins, who was my director of communications, he and I went back and reinterviewed a lot of people to refresh my recollection and to get different views. I talked to the doctors at Parkland Hospital in Dallas. One of the interviews we had was with Dr. Humes and Dr. Thornton Boswell. They came to the Senate dining room for lunch about three years ago and we sat and talked . . . and Dr. Humes told us a story.

The story was that Dr. Humes had been on a site where they had a recreation of President Lincoln's office. On the desk there was a doily that they used to cover furniture and the representation was made, falsely, that some of the staining on the doily was blood from the Lincoln assassination. It turned out to be some sort of hair tonic. But Dr. Humes was so offended by that. When he took his notes—an autopsy surgeon wrote his [own] notes during the course of the autopsy—there was a lot of blood on the notes. He didn't want anybody seeing those notes. So, from the bad reaction he had to the Lincoln situation, he burned his notes.

Even as I recite what Dr. James Humes told me, I know many people are going to be doubting it. . . . There has been a lot written about Humes having burned his notes, and people will be speculating about that and the whole Kennedy assassination for years. It's been more than one hundred years since President Lincoln was shot, 136 years, and there are still conspiracy stories. They'll be talking about President Kennedy for who knows how long, centuries.

We should look at [the Kennedy autopsy photos and X rays]. There has grown a tremendous distrust of the Warren Commission. . . . In writing this book, [I'm] trying to tell people in America that there are ways of dealing with the government. [I'd like to stem] the free fall we've seen in voting and the tremendous skepticism. . . . These are issues that we need to deal with to restore public confidence.

The RFK–LBJ Feud

by

JEFF SHESOL

*Lyndon Johnson and Robert Kennedy were men of common political inter-
ests and similar political sentiment. But few political rivalries could match
the intensity of the one that existed between these two giants of the Democratic Party. Jeff Shesol's* Mutual Contempt: Lyndon Johnson, Robert
Kennedy, and the Feud That Defined a Decade, *published by W.W.
Norton in 1997, tells more stories about their difficult relationship. Mr.
Shesol, a writer in Washington, D.C., appeared on* Booknotes *on October
21, 1997, to discuss his work.*

THE RELATIONSHIP BETWEEN Robert Kennedy and Lyndon Johnson pre-
sents] a very valuable prism through which to view the events of the 1960s
and to view the two most powerful leaders of the decade. These two were in
combat for the whole course of the 1960s over a whole variety of contentious
issues. [The rivalry was] not just one of petty slights on both sides, not just
one of nasty words being thrown back and forth, but one of issues that had a
real impact on the 1960s.

Johnson said in his memoirs that [the conflict] was a matter of chemistry.
That only goes part of the way in explaining the intensity of this rivalry. He
denied that there were any issues really at stake between the two of them,
which was certainly disingenuous. It's the kind of thing that a president
writes in a president's memoirs. Robert Kennedy had spoken very frankly in
some oral histories. . . . I was utterly struck by the language Kennedy used to
describe LBJ. He describes him as an animal, in many ways: "mean, bitter,
vicious." As someone who was weaned on the standard survey histories of the
period, this was a shock to me.

I went into this project believing that Kennedy was in the right more often than not. But what I came to understand was that it was quite a bit more complicated than that. Drawing clean lines between good and bad and right and wrong can be done in some cases, but not in most of them. What makes this so interesting is that it's such a complex interweaving of ideas and ambitions and personal slights and pettiness and so forth.

Upon reflection, how much had to do with Lyndon Johnson, and how much of it had to do with Johnson's policies? Can we separate those two things? It certainly was very hard at the time for Robert Kennedy to separate those things. . . . I have often wished I could ask the two men, not that you could be sure that you get a straight answer or that they even would know the answer. Sometimes these things are complicated in our own minds. Is it an honest difference on the issues, or is it a personal grudge? It's all blended together.

THE 1960 DEMOCRATIC Convention . . . was a very turbulent couple of days. Johnson had arrived at the convention having not taken the Kennedys seriously at all as a political threat, until the very end when it was clear that John Kennedy had run away with the primaries and was about to win himself a first-ballot victory. Johnson had bitterly attacked not just John Kennedy but the whole Kennedy family. He called Joe Sr. an "appeaser," a reference to his work as ambassador to Great Britain during the early part of the Second World War. Johnson actually said to a group of delegates at that convention, "I never thought Hitler was right." These are the kinds of comments that just burned in Robert Kennedy. John Kennedy shrugged them off, but Robert Kennedy was a more intense individual.

One Boston politician said that "Jack Kennedy was the first Irish Brahman and Robert Kennedy was the last Irish Puritan." Certainly they responded to political mudslinging in that way, . . . so [Robert Kennedy and Johnson's relationship] got off on a very bad foot. Then the issue of the vice presidency arose and threw the relationship into turmoil from which it never recovered.

John Kennedy was ambivalent, and so was Lyndon Johnson, about Johnson taking a second seat on the ticket. Johnson, obviously, wanted the first seat. That was not going to happen. But he had been sending some signals to John Kennedy through some political intermediaries, people like Tip O'Neill and Hale Boggs and some of the big power brokers on Capitol Hill, telling Kennedy that maybe Johnson wanted it after all, which was a shock to Kennedy.

Johnson had been the most powerful majority leader in the history of the U.S. Senate in the 1950s. Some even said he was the most powerful man in the United States. The Eisenhower presidency was not a particularly activist presidency, and some thought it was actually Johnson and Sam Rayburn,

Speaker of the House, who were driving events. So, few believed that Johnson would actually willingly accept such a powerless role as vice president. But he was tiring of the job of majority leader. The Democrats were no longer as easy to control. He was worried about his health and thought maybe the vice presidency might be an acceptable role.

John Kennedy saw the obvious strength that Johnson added to the ticket in Texas and in the South, so he went to the Johnson suite and made a very tentative offer, just to see what Johnson was thinking. . . . John Kennedy later described it as "holding the offer out to here, and Johnson reached and grabbed it." Johnson took this offer; he said that he would be happy to be vice president. John Kennedy was shocked and went reeling back up into the Kennedy suite. He told his brother, and Bobby said, "Oh, my God, I can't believe he took it."

The two of them spent the next several hours debating whether or not they could possibly live with Johnson on the ticket, decided they couldn't, and JFK sent Bobby down to talk Johnson off the ticket. That is when the relationship was dealt its final blow, that early on. It never recovered from Robert Kennedy's visit down to the Johnson suite when he tried to talk LBJ off the ticket.

Labor was very dubious about John Kennedy to begin with because he had supported labor reform in the 1950s and Johnson had as well. So there was the feeling that putting the two of them together on the ticket—rather than combining, say, John Kennedy and Hubert Humphrey, who was adored by organized labor—would be the death knell to the Democratic ticket.

So there was a lot of outrage [about Johnson's selection] and a lot of it also had to do with simply a general disdain for Lyndon Johnson's personality and his alleged lack of cultural grace, . . . all the things that would emerge during the Kennedy presidency as bones of contention between the Kennedy circle and LBJ.

[ON NOVEMBER 22, 1963] Lyndon Johnson was in the limousine behind the president's in the motorcade when the shots rang out in Dealey Plaza in Dallas. A secret serviceman threw himself on top of Lyndon Johnson, and they all sped together toward the hospital. Johnson was with the dying president from moment one and then spent much time sitting in *Air Force One* . . . on the tarmac at Love Field in Dallas.

Robert Kennedy was at Hickory Hill and had received the news from J. Edgar Hoover in a rather insensitive phone call. Hoover was not a big fan of Robert Kennedy, who was attorney general during those years. . . . The two of them had overlapping jurisdictions, and Robert Kennedy was in some senses Hoover's political senior. Johnson placed a phone call to RFK from *Air*

Force One, reaching Robert Kennedy by the poolside at Hickory Hill, where he was in a state of utter shock, and asked Bobby, as attorney general and as the leader of the Kennedy family now that JFK was dead, whether it was appropriate or even constitutionally necessary for Johnson to be sworn in on *Air Force One* before it left the ground.

Robert Kennedy was not in a state to really assess these constitutional matters. He passed it on to his assistant, Nick Katzenbach, who said, "Well, the president can do whatever the president wants to do." Johnson then called for a district judge to be brought to the plane, and the plane sat and waited and waited for Judge Sarah Hughes to arrive and give the oath.

People were getting very, very upset. Johnson told them all, "Well, it's all right. Bobby says that I have to be sworn in now." This was a bitter bone of contention between them in the days afterward. He had gotten Bobby's professional advice, had then twisted it a bit in order to calm very frayed nerves on the plane, and said, "This was actually Bobby Kennedy's idea, not mine." And that was a great cause of bitterness later.

The most valuable resource [for this account of Johnson's swearing-in] is a book called *The Death of a President,* written by William Raymond Manchester. . . . That book itself became a matter of great contentiousness between Johnson and Robert Kennedy when [it] came out in 1967. Johnson saw it as an attempt to undermine the Johnson presidency right in time for the 1968 presidential race.

Nonetheless, Manchester did some incredible research and interviewed Jacqueline Kennedy, among many others. . . . Manchester was both a historian and a novelist. [He] had written a very, very flattering book about President Kennedy while President Kennedy was alive that had been cleared through the White House press office and given the stamp of approval. So his objectivity as a reporter was really in doubt from the very beginning, which is exactly what the Kennedys wanted. . . . Robert Kennedy and Jacqueline Kennedy [were afraid] that there would be . . . a glut of books about the Kennedy assassination. They wanted one definitive volume about the events of November 22 and the surrounding days that would be written . . . so decisively that it would scare everybody off [so] no one else would even want to get into the subject because it had been covered so thoroughly.

They signed on Manchester because they trusted him and they knew that he would do nothing to discredit the family. Manchester actually signed a contract that said that he would not publish the book until it had been approved by both Robert Kennedy and Jacqueline Kennedy. . . . When the galleys of the book were circulated in late 1966, readers . . . were just shocked at the portrayal [of President Johnson]. Even Kennedy men, like Arthur Schlesinger, were shocked at the portrayal of Johnson. He came across horribly, as a boorish, insensitive, callous man who had treated Jackie Kennedy with utter disregard and treated all the Kennedys with contempt during those days, that he had just grabbed for power.

It was a terrible portrait of LBJ and an inaccurate portrait of LBJ. Those who were on the plane, reporters and neutral observers, said that Johnson acted with dignity and restraint. And that is certainly what most of the ·accounts bear out.

[According to Manchester] on the plane [from Dallas to Washington], there was Johnson's allegedly rough treatment of Jacqueline Kennedy, which is really unfounded in truth. Jacqueline Kennedy never argued that it had actually happened that way. . . . Then [according to Manchester] as soon as Johnson got to Washington, he wanted to move into the Oval Office. In fairness, he had been advised by Secretary of State Dean Rusk and Secretary of Defense Robert McNamara that he really needed to move in right away and assume the reins of the presidency, so that there was no question in the world, particularly in the Communist world, that there was order and continuity in the United States.

So Johnson wanted to move into the Oval Office and very callously told John Kennedy's personal secretary, Evelyn Lincoln, to get her stuff together by 9:30 so his girls could come in. That's the way he put it. Robert Kennedy walked into the Oval Office moments later to get some of his brother's belongings out of the desk, found Evelyn Lincoln weeping, and was just enraged at Johnson. He just couldn't believe that Johnson could be so callous. He stormed into the Oval Office and attacked Johnson for it. Johnson blithely waved his hand and gave Evelyn Lincoln another hour to get her things together.

When excerpts of [the Manchester book] began to be run in *Look* magazine at the end of 1966, it was . . . a political bombshell. Johnson's White House was being forced to respond . . . to all these horrible charges. [Johnson's White House] telephone tapes reveal exactly how upset Johnson was about this whole thing, and he traced it back to RFK.

The Kennedy family, interestingly, had its own problems with the Manchester book. They thought that the portrait of Johnson made them look bad. Also, Jacqueline Kennedy had told Manchester a lot of things in confidence in the first couple of days or weeks after the assassination. Actually, she had told these things to Theodore White, the historian, in the privacy of Hyannis Port, and White had been given permission by her to pass those notes along to Manchester. She, on second thought, wasn't so happy that these things were actually in the text, and so they sued Manchester to stop publication of the book. So you had Johnson upset and the Kennedys upset, but they were also upset at one another.

IT'S WIDELY BELIEVED that [early on] Robert Kennedy was gung-ho about
the [Vietnam] war; he certainly was not particularly restrained during the
Kennedy years and [he had] enthusiasm for military action, particularly in
Cuba. He was very eager to foment a counterrevolution in Cuba to bring
down Castro. He saw Vietnam as a similar test case for counterinsurgency,
using the Green Berets to go in, as they put it at that time, "using knife
thrusts, not tank blasts." He did not foresee Vietnam as a battleground for
massive army units and a massive bombing campaign.

Robert Kennedy thought that the weak political structure of South Vietnam needed to be shored up by an American presence, but he did not foresee
Americans leading that fight, and he was very uneasy about it from the very
beginning. There's a conversation from the Johnson tapes which is so important that I quote it verbatim. It's a conversation between Robert Kennedy
and LBJ in May of 1964. This is several months before the Gulf of Tonkin
incident, and it is a full year before Johnson really beefed up American forces
in Vietnam.

Robert Kennedy . . . quite frankly and boldly [told] the president, "We're
not going to win this war militarily." And Johnson agreed with him. Johnson
did have a tendency to agree with whomever he was speaking to at the time.
He saw the wisdom of Kennedy's comments, but he also saw the wisdom of
the others who said that there was no way to withdraw and there was no way
to avoid a bigger military commitment.

Robert Kennedy came down very early, not on the side of the doves or a
unilateral withdrawal—nobody was talking about unilateral withdrawal at
that point in time—but he was . . . expressing serious doubts about a military
course in Vietnam, and Johnson knew this.

Later, as the disputes over Vietnam became more fractious between Johnson and Robert Kennedy, Johnson always argued, and so did Dean Rusk and
the others in that White House, that Robert Kennedy's opposition on Vietnam was just purely political, that he didn't really believe this stuff. If Johnson were pulling out of Vietnam, Robert Kennedy would become a hawk
and outflank him on the right. A number of Johnson's men told me that.
George Reedy, one of Johnson's press secretaries, said to me that Kennedy
cultivated the antiwar issue because it was anti-Johnson. That's just a little
too simple. There were doubts that went way back, and Robert Kennedy was
not at all enthusiastic about the big troop buildup in July of 1965.

[JOHNSON AND ROBERT Kennedy held] what was called a unity meeting on
April 3, 1968. Johnson, just a few days earlier, on March 31, had withdrawn
from the presidential campaign of 1968. Kennedy immediately requested a
meeting with Johnson so they could discuss the important issues of the day

and to make sure that Johnson was not going to interfere with Kennedy's run for the presidency after that point. Johnson invited him to the Oval Office. They actually sat in the Cabinet room and . . . Johnson and Kennedy talked about a whole range of issues. [Their discussion] was not only not contentious, but it was, actually, in a way, pleasant. It seemed that the two men had actually put all the fractiousness of the past five years, in particular, behind them. That was not the case, but it was actually a very productive meeting, and they talked about everything from the campaign itself to Vietnam, to the problem of the cities and the economy.

There was a cartoon of the day that summed up [Johnson's belief at the time] perfectly well. It pictured a thick, handsome, leather-bound volume that said "The Johnson Years" on the spine, but it was flanked by these absolutely beautiful baroque bookends. On one side, it said "JFK" and on the other, it said "RFK." This was before RFK was killed. [It] was very much Johnson's understanding that he would be this dull leather book between these two beautiful bookends of the Kennedy presidencies.

When Robert Kennedy was killed, [however,] it did not necessarily solve that historical problem for Lyndon Johnson. All the questions of what might have been that lingered after JFK's death would now linger after Robert Kennedy's death as well. The ugly reality of the 1960s and the riots and the war and the student protests . . . that clung to Lyndon Johnson's historical reputation were not problems for either Kennedy because they were both dead; they were both beyond reproach. They both stirred up so much hope and optimism in the country that it did seem that whatever they would have done, it would have been far grander than what Johnson himself had done. He understood that this would forever tarnish his historical legacy.

Robert Kennedy's grave site is a grim footnote to the relationship between Johnson and Robert Kennedy. Johnson told Ethel Kennedy very warmly the day of the funeral, "Anything that I can do for you, you just let me know." Well, the one thing that she had wanted to do was to have Robert Kennedy buried at Arlington Cemetery. Little did she know that in the couple of days prior to this, Johnson had been trying to keep Bobby's body out of Arlington. Bobby was neither a president nor a war hero, Johnson reasoned, and there was no reason to give him a hero's burial. But, of course, the country and the family wanted him to be buried there by his brother's side, and there was nothing Johnson could really do politically to stop it. It would have looked absolutely petty and would have blackened his image even further. So he allowed that to go ahead, but he refused to allocate [the] $400,000 to maintain the grounds around Robert Kennedy's grave site in the way that they had maintained the grounds around JFK's grave site. . . . As a result, it was left to Richard Nixon to allocate that money, and he did so on the first day of his presidency.

New York Times Co. v. Sullivan

by

ANTHONY LEWIS

There have been several cases in the second half of the twentieth century in which the U.S. Supreme Court has upheld the right of the press to pursue its mission: New York Times Co. v. United States *(1971) made it possible for the* New York Times *and the* Washington Post *to publish the then classified Pentagon Papers without government censure;* Miami Herald Publishing Co. v. Tornillo *(1974) prevented the government from telling the press what it must report; and* Hustler Magazine v. Falwell *(1988) allowed the press to parody public figures. Anthony Lewis, who covered the Supreme Court for the* New York Times, *appeared on* Booknotes *on September 10, 1991, to discuss another landmark case covered in his book,* Make No Law: The Sullivan Case and the First Amendment, *published by Random House in 1991.* New York Times Co. v. Sullivan *(1964) protects the press from being charged with libel for printing false or misleading statements unless it can be proved that those statements were made with "actual malice."*

L. B. Sullivan was a city commissioner of Montgomery, Alabama, in the '60s who sued the *New York Times* and some others, . . . [including] four black ministers, . . . after we carried an advertisement for Dr. Martin Luther King and the civil rights movement in 1960. . . . [The ad did not criticize anyone by name; it spoke, rather, of "Southern violators of the Constitution."] Sullivan said that though he wasn't named in the ad, it reflected on him.

[The ad] ran a full page in the *New York Times* on March 29, 1960. . . . We forget, or some of us are too young to remember, what it was like in the

American South in 1960. . . . You had a situation in which blacks in the Deep South could not vote, that even trying to register and vote in Mississippi was to risk your life. People were lynched for trying to run voter campaigns to get the right to register. And strict segregation was imposed by the state, not only in schools in all the Deep Southern states but on buses, in restaurants, in hotels. It was a very different country then, and it was Dr. King's protest, his attempt to change that system that led to this ad.

[The bottom half of the ad read, "The Committee to Defend Martin Luther King and the Struggle for Freedom in the South," and it listed several names, including famous entertainers.] But not just entertainers, Eleanor Roosevelt and Jackie Robinson [were also listed]. They were believers in the civil rights movement who were rallied to this ad, I suppose. . . . But as usual, you want to get famous names to support your cause. . . . The *Times* didn't place the ad; we just took their money and printed it.

[The ad was published in the *New York Times* for one day only and cost] just under $5,000. [The suit was brought] quite soon [after that]. The judge who handled the case in the circuit court of Montgomery, Alabama, was quite an extraordinary character named Walter Jones. Judge Jones was a deep believer in the Confederacy with strong views on racial matters, who, on the anniversary of the Confederacy, seated the jurors in his courtroom in Confederate military uniforms. So he hustled the case through and rejected all the *New York Times'* arguments and put the case to the jury on Alabama law of libel.

Libel is a very old form of law, coming down from English common law, which means a damaging statement about somebody. Slander is oral and libel is written—printed or, now, broadcast. If I, simply in a conversation, say something mean and untruthful about you that's slander. But the difference has eroded over time.

I [remember when this ad was taken out] but it didn't really . . . grip my mind until the lawsuit began. It was a lawsuit that was very intimidating to the *New York Times*. Mr. Sullivan asked for $500,000 in damages, and an all-white jury awarded him every penny of the $500,000—I repeat, although his name wasn't mentioned in the ad. Others sued over the ad, including Governor John Patterson of Alabama, and the total sum demanded [of all five lawsuits] was $3 million. It was quite clear that if it were up to the Alabama juries, the paper would be $3 million in the hole. The *New York Times* could not afford that kind of money then; it was a barely profitable newspaper.

The Alabama law of libel [said that] if there were any mistakes in a statement, however trivial, the defendant—the publisher—loses the defense of truth, and there were mistakes in this advertisement. For example, it said that Dr. King had been arrested seven times, and he'd only been arrested four times. I remind you that Mr. Sullivan's name was not mentioned in the ad, but the judge charged the jury that they could find that the ad referred to Sullivan even though he wasn't mentioned. The jury so found, and it had the power to set the damages. It awarded all the damages he asked for—a half a million dollars. That all had happened by the end of the year in 1960.

[Herbert Wechsler, the attorney for the *New York Times*] was asked to come into the case shortly before the case was put to the Alabama Supreme Court. He began then to shape an argument that was novel for its time—that the First Amendment had something to do with this libel suit. It was fortunate that the question was raised. . . . Unless you raise it in the lower court, it's an afterthought; you can't raise it in the United States Supreme Court. The Alabama Supreme Court rejected that argument on the First Amendment in one sentence, which said libel has nothing to do with the First Amendment. That was a correct statement of the law at the time.

The Supreme Court of Alabama upheld the logic of the case and of the [circuit court] judge's decision. It indeed broadened [the decision] and made it, from the point of view of the right of public criticism, even more dangerous. It said whenever a newspaper or a citizen makes reference to a governmental action, a department of government, . . . then any official who has to do with [that department] can take that as a criticism of him and he can sue for libel. . . . The ad used the word "police" at one point, and the Supreme Court of Alabama said this ad was critical of the police—just generally, the police. It didn't focus on a particular police force or the southern police, although it did focus at one point on Montgomery, Alabama. . . . Now, that in effect is to say that there is such a thing as libel on government, that government as such can be immune from criticism, which exists in some other societies. But to say that this exists in the United States would be to change our culture.

[After the Alabama State Supreme Court upheld this decision] there was only one recourse left, and that was to ask the Supreme Court of the United States to review this. It only has the power to review such a decision if there is a federal constitutional issue. The Supreme Court has no power to say, "We don't like that state court decision. We're going to reverse it." It only has jurisdiction under the Constitution and laws if there's a federal constitutional question. What made it a very hard case for us was that people then thought that libel had always been considered outside the First Amendment, just as a matter of tradition. No libel suit had even been held to violate the First Amendment. After the jury verdict, the lawyer who represented the *Times* wrote a piece for the magazine for employees of the *New York Times, Times Talk,* about what we would do on appeal to try to reverse this judgment, and he didn't mention the First Amendment.

[THE *NEW YORK TIMES v. Sullivan* case resulted] in very dramatic circumstances. The Supreme Court reversed that $500,000 judgment and said . . . that you have the right to criticize political figures in an ad. Whether they called it libel, or whatever they called it, there is a very fundamental right to criticize politicians. [With this finding] many other newspapers, magazines, and broadcasters were out from under this threat.

[The nine members of the court were William Brennan, Hugo Black, Arthur Goldberg, Byron White, William O. Douglas, John Marshall Harlan, Tom Clark, and Potter Stewart; the chief justice was Earl Warren.] I think it is fair to say that in our entire history, this may have been the Supreme Court that was the most devoted to individual liberty. It had the strongest impulse to read the Constitution for individual rights.

Justice Byron White asked Professor Wechsler, "Are you saying that you would protect deliberate mistakes?" He asked a whole line of questions about whether the Constitution—if it protected libel at all—whether it should protect statements that are deliberately false. The way the case came out was making that distinction. The Constitution protects statements made about political figures, even if you make a mistake, but not if it's deliberately false; if you are intentionally lying, you're not protected.

I think [Professor Wechsler won this case even before he got in the courtroom]. . . . His brief was a very compelling brief; it was a historical brief. . . . The problem for him in this case, the psychological problem that is very important with the court, was that history went the other way; that there had never been a libel case held to come within the First Amendment. The Supreme Court and judges generally don't like, on the whole, to do novel things. They don't want to make sudden breaks with history. What he did was to use history himself in a very powerful way. He told the story in that brief of what happened when Congress in 1798 passed a Sedition Act that made it a crime to say false, malicious, unpleasant things about President John Adams and Congress. It was used by Adams and the Federalist Party, which was then in power, to try to suppress the Anti-Federalists—the followers of Thomas Jefferson, the vice president—in the newspapers.

Chief Justice John Marshall was a candidate for Congress. He ran as a Federalist, and he naturally, inevitably supported the Sedition Act or defended it. He said the Sedition Act was necessary to defend the government from wicked citizens. That's a quote: "wicked citizens." It's a very sort of English view, today as then, that the government has to be protected from these unruly citizens. If that view had prevailed, we'd be living in a different country.

[The Federalists] prosecuted the editors and the publishers of those newspapers before the presidential election of 1800. They tried to shut up the opposition. There was a very adverse public reaction. Jefferson and company said, "Hey! Look what they're doing. They're trying to turn this country back into a tyranny. George III! They're trying to tell you what you can read and hear." That caught on politically, and Jefferson was elected. The first thing he did after his election was to pardon all the editors who had been convicted. That historical episode was seized on by Professor Wechsler and then by Justice Brennan as indicating the meaning of the First Amendment—that in this country we allow criticism of political figures.

THE PRACTICE IN THE 1960s was that on the Friday of each week of arguments, the members of the court held a private conference. They met in the room adjoining the chief justice's chambers and they sat around the table, just the members of the court, never anybody else. . . . They discussed and voted on all the cases that were argued that week. . . . The members of the court all agreed that the libel judgment, the $500,000 verdict against the *Times* and the four black ministers, had to be set aside. But the ground was not at all clear. There was a rather murky ground suggested, in fact, by Justice Brennan. That was the end of the discussion. Then the court's practice was for the chief justice, if he was in the majority, to assign the writing of the opinion to himself or one of the other members of the court. He wrote a note to Justice Brennan saying, "Will you please write the opinion in *New York Times v. Sullivan?*" That's when the real work begins—the work of analyzing, deciding the ground of decision, and circulating your drafts to the other members of the court to see whether they agree with your analysis of the case, which they may not.

I obtained [the first draft of William Brennan's decision] with his permission, from the manuscript division of the Library of Congress—all his written materials on the case, which included eight drafts of his opinion. In fact, there was even some tinkering with the eighth draft at the last minute, so you could say nine drafts. It gave me a very interesting insight . . . into the process of decisionmaking at the court because each of those drafts was circulated to the other members of the court and got comments. Of course, Justice Brennan's object was both to write for history and to get a majority of votes on his side. That's the game. You've got to get a majority if you hope to make an impression.

Justice Harlan was the most crucial and the most important, from the point of view of the legitimacy, the weight, of the decision. He was the conservative voice, the man who had the respect of New York, Wall Street, and that whole position. He differed from Justice Brennan. Harlan told him that he had to write a different opinion and that he would not agree entirely with what Brennan wrote. The case was scheduled to come down on a Monday, and Justice Harlan, right through eight drafts of the opinion, wouldn't agree. On Sunday night he telephoned Justice Brennan at home and said, "Bill, I've decided to join your opinion." First thing Monday morning he circulated a note to all the other justices saying, "My dear brethren, I have decided to join Brother Brennan's opinion without reservation." This was a remarkable thing, . . . illuminating human history about the relationships on the court.

Six members of the court joined in Justice Brennan's opinion and three others took a more all-out absolutist view of the First Amendment. They were Justices Black, Douglas, and Goldberg.

[FROM THE DAY the ad ran until the case was decided by the Supreme Court, it took] just short of four years.

This was not a case about newspapers. This was a case about the right of every citizen to voice disagreement with politicians. Justice Brennan's phrase was, "the citizen critic of government," that's what he focused on, not newspapers or broadcasters. But the decision has had a big effect for the press, no doubt, freeing us. There's always a chance that a rotten press, an abusive press, will misuse freedom. The press is not always the good guy. I've never believed it always is. We have bad apples like other professions.

[At the time, people didn't realize how important this case was going to be.] They understood it was important for the civil rights movement and for the *New York Times*. I know the case was not seen then as the fundamental building block of free speech for everybody in this country, which it is now. Now it's universally recognized by commentators, law professors, and so on as one of the great free speech cases ever.

We tend to assume that the First Amendment is where "Congress shall make no law abridging the freedom of speech or of the press"—nice, clear-ringing things, and ever since that was written into the American Constitution two hundred years ago, December 1791, we've been free. But it's not like that, not at all. That's what gradually got hold of my consciousness because it really wasn't until very recently that the courts, and the Supreme Court particularly, gave concrete meaning to those words and put back into the First Amendment what James Madison, its principal author, thought was there. For most of its history the amendment was not enforced, and no person who made claim of a right to free speech under the First Amendment won a case in the Supreme Court until [*Gitlow v. New York* in 1925]. That's pretty late.

THE PURPOSE IN my writing is to show the human drama on which the Supreme Court actually decides cases. The Supreme Court does not sit there, and is not constitutionally able to sit there, giving abstract judgments, saying [to itself] "Please, Court, tell us what the First Amendment means."

It's also a book that celebrates our right of free speech. . . . After a lot of years of dealing with issues of law and democracy, I came to realize rather belatedly how fundamental our right to criticize and disagree with our politicians is; how it makes all the difference in the nature of this country. . . . I don't think [any other country in the world is as free as this country is to speak]. Certain kinds of speech—the raucous, uninhibited American habits of razzing our politicians and our public figures, the right to have fun with Jerry Falwell, which the Supreme Court said was protected by the First Amendment; hate speech, "freedom for the thought that we hate," Justice Holmes said—is more deeply rooted in our culture and our law than in any other country I know.

Stories from 1964

by

JON MARGOLIS

A year packed with events that changed America and the world—that was 1964. The nation's involvement in Vietnam and the civil rights movement were both growing, and these two trends helped make it a year of banner headlines. Jon Margolis, who covered politics for the Chicago Tribune, *appeared on* Booknotes *on June 27, 1999, to discuss the many changes and events examined in* The Last Innocent Year: America in 1964, *published by William Morrow in 1999.*

THERE WAS NO INNOCENT YEAR, ever. This myth of American innocence is something of a delusion. But 1964 may have been the last year it was a believable delusion; ever since then, it's been harder to convince ourselves that we were ever innocent.

In 1964 the country had about 190 million people. It was the first time that more people lived in California than in New York. Unemployment was 5.2 percent. Inflation was quite low. . . . We had over 15,000 [American soldiers] advising in Vietnam. And before the year was out, we had more. But aside from that, it was sort of the postwar status quo. In February of that year, the Beatles came to America. "A Hard Day's Night" had become popular very late in '63, in December; it revolutionized popular music. . . . Nineteen sixty-four was the year of the quarterback, and Roger Staubach was the quarterback of the year. . . . The World Series that year was the Cardinals beating the Yankees. . . . And of course the major sporting event was Cassius Clay, as he was then known, defeating Sonny Liston on February 25, in Miami.

OBVIOUSLY, THE MOST dramatic and tragic event of 1964 was the murder of three civil rights workers in Mississippi. Three young men knowingly risked their lives, especially the two middle-class young white men from the New York area. They went down, did a noble task, and were cruelly murdered. Their names were Mickey Schwerner, James Chaney, and Andy Goodman. They were shot on a side road outside of Philadelphia, Mississippi, essentially by sheriffs' deputies or by Klansmen, some of whom were law enforcement officers.

It happened because, at that time, Mississippi was the closest thing this country has ever had, I believe, to a police state. As we learned later in South Africa, in order to suppress a large number of people, you cannot have political and intellectual freedom. There was a secret police force, of which the records are only now coming out, and a sovereignty commission, which was part of the state government. The county sheriffs in many counties were effectively terrorist organizations to scare people against coming down and helping blacks register to vote. Very, very few black people could register to vote in Mississippi. It was really a reign of terror.

The [locals] considered this an invasion from the North. They were right, it was an invasion from the North, carefully planned and carefully executed in order to bring elementary democracy to Mississippi. There was armed and violent resistance against it.

[This incident] was planned only by the White Knights of the Ku Klux Klan of Neshoba County and the adjacent county where [the city of] Meridian is. They had been meeting as soon as Mickey Schwerner and his wife, Rita, got down there [because] they were very noticeable. Mickey had a little goatee and wore a Mets cap. They were obviously Jewish, and they were obviously sort of Bohemianish in their dress. They hung around with "Negroes," to use the term that people said in 1964.

They were integrating the area, and they very quickly came to the attention of the Klan and were sort of a recruiting tool. The Klan would drive some young toughs past and see the Schwerners having a cup of coffee in a black restaurant, together with mixed races, and that would enrage people. And that was a good recruiting drive for the Ku Klux Klan.

They were after them. Whether at one point people decided actually to kill them is a little unclear. Some of the people involved didn't really think it would end in murder. They thought it would be some slapping around . . . as a "get out of town" message. But for some of them, obviously, that was not enough.

The bodies were not discovered for some time thereafter. The Mississippi establishment's first reaction was to say that it was a fraud before the bodies were discovered, that they had run away, that it was all a fake. Senator James Eastland even told Lyndon Johnson that he didn't believe that they were dead at all; he thought they had run to Chicago or something like that.

Then the bodies were found. The FBI had been very, very slow in this entire area; they had no office in Mississippi. But when the FBI did step in, under pressure from President Johnson, they did quite a good job, and they found out who did this. Of course, nobody has ever been charged with murder for it; people were charged with violating civil rights. But the state of Mississippi, to this day, has never brought a murder charge against anyone.

IN POLITICS IN 1964, the big names were Lyndon Johnson, Hubert Humphrey, and Robert Kennedy. For the Republicans, Barry Goldwater, Nelson Rockefeller, William Scranton. . . . [Jacqueline Kennedy was] an icon. . . . In 1964 she was the bereaved widow and the whole country felt sorry for her and looked up to her because of the way she had acted in those four days from the assassination to the funeral, which was, indeed, quite admirable. She was a woman who knew that history was stopping here and would take note, and she acted accordingly and perfectly.

Barry Goldwater comes out of this book as rather an admirable fellow. Toward the end, he refused to do things that some of his more hotheaded advisers wanted him to do to try to win the election, I think because he knew he wasn't going to win it, anyway. He refused to allow the showing of a film that some of his supporters had created, which was really, when you look at it now, a rather silly, unsophisticated film, called *Choice*. It tried to scare people into thinking that the world was coming to an end; there was going to be crime and America's way of life was in grave danger. It was less racist probably than the Willie Horton ads of 1988, but Goldwater looked at it and said, "This is nothing but a racist film. I won't have it shown."

And then after Walter Jenkins, President Johnson's chief of staff, was caught in a homosexual encounter in the men's room here in Washington at the YMCA, some of Goldwater's staff wanted him to use this and he refused to do it. He knew that if you were going to lose, you might as well lose like a gentleman. And Goldwater was a gentleman.

NINETEEN SIXTY-FOUR was the year Nikita Khrushchev was ousted by Leonid Brezhnev, in October. It had tremendous impact later for the Europeans and the Russians and, therefore, the Americans. But at that time, its main impact was to knock the Walter Jenkins story off page one very quickly. And also the Labor Party took control in Britain for the first time in quite a number of years. Those two events together knocked the Walter Jenkins story off page one.

VIETNAM [WAS] only mildly prominent. . . . But behind the scenes, many people really knew that it wasn't going well at all, including Lyndon Johnson, who knew from the beginning that it was not winnable but couldn't figure out how not to get more and more involved.

The assumption was that the Russians had started this, that if we lose here—it was the domino theory, which Johnson could believe. [In the] first place, he liked to play dominos, so it was a metaphor that he could accept readily. And, really, almost nobody doubted it, neither the liberals nor the conservatives. Remember, these were the liberal foreign policy experts who inadvertently, step by step, got the country more deeply involved in Vietnam.

Most of the Republican conservatives were for either going in strongly or for not doing anything. The problem was almost nobody was against it from what we would now call the left. Almost nobody said, "This is not worth it, this is not a good idea, this is not winnable." One of the few people who did say that was Richard Russell, a senator from Georgia, chairman of the Armed Services Committee, a veteran, a highly respected senator, who had been in the Senate for many years and was one of the most powerful men in the country. And at one point, he gave Lyndon Johnson what I thought might have been great advice. He said, "Let's arrange for another coup" (there had already been about two by then) "and have the new guys tell us to get out, and then we can get out."

The Gulf of Tonkin incident was on August 2, 1964. Two American navy ships were, or were not, perhaps, fired on by North Vietnamese torpedoes. That was the incident that got the president to go to the Congress and ask for a resolution giving him the authority to take all necessary steps to protect American military people and military facilities in and around Vietnam. It was the functional equivalent of a declaration of war. And it was the basis by which Johnson, and later President Nixon, waged war in Vietnam. And it probably never happened. As Johnson himself said, "Those sailors were probably shooting at a bunch of fish." Besides which, even if it did happen, they were not unprovoked, because we were supporting South Vietnamese commando raids on North Vietnamese islands and North Vietnamese coastal outposts.

THE EXACT DATE of the election that year was November 3. Lyndon Johnson was running against Barry Goldwater. . . . He was way ahead all year, but he was afraid all year. He was always afraid he was going to lose; he was afraid he wasn't even going to get nominated. Two days before he was going to be nominated by acclamation, he called up two or three of his friends and his wife and said, "I'm going to withdraw. I don't want to run again." And they didn't think he was kidding.

The president was really worried about this Mississippi Freedom Democratic Party protest. This was a group of people who had organized their own shadow Democratic Party in Mississippi, which was integrated. It was actually much more of a loyal Democratic Party than the official Democratic

Party, which came out for Barry Goldwater and against the United Nations and was not at all loyal to the president. But Johnson was very upset about it, so he called the FBI, and the FBI sent a group of people up to [the National Democratic Convention in] Atlantic City. Some of them, using NBC press credentials, masqueraded as newspeople and went to press conferences.

They infiltrated the civil rights organizations. I don't know whether they actually infiltrated the party itself. . . . And they put a tap on Martin Luther King's phone in his hotel room and on a couple of other of the leaders of the civil rights organizations that were having meetings with this Mississippi Freedom Democratic Party contingent.

The FBI was working for Lyndon Johnson on his behalf, wiretapping his own Democratic politicians, putting a tail on his own attorney general, Robert Kennedy, who was their boss. [They were] acting as the president's political secret police force, reporting four times a day to Bill Moyers, among others. Moyers is the only person who wouldn't talk to me . . . but it's all in the Senate investigation headed by Senator Frank Church of Idaho in the '70s. So much stuff came out there that a lot of it was not paid too much attention to. But that's when we first knew about this. It's all in documents from those committee hearings and elsewhere.

Nineteen sixty-four was also the year that Strom Thurmond became a Republican, part of the whole transformation of the South from solid Democratic to what is almost solid Republican today. Perhaps that's changing a bit now for various reasons, but certainly, it has been more Republican than Democratic for the last couple of decades. And this was really the beginning of it, and it was basically all over civil rights.

John Marshall Harlan
and the Warren Court

by

TINSLEY YARBROUGH

John Marshall Harlan was born in Chicago in 1899. He sat as a justice on the U.S. Supreme Court for sixteen years, from 1955 to 1971. He was the grandson of another Supreme Court justice named John Marshall Harlan, who served on the court for thirty-four years, from 1877 to 1911. The second Justice Harlan was considered to be among the Warren court's more conservative justices and served in an era of many high-profile decisions, including the landmark First Amendment case New York Times Co. v. Sullivan. *Tinsley Yarbrough, of East Carolina University, appeared on* Booknotes *on April 26, 1992, to discuss* John Marshall Harlan: Great Dissenter of the Warren Court, *published by Oxford University Press in 1992.*

THERE IS A TENDENCY, when one thinks of Warren court critics, to focus on Justice Felix Frankfurter. But we have to keep in mind that the most liberal period of the Warren court was from about 1962 to 1969, and Frankfurter left the court in 1962. In fact, it was Frankfurter's replacement, Arthur Goldberg, who helped give the liberal activist side the votes needed to do all that the Warren court did in the '60s, in terms of criminal procedure rights, rights in the area of erotic expression, separation of church and state, reapportionment—all of those things. So, Justice John Marshall Harlan was a very significant figure. He may not have been the scholar that Felix Frankfurter was, but he was the critic on the court during the most productive period or activist period of the Warren court's tenure.

During his sixteen years on the Supreme Court (1955 to 1971), a tenure less than half the length of his illustrious grandfather's, Justice John Marshall Harlan wrote 613 opinions—more than any other justice of his era. One hundred and sixty-eight were opinions for the court and 149 were concurrences, but nearly half—an impressive 296—were dissents.

Different chief justices have had different views on [the value of dissenting opinion] and at some times in the past, dissent has been discouraged. There has been a feeling that the court's decisions will have more impact if dissenters either don't dissent or don't express their views and opinions. My own feeling, though, is that it's very healthy. And, of course, the dissents of Justice Harlan are now being quoted with some frequency on the Rehnquist court as justifications for particular interpretations of the Constitution. So, though he was a lonely figure in the latter part of the Warren years, his decisions [had] an impact then [and] may be having an impact now.

Some people suggested that Harlan did not have much respect for Chief Justice Earl Warren, that he thought Earl Warren tended to take positions based too much on his own personal notion of what was fair, what was moral, and he had trouble with that. On one occasion, at the time a decision was being announced in open court, around the time Chief Justice Warren was getting ready to leave the court, Harlan mentioned that this issue was not dead and that there would be other terms of the court and other considerations of this particular issue. Warren sent him a sharp note to the effect of, "I got your message loud and clear." Well, Harlan was really stricken by this, and he did everything he could to try to patch relations with Warren.

HARLAN'S PRINCIPAL mentor was Felix Frankfurter, who had served on the court from the late '30s. Another close friend of his on the court was Alabamian Hugo L. Black. Justice Black and Justice Harlan differed on a lot of constitutional issues and on their approach to interpreting the Constitution, but both of them were concerned about excesses of judicial power. They had warm personal feelings [toward one another] particularly after Felix Frankfurter left the court in 1962. They agreed increasingly on some of the constitutional issues too, but they were also close personal friends. Harlan probably had a closer personal relationship with Black than he did with Felix Frankfurter, even though he and Frankfurter thought more alike on constitutional issues and the role of the judges.

Felix Frankfurter was one of the major antagonists on the court during the later Warren years. He was a strong advocate of judicial self-restraint. He was an accomplished scholar and Harvard law professor before going on the court, a strong intellect. He attempted to exert influence on other justices, both those who generally agreed with him and those who did not. He viewed the court as a continuing seminar in constitutional law.

Hugo Black had a different career. Prior to going on the Supreme Court, he was a lawyer in Birmingham. He had been a member of the United States Senate from Alabama, and he was a politician. He had had that sort of life. On the court, though, he attempted to develop an approach to constitutional interpretation that he thought would limit the ability of judges to abuse their authority. He tried to get the justices to tie their decisions and interpretations of the Constitution to the language of the Constitution and its historically intended meaning, at least as Hugo Black viewed that.

It's true that in the last years, in the mid- and late sixties, [Harlan and Black] were in agreement more often than they had been. . . . Justice Black's approach to the Constitution, and his attempt to base the Constitution on the language of the document, not only meant that he handed down some pretty liberal positions, such as the view that there could be no obscenity controls and no libel controls over freedom of speech and freedom of the press; his approach also meant that the court would have a limit to the extent to which it could expand civil rights and civil liberties. When the court began to go beyond what Black thought the Constitution's language and history required, then he began to dissent and sometimes—not always, but sometimes—he and Harlan would be together in dissent, taking, if you will, a conservative position on a particular civil liberties issue. Also, interestingly enough, at times, Harlan would be taking the more liberal position than Black, because Harlan's approach to the Constitution, while essentially a restraintist approach that would limit the degree to which judges would exercise judicial review, was also a rather flexible approach, which did allow judges to read into the Constitution rights that were not necessarily stated there.

One area for illustration is the right of privacy. In 1965 the Supreme Court held that the Constitution implies a right of privacy, and it struck down a Connecticut law that prohibited the use of birth control devices, which was the famous *Griswold* case. Justice Harlan not only joined that decision, but four years before, when the court, in another case, *Poe v. Allman,* had dodged ruling on the constitutionality of the Connecticut law, Justice Harlan had gone on record as including that there is a right of privacy in the Constitution and that this law violated the right of privacy. Justice Black, on the other hand, dissented vehemently in the *Griswold* case, not only in print but in the court that day when the decision was handed down.

In the later years, Harlan became more and more isolated. Byron White often voted, if you will, conservatively with him in the later years. But it became an overwhelmingly liberal court from about 1962 on. There were people like Goldberg, who was then replaced by Abe Fortas; there was also William Brennan and William O. Douglas through the whole period—and Douglas's position was typically liberal activist. So Harlan was more and more isolated during the later years.

JUSTICE HARLAN'S FATHER was John Maynard Harlan, who was an interesting personality himself, but his grandfather was John Marshall Harlan. When Harlan was born, he was given the name John Marshall Harlan. It was a name closely connected not only with the great Chief Justice John Marshall but also with [his grandfather] the great Justice John Marshall Harlan. By 1899, when Harlan was born, [his grandfather] had been on the Supreme Court for a long time and had established a very significant reputation. One of [his grandfather's] friends wrote him that this young man would have a difficult time living up to the name that he had been given, John Marshall Harlan.

[The first John Marshall Harlan] was from Kentucky. . . . He served on the Supreme Court from 1877 until 1911. . . . Interestingly, he was the son of a Kentucky slaveholder and he himself had a few slaves. They freed most of their slaves prior to the Civil War period, or the period when federal law would absolutely have required it. This is ironic because he, of course, was the only justice to dissent in the *Plessy* case.

The *Plessy* case upheld the power of states to segregate the races. He dissented there. He said that the Civil War amendments had made ours a color-blind Constitution, and he warned the court that they would come to regret that decision as much as the nation had come to regret the *Dred Scott* decision of the 1850s, which had held, among other things, that blacks were not citizens and could not become citizens of the United States. *Plessy* was not an exceptional case for the first John Marshall Harlan. He took a strong civil rights position in a lot of cases.

[The second] Justice John Marshall Harlan and [his grandfather] would not have agreed on a lot. [His grandfather] believed that the Fourteenth Amendment, which forbids states to take away the privileges and immunities of U.S. citizens and to take away life, liberty, or property without due process of law, embodied the great guarantees of the Bill of Rights, the first state amendments. He believed in what the scholars called "total incorporation." When the Fourteenth Amendment was adopted, one intention of that amendment was to make all the guarantees of the Bill of Rights—freedom of speech, freedom of the press, trial by jury, etc.—fully binding on the state governments. [But the second] Justice John Marshall Harlan, through his entire career, challenged that view. . . . In the area of civil rights—in terms of race relations—they might have agreed on a good bit. Justice Harlan wasn't on the court when the first *Brown* decision of 1954 came down, but he was on the court for the 1955 decree decision in which the court remanded the school segregation cases back to the trial courts with the notion that they proceed with all deliberate speed to dismantle segregated schools. So he and [his grandfather] were of a single mind on that issue and a goodly number of other race issues.

His father, John Maynard Harlan, was also born in Kentucky, but after schooling at Princeton, he settled in Chicago and was a Chicago lawyer. He was briefly a member of the city council and a candidate for mayor—never successful. In personality, he was quite different from his son. Justice Harlan [had] a very reserved personality, very discreet. He was an extremely cautious person. It was hard to read in his papers or find any personal hostility or personal gossip. He was so restrained and refined.

I believe—though I try not to be a psychohistorian in writing these things—that some of Justice Harlan's restraint came from the fact that his father was such a bombastic personality. John Maynard Harlan had a hot temper. He was the kind of political candidate who, if challenged by someone in the audience, would invite the person to come up onstage to fight it out man to man. In part because of that bombastic personality, in part because he dabbled so much in politics rather than paying close attention to his legal practice, relations [with his wife] Elizabeth were rather tense. They never divorced, but they were not together a good deal, as one of Justice Harlan's sisters put it. The turmoil in the family, caused in part by the father's personality, may have had the effect of making John Harlan the kind of low-key, restrained, dignified person that he was. Some people would say it was his experience in Oxford as a Rhodes scholar, but I think it probably went back in part to his father and mother and their relationship, and some other incidents from his early life.

Very early on, Harlan was sent away to Canada to boarding school. From his sisters, I gathered that he was sent away in part because his father thought he just wasn't manly enough, he wasn't hard enough. So his father wanted him to be sent to a boarding school where conditions were pretty spartan, and he selected one in Canada. After some period of real homesickness, he thrived in the boarding school, and then from the boarding school went to prep school—also in Canada. For his last year of prep school, he went to the Lake Placid School in New York, in part so that he could associate with some of the children of major American families. Then he went to Princeton for his undergraduate work and to Oxford for study on a Rhodes scholarship, but that wasn't the last of his formal education.

When Harlan got back from Oxford, he decided that he wanted to be a lawyer. His sister Elizabeth's husband arranged an interview with him at Root, Clark, which is now Dewey Ballantine, one of the most prominent New York law firms. They wanted him, but they said that he hadn't gotten enough practical legal study at Oxford, and so, in a year, he took a two-year program of study at the New York Law School and passed the bar on the basis of that study.

He met his wife, Ethel, at a Christmas party at Root, Clark. Ethel's brother was a young associate there. She was divorced at the time; she had been married to a very interesting man, and that marriage had not worked out. It was not long after the divorce that she and Justice Harlan married. Their daughter, Eve, shared with me a wonderful letter that Harlan wrote to his mother to inform her that he was in love with Ethel Andrews and that they wanted to marry. He [wrote] about what a wonderful person she was, and then he broached the sensitive subject, for that period of time—we're talking about the 1920s—that she was divorced. He did a beautiful job of that, and the mother did accept this and they were married. They were apparently devoted to each other throughout their lives.

For about the last seven years of Harlan's life, Ethel apparently suffered from what now is generally labeled Alzheimer's disease. She would become lost in time and space. Sometimes she would be perfectly normal, sometimes not. Harlan couldn't bear the thought of having her institutionalized, so he simply had a nurse in the home, as well as some other servants. He did his best to stay with her through all the times that he was not on the court and tried to shield her from the embarrassments that her condition created.

TOWARD THE VERY end of Harlan's career, he was almost entirely blind. The court tried to deal with this by giving him an extra clerk so that the clerk could do a good bit of reading to him. He also experimented with various kinds of magnifying glasses. He worked up huge charts of cases that he would take into conference with him so that he could write out his own notes, . . . but it was still a problem.

Toward the end, according to one clerk, they were spending around sixty hours per week reading to him because he simply wasn't able to digest the material with his own eyesight and he was not willing simply to let them summarize a lot of it. He wanted it read to him. It was a terrific problem, but he took it with good humor. Paul Burke, his messenger, mentioned that one morning they were getting ready to leave for the court and he heard the justice say "good morning" to someone and Burke hadn't noticed anyone at all on the street. Then the justice said, "Damn, Paul, I just said good morning to a tree." But it didn't bother him. He took that kind of thing with good humor and, I thought, handled it as well as he could possibly have. [Justice Harlan died of cancer in 1971.]

I ALWAYS HAD a great admiration for Justice Harlan. I had an admiration for the style of his opinions and the degree to which he could write internally consistent opinions and opinions that I thought very persuasive, even though politically and philosophically we might have differed. Also, I had some sense before starting the project that this was a very decent man, a very fine human being.

Getting to Know
Richard M. Nixon

by

LEONARD GARMENT

Leonard Garment's relationship with Richard Nixon began at a New York City law firm in 1963. Nixon joined the firm after losing an election for the governorship of California in 1962. Garment and Nixon worked on a case together, which Nixon argued before the U.S. Supreme Court, and Garment later became White House counsel to Nixon during his presidency. Mr. Garment talked about the country's thirty-seventh president during a Booknotes *interview on March 13, 1997, as he discussed his memoir,* Crazy Rhythm: My Journey from Brooklyn, Jazz, and Wall Street to Nixon's White House, Watergate, and Beyond . . . , *published by Times Books in 1997. Mr Garment is an attorney in Washington, D.C.*

ELMER BOBST was the chairman of Warner-Lambert Pharmaceutical Company. He was the chairman of a lot of other things before that. He was a great big, heavyset man who built that company up. He had a very formal manner; he managed to say, "Hello," and make it sound like the opening of a speech to the board of directors.

Elmer Bobst lived in New Jersey—Warner-Lambertville—and he had Richard Nixon and myself come down to visit him for dinner and to stay over at his place in 1965. We were preparing an argument for the United States Supreme Court in *Time Inc. v. Hill*. And Nixon had a date to speak at a housing facility that was financed by Investors Diversified Services. He was going to talk politics there. So we had dinner with Elmer and his wife—a very pleasant dinner—and then the driver took us down to this development. We were going to stay there for the night and then Nixon was going to speak in the morning, and then we would drive back to Bobst's home, about forty miles away.

Richard Nixon had a nose for political manipulation—by himself, as a politician, or by others trying to manipulate him—that was second to none in the world. He looked around and realized that the next day, he was going to walk out of this house where he and I spent the night, and on the porch would be photographers from the [housing facility] and that he was going to become a prop in a merchandising promotion. So he said, "Let's get back in the car. We'll go back, and we'll come here in the morning." And we got back in the car and drove back to the Bobst estate. By now it was later than midnight; everything was closed; and there was a relatively high stone wall around the place.

They locked the gate, there was no way of pressing buttons, and he wouldn't do that anyway because the folks were sleeping. The lights were out. So he said, "Come on, Garment. Over the wall we go." And, you know, we got over the wall. It was one of the first walls he climbed on his way back to the presidency with me, as we would say in Brooklyn, schlepping along.

In any event, we weren't going to go into the house. He knew that there was a little guest house right by the swimming pool and there were two camp-size beds there. So we got into our little camp beds. As I later found out in much more somber and important detail, he had great trouble sleeping. I mean, he was an insomniac and the way he generally went to sleep was to talk, or maybe he'd have a drink, or take a sleeping pill, like most of us do in times of tension or illness. In any event, he did quite a bit of talking, sort of free association. I was in the other bed, and it was like being at camp and having a friend telling about his life and problems. He did a lot of talking to me that night.

He talked about his life, talked about his mother and father, those were prime themes in his life. What was interesting was that we had been partners now for a year and a half and we worked a lot on this case and we were talking about politics. Of course, from the day he reached the law firm—the first time I sat down with him, I had a long head-to-head talk—an hour and a half, two hours—it was clear to me that he was running for the presidency, somehow, if it were humanly possible. And if it were not humanly possible, I think he felt that he wouldn't live very long. He had to get back into his famous "arena."

So he talked about his ambitions and he talked about his mother and her love of peace and the trouble with his father and brothers [which] everybody knows so well. And he made it very clear that he would do anything to enhance his energy and his ability to maintain a footing in public life. He had a view to doing the things he felt he was destined to do, . . . in the world of foreign affairs and in bringing about a greater stability and more hope for peace in the world. He wasn't kidding around that night. There was no point to it. He gradually tailed off; became more personal about his hopes and aspirations and he and I fell asleep.

He left early in the morning. I woke. He was gone. The car came back; he had told the chauffeur to come back at a certain time—8:00 in the morning. I guess he had seen Bobst before he left. And Elmer Bobst came and we had breakfast and then we sat by the pool and we talked for the whole morning until Nixon came back.

A LITTLE NIXON phrase was "Never rush into a public place." When we were going to the United States Supreme Court, I was "Mr. Anxious" and he was "Mr. Anxious-but-Disciplined" with a sense of his own status and rank. We were law partners and he was going in for his first argument and last argument before the Supreme Court. He did it magnificently, truly.

We weren't the first case scheduled for argument that morning. And we were out in the lawyers' room and he was going over his notes on yellow pads, he was reading them right up until the very last split second. Everybody was in the courtroom and the justices were about to enter, and it was a question of decorum that all of the counsel be present, particularly he should be present, when the court came in. And so I was sort of bustling him, "Come on, Dick, let's get in there. They're about to sweep through. You're not going to be there and you'll come in and they'll say you're showboating." And as we were walking along, he whispered to me out of the side of his mouth, "Len. Never rush into a public place." Good lesson. I still rush into public places.

That was in 1966. We argued it twice. The case was argued in the spring and was argued again in the fall. After the first case was over, he wrote a memorandum the night we got back from Washington after a fourteen-hour day. I went to my home and he went to his apartment. I was in Brooklyn Heights, had moved up in the world. He was out on Fifth Avenue. There was no reason to believe the case was going to be reargued. It was the end of it. Done. Finished. Presented the argument. He dictated this memorandum—I suppose it was between midnight, 1:00, when he woke up; he didn't have anybody to call on the phone to help put him to sleep.

I got to the office about 10:00 the next morning, and there on my desk was a five-page, single-spaced typewritten document, a memorandum to me from Richard Nixon, "The things I should have done that I didn't do right in the argument today." He had dictated this impeccable memorandum before he went to sleep, whenever he went to sleep, and when he came in the next morning at 7:30, he gave it to Rose Mary Woods and she typed it up and it was on my desk. I knew that there were no little dancing gremlins preparing memoranda, and the memorandum is kind of startling for its active legal prophecy about *Roe v. Wade* and *Griswold* and what have you. You've got to read it to believe it.

I WAS IN THE Nixon White House from beginning to end, except for a few months at the beginning of President Nixon's time in office. He asked me to come down to Washington and he put me in that huge basketball-court office overlooking the White House. So I saw all these fellows that I had recruited marching in and out and running the world, and I was up there just sort of looking at them.

I was undertaking to become, at his instructions, the "Republican Clark Clifford." Now, I wasn't a Republican, wasn't then, am not now; I'm more independent than politically affiliated. I knew the name Clark Clifford, but I didn't know what he did. People thought that's what I was going to be and so a lot of clients and others started calling me to go to the agencies with acronymic titles—I didn't even know what they were or where they were. I called [the highest ranking of my personal friends at the White House] Peter Flanagan. I said, "Look, Peter, I'm either going to go into the [government] and work there," which is what I really wanted to do, "or I'm going back to New York and try lawsuits, because the only other place I could possibly go would be to jail."

And we got some things done [regarding] domestic policy. People don't talk much about that. . . . Richard Nixon [and his top domestic adviser] John Ehrlichman . . . freed me up to go over in the old executive office building and do my thing, which was to work in civil rights and work for reform of Indian policy and [with the] arts and humanities and what have you.

[LATER, AFTER WATERGATE and Nixon's resignation from the presidency] I was working for President Ford. I wrote a memorandum for the president [that concerned a possible presidential pardon for Nixon]. I gave it to Philip Buchen, the president's counsel, and then to [White House chief of staff] Al Haig. An hour after it was delivered, Al Haig called me and said, "It's all—it's done." . . . I'm telling you exactly what my ears heard and what my mind recalls. I said, "Al, that's terrific." He said, "Don't leave your office." President Ford's first press conference was scheduled for that afternoon.

I had submitted my memorandum, along with a suggested opening statement . . . that was drafted by Ray Price, who was President Nixon's principal speechwriter. [My memorandum was written] with a view to giving Jerry Ford and his colleagues a sense of how [a pardon] would sound. And, of course, it sounded very good, the logic of law. The essence of the law is experience, doing not just the letter of the law but what represents the common sense of the people and what should be done.

An awful idea was being pressed, as I knew, by a number of independent counsels, special prosecutor Leon Jaworski's associates—Jaworski was the successor to Archibald Cox—which was to indict President Nixon and try him.

It would have been like a national freak show, just calamitous for the world and for the country. And my own feelings were, it was a good chance it would end in a personal calamity for Richard Nixon because he was just not about to be presented as a human geek biting off the heads of chickens for the entertainment of people who hated him.

[I had gone for counsel to three men.] One was somebody who combined wisdom and political intelligence and we both have a natural devotion to the country, and that was [retired Supreme Court justice] Abe Fortas. We went over to his house; he poured me a drink and said, "What's on your mind?" I told him what was on my mind. He said, "By all means," he said, "this is Ecclesiastes time. This is not the time for that kind of catastrophic flogging of the country through the vehicle of Richard Nixon. It's a time to get it behind us and go on."

So that's what led to my writing the memorandum and I'm presuming that it went to the president from Philip Buchen in some form or other. And I'm happy that Nixon was pardoned.

There were people who truly hated Nixon and wanted him to be savaged. It goes all the way back, in a sense, to a geological fault in American politics, to the time of Alger Hiss and Richard Nixon's campaigning and the hatreds that were formed and then were either institutionalized or internalized by the media.

Ford did the right, proper, generous, patriotic, and presidential thing. He didn't have a clue about the kind of explosion that would set off in the media, generated a lot by the young prosecutors and investigators for the House committee and others. . . . The big show, the final act, the grand plunge in a barrel off Niagara Falls suddenly was preempted and ended by Jerry Ford.

IF SOMEBODY ASKED me, "Did you like Nixon?" I'd say, "Of course, I liked him. I admired him." They'd say, "Well, what was there about him that you liked?" I'd say, "Well, the first and foremost thing I liked about him was that he had a spacious, immense intelligence." A lot of his troubles came from the fact that he couldn't contain himself.

The Life and Career of
Adam Clayton Powell Jr.

by

CHARLES V. HAMILTON

Adam Clayton Powell Jr. was born in 1908 in New Haven, Connecticut. He succeeded his father as pastor of the Abyssinian Baptist Church in New York City in 1937 and quickly earned a reputation as a powerful black leader. Powell was elected as a Democrat to the U.S. Congress in 1945, and in 1960 he became chairman of the House Committee on Education and Labor, at the time the highest position ever held by an African American in the U.S. government. In March 1967, he was "excluded" by the House of Representatives, which had accused him of misuse of House funds, contempt of New York court orders concerning a 1963 libel judgment against him, and conduct unbecoming a member. He was reseated in 1969 after a special election but was fined and deprived of his seniority. Although the Supreme Court ruled that Powell's exclusion had been unconstitutional, he failed to win reelection in 1970. Charles Hamilton appeared on Booknotes *on January 5, 1992, to discuss* Adam Clayton Powell, Jr.: Political Biography of an American Dilemma, *published by Atheneum in 1991. Mr. Hamilton taught courses in government and political science at Columbia University.*

ADAM CLAYTON POWELL was a civil rights leader; he was a congressman; he was a preacher; he was a playboy. He was terribly controversial throughout his career.

He was a fellow who, for about thirty years, was one of the more important and interesting figures on the American political scene, locally and nationally, and not much was known about him. I wanted to make sure I could capture that career, with all of its controversies and dynamism.

He went to Congress in 1945, was elected in '44, sworn-in in '45, and stayed until 1967 (at which point they excluded him), and he came back in '69. The Supreme Court ruled that his exclusion was unconstitutional, so then he was in Congress from 1945 to 1967 and then from 1969 to 1970.

He was most powerful in Congress from January 1961 to September 1966, when he was chair of the House Education and Labor Committee. He had, during that period, what no other African American politician had—institutional power. He was chair of a major, substantive committee. [In the] 1960s, the committee handled roughly 40 percent of the domestic legislation of the United States, and [this was] . . . the period of the New Frontier and the Great Society. When Lyndon B. Johnson, especially as president, was churning out all that legislation—Medicare, elementary and secondary education, Office of Equal Opportunity Programs, National Defense Education Act—all that legislation came through Powell's committee. He was the chair of that committee, and, for that period, he ran a good ship. . . . He was an effective chairperson in accounts from not just his staff and his friends, which you would expect, but from [other members of Congress] on his committee, John Brademas, for instance, and Frank Thompson.

POWELL WAS BORN in New Haven, Connecticut, and bred in Harlem. . . . His father took over Abyssinian Baptist Church in 1909. . . . He was a child of privilege and a child who was terribly pampered in a time when few people—black or white—in this country had much in the way of resources. He had a nanny. . . . He always grew up in a very comfortable circumstance. He never had a day of poverty or want in his life growing up in Harlem. They dressed him in Little Lord Fauntleroy suits. . . . To give you a little indication of the privileged nature of this man, . . . when he graduated from Colgate in June of 1930, pretty bad times, his parents sent him on a three-month cruise to the Mediterranean.

If he were to walk in here now, he'd have to tell us he was black, because he looked white. . . . For a while, he passed for white, to use the lexicon of that process. He passed for white when he was in college at Colgate University. He pledged a white fraternity. He lived in a white dormitory. He was found out by the fraternity when they investigated his background.

From that point on, he never attempted to cross that racial line. However, his sister who was ten years older did pass for white in the 1920s when she worked on Wall Street in a secretarial job. That was not an uncommon phenomenon for people of his complexion, then and, I assume, now, but his father and his whole family [were] quite white-looking. It's also clear that, while they did not deny their racial identity, there were times when they would go on summer vacations to the South. His father and he loved fishing. They would take the train south. . . . After you came to a certain point on the Mason-Dixon Line, they separated the races—colored in this place, white here. The Powells never moved, and no one ever questioned them, and they never called it to anyone's attention. So there was always this subtle aspect of "passing." It was a kind of game that people played then, which also contributed to his cynicism.

I HAD THREE [personal] contacts with Adam Clayton Powell. The first contact . . . came when I was a young nineteen-year-old recruit in the army. It was in 1949. I was in Camp Hood, Texas, . . . and Mr. Truman had just issued orders desegregating the military. As a Negro—and I like to use the lexicon of the times; it helps [people] understand the atmosphere—I couldn't use the darkroom, the photographic facilities, except during limited periods of time: Sunday mornings, 6:00 to 11:00. I wrote to Adam Clayton Powell [to protest this]. Now keep in mind, I'm from Chicago. My congressman was a black congressman, William L. Dawson. I didn't write to Dawson because I didn't think I'd get an answer. I wrote to Congressman Adam Clayton Powell from Harlem. About three weeks later, my company commander called me in and said, "You should be careful about rabble-rousers you're corresponding with. Do you know that this congressman you wrote to called Mrs. Truman, the president's wife, 'the last lady of the land?'" Bess Truman had refused to turn down an invitation from the Daughters of the American Revolution, which had just excluded Powell's wife, Hazel Scott, from performing in Constitution Hall. So Powell called her "the last lady of the land."

My company commander [said], "That's not the kind of person you'd want to correspond with. This is a rabble-rouser, troublemaker, disrespectful." I looked on the desk, and there was a letter, a memo from the Department of the Army. Now, I was standing at attention. Right under that was a letter from Adam Powell to the Department of the Army. "If you have any problems," the company commander said, "with this man's army, you come to us. Now you can go ahead and use the darkroom anytime you want to use it." I never heard from Adam, but he and I got the results.

The second time was ten years later. I was then . . . an assistant professor at a major black college in Tuskegee, Alabama. I was very involved in voter registration. We wanted several senators and congresspeople to introduce a bill, and we had Powell on that list. I had an occasion to talk to him on the phone then. [It was the] first time I ever talked to him, [and I] still hadn't met him.

The third and last time [I had contact with Adam Clayton Powell, I was] a professor at Columbia. It was now 1970. He and I were invited to appear at a major civil rights rally in Cleveland as the two main speakers. He was running for reelection against Charlie Rangel, and it was very clear he was dying of cancer. He was not spending much time back in the district. He had five opponents (Rangel was just one of them), and that was ideal for him. That was the first time I'd really met him. We were sitting up late one night in his hotel room and I said, "Mr. Congressman, shouldn't you be back in the district? I hear this is a close race." He looked at me incredulously. He said, "I can't lose. They'll vote for me because they'll remember how effective I was." As a matter of fact, he was [effective, but he lost that race in 1970].

[WOMEN PLAYED a large role in his life] by his own account. He was married three times, and each marriage had a particular flair about it. His third wife was from Puerto Rico. His youngest son, Adam Clayton Powell IV, was elected to the City Council of New York in the footsteps of his father in October [1991], representing a district in East Harlem. Hazel Scott [was his second wife and] Adam Clayton Powell III was their son. He is in the media, in journalism, and apparently has no interest in the political realm.

Adam Powell would never admit to having a worst side. But clearly [he had a] rather careless disregard for certain things, like misuse of committee funds. That was in the record, and there was no doubt of that. Some of his personal activities by his own admission [reflect his worst inclinations, for instance] the way he disregarded the court warrants against him and a libel suit against him in Harlem. He [would say], "I was inattentive. I was neglectful on that. That was not good." His absentee record, which a lot of us excused at the time, worked against him. Finally, the part I found to be as intriguing was from friend and foe. They simply felt they couldn't trust the man. He would enter into a deal, and then you'd find out you didn't have a deal. He was a very complex fellow in that regard. . . . We're not talking here about a saint, and neither are we talking about a sinner. We're talking about a complex politician who had some very, very serious negatives about him that people didn't like.

I don't think there was anything Mr. Powell did for which there were not at least multiple reasons. [He supported the Republican, Dwight Eisenhower, instead of the Democrat, Adlai Stevenson, for president in the 1950s.] A lot of people said, "Oh, look at that. He's under investigation for his income taxes. If he cuts a deal with the Republicans, the Republicans will ease up on investigating his income taxes." That's one reason. Another reason was his own. "You want to know why I supported Eisenhower? Because he's better than Stevenson on civil rights." Well, not many civil rights people believed that. There were a lot of reasons why he supported Eisenhower, and they are always mixed up with political, professional, and personal explanations. But he survived it. He almost got in trouble with it, in terms of denying his seniority in Congress, but he survived. That's something else that was intriguing about this man. You would say, "Oh, there goes Adam jumping off a roof again." And you would be right. But he would land on his feet.

Most of the time, he could turn what some people would call negatives into positives. That was very important in the sense of trying to understand who this terribly complex political figure was . . . . His main issue throughout his career was civil rights and economic justice. He always knew that he had those two issues going for him, and he brought them home always to the pulpit of Abyssinian Baptist Church. Whenever he was under attack for these negatives, for these faults, for these bad qualities, he could say, "That's why they're doing it, because I am such a forceful champion of civil rights. That's why they're out to get me."

[In the pulpit, he was] dynamic, unheralded, an excellent orator and preacher. Like a lot of Baptist preachers, he could take a text and weave it into either a religious theme or a political theme. He captured the parishioners emotionally and in every other way, in a very superb manner. [He had] one of the major churches too. It's a very impressive congregation.

THIS MAN WHO spanned all these years, who saw the evolution of the civil rights movement—the Kings, the Malcolm Xs—had a little bit of a time adjusting to it. He could see in them his earlier self because he was the fiery, stomping platform speaker in the '30s and '40s and, indeed, into the '50s. Now new leaders came along—King, Malcolm, many others—and the TV cameras weren't on him. Where was he? He was in Congress doing very important things, running committees, getting legislation passed, [being] liberal and progressive. But that's not where the cameras were.

Where were the cameras? They were at Lincoln Memorial in August of 1963. Where was Powell? He was assigned to leading a little congressional delegation to sit on the platform. The cameras were in Birmingham. Where was Powell when the dogs were jumping and biting people? Powell was holding a subcommittee meeting. [Same with] Selma, Alabama, and so forth and so forth. He was angry because of that, jealous. It was the dynamism of the movement. A lot of people said, "Ah, the movement's passing Powell by." He didn't like that.

[MALCOLM X WAS] assassinated in February 1965. [He was] on the scene a much shorter time than Powell. There was something very dynamic about both his life and death. He was articulating a message—particularly in the earlier part of his life before the break with the Nation of Islam—that was quite appealing to an awful lot of people. [As with] Martin Luther King, there is something very intriguing—and I hope I'm not misunderstood—about the dynamic martyr-type way they were killed, by assassination. Snap, snuffed out like that.

Malcolm X apparently was undergoing a transformation after his break with the Nation of Islam. Where was he going? . . . Malcolm X's career lends itself to analysis. It's a very different career than Powell's. You look long and hard, and Malcolm X never registered anybody to vote, never got a piece of legislation through Congress, and yet I would never denigrate his career. But it's a very different impact. And, incidentally, that's what made Powell angry and jealous of those people. Why all this attention to Malcolm? He didn't even lead a march. It's a very interesting aspect of the story of the black struggle. [Marches are] what the cameras are turned to [in the] early '60s. Even with his power in Congress, Powell was perhaps a little apprehensive [about] this young man, Malcolm X, a fiery speaker.

ADAM CLAYTON POWELL died April 4, 1972, the same day, four years [after,] that King was killed. . . . I would like to see a reexamination of him and his life. Not just biographies, but other complex stories about the movement. We've been very simplistic in explaining this very important American struggle—good guys against the bad guys, right or wrong. His life is simply an account of the complexity of that struggle.

Richard J. Daley and
Chicago's Political Machine

by

ELIZABETH TAYLOR

Richard J. Daley served as mayor of Chicago for twenty-one years, from 1955 until his death in 1976. He also was chairman of the Cook County Democratic Party from 1953 until 1976. From these two positions, Daley ran one of the most effective political machines this country has ever seen, delivering votes, jobs, and other forms of patronage to those who cooperated. When protesters and police clashed in the streets during the National Democratic Convention in 1968, Daley's national reputation was damaged. Thus the nation had one more very public trauma to endure in a year that had already seen the assassination of Martin Luther King Jr. and Robert Kennedy. Chicago Tribune *literary editor Elizabeth Taylor appeared on* Booknotes *on July 23, 2000, to discuss* American Pharoah: Mayor Richard J. Daley, His Battle for Chicago and the Nation, *published by Little, Brown & Company in 2000, the book she coauthored with the journalist Adam Cohen.*

MAYOR RICHARD J. DALEY WAS A pharaoh in many senses of the word. He was powerful. He was autocratic. He ruled Chicago for twenty-one years, from 1955 until his death in 1976. In another way, he was also a builder. He built all of the great things [associated with] Chicago: the world's busiest airport; the world's tallest building, Sears Tower; the beautiful Magnificent Mile; the skyline. It's all his. He also built some of the worst buildings in Chicago—some of the public housing projects. Finally, the word "pharaoh" was his nickname from civil rights leaders who dubbed him that in the '50s and '60s because of his resistance to civil rights, particularly his resistance to Martin Luther King, who actually moved to Chicago and lived there for eight months.

DALEY HAD CAMPAIGNED hard [to have the 1968 Democratic National Convention in Chicago]. He had wanted the convention brought to Chicago so he could showcase this beautiful city he had rescued from the brink of despair. He left no detail untouched. He looked at the convention hall and focused on everything from the ashtrays to the banners—simply every detail. He was extremely worried about violence in the aftermath of the death of Martin Luther King and Bobby Kennedy. He did not want anything upsetting his city. The protesters had their sights on Chicago. He was determined not to let them get any attention. They approached him consistently for all sorts of permits, and he denied them those permits. This wrangling went on for months. Meanwhile, Daley was dressing up his city and making it look really beautiful.

Daley defended his city [as well as he could]. Senator Abraham Ribicoff had just said [to the convention], "If we elect McGovern, we will not have Gestapo tactics in Chicago." He was referring to the extraordinary protests that were occurring on the streets of Chicago. This was Daley's lowest moment.

Finally, in this terrible twenty minutes, everything exploded. The police went wild, attacking protesters, and protesters were also violent. Daley just didn't know what to make of it. There were these people who nominated Pigasus, a 125-pound pig, for president. They had threatened to poison the water. They had said they were going to pull down Hubert Humphrey's pants onstage. These were things that he couldn't deal with. He didn't understand the idealism of the protesters. He kept saying, "What do they want? What programs do they want?" But in the end, Daley was really underestimated, and he came out of it all brilliantly.

PRECINCT CAPTAINS had been so important [to Daley's political success]. Daley [once described someone to Lyndon Johnson by saying,] "This guy has a great education, he's a great lawyer, he's a great American. Best of all, he's a precinct captain." To him, it was the highest calling. The precinct captain was the guy—and it usually was a guy—who got out the votes.

There were lots of different ways [to deliver votes]. There was something called "four-legged voting," where the precinct captain would literally walk into the voting booth with a voter and help them pull down a lever. A reporter who covered elections told us he saw one precinct captain pull down the lever seventy different times at the start of the day. They would go into flophouses and get the names of the winos and register them as voters. They would offer them everything from nylons to Christmas trees to eyeglasses to get them to vote. They really worked hard. If they didn't turn out the vote, they were, as it was called, "viced." That meant that they lost their paycheck and their job.

People would tell us stories of paying people [to vote]. . . . Liquor stores were closed on election day, so [precinct captains would] give booze to winos so they would vote. One woman said [to a reform candidate], "I can't vote for you, because I got a Christmas tree from my precinct captain. He gives everyone a Christmas tree. You can't afford that." So, it was a lot of gifts in-kind. There was a lot of that sort of thing going on.

Election honesty was totally flouted in Chicago. The precinct records were erased and made up and precinct captains threatened Republicans. It was not an honest, open system at all.

[IN 1960 JOHN KENNEDY narrowly defeated Richard Nixon in the popular vote.] Mayor Daley [helped Kennedy win the state of Illinois by 8,858 votes] and so many votes were stolen that it's probable that Kennedy got enough to win the election.

Daley felt an affinity for John Kennedy. He had had a long relationship with his father, Joe Kennedy. The Kennedys owned the Merchandise Mart, this huge piece of real estate in Chicago. But Daley really cared about the state's attorney race. . . . He was determined that the Republican candidate, Benjamin Adamowski, would not be elected. Adamowski had been a friend of Daley's, [but] he turned Republican and was just bashing the machine constantly. Adamowski posed a threat to Daley, and many people believed that Daley worked very hard not just for Kennedy, but against Adamowski.

[DALEY'S CITY COUNCIL] floor leader, Tom Keane, who actually ended up going to jail . . . said that he wanted money and Daley wanted power. Daley was honest. He tolerated corruption around him, but he wasn't about money. He was about power.

Tom Keane was one of the people who was closest to Daley and he was kind of irreverent. He would just say whatever was on his mind. . . . After Martin Luther King had lived in Chicago for eight months, Daley and some realtors and some legislators all sat down and had a summit agreement where they agreed on open housing. Then King got on a plane, went back to Alabama, and Keane said, "What agreement? We never had an agreement." Keene was really a wily guy. He helped Daley out a lot.

RICHARD J. DALEY lived his whole life in Bridgeport. It's a totally fascinating place. It's a neighborhood in Chicago, and it's an Irish-Catholic enclave.

The neighborhoods in Chicago are very strong. . . . It really was a separate world. He lived on Lowe Street his whole life, always within a block from his mother. He went to church just a block or two away. He grew up in the shadow of the stockyards. It was a really violent place. Upton Sinclair wrote about it in *The Jungle*. Daley actually worked in the stockyards a little bit. In one of his campaigns, he showed himself riding around and working in the stockyards.

Bridgeport was this little enclave, and there were no blacks there. . . . Daley was not comfortable with blacks. He really saw himself as being Irish and one of the "out" groups. He just thought that blacks should pull themselves up by their bootstraps.

But Daley operated the [political] machine and he really depended on [a submachine of] loyal black voters. They really stuck with him over time. The first one was William L. Dawson, at one point the most powerful black [elected official] in America. He really supported Daley and was, in fact, opposed to integration, [which was] ironic because he had fled Georgia because his family was threatened over a racial incident. He continued to be a loyal soldier for Daley.

Daley was brilliant at playing ethnic politics, [playing] people off each other. It's also important to understand that even within Irish Chicago, it wasn't all monolithic. . . . Even within the parishes, or even within neighborhoods, there were distinctions.

Daley actually held onto a lot of white people, keeping them from fleeing to the suburbs. He did a much better job of that than, say, Detroit or Cleveland or St. Louis. One of the brilliant ideas he had was that if you worked for the city, you had to live in the city. That really was pretty effective. He also made the Loop a thriving place, kept a lot of industry in Chicago when it could have left. We give him a lot of credit for saving Chicago.

We owe Richard J. Daley a big credit for [the state of the city today]. It's a thriving, wonderful city, with a downtown that's bustling. People have stayed in the city. They haven't fled to the suburbs. But there are these lingering problems, and the worst of these is public housing.

The Robert Taylor Homes is one of the most famous public housing projects in the country. It's miles and miles of tall brick buildings, separated by one of the world's widest highways. . . . That highway separates these housing projects from Bridgeport. [Daley had the highway built there] as a dividing line. . . . It could have gone in different places, but it went there to bisect the city. The public housing projects were Daley's effort. They were described as "human filing cabinets into the sky."

At the beginning, [public housing was] envisioned as a way station for the

poor. There's this wonderful woman, . . . Elizabeth Wood, this poetry professor from Vassar who was the first head of the Chicago Housing Authority
[for twelve years]. She was for low-rise, integrated public housing. . . . She
was kicked out in 1954 when Daley was head of the machine, which is a very
powerful job, which he promised to give up when he was made mayor, but he
never did. Elizabeth Wood got herself into some trouble because she was
resisting these high-rises. Also, she resisted the appointment of one of Daley's
relatives to the staff of the CHA. She said they shouldn't hire somebody who
had finished last in his law school class.

These housing projects were very important for several reasons. Daley
wasn't the only one who wanted them. The black [political] submachine was
for them too, because they were a way to consolidate votes. It was very easy
for a precinct captain to march up and down the towers. There was so much
dependency. People felt that they would have to vote the machine ticket or
they'd be thrown out of their apartments.

JAMES THOMPSON, who was the Republican U.S. attorney, [made an] effort
to put the machine officials in jail. Some of the biggies were [former Illinois
governor] Otto Kerner; Tom Keane, who was Daley's floor leader; Paul
Wigoda, who was a city councilman and a Daley ally. He also [targeted] Earl
Bush, who was Daley's speechwriter and known as the intellectual on the
staff. He was the only Jewish person on Daley's staff . . . . He had gotten
involved in a company that sold airport signs. It was really Mickey Mouse
stuff. He was benefiting from the airports.

[After conducting this campaign against the political machine, Jim
Thompson was] elected governor. He was . . . seen as somebody who was
politically ambitious and wanted to be governor. In fact, some people
thought he could be a presidential candidate.

[A 1972 CHICAGO TRIBUNE series on vote fraud] really started the reform
movement in Chicago politics. It started people criticizing the machine.
Later, there was something known as the Shakman Decree, which started to
dismantle patronage, which was a key part of the machine and how it operated.

Patronage was eviscerated by the decree. Patronage essentially entailed
some 40,000 jobs that were at the disposal of the mayor. He could dispense
them as he liked, or he could punish people. [If a] precinct captain . . . didn't
deliver, [the mayor could] take away their patronage jobs. It was pretty serious stuff. [The patronage system today is] a shell of what it used to be.

A generation or two ago, [Chicago politicians] did more of what they
wanted. Now they really do have to be more sensitive to the media, and espe-

cially television. That's the real change. Daley met with newspaper reporters all the time when he was mayor. Over the years, with the increase of television and with his famous malapropisms, he avoided television more and more.

[Chicago's current mayor, Richard M. Daley, is] Richard J. Daley's eldest son and, like in all good family businesses, he went on to run the family business. He [has served as] mayor of Chicago since 1989. . . . Richard J. Daley operated this huge machine. [His son] is making the widgets in the factory that his father built.

Reporting from Vietnam

---

by

PETER R. KANN

FRANCES FITZGERALD

The American government first became involved in Vietnam during the Truman administration. President John F. Kennedy increased the number of U.S. military advisers from around 900 to over 16,000 during his time in office. On August 7, 1964, following a disputed attack on American naval forces in the Gulf of Tonkin by Vietnamese torpedo boats, the U.S. Congress passed the Tonkin Gulf Resolution, allowing President Lyndon B. Johnson "all necessary measures to repel any armed attack against the forces of the United States and to prevent further aggression." By 1966 there were 190,000 U.S. troops in South Vietnam, and by 1969, during President Richard Nixon's administration, there were 540,000. U.S. troops began to withdraw in 1969 and a peace agreement was signed in Paris on January 27, 1973. Within several months, the last American troops had left the country. America's role in Vietnam was, and remains, extremely controversial, and the journalists who covered it found their news reports had an enormous impact on the public debate. Reporting Vietnam: American Journalism, 1959–1969, *published by the Library of America in 1998, collected these war correspondents' articles. In a* Booknotes *interview on January 12, 1999, Dow Jones chairman Peter R. Kann and Frances FitzGerald of* The Nation *discussed the war and what it was like to cover it.*

Kann: Vietnam was where the action was. If you were a journalist in the mid-sixties and you had the opportunity to get there, it clearly was the great story and to some extent, probably still would rank as the great journalistic story of our generation.

Most reporters in Vietnam were not hawks or doves in the sense that the American public lined up. . . . Most reporters who covered Vietnam for any length of time became critics—some more, some less, but all, to some extent—of the way the war was being waged. We weren't in a position to be critics of what the Communists were doing because we couldn't follow their troops around and we couldn't see the destruction they were causing and we couldn't see the suffering that they caused. But we certainly could see that which our own troops and our allies caused. So in one way or another, we all became critics, but we weren't, by and large, ideologues on the war. I don't think we started, or even ended, in most cases, with the proposition that one side was evil and one side was good.

CLEARLY, [THE November 1968 massacre of civilians at] My Lai happened. I presume on a lesser scale there were some other [similar incidents]. But the main suffering that America caused was much more mindless, random suffering. It was free-fire zones; it was search-and-destroy missions; it was someone sitting at a map declaring a certain part of a certain province Vietcong territory, which then permitted any amount of firepower being directed at that portion of a province. And in that portion of the province, not all the people would have been Vietcong or North Vietnamese combatants. There would have been civilians. That gets at how difficult it is to fight a fundamentally guerrilla-type war.

The suffering we caused there tended to be much more from thousands of feet up with the bombs and with the artillery pieces than it was a small group of soldiers going off and committing some specific act of violence against a particular civilian. [Events like My Lai] happened, but I don't think that was in any way typical of the American GI in Vietnam.

FitzGerald: Unfortunately, I think the press appetite for these kinds of stories was so great that they actually neglected this other and far more destructive behavior. I remember when Kevin Buckley discovered that the U.S. Ninth Division went down to the Mekong Delta for a period in '68 and caused horrendous civilian casualties. No American division had been in the delta before because it was so thickly populated. They just went about, bombing and artillery, and so forth. Kevin could hardly get this piece published because it wasn't My Lai II. And yet it was far more destructive.

Kann: The other thing one does have to keep remembering is that when it came to specific acts of violence, that was a tactic [used by] the Vietcong and the North Vietnamese. They did assassinate village leaders. That kind of thing happened on both sides. We, to some extent, then copied them with things like the Phoenix Program and the Provincial Reconnaissance Units. So there was another level of quite targeted, very nasty violence on both sides.

FitzGerald: I saw [this chapter in American history] as a criminal waste, and I was angry a good deal of the time because it seemed to me that we were destroying ourselves and destroying the Vietnamese. And the fact that the casualties in Indochina as a whole were just so enormous, it seemed to me that none of this was necessary. . . . Where we failed was politically and diplomatically, early on. We were driven by internal domestic demands of, "Don't lose China. Don't lose Vietnam." We just never even considered the possibilities of a neutral South Vietnam.

What is so surprising about this war, as compared to any other war that the U.S. has fought, was how little we understood the other side or knew anything about them. We made little effort to see whether, in fact, it was possible to achieve at least some of our objectives without fighting a war.

[The Johnson administration was reported to not] have enough [experts about Asia]. They didn't have enough, but they had some. And certainly, Bernard Fall's books would have told them something. My belief is that their estimates were pretty good, certainly much better than we thought they were. If they wanted more expertise, they could have gotten it. They just didn't want to hear that. They didn't want to hear, "No, this can't be won."

The U.S. government got in there without ever making a coherent decision of what they were going to do, what their policy was going to be. It was essentially always a holding action. And getting out was a holding action as well. It was about not losing as opposed to winning. Nobody knew what [disagreement] might mean because the Saigon government was never a successful political entity. If it had been, the war would have been totally different. As it was, it was simply an administration and an army as opposed to a real government.

What staggered me was reading the Pentagon Papers, where I discovered that in 1961 [Secretary of Defense] Robert McNamara thought that it would require a quarter of a million troops to keep us from losing. . . . In fact, there were double that number. But I had no idea at the time, when I was reporting there in '66, that the estimates were really so pessimistic internally. I think that there were a lot of people who really understood this quite well. . . . The CIA estimates were always very pessimistic. So [we] got in incrementally, largely for political reasons. Not in the sense that if it's not going to work out well, you've got a real decision to make. And they got out, just hoping that the Saigon government could keep on going until there was a so-called decent interval. And that's what they achieved.

Only now are we beginning to get some understanding of the kinds of debate that went on in Hanoi, the problems they were having with the Soviet Union and with China which prevented them from moving towards any negotiation with us. We're now seeing the struggles that went on between Ho Chi Minh and [his party's successor] Le Duan, for example, about their different policies. When Ho Chi Minh died, or even before his death, the policies become much harder.

Kann: [The demonstrations at the 1968 Democratic Convention] were clearly part of a deep division in the American psyche and social fabric. I remember coming back here on a brief visit somewhere around that time, going to speak on the very quiet little campus of Bryn Mawr. I tried to talk . . . about how the war wasn't being fought right, about how we were causing too many civilian casualties, about how search-and-destroy missions didn't work and so on. What I didn't do was say America was an evil force or an imperialist, a conquering power in Vietnam. At the end of my little speech, a young woman stood up and said, "You know, that was very interesting, but none of us believe a single word you said." Someone else came up and said, "Why aren't you supporting those groovy little people in the jungle?" That was the Vietcong. Well, they weren't groovy little people in the jungle, but that is how some people in this country saw them at the time.

FitzGerald: Almost everybody [lied to the American people back then] from Johnson on down. We'll start with Kennedy because our political leadership would simply not face up to the serious decisions that they were making at the time and pretended it wasn't happening. That led to a lot of other lying, all the way down through the bureaucracy and the military.

Kann: The politicians lied, particularly in terms of how well the war was going. The military lied to itself within its own chain of command, which was a sad thing. Military people out in the field knew how it was going, but those reports never quite reached the top. But having said all that, the North Vietnamese lied too, and in a way with even bigger lies if you look back and say, "What did they say Vietnam was going to be like after the so-called liberation, and what did it turn out to be like?" They lied too.

FitzGerald: The first reporters who went there in 1959 tended to come from World War II and to have certain assumptions about what reporters ought to do when America goes to war. Those assumptions were broken by Neil Sheehan and David Halberstam, Mal Browne, and others. They found that they had to become critics because they were lied to a lot of the time by Americans on the ground. They became very unpopular with the embassy and with the military command and so forth. There was this antagonism between reporters and the higher officials throughout the war because they were essentially trying to say, "We're doing fine. We're winning. There's nothing going wrong at all." Therefore, you found that you had to examine every single statement that was made, practically, to see whether it was really the case or not. It made reporting very difficult. You kept having to go to the Mekong Delta to find out whether what they were saying about it was so or not.

This antagonism created more of a sense that reporters were on one side or another, whereas I don't think they really were. They were just trying to do their jobs. The antagonism did not extend to GIs or to anybody who was on the lower levels. It was really high-level policy.

Kann: If [the two of us] might disagree on anything, it might be with the benefit of all this hindsight now the two decades later. I would take, these days, somewhat the position that Vietnam was a battle we lost in a larger war that we won—the Cold War or the war for the future of Asia. If you look at Asia today, leaving aside a current economic or financial crisis, fundamentally Asia turned out very well. The so-called dominoes held. If not totally free, Asia is essentially composed now of freer societies and largely free markets. One can argue that the ten years America spent in Vietnam actually wound up buying time for Asia to achieve a level of stability and prosperity that lasts today. Then, in a larger sense, Vietnam was one of many battles we fought in a very long Cold War. So maybe in this we have a somewhat different perspective, but I don't think we would have had a very different perspective on what was going on on the ground in Vietnam.

FitzGerald: I didn't cover large troop movements and I didn't cover GIs. My interest was always with the Vietnamese government, with the civilian population and so forth. I would travel outside of American circles most of the time. Insofar as there were Americans, they would be with advisers to provinces and so forth. So, really, violence was a question of timing. You never knew. You'd drive along a road and have no idea whether it was mined or not, no idea whether you'd run into a battle or not. But I certainly wasn't seeking it out.

Kann: The *Wall Street Journal* gave me the luxury not to have to write the daily war stories. I didn't spend a lot of time with the big American troop units and so on. If I went out with American troops, it wasn't to cover a battle per se; it was to get some sense of what they were thinking and doing on a kind of normal day; similarly with South Vietnamese units. I did see people shot, not because I wanted to be where someone was being shot but because I happened to be in the wrong place at the wrong time and something happened—a mortar landed or something.

FitzGerald: Neil Sheehan is one of those reporters who went back many times over the years, and that's an important point, that the war was not one thing at one time. It had no dramatic unity so that if you went in any given year, you would see something quite different and that would probably form your impression. But Neil, who had long experience, was one of the few people who was able to make a statement like ["I, while not a dove, am no longer a hawk."] Others of us would have been shy about doing so. But he had seen so much that he had the authority to say, "This is the way I feel about it."

Kann: George Esper was [with the] Associated Press [AP] and George sat for years and years in the AP office and wrote the daily war story for AP. He went to the briefings, he listened to the usually inflated figures from the military briefers. He tried to put it into some kind of context, with reports coming in from AP people in the field. Day after day, he wrote that daily war story that was probably the mainstay of most newspapers throughout the war.

FitzGerald: Gloria Emerson was there in the '69, '70, and '71 period. She covered the Lan Som 719, which was the Vietnamese incursion into Laos, and did some of the great reporting of the war. Of all the pieces that annoyed the military brass, hers was it. She discovered that some general was faking his own medals and citations and so on. . . . To a military man, [this kind of discovery] is the worst thing that can happen.

Peter Braestrup, I think you could say, was politically conservative. And he was also a really good reporter.

Kann: Peter's main contribution, beyond good reportage, was a book [that] really does try to dissect the Tet Offensive and get beyond the somewhat stereotypical idea that this was a total disaster for the South Vietnamese and the Americans. He looked at it from a more historical prospective and said that the Vietcong and the North Vietnamese suffered enormous casualties; that, in a military sense, it really was much more of a defeat for the Communists even though, politically, it wound up being a great success for them.

There was some evidence to support this. Vietnam, in the several years after the Tet Offensive, had the American and the South Vietnamese army on the offensive and the North Vietnamese and the Vietcong quite desperately trying to rebuild their forces. Then, of course, we started leaving Vietnam and we left our allies somewhat alone with our tactics but without our support and, eventually, they lost.

FitzGerald: You can see the legacy of Vietnam in the way we approach military intervention in other countries, for good or for ill. There's a great reluctance to send American troops into harm's way, a great reluctance even to send in peacekeeping forces, often. It determined the way the war with Iraq was fought, namely, by high-tech weapons and so forth. Vietnam left a permanent scar, and maybe for good in many, many cases, because it certainly warned us not to go lightly into other people's civil wars and make that kind of a disaster again.

Kann: The legacy of Vietnam clearly has left a scar on America, particularly in the area of trust of our institutions. For a period of time, it had a quite devastating effect on morale in the U.S. military. I think the morale in the U.S. military has turned around and is very strong these days, again. And I think the other scars of Vietnam, by and large, are healing. To some extent, Ronald Reagan deserves some of the credit for that.

Even all these years later, it's very hard to be totally clear about what Vietnam was all about, much less how it turned out and why. It's a little like blind people touching parts of an elephant. No reporter saw the whole story or understood the whole story, but this collection has so many stories by so many, by and large, terrific journalists that someone who goes through it does collectively get a sense of what Vietnam was all about.

American POWs in Vietnam

by

STUART I. ROCHESTER

Fifty-eight thousand Americans soldiers were either killed or went missing in action during America's involvement in the Vietnamese conflict. Over eight hundred soldiers became prisoners of war, often enduring years of physical and mental torture. Stuart I. Rochester, a Defense Department historian, appeared on Booknotes *on October 10, 1999, and told us some of these POWs' stories from his book,* Honor Bound: American Prisoners of War in Southeast Asia, 1961–1973, *co-written with Frederick Kiley and published in 1999 by the Naval Institute Press.*

THERE WERE FIFTEEN prisons in North Vietnam. In South Vietnam, there were not so many prisons as simply locations, often jungle stockades. The captivity for [U.S. prisoners of war] in the South was more of an itinerant, nomadic captivity where often just one or two prisoners in a cluster, later on in the war, would be brought together. But during much of the period of captivity in the South, you did not have formal enclosed prison structures as such, as much as you had camps that would be moved every few days, and stockades would be set up with cages.

In many cases, lower-ranking enlisted men, marines and army enlisted, who were captured in the South, had to go and endure this itinerant captivity. . . . In many cases, they had, in some ways, a lonelier, certainly, but also a more challenging experience [than the officers in the northern camps] because they had to deal more with of the elements. Being outdoors and often in a mountainous jungle location, where there would be leeches and scorpions and snakes, and having to deal with probably a more precarious food and water situation as well.

Altogether, there were at least eight hundred documented cases of U.S. prisoners during the Vietnam War. . . . The average age . . . was thirty-nine [and] rank was 04, meaning major or lieutenant commander. They were fathers of three children on average. They spent forty-five months in confinement and six to twelve months in solitary confinement.

AIR FORCE CAPTAIN Konrad Trautman . . . a senior ranking officer at the Zoo, one of the POW camps that was located about three miles southwest of Hanoi, [gave] a good summary of his torture experience, particularly the rope torture. He describes how the prisoners were literally strung up from the ceiling with their arms behind their back and cinched up to the point where their shoulders were almost dislocated; in some cases they would be. They would be put through this periodically, in two or three sessions, and it was one of the worst of the tortures. Some were maimed in the process.

Few got through it without giving up some information, without in some way giving the enemy what he wanted. . . . By all accounts, it was the worst of the many kinds of torture they were subjected to. But, curiously, some managed to get through. As with all things with the POWs, what some found to be the worst case, others found to be more tolerable. And there were some who found other tortures to be more vicious and more difficult to tolerate.

The so-called middle years were the most difficult ones, when the torture program was fairly regularly practiced to extract information, and also for punishment purposes. Most of the POWs had at least one session in the ropes. Later on, as you got toward the end of the captivity period and closer to homecoming, fewer and fewer of them would be subjected to the rope torture.

PROBABLY THE TWO worst torture cases would be Edwin Atterberry and Earl Cobiel. Atterbury made a mistake of trying to escape with John Dramesi, an air force captain, in May of 1969. Atterberry and Dramesi had an elaborate escape plan, a good plan, actually, although no one ended up successfully escaping from the North. You could escape from the prison maybe, but they would usually be able to find you after a short while.

Atterberry and Dramesi were captured soon after getting out of the Zoo Annex, which turned out to be a terrible thing for the other prisoners, who took tremendous punishment in retaliation. But the worst case was Atterberry, who was put in a torture cell. [In the book, there is a] description of what he underwent, the shrieks were heard from the equivalent of several city blocks away. He died in that torture cell. This is one of the very few cases where a man was tortured to death, and that was in direct retaliation for the escape effort.

Dramesi also took terrible punishment but survived, and some of the other POWs took awful punishment. Eugene "Red" McDaniel took [approximately] seven hundred lashes. There was even some electroshock treatment that they didn't usually resort to.

McDaniel took tremendous punishment because he was a senior in the Zoo area, in that complex. The POWs assumed that the Dramesi-Atterberry escape had been organized and directed by the seniors, which really wasn't the case. Dramesi pretty much went on his own. Although he finally got the order that it was okay to go, there was a lot of reluctance on the part of Konrad Trautman, who was the senior, who said, "Okay, you want to try it? Go ahead." But there would always be the concern that if the guy didn't make it, or for that matter, even if he did make it, the repercussions for the guys left behind would be punishment in retaliation.

And it came true. In every camp in the North, for two months, it was probably the worst sustained torture period. There were at least four or five main prisons. So [there was sustained torture of prisoners] not only the Zoo and the Zoo Annex, but at Hoa Lo, [known as the] Hanoi Hilton, at Plantation, Son Tay, and all the other camps in the North. The other severe torture case would have been Earl Cobiel, who was a victim of what was called the "Cuban program," the "Fidel" program.

We still don't know exactly who Fidel was. It's one of the remaining mysteries of the POW story. We think Fidel was a Cuban, a Spaniard of some type, probably Cuban from his appearance and from the language. He showed up one day along with an entourage of a few other Cubans, in August of 1967. Fidel showed up rather suddenly and was given special deferential treatment by the Vietnamese. It's hard to tell whether he was considered a Communist superior to the Vietnamese, or if the Vietnamese were just indulging this foreign visitor.

He was given free rein for almost the course of a year with about twenty POWs, two groups of ten each who were taken out of the Zoo Annex and put in a special part of the compound. It's hard to know exactly what the purpose of the program was. It appears that it was to turn out Manchurian candidates for early release, to punish guys so severely and indoctrinate them to the extent that they could be prepped for early release and then would just recite the Communist line when they got out. We don't know the details of this program because no one has ever determined Fidel's identity or the Cuban identities because they left after a year. Defense Intelligence Agency analysts have been trying to track this guy for years, trying to locate him.

All we know is that several of the POWs in this program, in particular Cobiel, were viciously tortured in kind of an alternation of the carrot and stick over a period of time. Cobiel's mistake was to be in bad shape to begin with, and Fidel assumed that Cobiel was faking insanity. He said, "We've got a faker here," and he just continued to beat the hell out of the guy in session after session until Cobiel was mindless, was just completely numb. He didn't know where he was, who he was, could not eat. He had to be force-fed by some of the others at the Zoo. He would die two years later.

SOLITARY WAS THE worst kind [of isolation] with darkness in a small cell, often with vermin and rats and things that you could hear but could not see. Occasionally, you might be let out for a half hour a day. The only break would be in receiving food, usually two meals a day around 10:00 and 3:00. The longest [to be] held in solitary would have been probably the seniors, Jeremiah Denton, James Stockdale, and Robinson Risner. Ben Purcell, who was an army lieutenant colonel in the South, spent a long time in solitary. Ernie Brace, a civilian captured in Laos, also spent a lot of time in solitary. Solitary required as much as anything, obviously, the ability to cope, to distract yourself, to kill time, to learn some way to survive, what Red McDaniel called the inner struggle, the mental struggle that all the POWs really had to go through. Torture occurred fairly regularly, but there were long periods in between where the real challenge was to mentally stay together and survive just the monotony of the routine and the boredom . . . . You used that time in solitary to restore yourself physically by just walking and pacing back and forth.

THEY WERE ROUTINELY afflicted with dysentery, with worms. In the South, again, there were even worse conditions because of the lack of fruit and vegetables—beriberi, scurvy type of diseases. In the North, they did have at least occasional access to, even if it was rotten, some fruits and vegetables, like pumpkin. One new arrival came and was delighted to see that there was actually some rye bread on his plate, until he noticed that the seeds were starting to move. There was very little in the way of palatable food, except during holidays and toward the end. Then they were being fattened up so that at the time of release they would look better and would reflect the so-called humane and lenient treatment that the Vietnamese had maintained that they had always extended to the POWs.

Food rations at the Zoo were cut drastically, and kitchen staff were no longer washing off the human fertilizer the Vietnamese used for their crops. In the South, in fact, the food was so bad that oftentimes the Vietnamese themselves were eating this tainted stuff. . . . Cat, who was the head of the North Vietnamese prison system, said, "Do you know you're eating shit?" And Denton, who was as tough as they come, said, "Does it have any protein in it?" Somehow they adapted. They were able to do this. They were able to down this stuff and eat it. [There were] problems with disease. Some of them died from disease. In fact, there were 113 POWs who died during the course of the captivity, during the course of a decade, and most of them from disease—dysentery, malaria, beriberi, food and stomach problems—rather than from torture.

Usually, when David Dellinger or Tom Hayden and Jane Fonda would come over there, the prisoners would be trotted out with trays of cookies and put in a fairly nice circumstance or might get a break in terms of some decent food and a break from monotony. . . . They were being exploited for the purposes of showing the humane and lenient side of the Vietnamese. The Haydens and the others would go back to the United States and then say that these guys were being treated fine, that there was no reason for concern. The effect of them being over there was to really enhance the propaganda campaign of the North Vietnamese, and it angered the POWs tremendously. Then they would hear Jane Fonda or Tom Hayden on the radio spouting about the American imperialists and the Vietnamese being so humane and lenient in the treatment of their prisoners, giving the wrong impression.

JEREMIAH DENTON, one of the top-ranking seniors, was captured early in the war in 1965. Denton had a reputation, even among the seniors, as being one of the strictest and one of the staunchest in terms of his adherence to the [U.S. military] Code of Conduct and requiring that the others adhere to it. Every now and then, Denton would get into some conflicts with Stockdale and Al Brudno and some of the others who had a slightly different interpretation of the code.

The so-called tap code was a system whereby the POWs communicated. Denton contributed an important new nuance or aspect, a so-called vocal tap code, whereby prisoners would be able to communicate, not just by a tapping on the wall but through coughing or sneezing. Which was very important because it was very easy to disguise that form in an environment in which everyone had either some form of malaria or some kind of coughing, some kind of lung disease from the chill of winter or the dampness. These places sounded like tuberculosis wards anyway, the various compounds, but they were often coughing in a certain code that Denton had developed.

There was a matrix for the tap code, which was probably the primary form of communication. It's a five-by-five matrix of the alphabet containing all the letters except the letter K, for which they substituted the letter C. They used this matrix and they could rotate the letters in which they were able to tap almost any kind of a message, often using an abbreviated form. For example, one of the early sign-offs that appears in almost all the messages was, "God bless you." The G would be in the second line, A-B-C-D-E-F-G—it's second row and the second vertical column. So it would be a two-two. The B would be one-two, first row across, second row down. They got to the point where they could do this with an almost blinding speed, and they were able to use this system of tapping either through the wall or they could apply it, as Denton did, to sneezes and coughs or even sweeping with a broom.

There was a lot of black humor. They were sustained by humor, and they each would have kind of a signature sneeze in which they would sneeze saying "bullshit," or worse obscenities, in their sneezes.

JAMES STOCKDALE, by all accounts, even when compared with Denton and the other leaders, was probably the most respected of the POWs. He was a Congressional Medal of Honor winner who was willing to slash his wrists and kill himself before giving information on the communications system at Hoa Lo, in this particular compound called Vegas. Stockdale also was very important in terms of developing a version of the Code of Conduct, a rendering of it, an interpretation of it that would be conveyed and communicated throughout the whole prison system. It was considered a reasonable, commonsensical approach to how much torture the POWs could be expected to take. [It helped shape] attitudes, [for example,] Do you have to try to escape, even if it means risking your life and the lives of others?

The Code of Conduct, which is what Stockdale's and, for that matter, other senior leaders' instructions were based on, is a rather short Code of Conduct. It came after the Korean experience. The basic concept was stick to the big four: your name, your rank, serial number, date of birth. Stockdale developed [another] system. . . . that dealt with some of the main experiences that the POWs would face and how they should deal with those experiences.

DIETER DENGLER was a naval aviator who was captured in '66, in Laos. There were very few POWs who got out of Laos alive; even at the end of the war, at homecoming nine POWs came out of Laos. . . . The big question about MIAs and the big mystery about how many were ever in the prison system really is in the case of Laos. We just don't know because they were held singly and [were] very isolated cases. One or two would be held in a cave. We know a lot of guys went down in good parachutes—or at least three hundred cases where guys who were downed in Laos appeared to be in a position to survive and to become prisoners. But we only know of nine who came out in 1973 and several who escaped, including Dengler, along the way.

Dengler had a phenomenal story, and it is told in a book that he has written. It's so phenomenal a lot of the analysts who reviewed it were not sure of its accuracy, partly because Dengler had been so dehydrated and may have been hallucinating and was not sure himself of exactly what he experienced. In any case, he did manage to get out. He managed to escape, along with several others who were in this one group. He was the only one [to survive the attempt]. Duane Martin was an army helicopter pilot who joined Dengler in this escape, and we know that Martin died along the way when they encountered—literally—villagers with machetes.

What remains a discrepancy . . . is the case of Eugene DeBruin, who went out with Dengler; his body has never been recovered. We don't know what happened to him. We just know that he didn't make it out. There were reports that DeBruin would be spotted in certain sites, certain areas in Laos, but he did not come out in 1973. He is one of the remaining really intriguing discrepancy cases. DeBruin's brother, Jerome DeBruin, is a professor at the University of Toledo, who has made it his life's work . . . to try to get more information on DeBruin. But we don't know what happened.

DeBruin didn't make it out, but Dengler did. He was on a mountaintop and had just about run out of food; he was eating frogs, he was eating leaves, and finally he was spotted by a rescue aircraft and taken out.

THERE WERE MANY others. George "Bud" Day, who won the Congressional Medal of Honor and who was as tough a nut as anyone over there, as tough a resister, and had as much fortitude and strength as anyone. Bud Day had the most problems with what was called a kneeling torture, where they would simply have to kneel for long periods of time, often on a pebble or a stone. As he said in his memoir, "Try that sometime for four or five hours and see what it feels like." Day had more problems with that than with the ropes.

JOHN MCCAIN was unquestionably a hard resister, hard-line, courageous, with tremendous fortitude, just to have survived his initial injuries. McCain landed in prison in Hanoi after a shoot down in as bad a condition as any prisoner who survived a crash or a shoot down—a bailout. He had a bad back. He had a broken leg and arms. He would be in casts for much of his captivity, in fact. He almost drowned on landing in Hanoi—he landed in a lake in the city and with his equipment on. Somehow, despite his injuries, he got out of the lake and ended up at [a prison called] the Plantation and resisted indoctrination and resisted interrogation. The Vietnamese knew that he was the son of an admiral, Admiral John McCain, in the Pacific; they knew they had a prize. They tried desperately to get him to tape or to write something that they could use for propaganda purposes. He refused. He was punished repeatedly. Somehow, he recovered from his injuries with the help of a couple of cell mates who nursed him along. He would become one of the leaders in the resistance.

EVERETT "Ev" ALVAREZ Jr., of course, is famous as the so-called "Old Man of the North." He was the first pilot captured over North Vietnam in August of 1964, so Alvarez was there almost a decade altogether. He came out in 1973. Around 1966, Alvarez was taken through the town. They often would take prisoners on a tour of bombed-out sites as part of the indoctrination process. They would take prisoners out "on the town." Many of the POWs actually welcomed this as a change of pace from the monotony of being in their cell for all but twenty, twenty-two hours a day.

MANY GUYS CAME out with injuries that never healed—back injuries, leg injuries, of course, all kinds of scars and other effects. The ratchet cuffs were another very difficult thing for them to handle, along with the rope torture. Sometimes the degree or the severity of the torture would be inadvertent. The Vietnamese didn't realize that at times they were using some cuffs and manacles that had been used on Vietnamese prisoners; they had smaller wrists and so these things tended to be a lot smaller in dimension. So, for the Americans, even when these things would be clamped on and were not ratcheted, they caused tremendous pain that the Vietnamese didn't even realize. Using manacles and shackles . . . created pain from the beginning and then these things would be ratcheted.

What was really significant here is the longevity. These guys were the longest-held POWs in American history. There were some who were POWs almost a decade: Alvarez and Floyd "Jim" Thompson, called the "Old Man of the South." He was captured in '64 and he came out in '73. These were POWs who underwent repeated instances of torture and of just having to withstand some very difficult conditions in terms of the climate, in terms of sanitation, hygiene, malnutrition over a period of time.

[Some of the POWs were] on one of the aircraft finally taking off from Hanoi in March 1973. They were stoic almost up to that point. They were told not to show any emotion until they got on the plane, not to give the Vietnamese any satisfaction, but they were also pretty enervated by that time. Finally, when they realized they were leaving captivity, some of them perhaps after seven or eight years, they just let it all out in absolute joy and elation.

We decided on the title, *Honor Bound*, because it captured both concepts of the captivity, their being bound, but also the importance of honor. That was the key thing, to retain your honor and to observe the Code of Conduct. Their symbolic phrase was to return with honor.

The Culture Wars
1975–2002

The Rise of the Neoconservatives

by

IRVING KRISTOL

NINA J. EASTON

Like Norman Podhoretz, his former fellow colleague at Commentary *magazine, Irving Kristol has moved politically from the left to the right during his long career as a writer and thinker. He told us his own story when he appeared on* Booknotes *on September 5, 1995, to discuss* Neo-Conservatism: The Autobiography of an Idea, *published by The Free Press in 1995. Washington, D.C. writer Nina J. Easton told us more about the growth of neoconservatism when she visited us on September 12, 2000, to discuss* Gang of Five: Leaders at the Center of the Conservative Crusade, *published by Simon & Schuster in 2000. Ms. Easton's book covers the careers of five leaders of the neoconservative movement. A generation younger than Norman Podhoretz and Irving Kristol, this small group of ideologues, including Kristol's son Bill, mobilized against what they saw as the overwhelmingly liberal social environment of the 1960s and have since become some of the power players of modern conservatism.*

IRVING KRISTOL

[I FIRST HEARD the term "neoconservatism"] sometime in the mid-1970s. It was not my term; I did not invent it. I believe it was invented by someone who was criticizing me and thought it was a term of opprobrium. I decided that it was a pretty good description of what I was thinking and feeling, so I ran with it. Neoconservatism refers to a constellation of opinions and views not traditionally conservative but [which are] conservative and certainly not liberal. Since I and others who have been called neoconservatives moved from being liberals to being a kind of conservative, then "neoconservatism" seemed like a pretty good term.

Intellectual and political ideas were more in flux in the 1970s than either before or after. That was the decade of transition. In 1968 I still voted for Hubert Humphrey, but by 1974, I realized I was going to become a Republican.

[I've been a neo-Marxist, a neo-Trotskyist, a neosocialist, a neoliberal, and now a neoconservative.] That pretty much traces the trajectory of my political beliefs. I've never been comfortable with any of those doctrines because I always saw problems inherent in [them]. I even see problems inherent in conservatism today. Anyone who has studied the history of political thought would be bound to see problems with conservatism today, which is why I still call myself a neoconservative, though in truth, those who ten years ago would have been called neoconservatives, these days simply call themselves conservatives. The conservative movement has expanded to include us.

One of the reasons I have always looked back with some good feelings toward my rather brief period as a Trotskyist is that I met my wife there. I was twenty and she was eighteen. We were married a year later and have been married now for fifty-three years, so that successful marriage came out of the Trotskyist movement. Also I met many of my lifelong friends there, and I got a very good, intensive, early education in Marxism and Leninism, which carried me right through the Cold War. I really didn't have to do any studying in Marxism and Leninism after I left the Trotskyists.

[I WENT TO] City College [in New York in the 1930s]. It was a wonderful place. It had a lot of very bright students, very much interested in politics and very much interested in ideas. . . . The faculty, I don't think, was all that distinguished, but it didn't matter. Most of us students ended up educating each other, and we learned a lot. I got a very good education at City College, not all of it in the classroom.

[I sat in] alcove no. 1, the anti-Communist or anti-Stalinist alcove, where socialists of various kinds and some liberals would congregate and argue and exchange ideas, and it was a very nice alcove. It was my second home. All the alcoves were in an arc around the cafeteria. [Those who joined me in alcove no. 1 included] Daniel Bell; Melvin Lasky; Philip Selznick, now professor emeritus of sociology at Berkeley; and Seymour Martin Lipset, also a professor for many years at Berkeley. A lot of people who became fairly well-known academics were [there]. Irving Howe was in that alcove; he became a well-known literary critic. In terms of subsequent careers, the alcove produced quite a lot of people of some distinction.

The Communists—that is to say, the Stalinists, the people who were apologetic for the Soviet Union, [sat in alcove no. 2]. They did not produce as many distinguished people as we did, because they didn't have the kind of intellectual stimulation we had. Alcove no. 2 was forbidden to even argue with us; that was the way the Communist organization worked. Young Communists dominated alcove no. 2, and they felt bad having conversations or even disputes with Trotskyists or socialists or any sort of non-Communist, left-wing person.

[TO BE AN INTELLECTUAL] means you have to be able to cope with abstract ideas comfortably, or uncomfortably sometimes, but that's all right too, wrestling with them. I suppose most people can get along very well without coping with abstract ideas, and that's okay too.

[Reading theology] is a way of being introduced to and getting acquainted with very deep and large ideas, and I like those deep and large ideas. I'm no theologian, though I've written about religion. I like being stimulated by those very large ideas, about the meaning of life and whether there is God and what is God, if there is God, and what is the relation of organized religion to morality. All of those questions tantalize me.

I've never had a problem with God, never. Even when I was a young Trotskyist, I never had a problem with God—the so-called existence of God was never a problem for me. However you define God, what you mean when you use the word "God" is a serious theological matter. But I had no doubt, ever since I read the opening of the Bible, that, yes, there is such a thing as original sin, and we all live with it. And if you want to understand the human condition, reading the opening of the Bible is as good a place as any, the best, I think. And so that part of religion has simply never been a problem for me.

COMMENTARY WAS FOUNDED in 1945. It was published by the American Jewish Committee, and it aimed at reaching both a Jewish and non-Jewish audience. We would now call it a somewhat highbrow magazine, and it published a lot of the intellectuals from *Partisan Review*. It published a lot of non-Jews, of course, and I was an editor there for five years.

During the McCarthy goings-on [in the 1950s, I wrote a piece on Senator Joseph McCarthy]. I was anti-McCarthy, as we all were at *Commentary* magazine, where I was then the managing editor. I wrote this piece attacking a lot of the Communist fellow travelers, who were being either fairly or unfairly attacked by Senator McCarthy. Some of them were being fairly attacked, I do believe. I explained why McCarthy was so popular, whereas the liberal intellectuals were having so much trouble. I wrote one sentence that did the trick.

The sentence was to the effect that the one thing American people know about Senator McCarthy is that he's an anti-Communist. They don't know this about the liberal intellectuals, with some good reason, because so many of the liberal intellectuals were fellow travelers at the time. And for some reason, that got me into disfavor with a lot of people for calling McCarthy an anti-Communist—they said he wasn't sincerely an anti-Communist. I don't know that he was sincere about anything, but that's not the issue. He was certainly perceived to be a sincere anti-Communist. A lot of the intellectuals thought I was being unfair to liberal intellectuals. On the whole, I don't think I was. I wasn't attacking all liberal intellectuals. That particular article . . . exposed liberals, in general, to a lot of ridicule and considerable scorn.

[IN 1976] I TOOK a leave of absence from my teaching at NYU, a sabbatical, to learn economics. I felt that economics was becoming important. Up until that point, I assumed that John Maynard Keynes had said everything there was to say about economics. But once we got stagnation and inflation at the same time, it was quite clear that someone had to revise economics. Although I knew I couldn't do it myself, at least I wanted to understand what was going on.

I took the year off, and I came to Washington to the American Enterprise Institute (AEI). Mr. Ford had just lost the election, [and Ford administration staffers] Laurence Silberman, Bob Bork, and [Antonin] Scalia all came out of the government. Before going on to their other careers as judges or as professors, they spent something like six months at AEI. We had no cafeteria then, we had no lunchroom, so the four of us brown-bagged it every day and just talked. Then Jude Wanniski came down on a fellowship—he was writing his book [*The Way the World Works*] then—and he started talking to us about supply-side economics, which was very interesting and about which we knew nothing, and that was a very stimulating period for all of us.

At our luncheons, we never talked about law, about which, of course, I knew very little. We talked mainly about religion and economics, religion being my subject and economics being Jude Wanniski's subject. Everyone was interested, and we became very good friends and have been very good friends, all of us, since then. . . . These are not just lawyers, these are not just legal thinkers. All of these people are what we would call intellectuals, namely [people who] have a very broad interest in ideas. And the thing they liked about being at AEI is they were able to indulge that interest in ideas.

RONALD REAGAN WAS persuaded to adopt supply-side economics by [Republican congressman from New York] Jack Kemp, who got it from Wanniski and, to some degree, from myself. And he had a Council of Economic Advisers during his campaign. Of the twelve members of that council, one was in favor of supply-side economics. All the other very distinguished economists were originally against it. But Jack Kemp persuaded Ronald Reagan this was the way to go, and in the end, they all fell into line, and that's the way ideas have impact.

I ADMIRED JOHN F. Kennedy and voted for him, but the importance of Ronald Reagan for someone like myself, a neoconservative, is that he brought neoconservatism into the conservative spectrum. Ronald Reagan was the first Republican president to praise Franklin D. Roosevelt. Newt Gingrich has since followed him in that. This was a breakthrough. It meant that the Republican Party, unlike, say, the Goldwater Republican Party of 1964, was no longer fighting against the New Deal; that it was possible to think of reforming many of the institutions bequeathed to us by the New Deal, but that the issue of the New Deal was behind us. And acceptance of the New Deal in principle, if not in all of its details, was one of the basic differences between neoconservatives and traditional Republican conservatives, who were still fighting against the New Deal. Once Ronald Reagan began praising Franklin D. Roosevelt as a kind of predecessor, . . . the Republican Party changed. Not everyone in the Republican Party has changed, but it is an important fact that these two leaders who helped define the modern Republican Party spoke so well of Franklin D. Roosevelt.

IDEAS DO MATTER. The right has rarely understood that, the right being more interested in pragmatic affairs: business and government as an administrative organism. One of the things I think neoconservatism has contributed to contemporary conservatism is a strong belief and a strong acknowledgment that ideas do matter. . . . The presidency of Reagan and the current control of Congress show that ideas do matter.

Ideas filter down through the educational system, through the media, through a few politicians who are always hungry for ideas by which to distinguish themselves from the crowd of other politicians. Before you know it, an idea has gained some momentum, and there it is on the agenda. A lot of it is accident. You never know how and where and when ideas are going to impinge on reality.

NINA J. EASTON

Bill Kristol, Ralph Reed, David McIntosh, Grover Norquist, and Clint Bolick compose my gang of five. I tried to look at what I call the flip side of the baby boom generation. These are folks who emerged on campus in the 1970s and [were] social pariahs on campus . . . at that time. They came to Washington with Ronald Reagan, behind a victor. They were part of the baby boom generation, so they have the same personality qualities that you find among '60s leftists, that sort of contrarianism. They were rebels; they were insurgents. And they remain so today.

Each of these men represents a different piece of the movement, a different school of thought. . . . Kristol represents the Straussians, . . . Bolick represents libertarians . . . David McIntosh, the University of Chicago Law School [group, Reed the Christian right, and Norquist the antitax, big-tent combatants]. They're that tail end of the baby boom generation, and they tell a generational story. Their stories are interwoven enough that I can narrate a story through the 1970s, '80s, and '90s.

I call [my book] a hidden history of American politics because this particular generation of conservatives has tremendously influenced the political debate, . . . everything from political muckraking to abortion politics to the budget battles of the '90s. These guys were very key in helping shape those debates. They all got involved in college. The one thing that motivated them was the fact that they felt like they were not able to speak, that they were being shut out of the process. They went in and they made themselves a part of the process.

BILL KRISTOL FREQUENTLY gives opinions on the major [television] networks. He's the publisher of the *Weekly Standard*, quite an influential conservative magazine. Grover Norquist is an antitax lobbyist. But that's only one piece of his claim to fame because this mythical right-wing conspiracy we hear about so much from Hillary Clinton and others would probably be taking place in Grover Norquist's conference room every Wednesday morning when he gathers dozens of activists from the right to plot strategy. David McIntosh [was a] congressman from Indiana who graduated from the University of Chicago Law School. He's very smart and came to Congress with the so-called Republican revolution in 1995. He was a coleader of that freshman class, who, we all remember, raised quite a ruckus in Washington. Clint Bolick is a constitutional lawyer. He's at the Institute for Justice here in Washington, which he cofounded. He is a leader of the school choice movement throughout the country and is also famous for sinking the nomination of Lani Guinier, a civil rights appointee, during the early years of the Clinton administration. He's an anti–affirmative action activist as well. Ralph Reed . . . built the Christian Coalition into a major political powerhouse in the 1990s.

THIS [GROUP] PLAYS to win. They think they're going to win, as opposed to the Barry Goldwater generation, who played on the fringe of politics for so long. Or [conservative activist] Paul Weyrich, who after the last election and the impeachment battle . . . wrote that memo basically saying he was going to check out of politics. He was through with it. These guys don't play like that. They want to return to the days of Ronald Reagan, and they think they will. Even though there's somewhat a sense of being an underdog and they feel they've battled a liberal press and liberal groups that are well funded and [have] a better standing with the press in Washington—they also believe themselves part of the process, winners. It's not an accident that they became an important part of the Republican Party.

Some [in this group are] friends and some are bitter rivals. The biggest rivalry is between the circle around Grover Norquist and the circle of thinkers around Bill Kristol, partly because Grover Norquist tends to be a populist type. He tends to draw the gun crowd around him. He tends to talk in a language that we heard a lot in the mid-nineties, revolutionary rhetoric. Kristol talks more about virtue and the importance of family, and the coarsening of the culture. Grover Norquist listens to Janis Joplin. He doesn't care about those things.

Norquist feels like the thinkers around Kristol "write and they talk and they get on these big TV shows, but what have they done for the cause lately?" [Kristol's faction is] also viewed as a bit disloyal because he's willing to criticize fellow conservatives, which does not go over very well in the Norquist camp. Frankly, that's probably the biggest division, the iconoclasm of somebody like Bill Kristol, who is willing to criticize. During the [1996] Bob Dole presidential campaign, Kristol was a thorn in that man's side through the entire campaign. That really rankled a lot of loyal Republican conservatives.

They're from very different backgrounds. Bill Kristol is from a very elite background. His father is Irving Kristol, the neoconservative; his mother, [Gertrude Himmelfarb,] is a well-known Victorian scholar. He grew up in Manhattan . . . and went to a very tony, upscale, and intellectually rigorous prep school, [then] to Harvard. [He is] very much a part of the establishment. . . . Clint Bolick [by contrast is] the son of a welder from New Jersey.

NORQUIST IS ACTUALLY famous for his bachelorhood. He has a group house on Capitol Hill that has served as a nesting ground and party central for his fellow comrades, as he calls them. He borrows a lot of Leninist-Marxist rhetoric to make his point. Norquist is interesting because he's the son of an engineer, and he looks at politics as systems. When he was fighting the Clinton health care plan, for example, he said, "Clinton's health care plan was an attempt to put more Democrats on the payroll," because government workers vote Democratic and it's going to expand the government. That's how he views politics, like systems.

Norquist went to Harvard. He came down to Washington, started with the National Taxpayers Union, and went back to Harvard to finish his MBA, really just to satisfy his father. He grew up in a very, very tiny suburb of Boston, a beautiful area, with the kind of regulation that Grover hates; a lot of very nice suburbs without the trash you usually see with suburbs, a lot of strict zoning, two-acre plots.

DAVID MCINTOSH comes from a small town in Indiana. He lost his father when he was five years old. . . . His mother's a nurse. . . . A lot of liberals think that Republicans and conservatives just come from elite backgrounds. [That's not necessarily true.] McIntosh is a good example. His mother struggled. She had four children. He was the oldest, and he was kind of in charge of them. He was a very unathletic boy, but brilliant. He would sit in his room reading math books while the kids outside were playing. They'd say, "David, come out," and he wouldn't come out.

His mother expected her children to be able to debate, to build a fine argument, a reasoned argument. This was a trait handed down from her side of the family; Slows was her last name. They were called the Slows Slayers, the folks in the family who could really argue the best. If you couldn't make a good argument at the table and stand up and reason your way out of an issue that you wanted to defend, you could be laughed off the table. So that trait is part of his family and led to him being quite articulate, but also a bit combative . . . in debate.

McIntosh went to Yale. Like a lot of conservatives on campus in the '70s, he moved into the debate society, because on campus in the '70s, liberalism really did hold sway. It held the moral high ground and a lot of conservatives were written off. This idea of political correctness that we talked about in the '80s and '90s [was] a term that wasn't even invented in the '70s. The most striking thing about my research was to what extent liberal orthodoxy held sway on particularly elite campuses. If you had conservative views, you could be dismissed, ignored, laughed at. David actually started as a Democrat, but because of the liberal orthodoxy he and like-minded colleagues felt [existed] at Yale, they moved in the direction of what was known as the Party of the Right in the Yale Political Union. [The Party of the Right] was willing to debate really fundamental issues, was willing to have adventurous debates, and was willing to risk being called even anti-Democratic or racist, for example, if they challenged affirmative action policies. This appealed to David, this challenging of conventional wisdom.

[After Yale] he went to the great University of Chicago Law School, where great minds do challenge conventional wisdom, particularly in the '70s. [It was a] very free market–oriented school. He graduated from there and went on to become a foe of regulation. He worked for Vice President Quayle on the Competitiveness Council. Doing away with the regulation became his kind of forte.

McIntosh was a cofounder of the Federalist Society with some of his colleagues from Yale, Steven Calabresi and Lee Liberman. It started as a student group, but it soon got funding from former Treasury Secretary Bill Simon's organization, the Olin Foundation, a very big conservative funder. Irving Kristol was also involved in getting funding into this group early on. In the '80s, it became a real clearinghouse for anybody who was conservative, who wanted to work for the Reagan administration as a judge or clerk. It became much more of a professional society as well as a campus society. Today, it still is an important fixture on the Washington scene and in the conservative legal movement.

CLINT BOLICK['S] . . . father died when he was twelve, and his family also struggled financially. Interestingly, Clint went to UC–Davis Law School the year after the famed Bakke decision. [Allan Bakke had applied to the UC–Davis Medical School and was denied admission in both 1973 and 1974. He filed a lawsuit,] the so-called angry white male challenging affirmative action programs. The Supreme Court eventually said the UC–Davis Medical School program went too far, but that generally affirmative action programs, taking race into consideration, is okay.

Bolick went to Davis at a time when the campus was very prickly and sensitive about issues of race and really wanting to prove its commitment to diversity. He got caught up in a very interesting subplot going on at the Davis Law School, where he was the lone opponent of the affirmative action program. It was a very lonely, very bitter battle for him. He's actually a very idealistic person. I know we're not supposed to find idealists on the right, but he is. He's somebody who tends to wear his heart on his sleeve, and he tends to not let these kind of battles roll off him; they hurt.

He's a libertarian. . . . Libertarians don't always like to be called conservative. Libertarians believe in a limited government; that people should be left alone. Sometimes, especially in the '70s and when Clint ran for a state assembly seat as a libertarian in 1980, they would veer left on issues like drug legalization, for example, or Carter's draft registration, and they'd veer right on budget issues. So he is a libertarian, although he's come to call himself a big-government libertarian in that he does view more of a role for government than a lot of the libertarian purists, and often he gets in trouble with them for that reason.

Bolick likes [Thomas Paine, a pamphleteer during the American Revolution] because he coined an important antigovernment sentiment that Bolick has latched onto. Paine was willing to stand up to the king. He was willing to stand against slavery. He was also, however, a proponent of the French Revolution. He was this rootless guy. He was hardly a symbol of traditional family values. That's why a lot of conservatives keep saying to Clint, "Don't use Thomas Paine." But Clint loves Thomas Paine's revolutionary phrase, "We have the power to begin the world over again." Clint uses that a lot.

THERE ARE TWO sides to Ralph Reed. There's this hardball, play-to-win-at-any-cost politico on one side, and there's this very considered, brilliant strategist with good motivation on the other. They kind of run together. . . . He spent most of his youth in Miami. His father was a military man and they moved around. He moved to a small town in Georgia for the last three years of high school. He's often seen as somebody from the South, small town, Bible Belt. In fact he did not fit in with this Bible Belt town at all. They saw him as this mouthy little guy who was just willing to elbow anybody aside to get where he wanted to go. He was not well liked at high school.

He went to the University of Georgia. In 1980, when Ronald Reagan came in, he built the College Republicans from about five people. They used to call themselves the "closet Republicans"—they could all fit in a closet. He built them into a powerhouse on campus, and he was brilliant at doing this. At the same time, there was the other side of Ralph. He stole the College Republican election. He packed the room. He changed the constitution for the group so that you could sign up that day and become a member and therefore vote. He went out and he solicited, particularly fraternity brothers. He wasn't in a fraternity, but he'd solicit from the frats and promise them a beer keg party afterwards. [They either paid five dollars apiece] or he even apparently kicked in the five bucks if they couldn't pay.

It was legal that he got the constitution [of the College Republicans] changed. It was very upsetting to the people around him, though. He was trying to get his ally elected. [It was] very upsetting, that meeting at which they voted his ally in instead of the original candidate. There were tears; there was anger. The main group of College Republicans broke off and became Young Republicans, they were so angry.

He was the lamp-shade guy, the guy who was wilder, edgier. There was this danger in Ralph, which in a bigger boy might have been siphoned off into sports, but he wasn't athletic. He was small, and there was this dangerous edge to him. One friend of his told me a story. They were in the back of a pickup truck and Ralph was shooting blanks at people with his rifle to scare them on a Saturday night. There was the other story about him walking along a ravine with a couple friends and he just threw himself over the ravine just for laughs, to shock everybody.

It was an ugly period for him. He was fired for plagiarism from the school newspaper, where he wrote some terrific, brilliant columns, but also some that just went over the edge. . . . He plagiarized a review of the movie *Gandhi*, the Richard Attenborough movie that came out in 1982. He quoted verbatim a review in *Commentary*. I actually went back and checked both, and it's a pretty fair assessment that he took huge pieces of it. That was a very difficult time for him.

The debate society [at the University of Georgia] was known as the Demosthenian Society. He was distrusted enough on campus that the debate society blackballed him the first time he wanted to get in. Literally, they voted members in by placing in black balls and white balls. Here was the guy who wrote brilliant columns, could debate circles around anybody, should have had a lot of friends in the society, and should have been elected. But one of his friends stood up and said, "We can't trust him. We don't trust him."

I [found all this out because I] interviewed classmates of his, most of his friends. I was really surprised for all the profiles that have been done of Ralph, how many people hadn't been interviewed. These are very close friends of his from that time. The friend who stood up to give the speech said, "This was the hardest time in my life because I felt like he was a friend. And I knew him to be a friend, but I was worried that he would drag the society down into the mud." To be fair to Ralph, he mended his ways in the eyes of the society, and they did elect him in a year later.

The fact that he was drawn to this kind of edgy side made a lot of his friends nervous about him, even in the College Republicans. He [joined] Grover Norquist at the national College Republicans and basically turned it into a Communist cell of the right. They purged the leadership of all the moderates. They built up a system where the hard-core conservatives would be in control. They changed the constitution to eliminate entire bodies where the moderates were. . . . In fact, they convinced moderates to vote themselves out of office. So before you knew it, in the '80s you had this College Republican organization with 1,000 members nationwide, access to Republican money, . . . and running some real hard-core campaigns. The Republican Party wasn't very happy about the College Republicans' access to money, by the way, because they felt like they were wasting money.

A VERY IMPORTANT thing to understand about the school of philosophy that Kristol comes from is that these are not people of faith. They believe in religion for other people but not for themselves. There's a whole crop of graduate students [who called themselves] Straussians, followers of Leo Strauss, the philosopher, who believed that a virtuous citizenry is much more important than equality or opportunity. . . . Harvey Mansfield, a very preeminent Straussian at Harvard, taught Bill, and that was key. What's interesting about the Straussians—and very much not known—is they've defended religion, even in the creation battle [between] the pro-creationists [and others] in Kansas. They defended the religious right in the '90s, but they themselves are not religious.

Clinton Bolick, for example, was an atheist most of his life. He now describes himself as a recovering atheist, but he was very much in the Ayn Rand libertarian school. Ralph Reed found faith in 1993; he became born again. He decided to turn his life over to Jesus and that became his motivating factor in life. He was not a big churchgoer before that. He was, at the time, really living dangerously. . . . He is still religious; [he and his wife] go to a Protestant evangelical church.

THEY'RE ALL GOING to continue [being influential], and that's why I chose [to write about] them. . . . Bill Kristol will remain exceedingly visible. He knows how to stay visible. He got fired from ABC and he's now on *Meet the Press* all the time. [We'll continue to see] David McIntosh, [who left Congress to run for governor of Indiana and lost] in politics—he likes it, he thrives on it. Clint Bolick is looking forward to the day where he can walk the steps of the Supreme Court to fight a school choice case that he is convinced will change the lives of inner-city children throughout America. Maybe Ralph Reed will run for office someday, who knows?

The Forgotten Radio Scripts of
Ronald Reagan

by

KIRON K. SKINNER

Before Ronald Reagan was elected president in 1980, he delivered a daily radio broadcast heard on more than three hundred radio stations. Kiron K. Skinner, doing postdoctoral research on the Cold War, discovered handwritten drafts of these broadcasts among boxes of documents at the Reagan Library. Her discovery led to a book, Reagan in His Own Hand: The Writings of Ronald Reagan That Reveal His Revolutionary Vision for America, *published by The Free Press in 2001, which Ms. Skinner coedited with Martin and Annelise Anderson. In a* Booknotes *interview on March 21, 2001, Ms. Skinner, an assistant professor at Carnegie Mellon University, talked about her discovery and the portrait of Ronald Reagan that emerged from his handwritten scripts.*

RONALD REAGAN gave radio broadcasts between 1975 and the end of 1979. After he stepped down as governor at the end of '74, he went into private life, but not really. He wasn't in an elective position but he worked very hard in the public space. He decided to give a radio broadcast to support himself. It was daily, five days a week, about three minutes a day. He gave over 1,000 in the late 1970s. He stopped them to campaign for the presidency in late '75 and '76. When Gerald Ford defeated him at the Republican Convention in '76, he turned back to the radio broadcasts and continued them until the fall of 1979.

Reagan also had a [syndicated] newspaper column. . . . They were biweekly by the late '70s. The radio broadcasts were, many of them, written by Reagan. We found over 670 in his own handwriting in the archives. He probably wrote more. That's what we found in the archives where they were saved. . . . Reagan says in the archives in several letters that between the radio broadcast and his newspaper column, which went to, at its height, 226 newspapers, he was reaching 20 million Americans a week.

He wrote about fifteen [scripts] at a time. Every three weeks, he would go into a taping studio in Hollywood . . . and go through fifteen of them so that they would last for three weeks. Peter Hannaford, who helped Reagan with all of them, said that Reagan early on made a commitment to arrange his life around his taping schedule. So although he was giving [several] speeches a month around the country on behalf of conservative causes, he was always in the radio studio to do the broadcasts. He would write them on planes, at the ranch, in the back of cars, wherever he could write them.

He wrote most of them on yellow sheets, legal size, though some were on letter size. . . . What was convincing to our editors, eventually, was the actual drafts; when they saw Reagan's writing, when they saw the range of issues that he thought about, when they saw the sources he used, his notes in the margins, and the clarity of his thought. That's what eventually got a book contract for us. Reagan sold the book.

IN 1996 I WAS working in the Reagan Library [where I found these documents]. Most of the research in the 1990s that I saw in the scholarly literature [about the end of the Cold War] focused on the Soviet side and on Eastern Europe, and for good reasons. The revolutions were fascinating to people, and all of a sudden, documents were opening up that scholars had never seen before. But I was interested in the American contribution so I wrote Nancy Reagan and said, "I don't think there's enough reporting on the American side of the story, and I'd like to look at the president's private papers." I didn't know what would be there, but I thought there might be something to help me to unravel the American contribution. She granted me access to the papers and hundreds of archival boxes. [After about two years] I came upon, . . . literally, thousands of pieces of paper of Reagan's handwriting. It took a while to figure out what it meant. Some of it was disorganized. Some of it was organized in file folders. . . . It was fascinating.

I had to pause from my own work . . . to figure out what to do with these. I went to Martin and Annelise Anderson and we decided to join forces and produce this book, that it was so important. We all had major projects on our own that we were working on, but we decided that this was such a special set of documents we had to bring it to light. . . . The Andersons brought a special quality to the project because they'd worked with Reagan; they'd seen him write. But even they were surprised at the breadth and diversity of what he wrote.

Martin Anderson and Annelise Anderson are economists who worked very closely with Reagan in the '76 and '80 campaigns. Martin traveled with Reagan on the plane and was a close adviser. I saw his name quite often in the archives, and Annelise's as well. They're fellows at the Hoover Institution, and since I was there, I could go to them and show them documents, and they helped me understand what I was seeing. That collaboration became central because Reagan . . . covered almost every issue facing the U.S., domestic and foreign: abortion, Africa, arms control, weapons systems, taxation, regulatory policy. He was doing this all by himself, but we, as scholars, . . . focus narrowly on a single area that we specialize in. So the Andersons and I really needed each other for this story. They could do the domestic and economic issues and I could focus more on the foreign policy side, and then we did [some] parts together. They also had the confidence of Mrs. Reagan.

REAGAN WROTE privately and he never talked about it. He thought and he read privately and he didn't try to expose it. He never told people that he'd done all of this work before the presidency. If you look at some of the head notes we wrote, we tried to link things that Reagan wrote about before the presidency to actual things he did as president but never told people about. He just felt that they either knew him or they had heard him on the radio, and he felt no reason, no need to brag or expose his intelligence. I think it fueled the assessment that he didn't know very much.

When you read what he wrote in the margins and when you listen to what he said, it's really authentic Reagan. We interviewed so many people [who] were with Reagan all the time. Many of the speechwriters during the presidency, they know this story; it just never came out. One thing that Martin Anderson did in the interviews with Nancy Reagan and some of the others, . . . at the end of the interviews, he would say, "Who has asked you these questions?" For the most part, they would say, "No one's ever asked us about this, about his writing life, about his thinking life, about his reading life." So this is not a surprise to those who know him.

[This book] changes everything [about his legacy]. What's surprising is how fast the reassessment has begun. This really does change our understanding of Reagan, of the idea, the notion that he didn't know very much, that he didn't do very much, that he was handled by advisers. It now means we've got to look at him differently and at his mode of operation. It changes our understanding of him and also of the American presidency.

What's interesting about this book is that it's about the presidency, in a way, but there are very few documents from the presidential period. We look at the period right before the presidency, that five years about which I've watched television programs, specials on Reagan, that said, "Oh, in the late

'70s, he was at a Santa Barbara ranch chopping wood, relaxing." I think it suggests that we [must] begin to look at different periods [of a president's life] to understand what a president will do and follow [their] paper trail very closely.

Most scholars have not looked at Reagan's activities when he was not in office. His gubernatorial years have been mined and the presidency hasn't been completely mined, but there is work [that's been done] there. But this [discovery] sheds light on the presidency in a period where Reagan wasn't in office. To understand him, we looked, in much the way that social historians do, in a kind of bottom-up way. We were looking at documents that were outside of the government channels, that Reagan wrote himself, that were in his private possession. I think we get a sense of his mode of operation, how private he was, how contemplative he was, and we did that without focusing on the presidential years and the big events that happened.

He could take a speech or a document or a piece of material, and work with it and develop a story. And so he did on the foreign policy side. He would really rely on experts . . . to help him make the case he wanted to make. He went everywhere and he would use almost any source he felt was credible, but [also] was helping him make his point. He joined the Committee on the Present Danger, which was led by neoconservative Democrats in the late 1970s, and they actually came to his camp . . . . He would use sources from all over the place, not just conservative sources. He cites *Human Events* and *National Review* and those conservative publications, but other things as well, the *Economist*, the *Los Angeles Times,* of all things, but also government documents. That was surprising for many who've seen the book who were even close to Reagan.

NSC-68, National Security Council 68, was a centerpiece document of containment for the U.S. in the Cold War, drafted by Paul Nitze [director of the] Policy Planning Staff in the State Department and presented to President Truman in 1950. It was declassified in 1975. Reagan devoted two radio broadcasts to *NSC-68*. I actually went back and looked at that huge government document to see what Reagan was quoting, and he was quoting from all over that document, trying to talk about what rearmament means in peacetime and why it was important and what the Soviet threat was like.

Around 1978 Richard Allen came on as a foreign policy adviser to Reagan, so he did have more people helping him by the late '70s and giving him advice, but he put these things together in his own voice, the way he wanted to. Some of the most important radio broadcasts were written in 1975 right when he started them, a few months after he stepped down as governor. . . . This is Reagan without advisers. He's just mapping out his own philosophy, his own understanding of world politics, of democracy, of domestic life.

Reagan didn't have everything right. . . . He functioned as a one-man think tank. He did not have time to master the nuances of every foreign and domestic and defense issue that he wrote about, and very few political analysts or writers or pundits can predict the future and come out with a perfect record.

We try to point out some contradictions in things that he said in the broadcast in the '70s and things that happened later in the presidency . . . . He talked about, in very negative terms, U.S. ambassador to the United Nations Andrew Young's visit to Southern Africa, where he met with Samora Machel, the leader of Mozambique. He talked about this Marxist-oriented leader that Andrew Young met. I put in the head note, "But years later, as president, Reagan had one of his most convivial meetings with a foreign leader with Samora Machel in the White House."

On the section on Southern Africa, and South Africa in particular, where he talked about apartheid he thought sanctions wouldn't work; he made that argument very clearly in the 1970s; that it wouldn't work to get rid of apartheid. He did say, "We find apartheid to be morally repugnant," but he didn't see the direction the American people would go in the 1980s on that, so he didn't see the future better than most people who do this kind of work. But he did seem to understand the big game of the Cold War story better than most.

WHAT MARTIN HAS said before, and it's a good way of describing this book: this is the first book by Ronald Reagan. We know that in earlier books that his name was attached to, like his official biography and an earlier one, they were ghostwritten or cowritten. But this is really Reagan's writing. It was never intended for publication, but it ends up being a coherent body of work on policy issues in the late 1970s and some before and after. So it is unique. It is his first book.

The Political Lore of Tip O'Neill

by

JOHN A. FARRELL

Before being elected to the U.S. House of Representatives, Thomas P. "Tip" O'Neill was the first Democrat to serve as Speaker of the Massachusetts State House. O'Neill was elected to the Eighty-third Congress in November 1952 and served seventeen terms. He was Speaker of the House for ten years, from 1977 until his retirement in 1987. Boston Globe *Washington editor John A. Farrell appeared on* Booknotes *on April 4, 2001, to discuss O'Neill's fifty-year political career as chronicled in his biography,* Tip O'Neill and the Democratic Century, *published by Little, Brown in 2001.*

TIP O'NEILL was a Speaker of the House who would have gone down in history as one of thirty, forty, fifty semi-anonymous Speakers, had it not been for Ronald Reagan. Together, they made history in 1981. Between the two of them, they laid down a line that influenced our politics for the following twenty years; we're still squaring off on that line today.

His [relationship with] Reagan was exaggerated [by observers in] both directions, that they either hated each other totally or that they really were bosom buddies. I think they respected each other and I think they liked each other. The way it finally boils down is they liked each other enough that they could hurt each other's feelings.

THE NEW DEAL began to move America away from laissez-faire in the 1930s toward a more collectivist state, toward European-style social democracy. That trend continued, and in the 1970s, the Democrats ran out of steam, they ran out of ideas, they ran out of unity. They squabbled about a lot of different things. Their own constituents began to be dissatisfied with them on issues like race and taxes. Reaganism was the response, the correction, and the question was: Would we go back to the days before the New Deal, or could the Democrats draw that line in the sand and preserve Roosevelt's values and most of the heart of his programs? Tip was the leader for the Democratic Party when that happened. . . . Tip believed in the New Deal and he saw Republicans as basically evil creatures.

Tip wielded his personality as a political tool. Some of the most interesting interviews I had were with people either from the other side of the aisle or his own lieutenants, like Dan Rostenkowski or Tony Coelho, whom Tip had nudged aside in the rise to power, who felt that perhaps he had picked their pocket. He employed this great personality and this great feeling of friendship with these people and, to an extent . . . with Reagan as well. For better or for worse, some of them fell for it and some of them didn't.

Newt Gingrich was one who did not, and I quote Newt saying, "It's time the Republicans stop being Boy Scouts and stop playing golf with the Speaker on weekends and pay a little bit more attention to the fact that the Democrats have had this chamber for sixty years, and we're going to have to play a little tougher to get it back."

O'NEILL WAS ELECTED [to the U.S. House of Representatives] in November of 1952, and he left at the end of the 1986 term. He was Speaker of the House for ten years, the longest consecutive term. Speaker Sam Rayburn compiled many more years, from a period in the 1930s through the early 1960s, but it was interrupted by the Eisenhower landslides, when the Republicans had the House for two two-year terms in the late '40s and early '50s.

I knew him only in retirement. I covered him three or four times. In fact, I can remember coming down to Washington in 1990 and going to an event he had. At the end of the event, he turned to Andy Miga from the *Boston Herald* and me, and said, "Gather around, boys, and I'll give you a couple of minutes." I thought, "I've been in journalism for twenty years, and it's still fun to be called 'boys' by Tip O'Neill." So I had a couple of very good interviews with him.

I think my biggest surprise was the fact that in later years, in private, he credited his great empathy to the fact that he had grown up in this motherless home. In a closed-door confrontation with the members of the Black Caucus they said, "What do you know about prejudice and discrimination and hard times?" He had instantly gone to that and said, "I was shuttled from aunt to aunt and never had a life when I was a kid."

That's the Tip O'Neill creed. I mean, that basically is the core of the book. . . . I think that was a great motivating factor, the fact that his mom died when he was that young, that his father worked so hard, such long hours. He called his father a bricklayer [but] his father, when he was growing up, was actually a civil servant; his job was protected during the Depression and the family was basically middle class, not hardscrabbling, blue collar. So there's a little bit of the O'Neill myth in there as well.

TIP O'NEILL PROBABLY would spin in his grave to hear me describe him as this, but he had a little bit of the reformer to him. Even when he first ran for the Massachusetts State House of Representatives in the 1930s, he was not part of the old Michael Curley–style Irish American politician, "We're going to get elected on grievances." He was a college graduate. He had a little sheen, a little step of something extra. Throughout the reform era in Congress, he was open and amenable to the young guys who came and said, "We want to vote for committee chairman. We want to change this. We want to change that."

James Michael Curley was the great rascal king of Boston, who dominated Massachusetts politics for the first half of the century, basically, by preying on the Irish grievances against the Yankees. He was also the model on which the book *The Last Hurrah* was based. Later on in his career, when Tip was running for reelection [in the U.S. Congress] in 1955, Curley came to him and said, "'I'd like to raise money for you." And Tip said, "Well, fine."

He was glad to do whatever Curley wanted because he was always afraid Curley would run for the seat. So Curley went out and raised money, came in and gave Tip an envelope and said, "Here's $1,000." Tip opened it up, looked at it. It was only $900. This pattern continued. Tip finally said, "Well, who are the contributors? I'd like to thank them." Curley said, "Ah, that's okay. Don't worry about that," and sort of vanished from the scene.

After the election, this businessman came up to Tip and said, "I'd like a little bit of help for this favor." Tip said, "Who are you? I don't think we've ever met." And he said, "I contributed to your campaign. I contributed thousands of dollars to James Michael Curley on your behalf to raise money for television ads." And Tip said, "Well, let me tell you a story about that. Curley used to come in, used to give me an envelope with $1,000 it and I'd open it up and it was only $900. So, Curley was keeping 10 percent." The businessman laughed and said, "I know how much I gave James Michael Curley. You were the one who was working for 10 percent."

IT'S A LITTLE HARD to imagine now what a bonanza the television license was in the early 1950s. Of course, television had been with us for a couple of years, but the true potential of commercial television was a mystery. Robert "Beanie" Choate, from the *Herald*, was the first one to catch on that it could mean a great deal. At that time, the *Boston Herald* was the predominant paper in New England, and it was a Republican paper and it was a Republican administration, with the Eisenhower administration. Choate got the license, and there was a Federal Communications Commissions rule which said that if you had a predominant media outlet in a city, you shouldn't be getting a television license as well. When it turned out that they were Republican papers asking for television licenses, that rule was waived; and when it was Democrats, it was not.

The Taylor brothers, who owned the *Boston Globe,* came down to Washington and, at first, were very unsuccessful trying to get some sort of countervailing influence in this Republican administration. At that time, it was sort of a sleepy Democratic, Irish paper, not known for taking bold stands, not courageously liberal. It was very much like the Irish American population of New England at the time, which was very slowly climbing into conformity and respectability and not known as it was to be known in the 1960s and is known today as a more aggressive newspaper.

It was 1954 and this was Tip O'Neill's first term. He got into the act because the Taylors sent down a young guy named Bob Healy, who had been a reporter, gone away to war, flew something like twenty-five missions in the air force, came back, and was a very bright, aggressive guy. They called him in and said, "Look, Choate is threatening to put us out of business with the television stations. You have to go down to Washington and see what you can do." He was a reporter, and he was acting sort of as a private detective as well. Anything that he found, he would put in the paper, so he was actually reporting. But at the same time, the point of the reporting was to expose what they thought was a crooked deal with the television license.

He went to Tip because Tip was the only person he knew in Washington, and Tip had a patronage appointment on the committee that had oversight responsibilities for the communications licenses, a guy named Frank McLaughlin. Together, they worked with a young committee counsel whose name was Bernie Schwartz and began to expose this pattern across the country that the television licenses were being awarded to political favorites. The next thing that happened was that Schwartz and McLaughlin and the other staff members began to plug away; they got sidetracked momentarily on another thing that Tip told them, that the White House chief of staff, a very powerful position then, as now, was a guy from New Hampshire named Sherman Adams, and he had been dallying with a rich Boston industrialist and receiving gifts. This had nothing to do with the television channel, but it was something that Tip told them; within a year, that became a big national story, and Sherman Adams ended up resigning.

[The TV license issue] began to become a much bigger national story.

They had a series of hearings in Boston. The Federal Communications Commission finally said that they would hold the license in abeyance. It went to court for about a dozen years, and it was finally resolved in the favor of the *Globe*. The *Globe* went on to become the predominant newspaper in the region, became much more aggressive and actually pushed Tip to be more liberal and antiwar during the Vietnam era. So that whole little episode had great repercussions for what would happen over the next twenty years.

IN 1964 HE HAD a very important role in Congress. He [could act as the] swing vote . . . on the Rules Committee. At that time, the Rules Committee was much more important, and it served as a traffic cop that kept the legislation on or off the House floor. And so if he voted with the Republicans and the southern Democrats on the committee, he could stop legislation from going to the floor.

Everybody thinks he was an insider with the Kennedys, and he was not. He had a very conflicted and strained relationship with the Kennedys over the years. During the Kennedy administration, because he was old school and because he was something of a political rival for some of JFK's aides, he was effectively kept out of the Oval Office. [When] Kennedy was assassinated and Lyndon Johnson came in, he had this big, broad program and one of the first things Johnson did was announce that he was closing the Boston navy yard.

O'Neill was determined that he was not going to be taken for granted again, and he knew that his clout . . . was on the Rules Committee. In a series of votes throughout the spring of 1965, he rallied different coalitions of forces to stop Johnson's legislation from reaching the House floor. . . . Johnson was just driven to distraction by the fact that Tip O'Neill was casting these votes; . . . Tip played for high stakes.

Johnson finally said, "Give O'Neill what he wants. I'm tired of playing this game." Tip wrote a letter that was the most obvious quid pro quo ever put to paper by a Boston politician to [Johnson aide] Larry O'Brien saying, "I will vote for this bill to get to the floor if you agree to put $9 million worth of defense contracts to the navy yard and other shipyards in the Boston area. Please make sure the president sees this letter." And then there was a letter to the Pentagon from the congressional liaison people at the White House saying, "Make sure that O'Neill gets what he wants." So what he was doing was holding them up.

JIM WILMOT WAS a big contributor when Tip was rising in power in the House. . . . Marty Tolchin of the *New York Times* wrote a story exposing the fact that Wilmot had gotten a break from the Housing and Urban Development Department at the request of Tip O'Neill. The great part about that story was that Marty was banned from the Speaker's office until a calendar year had passed. And on that date, he was allowed back in. Tip obviously marked it on his calendar: "From this day on for one year Tolchin is not allowed back in my office." That shows the dark side, the black Irish side of Tip O'Neill, that he had a way of taking you to task as well. The year was up. Tip said, "Marty, the Irish are a forgiving race."

HE HAD A MODESTLY successful insurance business when he was in Massachusetts politics that he gave up when he came down to Washington. [When he died in 1994] he was worth a ton, thanks to the media, because he had sold his memoirs—they were a huge best-seller, *Man of the House.* And he appeared in a number of commercials, not without criticism, hopping out of suitcases and doing Miller Lite beer ads and made a lot of money, and then he went around the country doing the speaking circuit as well. So he cashed in at the end. It was interesting, because some of his critics were liberals, like Mary McGrory, and his defenders were conservatives, like Roger Ailes, who was a great adviser to Republican presidents.

He wasn't really ready for retirement when he left, but his timing was good. There was enough dissatisfaction and restlessness within the Democratic Party—the advent of the new Democrats, Dick Gephardt in the House, Gary Hart in the Senate—that it was time for him to go. . . . He still wasn't somebody who wanted to go back to Cape Cod and stroll the beach and watch birds.

George H. W. Bush [offered him the ambassador's post to Ireland]. By that time, he had developed [colon] cancer and his wife, Millie, was suffering from emphysema. They just thought that it would have been too much, and it also would have been tough being an ambassador for a Republican administration.

[His last years] in some ways were typical O'Neill. . . . When told that he would have a colostomy, [he] was terror stricken and went into a great depression. He was cheered by the fact that he had so many friends, including President George W. Bush's brother Marvin, football great Otto Graham, other people who had had colon cancer, and went public with it. He testified before Congress, and he did cassette tapes that could be sent out to colostomy patients. He didn't try to hide it. There's one sad story that Chris Matthews told me, which is that he would go visit O'Neill in his office and O'Neill would be sitting there watching C-SPAN. He missed the House so much that he would spend large hours of his day just watching what was going on on the floor of the House. He gradually deteriorated. . . . He had given a public speech in early December. Over Christmas, his family said he was grumpy and he went into the hospital just for a checkup. He was watching a basketball game on television and eating some ice cream with his son Tommy, and he suffered a massive heart attack and passed away. . . . Tip O'Neill died on January 5, 1994.

TIP WAS VERY proud of what he had done to help create a middle class. That being said, in the 1970s, the Democrats had run out of steam and their answer to everything was tax and spend. Tax, tax, spend, spend. There's unemployment, let's create the Comprehensive Education and Training Act, a make-work jobs program. Reaganism was absolutely a necessary correction. Part of the great fascination I had in writing those chapters was the fact that you had a revival of the individualism and the entrepreneurial spirit that the country desperately needed in the 1980s. Everything was up for grabs and the whole country had to come together again and say: Okay, who are we? What do we believe in? How much of Roosevelt do we keep? How much do we throw away? That's why I think there was such a great story between Tip and Reagan.

A Symposium on Race

SHELBY STEELE

CORNEL WEST

THOMAS SOWELL

RANDALL ROBINSON

The subject of race inspires debates as spirited as any topic in American society. Since the landmark legal achievements of the civil rights movement in the 1950s and 1960s, racial issues have remained at the center of political discourse. Many members of a generation of African American intellectuals and public figures have appeared on Booknotes *over the years to discuss their differing views on race in America. Shelby Steele, based at the Hoover Institute and author of* A Dream Deferred: The Second Betrayal of Black Freedom in America, *published by Harper-Collins in 1998, appeared on* Booknotes *on November 17, 1998, and discussed his political views. Harvard University professor Cornel West, author of* The Cornel West Reader, *published by Basic Civitas Books in 1999, discussed his collection of writings on* Booknotes *on January 13, 2000. Thomas Sowell, also at the Hoover Institute and author of* Preferential Policies: An International Perspective, *published by William Morrow in 1990, talked about the cultural effects of civil rights laws on* Booknotes *on May 24, 1990. TransAfrica Forum founder Randall Robinson appeared on* Booknotes *on February 10, 1998, to discuss his life and the status of African Americans today as recounted in his book,* Defending the Spirit: A Black Life in America, *published by Dutton in 1998.*

SHELBY STEELE

[My father, who was black, and my mother, who was white] met in the civil rights movement. They were both founding members of CORE in Chicago, the Congress of Racial Equality, in the very early '40s. . . . I grew up in that milieu and it was a subject that we constantly talked about and explored in family life. Their attitude was very much of the classic civil rights attitude, that race was something used to defeat the humanity of people, and that it was an emptiness in itself and something that was used against human beings. In my own work, I still have that spirit, so when I say "a dream deferred," I suppose my sense is that we're still not quite there. We still, in America, have uses for race. So I think the dream of being fully human has been deferred a bit.

If my parents came back [to witness my] evolution to [black conservatism] they would be absolutely shocked. They were, obviously, in that day and age, clearly liberal in their point of view. But I try to make a distinction. They were liberals of what I call a "freedom focus" kind of liberalism, where the focus is on providing the maximum amount of freedom to the individual. I'm not sure they would have signed onto what I call "redemptive liberalism," where we focus more on groups and identities. They might well have seen why what is conservative to me today is what was liberal to them then. . . . I don't know if I'm ever entirely comfortable with [the label "black conservative"] or any other label. I was called that relentlessly; I did not start out calling myself that.

The idea of a black conservative is disturbing to liberals. It does not confirm their sense of their own virtue. Their virtue is, in many ways, tied to this idea that blacks are victims who have to be helped. The black conservative is someone who in a sense, says, "No, we have to really be responsible for ourselves, whether or not you help." So the black conservative makes the liberal feel obsolete, irrelevant on some level, aside from the obvious surface disagreements, the ideological disagreements that the two might have. There's this sense of "if I really go along with you and accept that, then in a sense, my own politics, my own idea of virtuousness, becomes obsolete." . . . The great failure of this redemptive liberalism is the fact that it asks nothing of the people whom it seeks to help.

I was a liberal. In college, I started the local chapter of Martin Luther King's group, Southern Christian Leadership Conference. . . . After that, I went through a black nationalist phase, so my change has been very gradual and over time. . . . I didn't know anybody who was conservative. I had a mythology built up around conservatives as just sort of insensitive, cold-hearted, and often bigoted people.

It cannot be coincidental that in those areas of greatest black achievement—music, literature, entertainment, sports—there have been no interventions whatsoever, no co-option of agency, no idea that some opportunity structure will enable blacks to participate.

My point is that what transforms you from poverty to a better way of life in America is entirely the assumption of responsibility for your own development. If you take that kind of responsibility, you will inevitably do better. If you don't take that kind of responsibility, no intervention will help. It won't work. Because of our racial history and our guilts and our grievances and our grudges, we have been unable to appreciate that simple truism of human nature when it applies to black Americans.

CORNEL WEST

[My book, *The Cornel West Reader*] is a testament of a particular human being, of a particular brother who's trying to make sense of the world and leave the world just a little bit better than he found it when he makes his exit. [I am] very much a product of the black church, a product of a loving black family, a mom, a dad, and my older brother and two younger sisters. [I was] deeply empowered by Harvard College, Princeton University, and philosophy—and highly privileged, in terms of being able to have access to time to write and lecture, and run my mouth around the country. But in the end, I think I'm still first and foremost a bluesman in the life of the mind; first and foremost, a jazzman in the world of ideas.

What I mean by that is always keeping track of the unjustified suffering in the world, the unnecessary social misery; keeping a limelight on the plight and predicament of what Frantz Fanon called the wretched of the Earth. How do we broaden the scope of human dignity? I guess that's what I'm after. . . . John Coltrane, for me, is a culminating figure in a very rich tradition of blues and jazz—a blues that injects a blue note into Western history, into Western musical harmony, a note of dissonance, disturbance, defiance, wrestling with darkness, but always sustaining a sense of endurance and stamina, rooted in a deep love of self and a love of others. And be it a Ma Rainey, be it a Billie Holiday, a Sarah Vaughan, a Miles Davis, Thelonious Monk, or John Coltrane, you have this story of a people, who up against institutional terrorisms—slavery, Jim Crow, lynching, police brutality—still forge a sense of self with integrity and dignity. That's what I hear in John Coltrane. He vocalizes a European instrument, the saxophone, but it's expressing a spirituality rooted in black struggle that reaches out for the struggle of others, be they in Russia, be they in Kurdistan, be they in Greece, be they in Guatemala, be they in Chile. One has to be silent in the face of that kind of depth, actually. [Coltrane is] somebody who represents something that is both quintessentially American and quintessentially African American.

The blues and jazz are so very important because it's one of the few examples in American civilization where it doesn't believe the hype about the melodramatic, sentimental stories of the happy ending, nor is it cynical. It tries to tell the truth about America, but also sustain the possibility of America. . . . This is a tradition with a variety of different voices, you see, but is rooted in craft, technique, and discipline on the one hand, and wrestling with the dark side of America on the other: pain, suffering, grief, oppression, domination.

Here you have the land of dreams and possibility and yet slavery, lynching, Jim Crow, segregation, discrimination. What's going on? We do love the ideals of freedom, yes. But we're unfree. We love the ideals of democracy, but we're voiceless. James Weldon Johnson in the Negro National Anthem says, "Lift Every Voice and Sing." What a democratic ideal!

I have been privileged in an excessive manner. But at the same time, I've had to deal with the cost, you see. I had to deal with the cost, because one of the most dangerous persons in the world is a self-loving, self-respecting black man who tells the truth about America. So you've got death threats every day. [The market culture is] deeply hedonistic, self-indulgent, pleasure, instant gratification, violence—unbelievable in terms of not just physical violence but the psychic violence that creates a coldheartedness and a mean-spiritedness toward one another. We see this more and more among young people.

Black kids have been dealing with bullets for a long time in junior high and high school, but when black children point guns at other black children, that is less news than when white children point guns at other white children. Unfortunately, that's still the case in our society.

It's harder to sustain the webs of care these days with the families divided and shattered, with the communities much more dispersed. I grew up in a neighborhood. The young brothers and sisters [today] the hip-hop culture and rap music, say they're growing up in a hood. There's a big difference. A "hood" is social Darwinian space. It's . . . hard to forge bonds of trust and ties of sympathy. The neighborhood where I grew up [had] tremendous care, love, nurture overflowing, everybody keeping track of me—Mrs. Durham and Mrs. Burton and my mother and the Reverend Willoughby Cooke and Deacon Hinton—all these folks keeping track of me. In the hood, young folks [are] out there, rootless, dangling, deracinated, drifting. What changed was they don't have enough adults in their lives. They don't have enough love and nurture that's targeting them. They don't have enough people who are concerned about them, who believe in them, keeping track of them.

What we have . . . here now is a low quality of life of children, in terms of the state of their souls, spiritual malnutrition, existential emptiness, hungry, thirsty for something bigger than themselves, but more and more finding themselves obsessed with instant gratification, obsessed with putting others down in order for them to feel like they are somebody. And that cuts across race.

The important thing to keep in mind, though, is that, historically, enslaved Africans were not allowed to read. It was against the law. So we brought the rich oral traditions of Africa—the drums, which themselves were also outlawed, but we began to clap. At the same time, [we were] exposed to European instruments or brought African instruments, so that early on in America, you get this original, indigenous form of cultural expression in spirituals, blues, jazz. Gaining the right to read after the Civil War, we've gone on to produce a very rich literary and intellectual tradition.

The advantage of reading is that there is a connection between cultivating the art of living and fighting courageously for the expansion of democracy. See, the art of living is learning how to die, and what I mean by that is that if you're really going to live life intensely, then something in you every day ought to die—some bad habit, some prejudice, some faulty presupposition—so that you're continually involved in a struggle to better yourself, become more mature, more compassionate, more courageous. We need that compassion and courage and maturity to expand democracy because in the end, that is still the best ideal that we fragmented, cracked vessels called human beings have been able to come up with.

THOMAS SOWELL

I'm a great believer in maximum freedom. [I'm a civil libertarian, but] certainly not in the sense in which the American Civil Liberties Union is. I don't believe that hoodlums should be kept in school because of some strange reading of the Constitution. People have to recognize that all people owe their lives to the surrounding society. They cannot simply demolish it because it is unjust, because everything human has always been unjust. What you're going to do to make it better will have to be within that context, so my tendency is to want more freedom for the individual. . . . I don't want people making decisions who don't pay the price of their decisions, and that's what politics is all about. You don't pay the price of the decisions.

One of the reasons we had a Jim Crow era in this country was because the politicians didn't pay the price of that. It was enormously costly to the white as well as the black population, but the politicians who put that in didn't pay any cost for that. They drew their full salaries irrespective of all that. I want someone who discriminates to have to lose money discriminating because people tend to back off when they start losing big money. Harlem was an all-white community. It became a black community despite organized efforts to keep blacks out because people were losing money trying to keep it a white community. People in the civil rights area missed a bet by not trying to promote more free markets because that makes discrimination the most costly it can be.

One of the ways that the organized noisemakers have succeeded is by saying that what they're saying is what their race is saying. . . . The black intellectuals are no more typical of the black population than white intellectuals are of the white population, but they have a very large vested interest in certain beliefs that underlie various programs from which they benefit enormously. This is common around the world, that the elites benefit from preferential programs. Even when those programs are in the name of the masses, the masses do not benefit.

If you went back into the '60s, you'd find people with different views, like Martin Luther King and Malcolm X, but both those men believed in what they said. Whereas today, you have people who are simply professional hustlers. Again, this is not peculiar to blacks or peculiar to the United States, or even peculiar to racial issues. Many movements are set off by idealistic people who want to promote some good for mankind or for some group. But as time goes by and as they succeed, they will be followed by people who can use these things for their own self-interest. That's been the history of regulatory agencies in the government. It's been the history of religions. The first Christians who were being persecuted by the Roman Empire were not in it for what they could get, because all they were going to get was trouble. But once Christianity became the state religion, it became a very lucrative career for some people. Then you get an entirely different kind of person coming in at that point, and we have an entirely different kind of movement.

THERE ARE SOME reactions that are self-equilibrating, but there are some that keep feeding each other. Let's say an ugly racial incident happens on campus, at one of the elite colleges. Invariably, the first thing that will be said is, "We must have now a larger quota of minority students, a larger quota of minority faculty, and we must now subject the white students to these sensitivity courses, or ethnic courses, or what have you." [These are] courses that they have rejected taking, otherwise it wouldn't be necessary to force them. That is not going to make things better; that's going to make them worse. But as they get worse, then you keep doing that, and so it's just an upward spiral. I don't know where that spiral is going to end. I don't see anybody with the courage to end it, and I see it leading only to bad things.

RANDALL ROBINSON

If we're going to have a racial discussion in the country that's useful and productive, at the very first, it must be honest. . . . If we are going to have an honest dialogue about race in the United States, we have to talk about our feelings and our sense of injury and the graphic enduring unfairness of this thing. If we don't use that as a starting point for this discussion, at the end of the day, we will have gotten nowhere.

America is a country that is extremely uncomfortable with its past and its less laudable side. It causes us, as a society, to lie to ourselves about what we've stood for. We don't look into any mirror reflecting ourselves accurately as a country, unlike other countries that now are in a kind of atonement trend. [Other] countries are honestly looking at their past, apologizing, often making restitution, reparations.

The French are apologizing to . . . French Jews for the Vichy–Nazi collaboration during World War II. South Africa has a Truth and Reconciliation Commission. Europeans are apologizing for colonialism. The Canadians are apologizing and making reparations available to an Indian population . . . that has been abused since the fifteenth century. The U.S., of course, extended reparations to Japanese Americans for a World War II internment.

But our country is disinclined to even apologize for slavery—as inadequate, as incomplete an answer as that would constitute to what has been done to African Americans. [The U.S. government] not only refuses to apologize but to even make that chapter in our history a constant component in this country's telling of its own story to all of its people. There's no museum on the Mall [in Washington, D.C.], there's no slavery memorial on the Mall. When the memorial is built to Native Americans on the Mall, the only major group that will then remain excluded from representation on the Mall will be African Americans.

I AM NO MORE and no less angry than any other African American. It is simply that this abuse of which I speak that has been lifelong cannot be a lifelong diet without a price. It accumulates in your craw. And it can't be safely vented because all African Americans know if you're going to be successful in our society, an expression of anger is the best road—the easy road—to failure. It's unattractive. No one wants to hear it vented. So we mask it.

There is a pressure on African Americans who aspire to reach the upper echelons of policymaking and great public success. There's a pressure to choose. I describe [it as] the city of privilege. It's an allegorical city where blacks are caused to choose. How do you deal with the anger that we all feel? Do you mask it and accommodate to the system or are you driven out because of an honest and unattractive constant, relentless expression of this kind of anger? Louis Farrakhan can bring one in every ten blacks over the age of fifteen to Washington in a Million Man March and still not be a policy factor in this town, which would roundly disregard anything he would have to say. He would be locked out of this allegorical city.

But those of us who function in the city, of whom I am one, are forced to cut deals. We make compromises. What can we say and survive, and what are we pressed not to say? How brave and honest can we be? How much, implacably, can we stand for? Where do we stop before it becomes counter-productive? But where do we start so that we salvage some sense of self-esteem and self-respect?

The Reagan–Gorbachev Summits

by

DON OBERDORFER

President Ronald Reagan and General Secretary Mikhail Gorbachev of the Soviet Union held four summit meetings during Reagan's second term in office. These meetings, resulting in the most far-reaching arms reduction agreement of the Cold War, along with Gorbachev's commitment to his programs of perestroika (restructuring) and glasnost (openness), led to a dramatic decline in tensions between the two nations. On his first official visit to West Germany in May 1989, Gorbachev informed Chancellor Helmut Kohl that the Brezhnev doctrine had been abandoned; Moscow would no longer use force to prevent the democratization of its satellite states. This news sent shock waves through the Soviet Union, Eastern Europe, and beyond. By November the Berlin Wall, perhaps the most infamous symbol of the Cold War and the Iron Curtain, was being dismantled. The United States and the Soviet Union would remain giants on the world stage but the long, divisive, and dangerous Cold War was over. In a Booknotes *interview aired on October 27, 1991, Don Oberdorfer discussed* The Turn: From the Cold War to a New Era, *published by Simon & Schuster in 1991. Mr. Oberdorfer spent seventeen years as the diplomatic correspondent for the* Washington Post, *and during his visit he told us stories from this intense, and productive, era of U.S./Soviet negotiations.*

FROM 1983 to the middle of 1990 is the period when we went from an intense confrontation with the Soviet Union to almost a partnership with the Soviet Union.

If I had to pick one date as the epicenter of the turn, it would have been the Reykjavik summit in October of 1986. . . . In this remarkable event, probably the most remarkable meeting of U.S. and Soviet leaders certainly since

Kennedy's meeting with Nikita Khrushchev in Vienna, [President] Ronald Reagan, [General Secretary] Mikhail Gorbachev, [Soviet Foreign Minister] Eduard Shevardnadze, and [U.S. Secretary of State] George Shultz sat down in a small room in Reykjavik, Iceland, over a dining room table and started negotiating over their entire nuclear arsenal. The entire stock of ballistic missiles in the arsenals of both governments, which were the basic weapons underpinning their national power, were to be bargained with on the table. At the end of the summit Reagan even said, . . . "Why don't we just get rid of all nuclear weapons? Just get rid of them all." And Gorbachev said, "Yes, let's do that. Let's just get rid of them." It broke up in its final hour over Strategic Defense Initiative, [also known as "Star Wars"]. But it was the most spectacular event, deemed to be a failure in its immediate aftermath, but it opened the way, in a way, toward a degree of trust and a degree of willingness to bargain that was not the case before that meeting.

There were a lot of people [who made a difference] but you have to really look first and foremost at the leaders. We tend to forget this, but when Gorbachev came to power in 1985, it was the first time since 1972 that you had a politically and physically healthy Soviet leader and a politically and physically healthy American leader in office at the same time. After Richard Nixon's summit with Leonid Brezhnev, his first summit in '72, Nixon was weakened by Watergate. Then came Gerald Ford, who was an unelected president, then came Jimmy Carter. By the time Carter was well ensconced in office, Brezhnev was in a decline. If you will remember, at the summit with Carter in 1979, he was almost like a vegetable. He had to be carried around. He was succeeded by Yuri Andropov, a Soviet leader who had only about four months of decent health in office before his kidneys failed, and then by Konstantin Chernenko, who had emphysema so bad when he took office that he could barely complete a speech.

When Gorbachev came [to power] in 1985 and Reagan had just been reelected by a tremendously big majority in the United States, you had two strong guys who could interact. Gorbachev, in my opinion, is going to be one of the great historical figures of the twentieth century. We've seen his deficiencies and difficulties and weaknesses, but, with all that, this could not have happened without him and he is going to be a very important figure in history. He's certainly a very important figure in my chronicle of what happened.

Ronald Reagan was much readier than we knew, certainly much readier than I knew as a reporter, to engage with the Soviets, to get in there and bargain with them even while he was condemning them in the harshest terms. So Reagan was an important figure. Shultz and Shevardnadze in their own right were extremely important. George Shultz was a steady, methodical sort of bulldog figure who knew how to get things done. And as an economist, which is rare in the political side of government, he was a man who believed in the long gain and in steady inputs—in putting things on the table and keeping at it.

Shevardnadze is just a truly remarkable person. He is a man who had absolutely no experience in diplomacy, none in democracy, and he became one of the important diplomats of our time and, in my opinion, a small-D democrat. How he got that way is an incredible puzzle, and he was more important than we knew to lots of things that took place in the Soviet Union.

As best I can tell, Secretary of Defense Caspar Weinberger and George Shultz never liked each other in the first place [and they feuded while in office]. They worked together at the Office of Management and Budget back in the Nixon administration. Shultz was head of it, Weinberger was his deputy, and they didn't really get along that well. Then they went to Bechtel Corporation. Shultz, again, was president of the company; Weinberger was the general counsel. Then in the Reagan administration Weinberger was there first as secretary of defense. Shultz only came in after Alexander Haig resigned in the summer of 1982. They're two very, very different people. Shultz is a very methodical, steady, thoughtful person who is not a person that likes to battle over things, and he will fight on his turf. Weinberger is much more the guy who enjoys combat.

I don't think it was [healthy to have the secretary of defense and the secretary of state disagreeing strongly or having a feud]. It's healthy to have differences of opinion and to have honest differences, either from a bureaucratic position or from your own philosophical or political position, but to carry it to the extent that the Reagan administration did and that President Reagan tolerated is not healthy. I don't think it was healthy to have [National Security Adviser] Zbigniew Brzezinski and [Secretary of State] Cyrus Vance battling for years during the Carter administration [either]. At the end of the day, the government needs to have a policy—not two policies or three policies.

WHEN IT COMES to ministerial meetings between the U.S. and the U.S.S.R. or summit meetings, reporters are dependent on second-level briefings and dribs and drabs of what people will tell us. We just don't have the kind of access to what really went on that people are willing to provide several years after the fact, especially after an administration is over. So there was not one moment—there were many moments—when I said, "Oh, if I had only known that!"

One example of the difference between daily journalism and what is actually happening: George Shultz went to Moscow in early November of 1985, a few weeks before the Geneva summit. . . . All we had in our heads as members of the press was that Shultz had better make a deal with Gorbachev or the summit coming up in Geneva was going to be a disaster because we had no confidence that Reagan and Gorbachev would be able to iron out anything.

Shultz had a press conference after the meeting was over. . . . Then they shooed us [reporters] out, and for the next three hours or so they had a meeting, which I later learned was an extremely tumultuous meeting. Gorbachev was attacking Shultz and Reagan. He was saying, "You're afraid to tell me the truth. You'll be fired from your job!" Shultz says, "I've got news for you. I'm a tenured professor at Stanford University. I don't have to worry about a job. I'll tell you anything that's on my mind." They went back and forth in absolutely extraordinary terms we were not told anything about.

At the end of the meeting, though, Shultz had a press conference and he said, "We made absolutely no progress. There was no narrowing of the gap at all." I'm saying to myself, "Oh my God. Geneva is going to be a disaster!" I'm sitting there in the American ambassador's house, where they had set up a temporary press room, writing on this laptop computer for the *Washington Post,* saying disaster was coming up in Geneva. I looked up and Secretary Shultz has come to the door of the press room and was looking in at us typing our stories. He had a drink in his hand and he looked extremely pleased. I looked down on my story, I looked up at the secretary, I looked down on my story—I don't know if you've ever had this feeling, "there's something wrong here and I don't know what it is"—but with the instinct of a lifetime of journalism, I toned down my story. It was now not a disaster; it was just a very difficult meeting.

Much later I learned that Shultz had had this fiery meeting with Gorbachev. Then he came to the conclusion he had faced down Gorbachev, didn't give an inch, and that Gorbachev was going to blink, that he would not come to the Geneva summit and try the same kind of tactics on Reagan. After the meeting was over, Shevardnadze said to Shultz very confidentially, "Listen, we now have to work together and make sure that the Geneva meeting is a big success." Had we known all that happened, and why Shultz was so contented, and what happened in the meeting, we would have reported the whole thing completely differently. But we didn't know.

GEORGE SHULTZ IS very much like what you saw as secretary of state except that he is also a witty guy. He's a very shrewd observer of people and of things. There's one incident that tells a lot about Shultz. In October of 1987 he had a meeting with Gorbachev in Moscow in the Kremlin, a meeting at which Gorbachev was supposed to agree to the dates for the Washington summit. Gorbachev suddenly balked and refused to set a date. You've probably forgotten about it now—I'm sure most Americans have—but it was a rather sensational story for a day or two in the press. When Gorbachev came into the meeting, Shultz, who had been a veteran of labor–management negotiations, saw something different about Gorbachev.

When the meeting was over, . . . there were a few people around him; again, this did not reach the ears of the press. He said Gorbachev reminded him in that meeting of a poem by Carl Sandburg in which Sandburg talks about a fighter who had never been hit. Shultz said Gorbachev had always reminded him of a fighter who had never been hit. It's from Sandburg's great poem "Chicago." George Shultz said, without knowing any more, that when he came into that meeting he thought Gorbachev had been hit. This wasn't the same man. Somehow, someone had hit him. It turned out a week later, that the day before this meeting with Shultz was the first big blowup in the meeting of the Central Committee in which Boris Yeltsin had made attacks on [his Politburo colleagues,] Yegor Ligachev and Gorbachev.

"Gorby" came into this meeting having been battered around by Yeltsin and the right-wingers, and he really lost some of his confidence. It is remarkable that Shultz could sit there and watch this guy and make the analysis that there was something different, something about him that suggested that somebody was closing in on him and that this accounted for his behavior. He's a very shrewd observer.

ANDREI GROMYKO [was] the veteran foreign minister of the Soviet Union . . . . When Gromyko came to the White House in 1984, it was a big thing for Reagan. He had never met a senior Soviet leader before. I was sitting at my desk at the *Washington Post* the day after the meeting and received a telephone call from the secretary of the Soviet ambassador, Anatoly Dobrynin. He said, "Mr. Oberdorfer, Foreign Minister Gromyko is going back to Moscow this afternoon and he wonders if he could have as a souvenir a picture that appeared in the *Washington Post* today."

I said, "Well, I'll see what I can do, if I can get it for him. Which picture?" It was that picture of Gromyko with Reagan [in the Rose Garden at the White House], Reagan with his arms, in effect, around Gromyko. It stunned me that he wanted to take that back and, I guess, show it to the Politburo or hang it on the wall or do whatever he did with it. [He and Reagan] got along fairly well. Gromyko is a sort of old-line tough guy, but he was on his good behavior for Reagan, and Reagan was on his good behavior for Gromyko.

[Gromyko served almost fifty years] the longest time of any foreign minister that the Soviet Union has ever had, and almost anybody ever had. He was foreign minister in 1960 when Khrushchev came to the United States and went to the UN and pounded his fists on the table; he was foreign minister long before that. [Khrushchev once] said that if you wanted Gromyko to sit on a block of ice, you'd tell him to sit on it and he'd sit there until you told him to get up "even if he was told to take his pants off and sit there." Khrushchev said that publicly. He was ridiculing Gromyko. But Gromyko was quite a person too. He is clearly partly responsible for the selection of Gorbachev. He had a big role in '85 in making Gorbachev the Soviet leader.

There's one other story about Gromyko that's priceless. In this meeting in 1984 when he came to the White House, the U.S. government wanted Reagan to impart some particularly important piece of information through Gromyko—some arms control position or something. People can't remember it, but at the time it seemed very important to get this across. It was decided that after the meeting in the Oval Office and before the luncheon where Gromyko met Nancy Reagan, that Reagan would keep Gromyko back—say, "Stay back a minute, Andrei. I want to tell you something," and he would tell him this vital thing and then they'd go to lunch.

The next day, the State Department began checking with the Soviet delegation, and no one had heard about this big, important information. So they began checking back, and they found the secret service agent who has a peephole that looks into the Oval Office to make sure that the president is not having a heart attack or that something untoward is happening.

What the agent saw was the two men talking for just a minute, and then Reagan saying to Gromyko, "Would you like to use the bathroom?" So this seventy-five-year-old foreign minister goes in to use the bathroom, then Reagan says, "Now I will." He went in to use the bathroom, the seventy-three-year-old Reagan, and he came out and the two guys went to lunch. Apparently, Reagan forgot to tell him this vital piece of information because the two fellows used the bathroom and then went to lunch. So that's the way diplomacy really works.

THE REAGAN ADMINISTRATION, though it sometimes didn't articulate it very well, had two points to its policy about dealing with the Soviet Union. One of them was to deal from a position of strength. President Reagan made that very clear—his military buildup, Strategic Defense Initiative, and all the rest. How much of that was necessary, people are going to be debating for a long time, but certainly you do have to be strong.

The other side of his policy, which was not known for quite a long time, was to engage them, to have dialogue with them, to negotiate with them, and to try to work things out with them. So the two things fit pretty well, and both things were necessary. If you'd have had a policy of being strong but not of talking to the Soviet Union, you would have just had a heightened confrontation between the two countries. And if you'd have had a policy of being conciliatory and being engaged without the sense that the United States was a strong power that could not be pushed over, it would not have been a particular success either. I'm not judging whether this particular move, domestically or in foreign policy, was good or bad, but overall you needed to have both of those sides for your policy.

[THE FIRST BUSH] administration started off very slowly with the Soviets, and it took them quite a few months to get going, to get the traction up that the Reagan administration had at the end. . . . [Secretary of State] James Baker hosted Foreign Minister Shevardnadze at Jackson Hole, Wyoming. . . . It was Baker's idea to get Shevardnadze out of Washington and see some of the real country and the beauty of the United States. It really was an idea that worked brilliantly.

The big change—the coup, the demise of communism, and the threatened breakup of the Soviet Union—presented [the first Bush] administration with a different sort of problem than anyone had predicted. Not the question of managing a partnership, a friendship, but managing a world in which the Soviet Union simply, probably was not going to be a major player at all. It's a country in great disarray. Its economy is dropping like a stone. It does not have a stable political situation. Even if Russia and some republics join in, they're going to be so tied up with their internal problems, probably for decades, that they're unlikely to be a major player on the international scene.

Reagan, Bush, and the Press

by

MARLIN FITZWATER

Marlin Fitzwater worked at the White House for ten years, from Ronald Reagan's first term in office through the presidency of George H. W. Bush, making him one of the longest-serving presidential assistants in history. In the course of his tenure as White House spokesman, Mr. Fitzwater conducted more than 850 briefings with the members of the press corps. His book, Call the Briefing! Reagan and Bush, Sam and Helen: A Decade with Presidents and the Press, *published by Times Books in 1995, chronicles both the everyday activities behind the scenes and the historic public events of the Reagan and Bush administrations.* Booknotes *aired our conversation with Mr. Fitzwater on November 5, 1995. Mr. Fitzwater is now a writer living in Deale, Maryland.*

I FIRST WENT TO the White House as deputy press secretary to Larry Speakes under President Reagan in September of 1983. I had not been involved in politics in any way and didn't know any of the Reagan people. I never met the president until the day he hired me.

[There were differences in how one worked for President Reagan and President Bush though both were] men of extraordinary dignity and kindness in the way they dealt with staff and the way they conducted their business; both were a pleasure to work for in that sense. But Ronald Reagan liked his briefing materials in writing—on paper—and every decision would go to him with an explanation and with options—one, two, three, four; pick the one you want. He would come in the next morning and say, "I pick option three" and that was it. The result for a press secretary was that I could be with President Reagan maybe 20 percent of the day and know 80 percent of what he knew by reading all of his briefing papers. I would know what he considered, what the options were, what he chose, and usually why.

It was a very effective way for a press secretary to stay on top of what the president was doing. With President Bush, he liked to have oral presentations. He would have people come in and talk to him about what the options were, and he would often decide on the scene. "Okay, let's do this. Let's do that." So I would have to spend 80 or 90 percent of my day with the president to get the same amount of knowledge that I could get by reading briefing papers under President Reagan. They had a totally different way of doing business that caused me to do business in a different way also.

President Bush was most interested [in the day-to-day progress]. He was really a news junkie. He would read all the papers before I ever got in. I'd check with him about 7:15 in the morning. He'd say, "'Did you see this *Times* story? Did you see this *Wall Street Journal* piece?" I'd say, "Mr. President, I haven't seen anything. I've been on the road driving in all morning." And he'd been up since 5:30, reading the papers. At night, he had four television sets in his study in the private quarters of the residence, and often he would invite me up there, and we'd watch all the newscasts simultaneously. He would compare the newscasts from each correspondent and each network.

President Reagan viewed the press conferences as a very formal opportunity, and one that he was good at. It accentuated his talents, his experience as an actor. He had presence. He had the aura of the presidency about him, and he liked to study his questions and, in effect, script them out for himself. President Reagan really memorized the answers to various problems and issues that you could identify were going to come up at a press conference and delivered them almost like he was an actor. He had the ability to do that in a way that people loved and appreciated and felt really warm about.

President Bush, on the other hand, didn't like that kind of formality and eschewed the big East Room evening press conferences. He only did two, one in the beginning of his administration and one at the end—and he just did those to show he could. Most of the rest were held in the briefing room or in more informal settings—in the Rose Garden or on the driveway or somewhere. He didn't have very much preparation at all. He was very much a student of the presidency; he stayed on top of all the issues all the time.

About every two weeks, President Bush would say, "Marlin, what are those reporters yelling at me about?" I'd say, "Oh, Helen Thomas [then of United Press International] is crazy down there. She's got it in her mind that we don't know what we're doing on this issue or that issue." And he'd say, "Well, let's go talk to them." And I'd say, "Well, fine. When?" He'd say, "Right now." I'd say, "I can't do it right now. Give me a half an hour." He'd say, "Okay, in a

half an hour." And we'd call a press conference, and he'd go down to the briefing room and spend half an hour explaining an issue.

President Reagan had forty-eight press conferences in eight years. President Bush had 280 in four years. . . . I think they both had it right for themselves, and they both couldn't do it the way the other did it. President Bush
did not have the background, the training, the confidence in scripts, and the
presence to do the big East Room press conferences. And President Reagan
didn't have the kind of intellectual curiosity that allowed him to want to get
into all these issues and answer every reporter's question on every issue.
Therefore, he didn't like to do it and really could not have done the more
spontaneous things.

A BRIEFING IS the ordeal that every White House press secretary goes
through every morning, usually at 11:00 or thereabouts, to explain the news
of the day, what the president's doing, his schedule, and answer any questions
that the press may have on their minds. It's the focal point of the whole day
for a press secretary, and everything you do is geared toward it. There had
been a long tradition of not having television cameras on [during the briefings, which I continued]. I tried it for a few minutes, but when you're on
camera, they can record every stupid thing you say. If you make a slip—as I
often did—it gets replayed over and over. So, it was a form of self-protection.
I would sometimes leave the cameras on for a few minutes for networks to
get the top story of the day and get some film of me and then turn them off. I
could then be more relaxed and have more freedom to make a mistake without that worry.

I WROTE THIS BOOK to describe how the presidency works and how it
relates to the press corps, and I did it by episode. In other words, episodes
that happened demonstrate various aspects of the press operation, or how the
press thinks, or how they relate to the president, and so forth. Andy Rosenthal [of the *New York Times*] was involved in one of the most harmful, or significant, press episodes in the Bush administration, which was the
supermarket scanner story. I came out pretty critical of Andy, but I really like
him personally.

President Bush during the 1992 campaign went to a convention in Florida
of grocery manufacturers, and before the speech, he was shown some demonstrations and displays. He walked up to a new checkout scanner that was
being displayed by National Cash Register Company, and the fellow who was
at the cash register said, "This is our latest thing. This can do everything but
slice bread, and it reads credit cards, and does billing, and everything." That
fellow—the cash register guy—said, "That's amazing!" President Bush, to be

gracious, said, "Yes, it is amazing," and we just kind of withdrew. Nobody paid much attention to it. Then later on, when the president was asked about the technology, he said, "I saw some amazing technology on the cash register." Andy wrote up the story as if the president was so out of touch with American life that he'd never seen a supermarket scanner before. It was one of those tragic situations where we could never catch up with the story.

It painted the president as being out of touch, and it was also interesting that, in a sense, it touched on a truth—which was why this story had legs—we were out of touch on the economy. We really didn't know where the American people were hurting and how they were reacting to economic problems at that time. The problem was that this scanner didn't awe the president; it wasn't really true. He hadn't expressed his amazement over something he had never seen before, and it wasn't the case that he'd never been in a grocery store before. It was a case where the story that Andy wrote—which was from a pool reporter—was not true or accurate in the sense of what the president did.

Andy was at the filing center, which was another kind of phenomenon of the White House press corps. When you take three hundred reporters with you on a trip, for example, they can't all be with the president all the time. What they'll often do is stay in a hotel ballroom that we rent for them. A pool of reporters, usually fifteen, goes with the president and records everything he says and does. Then they write up a report of what he did and give that to the other reporters. So the three hundred who stayed at the hotel are really rewriting a report by that fifteen-man pool. That's what Andy Rosenthal did in this case, and he described this event in a way that no other reporter described it. It turned out to be a major problem for the Bush campaign.

On February 11, 1992, Christopher Connell of the Associated Press wrote the single most courageous story of my White House years because, essentially, he pointed out that Andy's story was wrong, and that the facts as described were not what happened. There's an unwritten rule of journalism that you don't criticize other publications, and you especially don't take on the *New York Times,* which is, after all, the biggest and perhaps most powerful newspaper in America. For anybody, a reporter or otherwise, to challenge a *Times* story showed a lot of courage and a lot of ability to overcome peer pressure.

I FIRST BECAME press secretary to President Reagan, the full press secretary, after Larry Speakes left in 1987. [White House chief of staff] Don Regan had hired me. I worked for him at Treasury also; I thought very highly of Regan and liked him a great deal. When I first got in the job, there were all of these stories appearing about how he was hurting the president, and how

Regan was in trouble with the first family. I went to the president and the president said, "No. Don Regan and I have talked about these stories. There's no problem."

So I defended Mr. Regan in the press, and there were some stories that appeared that had Marlin Fitzwater saying there was nothing to these stories, and that Don Regan was doing a good job. Then Mrs. Reagan called me with this colloquy: "Hello, Mrs. Reagan," I said meekly. "Hello, Marlin," she said. "What can I do for you?" I said. "Well, Marlin, you know those stories about Don Regan?" she said. "Yes," I replied. "Well, you should just stay out of them," she said. "Yes, ma'am," I said. "Good-bye, Marlin," she said. Then it was clear that indeed she was involved in telling these reporters that there was a problem, and that Don Regan was going to be leaving.

How the game worked was that Mrs. Reagan would tell Paul Laxalt, who was known by everybody to be a close friend of the family's. . . . He was a former senator who was working in Washington as an attorney with a law firm, a widely known friend of the president's. Mrs. Reagan would let him know there were problems, or they wanted to make changes, or just to talk about what was going on in the presidency with a couple of his close advisers.

Paul Laxalt [would then talk to] Stewart Spencer, a political consultant in California who helped engineer many of the Reagan victories over the years and also remained close to the Reagans. Then Paul Laxalt to Lou Cannon, a *Washington Post* reporter who had also covered President Reagan in California and knew all of the people close to the party. In that kind of amorphous way, Lou Cannon got the story, which appeared in the *Washington Post,* that said, "The Reagans are known to be dissatisfied with the chief of staff's performance, and his days may be numbered." When the chief of staff sees those stories, he knows that process too. He knows basically where they come from.

I wasn't privy to all those conversations, but there was a process whereby—and that works with every president—every president has friends that become their private confidants or their family's confidants. They talk about so-and-so's hurting the president or so-and-so's not helping the president, and that's usually the way these things start.

Don Regan had gone to the president earlier, a month or two earlier, and said, "I think it's probably time for me to leave" (this was the time Iran-Contra was breaking), and the president had agreed. So they had talked about his leaving. But then the chief of staff said, "But I'd like to wait until the Tower Board comes out and clears me, so I can leave with a clear conscience and a good name." And President Reagan said, "Fine."

That was what Don Regan really was resentful of—that he didn't get a chance to play out that scenario. I think President Reagan probably wanted him to, but events took over, and the public pressure [was] to replace Don Regan. So he never got the chance to get his side of the Iran-Contra story out. He felt he'd been treated badly because he saw on CNN that he was going to be replaced.

I'm sure the Reagans had conversations about the chief of staff and his impact on the presidency, and the impact on the Reagans. Mrs. Reagan had served in this capacity, in essence, in other ways as it related to staff. She was very protective of the president, and I wrote this story with Mrs. Reagan having very noble purposes. Her purpose was to protect the presidency, to protect Ronald Reagan personally, and to protect her husband. As she saw it, he was not being well served by Don Regan. And there were other times in the president's career where Mrs. Reagan had been involved in, if not guiding people out the door, at least making sure the president understood that not all these people were as helpful as he might have thought.

MOST REPORTERS NEVER reveal or don't want to reveal their personal attitudes toward the president or towards any political ideology. For example, I never knew whether most reporters were Republican or Democrats, or liberals or conservatives, or how they felt about the president personally. That was not always the case. There were some who wore their politics on their sleeve and said, "I'm adversarial to what you're trying to do." But that was a pretty rare case.

Reporters [usually] have fairly large egos because, after all, the profession calls for you to make judgments about other people, and that requires a pretty healthy sense of self in most people. I suppose Sam Donaldson of ABC News had the most obvious large ego and liked to display it the most—but he was also a very good reporter. It helps when you can back it up.

The press holds a press secretary and a president to some pretty high standards and I think it's good that they do. I firmly believe we should not try to lower press standards; rather, we should raise standards for the presidency and the people who are in it. But by the same token, I think the press has to understand that they can be held to some high standards also. They don't always tell the truth. One of the cases where they didn't tell the truth to me was on the "Man of the Year" cover for *Time* magazine, because they wanted an interview with President Bush. They knew damn well that we wouldn't grant one if we knew it was going to be a mocking cover showing him to be a two-faced politician—which was what they had in mind. I was really resentful that we were duped into granting an interview and granting a photo session which was used for those purposes.

"Those bastards!" I screamed. "They lied to me. This whole thing was a setup. Those dirty, rotten bastards." I never said those things in public—[just to my staff]. I had a rule that in my office we could let go with all the frustrations and dealings with the press.

The fact is that in the course of a day, a press secretary and his staff will come to hate the press, hate the president, hate each other. So I had a rule that anybody on my staff could come in my office at anytime, close the door, and scream any fool thing that came into their head. You had to have a release for this pressure. And that's what happened in that case. I never said a word to *Time* magazine. I never said a word to the correspondents who covered us or the editors or anybody else because I felt that, professionally, you deal with reporters in a professional way.

Planning the Persian Gulf War

---

by

BOB WOODWARD

President George H. W. Bush engaged two large forces of American troops in conflicts during his presidency. In December 1989, American soldiers invaded Panama and removed the nation's leader, Manuel Noriega, to the United States to stand trial for drug trafficking and other alleged crimes. On August 2, 1990, Iraq moved troops into neighboring Kuwait. The United Nations Security Council called for Iraq to withdraw. By November the UN set a January 15, 1991, deadline for the removal of Iraqi troops and, when this deadline was not met, Operation Desert Storm, a military operation consisting of a coalition of thirty-two nations led by the United States, was launched. Air strikes continued into the next month, and on February 24 ground troops invaded Kuwait and southern Iraq, driving the Iraqi forces from Kuwait. President Bush declared a cease-fire on February 28. Bob Woodward's The Commanders, *published by Simon & Schuster in 1991, examines the foreign and military policy decisions of President Bush's administration. In a Booknotes interview on June 23, 1991, Mr. Woodward, Assistant Managing Editor of the* Washington Post, *discussed the stories of these decisions and the men who made them.*

IF YOU LOOK at the [first] Bush presidency, it is quite evident that . . . the most successful things—that is, the Panama operation and the Gulf War—were operations really overseen by Colin Powell. I was talking to somebody the other day from that White House who said, "You take away Panama and the Gulf, and the Bush presidency is really reduced to a lagging economy and lots of uncertainty about a legislative agenda." So, in a sense, you could argue that Bush needed a strong military man, needed to identify [that man] as a symbol of the successful operations.

Colin Powell was not negative on going to war. In October [1990] midway through the period leading up to the war from the invasion of Kuwait [in August of that year] what Powell said to the president; Brent Scowcroft, the national security adviser; Dick Cheney, his boss; the secretary of defense; and Jim Baker, the secretary of state, was, "Look, there are two alternatives here: war or continuing the economic sanctions. Both will achieve the objectives. Economic sanctions may take a year or two, but it will work." Bush rejected that and said, "No, we're going to develop the offensive capability" . . . and eventually decided to go to war. . . . The president felt the alternative would not succeed or that the political consequences would be so great internationally and domestically that he would not proceed on the sanctions-only option.

The book demonstrates that there was no one more active [than Powell] in making sure that we had adequate force [in the Gulf], that we had the best equipment, were the best trained, and that all of the details of the war plan were worked out to succeed.

The details I have of what various individuals thought, what Bush said, his key decision points, are all laid out in the book. . . . Some people have said it makes Bush look terrific, decisive, and forceful. [That he] knew the moral imperative and had a grand strategic vision. Then there were other people who have read it and said, "The Bush White House was not well run. He was not sure," that the procedures were very random, that the discussion among the key Bush advisers was way too informal, and so forth. [This book is] the best version I could get and it's laid out, and people have entirely different reactions to it.

"When the principals met, Bush liked to keep everyone around the table smiling. Jokes, camaraderie, the conviviality of old friends—positions and alternatives were not completely discussed. Interruptions were common." That is a description of Powell's concern about the informality of the process at that point in the decisionmaking. It's a criticism. It's something he felt and there it is.

There was some criticism that this group [Bush, Scowcroft, Powell, Cheney, and Baker] knew each other too well. They went back in some cases twenty years and there was not a rigor where somebody would come in and say, "Look, we can do this or we can do this or we can do that:" the classic option paper. It was a kind of feeling for each other; they knew where things were going, they understood Bush, and so views were not fully aired. I think that's probably a valid criticism.

George Bush was not interviewed. I asked to interview him and he, through his press secretary, Marlin Fitzwater, declined in an interesting letter. This was while the war was going on in the Gulf and Fitzwater said that Bush was not giving interviews during the war. He also said that the president wouldn't give interviews for books—a policy I was not aware of—because of the book's commercial value. Which, if you really think about it, doesn't make a whole lot of sense because he certainly gives interviews to newspapers and magazines and television, and they're all commercial enterprises. But that's what he said.

GENERAL NORMAN Schwarzkopf received a lot of notoriety before, during, and after the war, the symbol of this victory, obviously a talented man. He was at a backwater command. The central command had no troops before the invasion of Kuwait—just a staff of about seven hundred down in Florida. He was headed for retirement and, if you will, oblivion. He was the commander in the region. He knew the area and they kept him. He obviously brought a lot to the job, but the book also describes how much Cheney, Powell, and the White House brought to him and insisted that certain things be done. It lays broader responsibility for the success and makes it pretty clear, for instance, that the first war plan that he presented to the Pentagon and the White House was not this famous "Hail Mary, go around" maneuver. Granted, he had a very short period of time to present it and develop it; about forty-eight hours initially—but his plan was right up the middle; it would have been disastrous. It would have been something that would have killed certainly thousands of Americans—something that clearly did not withstand review. In fairness to Schwarzkopf, when he had his chief of staff present it, his chief of staff in the last slide in the briefing said, "These are General Schwarzkopf's caveats," and one of them essentially was, "We don't have enough troops and this is very preliminary and we don't think it would work and we're not saying we should do this, but here's an idea."

Key portions of the grand campaign were developed by a half dozen junior officers in their second year at the Army Command and General Staff College at Fort Leavenworth. These majors and lieutenant colonels, nicknamed the "Jedi Knights," had been sent to Saudi Arabia to apply the elements of advance maneuver warfare—probing, flanking, surprise initiative, audacity—to the war plan. . . . These ideas, . . . that you come at something not necessarily from the front door are all laid out in a very unclassified army operations manual, which is the Bible for them. In chapters six and seven it takes the [1863] Battle of Vicksburg in the Civil War as a model of how to do that. What really is surprising is that Saddam Hussein or some of the majors and lieutenant colonels in the Iraqi army didn't study our army and realize what we were likely to do.

PROBABLY THE PERSON who surprised me the most was [then] Secretary of Defense Dick Cheney. He came in very much a conservative, a Republican who had been Gerald Ford's White House chief of staff during the last year of the Ford presidency. He had been in Congress for ten years as a U.S. representative from Wyoming; he'd been in the Republican leadership, [was] thought of as the conservatives' conservative, and had never served in the military. He was sent to the Pentagon at the last minute by Bush when the nomination of John Tower was defeated [in the Senate]. Cheney learned the ropes at the Pentagon; he learned the system and got into detail. In a sense, if you would look for a model of civilian control of the military, he might represent it.

Cheney learned about war plans, he learned about weapons systems, he knew the White House, the Congress, and made sure that he was not making [a hasty] decision, say, about war plans in the Gulf. But he spent the hours to learn all the details and made sure that they answered all of his questions. He was feared, respected, not one of the boys, not inclined to go down and have a beer on Friday afternoon with the joint chiefs of staff or his own staff, but somebody who was very business-oriented in the sense of the business of the Pentagon. He was somebody, who if you look at the constituencies a secretary of defense has to serve—the military, the White House, the Congress, the world diplomatic scene—he mastered them all.

WARS AND THE USE of force are very emotional issues in this country. Even people who are wildly enthusiastic about it know that we killed lots of people and we risked a great deal in both Panama and the Gulf. The people who were passionately opposed to it often are the people who want more information on it. Both sides actually want more information on it. I have found when you write a book like this, you get calls and letters and talk to people [who think] the war is a big deal. The average person who might buy or read this book realizes what we were risking, how we were defining not just a foreign policy or the Bush presidency, but how we were defining what this country is. There is a deep awareness of the trauma of Vietnam among a whole age range in this country and, in a sense, this is the other side of Vietnam. People feel good about it but still feel quite hesitant and not exactly sure where it all fits in, and they want to know more.

Last Days of the First Bush White House

by

JOHN PODHORETZ

Despite record high approval ratings after the Persian Gulf War, President George Herbert Walker Bush lost his bid for reelection in 1992 to William Jefferson Clinton. John Podhoretz, a journalist and former speechwriter for Ronald Reagan, examined the inner workings of the first Bush White House in Hell of a Ride: Backstage at the White House Follies, 1989–1993, *published by Simon & Schuster in 1993. Mr. Podhoretz told us several stories from the end of President Bush's term when he appeared on* Booknotes *on December 19, 1993. Mr. Podhoretz is currently a freelance writer working at the* New York Post.

THE ANIMATING THEORY of this book is that the Bush presidency was largely the result of his running on the record of Ronald Reagan and then [when] in office, turning away from the policies and style of governing that made Reagan successful. George Bush began to stumble through a series of errors that eventually cost him his reelection.

[I use eight] freeze-frames, portraits of Bush White House staffers over the course of the last eighteen months of the presidency. . . . Every one of these freeze-frames is an unnamed specific staff [member] a real person—not a composite—someone whom I interviewed extensively. . . . They are interior monologues that are reflections of many hours of interviewing each one of the players portrayed in the freeze-frames.

The book is about the . . . midlevel staffers, people in their twenties and thirties who are the ones who basically run the White House, who work under the big guys: the [president's] chief of staff and [the budget] director. [My subjects] work in the West Wing in proximity to the president, but are the ones who stage the events, write the speeches, deal with the fallout from the public. The book is written . . . from their perspective and not from the perspective of what was going on inside the Oval Office, why Bush made the decisions that he made. It's about what life is like for people who work in a White House that is beginning to fall apart.

People who work in the White House at this level generally work ninety to one hundred hours a week. It means that if they are married, they never get to the Little League game, they don't get to the parent–teacher conference, they don't get home to dinner very often. When they make promises to go to the school play, they often have to break them. It's an interesting complement to the idea of family values. . . . The White House staff I'm talking about comprises about 350 people, so they must be on call to help the presidency run, and they live a kind of Washington life that can be very grueling on families.

[THE STORY] BEGINS at the parade honoring the American victory in Desert Storm in June of 1991 and ends with the last week in office as a young staffer has to take down a banner that he hung outside his office window. In between, I chart what happened, from the 91 percent approval ratings that Bush had in March 1991, to 38 percent on November 3, 1992, and then out of office January 20, 1993.

At the close of the Gulf War, there was an atmosphere of self-congratulation and excitement around the Bush White House, which largely contributed to their defeat. Everyone in the White House believed and assumed that because Bush's popularity had skyrocketed so extraordinarily and because he was seen to have had such a decisive victory, there was no way he was going to lose [the 1992 election]. This atmosphere moved down from the Oval Office to capture the hearts and minds and souls and gait of the staff who worked in the White House complex itself.

Most of the people who worked in the Bush White House were bound to George Bush by a kind of personal fealty. Bush is a man of extraordinary personal qualities: charismatic, friendly, very much present when people talk to him, people from his closest aides to the lowliest campaign worker. Bush [was] unique in the annals of the modern presidency and in the annals of Washington. He had built this ferociously loyal relation to the people who worked with him. The problem, of course, is that it does not necessarily get you very far. Bush's staff did not write books about him, did not leak about him, did not do all the things that the Reagan staff did against Ronald Reagan, who was a stronger and more decisive and more charismatic leader but was quite distant and aloof from his staff. His staff eventually sort of took revenge against him in large measure. But Bush's staff . . . loved him in a way that is very rare among Washington staffs. They thought and Bush thought that their love for him was reflective of the mood of the country. He lived in an atmosphere that was so friendly to him that he transmuted this and imagined that his daily life reflected the spirit of the country and reflected the spirit of the country toward him. It was the fundamental miscalculation that proved to be so disastrous to him.

[IN ONE FREEZE-FRAME, I wrote about a freak storm that tore apart President Bush's home in Kennebunkport, Maine, in November 1991.] It's almost novelistic how life unfolds. . . . There were almost Shakespearean signs that George Bush was not going to win reelection; that is, that nature in a peculiar way was turning against him.

Bush was rained on constantly—terrible freak storms. There was a barbecue in Illinois on what was supposed to be a sunny day in August and there was a rainstorm. The day after he left the Republican Convention to do a rally in Louisiana—a downpour. He had the famous gastrointestinal bout when he met the Japanese prime minister at a banquet and had an unfortunate incident there. There were all sorts of things that don't happen to people for whom things are going well, but seem to happen to people for whom things are going badly. This incident at Walker's Point when a freak storm destroyed his mildly ancestral home in Kennebunkport was almost a portent of what was to come.

MANY PEOPLE remember [the banquet in honor of the president of Japan] because it was a staple of humor on the late-night talk shows. President Bush was stricken with a bug and vomited into the lap of the Japanese prime minister, a sight that was frightening for the first couple of minutes because it really looked as though he might be terribly, terribly ill, and then subsequently it became inadvertently comic. This trip . . . to Japan was itself a comedy of errors. Scheduled to take place as a foreign policy trip in November of 1991, the failure of Republicans, primarily Richard Thornburgh in the Senate race in Pennsylvania in November of 1991, created a panic inside the White House that Bush was spending too much time on foreign policy. The trip was canceled; it was then rescheduled, and it was decided it would become a domestic [policy] trip to Japan in which Japan would be asked to change its policies on car imports and exports.

Many people in the White House were very angry because they thought this was a valuable trip. [They felt that commerce secretary] Robert Mosbacher was coming in seizing and hijacking control. "Mosbacher had his grubby paws all over the trip"—this is the way White House people talk and think; these are relations of power. They thought that what they were doing was life-and-death work. They were not modulated, they were not calm, they did not take things in stride. It's a very embattled atmosphere, and people got very heated in their views of each other.

[ANOTHER FREEZE-FRAME in the book features a controversial figure in the Bush White House.] "The French breakfast-roll man" was a man named Eugene Croisant; many different pronunciations of his name were attendant. He was a management consultant brought into the White House by Samuel Skinner, the second chief of staff, to advise Skinner on how to organize the White House. This was an act almost unparalleled in White House history— the notion that the guy who was running the president's political operation and personal staff would need a professional business consultant from Madison Avenue to tell him how to run politics in Washington. It was viewed with a kind of despair and contempt that this had happened in the first place— that the chief of staff to the president of the United States, one of the most powerful jobs in America, was being performed by somebody who was admitting to his staff upon coming in that he did not know how to perform his job.

BOB TEETER, the chairman of the president's reelection campaign, constantly shifted his own opinion of what issues were and were not playing with the public. One week he would tell people that education was very important; the next week he would tell them that a reform agenda was important. When speechwriters tried to then reconcile his directive of the week, he would then announce that, no, in fact thus and such was more important. Every single poll that came out changed his mind. It was very frustrating for these guys because they did not know exactly what line was going to be taken by the reelection campaign.

"THE LONGEST DAY," [another] freeze-frame [describes one speechwriter's view of] Bob Grady, the number two official in the Office of Management and Budget run by Richard Darman, who was the most powerful staffer in the four years of the Bush White House. The speechwriter said, "You really like him; he's terrifically smart and lively, but you do find his office a little disconcerting. Its walls are covered with every award he has ever received, dating back to high school, not to mention two dozen photos of him shaking hands with every dignitary he has ever met—not only the traditional photos of Grady with Bush and Barbara and Reagan but also Grady with Jesse Jackson."

There is a kind of White House etiquette and style of personal self-congratulation. It's very odd; . . . it is a matter of style that people hang photos of themselves with celebrities, political celebrities . . . . This generic White

House style has been the case through administrations, since the invention of the photograph. . . . Grady was an exceptional example of this. Grady had almost created a museum effect. That was why it was so startling, because he did have, I think, twenty-four photos of himself with President Reagan, with the governor for whom he'd worked, with Arnold Schwarzenegger, with all sorts of people, including Jesse Jackson, which was a startling thing to have on the wall of a Republican White House.

THE WHITE HOUSE is a totalistic atmosphere. Someone who is in the senior echelons of the White House drives in, probably 7:00 in the morning, goes up to the gate, pops his trunk, the Secret Service looks in his trunk, finds there are no bombs in it, lets him go through onto West Exec, which is the street that separates the White House from the Old Executive Office Building. [He or she] parks in the parking space, goes into the White House mess, the dining room of the White House for the White House senior staff, for breakfast, goes to the senior staff meeting and then from 9:00 in the morning until probably 7:30 at night is on the phone constantly—seventy, eighty, ninety phone calls, a couple of meetings maybe, maybe sneaks a little lunch. And people love this. Peggy Noonan, in her book *What I Saw at the Revolution*, says, "Everybody in the White House is happy." It's true. People do not quit; people do not resign out of frustration. People leave the White House when their hands are pried loose from the fence.

[As a White House staffer, you have "arrived" when you are given a] beeper and cellular phone. You have a beeper, you have a White House cellular phone in your car, and, most significantly, you have what is known as a drop in your house. A drop is a phone line that is directly connected to the White House operator so that when you pick it up, rather than getting a dial tone, you get a voice saying, "Can I help you, Mr. Podhoretz?" You say, "Yes, I very much need to speak to Chief of Staff Sam Skinner." The operator says, "Just a moment, please." I think about twenty-five [White House staffers receive this perk].

[On the road] White House staffers have a White House phone so they can communicate with their superiors in the White House. However, it is illegal to conduct business for a convention or for Bush's reelection campaign on the taxpayer's dime. So if [a staff member] picked up this phone and called a local number in Houston to say somebody in the campaign wanted X, that was campaign business. He would be violating federal campaign law. So they gave him a second phone, [to wear] on his hip, and this was the phone he used to call and say the campaign needs thus and such. Then on the first phone he would conduct his White House business. It was a very elaborate way of dealing with federal election law. . . . Maybe fifty to one hundred [staff members] had two phones [at the 1992 Republican National Convention].

[IN THE BOOK'S final freeze-frame, I describe a staff member who hung a big banner on the outside of the Old Executive Office Building] hanging off 17th Street. . . . It was the last week before the Clintons were arriving to take up residence, and this fellow had had this banner printed up that said, "We Will Be Back." A man from the General Services Administration, whose office was down the block from this, took one look at it, stormed into his office and said, "You've got to take this down. How dare you do something so . . . outrageously partisan." The fellow who is the subject said, "You have no authority here; only the White House staff has authority to deal with this." Tim McBride, who was once Bush's closest personal aide and was in charge of White House administration, was called. Tim McBride said, "Take the sign down."

[About the staffer who hung the banner, I write,] "Standing in this office which has been emptied of all its files so they can be carted away to the future Bush library where no one will ever look at them, the feeling comes over you in a nihilistic rush. He is the reason that things were never quite right, never ever. George Bush, empty man." By the end of the administration, a number of people looked at George Bush and said, "There's no there there," rather like Gertrude Stein said of Oakland. There was no core there; there was no core of conviction, and it was the lack of this core of conviction that had cost Bush the presidency.

It's a sad experience to write about failure. This is a book about a failure. It gets to you; it washes over you, the melancholy, the sense of wasted opportunity that it provided every day.

Dan Rostenkowski's
Fall From Power

———————

by

RICHARD E. COHEN

Dan Rostenkowski was born in Chicago, Illinois, on January 2, 1928. He was elected to the U.S. Congress in 1959 and served as a congressman for the next thirty-six years. Rostenkowski was held in high regard through most of his political career. However, his career in public service ended when he was indicted for misuse of official funds, lost his congressional seat, and was sentenced to seventeen months in prison. National Journal *reporter Richard E. Cohen appeared on* Booknotes *on September 19, 1999, to discuss* Rostenkowski: The Pursuit of Power and the End of the Old Politics, *published by Ivan R. Dee in 1999.*

DAN ROSTENKOWSKI [as a Democratic U.S. representative from Illinois] was chairman of the House Ways and Means Committee for thirteen and a half years. It's the most powerful committee in Congress. Their job is, in effect, to originate all tax legislation, and they control most international trade issues. They have jurisdiction over Social Security, Medicare, and welfare. The Ways and Means Committee has control over most entitlement programs and aspects of revenue raising. . . . Dan Rostenkowski, after serving thirty-six years in Congress, ended up in federal prison because he pleaded guilty to two offenses.

The U.S. attorney's office here in Washington, D.C., spent two years, from 1992 until the indictment in May of 1994, investigating all aspects of Dan Rostenkowski's finances. The seventeen counts included many other charges of basically, in one way or another, ripping off the taxpayer, and as the U.S. attorney said, betraying the public trust.

His view when he pleaded guilty and his view now is that he continued to play by the rules in place when [he was] first elected to Congress in 1958. Under those rules, he believed his practices and the way he ran his office was proper. . . . Jack Murtha [a Democrat] from Pennsylvania, like Rostenkowski, opposed many of these new rules, but as Murtha said to me, "When the rules change, members of Congress have to adapt." Murtha adapted to the rules changes. Rostenkowski . . . was too arrogant to think he needed to change his life.

Another member of Congress, Dennis Eckart, who was a younger [Democratic] member from Ohio . . . said, "During Rostenkowski's years, the road curved, but Rostenkowski kept driving straight." Rostenkowski was old-fashioned. . . . He thought these rules were silly, frankly, and that it was more important that he legislate in the national interest. That was his view.

THE MAIN COUNT [in the indictment against him] the one that is most often described to the public in newspaper articles and by the prosecutors, was that he illegally exchanged postage stamps he received as a member of the House for cash. The prosecutors suggested that he pocketed the cash. But because the prosecutors never presented their evidence in this case; all we had were maybe twenty pages of an indictment. We never saw the government's evidence. Rostenkowski firmly denied that he ever received cash in exchange for stamps. There were a number of individuals—House officers, one other member of the House; Joe Kolter [a Democrat] from Pennsylvania—who said they were guilty of stamps for cash or other violations at the post office. That was the centerpiece of the indictment.

He confessed to the two counts to which he ultimately pleaded guilty in April of 1996, although he said that what he did was no different from what many or even most other members of Congress did. The [first of the] two actions to which he pleaded guilty was payroll padding, putting individuals on his payroll, like teenage kids who were children of friends, for summer jobs. Rostenkowski was up front about the fact that these individuals didn't do a lot of work, but that it was good for them to see government in operation. It's clearly illegal under the law to be on a government payroll and not do work. But it's something that goes back decades in American government and politics.

The other offense to which he pleaded guilty [involved a perk]. All members of Congress have allowances to make purchases, for example, at the [House or Senate] stationery store. He used his allowance to purchase crystal sculptures and other kinds of china, which he gave to friends rather than using those sculptures as part of his government work.

AT FIRST HE reported to the Bureau of Prisons Federal Medical Center in Rochester, Minnesota, which is affiliated with the Mayo Clinic. The reason he went to the federal prison hospital in July of 1996 is because he had had prostate surgery and needed aftercare. So he was in Rochester, Minnesota, at a higher-security prison for inmates with health problems. He was there between July and December of 1996, and then he was transported in December to [the federal penitentiary in] Oxford, Wisconsin, and remained there [for the next eight months].

He told me—and I believe him—that I was the only person who visited him while he spent more than a year in jail. Even though his wife and his four daughters were in Chicago, maybe a three-hour drive from the federal prison, he didn't permit them to visit him. There were lots of friends from Washington and Chicago who wanted to visit him. [But] he said no. He didn't want anyone to see him while he was in jail.

He was [dressed] in prison fatigues, which were very drab green. He had on glasses that may have been prison issue. . . . Rostenkowski's job while he was in prison . . . was to read the meters on the boiler. He did that fine; it wasn't very onerous, [but] it showed how much he had fallen.

I saw a guy who then and now refused to be beaten down by a very unpleasant turn of events, being sent to jail and having a very painful end to his political career. Even in prison, he enjoyed his life, as he said to me then. Even while he was in prison, he wanted to get it over with so that he could resume his life in Chicago, where he was respected as a member of the community. And he thought he could do that. He wanted to get to it.

There weren't bars [on the doors or windows]. However, it would have been very ill-advised for individuals to have walked away. The inmates wanted to serve their time, follow the rules, and leave. There were just a couple hundred male prisoners there. I talked to Rostenkowski in what was a very, very modest cafeteria. Let me assure everyone there were no golf courses there, there were no tennis courts. He got his exercise; he lost about seventy pounds while he was at Oxford by eating better and by doing a lot of walking. This minimum-security prison in Oxford was immediately adjacent to a much higher-security prison a quarter mile away with a high barbed-wire fence, some rolled wire at the base.

[He served] thirty-six years [in Congress, representing Chicago's] Eighth District; it's now the Fifth District. It started off on the northwest side of Chicago, which in 1958, when he was first elected, was a heavily Polish, largely white district. . . . Milwaukee Avenue was the center of the district. Over the years, as Poles moved out to the suburbs, a lot of Hispanics, Mexicans, and some Asians moved in. The district changed, not only in the demographics but the geography. He moved east to the lakefront, and that was his [district in his] closing years.

Rostenkowski loved the camaraderie, the bonhomie, the life's blood, of politics and engaging with colleagues, with other politicians, with friends. It used to be said of him, and largely correctly, that he'd conducted a lot of business over steak and martinis. Morton's is a restaurant chain\originally started in Chicago—Rosty knows the original owner. Morton started up restaurants here in Washington and elsewhere. It was Rosty's kind of restaurant. When he was a young politician, he would have dinner with older men, white men typically, and they would share stories, have a good time, and that was his political life.

When he went to dinner at Morton's or other places in Washington, if it was just a bunch of politicians, fellow members of Congress, they probably shared the tab among each other or maybe back in the '60s, when the political money routine and the rules were different and much looser than they are now, one of the members of Congress or politicians might have gone into a personal fund to get the money. They might have had a lobbyist come with them . . . the rules permitted that in those days. The rules would not permit that now. He also did a lot of traveling, where companies wanted him or interest groups asked him to speak to their members. . . . The restrictions got tighter over the years.

IN 1989, IN THE middle of Rostenkowski's chairmanship, he put on a big shindig, a party to celebrate the committee's two-hundredth anniversary. He had to raise [$800,000 to pay for it all]. In the common practice in Washington, he went to interest groups, to big companies, perhaps to some labor unions that have issues before the Ways and Means Committee, and he and his staff and fund-raisers raised money in $10,000 and $20,000 chunks from these groups. That $800,000 put on a big private dinner that was held in the Ways and Means Committee hearing room in the Longworth Building. They produced this fairly impressive book, a history of the Ways and Means Committee, a commendable book. Not many people ever read it; it had a very limited circulation, but it was a pretty good book about the committee.

You don't need [a party to mark the bicentennial of the House Ways and Means Committee]. Rostenkowski wanted to do it to make the members of the committee feel a sense of history, feel important. And, frankly, it was a way for Rostenkowski to show his importance to others. . . . He wanted to bring many of its current members and former members together. Among the former members of the committee who attended that dinner in July of 1989 was the then president of the United States, George H. W. Bush, who was a good friend of Rostenkowski's.

[Journalist Cokie Roberts emceed that evening.] Her late father was Hale Boggs, a Democratic member of Congress and a member of the Ways and Means Committee. . . . In 1970 Hale Boggs had just been elected majority leader. [Democrat] Carl Albert of Oklahoma had just been chosen Speaker of the House. Dan Rostenkowski, who'd been in the House for twelve years, very much thought he was in line to be majority whip, and he had the support of Hale Boggs. But it was the decision of Carl Albert. Albert was unhappy with Rostenkowski for various reasons, some of which go back to the 1968 [Democratic National] Convention in Chicago, where Rostenkowski showed up Albert [when he "took charge" and "brought order" to Albert's convention].

[Becoming] majority whip would have put Rostenkowski on the track to be Speaker of the House, which was his goal. Albert said no, he wasn't going to give it to Rostenkowski. Rostenkowski was surprised. . . . Rostenkowski, even though he wanted to be whip, ran for a third term as Democratic caucus chairman, and he thought he had no opposition. But Albert . . . put up Tiger Teague, a Texas Democrat, to run against him and Teague won. Rostenkowski was stunned. He was in tears because he thought his move up the ladder of power in Congress was over.

[Boggs later] died in an airplane crash in Alaska in 1972, when he was the [House] majority leader. [His daughter] Cokie Roberts was raised as a kid in Washington. Even as a kid, she was very well connected to the House of Representatives and she was friendly with members, including Dan Rostenkowski. She's become something of a media celebrity and she enjoys emceeing various events on Capitol Hill.

THE COMMITTEE assignment process in which senior members of the House determine which junior member gets appointed to which influential committee used to be done by the Ways and Means Committee, Rostenkowski's committee. But the Democratic reforms of Dick Bolling [from Missouri] and David Obey [from Wisconsin] and others took the power away from the Ways and Means Committee. Democrats [instead] gave it to the leadership. But Rostenkowski really loved that process, acting like a boss. And he worked very closely and effectively with Jack Murtha in determining who got on the Ways and Means Committee, who got on the Appropriations Committee. . . . It was good old-fashioned politics.

David Obey was a leader and remains a leader of the reformers. He, as a leader of the reformers, achieved most of the changes that they wanted. Has it made the House a better institution? Dan Rostenkowski would say no. Changes, reforms, probably were inevitable, but even after the reforms were made [and] the Democrats accommodated themselves to change, some of the old practices in which members could gain more influence by being around for a while—the influence of committee and subcommittee chairmen—never really quite disappeared. . . . Obey himself would say, "Yes, we achieved most of the reforms—not all, but most of the reforms—but there are still serious problems in the way the House operates."

MR. ROSTENKOWSKI doesn't talk to me or . . . many others about precisely what he does [now that he's out of prison]. He did tell me once that since leaving Congress in 1994, he has made more money annually than he ever made when he was in government. He also continues to receive his pension. With the assistance of his longtime secretary, Virginia Fletcher, he has a Washington office across the river in Arlington, Virginia. He also does work out of an office out of his home in Chicago. He spends more of his time in Chicago, actually, than he does in Washington. But essentially, what he does, I gather, is advise big companies, mostly Chicago-based companies and other groups in Chicago, about their corporate business, advises them about what might be going on in Washington. He does not do any lobbying as far as I know. He has not registered as a lobbyist. He comes to Washington on occasion to visit with old friends, but he's kept an extremely low profile here. And he tries to enjoy life.

A Half-Century of Meet the Press

TIM RUSSERT

NBC's Sunday morning interview program Meet the Press *is the longest-running show on network television. After two years on the radio,* Meet the Press *made its television debut in November 1947. In the more than fifty years it has been on the air, the show has hosted political leaders, journalists, and newsmakers from across the globe, including eight U.S. presidents. Moderator Tim Russert discussed the program and its history on* Booknotes *on December 7, 1997.* Meet the Press: 50 Years of History in the Making *was published by McGraw-Hill in 1997 to mark the show's fiftieth anniversary.*

[LAWRENCE SPIVAK, the founder of *Meet the Press*, died in 1994] at age ninety-three. He was remarkable. . . . The first call I made when I became moderator [of the program in 1991 was to Mr. Spivak]. He invited me to lunch. I said, "What's the mission of *Meet the Press*? What do you do each and every Sunday?" He said, "That's simple. You learn everything you can about your guest and his or her positions, and take the other side. If you do that each and every Sunday, you'll demonstrate the requisite objectivity and balance and deference of guests, and no one will ever complain, and you'll have a long and illustrious career." He said, "You know, because when you engage people in that kind of intellectual exercise, you create a little tension and you make a little bit of news." Wonderful advice.

Martha Rountree was the cofounder of *Meet the Press* with Lawrence Spivak. She came to Lawrence Spivak in the early 1940s and said, "There ought to be a television program where each week the nation's journalists sit down with a national or international newsmaker. And we can interview people like Joseph Stalin." . . . Spivak said, "Well, you'll never get Stalin and people won't watch that kind of news setting." She said, "Let's try it."

The first guest was James Farley, the postmaster general to Franklin Roosevelt, [Roosevelt's] real political conscience in many ways. The show was an instant success. Martha Rountree stayed with the program for a few years and then Lawrence Spivak bought her out.

[EARLY HIGHLIGHTS of the program include] Lawrence Spivak in his first interview with Senator Daniel Patrick Moynihan. This was a very important interview in Senator Moynihan's life and probably in the history of discussion of race relations. He had written the "Negro Family" report, and it talked about how three out of every ten births in the black community were to a single parent. He said, "This could be an impending crisis unless we deal with it." It's now seven out of ten, and many people who were critical of Senator Moynihan have now praised him for being prescient on that particular issue.

[In 1948] Whittaker Chambers had said Alger Hiss was a spy in Congress, [where Chambers was guaranteed] immunity from prosecution. Hiss said to Chambers, "You do that in open forum and I'll sue you." Chambers went on *Meet the Press* and did it and Hiss sued.

Joseph McCarthy came on *Meet the Press* several times. One time he brought a gun to the studio and put it on his thigh. Mr. Spivak said, "What is that for?" Joseph McCarthy said, "Who knows?"

May Craig was . . . a reporter from Portland, Maine. She became such a fixture on *Meet the Press* [with over 260] appearances. She wore a hat. She said, "So people will remember me." She wore white gloves and used to—a wonderful [gesture]—wave her finger. When Fidel Castro came on the program in 1959, he said, "Where is May Craig? I've had a crush on her for all these years."

[IN THE EARLY years of *Meet the Press* each program had four reporters, a moderator, and a guest.] We found that trying to do a moderator and four questioners, five people questioning, gave the newsmaker an unfair advantage in the following way: When the program began in 1947, people were not schooled in television. They would appear on the set of *Meet the Press* and regularly tell the truth in simple and plain language. Many of the political leaders now are seasoned and trained and coached by media advisers, some would say even manipulators. And it's very hard to get beyond the boilerplate, and it sometimes takes the fourth or fifth or sixth . . . follow-up question on one particular area to find out what the newsmaker is really thinking or what his plans really are for the country. And if you have five people asking questions on five different subjects, you never get beyond the boilerplate.

So we decided to step back and have some flexibility with the format, and we think it's paid off.

THIS IS MY SIXTH year as moderator. Favorite shows would have to be . . . Ross Perot, Newt Gingrich, and Bill Clinton.

Ross Perot was 1992. He had been quite successful in defining the deficit as the important issue in the '92 presidential campaign. He came on as a candidate and said that we had to balance the budget. I said, "Many people agree with you. How are you going to do that?"

He said, "There's $180 billion in waste, fraud, and abuse." I said, "Well, is that a line item on the budget?" He said, "No." I said, "Then let's go through it in great detail, find the $180 billion, because, as you would say, Mr. Perot, that's where the rubber hits the road." He said, "Well, if you had told me you wanted to ask me questions like that, I would've brought my charts and I would've been prepared. But I don't wanna play this gotcha game."

I said, "It's not a gotcha game, Mr. Perot. If you're saying that we have to balance the budget, there's a responsibility to have a plan to do just that." It was very civil but testy. The next day he withdrew as a candidate for president for about eight weeks and then got back into the race. . . . He went out and hired a fellow named John White and they put together a book, which actually probably was the most honest way to balance a budget produced during the entire '92 campaign. I believe it was a direct result of his interview on *Meet the Press.*

Newt Gingrich was a remarkable day. The day after the interview, there were five front-page stories and five different subjects from the same interview. The *Los Angeles Times* talked about immigration and [California's Proposition] 209 [which would limit services available to illegal immigrants]. The *Washington Post* talked about the use of drugs by the White House staff. The *New York Times* talked about Bosnia. *USA Today* talked about Newt Gingrich advising the first lady to rent the movie *Boys' Town* about orphanages. It was just one of those most amazing days where Newt Gingrich decided that he was going to put forth the world according to Newt Gingrich. The headline writers across America enjoyed it thoroughly.

In 1993, on the forty-sixth anniversary of *Meet the Press*, President Clinton was our sole guest. It was in the middle of a minicrisis with Korea. . . . Many people thought we were on the verge of armed conflict with Korea. They were continuing to develop nuclear weapons.

I asked the president, "Just where do you draw the line? If the North Koreans insist on developing nuclear weapons, or if they would, God forbid, go into South Korea, what are the obligations of the United States?" He sat back in his chair and he put his finger up, and he said, "An attack upon South Korea is an attack upon the United States." That was a banner headline all across the world. The president of the United States had once again reaffirmed our alliance with South Korea and put the North Koreans on notice.

In the second half of the program, we talked about out-of-wedlock births and the underclass. The president [employed] a new term; he said, "I some-times believe now we have created a group called the outer class, a group of children who are so far removed from normal society that they're almost impossible to reach." It was really breaking out of the mold of liberal Demo-crat and, I think, really solidifying his view as a New Democrat, looking at the problems of race and children in a whole new context. He received enor-mous response from that interview on that particular issue.

BOB DOLE WAS on *Meet the Press* fifty-six times during his political career, which spanned [several decades]. He came to Washington in 1961. . . .

He was on television practically every other Sunday on one of the chan-nels or networks. It was a format that was made for Bob Dole. He was com-fortable sitting at the table, bantering back and forth, showing occasional humor, engaging [the audience] with the legislative process, talking about political tidbits and strategy.

When Dole ran for president in 1996, his advisers told him, "Stay off the Sunday shows. They're too dangerous." He appeared on *Meet the Press* in Jan-uary of 1996 and he talked openly about wanting Colin Powell to be his vice president and he talked openly about wanting to achieve a compromise on the issue of abortion in the party platform. And his handlers said, "That's it. No more, because he's gonna make news. Those darned Washington journal-ists are gonna get him in a corner and he's gonna say something he regrets saying."

I thought it was a terrible mistake. It was the one format, the one area, where Dole shined. The American people were comfortable watching Bob Dole on Sunday morning TV. He's not comfortable behind a podium. He's not comfortable in some of the more relaxed interview settings or the prime-time aspects of them. That's not who he is. He is from Russell, Kansas. He is the former majority leader of the United States Senate. If you asked anyone involved in any of the Sunday shows, they will tell you he was their favorite guest. The American people grew to like and respect him in that format. For [his advisers] not to have enough confidence in their candidate to continue that during the campaign, I believe was a blunder.

I wrote him a note and said, "If you win the presidency, will you do the fiftieth anniversary program from the Oval Office?" and he said, "Yes, I will." He lost the election, so I wrote him another note. I said, "Well, you lost the election and President Clinton has agreed to do the fiftieth anniversary pro-gram. Will you come on the week before, November 2, the first anniversary of your defeat, in effect, and talk about politics, past and future?" And he did. It was very reflective. He talked about the campaign and why he thinks he lost, largely because of the economy.

He talked, also, rather aggressively about his wife, Elizabeth, as a candidate for the presidency in the year 2000. He joked that if she won, he would be the first husband and his only demands were a car, driver, and beeper. He'd be in charge of movies and entertainment. But he was quite serious when he began to evaluate her chances in the year 2000 as a Republican candidate for president.

[THOUGH EARLIER in my career I worked for Democrats Senator Moynihan and Governor Mario Cuomo of New York, I work very hard to maintain my objectivity and believe I am able to do so.] My view is simple. When I sit in the moderator's chair of *Meet the Press*, I am there as a surrogate for the American people, for American journalists, and I must ask the best questions of my guest. My own personal political views are secondary and really don't come into play. One of the difficulties I've had, frankly, in studying up on both sides of an issue, I don't know what I believe anymore. I've become so well versed, I believe, on so many different subjects and understand each argument so well, I'm very confused and undecided on a whole variety of issues.

[The only time I believe I became too emotional in my questioning was with former Ku Klux Klan leader and Nazi sympathizer David Duke.] I was a panelist and David Duke was running against Edwin Edwards for governor of Louisiana. I said to Governor Edwards, "There are two issues that have been placed against you: that you're a womanizer and a gambler." He said, "Mr. Russert, I have never gambled illegally. And secondly, I'm sixty-five years old with white hair. For you to call me a womanizer is a compliment."

I then turned to David Duke and said, "Mr. Duke, the charge against you is that you are a Nazi sympathizer. What was it about the United States of America that made you want to be a Nazi?" He froze and he couldn't answer. He said, "It's unfair for you to keep focusing on my past. I want to be governor of Louisiana on a program of economic development. Why can't we talk about that?"

I took a chance. I had not prepared this question and I said, "Fine. Can you tell me that if you want to be the governor of Louisiana on a platform of economic development, what you will do and who are the three largest employers of the state of Louisiana?" He couldn't answer, and you could feel a hush come over the audience.

Rather than leave it at that, I leaned in and I said, "You mean to tell me you want to be governor of Louisiana and you can't name the three largest employers?" He said, "Well, there are lots of 'em." "Go ahead, Mr. Duke, name one. Just give me one." I watched the tape the next day and I said, "My God, I wasn't a moderator, I was a prosecutor."

I talked to Big Russ, my dad, and he said, "That was great." I said, "Dad, I went too far. I crossed the line. You can't be jabbing your guest with your finger and demanding answers and I made the point. He didn't know who the three biggest employers are. I made a mistake and I feel awful."

He said, "Oh, don't feel awful. If you're gonna make a mistake, make a mistake with a Nazi." My dad tried to make me feel better. But I learned a valuable lesson. Even though David Duke was a Nazi sympathizer and not someone that people have very much patience with, I shouldn't have done that. I crossed the line. I went too far. And I have never made the same mistake again.

Modern Presidents' Mothers

BONNIE ANGELO

In First Mothers: The Women Who Shaped the Presidents, *published by William Morrow in 2000, Bonnie Angelo, a writer living in Bethesda, Maryland, profiled eleven mothers of U.S. presidents. Ms. Angelo appeared on* Booknotes *on November 5, 2000, and spoke about Virginia Kelley, Bill Clinton's mother, and Barbara Bush, wife of the forty-first president and mother of the forty-third, as well as other mothers of modern presidents.*

I HAD COVERED the White House for a long time for *Time* magazine, but I remember the exact day [the idea for this book] came into my head, in 1968. I was covering the California primary with Robert Kennedy. The family was deployed all over the state campaigning for him, and I said, "With all the tragedy that your family has suffered at the hands of politics, how do you account for the fact that they're out there again?" He kind of looked at me under his eyebrows and said, "Have you met my mother?"

So I spent a couple of days with that formidable Rose Kennedy and saw just how resilient she was, how interested she was in all of the things connected with [politics] how devoted she was to Robert Kennedy, how she said at the time she would campaign for Teddy when his time came around. I began to think about it then, and back in my daily rounds at the White House, I kept hearing presidents mention their mothers and almost never mention their fathers. It began to impress me very much.

We all remember that day in August of 1974 when Richard Nixon was struggling through his resignation speech in the East Room of the White House and, in this real effort to keep himself together, blurted out, "My mother was a saint." I thought, "There it is again, thinking of his mother at this most traumatic time for himself."

LILLIAN CARTER [Jimmy Carter's mother] was a Georgia original. . . . I feel confident that Jimmy Carter could never have been elected president had it not been for her. From her earliest days, she was totally open-minded on race, and in south Georgia, that was not an easy thing. Jimmy Carter said, "My mother knew no color line." That was implanted in him. His father was a classic Georgia segregationist who died before the Supreme Court decision [in *Brown v. Board of Education,* desegregating public schools]. She was a great baseball fan; her great hero in 1947, that early, was Jackie Robinson. Now in Plains, Georgia, that was not a popular hero, but that's how strongly she felt about racial equality and tolerance. Without that, Carter could not have been nominated, much less elected.

VIRGINIA KELLEY [Bill Clinton's mother] was a totally different kind of creature. She was the only real twentieth-century girl [I wrote about]. She wrote an autobiography that was so candid and spared herself not at all. She was a rhinestones-and-racetrack lady. She loved nightclubs and she loved partying. [She had her hair done in a] skunk stripe because [as] she said, "When I walk in a room, I want everybody to look at me." She said, "If everybody but one person likes me, I've got to have that other person like me." Bill Clinton is just like that. Everybody's got to like him.

She had four husbands. She was actually married five times because she married Roger Clinton twice. Bill Clinton's father was killed in an automobile accident before he was born, so that was a very, very brief wartime marriage. [She had two sons.] She went to see [her younger son Roger Jr. once] in prison on a Christmas Eve because she felt he had to have something for Christmas. A friend went with her. They couldn't find anything but a sorry roadside motel, and she said, "It was Christmas Eve. There was nowhere we could get food. We got a Snickers bar out of the machine. We ate the Snickers bar, and I guess a Pepsi-Cola, waiting to see my son in prison. That was when I realized my life is like a country song." And it was. It was all of these terrible things that happened: bad husbands, abuse, alcoholism, one son who was a tremendous success beyond anybody's dreams, and one son who went to jail.

I think she gave Bill Clinton the sense that he could do anything. She backed him in every way. He wanted to go to Georgetown University, an expensive university in Washington. It would have been much cheaper to send him to the university in Arkansas, but she sent him there because she was the breadwinner in the family as a nurse-anesthetist. She said about herself, "Rules are not meant for me." Maybe she imbued that a bit with Bill Clinton, that he didn't have to play by some rules.

BARBARA BUSH IS in the category quite apart from the others in that she is the only woman, since Abigail Adams, to be both first lady and first mother.

. . . [She is a] very strong woman. Even George W. Bush's wife, Laura, says that he is just like his mother. She said they're both feisty. They are just like each other in that they say funny things. They used to fight when George W. was just a boy because they were so alike. At one point, recently, he said, "She gave me a lot of love and advice, and I gave her white hair."

ALL OF THESE [women] were daddy's girls. . . . There was such a special bond, with every one of these women and their own fathers. That's where their self-confidence and their sense of independent thinking came from, which enabled them to feel confident about bringing up these boys without a Dr. Spock, without anybody telling them what to do. They just did it on their own gumption. It was the father to the daughter to the son.

The 2000 Election

by

JEFF GREENFIELD

RALPH NADER

The 2000 presidential race between Texas Governor George Bush (R) and Vice President Al Gore (D) was the closest election in a generation. The outcome hinged on the state of Florida, which was deemed too close to call on election night, setting in motion a chain of events that culminated with a 5–4 decision by the Supreme Court to end a manual recount in Florida. On January 6, 2001, Vice President Al Gore presided over a meeting of Congress in which the electoral votes were tallied and George W. Bush was declared the winner. Also playing a role in the 2000 contest was longtime consumer advocate Ralph Nader, who garnered just under three percent of the vote as the Green Party's candidate. He described the experience in his book Crashing the Party: How to Tell the Truth and Still Run for President, *published in 2002 by St. Martin's Press. He appeared on* Booknotes *on February 3, 2002. Jeff Greenfield, political analyst for CNN, discussed the media coverage of this historic election in* Oh, Waiter! One Order Of Crow: Inside The Strangest Presidential Election Finish in American History, *published by Putnam in 2001. He appeared on* Booknotes *on July 22, 2001.*

JEFF GREENFIELD

Both of these fellows [George Bush and Al Gore] could have been presidential candidates fifty years ago. People talk a lot about how television has changed politics at the root, and I'm a little bit skeptical about that. After all, what is so weird about the son of a senator from Tennessee ascending through the ranks to become a senator from Tennessee, displaying at a young age a lot of ambition, a lot of intelligence, and over a long period of time building alliances?

BUSH IS A LITTLE different because he did do this in a much more accelerated fashion. But, again, he's the son of a president. We have a lot of politicians who get into the family business. You look at the folks in the House and Senate and ask how many of them had fathers in politics, it's an astonishingly high number. In Bush's case, it would be a little harder to predict going from a private citizen to president of the United States in six years. I think you've got to go back to Grover Cleveland and Woodrow Wilson to find those examples.

IF YOU HAD told me, at the start of my life, "Someday you will see an election, not only where the popular vote loser gets elected, but where it takes a month and a half or so to figure out who won," I'd have said, "That sounds like an implausible story to me."

In the first post-election blush, within forty-eight hours, it struck me that both sides were picking up rhetoric and banging away, without any regard to its reality. The Bush people were saying, "No, that Palm Beach ballot was fine. Palm Beach is a hotbed of support for Pat Buchanan." Well, no. It's clear that those votes—thousands of those votes—were cast mistakenly. And the Democrats were saying, "Well, we know what to do. Let's have a re-vote, or let's have a judge look at those ballots and allocate them to the guy really meant to have those votes." You can't do that. . . . Maybe they were over-zealous, but clearly neither of those arguments could stand the cold light of day.

ONE OF THE reasons the Supreme Court has historically been held in high regard and why, toward the end of this campaign, a great majority of Americans named it as the one institution they had confidence in to deal with— this was before their election decision—was because we don't see them on television. How many people have ever seen the Supreme Court? I never have seen a Supreme Court case argued, never. If you're a tourist or a reporter, you go there and the curtain opens and these nine folks in black robes step out. The very fact that they don't come to us through this incredibly intimate, familiar medium of television has given them a certain kind of stature. Now, how much they lost because of this [election] decision, we'll find out. . . .

[THE TITLE of my book comes from] something that I actually said on election night. CNN had given Florida to Gore. The Bush people were on all the networks frantically trying to say, "This is premature"—for good political reasons. [Bush adviser] Mary Matalin had just finished her explanation, and I said, somewhat dismissively, "Well, it's true, Mary, that sometimes we in the media have to eat crow." At that precise moment, [CNN anchor] Bernard Shaw broke into our conversation to say, "Hold it, hold it. We're pulling Florida back from Gore." And I said the only thing that came to mind, in that first of the two wretched moments, "Oh, waiter, one order of crow."

RALPH NADER

Out of all my votes, 25 percent came from Bush, 38 percent came from Gore, and the rest wouldn't have voted. We got over a million new voters, in effect.

Gore slipped on a lot of bananas. The question is, which banana do you want to blame? You could blame his loss of Tennessee, where he had his national headquarters for thirteen months, [or Bill Clinton's] home state, Arkansas. You could say that his own Democratic leaders in the counties in southern Florida did him in. There are a lot of reasons he lost. He didn't do all that well on the debates. He came across as stiff.

[Yet] this argument goes on with the Democrats that we cost Gore the election. A lot of them are still angry with me. . . . I met with [House Democratic Leader] Dick Gephardt in February of 2001. He didn't say I cost Gore the election; he said we ran a terrific campaign. And I met with Senator Harry Reid, the number two Democrat in the Senate. He acknowledged that the Green Party's spillover votes elected Maria Cantwell [as U.S. Senator from Washington]. She won by 2,300 votes. I got 103,000 in Washington state, and there was no Green Party Senate candidate. Our folks went overwhelmingly for her. That brought the Senate to 50-50 and set the stage for Senator Jeffords to turn independent and flip the Senate to the Democrats. I haven't gotten a single letter of thanks from any Democratic senator.

[I went to all fifty states during the campaign] and some more than once. I felt if I was going to run for president of the United States, I should go to every state. And in those states where we weren't on the ballot, I wanted to point out the terrible ballot access obstructions of these state laws, like Oklahoma and especially North Carolina and Georgia, where you have to get tens of thousands of signatures—many more than are required. In North Carolina, it was 53,000 or so—because they pick at them. They say, "Oh, no. This is an avenue. This is a street. This was not done by someone who has a residence in the county. It's just a petitioner." There are an unbelievable number of obstructions.

[My campaign raised $8 million] by letters in the mail, which means the contributions came in at $50, $100 or so. We did it by having huge rallies, filling Madison Square Garden and the Boston Garden and Portland and Seattle and L. A. and Chicago. They paid anywhere from $7, $10, to $20 for those rallies. We had the biggest paid rallies of any of the presidential candidates, including Bush and Gore. Thirdly, [we raised money] by maximum contributions by individuals who had no ax to grind: $2,000–$1,000 in the primary, $1,000 in the general. [We raised funds by] selling memorabilia and things like that—t-shirts. That was basically the way we did it. And we had around $800,000 of federal matching funds.

The campaign had three goals: one goal was to get on the ballots, and we got on in forty-three states. Another was to get into the presidential debates, and it did not happen. And the other one was to get 5 percent of the vote so they could fund the primary next year, the convention for the next time, in 2004. None of that happened. But what happened was quite important.

The 5 percent for Federal funds—that's a convenience [for a campaign]; sometimes I think it's better to be self-reliant and get your funding in $5, or $10, $20 segments from large numbers of people. Our big failure was being blocked from the debates because, right now, our political electoral system is so skewed that if a presidential candidate does not get on those three presidential debates, it is impossible to reach the electorate.

I campaigned in fifty states and didn't reach more than 1.5 percent of the number of people that I could have reached interacting with Bush and Gore on these presidential debates. Poll after poll showed that the people of this country wanted me and Pat Buchanan in those debates—even though they wouldn't vote for us, perhaps, in large numbers. They didn't think the debates should be a cure for insomnia.

I call the debate [organizers] "a malignant species" because they are perpetuating a private tyranny. They are basically saying that there are just two candidates that can reach the American people and, in that, that they have gotten the cooperation of the press. . . . Why ration debates? They don't ration VCRs. They don't ration entertainment. Why ration the critical opportunity for the American people to mix it up in all kinds of debates—regional debates, debates between two candidates, between four candidates? That's what brings people out to the polls. When 41 percent of the people stayed home in the year 2000, you've got a real problem. We've got the lowest participation of voters in the Western world.

The debate commission is a private company created in 1987 to replace the League of Women Voters-sponsored presidential debates. It was created by the Republican and Democrat parties, and is controlled by the Democratic Party and Republican Party. Because the mass media, by default, don't have their own presidential debates, they have accorded this debate commission, this private corporation, an incredible amount of power to decide which candidate is going to reach tens of millions of people.

PBS's Jim Lehrer should never have [agreed to moderate the 2000 presidential debates]. . . . Those rules [set by the candidates] compromised the quality and the probing nature of his performance. They tied his hands. He should have really said, "Look, I know we have to come to agreement on some format here, but if you tie my hands, I'll see you later."

As a result, the questions really were not varied enough. . . . There was never a question on globalization and GATT and NAFTA because they agreed on it. There was never a question on corporate crime because both

Bush and Gore were soft on it, or corporate welfare or even national health insurance. . . .

REPUBLICAN AND DEMOCRAT state legislators . . . have an interest in excluding third parties, excluding competition, excluding choice to the voters, even though . . . it was third parties [which led] the fights against slavery, for women's right to vote, the trade union movement, the farmer-populist-progressive movement—right into the twentieth century. It's a great record, even though only one third party ever won major party status: the Republican Party, which started in 1854 and elected a president in 1860. But they've really pushed the major parties into more humane, progressive, responsive postures.

It's really a disgrace that the two parties can't deliver more than half of the voters for themselves. I think if we had more initiatives and referenda on the ballot, more people would come out. Maybe if election day was a national holiday, more people would come out. Maybe if you didn't have the Florida-type obstruction problems and precinct address changes and so on, more people would come out.

A lot of the reason people don't vote is they don't think it means anything to them. They think that "they," whoever the powers that be, are going to decide what they're going to decide, and so why waste their time? That's one reason. There are other reasons. Some people are working the wrong hours, and they're commuting. They don't get there. Some people are so beset by poverty and by all kinds of illness and so on that they just don't get there.

The one thing that would get most people out is a "None of the above" option on every ballot line—for governor, or president, whatever. And if binding "None of the above" got more votes than anyone else on that line, say for mayor, it would cancel the election, send the candidates packing, and order new elections in thirty or thirty-five days with new candidates. That gives people an opportunity to say no. You can't say no when you vote in America. You have to vote for a Republican or a Democrat or whoever is on [the ballot]. A "no confidence" vote is very important.

It's gotten so bad that our democracy's at stake. And as Jefferson said, and Lincoln and Woodrow Wilson and Teddy Roosevelt said, when the concentration of power in fewer and fewer hands becomes extreme, the people have to become much more engaged.

IT'S TOO EARLY to say [if I'll run again in 2004, but] I do want to help build the Green Party. I'd like to see thousands of Green Party candidates at the local level. They're winning now. In fact, in November 2000, they won 25 percent of the seats that they were contesting at the local level. You can really win at the local level, and that's the best way to build a party.

September 11 and Osama Bin Laden

by

PETER BERGEN

On September 11, 2001 the United States experienced the greatest act of terrorism ever perpetrated on its homeland when four commercial airliners were hijacked and used as missiles. Two were flown into the World Trade Center Towers, one into the Pentagon, and the fourth crashed into a Pennsylvania field. More than 3,000 people died. For the first time, many Americans heard of Osama bin Laden, described as the mastermind of the attack, and of his Islamic fundamentalist followers, the al Qaida. On December 16, 2001, journalist Peter Bergen was asked to tell Booknotes *viewers what he had learned about bin Laden, described in his book* Holy War, Inc.: Inside the Secret World of Osama bin Laden, *published by the Free Press in 2001. Bergen detailed the environment that shaped Osama bin Laden and discussed the roots of Islamic fundamentalism and the response of the U.S. intelligence community.*

OSAMA MEANS "lion" in English. Al Qaida means "the base." He started it in 1989. After the Soviets withdrew in February of '89 from Afghanistan, bin Laden recruited people from around the world for holy wars, and they all got some sort of military experience and rubbed shoulders and got to know each other. This international cast of holy warriors, as it were . . . all of them wanted to change the governments in their native countries, like Egypt, or foment rebellion in various other places or eventually, in bin Laden's case, attack the United States. Al Qaida sprang out of all those people who traveled to Afghanistan.

OSAMA BIN LADEN lived in Afghanistan, Pakistan, Sudan, and Saudi Arabia. He studied economics and public administration in Saudi Arabia. His father died in '67. All the kids were pretty young; even Osama's oldest brother at that time would have only been only twenty. And so the family company was put in trust, and the estate was only divided in the '80s, and bin Laden apparently got about $35 million.

At a certain point, he became the biggest businessman in Sudan between '91 and '96. . . . It really was Holy War, Inc., in the sense that he had this huge array of businesses—from tanneries to bakeries to banks to construction businesses to trucking companies to import-export—cornering the market in certain Sudanese agricultural products, but at the same time running these paramilitary camps.

Money has been important, but it's not been vital to bin Laden's project. What's been vital is his ability to transfer a lot of rage against the United States, taking the localized rage of people against Middle Eastern governments which are authoritarian and corrupt, etc., and making the analysis that it's the United States' fault for all these problems. Getting people to go along with that idea and being able to organize them and recruit them and giving them the training to become quite deadly, that's bin Laden's genius. It's not his money.

He's always had access to some money, but at the end of the day the money's a bit of a red herring in the sense that it's not about money. It's about belief. The people that he recruits to him aren't paid. They're volunteers, they're not mercenaries. And the people who die in these operations . . . clearly there's no amount of money you can give to somebody like Mohamed Atta, who came from a prosperous Egyptian family anyway, to persuade him to fly a 747 into the World Trade Center.

[I WENT TO the village of Osama bin Laden's father.] It's a beautiful place in Hadhramaut, which is a very remote area of eastern Yemen. It looks perhaps a little bit like Arizona, the mesas and honey-colored cliffs. At the end of one of these valleys, you can find the town of Al-Ribat, which is bin Laden's ancestral village. It's about 5,000 people. If you go there as a westerner, you're a big deal. All the kids in the village just start running after you. It's not a place that's regularly visited.

Bin Laden's father left the village when he was a young man to go and seek his fortune in Saudi Arabia, but the family retains some links to the village. They gave some money for irrigation projects. There is a house there which is on bin Laden Street, which is this rambling, old, decrepit place that now houses an extended family—some of the more distant relatives of Osama bin Laden. It's so big that part of it is the village school. I went there with John Burns of *The New York Times* and we went talk to some of the remaining cousins.

To the south is the Arabian Sea, and then to the north is Saudi Arabia. A lot of Yemenis went to Saudi Arabia because Yemen is a very, very poor country. I think it's the poorest country in the Middle East, and so you get a lot of emigration, and one of the people who emigrated was Mohammed bin Laden, the father of Osama. But he was part of a pretty big movement. And one thing that's interesting about bin Laden's organizations, you'll find that some of the key people are Saudis, but they actually have Yemeni backgrounds like bin Laden himself. For instance, the person who's regarded as being the mastermind of the bombing of the *USS Cole* in Yemen is somebody whose family originates in Yemen, but grew up in Saudi Arabia and fought in Afghanistan, like bin Laden, against the Soviets.

The population of Yemen is seventeen or eighteen million; the number of guns in Yemen may be sixty-five million. . . . It's tribal. . . . It's really like stepping back into the Middle Ages. You see camels wearing blinkers; they make sesame oil in those giant mortars and pestles. It's like a scene out of some medieval painting.

Unfortunately, bin Laden's group managed to function pretty well there. They were able to bomb the *USS Cole,* and there were plans for some of bin Laden's followers to bomb the U.S. Embassy there. So it remains a place where pockets of al Qaida exist, although the Yemeni government has been apparently quite cooperative with the United States government in terms of trying to close al Qaida down there.

THE *USS The Sullivans* was a dress rehearsal for the *Cole* that occurred on January 3, 2000, which was towards the end of Ramadan. Basically, what happened is that the bombers overloaded their boats with explosives, and it sunk. But they learned from their mistakes and they came back and did the *USS Cole*. But the interesting thing about the planned attack on *The Sullivans* was that it was going to be part of a terrorist spectacular involving the bombing of Los Angeles International Airport (LAX), and also the bombing of tourist sites in Jordan. All of these things were going to be related for the new millennium. None of them actually worked out, either because of the incompetence of the plotters or good police work.

But it shows a) that al Quaida has had its share of failures, as it were, luckily and, b) it shows these rather grand-scale plans. This was a plan within the same time period to blow up an airport in America, blow up a U. S. warship in Yemen, and also blow up places associated with American tourists in Jordan. It would have been pretty devastating.

IT'S VERY EASY to Monday-morning-quarterback U. S. intelligence because, obviously, September 11 was the biggest failure of intelligence-gathering in American history. No one can argue with that fact. On the other hand, it has to be said that U. S. law enforcement and the intelligence community knew that bin Laden was a pretty serious character quite early on. As early as 1995, the prosecutors in the Southern District of New York, which has handled a lot of the terrorism cases—they worked for the initial Trade Center bombing in '93, for instance—were asking people in some terrorism trials, "Do you know Osama bin Laden?" Lawyers who were in the case at that time said they were kind of mystified—who was this Osama bin Laden? Even though they knew a lot about the case, why was it the prosecutors were asking about him? So his name was beginning to surface in '95 for American law enforcement and prosecutors.

By 1996, the U. S. State Department was calling him the most significant financier of Islamic extremism in the world, and actually had a very detailed white paper about who this guy was that he had training camps in Afghanistan and Sudan. Around about the same time, the CIA founded its own separate unit devoted to bin Laden . . . which was allowed to function, apparently, without having to deal with the Washington bureaucracy so much. So, the United States government was well aware that bin Laden was a very dangerous man.

On September the 10th, he was already on the Ten Most Wanted list and he had a $5 million reward on his head—unprecedented. So it's easy to say, "Well, that was a huge failure." It was an intelligence failure, but also the U. S. government had put a lot of effort into going after him. The fact is that he and his group were sort of *sui generis*, very unusual, in the sense that they were very disciplined and very organized. If you think about the terrorism that happened against American targets in the '80s, there was the Marine barracks bombing that killed more than 200 Americans in 1983. But it was never on this scale. The thing about this group is they kept making their plans more and more complex and more and more deadly as time went on. One can only hope that the Trade Center represents the apex.

[IN 1997, I interviewed bin Laden in Afghanistan.] We had a meeting with his media adviser, who looked at our camera equipment and said, "You can't take any of this" [into the interview] because they we're concerned about bin Laden's security and any kind of electronic device that might give away his location. They were very paranoid. He said, "Well, you can do your interview, but it'll have to be with our equipment." There was no point in arguing the matter; it was either that or no interview.

We [were transported in] a series of different trucks and we were blindfolded and it was the middle of the night. We went through various concentric rings of security around bin Laden. We were searched in a professional manner. They made it clear at a certain point that if we had a tracking device and we told them now, it wouldn't be a problem, but if we told them later, it would definitely be a problem.

We didn't really know how the whole thing was going to end, but we'd all spent a lot of time and effort trying to get to that point. We didn't know exactly where we were, but I'm pretty sure we were in the White Mountains where that al Qaida base was located; somewhere near there.

We weren't allowed to even take watches, so we had no idea of what time it was, exactly. I estimated it was some time before midnight when bin Laden finally showed up. He wasn't going to hang around. He just wanted to do the interview and go. He was with his entourage. I counted a total of maybe thirty people that I saw over the course of the night around him. In the direct entourage there were, maybe, ten. Everybody was armed, and some of them spoke pretty good English.

The interview itself taped for about an hour. Peter Arnett (then of CNN) and I had worked up a lot of questions for bin Laden. He didn't want to answer anything about his personal life, his family, or his finances. He just wanted to talk about why he was declaring war against the United States, which, after all, was the reason that we were there.

In a nutshell, his main gripe was the continued presence of American troops in Saudi Arabia, which he regarded as "infidels" trespassing on the Holy Land.

He had an almost feline aspect. He was not a very macho kind of guy at all. He was pretty low key, and he didn't strike me as being particularly charismatic. I don't speak Arabic, so maybe there's more charisma when you can understand him in the native tongue. But he didn't have this light bulb-like personality; he didn't swagger. You could barely hear him speaking because he was so low key.

Peter Arnett talked to him about Saddam Hussein and he said a very interesting thing. He said Saddam Hussein was a "bad Muslim," and that he had seized Kuwait for his own self-aggrandizement. Both are factually correct statements. But it was an early indicator to me that bin Laden regards someone like Saddam Hussein as basically a heretic.

BIN LADEN HAD been anti-American for a long time. But . . . on August 7, 1990, he was living in Saudi Arabia, and that was the day that President Bush announced Operation Desert Shield, which effectively meant the introduction of several hundred thousand Americans into Saudi Arabia. There were women soldiers trespassing on the Holy Land of Saudi Arabia; that was terrible, as far as bin Laden was concerned.

Eight years later to the day, bin Laden's men blew up two U. S. embassies in Africa within nine minutes of each other. That was sending a very clear signal. He's been very consistent about the fact that these [Americans] need to be expelled [from Saudi Arabia]. . . . His public statements usually mention this.

On September 11, he wanted to provoke some sort of trashing of our civilization. It was a total failure. The striking thing to me is that you can't justify the September 11 attacks in Islam because there is no language to justify it. Bin Laden doesn't even try and justify it. When people ask why the assault on American citizens, he says, "Well, they're Americans—they pay taxes and, therefore, they're complicit." That's hardly a religious justification. His message has had very little resonance in the [larger] Muslim world. You have not seen millions of people getting on the streets saying, "Osama, Osama, Osama." On the contrary, the demonstrations have been tiny, and you've seen every Middle Eastern government lining up to help against bin Laden because they understand he's a threat to them.

We've seen a lot of his type in the past century . . . whether it was Pol Pot or Stalin or Mao. These are all very different people. . . . But these men all share one absolutely common thing, which is "I know how to create paradise on Earth, and I'm absolutely certain about it, and if other people don't understand that, they're wrong and we should be able to kill them." The worst person in my view is the person who thinks that they have the perfect answer. They think they're going to create paradise here on Earth if their solutions are implemented. As it happens, they tend to create hells on Earth for people. Anybody with that level of certainty is almost certainly wrong, and will probably do a lot of damage.

September 11 and
the Roots of Islamic Terrorism

by

BERNARD LEWIS

Following the September 11 terrorist attacks on the World Trade Center and the Pentagon, attention focused on Muslim extremism in the Middle East. Historian Bernard Lewis appeared on Booknotes *on December 30, 2001 to discuss the history of the region and the roots of its conflicts. In his book* What Went Wrong?: Western Impact and Middle Eastern Response, *published by Oxford University Press in 2001, Lewis explores the complicated relationship between politics and religion in the Islamic world.*

ANYONE WHO FOLLOWED the Middle East could see which way things were going . . . Let me put it this way: here you have the Middle East, a very ancient and a very great civilization, which for 1,000 years or so was in the very forefront of human endeavor. It was the richest, strongest, most powerful, most wealthy of all living societies. It was also on the cutting edge of science, technology, in virtually every field. And then, suddenly, within a very short period, this society is overshadowed, outperformed in almost every respect, by what they had hitherto regarded as the ignorant, barbarous infidels beyond the northwestern frontier—namely, Christian Europe.

Suddenly, instead of winning every war, they lost every war. They were beaten in battle again and again, they who had been accustomed to unending triumphs and victories. The defeats on the battlefield at the peripheries didn't matter so much. But when they were defeated at the very center and when the greatest of the Muslim powers, the Ottoman Empire, was forced by victorious enemies to surrender and sign a peace treaty, in effect imposed by the enemy, that concentrated the mind wonderfully and began a debate. This was just over three hundred years ago, in 1699, and the debate has been going on ever since.

IT BEGAN WITH the military. The question was asked at the time, "Hitherto, we have always defeated the infidels. Now the infidels are defeating us. Why? What went wrong?" Then, defeat in the battlefield was matched by defeat in the marketplace. Suddenly, Western economies began to develop while theirs became stagnant, and even things which they regarded as peculiarly their own were better done elsewhere. Then they found themselves outperformed politically, and they looked to the reasons for their relative failure compared with Western success, and they tried a number of things. They started with the military: they modernized their armies, they adopted Western methods, Western weapons, Western drill, and so on. But it didn't help. They still lost war after war.

They decided that it must be the economy. So, they tried to industrialize, forced industrialization by the state, and that didn't work very well, either. Then they decided that it must be the political systems of the West. The magic talisman of Western wealth and power was elected assemblies, something entirely alien to their experience. So they tried that. None of it has worked, and this has been going on now for three centuries.

And it got worse and worse; not only were they outperformed by the West, they came to be dominated by the West as most of the Islamic world, with very few exceptions, came under the rule of one or other of the great European imperial powers—Britain, France, Holland, and Russia.

WHEN OSAMA BIN LADEN, in one of his pronouncements, said, "We have suffered this shame and humiliation for more than eighty years," I haven't the slightest doubt that all his intended audience knew exactly what he was talking about. They didn't have to start scurrying around and looking up reference books and saying, "Eighty years? What happened eighty years ago?" Now, we did that here; they didn't.

Slightly more than eighty years ago was the fall of the Ottoman Empire. The Ottoman Empire was the last great Islamic empire. In 1918, along with its German and Austrian allies, the Ottoman Empire was defeated; not only defeated, but occupied, partitioned, its capital occupied, its sultan a prisoner, and so on. This was seen as the ultimate point in the degradation and humiliation of the Islamic world. [It was defeated by] the Allies; that's to say Britain, France, and the United States.

At its height, the Ottoman Empire extended from the suburbs of Vienna to the frontiers of Iran and the Persian Gulf in the East, across north Africa, as far as the frontiers of Morocco, and a large part of southeastern Europe. It was a very mighty power.

IT WAS A SLOW and painful process, and the end result was that they were driven from one province after another and eventually lost control, even of their capital and their heartlands. Later, they were able to get out of that because of a remarkable man called Mustafa Kemal, later surnamed Ataturk, who led a rising in occupied Anatolia and was able to drive out the allied occupation forces and reassert Turkish independence. But this was not an Islamic victory. This was another Islamic defeat because Kemal Ataturk was a secularist and a modernist and believed in separation between religion and the state. So . . . from the Muslim point of view, it was a worsening of the situation because the Kemalists, having restored the independence of Turkey, proceeded to abolish the sultanate and the caliphate.

Ataturk, in the early '20s when he founded and became first president of the Turkish Republic, began with a campaign for women's rights. He was an unlikely advocate, an Ottoman general campaigning for women's rights. But he put his case very clearly and simply. He said, "Our task now is to catch up with the modern world. We will not catch up with the modern world if we only modernize half the population." I think he had a point. The Taliban might take note of that.

ISLAM IS SEEN as a single community. We in the Western world tend to think of a nation subdivided into religions. There, it's rather a religion subdivided into nations. The basic identity is the religious identity. One is first a Muslim or whatever other religion it may be and then subdivided. These nation-states in that part of the world are very new, very recent, and many of them are creations of the Western imperialist powers, invented by Britain and France for the most part. But that doesn't mean to say that they are not ancient civilizations. They are very ancient civilizations, but they did not define themselves in national or territorial terms. They defined themselves by religious identity and political allegiance.

Mohammed is revered because he was the founder of this religion. He wrote them a book called the Koran. According to Muslims, it is of divine authorship, divine, eternal, and uncreated. It was revealed to Mohammed through the archangel Gabriel, and he brought it to the people who became Muslims.

He was born in Arabia, in Mecca. Life in Mecca became difficult for him and he was oppressed by the pagan rulers of Mecca. So he moved to Medina, where he managed to build up his strength and eventually returned to Mecca. This theme of exile and return is a recurring theme in Muslim history.

For Muslims, Mohammed is not divine. He is a prophet—the chosen, the last, the greatest prophet of God, but not more than a human being. This is very clearly stated in Muslim teachings. They also revere Jesus as a prophet, but they say that the Christians made a monstrous error in calling him the son of God. That, from a Muslim point of view, is blasphemy.

So you have a prophet, the founder of religion, who was also a statesman, who during his lifetime became a head of state, which means that he promulgated and enforced laws, that he made peace and made war, and did all the other things that a head of state does, and those events formed part of the core of memories that Muslims all over the world share. This is the sacred history, the structural history of Muslims, and it is, therefore, political in a sense that Christianity never was and that Judaism has long ceased to be.

FOR A MUSLIM—not only Osama bin Laden, but for any Muslim—a non-Muslim military presence on the Arabian peninsula is, shall we say, troubling to say the very least, and for many, much worse than that. Even in the greatest days of the British empire, the British empire nibbled around the edges of Arabia—Kuwait, Bahrain, Oman, Aden—but they took good care not to get involved in the mainland of the Arabian peninsula because they realized that this would really stir up a hornet's nest.

ONE DEFINING American interest in the Middle East [is] oil, and I think probably in many respects, it is the main problem of the region, both for its people and for outsiders. And the other is Israel, the small country which is surrounded by hostile neighbors and in which clearly the United States has an interest.

The development of oil made a tremendous difference in every respect, one of which I think is important and has not been generally mentioned. The kind of Islam that is represented by Osama bin Laden, this radical, extreme kind of Islam, *did* originate in Arabia—as far back as the eighteenth century—and it would have remained in Arabia, had it not been for oil.

Imagine that some such group as the Ku Klux Klan or the Aryan Nation was suddenly to come into the possession of unlimited wealth and use that money to set up schools and colleges all over the world, promoting their particular version of Christianity. Then you get an idea of what has happened to Islam as a result of the enormous wealth that oil has brought to some people in Saudi Arabia. . . . Without oil money, this kind of Islam would have remained a fringe group in a marginal country.

And, of course, it suddenly transforms these rather simple pastoral economies with an injection of immense wealth. It has a very disruptive effect, and on the whole, I should say that oil has been a curse to the Arab world.

There's this old American dictum: no taxation without representation. What is sometimes overlooked is that the converse is also true: no representation without taxation. With our oil revenues, they didn't need taxes; therefore, they didn't need assemblies to levy taxes. And they were made independent of public opinion in their own countries with this untold wealth accruing from oil revenues. This greatly strengthened the power of autocratic governments, far greater than it had ever been in the past. Traditional Islamic government is authoritarian, but it is not dictatorial or despotic—it is governed under certain rules. In modern times, the power of the ruler has been vastly augmented by these huge revenues so that he doesn't need public support or public approval of his taxes. It has also been increased by all kinds of modern devices for surveillance and repression so that any tin pot dictator today wields far greater powers than were ever wielded by Suleyman the Magnificent or Harun al-Rashid or any of the legendary rulers of the Islamic past.

[REGARDING ISRAEL:] If you look at the published statements, you would think that the Israel/Palestine question is of primary importance [to the fundamentalists]. Certainly, it is important, but I don't think it's of primary importance. It is given importance because it is the only grievance that can be freely and safely expressed in Arab countries. Other grievances against the policies and behavior of their rulers cannot be expressed. That and also anti-Americanism; these are the two safety valves for letting it out.

Now why do I think that the Israeli-Palestinian issue is exaggerated? Because if you look at bin Laden's earliest statements, his first major grievance is the American presence on the holy soil of Arabia, infidel soldiers on the heartland of Islam. The second grievance is using that place as a base from which to attack Iraq. Iraq is not holy from a Muslim point of view, but for half a millennium, it was the seat of the Khalifate, the greatest and most glorious period of Islamic history. And only in third place does he mention Jerusalem—not Palestine, just Jerusalem. I think that is an honest statement of his priorities and a fairly general one. Since then . . . he has given more emphasis to Palestine, knowing that this will raise support for him in Europe and some other places.

THE QUESTION people are asking is "Why do they hate us?" That's the wrong question. They've been hating us for a long time. In a sense, they've been hating us for centuries, and it's very natural that they should. You have this millennial rivalry between two world religions, and now, from their point of view, the wrong one seems to be winning. And more generally, you can't be rich, strong, successful, and loved—particularly by those who are not rich, not strong, and not successful. So the hatred is something almost axiomatic. The question which we should be asking is "Why do they neither fear nor respect us?" This is what comes out very clearly in the writings of Osama bin Laden. In the past, there were always rival powers. If they were unhappy with the Americans, they could turn to the Russians. If they were unhappy with the British, they could turn to the Germans. They can't do that anymore.

Now, this has served not only to concentrate their minds wonderfully in one direction, but also to encourage them. Because as they see it, they destroyed the Soviet Union through the long struggle in Afghanistan, and finally the Russians were driven out of Afghanistan by people like Osama bin Laden—as they see it, to such devastating effect that the Soviet Union itself collapsed. They saw this as stage one of their major victory. They regarded the Soviet Union as by far the more dangerous of the two superpowers. They were really scared of them. They were always much more careful in doing anything which might offend them or even saying anything which might offend them.

Having, as they see it, destroyed the Soviet Union, they reckoned that dealing with the United States would be comparatively easy. This comes again and again in Osama bin Laden's writings and statements. He says, for example, "The Americans are paper tigers. They've grown soft. Hit them and they'll run." Then the same litany is always repeated—Vietnam, Lebanon, Somalia. That is a belief which, to any American, would appear absolutely preposterous. But that is how Osama bin Laden sees it. He saw this as evidence of American weakness and softness and was encouraged to go on.

Appendix

Readers can review an online appendix to
Booknotes: Stories from American History
on the World Wide Web at:

http://www.booknotes.org

Available on the C-SPAN Web page are
- *Complete transcripts of over six hundred* Booknotes *interviews*
- *Audio and video archives looking back at programs over the past twelve years*

Complete List of C-SPAN *Booknotes* (1989–2002)

SEPTEMBER 14, 1988
Pre-BOOKNOTES Interview
with Neil Sheehan
A Bright Shining Lie: John Paul Vann and America in Vietnam
Publisher: Random House

1. APRIL 2, 1989
Zbigniew Brzezinski
Grand Failure: The Birth and Death of Communism in the Twentieth Century
Publisher: Macmillan

2. APRIL 9, 1989
Judy Shelton
The Coming Soviet Crash: Gorbachev's Desperate Pursuit of Credit in Western Financial Markets
Publisher: The Free Press

3. APRIL 16, 1989
Bruce Oudes
From: The President—Richard Nixon's Secret Files
Publisher: Harper & Row

4. APRIL 23, 1989
Susan Moeller
Shooting War: Photography and the American Experience of Combat
Publisher: Basic Books

5. APRIL 30, 1989
Henry Brandon
Special Relationships: A Foreign Correspondent's Memoirs
Publisher: Atheneum

6. MAY 7, 1989
David H. Hackworth (with Julie Sherman)
About Face: The Odyssey of an American Warrior
Publisher: Simon & Schuster

7. MAY 14, 1989
James Fallows
More Like Us: Making America Great Again
Publisher: Houghton Mifflin

8. MAY 21, 1989
Gregory Fossedal
The Democratic Imperative: Exporting the American Revolution
Publisher: Basic Books

9. MAY 28, 1989
Stanley Karnow
In Our Image: America's Empire in the Philippines
Publisher: Random House

10. JUNE 4, 1989
James MacGregor Burns
The Crosswinds of Freedom
Publisher: Alfred A. Knopf

11. JUNE 11, 1989
Robert Christopher
Crashing the Gates: The De-WASPing of America's Power Elite
Publisher: Simon & Schuster

12. JUNE 18, 1989
Sen. Robert Byrd
The Senate: 1789–1989
Publisher: Government Printing Office

13. JUNE 25, 1989
Elizabeth Colton
The Jackson Phenomenon: The Man, the Power, the Message
Publisher: Doubleday

14. JULY 2, 1989
Nathaniel Branden
Judgment Day: My Years with Ayn Rand
Publisher: Houghton Mifflin

15. JULY 9, 1989
Roger G. Kennedy
Orders from France: The Americans and the French in a Revolutionary World (1780–1820)
Publisher: Alfred A. Knopf

16. JULY 14, 1989
Simon Schama
Citizens: A Chronicle of the French Revolution
Publisher: Alfred A. Knopf

17. JULY 16, 1989
George Wilson
Mud Soldiers: Life Inside the New American Army
Publisher: Scribner

18. JULY 23, 1989
Jeanne Simon
Codename: Scarlett—Life on the Campaign Trail by the Wife of a Presidential Candidate
Publisher: The Continuum Publishing Company

19. JULY 30, 1989
Michael Kaufman
Mad Dreams, Saving Graces—Poland: A Nation in Conspiracy
Publisher: Random House

20. AUGUST 6, 1989
Porter McKeever
Adlai Stevenson: His Life and Legacy
Publisher: William Morrow

21. AUGUST 13, 1989
Gary Paul Gates and Bob Schieffer
The Acting President
Publisher: E. P. Dutton

22. AUGUST 20, 1989
Bruce Murray
Journey into Space: The First Thirty Years of Space Exploration
Publisher: Norton

23. AUGUST 27, 1989
Jack Germond and Jules Witcover
Whose Broad Stripes and Bright Stars: The Trivial Pursuit of the Presidency, 1988
Publisher: Warner Books

24. SEPTEMBER 3, 1989
Walter Lacquer
The Long Road to Freedom: Russia and Glasnost
Publisher: Scribner

25. SEPTEMBER 10, 1989
Thomas Friedman
From Beirut to Jerusalem
Publisher: Farrar, Straus & Giroux

26. SEPTEMBER 17, 1989
General Ariel Sharon
Warrior: An Autobiography
Publisher: Simon & Schuster

27. SEPTEMBER 24, 1989
George Gilder
Microcosm: The Quantum Revolution in Economics and Technology
Publisher: Simon & Schuster

28. OCTOBER 1, 1989
Mort Rosenblum
Back Home: A Foreign Correspondent Rediscovers America
Publisher: William Morrow

29. OCTOBER 8, 1989
Barbara Ehrenreich
Fear of Falling: The Inner Life of the Middle Class
Publisher: Pantheon

30. OCTOBER 15, 1989
Harrison Salisbury
Tiananmen Diary: Thirteen Days in June
Publisher: Little, Brown and Company

31. OCTOBER 22, 1989
Kenneth Adelman
The Great Universal Embrace: Arms Summitry—A Skeptic's Account
Publisher: Simon & Schuster

32. OCTOBER 29, 1989
Reverend Ralph David Abernathy
And the Walls Came Tumbling Down
Publisher: Harper & Row

33. NOVEMBER 5, 1989
Vassily Aksyonov
Say Cheese: Soviets and the Media
Publisher: Random House

34. NOVEMBER 12, 1989
Felix Rodriguez (and John Weisman)
Shadow Warrior: The CIA Hero of a Hundred Unknown Battles
Publisher: Simon & Schuster

35. NOVEMBER 19, 1989
Robin Wright
In the Name of God: The Khomeini Decade
Publisher: Simon & Schuster

36. NOVEMBER 26, 1989
Peter Hennessy
Whitehall
Publisher: The Free Press

37. DECEMBER 3, 1989
Clifford Stoll
The Cuckoo's Egg: Tracking a Spy Through the Maze of Computer Espionage
Publisher: Doubleday

38. DECEMBER 10, 1989
Arthur Grace
Choose Me: Portraits of a Presidential Race

Publisher: University Press of New England

39. DECEMBER 17, 1989
James Reston Jr.
The Lone Star: The Life of John Connally
Publisher: Harper & Row

40. DECEMBER 24, 1989
Richard Rhodes
Farm: A Year in the Life of an American Farmer
Publisher: Simon & Schuster

41. DECEMBER 31, 1989
William Lutz
Doublespeak: From "Revenue Enhancement" to "Terminal Living": How Government, Business, Advertisers, and Others Use Language to Deceive You
Publisher: Harper & Row

42. JANUARY 7, 1990
Sig Mickelson
From Whistle Stop to Sound Bite: Four Decades of Politics and Television
Publisher: Praeger

43. JANUARY 14, 1990
John Barry
The Ambition and the Power—The Fall of Jim Wright: A True Story of Washington
Publisher: Viking

44. JANUARY 21, 1990
Fitzhugh Green
George Bush: An Intimate Portrait
Publisher: Hippocrene Books

45. JANUARY 28, 1990
Charles A. Fecher, editor
The Diary of H. L. Mencken
Publisher: Alfred A. Knopf

46. FEBRUARY 4, 1990
Jim Mann
Beijing Jeep: The Short, Unhappy Romance of American Business in China
Publisher: Simon & Schuster

47. FEBRUARY 11, 1990
David Burnham
A Law Unto Itself: Power, Politics, and the IRS
Publisher: Random House

48. FEBRUARY 18, 1990
Peggy Noonan
*What I Saw at the Revolution: A
Political Life in the Reagan Era*
Publisher: Random House

49. FEBRUARY 25, 1990
Michael Fumento
The Myth of Heterosexual AIDS
Publisher: Basic Books

50. FEBRUARY 27, 1990
Hedley Donovan
*Right Places, Right Times: Forty
Years in Journalism Not Count-
ing My Paper Route*
Publisher: Henry Holt and
Company

51. MARCH 4, 1990
Richard Barnet
*The Rockets' Red Glare: When
America Goes to War—The
Presidents and the People*
Publisher: Simon & Schuster

52. MARCH 11, 1990
Frederick Kempe
*Divorcing the Dictator: America's
Bungled Affair with Noriega*
Publisher: Putnam

53. MARCH 18, 1990
(Neil Livingstone and) David
Halevy
Inside the PLO
Publisher: William Morrow

54. MARCH 25, 1990
James Abourezk
*Advise and Dissent: Memoirs of
South Dakota and the U.S.
Senate*
Publisher: Lawrence Hill Books

55. APRIL 1, 1990
Fred Graham
*Happy Talk: Confessions of a TV
Newsman*
Publisher: Norton

56. APRIL 9, 1990
Leonard Sussman
*Power, the Press, and the Tech-
nology of Freedom: The Coming
Age of ISDN*
Publisher: Freedom House

57. APRIL 15, 1990
Helmut Schmidt
*Men and Powers: A Political
Retrospective*
Publisher: Random House

58. APRIL 22, 1990
Michael Barone
*Our Country: The Shaping of
America from Roosevelt to
Reagan*
Publisher: The Free Press

59. APRIL 29, 1990
Robert Caro
*Means of Ascent: The Years of
Lyndon Johnson*
Publisher: Alfred A. Knopf

60. MAY 6, 1990
Morley Safer
*Flashbacks on Returning to
Vietnam*
Publisher: Random House

61. MAY 13, 1990
Brian Duffy and Steven Emer-
son
*The Fall of Pan Am 103: Inside
the Lockerbie Investigation*
Publisher: Putnam

62. MAY 20, 1990
Allister Sparks
The Mind of South Africa
Publisher: Alfred A. Knopf

63. MAY 27, 1990
Bette Bao Lord
Legacies: A Chinese Mosaic
Publisher: Alfred A. Knopf

64. JUNE 3, 1990
Dusko Doder
*Gorbachev: Heretic in the
Kremlin*
Publisher: Viking

65. JUNE 10, 1990
Thomas Sowell
*Preferential Policies: An Interna-
tional Perspective*
Publisher: William Morrow

66. JUNE 17, 1990
Judith Miller
*One, by One, by One: Facing the
Holocaust*
Publisher: Simon & Schuster

67. JUNE 24, 1990
Kevin Phillips
*The Politics of Rich and Poor:
Wealth and the Electorate in the
Reagan Aftermath*
Publisher: Random House

68. JULY 1, 1990
Chris Ogden
*Maggie: An Intimate Portrait of a
Woman in Power*
Publisher: Random House

69. JULY 8, 1990
Denton Watson
*Lion in the Lobby: Clarence
Mitchell Jr.'s Struggle for the
Passage of Civil Rights Laws*
Publisher: William Morrow

70. JULY 15, 1990
Caspar Weinberger
*Fighting for Peace: Seven Critical
Years in the Pentagon*
Publisher: Warner Books

71. JULY 22, 1990
Teresa Odendahl
*Charity Begins at Home: Gen-
erosity and Self-Interest Among
the Philanthropic Elite*
Publisher: Basic Books

72. JULY 29, 1990
Michael Shapiro
*In the Shadow of the Sun: A
Korean Year of Love and Sorrow*
Publisher: Atlantic Monthly
Press

73. AUGUST 5, 1990
Dan Raviv and Yossi Mellman
*Every Spy a Prince: The Complete
History of Israel's Intelligence
Community*
Publisher: Houghton Mifflin

74. AUGUST 12, 1990
Roger Kimball
*Tenured Radicals: How Politics
Has Corrupted Our Higher
Education*
Publisher: Harper & Row

75. AUGUST 19, 1990
Tad Szulc
*Then and Now: How the World
Has Changed Since World War II*
Publisher: William Morrow

76. AUGUST 26, 1990
Christopher Wren
*The End of the Line: The Failure
of Communism in the Soviet
Union and China*
Publisher: Simon & Schuster

77. SEPTEMBER 2, 1990
Lee Edwards

Missionary for Freedom: The Life and Times of Walter Judd
Publisher: Paragon House

78. SEPTEMBER 9, 1990
Senator Robert Dole
Historical Almanac of the United States Senate
Publisher: Government Printing Office

79. SEPTEMBER 16, 1990
M. L. Farber
Outrage: The Story Behind the Tawana Brawley Hoax
Publisher: Bantam Books

80. SEPTEMBER 23, 1990
Janette Dates
Split Image: African Americans in the Mass Media
Publisher: Howard University Press

81. OCTOBER 14, 1990
Harold Stassen
Eisenhower: Turning the World Toward Peace
Publisher: Merrill Magnus

82. OCTOBER 21, 1990
Tim Weiner
Blank Check: The Pentagon's Black Budget
Publisher: Warner Books

83. OCTOBER 28, 1990
Pat Choate
Agents of Influence: How Japan's Lobbyists in the United States Manipulate America's Political and Economic System
Publisher: Alfred A. Knopf

84. NOVEMBER 4, 1990
Paul Taylor
See How They Run: Electing a President in an Age of Mediaocracy
Publisher: Alfred A. Knopf

85. NOVEMBER 11, 1990
Blaine Harden
Africa: Dispatches from a Fragile Continent
Publisher: Norton

86. NOVEMBER 18, 1990
Jean Edward Smith
Lucius D. Clay: An American Life
Publisher: Henry Holt and Company

87. NOVEMBER 25, 1990
Martin Mayer
The Greatest-Ever Bank Robbery: The Collapse of the Savings and Loan Industry
Publisher: Scribner

88. DECEMBER 2, 1990
Carol Barkalow (with Andrea Raals)
In the Men's House: An Inside Account of Life in the Army by One of West Point's First Female Graduates
Publisher: Poseidon Press

89. DECEMBER 9, 1990
Sally Bedell Smith
In All His Glory: The Life of William S. Paley, the Legendary Tycoon and His Brilliant Circle
Publisher: Simon & Schuster

90. DECEMBER 16, 1990
Shen Tong
Almost a Revolution: The Story of a Chinese Student's Journey from Boyhood to Leadership in Tiananmen Square
Publisher: Houghton Mifflin

91. DECEMBER 23, 1990
John Wallach and Janet Wallach
Arafat: In the Eyes of the Beholder
Publisher: Lyle Stuart

92. DECEMBER 30, 1990
Garry Wills
Under God: Religion and American Politics
Publisher: Simon & Schuster

93. JANUARY 6, 1991
Ben Wattenberg
The First Universal Nation: Leading Indicators and Ideas About the Surge of America in the 1990s
Publisher: The Free Press

94. JANUARY 13, 1991
Daniel Roos
The Machine That Changed the World
Publisher: Macmillan

95. JANUARY 27, 1991
Daniel Yergin
The Prize: The Epic Quest for Oil, Money, and Power
Publisher: Simon & Schuster

96. FEBRUARY 3, 1991
Carl Rowan
Breaking Barriers: A Memoir
Publisher: Little, Brown and Company

97. FEBRUARY 10, 1991
Theodore Hesburgh (with Jerry Reedy)
God, Country, Notre Dame: The Autobiography of Theodore M. Hesburgh
Publisher: Doubleday

98. FEBRUARY 17, 1991
Ronald Brownstein
The Power and the Glitter: The Hollywood-Washington Connection
Publisher: Pantheon

99. FEBRUARY 24, 1991
Robert Kuttner
The End of Laissez-Faire: National Purpose and the Global Economy After the Cold War
Publisher: Alfred A. Knopf

100. MARCH 3, 1991
Haynes Johnson
Sleepwalking Through History: America in the Reagan Years
Publisher: Norton

101. MARCH 10, 1991
Georgie Anne Geyer
Guerrilla Prince: The Untold Story of Fidel Castro
Publisher: Little, Brown and Company

102. MARCH 17, 1991
Leonard Goldenson (with Marvin Wolf)
Beating the Odds: The Untold Story Behind the Rise of ABC: The Stars, Struggles, and Egos That Transformed Network Television
Publisher: Scribner

103. MARCH 24, 1991
Richard Brookhiser
The Way of the WASP: How It Made America and How It Can Save It . . . So to Speak
Publisher: The Free Press

104. MARCH 31, 1991
Dayton Duncan
Grass Roots: One Year in the Life of the New Hampshire Presiden-

tial Primary
Publisher: Penguin

105. APRIL 7, 1991
Tom Wicker
*One of Us: Richard Nixon and
the American Dream*
Publisher: Random House

106. APRIL 14, 1991
William Strauss and Neil Howe
*Generations: The History of
America's Future, 1584–2069*
Publisher: William Morrow

107. APRIL 21, 1991
Robert Shogun
*The Riddle of Power: Presidential
Leadership from Truman to Bush*
Publisher: Dutton

108. APRIL 28, 1991
Caroline Kennedy and Ellen
Alderman
*In Our Defense: The Bill of Rights
in Action*
Publisher: William Morrow

109. MAY 5, 1991
Nick Lemann
*The Promised Land: The Great
Black Migration and How It
Changed America*
Publisher: Alfred A. Knopf

110. MAY 12, 1991 (PART ONE)
Lou Cannon
*President Reagan: Role of a
Lifetime*
Publisher: Simon & Schuster

111. MAY 19, 1991 (PART TWO)
Lou Cannon
*President Reagan: Role of a
Lifetime*
Publisher: Simon & Schuster

112. MAY 26, 1991
Robert Reich
The Work of Nations
Publisher: Alfred A. Knopf

113. JUNE 2, 1991
Robert Kaiser
*Why Gorbachev Happened: His
Triumphs and His Failure*
Publisher: Simon & Schuster

114. JUNE 9, 1991
George Friedman and Meredith
LeBard
The Coming War with Japan

Publisher: St. Martin's Press

115. JUNE 16, 1991
Dixy Lee Ray
*Trashing the Planet: How Science
Can Help Us Deal with Acid
Rain, Depletion of the Ozone, and
Nuclear Waste Among Other
Things*
Publisher: Regnery Publishing

116. JUNE 23, 1991
Bob Woodward
The Commanders
Publisher: Simon & Schuster

117. JUNE 30, 1991
Roger Gittines
*Consequences: John G. Tower—A
Personal and Political Memoir*
Publisher: Little, Brown and
Company

118. JULY 7, 1991
Donald Ritchie
*Press Gallery: Congress and the
Washington Correspondents*
Publisher: Harvard University
Press

119. JULY 14, 1991
Michael Beschloss
*The Crisis Years: Kennedy and
Khrushchev, 1960–1963*
Publisher: HarperCollins

120. JULY 21, 1991
Alan Ehrenhalt
*The United States of Ambition:
Politicians, Power, and the Pursuit
of Office*
Publisher: Random House

121. JULY 28, 1991
Clark Clifford
*Counsel to the President: A
Memoir*
Publisher: Random House

122. AUGUST 4, 1991
Elaine Sciolino
*The Outlaw State: Saddam
Hussein's Quest for Power and the
Gulf Crisis*
Publisher: John Wiley & Sons,
Inc.

123. AUGUST 11, 1991
Len Colodny and Robert Gettlin
*Silent Coup: The Removal of a
President*
Publisher: St. Martin's Press

124. AUGUST 18, 1991
Liz Trotta
*Fighting for Air: In the Trenches
with Television News*
Publisher: Simon & Schuster

125. AUGUST 25, 1991
E. J. Dionne Jr.
Why Americans Hate Politics
Publisher: Simon & Schuster

126. SEPTEMBER 1, 1991
Andrew Cockburn and Leslie
Cockburn
*Dangerous Liaisons: The Inside
Story of the U.S.–Israeli Covert
Relationship*
Publisher: HarperCollins

127. SEPTEMBER 8, 1991
Liva Baker
The Justice from Beacon Hill
Publisher: HarperCollins

128. SEPTEMBER 15, 1991
Reuven Frank
*Out of Thin Air: The Brief
Wonderful Life of Network News*
Publisher: Simon & Schuster

129. SEPTEMBER 22, 1991
Robert Dallek
*Lone Star Rising: Lyndon Johnson
and His Times, 1908–1960*
Publisher: Oxford University
Press

130. SEPTEMBER 29, 1991
Stephen Carter
*Reflections of an Affirmative
Action Baby*
Publisher: Basic Books

131. OCTOBER 6, 1991
Ken Auletta
*Three Blind Mice: How the TV
Networks Lost Their Way*
Publisher: Random House

[OCTOBER 13, 1991: PRE-EMPTED
BY U.S. SENATE]

132. OCTOBER 20, 1991
Anthony Lewis
*Make No Law: The Sullivan Case
and the First Amendment*
Publisher: Random House

133. OCTOBER 27, 1991
Don Oberdorfer
The Turn: From the Cold War to

a New Era—The United States
and the Soviet Union, 1983–1990
Publisher: Simon & Schuster

134. NOVEMBER 3, 1991
Larry Sabato
*Feeding Frenzy: How Attack
Journalism Has Transformed
American Politics*
Publisher: The Free Press

135. NOVEMBER 10, 1991
Tina Rosenberg
*Children of Cain: Violence and
the Violent in Latin America*
Publisher: William Morrow

136. NOVEMBER 17, 1991
Suzanne Garment
*Scandal: The Culture of Mistrust
in American Politics*
Publisher: Times Books

137. NOVEMBER 24, 1991
James Stewart
Den of Thieves
Publisher: Simon & Schuster

138. DECEMBER 1, 1991
Gary Sick
*October Surprise: America's
Hostages in Iran and the Election
of Ronald Reagan*
Publisher: Times Books

139. DECEMBER 8, 1991
James Reston
Deadline: A Memoir
Publisher: Random House

140. DECEMBER 15, 1991
Thomas Byrne Edsall and Mary
Edsall
*Chain Reaction: The Impact of
Race, Rights, and Taxes on
American Politics*
Publisher: Norton

141. DECEMBER 22, 1991
Martin Gilbert
Churchill: A Life
Publisher: Henry Holt and
Company

142. DECEMBER 29, 1991
Jimmy Breslin
Damon Runyan: A Life
Publisher: Ticknor & Fields

143. JANUARY 5, 1992
Charles V. Hamilton
Adam Clayton Powell Jr.: The

Political Biography of an American Dilemma
Publisher: Atheneum

144. JANUARY 12, 1992
August Heckscher
Woodrow Wilson: A Biography
Publisher: Scribner

145. JANUARY 26, 1992
Frederick Downs
*No Longer Enemies, Not Yet
Friends: An American Soldier
Returns to Vietnam*
Publisher: Norton

146. FEBRUARY 2, 1992
Robert Cwiklik
*House Rules: A Freshman Con-
gressman's Initiation to the
Backslapping, Backpedaling, and
Backstabbing Ways of Washing-
ton*
Publisher: Villard Books

147. FEBRUARY 9, 1992
Francis Fukuyama
*The End of History and the Last
Man*
Publisher: The Free Press

148. FEBRUARY 16, 1992
Senator Al Gore
*Earth in the Balance: Ecology
and the Human Spirit*
Publisher: Houghton Mifflin

149. FEBRUARY 23, 1992
(PART ONE)
Richard Nixon
*Seize the Moment: America's
Challenge in a One-Superpower
World*
Publisher: Simon & Schuster

150. MARCH 1, 1992 (PART
TWO)
Richard Nixon
*Seize the Moment: America's
Challenge in a One-Superpower
World*
Publisher: Simon & Schuster

151. MARCH 8, 1992
Robert Massie
*Dreadnought: Britain, Germany,
and the Coming of the Great War*
Publisher: Random House

152. MARCH 22, 1992
Linda Chavez
Out of the Barrio: Toward a New

Politics of Hispanic Assimilation
Publisher: Basic Books

153. MARCH 29, 1992
Nan Robertson
*The Girls in the Balcony:
Women, Men, and the New York
Times*
Publisher: Random House

154. APRIL 5, 1992
Robert Remini
*Henry Clay: Statesman for the
Union*
Publisher: Norton

155. APRIL 12, 1992
Orlando Patterson
*Freedom in the Making of
Western Culture*
Publisher: Basic Books

156. APRIL 19, 1992
Paul Hollander
*Anti-Americanism: Critiques at
Home and Abroad, 1965–1990*
Publisher: Oxford University
Press

157. APRIL 26, 1992
Tinsley E. Yarbrough
*John Marshall Harlan: Great
Dissenter of the Warren Court*
Publisher: Oxford University
Press

158. MAY 3, 1992
Earl Black and Merle Black
*The Vital South: How Presidents
Are Elected*
Publisher: Harvard University
Press

159. MAY 10, 1992
David Moore
*The Superpollsters: How They
Measure and Manipulate Public
Opinion in America*
Publisher: Four Walls Eight
Windows

160. MAY 17, 1992
Robert Bartley
*The Seven Fat Years and How to
Do It Again*
Publisher: The Free Press

161. MAY 24, 1992
Lewis Puller Jr.
*Fortunate Son: The Autobiogra-
phy of Lewis Puller Jr.*
Publisher: Grove Weidenfeld

162. MAY 31, 1992
Lester Thurow
*Head to Head: The Coming
Economic Battle Among Japan,
Europe, and America*
Publisher: William Morrow

163. JUNE 7, 1992
R. Emmett Tyrrell Jr.
The Conservative Crack-Up
Publisher: Simon & Schuster

164. JUNE 14, 1992
William Lee Miller
*The Business of May Next: James
Madison and the Founding*
Publisher: The University Press
of Virginia

165. JUNE 21, 1992
John Jackley
*Hill Rat: Blowing the Lid Off
Congress*
Publisher: Regnery Publishing

166. JUNE 28, 1992
David Savage
*Turning Right: The Making of
the Rehnquist Supreme Court*
Publisher: John Wiley & Sons,
Inc.

167. JULY 5, 1992
William Rehnquist
*Grand Inquests: The Historic
Impeachments of Justice Samuel
Chase and President Andrew
Johnson*
Publisher: William Morrow

168. JULY 12, 1992
Jeffrey Bell
*Populism and Elitism: Politics in
the Age of Equality*
Publisher: Regnery Publishing

169. JULY 19, 1992
David McCullough
Truman
Publisher: Simon & Schuster

170. JULY 26, 1992
Richard Ben Cramer
*What It Takes: The Way to the
White House*
Publisher: Random House

171. AUGUST 2, 1992
Gilbert Fite
*Richard B. Russell Jr.: Senator
from Georgia*
Publisher: The University of
North Carolina Press

172. AUGUST 9, 1992
Robert Donovan and Ray
Scherer
*Unsilent Revolution: Television
News and American Public Life*
Publisher: Cambridge University Press

173. AUGUST 16, 1992
Martin Anderson
*Impostors in the Temple: American Intellectuals Are Destroying
Our Universities and Cheating
Our Students of Their Future*
Publisher: Simon & Schuster

174. AUGUST 23, 1992
Mickey Kaus
The End of Equality
Publisher: Basic Books

175. AUGUST 30, 1992
Neil Postman
*Technopoly: The Surrender of
Culture to Technology*
Publisher: Alfred A. Knopf

176. SEPTEMBER 6, 1992
Terry Eastland
*Energy in the Executive: The
Case for a Strong Presidency*
Publisher: The Free Press

177. SEPTEMBER 13, 1992
James Billington
Russia Transformed: Breakthrough to Hope
Publisher: The Free Press

178. SEPTEMBER 20, 1992
Senator Paul Simon
*Advise and Consent: Clarence
Thomas, Robert Bork, and the
Intriguing History of the Supreme
Court's Nomination Battles*
Publisher: National Press Books

179. SEPTEMBER 27, 1992
Walter Isaacson
Kissinger: A Biography
Publisher: Simon & Schuster

[OCTOBER 4, 1992: PRE-
EMPTED BY U.S. HOUSE OF
REPRESENTATIVES]

[OCTOBER 11, 1992: PRE-
EMPTED BY PRESIDENTIAL
DEBATE]

180. OCTOBER 18, 1992
George Will
*Restoration: Congress, Term
Limits, and the Recovery of
Deliberative Democracy*
Publisher: The Free Press

181. OCTOBER 25, 1992
Susan Faludi
*Backlash: The Undeclared War
Against American Women*
Publisher: Crown

182. NOVEMBER 8, 1992
Barbara Hinkley and Paul Brace
*Follow the Leader: Opinion Polls
and the Modern Presidents*
Publisher: Basic Books

183. NOVEMBER 15, 1992
Derrick Bell
*Faces at the Bottom of the Well:
The Permanence of Racism*
Publisher: Basic Books

184. NOVEMBER 22, 1992
General Norman Schwartzkopf
It Doesn't Take a Hero
Publisher: Bantam Books

185. NOVEMBER 29, 1992
Charles Sykes
*A Nation of Victims: The Decay
of the American Character*
Publisher: St. Martin's Press

186. DECEMBER 6, 1992
Daniel Boorstin
The Creators
Publisher: Random House

187. DECEMBER 13, 1992
Brian Kelly
*Adventures in Porkland: How
Washington Wastes Your Money
and Why They Don't Stop*
Publisher: Villard Books

188. DECEMBER 20, 1992
Eric Alterman
Sound and Fury: The Washington Punditocracy and the Collapse of American Politics
Publisher: HarperCollins

189. DECEMBER 27, 1992
Michael Medved
*Hollywood Versus America:
Popular Culture and the War on
Traditional Values*
Publisher: HarperCollins

190. JANUARY 3, 1993
Michael Davis and Hunter
Clark
*Thurgood Marshall: Warrior at
the Bar, Rebel on the Bench*
Publisher: The Carol Publishing
Group

191. JANUARY 10, 1993
Jeffrey Birnbaum
*The Lobbyists: How Influence
Peddlers Get Their Way in
Washington*
Publisher: Times Books

192. JANUARY 17, 1993
P. F. Bentley
Clinton: Portrait of Victory
Publisher: Warner Books

193. JANUARY 24, 1993
Robert Gilbert
*The Mortal Presidency: Illness
and Anguish in the White House*
Publisher: Basic Books

194. JANUARY 30, 1993
Benjamin Stein
*License to Steal: The Untold
Story of Michael Milken and the
Conspiracy to Bilk the Nation*
Publisher: Simon & Schuster

195. FEBRUARY 7, 1993
Jack Nelson
*Terror in the Night: The Klan's
Campaign Against the Jews*
Publisher: Simon & Schuster

196. FEBRUARY 14, 1993
Nathan Miller
Theodore Roosevelt: A Life
Publisher: William Morrow

197. FEBRUARY 21, 1993
Richard Norton Smith
*Patriarch: George Washington
and the New American Nation*
Publisher: Houghton Mifflin

198. FEBRUARY 28, 1993
Kay Mills
*This Little Light of Mine: The
Life of Fannie Lou Hamer*
Publisher: Dutton

199. MARCH 6, 1993
Alex Dragnich
*Serbs and Croats: The Struggle in
Yugoslavia*
Publisher: Harcourt Brace
Jovanovich

200. MARCH 13, 1993
Paul Kennedy
*Preparing for the Twenty-First
Century*
Publisher: Random House

201. MARCH 21, 1993
Deborah Shapley
*Promise and Power: The Life and
Times of Robert McNamara*
Publisher: Little, Brown and
Company

202. MARCH 28, 1993
Michael Kelly
*Martyrs' Day: Chronicle of a
Small War*
Publisher: Random House

203. APRIL 4, 1993
Nadine Cohodas
*Strom Thurmond and the Politics
of Southern Change*
Publisher: Simon & Schuster

204. APRIL 11, 1993
Blanche Wiesen Cook
*Eleanor Roosevelt: Volume 1,
1884–1933*
Publisher: Viking

205. APRIL 18, 1993
Douglas Brinkley
*The Majic Bus: An American
Odyssey*
Publisher: Harcourt Brace

206. APRIL 25, 1993
Lisa Belkin
*First, Do No Harm: The
Dramatic Story of Real
Doctors and Patients Making
Impossible Choices at a Big-
City Hospital*
Publisher: Simon & Schuster

207. MAY 2, 1993
Marshall DeBruhl
*Sword of San Jacinto: A Life of
Sam Houston*
Publisher: Random House

208. MAY 9, 1993
Charles Adams
*For Good and Evil: The Impact
of Taxes on the Course of Civi-
lization*
Publisher: Madison Books

209. MAY 16, 1993
Anna Quindlen
Thinking Out Loud: On the

*Personal, the Political, the Public,
and the Private*
Publisher: Random House

210. MAY 23, 1993
George Ball
*The Passionate Attachment:
America's Involvement with
Israel, 1947 to the Present*
Publisher: Norton

211. MAY 30, 1993
Douglas Davis
*The Five Myths of Television
Power: Or, Why the Medium Is
Not the Message*
Publisher: Simon & Schuster

212. JUNE 6, 1993
J. Bowyer Bell
*The Irish Troubles: A Generation
of Violence, 1967–1992*
Publisher: St. Martin's Press

213. JUNE 13, 1993
David Brock
The Real Anita Hill
Publisher: The Free Press

214. JUNE 20, 1993
Howard Kurtz
*Media Circus: The Trouble with
America's Newspapers*
Publisher: Times Books

215. JUNE 27, 1993
George Shultz
*Turmoil and Triumph: My Years
as Secretary of State*
Publisher: Scribner

216. JULY 4, 1993
Joel Krieger
*The Oxford Companion to
Politics of the World*
Publisher: Oxford University
Press

217. JULY 11, 1993
David Halberstam
The Fifties
Publisher: Villard Books

218. JULY 18, 1993
Molly Moore
*A Woman at War: Storming
Kuwait with the U.S. Marines*
Publisher: Scribner

219. JULY 25, 1993
David Remnick
Lenin's Tomb: The Last Days of

the Soviet Empire
Publisher: Random House

220. AUGUST 1, 1993
Alexander Brook
The Hard Way: The Odyssey of a Weekly Newspaper Editor
Publisher: Bridge Works

221. AUGUST 8, 1993
Tom Rosenstiel
Strange Bedfellows: How Television and the Presidential Candidates Changed American Politics, 1992
Publisher: Hyperion

222. AUGUST 15, 1993
Lewis Lapham
The Wish for Kings: Democracy at Bay
Publisher: Grove Press

223. AUGUST 22, 1993
Harold Holzer
The Lincoln-Douglas Debates
Publisher: HarperCollins

224. AUGUST 29, 1993
Peter Macdonald
Giap: The Victor in Vietnam
Publisher: Norton

225. SEPTEMBER 5, 1993
Joseph Ellis
Passionate Sage: The Character and Legacy of John Adams
Publisher: Norton

226. SEPTEMBER 12, 1993
Ronald Kessler
The FBI: Inside the World's Most Powerful Law Enforcement Agency
Publisher: Pocket Books

227. SEPTEMBER 19, 1993
Madeline Cartwright
For the Children: Lessons from a Visionary Principal; How We Can Save Our Public Schools
Publisher: Doubleday

228. SEPTEMBER 26, 1993
Malcolm Browne
Muddy Boots and Red Socks: A Reporter's Life
Publisher: Times Books

229. OCTOBER 3, 1993
Peter Skerry

Mexican-Americans: The Ambivalent Minority
Publisher: The Free Press

230. OCTOBER 10, 1993
Alan Brinkley
The Unfinished Nation: A Concise History of the American People
Publisher: Alfred A. Knopf

231. OCTOBER 17, 1993
Christopher Hitchens
For the Sake of Argument
Publisher: Verso

232. OCTOBER 24, 1993
William F. Buckley Jr.
Happy Days Were Here Again: Reflections of a Libertarian Journalist
Publisher: Random House

233. OCTOBER 31, 1993
Andrew Nagorski
The Birth of Freedom: Shaping Lives and Societies in the New Eastern Europe
Publisher: Simon & Schuster

234. NOVEMBER 7, 1993
Charles Mee
Playing God: Seven Fateful Moments When Great Men Met to Change the World
Publisher: Simon & Schuster

235. NOVEMBER 14, 1993
Herbert Block
Herblock: A Cartoonist's Life
Publisher: Macmillan

[NOVEMBER 21, 1993: PRE-EMPTED BY U.S. HOUSE OF REPRESENTATIVES]

236. NOVEMBER 28, 1993
Betty Friedan
The Fountain of Age
Publisher: Simon & Schuster

237. DECEMBER 5, 1993
Margaret Thatcher
The Downing Street Years
Publisher: HarperCollins

238. DECEMBER 12, 1993
Richard Reeves
President Kennedy: Profile of Power
Publisher: Simon & Schuster

239. DECEMBER 19, 1993
John Podhoretz
Hell of a Ride: Backstage at the White House Follies, 1989–1993
Publisher: Simon & Schuster

240. DECEMBER 26, 1993
Willard Sterne Randall
Thomas Jefferson: A Life
Publisher: Henry Holt and Company

241. JANUARY 2, 1994
David Levering Lewis
W.E.B. Du Bois: The Biography of a Race, 1868–1919
Publisher: Henry Holt and Company

242. JANUARY 9, 1994
William Bennett
The Book of Virtues: A Treasury of Great Moral Stories
Publisher: Simon & Schuster

243. JANUARY 16, 1994
Carolyn Barta
Perot and His People: Disrupting the Balance of Political Power
Publisher: The Summit Group

244. JANUARY 23, 1994
Gary Hymel (with Tip O'Neill)
All Politics Is Local and Other Rules of the Game
Publisher: Times Books

245. JANUARY 30, 1994
William Chafe
Never Stop Running: Allard Lowenstein and the Struggle to Save American Liberalism
Publisher: Basic Books

246. FEBRUARY 6, 1994
Stanley Weintraub
Disraeli: A Biography
Publisher: Dutton

247. FEBRUARY 13, 1994
Bill Emmott
Japanophobia: The Myth of the Invincible Japanese
Publisher: Times Books

248. FEBRUARY 20, 1994
Peter Arnett
Live from the Battlefield: From Vietnam to Baghdad, 35 Years in the World's War Zones
Publisher: Simon & Schuster

249. FEBRUARY 27, 1994
Stephen Lesher
George Wallace: American Populist
Publisher: Addison-Wesley

250. MARCH 6, 1994
Nathan McCall
Makes Me Wanna Holler: A Young Black Man in America
Publisher: Random House

251. MARCH 13, 1994
Norman Ornstein
Debt and Taxes: How America Got into Its Budget Mess and What to Do About It
Publisher: Times Books

252. MARCH 20, 1994
Clare Brandt
The Man in the Mirror: A Life of Benedict Arnold
Publisher: Random House

253. MARCH 27, 1994
John Corry
My Times: Adventures in the News Trade
Publisher: Putnam

254. APRIL 3, 1994
Andrew Young
A Way Out of No Way: The Spiritual Memoirs of Andrew Young
Publisher: Thomas Nelson Communications

[APRIL 10, 1994: *BOOKNOTES* FIFTH ANNIVERSARY SPECIAL]

255. APRIL 17, 1994
James Cannon
Time and Chance: Gerald Ford's Appointment with History
Publisher: HarperCollins

[APRIL 24, 1994: ENCORE *BOOKNOTES* RICHARD NIXON (PART TWO)]

256. MAY 1, 1994
Howell Raines
Fly Fishing Through the Mid Life Crisis
Publisher: William Morrow

257. MAY 8, 1994
John Keegan
A History of Warfare
Publisher: Alfred A. Knopf

258. MAY 15, 1994
Forrest McDonald
The American Presidency: An Intellectual History
Publisher: University of Kansas Press

259. MAY 22, 1994
James M. McPherson
What They Fought For, 1861–1865
Publisher: Louisiana State University Press

260. MAY 29, 1994
Pete Hamill
A Drinking Life: A Memoir
Publisher: Little, Brown and Company

261. JUNE 5, 1994
Stephen Ambrose
D-Day: June 6, 1944: The Climactic Battle of World War II
Publisher: Simon & Schuster

262. JUNE 12, 1994
Mark Neely
The Last Best Hope of Earth: Abraham Lincoln and the Promise of America
Publisher: Harvard University Press

263. JUNE 19, 1994
Sam Roberts
Who We Are: A Portrait of America
Publisher: Times Books

264. JUNE 26, 1994
Lani Guinier
The Tyranny of the Majority: Fundamental Fairness in Representative Democracy
Publisher: Martin Kessler Books

265. JULY 3, 1994
Murray Kempton
Rebellions, Perversities, and Main Events
Publisher: Times Books

266. JULY 10, 1994
Cal Thomas
The Things That Matter Most
Publisher: HarperCollins

267. JULY 17, 1994
David Hackett Fischer
Paul Revere's Ride
Publisher: Oxford University Press

268. JULY 24, 1994
Dan Quayle
Standing Firm
Publisher: HarperCollins

269. JULY 31, 1994
Colman McCarthy
All of One Peace: Essays on Nonviolence
Publisher: Rutgers University Press

270. AUGUST 7, 1994
Peter Collier
The Roosevelts: An American Saga
Publisher: Simon & Schuster

271. AUGUST 14, 1994
Merrill Peterson
Lincoln in American Memory
Publisher: Oxford University Press

272. AUGUST 21, 1994
Hugh Pearson
The Shadow of the Panther: Huey Newton and the Price of Black Power in America
Publisher: Addison-Wesley

273. AUGUST 28, 1994
John Leo
Two Steps Ahead of the Thought Police
Publisher: Simon & Schuster

274. SEPTEMBER 4, 1994
Paul Weaver
News and the Culture of Lying: How Journalism Really Works
Publisher: The Free Press

275. SEPTEMBER 11, 1994
Shelby Foote
Stars in Their Courses: The Gettysburg Campaign
Publisher: Modern Library

276. SEPTEMBER 18, 1994
Irving Bartlett
John C. Calhoun: A Biography
Publisher: Norton

277. SEPTEMBER 25, 1994
Ben Yagoda
Will Rogers: A Biography
Publisher: Alfred A. Knopf

278. OCTOBER 2, 1994
Harry Jaffe and Tom Sherwood
Dream City: Race, Power, and

the Decline of Washington, D.C.
Publisher: Simon & Schuster

279. OCTOBER 9, 1994
Henry Louis Gates Jr.
Colored People: A Memoir
Publisher: Alfred A. Knopf

280. OCTOBER 16, 1994
Nicholas Kristof and Sheryl
Wudunn
*China Wakes: The Struggle for
the Soul of a Rising Power*
Publisher: Times Books

281. OCTOBER 23, 1994
Liz Carpenter
Unplanned Parenthood
Publisher: Random House

282. OCTOBER 30, 1994
David Frum
Dead Right
Publisher: Basic Books

283. NOVEMBER 6, 1994
Bill Thomas
*Club Fed: Power, Money, Sex,
and Violence on Capitol Hill*
Publisher: Scribner

284. NOVEMBER 13, 1994
John Kenneth Galbraith
*A Journey Through Economic
Time: A Firsthand View*
Publisher: Houghton Mifflin

285. NOVEMBER 20, 1994
Milton Friedman
Introduction to F. A. Hayek's
Road to Serfdom
Publisher: The University Press
of Chicago

286. NOVEMBER 27, 1994
Melba Pattillo Beals
*Warriors Don't Cry: A Searing
Memoir of the Battle to Integrate
Little Rock's Central High*
Publisher: Pocket Books

287. DECEMBER 4, 1994
Charles Murray
*The Bell Curve: Intelligence and
Class Structure in American Life*
Publisher: The Free Press

288. DECEMBER 11, 1994
Elizabeth Drew
*On the Edge: The Clinton
Presidency*
Publisher: Simon & Schuster

289. DECEMBER 18, 1994
Peter Robinson
*Snapshots from Hell: The Mak-
ing of an MBA*
Publisher: Warner Books

290. DECEMBER 25, 1994
Glenn Frankel
*Beyond the Promised Land: Jews
and Arabs on a Hard Road to a
New Israel*
Publisher: Simon & Schuster

291. JANUARY 1, 1995
Doris Kearns Goodwin
*No Ordinary Time: Franklin
and Eleanor Roosevelt: The
Home Front in World War II*
Publisher: Simon & Schuster

292. JANUARY 8, 1995
Robert Wright
*The Moral Animal: Why We Are
the Way We Are: The New
Science of Evolutionary Psychol-
ogy*
Publisher: Pantheon

293. JANUARY 15, 1995
Anthony Cave Brown
*Treason in the Blood: H. St. John
Philby, Kim Philby, and the Spy
Case of the Century*
Publisher: Houghton Mifflin

294. JANUARY 22, 1995
Marvin Olasky
*The Tragedy of American Com-
passion*
Publisher: Regnery Publishing

295. JANUARY 29, 1995
Steven Waldman
*The Bill: How the Adventures of
Clinton's National Service Bill
Reveal What Is Corrupt, Comic,
Cynical, and Noble About
Washington*
Publisher: Viking

296. FEBRUARY 5, 1995
M. Stanton Evans
*The Theme Is Freedom: Religion,
Politics, and the American
Tradition*
Publisher: Regnery Publishing

297. FEBRUARY 12, 1995
Philip Howard
*The Death of Common Sense:
How Law Is Suffocating America*
Publisher: Random House

298. FEBRUARY 19, 1995
Jimmy Carter
*Always a Reckoning and Other
Poems*
Publisher: Times Books

299. FEBRUARY 26, 1995
Alan Ryan
Author, Introduction
Democracy in America
Publisher: Alfred A. Knopf

300. MARCH 5, 1995
Lynn Sherr
*Failure Is Impossible: Susan B.
Anthony in Her Own Words*
Publisher: Times Books

301. MARCH 12, 1995
Donald Kagan
On the Origins of War
Publisher: Doubleday

302. MARCH 19, 1995
Neil Baldwin
Edison: Inventing the Century
Publisher: Hyperion

303. MARCH 26, 1995
James Loewen
*Lies My Teacher Told Me:
Everything Your American
History Textbook Got Wrong*
Publisher: The New Press

304. APRIL 2, 1995
Gertrude Himmelfarb
*The De-Moralization of Society:
From Victorian Virtues to
Modern Values*
Publisher: Alfred A. Knopf

305. APRIL 9, 1995
Stanley Greenberg
*Middle Class Dreams: The
Politics and Power of the New
American Majority*
Publisher: Times Books

306. APRIL 16, 1995
Alvin Toffler and Heidi Toffler
*Creating a New Civilization:
The Politics of the Third Wave*
Publisher: Turner Publishing, Inc.

307. APRIL 23, 1995
Robert McNamara
*In Retrospect: The Tragedy and
Lessons of Vietnam*
Publisher: Times Books

308. APRIL 30, 1995

Michael Klare
Rogue States and Nuclear Out-
laws: America's Search for a New
Foreign Policy
Publisher: Farrar, Straus &
Giroux

309. MAY 7, 1995
David Maraniss
First in His Class: A Biography of
Bill Clinton
Publisher: Simon & Schuster

310. MAY 14, 1995
Tim Penny and Major Garrett
Common Cents
Publisher: Little, Brown and
Company

311. MAY 21, 1995
Linn Washington
Black Judges on Justice
Publisher: The New Press

312. MAY 28, 1995
John Niven
Salmon P. Chase: A Biography
Publisher: Oxford University
Press

313. JUNE 4, 1995
Hanan Ashrawi
This Side of Peace
Publisher: Simon & Schuster

314. JUNE 11, 1995
Peter Brimelow
Alien Nation: Common Sense
About America's Immigration
Disaster
Publisher: Random House

315. JUNE 18, 1995
Yuri Shvets
Washington Station: My Life as a
KGB Spy in America
Publisher: Simon & Schuster

316. JUNE 25, 1995
Norman Mailer
Oswald's Tale: An American
Mystery
Publisher: Random House

317. JULY 2, 1995
Ari Hoogenboom
Rutherford B. Hayes: Warrior
and President
Publisher: University Press of
Kansas

318. JULY 9, 1995

DeWayne Wickham
Woodholme: A Black Man's Story
of Growing Up Alone
Publisher: Farrar, Straus &
Giroux

319. JULY 16, 1995
Armstrong Williams
Beyond Blame: How We Can
Succeed by Breaking the Depen-
dency Barrier
Publisher: The Free Press

320. JULY 23, 1995
Newt Gingrich
To Renew America
Publisher: HarperCollins

321. JULY 30, 1995
John Hockenberry
Moving Violations: A Memoir:
War Zones, Wheelchairs, and
Declarations of Independence
Publisher: Hyperion

322. AUGUST 6, 1995
Marc Fisher
After the Wall: Germany, the
Germans, and the Burdens of
History
Publisher: Simon & Schuster

323. AUGUST 13, 1995
Robert D. Richardson Jr.
Emerson: The Mind on Fire
Publisher: University of Califor-
nia Press

324. AUGUST 20, 1995
Cartha "Deke" DeLoach
Hoover's FBI: The Inside Story by
Hoover's Trusted Lieutenant
Publisher: Regnery Publishing

325. AUGUST 27, 1995
Robert Timberg
The Nightingale's Song
Publisher: Simon & Schuster

326. SEPTEMBER 3, 1995
Robert Leckie
Okinawa: The Last Battle of
World War II
Publisher: Viking

327. SEPTEMBER 10, 1995
Emory Thomas
Robert E. Lee: A Biography
Publisher: Norton

328. SEPTEMBER 17, 1995
Elsa Walsh

Divided Lives: The Public and
Private Struggles of Three Accom-
plished Women
Publisher: Simon & Schuster

329. SEPTEMBER 24, 1995
Irving Kristol
Neoconservatism: The Autobiog-
raphy of an Idea
Publisher: The Free Press

330. OCTOBER 1, 1995
Andrew Sullivan
Virtually Normal: An Argument
About Homosexuality
Publisher: Alfred A. Knopf

331. OCTOBER 8, 1995
Susan Eisenhower
Breaking Free: A Memoir of Love
Publisher: Farrar, Straus &
Giroux

332. OCTOBER 15, 1995
Nicholas Basbanes
A Gentle Madness: Bibliophiles,
Bibliomanes, and the Eternal
Passion for Books
Publisher: Henry Holt and
Company

333. OCTOBER 22, 1995
David Fromkin
In the Time of Americans: The
Generation That Changed
America's Role in the World
Publisher: Alfred A. Knopf

334. OCTOBER 29, 1995
Ben Bradlee
A Good Life: Newspapering and
Other Adventures
Publisher: Simon & Schuster

335. NOVEMBER 5, 1995
Marlin Fitzwater
Call the Briefing! Reagan and
Bush, Sam and Helen: A Decade
with Presidents and the Press
Publisher: Times Books

336. NOVEMBER 12, 1995
Pierre Salinger
P.S.: A Memoir
Publisher: St. Martin's Press

337. NOVEMBER 19, 1995
bell hooks
Killing Rage: Ending Racism
Publisher: Henry Holt and
Company

338. NOVEMBER 26, 1995
Sanford Ungar
Fresh Blood: The New American Immigrants
Publisher: Simon & Schuster

339. DECEMBER 3, 1995
James Baker (with Thomas DeFrank)
The Politics of Diplomacy: Revolution, War and Peace, 1989–1992
Publisher: Putnam

340. DECEMBER 10, 1995
David Brinkley
A Memoir
Publisher: Alfred A. Knopf

341. DECEMBER 17, 1995
Evan Thomas
The Very Best Men—Four Who Dared: The Early Years of the CIA
Publisher: Simon & Schuster

342. DECEMBER 24, 1995
David Herbert Donald
Lincoln
Publisher: Simon & Schuster

343. DECEMBER 31, 1995
Charles Kuralt
Charles Kuralt's America
Publisher: Putnam

344. JANUARY 7, 1996
Colin Powell
My American Journey
Publisher: Random House

345. JANUARY 14, 1996
William Prochnau
Once Upon a Distant War
Publisher: Times Books

346. JANUARY 21, 1996
Michael Kinsley
Big Babies
Publisher: William Morrow

347. JANUARY 28, 1996
Carlo D'Este
Patton: A Genius for War
Publisher: HarperCollins

348. FEBRUARY 4, 1996
Dennis Prager
Think a Second Time
Publisher: HarperCollins

349. FEBRUARY 11, 1996

Lance Banning
The Sacred Fire of Liberty: James Madison and the Founding of the Federal Republic
Publisher: Cornell University Press

350. FEBRUARY 18, 1996
Dan Balz (with Ronald Brownstein)
Storming the Gates: Protest Politics and Republican Revival
Publisher: Little, Brown and Company

351. FEBRUARY 25, 1996
H. W. Brands
The Reckless Decade: America in the 1890s
Publisher: St. Martin's Press

352. MARCH 3, 1996
Hillary Rodham Clinton
It Takes a Village: And Other Lessons Children Teach Us
Publisher: Simon & Schuster

353. MARCH 10, 1996
Johanna Neuman
Lights, Camera, War: Is Media Technology Driving International Politics?
Publisher: St. Martin's Press

354. MARCH 17, 1996
Clarence Page
Showing My Color: Impolite Essays on Race and Identity
Publisher: HarperCollins

355. MARCH 24, 1996
Robert Merry
Taking on the World: Joseph and Stewart Alsop—Guardians of the American Century
Publisher: Viking

356. MARCH 31, 1996
Fox Butterfield
All God's Children: The Bosket Family and the American Tradition of Violence
Publisher: Alfred A. Knopf

357. APRIL 7, 1996
Jean Baker
The Stevensons: A Biography of an American Family
Publisher: Norton

358. APRIL 14, 1996
Wayne Fields

Union of Words: A History of Presidential Eloquence
Publisher: The Free Press

359. APRIL 21, 1996
Robert Kaplan
The Ends of the Earth: A Journey at the Dawn of the 21st Century
Publisher: Simon & Schuster

360. APRIL 28, 1996
David Reynolds
Walt Whitman's America: A Cultural Biography
Publisher: Alfred A. Knopf

361. MAY 5, 1996
David Broder (with Haynes Johnson)
The System: The American Way of Politics at the Breaking Point
Publisher: Little, Brown and Company

362. MAY 12, 1996
Stanley Crouch
The All-American Skin Game, or the Decoy of Race: The Long and Short of It, 1990–1994
Publisher: Pantheon Books

363. MAY 19, 1996
Michael Sandel
Democracy's Discontent: America in Search of a Public Philosophy
Publisher: Harvard University Press

364. MAY 26, 1996
Noa Ben Artzi-Pelossof
In the Name of Sorrow and Hope
Publisher: Alfred A. Knopf

365. JUNE 2, 1996
James Thomas Flexner
Maverick's Progress: An Autobiography
Publisher: Fordham University Press

366. JUNE 9, 1996
Christopher Matthews
Kennedy and Nixon: The Rivalry That Shaped Postwar America
Publisher: Simon & Schuster

367. JUNE 16, 1996
Albert Murray
Blue Devils of Nada: A Contemporary American Approach to Aesthetic Statement
Publisher: Pantheon

368. JUNE 23, 1996
Seymour Martin Lipset
American Exceptionalism: A Double-Edged Sword
Publisher: Norton

369. JUNE 30, 1996
Glenn Simpson (with Larry Sabato)
Dirty Little Secrets: The Persistence of Corruption in American Politics
Publisher: Times Books

370. JULY 7, 1996
Paul Greenberg
No Surprises: Two Decades of Clinton Watching
Publisher: Brassey's

371. JULY 14, 1996
Ted Sorensen
Why I Am a Democrat
Publisher: Henry Holt and Company

372. JULY 21, 1996
Eleanor Randolph
Waking the Tempests: Ordinary Life in New Russia
Publisher: Simon & Schuster

373. JULY 28, 1996
James Lardner
Crusader: The Hell-Raising Police Career of Detective David Durk
Publisher: Random House

374. AUGUST 4, 1996
Denis Brian
Einstein: A Life
Publisher: John Wiley & Sons, Inc.

[AUGUST 11 AND AUGUST 18, 1996: PREEMPTED BY REFORM PARTY CONVENTION]

375. AUGUST 25, 1996
Eleanor Clift and Tom Brazaitis
War Without Bloodshed: The Art of Politics
Publisher: Scribner

376. SEPTEMBER 1, 1996
Drew Gilpin Faust
Mothers of Invention: Women of the Slaveholding South in the American Civil War
Publisher: University of North Carolina Press

377. SEPTEMBER 8, 1996
Donald Warren
Radio Priest: Charles Coughlin, the Father of Hate Radio
Publisher: The Free Press

378. SEPTEMBER 15, 1996
Lloyd Kramer
Lafayette in Two Worlds
University of North Carolina Press

379. SEPTEMBER 22, 1996
Michael Elliott
The Day Before Yesterday: Reconsidering America's Past, Rediscovering the Present
Publisher: Simon & Schuster

380. SEPTEMBER 29, 1996
Monica Crowley
Nixon off the Record: His Candid Commentary on People and Politics
Publisher: Random House

[OCTOBER 6, 1996: PREEMPTED BY PRESIDENTIAL DEBATE IN HARTFORD, CONN.]

381. OCTOBER 13, 1996
Louise Barnett
Touched by Fire: The Life, Death, and Mythic Afterlife of George Armstrong Custer
Publisher: Henry Holt and Company

382. OCTOBER 20, 1996
David Friedman
Hidden Order: The Economics of Everyday Life
Publisher: HarperBusiness

383. OCTOBER 27, 1996
Paul Hendrickson
The Living and the Dead: Robert McNamara and Five Lives of a Lost War
Publisher: Alfred A. Knopf

384. NOVEMBER 3, 1996
Andrew Ferguson
Fools' Names, Fools' Faces
Publisher: Atlantic Monthly Press

385. NOVEMBER 10, 1996
Leon Dash
Rosa Lee: A Mother and Her Family in Urban America

Publisher: Basic Books

386. NOVEMBER 17, 1996
Conor Cruise O'Brien
The Long Affair: Thomas Jefferson and the French Revolution, 1785-1800
Publisher: The University Press of Chicago

387. NOVEMBER 24, 1996
Mikhail Gorbachev
Memoirs
Publisher: Doubleday

388. DECEMBER 1, 1996
Robert Bork
Slouching Towards Gomorrah: Modern Liberalism and American Decline
Publisher: HarperCollins

389. DECEMBER 8, 1996
Nell Irvin Painter
Sojourner Truth: A Life, a Symbol
Publisher: Norton

390. DECEMBER 15, 1996
President Bill Clinton
Between Hope and History: Meeting America's Challenges for the 21st Century
Publisher: Times Books

391. DECEMBER 22, 1996
David Denby
Great Books: My Adventures with Homer, Rousseau, Woolf, and Other Indestructible Writers of the Western World
Publisher: Simon & Schuster

392. DECEMBER 29, 1996
Stanley Wolpert
Nehru: A Tryst with Destiny
Publisher: Oxford University Press

393. JANUARY 5, 1997
Edward Jay Epstein
Dossier: The Secret History of Armand Hammer
Publisher: Random House

394. JANUARY 12, 1997
Robert Ferrell
The Strange Death of President Harding
Publisher: University of Missouri Press

395. JANUARY 19, 1997

Alfred Zacher
*Trial and Triumph: Presidential
Power in the Second Term*
Publisher: Midpoint Trade
Books

396. JANUARY 26, 1997
David Boaz
Libertarianism: A Primer
Publisher: The Free Press

397. FEBRUARY 2, 1997
Henry Grunwald
*One Man's America: A Journal-
ist's Search for the Heart of His
Country*
Publisher: Doubleday

398. FEBRUARY 9, 1997
John Brady
*Bad Boy: The Life and Politics of
Lee Atwater*
Publisher: Addison Wesley

399. FEBRUARY 16, 1997
Katharine Graham
Personal History
Publisher: Alfred A. Knopf

400. FEBRUARY 23, 1997
(PART ONE)
Sam Tanenhaus
*Whittaker Chambers: A Biogra-
phy*
Publisher: Random House

401. MARCH 2, 1997 (PART
TWO)
Sam Tanenhaus
*Whittaker Chambers: A Biogra-
phy*
Publisher: Random House

402. MARCH 9, 1997
Sarah Gordon
*Passage to Union: How the
Railroads Transformed American
Life, 1829-1929*
Publisher: Ivan R. Dee

403. MARCH 16, 1997
John Fialka
*War by Other Means: Economic
Espionage in America*
Publisher: Norton

404. MARCH 23, 1997
Jon Katz
*Virtuous Reality: How America
Surrendered Discussion of Moral
Values to Opportunists, Nitwits,
and Blockheads like William*

Bennett
Publisher: Random House

405. MARCH 30, 1997
Claude Andrew Clegg III
*An Original Man: The Life and
Times of Elijah Muhammad*
Publisher: St. Martin's Press

406. APRIL 6, 1997
Keith Richburg
*Out of America: A Black Man
Confronts Africa*
Publisher: Basic Books

407. APRIL 13, 1997
David Horowitz
*Radical Son: A Generational
Odyssey*
Publisher: The Free Press

408. APRIL 20, 1997
Leonard Garment
*Crazy Rhythm: My Journey from
Brooklyn, Jazz, and Wall Street,
to Nixon's White House, Water-
gate, and Beyond*
Publisher: Times Books

409. APRIL 27, 1997
Stephen B. Oates
*The Approaching Fury: Voices of
the Storm, 1820-1861*
Publisher: HarperCollins

410. MAY 4, 1997
Christopher Buckley
Wry Martinis
Publisher: Random House

411. MAY 11, 1997
Richard Bernstein (with Ross
Munro)
The Coming Conflict with China
Publisher: Alfred A. Knopf

412. MAY 18, 1997
Anne Matthews
*Bright College Years: Inside the
American Campus Today*
Publisher: Simon & Schuster

413. MAY 25, 1997
Jane Holtz Kay
*Asphalt Nation: How the Auto-
mobile Took Over America, and
How We Can Take It Back*
Publisher: Crown Publishers

414. JUNE 1, 1997
Jill Krementz
The Writer's Desk

Publisher: Random House

415. JUNE 8, 1997
Pavel Palazchenko
*My Years with Gorbachev and
Shevardnadze: The Memoir of a
Soviet Interpreter*
Publisher: Penn State Press

416. JUNE 15, 1997
Walter McDougall
*Promised Land, Crusader State:
The American Encounter with
the World Since 1776*
Publisher: Houghton Mifflin

417. JUNE 22, 1997
James Humes
*Confessions of a White House
Ghostwriter: Five Presidents and
other Political Adventures*
Publisher: Regnery Publishing

418. JUNE 29, 1997
Walter Cronkite
A Reporter's Life
Publisher: Alfred A. Knopf

419. JULY 6, 1997
Jack N. Rakove
*Original Meanings: Politics and
Ideas in the Making of the
Constitution*
Publisher: Alfred A. Knopf

420. JULY 13, 1997
Tom Clancy
General Fred Franks (Ret.)
*Into the Storm: A Study in
Command*
Publisher: Putnam

421. JULY 20, 1997
Robert Hughes
*American Visions: The Epic
History of Art in America*
Publisher: Alfred A. Knopf

422. JULY 27, 1997
Sylvia Jukes Morris
*Rage for Fame: The Ascent of
Clare Boothe Luce*
Publisher: Random House

423. AUGUST 3, 1997
LeAlan Jones (and Lloyd
Newman)
*Our America: Life and Death on
the South Side of Chicago*
Publisher: Scribner

424. AUGUST 10, 1997

James Tobin
Ernie Pyle's War: America's Eyewitness to World War II
Publisher: The Free Press

425. AUGUST 17, 1997
Pauline Maier
American Scripture: Making the Declaration of Independence
Publisher: Alfred A. Knopf

426. AUGUST 24, 1997
Peter Maas
Underboss: Sammy the Bull Gravano's Story of Life in the Mafia
Publisher: HarperCollins

427. AUGUST 31, 1997
Frank McCourt
Angela's Ashes: A Memoir
Publisher: Scribner

428. SEPTEMBER 7, 1997
Brian Burrell
The Words We Live By: The Creeds, Mottoes, and Pledges That Have Shaped America
Publisher: The Free Press

429. SEPTEMBER 14, 1997
John Toland
Captured by History: One Man's Vision of Our Tumultuous Century
Publisher: St. Martin's Press

430. SEPTEMBER 21, 1997
Peter Gomes
The Good Book: Reading the Bible with Mind and Heart
Publisher: William Morrow

431. SEPTEMBER 28, 1997
John Berendt
Midnight in the Garden of Good and Evil: A Savannah Story
Publisher: Random House

432. OCTOBER 5, 1997
Howard Gardner
Extraordinary Minds: Portraits of Four Exceptional Individuals and an Examination of Our Own Extraordinariness
Publisher: Basic Books

433. OCTOBER 12, 1997
Geoffrey Perret
Ulysses S. Grant: Soldier and President
Publisher: Random House

434. OCTOBER 19, 1997
Nat Hentoff
Speaking Freely: A Memoir
Publisher: Alfred A. Knopf

435. OCTOBER 26, 1997
Alan Schom
Napoleon Bonaparte
Publisher: HarperCollins

436. NOVEMBER 2, 1997
Thomas West
Vindicating the Founders: Race, Sex, Class, and Justice in the Origins of America
Publisher: Rowman & Littlefield

[NOVEMBER 9, 1997: PRE-EMPTED BY COVERAGE OF THE U.S. HOUSE OF REPRE-SENTATIVES]

437. NOVEMBER 16, 1997
David Gelernter
Drawing Life: Surviving the Unabomber.
Publisher: The Free Press

438. NOVEMBER 23, 1997
Anita Hill
Speaking Truth to Power
Publisher: Doubleday

439. NOVEMBER 30, 1997
Jeff Shesol
Mutual Contempt: Lyndon Johnson, Robert Kennedy, and the Feud That Defined a Decade
Publisher: Norton

440. DECEMBER 7, 1997
Tim Russert
Meet the Press: 50 Years of History in the Making
Publisher: McGraw-Hill

441. DECEMBER 14, 1997
Susan Butler
East to the Dawn: The Life of Amelia Earhart
Publisher: Addison Wesley Longman

442. DECEMBER 21, 1997
Jim Hightower
There's Nothing in the Middle of the Road but Yellow Stripes and Dead Armadillos
Publisher: HarperCollins

443. DECEMBER 28, 1997

Sally Quinn
The Party: A Guide to Adventurous Entertaining
Publisher: Simon & Schuster

444. JANUARY 4, 1998
Paul Nagel
John Quincy Adams: A Public Life, a Private Life
Publisher: Alfred A. Knopf

445. JANUARY 11, 1998
Iris Chang
The Rape of Nanking: The Forgotten Holocaust of World War II
Publisher: Basic Books

446. JANUARY 18, 1998
Allan Metcalf (with David Barnhart)
America in So Many Words
Publisher: Houghton Mifflin

447. JANUARY 25, 1998
Daniel Pipes
Conspiracy: How the Paranoid Style Flourishes and Where It Comes From
Publisher: The Free Press

448. FEBRUARY 1, 1998
Roger Simon
Showtime: The American Political Circus and the Race for the White House
Publisher: Times Books

449. FEBRUARY 8, 1998
Carol Reardon
Pickett's Charge in History and Memory
Publisher: The University of North Carolina Press

450. FEBRUARY 15, 1998
Joseph Hernon
Profiles in Character: Hubris and Heroism in the U.S. Senate, 1789–1990
Publisher: M. E. Sharpe

451. FEBRUARY 22, 1998
William Gildea
Where the Game Matters Most
Publisher: Little, Brown and Company

452. MARCH 1, 1998
John Lukacs
The Hitler of History
Publisher: Alfred A. Knopf

453. MARCH 8, 1998
John Marszalek
*The Petticoat Affair: Manners,
Mutiny, and Sex in Andrew
Jackson's White House*
Publisher: The Free Press

454. MARCH 15, 1998
Randall Robinson
*Defending the Spirit: A Black
Life in America*
Publisher: Dutton

455. MARCH 22, 1998
Ernest Lefever
*The Irony of Virtue: Ethics and
American Power*
Publisher: Westview Press

456. MARCH 29, 1998
Douglas L. Wilson
*Honor's Voice: The Transforma-
tion of Abraham Lincoln*
Publisher: Alfred A. Knopf

457. APRIL 5, 1998
Paul Johnson
A History of the American People
Publisher: HarperCollins

458. APRIL 12, 1998
Taylor Branch
*Pillar of Fire: America in the
King Years, 1963–65*
Publisher: Simon & Schuster

459. APRIL 19, 1998
John S. D. Eisenhower
*Agent of Destiny: The Life and
Times of General Winfield Scott*
Publisher: The Free Press

460. APRIL 26, 1998
Molly Ivins
*You Got to Dance with Them
What Brung You: Politics in the
Clinton Years*
Publisher: Random House

461. MAY 3, 1998
David Aikman
*Great Souls: Six Who Changed
the Century*
Publisher: Word Publishing

462. MAY 10, 1998
Arthur J. Schlesinger Jr.
The Disuniting of America
Publisher: W. W. Norton

463. MAY 17, 1998
Patrick Buchanan
*The Great Betrayal: How Ameri-
can Sovereignty and Social Justice
Are Being Sacrificed to the Gods
of the Global Economy*
Publisher: Little, Brown and
Company

464. MAY 24, 1998
Jill Ker Conway
*When Memory Speaks:
Reflections on Autobiography*
Publisher: Alfred A. Knopf

465. MAY 31, 1998
Max Boot
*Out of Order: Arrogance, Cor-
ruption, and Incompetence on the
Bench*
Publisher: Basic Books

466. JUNE 7, 1998
Linda Simon
*Genuine Reality: A Life of
William James*
Publisher: Harcourt Brace

467. JUNE 14, 1998
Edward Lazarus
*Closed Chambers: The First
Eyewitness Account of the Epic
Struggles Inside the Supreme
Court*
Publisher: Times Books

468. JUNE 21, 1998
Ron Chernow
*Titan: The Life of John D.
Rockefeller Sr.*
Publisher: Random House

469. JUNE 28, 1998
Edward J. Larson
*Summer for the Gods: The Scopes
Trial and America's Continuing
Debate over Science and Religion*
Publisher: Basic Books

470. JULY 5, 1998
Andrew Carroll
*Letters of a Nation: A Collection
of Extraordinary American
Letters*
Publisher: Kodansha

471. JULY 12, 1998
John Lewis
*Walking with the Wind: A
Memoir of the Movement*
Publisher: Simon & Schuster

472. JULY 19, 1998
Ben Procter
*William Randolph Hearst: The
Early Years, 1863–1910*
Publisher: Oxford University
Press

473. JULY 26, 1998
Richard Holbrooke
To End a War
Publisher: Random House

474. AUGUST 2, 1998
F. Carolyn Graglia
*Domestic Tranquillity: A Brief
Against Feminism*
Publisher: Spence

475. AUGUST 9, 1998
Roy Reed
*Faubus: The Life and Times of
an American Prodigal*
Publisher: University of
Arkansas Press

476. AUGUST 16, 1998
Patricia O'Toole
Money and Morals in America
Publisher: Potter

477. AUGUST 23, 1998
Barbara Crossette
The Great Hill Stations of Asia
Publisher: Westview

478. AUGUST 30, 1998
Robert Sobel
Coolidge: An American Enigma
Publisher: Regnery Publishing

479. SEPTEMBER 6, 1998
Linda H. Davis
*Badge of Courage: The Life of
Stephen Crane*
Publisher: Houghton Mifflin

480. SEPTEMBER 13, 1998
Arnold A. Rogow
*A Fatal Friendship: Alexander
Hamilton and Aaron Burr*
Publisher: Hill & Wang

481. SEPTEMBER 20, 1998
Larry Tye
*The Father of Spin: Edward L.
Bernays and the Birth of Public
Relations*
Publisher: Crown Publishers

482. SEPTEMBER 27, 1998
Balint Vazsonyi
*America's 30 Years War: Who Is
Winning?*
Publisher: Regnery Publishing

483. OCTOBER 4, 1998
George Bush and Brent
Scowcroft
A World Transformed
Publisher: Alfred A. Knopf

484. OCTOBER 11, 1998
Juan Williams
*Thurgood Marshall: American
Revolutionary*
Publisher: Times Books

485. OCTOBER 18, 1998
Christopher Dickey
*Summer of Deliverance: A
Memoir of Father and Son*
Publisher: Simon & Schuster

486. OCTOBER 25, 1998
Dorothy Herrmann
Helen Keller: A Life
Publisher: Alfred A. Knopf

487. NOVEMBER 1, 1998
Charles Lewis
*The Buying of the Congress: How
Special Interests Have Stolen Your
Right to Life, Liberty, and the
Pursuit of Happiness*
Publisher: Avon Books

488. NOVEMBER 8, 1998
Simon Winchester
*The Professor and the Madman:
A Tale of Murder, Insanity, and
the Making of the Oxford English
Dictionary*
Publisher: HarperCollins

489. NOVEMBER 15, 1998
Eric Foner
The Story of American Freedom
Publisher: W. W. Norton

490. NOVEMBER 2, 19982
Philip Gourevitch
*We Wish to Inform You That
Tomorrow We Will Be Killed
with Our Families: Stories from
Rwanda*
Publisher: Farrar, Straus &
Giroux

491. NOVEMBER 29, 1998
Melissa Muller
Anne Frank: The Biography
Publisher: Metropolitan Books

492. DECEMBER 6, 1998
Shelby Steele
*A Dream Deferred: The Second
Betrayal of Black Freedom in*

America
Publisher: HarperCollins

493. DECEMBER 13, 1998
William Greider
*Fortress America: The American
Military and the Consequences of
Peace*
Publisher: PublicAffairs

494. DECEMBER 20, 1998
A. Scott Berg
Lindbergh
Publisher: The Putnam Publish-
ing Group

495. DECEMBER 27, 1998
Peter Jennings
The Century
Publisher: Doubleday

496. JANUARY 3, 1999
P. J. O'Rourke
Eat the Rich
Publisher: Grove Atlantic

497. JANUARY 10, 1999
John Morris
*Get the Picture: A Personal
History of Photojournalism*
Publisher: Random House

498. JANUARY 17, 1999
Dava Sobel
*Longitude: The True Story of a
Lone Genius Who Solved the
Greatest Scientific Problem of His
Time*
Publisher: Walker & Company

499. JANUARY 24, 1999
Michael Ignatieff
Isaiah Berlin: A Life
Publisher: Metropolitan Books

500. JANUARY 31, 1999
Peter R. Kann and Frances
FitzGerald
Reporting Vietnam
Publisher: Library of America

501. FEBRUARY 7, 1999
Harold Evans
The American Century
Publisher: Alfred A. Knopf

502. FEBRUARY 14, 1999
Virginia Postrel
The Future and Its Enemies
Publisher: The Free Press

503. FEBRUARY 21, 1999

Annette Gordon-Reed
*Thomas Jefferson and Sally
Hemings: An American Contro-
versy*
Publisher: University Press of
Virginia

504. FEBRUARY 28, 1999
Robert Famighetti
*World Almanac and Book of
Facts, 1999*
Publisher: World Almanac
Books

505. MARCH 7, 1999
Tom Brokaw
The Greatest Generation
Publisher: Random House

506. MARCH 14, 1999
Allen Weinstein
*The Haunted Wood: Soviet
Espionage in America—The
Stalin Era*
Publisher: Random House

507. MARCH 21, 1999
Richard Shenkman
*Presidential Ambition: How the
Presidents Gained Power, Kept
Power, and Got Things Done*
Publisher: HarperCollins

508. MARCH 28, 1999
Norman Podhoretz
*Ex-Friends: Falling Out with
Allen Ginsberg, Lionel and
Diana Trilling, Lillian Hellman,
Hannah Arendt, and Norman
Mailer*
Publisher: The Free Press

[APRIL 4, 1999: TENTH
ANNIVERSARY SPECIAL]

509. APRIL 11, 1999
Amity Shlaes
*The Greedy Hand: How Taxes
Drive Americans Crazy and
What to Do About It*
Publisher: Random House

510. APRIL 18, 1999
Max Frankel
*The Times of My Life and My
Life with the Times*
Publisher: Random House

511. APRIL 25, 1999
Randall Kenan
*Walking on Water: Black Ameri-
can Lives at the Turn of the*

Twenty-First Century
Publisher: Alfred A. Knopf

512. MAY 2, 1999
Mary Soames, editor
Winston and Clementine: The Personal Letters of the Churchills
Publisher: Houghton Mifflin

513. MAY 9, 1999
Betty Boyd Caroli
The Roosevelt Women
Publisher: Basic Books

514. MAY 16, 1999
T. R. Reid
Confucius Lives Next Door: What Living in the East Teaches Us About Living in the West
Publisher: Random House

515. MAY 23, 1999
Jean Strouse
Morgan: American Financier
Publisher: Random House

516. MAY 30, 1999
Bill Gertz
Betrayal: How the Clinton Administration Undermined American Security
Publisher: Regnery Publishing

517. JUNE 6, 1999
Roger Mudd
Great Minds of History
Publisher: John Wiley & Sons, Inc.

518. JUNE 13, 1999
Joseph E. Stevens
1863: The Rebirth of a Nation
Publisher: Bantam Books

519. JUNE 20, 1999
David M. Kennedy
Freedom from Fear: The American People in Depression and War
Publisher: Oxford University Press

520. JUNE 27, 1999
Jon Margolis
The Last Innocent Year: America in 1964
Publisher: William Morrow

521. JULY 4, 1999
Floyd Flake
The Way of the Bootstrapper
Publisher: HarperSanFrancisco

522. JULY 11, 1999
Michael Korda
Another Life: A Memoir of Other People
Publisher: Random House

523. JULY 18, 1999
Michael H. Cottman
The Wreck of the Henrietta Marie: An African-American's Spiritual Journey to Uncover a Sunken Slave Ship's Past
Publisher: Harmony/Crown Books

524. JULY 25, 1999
Dan Rather
Deadlines and Datelines: Essays at the Turn of the Century
Publisher: William Morrow

525. AUGUST 1, 1999
Richard Gephardt
An Even Better Place: America in the 21st Century
Publisher: PublicAffairs

526. AUGUST 8, 1999
H. W. Crocker III
Robert E. Lee on Leadership
Publisher: Forum/Prima Publishing

527. AUGUST 15, 1999
Elizabeth M. Norman
We Band of Angels: The Untold Story of American Nurses Trapped on Bataan by the Japanese
Publisher: Random House

528. AUGUST 22, 1999
David Atkinson
Leaving the Bench: Supreme Court Justices at the End
Publisher: University of Kansas Press

529. AUGUST 29, 1999
Mark Pendergrast
The History of Coffee and How It Transformed Our World
Publisher: Basic Books

530. SEPTEMBER 5, 1999
Leslie Chang
Beyond the Narrow Gate: The Journey of Four Chinese Women from the Middle Kingdom to Middle America
Publisher: Dutton

531. SEPTEMBER 12, 1999
Jay Parini
Robert Frost: A Life
Publisher: Henry Holt and Company

532. SEPTEMBER 19, 1999
Richard E. Cohen
Rostenkowski
Publisher: Ivan R. Dee

533. SEPTEMBER 26, 1999
Linda O. McMurry
To Keep the Waters Troubled: The Life of Ida B. Wells
Publisher: Oxford University Press

534. OCTOBER 3, 1999
James Glassman
Dow 36,000: The New Strategy for Profiting from the Coming Rise in the Stock Market
Publisher: Times Books

534. OCTOBER 10, 1999
Stuart I. Rochester
Honor Bound: American Prisoners of War in Southeast Asia, 1961–1973
Publisher: Naval Institute Press

535. OCTOBER 17, 1999
Witold Rybczynski
A Clearing in the Distance: Frederick Law Olmsted and America in the 19th Century
Publisher: Scribner

536. OCTOBER 24, 1999
Michael Kammen
American Culture, American Tastes: Social Change and the 20th Century
Publisher: Alfred A. Knopf

537. OCTOBER 31, 1999
Patrick Tyler
A Great Wall: Six Presidents and China, An Investigative History
Publisher: PublicAffairs

538. NOVEMBER 7, 1999
Eugene Robinson
Coal to Cream: A Black Man's Journey Beyond Color to an Affirmation of Race
Publisher: The Free Press

539. NOVEMBER 14, 1999
Fred Maroon
The Nixon Years, 1969–1974,

White House to Watergate
Publisher: Abbeville Press

540. NOVEMBER 21, 1999
Alfred F. Young
The Shoemaker and the Tea Party: Memory and the American Revolution
Publisher: Beacon Press

541. NOVEMBER 28, 1999
Winston Churchill
The Great Republic: A History of America
Publisher: Random House

542. DECEMBER 5, 1999
Edmund Morris
Dutch: A Memoir of Ronald Reagan
Publisher: Random House

543. DECEMBER 12, 1999
Michael Patrick MacDonald
All Souls: A Family Story from Southie
Publisher: Beacon Press

544. DECEMBER 19, 1999
Robert Conquest
Reflections on a Ravaged Century
Publisher: W. W. Norton

545. DECEMBER 26, 1999
Tom Wheeler
Leadership Lessons from the Civil War
Publisher: Current Books/Doubleday

546. JANUARY 2, 2000
Thomas Keneally (PART ONE)
The Great Shame and the Triumph of the Irish in the English-Speaking World
Publisher: Nan A. Talese/Doubleday

547. JANUARY 9, 2000
Thomas Keneally (PART TWO)
The Great Shame and the Triumph of the Irish in the English-Speaking World
Publisher: Nan A. Talese/Doubleday

548. JANUARY 16, 2000
William Least Heat-Moon
River-Horse: A Voyage Across America
Publisher: Houghton Mifflin

549. JANUARY 23, 2000
Isaac Stern
My First 79 Years
Publisher: Alfred A. Knopf

550. JANUARY 30, 2000
Robert Novak
Completing the Revolution: A Vision for Victory in 2000
Publisher: The Free Press

551. FEBRUARY 6, 2000
Arthur Herman
Joseph McCarthy: Reexamining the Life and Legacy of America's Most Hated Senator
Publisher: The Free Press

552. FEBRUARY 13, 2000
Arianna Huffington
How to Overthrow the Government
Publisher: Regan Book/HarperCollins

553. FEBRUARY 20, 2000
Cornel West
The Cornel West Reader
Publisher: Basic/Civitas Books

554. FEBRUARY 27, 2000
Gina Kolata
Flu: The Story of the Great Influenza Pandemic of 1918 and the Search for the Virus That Caused It
Publisher: Farrar, Straus & Giroux

555. MARCH 5, 2000
David Haward Bain
Empire Express: Building the First Transcontinental Railroad
Publisher: Viking

556. MARCH 12, 2000
Howard Zinn
A People's History of the United States, 1492-Present
Publisher: HarperCollins

557. MARCH 19, 2000
Loung Ung
First They Killed My Father: A Daughter of Cambodia Remembers
Publisher: HarperCollins

558. MARCH 26, 2000
John Dower
Embracing Defeat: Japan in the Wake of World War II

Publisher: W. W. Norton

559. APRIL 2, 2000
Philip Short
Mao: A Life
Publisher: Henry Holt and Company

560. APRIL 9, 2000
Tavis Smiley
Doing What's Right: How to Fight for What You Believe In—And Make a Difference
Publisher: Doubleday

561. APRIL 16, 2000
Allen C. Guelzo
Abraham Lincoln: Redeemer President
Publisher: William B. Eerdmans

562. APRIL 23, 2000
Walter Mosley
Workin' on the Chain Gang: Shaking Off the Dead Hand of History
Publisher: Ballantine Books

563. APRIL 30, 2000
Ward Connerly
Creating Equal: My Fight Against Race Preferences
Publisher: Encounter Books

564. MAY 7, 2000
David Wise
Cassidy's Run: The Secret Spy War over Nerve Gas
Publisher: Random House

565. MAY 14, 2000
Stephanie Gutmann
The Kinder, Gentler Military: Can America's Gender-Neutral Fighting Force Still Win Wars?
Publisher: Scribner

566. MAY 21, 2000
James M. Perry
A Bohemian Brigade: The Civil War Correspondents—Mostly Rough, Sometimes Ready
Publisher: John Wiley & Sons, Inc.

567. MAY 28, 2000
David Crosby
Stand and Be Counted: Making Music, Making History
Publisher: HarperSanFrancisco

568. JUNE 4, 2000

Zachary Karabell
The Last Campaign: How Harry Truman Won the 1948 Election
Publisher: Alfred A. Knopf

569. JUNE 11, 2000
Dan Baum
Citizen Coors: An American Dynasty
Publisher: William Morrow

570. JUNE 18, 2000
Joyce Appleby
Inheriting the Revolution: The First Generation of Americans
Publisher: Belknap/Harvard

571. JUNE 25, 2000
Francis Wheen
Karl Marx: A Life
Publisher: W. W. Norton

[JULY 2, 2000: PREEMPTED BY COVERAGE OF THE LIBERTARIAN PARTY CONVENTION]

572. JULY 9, 2000
James Bradley
Flags of Our Fathers
Publisher: Bantam Books

573. JULY 16, 2000
Brooks D. Simpson
Ulysses S. Grant: Triumph over Adversity
Publisher: Houghton Mifflin

574. JULY 23, 2000
Elizabeth Taylor
American Pharaoh: Mayor Richard J. Daley
Publisher: Little, Brown and Company

575. JULY 30, 2000
David Brooks
Bobos in Paradise: The New Upper Class and How They Got There
Publisher: Simon & Schuster

576. AUGUST 6, 2000
H. Paul Jeffers
An Honest President: The Life and Presidencies of Grover Cleveland
Publisher: William Morrow/Avon Books

577. AUGUST 13, 2000
Jane Alexander
Command Performance: An Actress in the Theater of Politics
Publisher: PublicAffairs

578. AUGUST 20, 2000
Harry Stein
How I Accidentally Joined the Vast Right-Wing Conspiracy (And Found Inner Peace)
Publisher: Delacorte Press

579. AUGUST 27, 2000
Ted Gup
The Book of Honor: Covert Lives and Classified Deaths at the CIA
Publisher: Doubleday

580. SEPTEMBER 3, 2000
Harold Bloom
How to Read and Why
Publisher: Scribner

581. SEPTEMBER 10, 2000
Lerone Bennett Jr.
Forced into Glory: Abraham Lincoln's White Dream
Publisher: Johnson Publishing

582. SEPTEMBER 17, 2000
Alan Murray
The Wealth of Choices: How the New Economy Puts Power in Your Hands and Money in Your Pocket
Publisher: Crown Business

583. SEPTEMBER 24, 2000
Michael Paterniti
Driving Mr. Albert: A Trip Across America with Einstein's Brain
Publisher: The Dial Press

584. OCTOBER 1, 2000
Nina J. Easton
Gang of Five: Leaders at the Center of the Conservative Crusade
Publisher: Simon & Schuster

585. OCTOBER 8, 2000
Diane Ravitch
Left Back: A Century of Failed School Reforms
Publisher: Simon & Schuster

586. OCTOBER 15, 2000
Rick Bragg
Somebody Told Me: The Newspaper Stories of Rick Bragg
Publisher: University of Alabama Press

587. OCTOBER 22, 2000
Karen Armstrong
Islam: A Short History
Publisher: Modern Library

[OCTOBER 29, 2000: PREEMPTED BY COVERAGE OF THE U.S. HOUSE OF REPRESENTATIVES]

588. NOVEMBER 5, 2000
Bonnie Angelo
First Mothers: The Women Who Shaped the Presidents
Publisher: William Morrow

589. NOVEMBER 12, 2000
William Duiker
Ho Chi Minh: A Life
Publisher: Hyperion

590. NOVEMBER 19, 2000
Maya Lin
Boundaries
Publisher: Simon & Schuster

591. NOVEMBER 26, 2000
Murray Sperber
Beer and Circus: How Big-Time College Sports Is Crippling Undergraduate Education
Publisher: Henry Holt and Company

[DECEMBER 3, 2000: PREEMPTED BY COVERAGE OF CAMPAIGN 2000]

592. DECEMBER 10, 2000
Frank Rich
Ghost Light: A Memoir
Publisher: Random House

593. DECEMBER 17, 2000
Harvey C. Mansfield, editor and translator of Alexis de Tocqueville's *Democracy in America*
Publisher: The University Press of Chicago

594. DECEMBER 24, 2000
Robert Putnam
Bowling Alone: The Collapse and Revival of American Community
Publisher: Simon & Schuster

595. DECEMBER 31, 2000
Peter Hitchens
The Abolition of Britain: From Winston Churchill to Princess Diana
Publisher: Encounter Books

596. JANUARY 7, 2001
Martin Goldsmith
The Inextinguishable Symphony: A True Story of Music and Love in Nazi Germany
Publisher: John Wiley & Sons, Inc.

597. JANUARY 14, 2001
Dinesh D'Souza
The Virtue of Prosperity: Finding Values in an Age of Techno-Affluence
Publisher: The Free Press

598. JANUARY 21, 2001
Robert Scigliano, editor
The Federalist
Publisher: Modern Library

599. JANUARY 28, 2001
Arlen Specter
Passion for Truth: From Finding JFK's Single Bullet to Questioning Anita Hill to Impeaching Clinton
Publisher: William Morrow

600. FEBRUARY 4, 2001
(PART ONE)
Kurt Eichenwald
The Informant: A True Story
Publisher: Broadway Books

601. FEBRUARY 11, 2001
(PART TWO)
Kurt Eichenwald
The Informant: A True Story
Publisher: Broadway Books

602. FEBRUARY 18, 2001
Maurizio Viroli
Niccolo's Smile: A Biography of Machiavelli
Publisher: Farrar, Straus & Giroux

603. FEBRUARY 25, 2001
Bernard A. Weisberger
America Afire: Jefferson, Adams, and the Revolutionary Election of 1800
Publisher: William Morrow

604. MARCH 4, 2001
Dick Gregory
Callus on My Soul: A Memoir
Publisher: Longstreet Press

605. MARCH 11, 2001
Jeffrey Meyers
Orwell: Wintry Conscience of a

Generation
Publisher: W. W. Norton

606. MARCH 18, 2001
Jason Epstein
Book Business: Publishing: Past, Present, and Future
Publisher: W. W. Norton

607. MARCH 25, 2001
Reese Schonfeld
Me and Ted Against the World: The Unauthorized Story of the Founding of CNN
Publisher: Cliff Street Books (HarperCollins)

608. APRIL 1, 2001
Don Hewitt
Tell Me a Story: 50 Years and 60 Minutes in Television
Publisher: PublicAffairs

609. APRIL 8, 2001
William J. Cooper Jr.
Jefferson Davis, American
Publisher: Alfred A. Knopf

610. APRIL 15, 2001
Andrew Burstein
America's Jubilee: How in 1826 a Generation Remembered Fifty Years of Independence
Publisher: Alfred A. Knopf

611. APRIL 22, 2001
Emily Bernard
Remember Me to Harlem: The Letters of Langston Hughes and Carl Van Vechten, 1925–1964
Publisher: Alfred A. Knopf

612. APRIL 29, 2001
Kiron K. Skinner
Reagan in His Own Hand: The Writings of Ronald Reagan That Reveal His Revolutionary Vision for America
Publisher: The Free Press

613. MAY 6, 2001
Susan Dunn
The Three Roosevelts: Patrician Leaders Who Transformed America
Publisher: Atlantic Monthly Press

614. MAY 13, 2001
Robert A. Slayton
Empire Statesman: The Rise and Redemption of Al Smith

Publisher: The Free Press

615. MAY 20, 2001
John Farrell
Tip O'Neill and the Democratic Century
Publisher: Little, Brown and Company

616. MAY 27, 2001
Diane McWhorter
Carry Me Home: Birmingham, Alabama—The Climactic Battle of the Civil Rights Revolution
Publisher: Simon & Schuster

617. JUNE 3, 2001
Rick Perlstein
Before the Storm: Barry Goldwater and the Unmaking of the American Consensus
Publisher: Hill & Wang

618. JUNE 10, 2001
Morton Kondracke
Saving Milly: Love, Politics, and Parkinson's Disease
Publisher: PublicAffairs

619. JUNE 17, 2001
Edward Said
Reflections on Exile and Other Essays
Publisher: Harvard University Press

620. JUNE 24, 2001
Alma Guillermoprieto
Looking for History: Dispatches from Latin America
Publisher: Pantheon

621. JULY 1, 2001
Daniel Schorr
Staying Tuned: A Life in Journalism
Publisher: Pocket Books

622. JULY 8, 2001
Alan Ebenstein
Friedrich Hayek: A Biography
Publisher: St. Martin's Press

623. JULY 15, 2001
Sally Satel
PC, M.D.: How Political Correctness Is Corrupting Medicine
Publisher: Basic Books

624. JULY 22, 2001
Jeff Greenfield

*Oh, Waiter! One Order of Crow:
Inside the Strangest Presidential
Election Finish in American
History*
Publisher: Putman

625. JULY 29, 2001
Jay Winik
*April 1865: The Month That
Saved America*
Publisher: HarperCollins

626. AUGUST 5, 2001
Tom Philpott
*Glory Denied: The Saga of Jim
Thompson, America's Longest-
Held Prisoner of War*
Publisher: Norton

627. AUGUST 12, 2001
Roger Wilkins
*Jefferson's Pillow: The Founding
Fathers and the Dilemma of
Black Patriotism*
Publisher: Beacon Press

628. AUGUST 19, 2001
Walter Berns
Making Patriots
Publisher: The University Press
of Chicago

629. AUGUST 26, 2001
Thomas Fleming
*The New Dealers' War: F.D.R.
and the War Within World
War II*
Publisher: Basic Books

630. SEPTEMBER 2, 2001
Herbert Bix
*Hirohito and the Making of
Modern Japan*
Publisher: HarperCollins

631. SEPTEMBER 9, 2001
Irvin Molotsky
*The Flag, the Poet, and the Song:
The Story of the Star-Spangled
Banner*
Publisher: Dutton

632. SEPTEMBER 16, 2001
(LIVE)
James Bamford
*Body of Secrets: Anatomy of the
Ultra-Secret National Security
Agency From the Cold War
Through the Dawn of a New
Century*
Publisher: Doubleday

and

Jeffrey Richelson
*The Wizards of Langley: Inside
the CIA's Directorate of Science
and Technology*
Publisher: Westview Press

633. SEPTEMBER 23, 2001
(LIVE)
John Steele Gordon
*The Business of America: Tales
from the Marketplace—American Enterprise from the Settling
of New England to the Break-Up
of AT&T*
Publisher: Walker & Company

634. SEPTEMBER 30, 2001
Hampton Sides
*Ghost Soldiers: The Forgotten
Epic Story of World War II's Most
Dramatic Mission*
Publisher: Random House

635. OCTOBER 7, 2001
Midge Decter
*An Old Wife's Tale: My Seven
Decades in Love and War*
Publisher: Regan Books

636. OCTOBER 14, 2001
Fran Grace
*Carry A. Nation: Retelling the
Life*
Publisher: Indiana University
Press

637. OCTOBER 21, 2001
Stephen Kinzer
*Crescent & Star: Turkey Between
Two Worlds*
Publisher: Farrar, Straus &
Giroux

638. OCTOBER 28, 2001
Ted Yeatman
*Frank and Jesse James: The Story
Behind the Legend*
Publisher: Cumberland House
Publishing Inc.

639. NOVEMBER 4, 2001
Michael Eric Dyson
*Holler if You Hear Me: Searching
for Tupac Shakur*
Publisher: Basic Books

640. NOVEMBER 11, 2001
Joseph Persico
*Roosevelt's Secret War: FDR and
World War II Espionage*

Publisher: Random House

641. NOVEMBER 18, 2001
Daniel Pink
*Free Agent Nation: How Amer-
ica's New Independent Workers
are Transforming the Way We
Live*
Publisher: Warner Books

642. NOVEMBER 25, 2001
Kirkpatrick Sale
*The Fire of His Genius: Robert
Fulton and the American Dream*
Publisher: The Free Press

643. DECEMBER 2, 2001
Laura Claridge
Norman Rockwell: A Life
Publisher: Random House

644. DECEMBER 9, 2001
Phyllis Lee Levin
*Edith and Woodrow: The Wilson
White House*
Publisher: Scribner

645. DECEMBER 16, 2001
Peter Bergen
*Holy War, Inc.: Inside the Secret
World of Osama bin Laden*
Publisher: The Free Press

646. DECEMBER 23, 2001
Vernon Jordan
Vernon Can Read! A Memoir
Publisher: PublicAffairs

647. DECEMBER 30, 2001
Bernard Lewis
*What Went Wrong?: Western
Impact and Middle Eastern
Response*
Publisher: Oxford University
Press

648. JANUARY 6, 2002
Bill Press
*Spin This!: All the Ways We Don't
Tell the Truth*
Publisher: Pocket Books

649. JANUARY 13, 2002
Jeffrey Hart
*Smiling Through the Cultural
Catastrophe: Toward the Revival
of Higher Education*
Publisher: Yale University Press

650. JANUARY 20, 2002
John Laurence
The Cat From Hue: A Vietnam

War Story
Publisher: PublicAffairs

651. JANUARY 27, 2002
Sandra Day O'Connor
Lazy B: Growing Up on a Cattle Ranch in the American Southwest
Publisher: Random House

652. FEBRUARY 3, 2002
Ralph Nader
Crashing the Party: How to Tell the Truth and Still Run for President
Publisher: St. Martin's Press

653. FEBRUARY 10, 2002
Steve Neal
Harry & Ike: The Partnership That Remade the Postwar World
Publisher: Scribner

654. FEBRUARY 17, 2002
Edward Steers, Jr.
Blood on the Moon: The Assassination of Abraham Lincoln
Publisher: University Press of Kentucky

655. FEBRUARY 24, 2002
R. Kent Newmyer
John Marshall and the Heroic Age of the Supreme Court
Publisher: Louisiana State University Press

656. MARCH 3, 2002
Randall Kennedy
Nigger: The Strange Career of a Troublesome Word
Publisher: Pantheon

657. MARCH 10, 2002
Richard Lingeman
Sinclair Lewis: Rebel from Main Street
Publisher: Random House

658. MARCH 17, 2002
Michael Novak
On Two Wings: Humble Faith and Common Sense at the American Founding
Publisher: Encounter Books

659. MARCH 24, 2002
Jon Ronson
Them: Adventures with Extremists
Publisher: Simon & Schuster

660. MARCH 31, 2002
Frank Wu
Yellow: Race in America Beyond Black and White
Publisher: Basic Books

661. APRIL 7, 2002
Leonard Downie, Jr. (co-author with Robert G. Kaiser)
The News About the News: American Journalism in Peril
Publisher: Alfred A. Knopf

662. APRIL 14, 2002
Ellen Joan Pollock
The Pretender: How Martin Frankel Fooled the Financial World and Led the Feds on One of the Most Publicized Manhunts in History
Publisher: Simon & Schuster

663. APRIL 21, 2002
Gordon Wood
The American Revolution: A History
Publisher: Modern Library

664. APRIL 28, 2002
Robert Skidelsky
John Maynard Keynes: Fighting for Freedom, 1937–1946
Publisher: Viking

665. MAY 5, 2002
Sarah Brady
A Good Fight
Publisher: PublicAffairs

666. MAY 12, 2002
Jennifer Toth
What Happened to Johnnie Jordan? The Story of a Child Turning Violent
Publisher: The Free Press

667. MAY 19, 2002
James Srodes
Franklin: The Essential Founding Father
Publisher: Regnery

668. MAY 26, 2002
Richard John Neuhaus
As I Lay Dying: Meditations Upon Returning
Publisher: Basic Books

669. JUNE 2, 2002
Richard Posner
Public Intellectuals: A Study of Decline

Publisher: Harvard University Press

670. JUNE 9, 2002
Jennet Conant
Tuxedo Park: A Wall Street Tycoon and the Secret Palace of Science that Changed the Course of World War II
Publisher: Simon & Schuster

671. JUNE 16, 2002
Samantha Power
A Problem From Hell: America and the Age of Genocide
Publisher: Basic Books

672. JUNE 23, 2002
Diana Preston
Lusitania: An Epic Tragedy
Publisher: Walker & Company

673. JUNE 30, 2002
John Leonard
Lonesome Rangers: Homeless Minds, Promised Lands, Fugitive Cultures
Publisher: The New Press

674. JULY 7, 2002
Sandra Mackey
The Reckoning: Iraq and the Legacy of Saddam Hussein
Publisher: W. W. Norton

675. JULY 14, 2002
Nguyen Cao Ky
Buddha's Child: My Fight to Save Vietnam
Publisher: St. Martin's Press

675. JULY 21, 2002
Daniel Stashower
The Boy Genius and the Mogul: The Untold Story of Television
Publisher: Broadway Books

Index